Gendering Post-1945 German History

Gendering Post-1945 German History
Entanglements

Edited by
Karen Hagemann, Donna Harsch,
and Friederike Brühöfener

berghahn
NEW YORK · OXFORD
www.berghahnbooks.com

First published in 2019 by
Berghahn Books
www.berghahnbooks.com

© 2019, 2022 Karen Hagemann, Donna Harsch, and Friederike Brühöfener
First paperback edition published in 2022

All rights reserved. Except for the quotation of short passages
for the purposes of criticism and review, no part of this book
may be reproduced in any form or by any means, electronic or
mechanical, including photocopying, recording, or any information
storage and retrieval system now known or to be invented,
without written permission of the publisher.

Library of Congress Cataloging-in-Publication Data

Names: Hagemann, Karen, editor. | Harsch, Donna, editor. | Brühöfener, Friederike, editor.
Title: Gendering Post-1945 German History: Entanglements / edited by Karen Hagemann, Donna Harsch, and Friederike Brühöfener.
Description: New York: Berghahn Books, 2019. | Includes bibliographical references and index.
Identifiers: LCCN 2019002794 (print) | LCCN 2019007420 (ebook) | ISBN 9781789201925 (ebook) | ISBN 9781789201918 (hardback:alk. paper)
Subjects: LCSH: Germany—History—1945-1990. | Sex role—Germany—History—20th century.
Classification: LCC DD257.2 (ebook) | LCC DD257.2 .G426 2019 (print) | DDC 305.40943/09045—dc23
LC record available at https://lccn.loc.gov/2019002794

British Library Cataloguing in Publication Data
A catalogue record for this book is available from the British Library

ISBN 978-1-78920-191-8 hardback
ISBN 978-1-80073-450-0 paperback
ISBN 978-1-78920-192-5 ebook

https://doi.org/10.3167/9781789201918

Contents

List of Illustrations	vii
List of Contributors	viii
Preface	x
Introduction. Gendering Post-1945 German History: Entanglements *Karen Hagemann, Donna Harsch, and Friederike Brühöfener*	1

Part I. Gendering the Historiography

1. Entanglements of Gender, Politics, and Protest in the Historiography on the Two Post-1945 Germanys — 21
   Karen Hagemann and Donna Harsch

2. Entangled Gender Relations and Sexuality in the Historiography on the Two Post-1945 Germanys — 45
   Jennifer Evans

3. Contact Zones and Boundary Objects: The Media and Entangled Representations of Gender — 67
   Erica Carter

Part II. Gender, Politics, and Policies

4. The Big Cleanup: Men, Women, and Rubble Clearance in Postwar East and West Germany — 93
   Leonie Treber

5. Children, Church, and Rights: East and West German Protests against Family Law Reforms in the 1950s — 115
   Alexandria Ruble

6. Gendering Health Politics: East and West German Healthcare Systems in Comparison, 1950–70 — 136
   Donna Harsch

Part III. Gendered Resistance, Protest, and Social Movements

7. Under the Habit: Resistance of Catholic Sisters against
East German State Authority in the 1950s   161
Kathryn C. Julian

8. Finding Feminism: Rethinking Activism in the West German
New Women's Movement of the 1970s and 1980s   184
Sarah E. Summers

9. Redefining the Political: The Gender of Activism in
Grassroots Movements of the 1960s to 1980s   207
Belinda Davis

10. Connected Differences: Black German Feminists and
Their Transnational Connections in the 1980s and 1990s   229
Tiffany N. Florvil

Part IV. Gender Relations and Sexuality

11. Domestic Abuse and Women's Lives: East and West Policies
during the 1960s and 1970s   253
Jane Freeland

12. Searching for Identity: 1950s Homophile Politics in
West Germany and Its Roots in the Weimar Homosexual
Movement   274
Clayton J. Whisnant

13. Contested Masculinities: Debates about Homosexuality
in the West German Bundeswehr in the 1960s and 1970s   295
Friederike Brühöfener

Part V. The Media and Representations of Gender

14. In the Presence of the Past, in the Shadow of the "Other":
Women Journalists in Postwar Germany   317
Deborah Barton

15. Entangled Femininities: Contested Representations of
Women in the East and West German Illustrated Press
of the 1950s   337
Jennifer Lynn

16. Gendered Orientalism: Representations of "the Turkish"
in the West German Press of the 1970s and 1980s   362
Brittany Lehman

Index of Names   382

Index of Subjects   383

Illustrations

Figure 15.1. *Die Frau von heute,* no. 14, 1 April 1953. Staatsbibliothek zu Berlin, Preußischer Kulturbesitz. — 343

Figure 15.2. *Die Frau von heute,* no. 25, 18 June 1954. Staatsbibliothek zu Berlin, Preußischer Kulturbesitz. — 344

Figure 15.3. *Constanze,* no. 3, February 1955: "Blusen, Pullis, Röcke!" (Blouses, Sweaters, Skirts!). Staatsbibliothek zu Berlin, Preußischer Kulturbesitz. — 347

Figure 15.4. *Neue Berliner Illustrierte,* no. 46, November 1953: "Die Monroe-Invasion" (The Monroe Invasion). Staatsbibliothek zu Berlin, Preußischer Kulturbesitz. — 350

Figure 15.5. *Die Frau von heute,* no. 21, 21 March 1952: "Schaufenster der Entwürdigung" (Showcase of Debasement). Staatsbibliothek zu Berlin, Preußischer Kulturbesitz. — 351

Figure 15.6. *Die Frau von heute,* no. 16, 19 April 1957: "Ihr Abendbrot? Milch und Kräcker" (Her Evening Meal? Milk and Crackers). Staatsbibliothek zu Berlin, Preußischer Kulturbesitz. — 354

Contributors

Deborah Barton, assistant professor of Modern German history at the Université de Montréal, Canada.

Friederike Brühöfener, assistant professor of Modern European history at the University of Texas Rio Grande Valley, United States.

Erica Carter, professor of German and film at King's College London, and chair of the British German Screen Studies Network, United Kingdom.

Belinda Davis, professor of history at Rutgers, The State University of New Jersey, United States.

Jennifer Evans, professor of history at Carleton University in Ottawa, Canada.

Tiffany N. Florvil, assistant professor of European history at the University of New Mexico, United States.

Jane Freeland, lecturer in modern German history at Queen Mary University of London, United Kingdom.

Karen Hagemann, James G. Kenan Distinguished Professor of History and adjunct professor of the Curriculum in Peace, War, and Defense at the University of North Carolina at Chapel Hill, United States.

Donna Harsch, professor of history at Carnegie Mellon University, Pittsburgh, United States.

Kathryn C. Julian, visiting lecturer of history at Maryville College, Tennessee, United States.

Brittany Lehman, visiting assistant professor of global history at the College of Charleston, South Carolina, United States.

Jennifer Lynn, associate professor of history and director of the Women's and Gender Studies Center at Montana State University Billings, United States.

Alexandria Ruble, assistant professor of European history at Spring Hill College, Mobile, Alabama, United States.

Sarah E. Summers, instructor of global and European history at Wilfrid Laurier University in Ontario, Canada

Leonie Treber, consultant for communication and research in the academic administration of the Technical University of Darmstadt, Germany.

Clayton J. Whisnant, Chapman Professor of Humanities at Wofford College, Spartanburg, South Carolina, United States.

Preface

Since German reunification in 1990, many studies on East and West Germany have been published, but even today the majority are gender blind. In the light of the increasing number of studies by women's and gender historians in Germany, Europe, and the United States on the two postwar Germanys, this is remarkable. This volume will present some of the most recent research on the subject. In October 2015, Donna Harsch and Karen Hagemann brought together a group of twenty scholars from Britain, Canada, Germany, and the United States for a series of four panels at the Thirty-Ninth Annual Conference of the German Studies Association (GSA) in Washington, DC. The main aim of the panel series was to produce a book that provides a critical review of the state of the research on postwar German history from a gender perspective. In this book we want to explore the wide-ranging variety of innovative theoretical and methodological approaches to contemporary gender history of the two Germanys. Our conceptual lens is "entanglement," which we interpret in a broad way as a form of interrelatedness. We will use it to explore and make sense of the complexity of continuity and change in the gender order of the two postwar Germanys.

For this volume we selected fourteen papers presented at the GSA and asked the authors to extend and rewrite them for publication. In addition, we invited two scholars to each write a paper on important subjects that we felt were missing. Most authors are younger scholars in the early stages of their career who just finished their dissertation or published their first book. Following our introduction, the volume begins with three shorter chapters on the development and state of research on the major themes that stand at the center of the volume: first, gender, politics, and protest; second, gender relations and sexuality; and third, the media and representations of gender. These three essays are written by established scholars. We hope the combination of new scholarship and thematic overviews will be useful for a broad academic readership of students, teachers, and researchers on both sides of the Atlantic.

We would like to thank all participants in the GSA panel series for their contributions and the authors of the volume for their wonderful collaboration. The comments of the two unknown readers were very fair and helpful. Chris Chappell from Berghahn Books was a very supportive editor. Last but not least we want to thank our excellent editorial assistants Björn Hennings and Derek Holmgren as well as the Berghahn copy editor Ryan Masteller for their help with the editing.

Karen Hagemann (University of North Carolina at Chapel Hill),
Donna Harsch (Carnegie Mellon University),
and Friederike Brühöfener (University of Texas Rio Grande Valley)
17 December 2018

Introduction
Gendering Post-1945 German History: Entanglements

Karen Hagemann, Donna Harsch, and Friederike Brühöfener

The reunification of Germany in 1990 prompted new questions and discussions among historians about how to research and write postwar German history. Is it possible and meaningful to construct one master narrative of post-1945 German history that systematically includes both states, the Federal Republic of Germany (FRG) and the German Democratic Republic (GDR)? Should historians pay equal attention to both states and societies, or should they treat the GDR as a mere "footnote in world history," as the much-cited GDR author Stefan Heym predicted in March 1990?[1] If scholars do want to do justice to each state and write a comprehensive German-German history, how should they conceptualize such a narrative?

Historian Christoph Kleßmann made a pathbreaking intervention into this discussion. In 1993, he argued that the histories of East and West Germany were marked by "demarcation and entanglement" (*Abgrenzung und Verflechtung*) and need to be analyzed as such.[2] Seven years later he reinforced this argument by asserting that post-1945 German history was shaped by "continuity, entanglement, demarcation, and division" (*Kontinuität, Verflechtung, Abgrenzung, und Teilung*) to an extent that became apparent only after the Cold War ended. He and his coauthors Hans J. Misselwitz and Günter Wichert suggested that research should focus intensively on the tensions inherent in the cultural tendencies toward integration in the two states and societies as well as on the conscious and unconscious trends toward demarcation. In addition, they proposed that the relationship between East and West Germany should be studied as an "asymmetrically entangled parallel history" (*asymmetrisch verflochtene Parallelgeschichte*).[3]

Kleßmann, Misselwitz, and Wichert issued an elaborate call for an integrated postwar history, which many other scholars have seconded.[4] The research by women and gender historians of the last two decades shows how fruitful it is to conceptualize contemporary German history as an asymmetrically entangled parallel past.[5] Since the 1990s, an increasing number of publications on women's and gender history of the two Germanys has appeared, especially in Britain, Germany, and the United States. *Gendering Post-1945 German History: Entanglements* offers a critical review of the state of the research from a gender perspective and presents new and innovative works by women and gender historians.

"Gender" and "entanglement" are the two central concepts of the volume. We use "gender" as a historically specific, context-dependent, and relational category of analysis and understand it as an amalgam of ideals and practices that give meaning to and socially differentiate male and female. As a contingent category, gender only works in connection with other "categories of difference" like "class," "race," "ethnicity," and "sexuality." Conceptualized in this way, gender is central to the entangled histories of the two Germanys. It shaped the gendered self-representation of the two states; informed their economic, social, and cultural policies; influenced the dominant ideas about the gender order and gender relations in politics, society, and culture, and with these ideas also shaped public representations of men and women; determined the space, content, extent, and forms of men's and women's political participation; and affected the practices, experiences, and identities of individuals in everyday life.[6]

Similarly, we use "entanglement" in multiple interrelated and historically specific ways. We apply the concept of entanglement, first, to the gendered histories of East and West Germany. Given that the two states and their societies were deeply interrelated historically and culturally, their gendered social structures too intersected in significant ways. Each state also made gendered policy decisions in reaction to discourse and policy of the state and society on the other side of the Iron Curtain. Yet, as several contributions to this volume show, these relations and reactions were asymmetrical, with the GDR in many cases making far more explicit references to West Germany than vice versa. We assume, second, that the postwar gender order and gender relations within each state were entangled with the shared past of the German Empire, the Weimar Republic, and Nazi Germany. We posit, third, that gendered ideas, policies, and practices were related to other social and cultural constructions of difference like class, race, ethnicity, and sexuality. The chapters in this volume pursue one or more of these three approaches to the concept of entanglement.

The volume focuses on gendered entanglements to explore and understand similarities and differences as well as continuities and changes in the gender order and gender relation of the two postwar Germanys. Following a brief exploration of gender and entanglement in the historiography on post-1945 Germany, this introduction discusses the approach, themes, and organization of our volume.

Gender and Entanglement in the Historiography on Post-1945 Germany

During the Cold War era, scholarship on East and West Germany was intensely invested in understanding the origins and significance of the real and ideological divide between the FRG and GDR. Initially, this scholarship almost exclusively focused on their political histories, but it later added social history to the mix.[7] The Cold War rift shaped historical interpretations and explanations, yet few scholars undertook careful comparative analyses based on primary sources, in part because of the limited access to archival material. Christopher Kleßmann broke new ground in the 1980s with his two comparative monographs on East and West German history between 1945 and 1970.[8] He was also one of the first male historians to point to the importance of the gender dimension for contemporary German history.[9] Most mainstream scholars treated women's contributions to the history of both German states and societies as peripheral at best. Unlike Kleßmann, they ignored studies by women and gender scholars of East and West Germany, even as these appeared in ever greater numbers from the 1980s onward. Blind to gender issues, the majority of historians, to whom we will henceforth refer as "mainstream," typically also overlooked the innovative character of women's and gender history.

A historiographical debate that could have cast light on the history of the GDR, for example, was the so-called *Historikerinnenstreit* (quarrel between female historians) that started in the late 1980s. Its central point of contention revolved around the role of "Aryan" German women under National Socialism. Given the Nazi regime's patriarchal character, should women be judged as, basically, "victims" and "innocent bystanders" of Nazi policy? Or, like the actions of men in a dictatorship, should women's behavior too be evaluated along a continuum from victims and active resisters to bystanders and perpetrators? The majority of the voices in this transatlantic debate argued that the simplifying dichotomy of victim and perpetrator had to be overcome so that women's and gender historians could explore the multiple and often ambiguous possibilities and limits that shaped women's conduct under National Socialism.[10] The methodological insights of the *Historikerinnenstreit* influenced the research on the Third Reich and Holocaust, but not on the dictatorial regime of the GDR. Only after the millennium did scholarly attention turn to the broad variety and ambiguity of relations between the East German populace and the socialist state controlled by the Socialist Unity Party of Germany (Sozialistische Einheitspartei Deutschlands, SED). In emphasizing the complex nature of popular involvement and arguing that the GDR was a "participatory dictatorship," historian Mary Fulbrook in 2005 stirred up a lively controversy about the extent and significance of popular engagement with the communist state. Yet, the gender of popular involvement was not considered in this debate.[11] Only in research on the operation of the Ministry for State Security (Ministerium für Staatssicherheit, MfS), the infamous Stasi, did several historians address women's direct entanglement with the organs of repression in the East German dictatorship.[12]

After reunification, scholarship on contemporary German history increasingly abandoned the dichotomist Cold War paradigm and began to pay closer attention to the gray areas in the histories of both the GDR and the FRG. The shift in the historiographic perspective was driven in part by the opening of archives: historians gained virtually unrestricted access to East German archival holdings after 1990. And, every year since 1980, they can look at previously inaccessible West German archival materials as another "thirty-year data protection" gate is unlocked. The new opportunities for historical research led to an outpouring of work on both German states and societies.[13] Rich in detail and nuanced in interpretation, these post–Cold War studies of specific regions, cultural encounters, or social groups challenged the older static, two-dimensional model of West German liberal constitutionalism versus East German totalitarian authoritarianism. They question the Manichean portrayal of Cold War Germany, with the FRG hailed, on one side, as the shining beacon of uninterrupted progress and spreading prosperity and the GDR excoriated, on the other, as a failed experiment that could not even effectively modernize the economy, much less deliver on its radical promise of social justice for all.[14] Historian Konrad H. Jarausch and others have argued that social and cultural liberalization in West Germany was, in fact, an uneven and contested process. The making of a democratic citizenry, the new scholarship has shown, was more incremental and more fraught than once assumed.[15] Researchers have traced the roots of West Germany's "1968"—a year that became the iconic representation of the cultural revolution of the 1960s and early 1970s—to the gradual spread and rising public defense of unconventional behavior and critical speech in the 1950s.[16] Thus, this scholarship has demonstrated that cultural and social liberalization in the FRG began earlier but was less sudden or complete than the self-congratulatory narrative about "1968" that presents the late 1960s as the transformative moment that created a liberal democracy with a thriving civil society.[17]

Although the immediate post-reunification period saw a boost in historical research on East and West Germany, comparative social or political histories of the GDR and FRG are still few in number.[18] This can be attributed to several factors: asymmetrical access to archival records after the complete opening of East German archives as opposed to the year-by-year lifting of restrictions on West German materials; the inclination of foundations to fund research on the GDR more readily; the methodological challenges and time demands of comparative or transnational research. Ironically, the postmillennial turn toward European and global Cold War studies has partially surpassed the German-German comparison as the global perspective has inspired historians of the FRG and the GDR to place their work in a broader transnational context.[19] In this volume, we adopt a narrower transnational lens, arguing that the study of the FRG and GDR is not the study of one nation but of two states, societies, and economies. There is still much to be learned and analyzed about their particular set of entanglements. The rise of transnational and global history has challenged the study of women and gender too. Exploring, for example, the gender of everyday life in the Cold War era, historians have revealed the entanglement of ideals and practices of consumption and fashion not only across the East-West divide but also across national borders within the West and within the East.[20] In its gendered perspective, too, this volume focuses largely on the entangled transnational history of the two German states and societies. This editorial decision influenced the composition of the volume. We invited mainly young scholars to write about their most recent, often still unpublished, work with the aim to present a variety of new conceptual and methodological approaches to the gender history of East and West Germany.

Women's and gender historians have made innovative contributions to the development of the post–Cold War scholarship on the FRG and the GDR. They fostered the poststructuralist and cultural turn in historiography. They belonged to the first group of scholars to advocate studying the history of everyday life (*Alltagsgeschichte*).[21] They asked new questions, turned to novel topics, and developed new theoretical and methodological frameworks to make sense of East and West German history. These innovations resulted in a host of publications focusing on three related subjects: paid work, housework, and family work; family, social, and labor policies;[22] and private consumption and fashion in both Germanys.[23] These studies pointed again and again to a highly visible paradox that mainstream scholarship overlooked: gender functioned in both German states and societies as a central marker of difference far beyond the political discourse on women's emancipation and roles in society. Gender images and family ideals were used in each German state to define its own political and social identity and distinguish itself from the Germany on the other side of the Iron Curtain. Yet this research simultaneously revealed the striking similarities between gendered practices in the authoritarian, communist state in the East and the democratic, capitalist state in the West.[24]

The shift from women's to gender history in the 1980s contributed to another innovation: the exploration of the history of men and masculinities. This new field of historical inquiry analyzes the social and cultural construction of notions of masculinity and studies men as "gendered subjects whose experience and behavior were crucially shaped by culturally and historically specific notions of masculinity." So far, scholars have mainly applied this focus to West Germany.[25] Inspired by the theories of Michel Foucault and other poststructuralists, gender historians furthermore have turned since the late 1990s to the sexual lives of East and West German citizens while paying close attention to official discourses and policies regarding sexuality. Studies of attitudes toward extramarital sex, pornography, and homosexuality have exposed the ongoing influence of the sexual mores and discourses of the German Empire, the Weimar Republic, and Nazi Germany on the history of sexuality in divided Germany.[26] The turn toward gender history and the history of sexuality also unearthed examples of subtle nonconformity and resistance to dominant gender roles and heteronormativity in both Germanys.[27] Growing interest in the history of homosexuality and investigations into the pervasiveness of patriarchal and heteronormative ideals have furthermore revealed examples of men's and women's resistance and outright protest against official discourses and legal provisions that not only regulated but often criminalized gay and lesbian expressions of gender and sexuality.[28]

In these multiple ways, women and gender historians have contributed to the historiography on post-1945 Germany. In the three chapters of the first part on "Gendering the Historiography," we discuss the development of the research by women and gender historians on the post-1945 history of both Germanys in more detail, position the chapters in this volume in this development, and suggest themes and topics for further research.

Gendering Post-1945 German History: Entanglements

This volume aims to offer a critical review of the state of the research on the postwar history of East and West Germany from a gender perspective and to present a selection of recent and innovative scholarship. By using the concept of gendered entanglement, its chapters contribute in multiple ways to the research on contemporary German history. Some authors use the concept of entanglement to shed light on how intertwined—politically, socially, and culturally—the gendered histories of East and West Germany were. By studying an entangled past from a gender perspective, these contributions integrate an important but often ignored dimension into the history of Cold War rivalry between the two German states. Gender, they argue, played a central role in a rivalry that was articulated through direct interaction with and explicit references to the other Germany as well as through indirect competition and observation. Cold War enmity shaped not only the foreign policy and gendered self-representation of each state but also their domestic policies. Healthcare policies, labor policies, or family, marriage, and divorce laws were oftentimes developed in reference to the other Germany, including its gender ideology and practices. Several studies in this volume establish gender as a central marker of difference in political discourse far beyond women's role and emancipation. They also, though, expose a contradiction between divergent policies and antagonistic rhetoric, on one hand, and popular and official assumptions about gender differences that were shared across the Cold War divide on the other.[29]

Other authors in the volume use the concept of entanglement to examine the triangular relationship between the GDR, the FRG, and their common German past. Cold War antagonism shaped East and West German self-representation, culture, and politics, certainly, but it did so in complex interaction with the histories and memories of the German Empire, the Weimar Republic, and especially Nazi Germany. In debates and decisions in all spheres of politics and policy, the room for maneuver (*Handlungsspielraum*) was limited by the need to demonstrate distance from both the Nazi past *and* the state on the other side of the Iron Curtain. Acknowledgment of the referential triangle between Nazi Germany, the FRG, and the GDR does not, however, preclude recognition of the Cold War era as its own period in German history. Posing the question of whether the 1950s and 1960s were merely a "post-fascist, post-war, post-Weimar and post-Wilhelmine" period or were also "anything in their own right," Elizabeth D. Heineman answered that they were both.[30] Such a dual approach allows scholars to identify the multiple pasts that influenced post-1945 German gender history and to explore continuities and discontinuities while identifying the new and specific character of the period that started at the end of the Second World War.

Furthermore, several chapters of the volume use the concept of entanglement to explore the intersection of gender with other categories of difference like class, race, ethnicity, or sexuality. In the construction of a hierarchical social order, each post-1945 German state and society interwove gendered discourses about politics, society, and culture with discourses about other social differences. Political rhetoric in the GDR, for example, typically paired gender and class. In both states, rhetoric tended to link homosexuality to insufficient masculinity. In postwar West Germany, discourse about the "fraternization" of German women and African American soldiers and about their children was shot through with biases about the intersection of gender, race, and ethnicity.[31] In later West German discourse about guest workers from Italy, Greece, the former Yugoslavia, and Turkey, assumptions about the conjunction of gender, ethnicity, and religion combined to produce a Christian-conservative definition of a "German identity" that demarcated it especially from the "Muslim other."[32]

In exploring these different lines of research on gendered German-German entanglements, the volume reveals an asymmetry in the relations and the actual and constructed power hierarchy between the FRG and the GDR. Christoph Kleßmann bluntly captured the essence of this imbalance when he asserted in 2001 that "the Federal Republic could, without difficulty, exist without the GDR."[33] Indeed, as the contributions to this volume attest, the Federal Republic of Germany seemed sure of itself and its claim to legitimacy. As a result, in its public discourse and its unpublished sources in many areas of politics and policy, East Germany rarely featured as an explicit reference point. In contrast, the FRG constantly functioned as an intensely observed and explicitly referenced comparison for both the leadership of the GDR and East German society. For the SED, the Federal Republic served publicly as the countermodel—and behind the scenes occasionally also as a prototype. For many in the East German populace, of course, West Germany stood for consumer heaven and political freedom.[34]

Finally, some chapters in this volume contribute to the scholarship that has questioned traditional periodization—such as "1961" as a turning point in the GDR's history or "1968" in the FRG's—and narratives of progress in the West—such as the steady march toward liberalization in the FRG. They examine, for example, different forms of activism and protest against political practices, legal systems, or gender, racial, and sexual ideologies. As such, they contribute to the ongoing discussions about whether the social and cultural upheaval of the 1960s contributed to an accelerated process of liberalization in West Germany or whether East German society became more or less resistant to SED policy over time.

We present the sixteen contributions to this volume in five parts. The first part, "Gendering the Historiography," focuses on important themes of women's and gender history on both Germanys since 1945. The three essays by Karen Hagemann and Donna Harsch, Jennifer Evans, and Erica Carter explore the development of research on "Gender, Politics, and Protest," the "Entangled Gender Relations and Sexuality," and "Media and Entangled Representations of Gender." They offer new perspectives on the intertwined but decidedly different histories of East and West Germany by addressing two central questions: What new insights can gender offer to the complicated, entangled history of the GDR and FRG? And, conversely, how did the entangled relationship of the two postwar Germanys inform gender relations in discourse and practice on both sides of the Iron Curtain? The four parts that follow this first section focus on the themes of "Gender, Politics, and Policies," "Gendered Resistance, Protest, and Social Movements," "Gender Relations and Sexuality," and "The Media and Representations of Gender."

Gender, Politics, and Policies

The major subject of the second part of the volume is the multiplicity of ways in which politics and policies in postwar East and West Germany were gendered. The contributions by Leonie Treber, Alexandria Ruble, and Donna Harsch examine three major topics: gender and politics in East and West German parties and parliaments; gender, the family, and work in East and West German policies; gender, health policy, and the female body. The chapters by Treber and Harsch highlight the impact of gendered assumptions about work and the body for the formulation, implementation, and perception of labor and healthcare policies. Treber writes about men, women, and the cleaning of the rubble in postwar East and West Germany, showing that not only economic exigencies but also different ideals of femininity determined the disparate deployment of women for rubble clearing in all four occupation zones and further shaped how "rubble women" (*Trümmerfrauen*) were remembered in the FRG and GDR. Discrepancies and parallels are the core of Harsch's comparative contribution on East and West German healthcare policies from the 1950s to the 1970s. By exploring responses to contagious and chronic diseases and to childbirth, the chapter reveals that the approaches of both healthcare systems converged from the late 1960s onward. Ruble places debates over the reform of marriage and family law in the GDR and FRG in the context of their tug-of-war for hegemony and political advantage. Throughout the 1950s and early 1960s, East and West German politicians relied on comparisons and contrasts to the other Germany to support their arguments for and against the new family laws.

Gendered Resistance, Protest, and Social Movements

The central theme of the third part of the volume with contributions by Kathryn Julian, Sarah Summers, Belinda Davis, and Tiffany Florvil is the ways in which grassroots activism redefined the "gender" and content of the "political" in resistance, protest, and social movements in the FRG and/or the GDR. Taken together, the chapters explore different ways in which female activists, whether in the East or the West, challenged limits placed on their social and political rights by their respective governments and how each state responded to the protest. Julian explores Catholic sisters' resistance against the East German state in the 1950s, demonstrating that their protests drew on their traditional female roles as nuns. Summers examines the different agendas and forms of feminist activism within the new women's movement in West Germany in the 1970s and 1980s and concludes that this movement was much broader than often assumed. Davis analyzes the impact of women's experiences in the extraparliamentary movement on feminist activism in the new women's movement and the wider grassroots movements of the 1960s to 1980s. In her chapter on Black German feminism and its transnational connections in the 1980s and 1990s, Florvil argues that the organization Afro-German Women (Afrodeutsche Frauen, ADEFRA) heightened the visibility of German Women of Color and confronted racial, gender, and sexual discrimination in Germany and beyond.

Gender Relations and Sexuality

The main themes of the three chapters in the fourth part of the volume by Jane Freeland, Clayton Whisnant, and Friederike Brühöfener are the entanglements between everyday gender relations and sexual practices, related public discourses, and state policies and the attempts to reform these policies in both German states. Freeland analyzes the discrepancies between women's experience of and political responses to domestic abuse in the FRG and the GDR in the 1960s and 1970s. She details difference and similarity in how each state constructed normative gender relations in the family. The chapters by Whisnant and Brühöfener contribute to our understanding of the history behind the uneven decriminalization of homosexuality in West Germany after 1945. Whisnant locates the roots of the limited but influential homophile discourse in 1950s West Germany in the language and ideas of Weimar's homosexual movement. Brühöfener analyzes the contested notions of military masculinity in the public discourse of the FRG in her chapter on debates about homosexuality in the West German defense forces in 1960s and 1970s. Unfortunately, in the long path of preparing this volume, we were not able to fulfill our hopes of including an essay on homosexuality in the GDR. To make up for this gap, Jennifer Evans kindly agreed to draw on her own research to discuss this subject in chapter 2, "Entangled Gender Relations and Sexuality in the Historiography on the Two Post-1945 Germanys."

The Media and Representations of Gender

Media in the East and West directly and indirectly shaped a gendered rhetoric of demarcation. The three chapters by Deborah Barton, Jennifer Lynn, and Brittany Lehman in the fifth part explore the entangled ways in which the press and television in both German states understood, constructed, and negotiated gender. In her contribution, Barton tells a little-known story about the experiences of German female reporters during the transition from the Third Reich to Cold War Germany. She explores how and why their journalism and their situation as women journalists did and did not change across the 1945 divide in East and West Germany.

Lynn deconstructs the contested gendered representations of women in the East and West German illustrated press of the 1950s, comparing and contrasting the ways in which the press used images of femininity not only to entertain their readers but also to promote specific labor and family policies, consumer practices, and visions of the modern woman. Lehman examines the evolution of the gendered orientalism manifested in the representations of "the Turkish" in the West German press during the 1970 and 1980s. She argues that by presenting Turkish men and women as the embodiment of Muslim otherness, the debates tended to essentialize them and to ignore the diversity of gender relations among various Islamic groups. We hoped to include a chapter on film but were unable to do so. Erica Carter graciously agreed to discuss some of her own film analysis in chapter 3, "Contact Zones and Boundary Objects: The Media and Entangled Representations of Gender."

Conclusion

Collectively, the contributions to *Gendering Post-1945 German History: Entanglements* confirm the pervasiveness of gender throughout all aspects of politics, society, and culture. They also demonstrate the critical ability of this perspective to reveal and illuminate the complexities of post-1945 German history. An entangled gender history, the volume shows, has the power to challenge Cold War master narratives of German history. Its contributions simultaneously move beyond political history and radically rethink the meaning of politics and "the political" in both Germanys. They prompt historians, for instance, to reconsider the scope, breadth, and success of political activism in both East and West Germany. They also work against historical determinism. Several chapters challenge the notion of the FRG as the consistently more progressive, liberalized state and society that was always slated to succeed. Other chapters undermine the idea that the GDR was uniformly more "backward" than the West, was never responsive to popular pressure, enjoyed no popular support for any policies, and was always doomed to fail. They reveal that various East German social policies, projects, and laws were inspired by the labor, health, education, and family policies of Weimar socialists and communists that remained innovative and even avant-garde after 1945—and, indeed, still today. One thinks of the reform of laws that criminalized abortion and homosexuality, the (quite successful) effort to end discrimination against single mothers and their children, the provision of all-day childcare and schooling to help working mothers, and, last but not least, special training and education for women so they could enter skilled occupations and the so-called male professions. The chapters also point to the tenacity with which men, whether out of self-interest or principle, held on to male privileges in the state, economy, and family in both the socialist East and democratic West. Given that the two Germanys shared patriarchal traditions—some unique to Germany, others Western, a few virtually universal—gender relations were not transformed in either Germany and were expressed in day-to-day practices, beliefs, and emotions that were often strikingly similar across the Cold War divide.

Karen Hagemann is the James G. Kenan Distinguished Professor of History at the University of North Carolina at Chapel Hill. She has published widely in Modern German and European history, combining the fields of the social, political, cultural, military and gender history. Her recent English books relevant for the theme of the volume include: *Gendering Modern German History: Rewriting Historiography* (ed. with Jean H. Quataert, Berghahn Books, 2007/2010, in German 2008); *Children, Families and States: Time Policies of Child Care, Preschool and Primary Schooling in Europe* (ed. with Konrad H. Jarausch and Cristina Allemann-Ghionda, Berghahn Books, 2011, in German 2015); *Gender and the long Postwar: Reconsiderations of the United States and the Two Germanys, 1945–1989* (ed. with Sonya Michel, Johns Hopkins University Press, 2014); *Oxford Handbook on Gender, War and the Western World since 1600* (ed. with Stefan Dudink and Sonya o. Rose, Oxford University Press, 2018) and started a new monograph entitled *Forgotten Soldiers: Gender, the Military and War in European History, 1600-2000*.

Donna Harsch is professor of history at Carnegie Mellon University, Pittsburgh. She is a social and political historian of twentieth-century Germany. Her recent publications include: *Revenge of the Domestic: Women, the Family, and Communism in the German Democratic Republic* (Princeton University Press, 2007); and "Women in Communist Societies," in *The Oxford Handbook of the History of Communism* (ed. by S. A. Smith, Oxford University Press, 2013). Currently she is researching the history of health and medicine in the Cold War Germanys. She is working on a book-length comparative study of infant mortality and efforts to reduce it in the German Democratic Republic and Federal Republic of Germany from 1945 to 1990.

Friederike Brühöfener is associate professor of modern European history at the University of Texas Rio Grande Valley. Her research interests include modern German and European history, cultural history, military history and gender with a special focus on the history of masculinities. She received her PhD in history from the University of North Carolina Chapel Hill in 2014. Currently she is transforming her dissertation to a book entitled *Forging States, Armies and Men: Military Masculinity, Politics and Society in East and West Germany, 1945–1989*. Her English publications include: "Sex and the Soldier: The Discourse about the Moral Conduct of Bundeswehr Soldiers and Officers during the Adenauer Era," *Central European History* 48, no. 4 (2015): 523–540; and "Politics of Emotions: Journalistic Reflections on the Emotionality of the West German Peace Movement, 1979–1984," *German Politics and Society* 33, no. 4 (2015): 97–111.

Notes

1. Quoted in, Hans-Ulrich Wehler, *Deutsche Gesellschaftsgeschichte,* vol. 5: *Bundesrepublik und DDR, 1949–1990* (Munich, 2008), 361.
2. Christoph Kleßmann, "Verflechtung und Abgrenzung: Aspekte der geteilten und zusammengehörigen deutschen Nachkriegsgeschichte," *Aus Politik und Zeitgeschichte,* B 29–30 (1993): 30–41.
3. Christoph Kleßmann et al., "Vorwort," in *Deutsche Vergangenheiten—Eine gemeinsame Herausforderung: Der schwierige Umgang mit der doppelten Nachkriegsgeschichte,* ed. Christoph Kleßmann et al. (Berlin, 1999), 9–13, 12, and 30.
4. See for example Günter Heydemann, "Integrale Nachkriegsgeschichte," *APuZ* B 3 (2007): 8–12; Konrad H. Jarausch, "Die Teile als Ganzes erkennen: Zur Integration der beiden deutschen Nachkriegsgeschichten," *Zeithistorische Forschungen/Studies in Contemporary History* 1, no. 1 (2004): 10–33; and Frank Bösch, "Geteilte Geschichte: Plädoyer für eine deutsch-deutsche Perspektive auf die jüngste Zeitgeschichte," *Zeithistorische Forschungen/Studies in Contemporary History* 12, no. 1 (2015): 98–114, and "Geteilt und Verbunden: Perspektiven auf die deutsche Geschichte seit den 1970er Jahren," in *Geteilte Geschichte: Ost- und Westdeutschland 1970–2000,* ed. Frank Bösch (Göttingen, 2015), 7–37.
5. See, as overviews of the research, Julia Paulus et al., eds., *Zeitgeschichte als Geschlechtergeschichte: Neue Perspektiven auf die Bundesrepublik* (Frankfurt/M., 2012), esp. 11–30; and Karen Hagemann and Sonya Michel, "Introduction: Gender and the Long Postwar: Reconsiderations of the United States and the Two Germanys, 1945–1989," in *Gender and the Long Postwar: The United States and the Two Germanys, 1945–1989,* ed. Karen Hagemann and Sonya Michel (Baltimore, MD, 2014), 1–27.
6. See AHR Forum: Revisiting "Gender: A Useful Category of Historical Analysis," *American Historical Review* 113, no. 5 (2008): 1344–430, esp. Joan W. Scott, "Unanswered Questions," 1422–30.
7. For a critical review of this Cold War scholarship, see also chapter 1 by Karen Hagemann and Donna Harsch in this volume. Early critical evaluations of this dichotomous approach were, Christoph Kleßmann, *Die Doppelte Staatsgründung: Deutsche Geschichte 1945–1955* (Bonn, 1982), and *Zwei Staaten, Eine Nation: Deutsche Geschichte 1955–1970* (Bonn, 1988); as well as Karl Dietrich Erdmann, "Drei Staaten—zwei Nationen—Ein Volk? Überlegungen zu einer deutschen Geschichte seit der Teilung," *Geschichte in Wissenschaft und Unterricht* 36, no. 10 (1985): 671–83.
8. Early comparative works are, Kleßmann, *Die Doppelte Staatsgründung,* and *Zwei Staaten*; and Rainer Geissler, *Die Sozialstruktur Deutschlands: Ein Studienbuch zur sozialstrukturellen Entwicklung im geteilten und vereinten Deutschland* (Opladen, 1992).

9. Kleßmann, *Zwei Staaten*, 56.
10. On the *Historikerinnenstreit*, see Atina Grossmann, "Feminist Debates about Women and National Socialism," *Gender & History* 3, no. 3 (1991): 350–58; Adelheid von Saldern, "Victims or Perpetrators? Controversies about the Role of Women in the Nazi State," in *Nazism and German Society, 1933–1945*, ed. David Crew (London, 1994), 141–66; Carola Sachse, "Frauenforschung zum Nationalsozialismus," *Mittelweg 36*, no. 6 (1997): 24–42; and Claudia Koonz, "A Tributary and a Mainstream: Gender, Public Memory, and the Historiography of Nazi Germany," in *Gendering Modern German History: Rewriting Historiography*, ed. Karen Hagemann and Jean H. Quataert (New York, 2007), 147–67.
11. See Mary Fulbrook, *The People's State: East German Society from Hitler to Honecker* (New Haven, CT, 2005).
12. See for example Elizabeth Pfister, *Unternehmen Romeo: Die Liebeskommandos der Stasi* (Berlin, 1999); Josie McLellan, *Love in the Time of Communism: Intimacy and Sexuality in the GDR* (Cambridge, 2011); and Jens Gieseke, *The History of the Stasi: East Germany's Secret Police, 1945–1990* (New York, 2014).
13. For East Germany, see for example Konrad H. Jarausch, ed., *Dictatorship as Experience: Towards a Socio-Cultural History of the GDR* (New York, 1999); Katherine Pence and Paul Betts, eds., *Socialist Modern: East German Everyday Culture and Politics* (Ann Arbor, MI, 2008); Mary Fulbrook, *Power and Society in the GDR, 1961–1979: The "Normalization of Rule"?* (New York, 2009); Mary Fulbrook and Andrew I. Port, eds., *Becoming East German: Socialist Structures and Sensibilities after Hitler* (New York, 2013); and for West Germany, Axel Schildt and Arnold Sywottek, eds., *Modernisierung im Wiederaufbau: Die westdeutsche Gesellschaft der 50er Jahre* (Bonn, 1993); Robert G. Moeller, *West Germany under Construction: Politics, Society, and Culture in the Adenauer Era* (Ann Arbor, MI, 1997); and Hanna Schissler, ed., *The Miracle Years: A Cultural History of West Germany, 1949–1968* (Princeton, NJ, 2001).
14. See for example Bösch, "Geteilt und Verbunden," 15; also Dagmar Herzog, "East Germany's Sexual Evolution," in Pence and Betts, *Socialist Modern*, 71–95; and Josie McLellan, "Did Communists Have the Better Sex? Sex and the Body in German Unification," in *Remembering the German Democratic Republic: Divided Memory in a United Germany*, ed. David Clarke and Ute Wölfel (New York, 2011), 119–30
15. Konrad H. Jarausch, *After Hitler: Recivilizing Germans, 1945–1995* (Oxford, 2006), 99–100 and 156–57.
16. See for example Schildt und Sywottek, eds., *Modernisierung im Wiederaufbau*; and Axel Schildt and Detlef Siegfried, "Youth, Consumption and Politics in the Age of Radical Change," in *Between Marx and Coca-Cola: Youth Cultures in Changing European Societies, 1960–1980*, ed. Schildt and Siegfried (Oxford, 2006), 1–35.
17. Jarausch, *After Hitler*; Konrad H. Jarausch, ed., *Das Ende der Zuversicht? Die siebziger Jahre als Geschichte* (Göttingen, 2008); and Ulrich Herbert, *Geschichte Deutschlands im 20. Jahrhundert* (Munich, 2014), 860–65.
18. See next to Kleßman, *Die Doppelte Staatsgründung*, and *Zwei Staaten, eine Nation*, for example, Jarausch, *After Hitler*; Wehler, *Deutsche Gesellschaftsgeschichte*, vol. 5; Udo Wengst and Hermann Wentker, eds., *Das doppelte Deutschland: 40 Jahre Systemkonkurrenz* (Berlin, 2013); and Bösch, ed., *Geteilte Geschichte*.
19. An overview of the research on the global Cold War provide, Melvyn P. Leffler and Odd Arne Westad, eds. *The Cambridge History of the Cold War*, 3 vols. (Cam-

bridge, 2010), esp. the introduction, 1:1–19; and Richard H. Immerman and Petra Goedde, eds., *The Oxford Handbook of the Cold War* (Oxford, 2012), esp. the introduction, 1–14.
20. See for example Paul Betts and David Crowley, eds., special issue, "Domestic Dreamworlds: Notions of Home in Post–1945 Europe," *Journal of Contemporary History* 40, no. 2 (2005): 213–36; Shana Penn and Jill Massino, eds., *Gender Politics and Everyday Life in State Socialist Eastern and Central Europe* (New York, 2009); Ruth Oldenziel and Karin Zachmann, eds., *Cold War Kitchen: Americanization, Technology, and European Users* (Cambridge, MA, 2009); Francisca de Haan, ed., "Gendering the Cold War in the Region: An Email Conversation between Malgorzata (Gosia) Fidelis, Renata Jambrešić Kirin, Jill Massino, and Libora Oates-lndruchova," *aspasia* 8 (2014): 162–90; and Philip E. Muehlenbeck, *Gender, Sexuality, and the Cold War: A Global Perspective* (Nashville, TN, 2017).
21. See Dorothee Wierling, *Geboren im Jahr Eins: Der Jahrgang 1949 in der DDR; Versuch einer Kollektivbiographie* (Berlin, 2002); Ina Merkel and Felix Mühlberg, *"Wir sind doch nicht die Mecker-Ecke der Nation": Briefe an das DDR-Fernsehen* (Cologne, 1998); and Ina Merkel et al., eds., *Das Kollektiv bin ich: Utopie und Alltag in der DDR* (Cologne, 2000).
22. See, for the extensive literature, chapter 1 by Karen Hagemann and Donna Harsch in this volume. Important monographs are, Robert G. Moeller, *Protecting Motherhood: Women and the Family in the Politics of Postwar West Germany* (Berkeley, CA, 1993); Elizabeth D. Heineman, *What Difference Does a Husband Make? Women and Marital Status in Nazi and Postwar Germany* (Berkeley, CA, 1999); Carola Sachse, *Der Hausarbeitstag: Gerechtigkeit und Gleichberechtigung in Ost und West 1939–1994* (Göttingen, 2002); Donna Harsch, *Revenge of the Domestic: Women, the Family, and Communism in the German Democratic Republic* (Princeton, NJ, 2007); Christine von Oertzen, *The Pleasure of a Surplus Income: Part-Time Work, Gender Politics, and Social Change in West Germany, 1955–1969* (New York, 2007).
23. See for example the following monographs: Erica Carter, *How German Is She? Postwar West German Reconstruction and the Consuming Woman* (Ann Arbor, 1997); Ina Merkel, *Utopie und Bedürfnis: Die Geschichte der Konsumkultur in der DDR* (Cologne, 1999); Judd Stitziel, *Fashioning Socialism: Clothing, Politics and Consumer Culture in East Germany* (New York, 2005); and Paul Steege, *Black Market, Cold War: Everyday Life in Berlin, 1946–1949* (Cambridge, 2007).
24. Chapter 1 by Karen Hagemann and Donna Harsch and chapter 2 by Jennifer Evans in this volume also discuss this paradox and the literature that has explored it.
25. Frank Biess, *Homecomings: Returning POWs and the Legacies of Defeat in Postwar Germany* (Princeton, NJ, 2006), 12; see also Robert G. Moeller *War Stories: The Search for a Usable Past in the Federal Republic of Germany* (Berkeley, CA, 2003); and Roy Jerome, ed., *Conceptions of Postwar German Masculinity* (Albany, NY, 2001).
26. For the extensive literature, see chapter 2 by Jennifer Evans in this volume. Important monographs are, Dagmar Herzog, *Sex after Fascism: Memory and Morality in Twentieth-Century Germany* (Princeton, NJ, 2005); Elizabeth D. Heineman, *Before Porn Was Legal: The Erotica Empire of Beate Uhse* (Chicago, 2011); Sybille Steinbacher, *Wie der Sex nach Deutschland kam: Der Kampf um Sittlichkeit und Anstand in der frühen Bundesrepublik* (Munich, 2011); Jennifer V. Evans, *Life among the Ruins: Cityscape and Sexuality in Cold War Berlin* (London, 2011); Clayton

Whisnant, *Male Homosexuality in West Germany: Between Persecution and Freedom, 1945–69* (New York, 2012); and McLellan, *Love in the Time of Communism*.
27. See for example Uta Poiger, *Jazz, Rock, and Rebels: Cold War Politics and American Culture in a Divided Germany* (Berkeley, CA, 2000); and Mark Fenemore, *Sex, Thugs and Rock 'n' Roll: Teenage Rebels in Cold-War East Germany* (New York, 2007).
28. For the literature, see chapter 2 by Evans in this volume.
29. For an examination of both East and West, see Gunilla-Friederike Budde, *Frauen arbeiten: Weibliche Erwerbstätigkeit in Ost- und Westdeutschland nach 1945* (Göttingen, 1997); Sachse, *Der Hausarbeitstag*; and Karen Hagemann, "Between Ideology and Economy: The 'Time Politics' of Child Care and Public Education in the Two Germanys," *Social Politics* 13, no. 2 (2006): 217–60.
30. Elizabeth D. Heineman, "Sexuality in West Germany: Post-Fascist, Post-War, Post-Weimar, or Post-Wilhelmine," in *Mit dem Wandel leben: Neuorientierung und Tradition in der Bundesrepublik der 1950er und 60er Jahre,* ed. Friedrich Kießling and Bernhard Rieger (Cologne, 2010), 229–45, here 234.
31. See for example Maria Höhn, *GIs and Fräuleins: The German-American Encounter in 1950s West Germany* (Chapel Hill, NC, 2003); Heide Fehrenbach, *Race after Hitler: Black Occupation Children in Postwar Germany and America* (Princeton, NJ, 2005); and Monika Mattes, *"Gastarbeiterinnen" in der Bundesrepublik: Anwerbepolitik, Migration und Geschlecht in den 50er bis 70er Jahren* (Frankfurt/M., 2005).
32. See for example Anna C. Korteweg and Gökçe Yurdakul, *The Headscarf Debates: Conflicts of National Belonging* (Stanford, CA, 2014).
33. Christoph Kleßmann, "Der schwierige gesamtdeutsche Umgang mit der DDR-Geschichte," *Aus Politik und Zeitgeschichte* B 30–31 (2001): 3–5.
34. Ibid.

Selected Bibliography

Bessel, Richard, and Ralph Jessen, eds. *Die Grenzen der Diktatur: Staat und Gesellschaft in der SBZ/DDR*. Göttingen, 1996.
Bösch, Frank, ed. *Geteilte Geschichte: Ost- und Westdeutschland 1970–2000*. Göttingen, 2015.
Brunner, Detlev, ed. *Asymmetrisch verflochten? Neue Forschungen zur gesamtdeutschen Nachkriegsgeschichte*. Berlin, 2013.
Crew, David, ed. *Consuming Germany in the Cold War.* Oxford, 2003.
Fulbrook, Mary. *The People's State: East German Society from Hitler to Honecker.* New Haven, CT, 2005.
———. *Power and Society in the GDR, 1961–1979: The "Normalization of Rule"*? New York, 2009.
Fulbrook, Mary, and Andrew I. Port, eds. *Becoming East German: Socialist Structures and Sensibilities after Hitler.* New York, 2013.
Geissler, Rainer. *Die Sozialstruktur Deutschlands: Ein Studienbuch zur sozialstrukturellen Entwicklung im geteilten und vereinten Deutschland*. Opladen, 1992.
Hagemann, Karen, and Sonya Michel, eds. *Gender and the Long Postwar: The United States and the Two Germanys, 1945–1989*. Baltimore, MD, 2014.
Herbert, Ulrich. *Geschichte Deutschlands im 20. Jahrhundert*. Munich, 2014.

Hoffmann, Dierk, and Michael Schwartz, eds. *Sozialstaatlichkeit in der DDR: Sozialpolitische Entwicklungen im Spannungsfeld von Diktatur und Gesellschaft 1945/49–1989*. Munich, 2005.

Jarausch, Konrad H. "Die Teile als Ganzes erkennen: Zur Integration der beiden deutschen Nachkriegsgeschichten." *Zeithistorische Forschungen/Studies in Contemporary History* 1, no. 1 (2004): 10–33.

———. *After Hitler: Recivilizing Germans, 1945–1995*. Oxford, 2006.

———, ed. *Dictatorship as Experience: Towards a Socio-Cultural History of the GDR*. New York, 1999.

Kleßmann, Christoph. *Die Doppelte Staatsgründung: Deutsche Geschichte 1945–1955*. Bonn, 1982.

———. *Zwei Staaten, eine Nation: Deutsche Geschichte 1955–1970*. Göttingen, 1988.

———. "Verflechtung und Abgrenzung: Aspekte der geteilten und zusammengehörigen deutschen Nachkriegsgeschichte." *Aus Politik und Zeitgeschichte*, B 29–30 (1993): 30–41.

———. "Spaltung und Verflechtung: Ein Konzept zur integrierten Nachkriegsgeschichte 1945 bis 1990." In *Teilung und Integration: Die doppelte deutsche Nachgeschichte*, ed. Christoph Kleßmann and Peter Lautzas, 20–37. Bonn, 2005.

Kleßmann, Christoph, Hans Misselwitz, and Günter Wichert, eds. *Deutsche Vergangenheiten—Eine gemeinsame Herausforderung: Der schwierige Umgang mit der doppelten Nachkriegsgeschichte*. Berlin, 1999.

Lindenberger, Thomas, ed. *Herrschaft und Eigen-Sinn in der Diktatur: Studien zur Gesellschaftsgeschichte der DDR*. Berlin, 1999.

Moeller, Robert G., ed. *West Germany under Construction: Politics, Society and Culture in the Adenauer Era*. Ann Arbor, MI, 1997.

Paulus, Julia, et al., eds. *Zeitgeschichte als Geschlechtergeschichte: Neue Perspektiven auf die Bundesrepublik*. Frankfurt/M., 2012.

Pence, Katherine, and Paul Betts, eds. *Socialist Modern: East German Everyday Culture and Politics*. Ann Arbor, MI, 2008.

Schildt, Axel, and Detlef Siegfried, eds. *Between Marx and Coca-Cola: Youth Cultures in Changing European Societies, 1960–1980*. Oxford, 2006.

Schildt, Axel, and Arnold Sywottek, eds. *Modernisierung im Wiederaufbau: Die westdeutsche Gesellschaft der 50er Jahre*. Bonn, 1993.

Schissler, Hanna, ed. *The Miracle Years: A Cultural History of West Germany, 1949–1968*. Princeton, NJ, 2001.

Wehler, Hans-Ulrich. *Deutsche Gesellschaftsgeschichte 1949–1990*. Munich, 2008.

Wengst, Udo, and Hermann Wentker, eds. *Das doppelte Deutschland: 40 Jahre Systemkonkurrenz*. Berlin, 2013.

PART I
GENDERING THE HISTORIOGRAPHY

CHAPTER 1

Entanglements of Gender, Politics, and Protest in the Historiography on the Two Post-1945 Germanys

Karen Hagemann and Donna Harsch

In "Gender: A Useful Category of Historical Analysis," historian Joan W. Scott argued thirty years ago that "gender" has the potential to destabilize conceptions of "politics and power in their most traditionally construed sense."[1] She defined gender as both "a constitutive element of social relationships based on perceived differences between the sexes" and "a primary way of signifying relationships of power."[2] Politics, Scott asserted, is an especially promising field for gender analysis because for centuries "gender has been seen as antithetical to the real business of politics" and "political history—still a dominant mode of historical inquiry—has been a stronghold of resistance to the inclusion of material or even questions about women and gender."[3]

Since the 1980s, feminist scholars have intensively studied gender and politics and demonstrated that, indeed, the usage of the category of gender in political history unleashed intertwined destabilizing effects. First and foremost, the examination of classically defined politics from a gendered perspective has exposed the exclusion of women from the direct exercise of political power in the state, parties, and parliaments. Furthermore, it has unveiled the gendered structure of political power as constituted by an age-old tradition of female exclusion from official political decision-making. With the emergence of the notion of a biologically justified and thus universalized bourgeois gender order in the time of the Enlightenment, the economy, war, and politics were constructed as "male domains" and household and family as "female spheres." Women's exclusion from active political participation made them into objects of men's politics. One important area of policy and legislation was the family, which was perceived as the basis of state and society. Family policies and civil law tried to enforce and protect the dominant ideal of the male-breadwinner/

female-homemaker family and regulated the duties and rights of men and women accordingly.[4]

With such insights, feminist scholarship unmasked the patriarchal interests that have undergirded the discourse and practice of political power. This research has challenged the classical definition of politics as confined, in the modern era, to international relations, the state, constitutions, parliaments, and political parties. Feminist scholars have asked, where were the women in politics? What kind of politics excluded the equal active participation of half of humanity? And which motives led to this exclusion? In order to answer these questions, they have proposed a new definition of politics—one that moves beyond the classic subjects and themes of mainstream political history and includes all areas of politics and policy. From this wider perspective, politics is intertwined with all areas of the economy, society, and culture and cannot be separated from private life, including the family and marriage, gender relations, sexuality, and reproduction. Feminist scholars, in other words, recognized that "the private is political," as did activists of the new women's movement and the gay rights movement that emerged in the late 1960s.[5] In addition, they broadened the understanding of political agency and activism. For them the latter encompasses a broad variety of gendered forms of activism in civil society, including the struggle of women and other disenfranchised social groups for equal rights.[6] In sum, the feminist transformation of the political-historical paradigm redrew the boundaries of politics, deconstructed the gendered meaning and foundations of political power, and challenged questions, approaches, concepts, and results of the dominant, gender-blind mainstream research in political history.

One can see this challenge at work in research on the political history of the two postwar Germanys. Before 1990, with the division of Germany—the geopolitical linchpin of the Cold War—high politics and foreign policy, the age-old kings of historical inquiry, sat atop the scholarly pedestal in mainstream research on the Federal Republic of Germany (FRG) and the German Democratic Republic (GDR). Even as scholars of other time periods and/or regions added the methods of, first, social history, then cultural history and discourse analysis, and finally women's and gender history to their toolbox of historical approaches, political histories of the two Germanys produced in the Cold War era usually ignored women. Oblivious to gender and with no historical concept of masculinity, they focused on systems set up and run by men and on decisions made by men, as if men were the universal subject who suddenly became sexless when exercising political power.[7] Certainly, pioneering research analyzed women's lack of political power in the conventional arenas of politics in both German states.[8] Women scholars also examined women's multiple roles in a more broadly defined political sphere beyond the state, parties, and parliaments, including the new women's movement.⁹ As significant as they were, these works were few and far between, and did not recast the history of Cold War Germany as a gendered history. Since the fall of the wall, with the paradigmatic transformations in the field of the study of the history of East and West Germany and the opening of the archives of the former GDR, the research on both German states and societies has flourished.¹⁰ This spate of historical inquiries has included a continuous increase in the number of studies on the FRG and GDR from multiple perspectives, including gender history.¹¹

In the following, we discuss the development of the research on the entanglement of gender and politics in post-1945 German history by focusing on five major themes: gender and politics in East and West German parties and parliaments; gender, the family, and work in East and West German policies; gender, health policy, and the control of the female body; gendered activism in West Germany; and gendered resistance, protest, and opposition in East Germany.

Gender and Politics in East and West German Parties and Parliaments

Beginning in the late 1950s, female scholars published a small number of studies on women in the political systems of the FRG and GDR. These studies focused on the representation of women in the state apparatus, parties, and the parliament and were informed by the Cold War paradigm that confronted the dictatorial communist system in the East with the democratic liberal system in the West.¹² Since the 1980s, however, works by women and gender historians have increasingly overcome the Cold War polarization and noted that, in fact, women were underrepresented in both political systems. In a review of this research, sociologist Ute Gerhard pointed to the "astonishing similarities" in the political and social situation of East and West German women.¹³

Strikingly comparable, for example, was the slow integration of women into political parties, parliaments, and social organizations. In the GDR, the percentage of female representatives in the People's Chamber (Volkskammer), the unicameral legislature of the GDR, fluctuated between 32 and 44 percent, a relatively high proportion that reflected the lack of real legislative power held by the Volkskammer. Women were heavily underrepresented in powerful institutions and leading positions in the GDR. They constituted about 24 percent of the membership of the ruling Socialist Unity Party of Germany (Sozialistische Einheitspartei Deutschlands, SED) in the early 1950s. In the 1980s, the percentage had increased to 35, but they only made up about 13 percent of the Central

Committee (Zentralkommitee, ZK).[14] No woman ever became one of the fifteen first secretaries of the SED, a much more powerful position than basic membership in the ZK, or a full/voting member of the Politburo of the ZK, the GDR's most powerful political body; only four were ever "candidate" members of the Politburo. From 1949 to 1989, only two women served as a minister in the central government, and only one held a position in the Council of Ministers of the GDR (Ministerrat der DDR). Only one woman ever served as chairperson of one of the fifteen district councils (*Räte der Bezirke*), one of the most powerful positions in state administration. In social organizations, the percentage of female members was usually higher than in political ones. In the Free German Trade Union Federation (Freier Deutscher Gewerkschaftsbund, FDGB), it came close to 50 percent in the 1980s, but here too the leadership was firmly in male hands.[15] The only exception was, not surprisingly, the leadership of the Democratic Women's League of Germany (Demokratischer Frauenbund Deutschlands, DFD). Founded in East Berlin in March 1947 for all of Germany and divided in 1949, the DFD's membership was very large throughout the life of the GDR, reaching some 1.5 million women in the 1980s, but the DFD enjoyed little political influence.[16]

In the FRG, women comprised from 6 to 10 percent of members of the Bundestag, the federal parliament, between 1949 and 1983. This percentage was similar to that of the Weimar Republic's parliamentary body, the Reichstag. With the rise of the new women's movement and of female membership in political parties since the 1960s, the demands for higher female representation in parliament grew in the major parties: the conservative Christian Democratic Union of Germany (Christlich Demokratische Union Deutschlands, CDU), its Bavarian sister party the Christian Social Union (Christlich-Soziale Union, CSU), the liberal Free Democratic Party (Freie Demokratische Partei, FDP), and the Social Democratic Party of Germany (Sozialdemokratische Partei Deutschlands, SPD). Especially notable was the expanding female membership in the SPD and CDU. Between 1962 and 1985 their percentage rose from 19 to 25 percent in the SPD and from 15 to 22 percent in the CDU.[17] After the election of 1986, the proportion of women in the Bundestag also leapt to 15 percent and in 1994 to 26 percent. Although this share of seats was still relatively low, globally Germany belonged to the ten countries with the highest proportion of women in their national parliament in the 1990s.[18] Until 1961 no woman had served as a cabinet minister in the federal government, whereas in the 1960s and 1970s there was always one female minister, in the 1980s and 1990s there were two.[19] As in the GDR, women's participation in West German social organizations was more developed than in political parties and the state. They joined the German Trade Union Confederation (Deutscher Gewerkschaftsbund,

DGB), where the level of female membership hovered around 30 percent in the late 1980s, and were active in the many women's associations founded after 1945. One of them was DFD West, which was banned as a "communist organization" in 1957, one year after the ban of the Communist Party of Germany (Kommunistische Partei Deutschlands, KPD).[20]

Clearly, the marginalization of women within the mainstream political institutions and organizations of the GDR and FRG was strikingly similar; in both states social activism of women found its place outside of the parliamentary system. Yet, even as the number of excellent publications on the gender of politics in East or West rises, comparative studies remain rare.[21] Remarkably, many scholars of contemporary German history still ignore all the new research on women in political parties, unions, and civic organizations after 1945.[22] It seems as if historians and political scientists take women's lack of power as the baseline of all political systems and, thus, unworthy of study. An additional factor presumably dampened interest in the gender of politics in postwar Germany. During the Cold War and through the first half of the 1990s, the scholarly bias leaned toward emphasizing contrast in the political functioning and ideology of the democratic West and the dictatorial East. Few students of politics or ideology adopted theoretical perspectives such as gender analysis that highlight resemblance or intersection between patriarchal political systems in both German states.

To move beyond the sheer fact of women's exclusion from political power and to challenge scholarly silence about the gender of politics, women's and gender historians have since the 1990s turned to social and cultural history and, in effect, introduced women and gender relations into the political framework through the side door of social policy or back door of political and social struggle. The historical reconstruction of society, culture, and popular protest is, of course, not new to historiography but came relatively late to the study of postwar Germany, in part because of the fixation on its political division. With this move in contemporary German history, scholars have explored an ever-growing array of topics. This work has contributed to an emerging history of Cold War Germany that is more realistic and interesting than the static story of democracy and economic success contrasted with socialist dictatorship and economic disaster or, alternatively, socialism and equality contrasted with capitalism and inequality.[23]

Since the 1990s, both scholars and the public have hotly debated the nature of the relationship between the party and the people or, in academic parlance, between state and society under communism. Especially motivated to understand this relationship were scholars who rejected the long-popular totalitarian theory of absolute top-down control of everything in the GDR (and other communist countries). Arguing that the

GDR did have a society that was, if not independent, still ineffectively controlled by the party/state, they put forward a theory of the "limits of dictatorship" and looked for archival evidence of social agency, *Eigensinn* (stubbornness), in the everyday life and individual and group resistance within the repressive confines of single-party hegemony.[24] This new research on the GDR inspired, as well, a fresh look at the history of the FRG and its evolving relations between state and civil society.

To write what historian Sandrine Kott calls a "social history of politics,"[25] historians have taken up all the tools of the "new history," including history from below, *Alltagsgeschichte* (history of everyday life), gay history, and the history of sexuality, and applied the methods of gender, cultural, and/or discourse analysis. Although sometimes accused of eliding or even avoiding politics, most practitioners of social and cultural history investigate the connections between social relations and public policy, private lives and political structures, and everyday resistance and political change in the history of both German states. The study of private lives has turned up evidence of indifference, nonconformity, self-fashioning, recalcitrance, and resistance by women and men to cultural norms, official discourse, and legal prohibitions regarding the body, sexuality, pornography, marriage, the family, religion, paid work and housework, private consumption, and the home in both East and West Germany from the late 1940s onward.[26] Research on income inequality, social hierarchy, and education has connected societal outcomes in both states to political decision-making.[27] Not all of this work has been driven by a gendered perspective, but its focus on society and culture has brought gendered behaviors and attitudes to the fore and highlighted their entanglement with state policy and political norms.[28]

Gender, the Family, and Work in East and West German Policies

Obsessed though they were with antithesis, political historians of the Cold War era ignored two important fields of politics that contemporaries used to mark differences between the FRG and the GDR: gender ideology and family and labor policy.[29] Both states (and their constitutions) insisted on their commitment to women's equality, but they disagreed about what constituted equality. Following the principles of socialist emancipation theory, the GDR propagated an approach to "women's emancipation" that championed women's equal right to participate in paid work as the path to female autonomy and integration into society and politics. For its part, the FRG touted women's freedom not to work and, instead, to nurture their children at home. The different notions of modern womanhood and the related family ideals—the dual-earner family in the East and the male-breadwinner/female-homemaker family in the West—influenced the respective family, welfare, and education policies. They led, for example, to an all-day system of childcare and schooling in the East, which encouraged mothers to take up full-time paid work, and a half-day system in the West, which deliberately prevented them from doing this.[30] The gender ideals also shaped health, housing, labor, and other social and welfare policies. Feminist scholars have exposed the centrality of gender to Cold War competitive discourse about democracy and socialism. Recently, comparative studies have uncovered the countless and constant gendered references and tropes in the rhetoric of political legitimation of "our" side and delegitimation of the "other" side.[31]

One of the first studies to disclose the centrality of gender ideology as a marker of differences that informed family and labor policies was Robert G. Moeller's groundbreaking 1993 book *Protecting Motherhood: Women and the Family in the Politics of Postwar West Germany*.[32] In its wake came studies of one of the two German states, as well as comparative works on family and social policy, which traced similarities and differences in West and East German policies and the ways in which hyperawareness of the other Germany affected decision-making—in some cases leading to ideologically motivated rejection of the alternative but in others to pragmatic adaptation.[33] German-German entanglement, they showed, was conditioned not only by Cold War rivalry but also by their shared past. They revealed the ways in which Nazi policies regarding, for example, women and employment had carved a path that was often difficult to leave. They also emphasized path dependency reaching back to the Wilhelmine Empire and Weimar Germany.

Cold War rivalry in East and West Germany, like the competition between the US and USSR, was informed by claims of each system's superiority. Politicians and media placed gender and the family in the center of such claims. Male and female roles, women's rights, family law, marriage and divorce law, maternal employment, the nurturing of children, and the quantity and quality of household consumption were key sites of contestation over the degrees of freedom and security provided by one political system relative to the other.[34] The understanding of "appropriate" gender relations reflected the contrasting gender ideologies. Touting the FRG's support of the family, West German commentators attacked GDR policies that allegedly undermined marriage, children's welfare, and domestic privacy. Celebrating the GDR's commitment to women's independence, East German publicists criticized FRG protection of paternal privilege over single mothers, wives, and children. No matter its content, however, gender ideology was central to discourse about political evil and good in divided Germany.

In this volume, two chapters focus on the contested subject of work and family. Leonie Treber's contribution, "The Big Cleanup: Men, Women, and the Rubble Clearance in Postwar East and West Germany," concentrates on the first postwar years and their importance to the construction of the gendered collective memory in East and West. Treber demonstrates the influence of the dichotomous gender ideology in both Germanys on economic policy and employment after 1945. She deconstructs the "myth of the rubble woman" (*Trümmerfrau*) as a central figure in the postwar cleanup of massive rubble piles in bombed German cities. Only in Berlin and the Soviet zone of occupation, however, did women play a significant role in the postwar clearing of the rubble. Their participation in the three Western zones was low for several reasons, including the shared belief of American, French, and British occupation powers as well as West German male administrators that rubblework was not for women. In the East, meanwhile, the print media turned a practical need for women laborers into a political symbol of women's equality and commitment to building a democratic Germany. The story of the idealistic female rubble worker persisted throughout the history of the GDR. In the FRG, the myth of the rubble women arose only in the 1980s as West German politicians and society looked for an icon of women's contributions to the reconstruction of postwar Germany. Treber's chapter thus illustrates change and continuity in gendered discourse about rubblework as Western rhetoric converged with the Eastern message.[35]

Alexandria Ruble's chapter, "Children, Church, and Rights: East and West German Protests against Family Law Reforms in the 1950s," explores debate and protest surrounding plans to reform marriage and family law in East and West Germany after 1949.[36] Both states sought to change the patriarchal Civil Code (*Bürgerliches Gesetzbuch*, BGB) that dated back to 1900. In the East, the SED aimed to replace the BGB with a more egalitarian socialist Family Code (*Familiengesetzbuch*, FGB) that supported the dual-earner family model. In the West, only the SPD and FDP, supported by many women's organizations, demanded reform of the BGB to achieve greater gender equality in family and marriage. The Christian-conservative parties and the Catholic and Protestant Churches wanted to reify the old male-breadwinner model in marriage and family, and opposed any far-reaching reform of the BGB in both German states. The debates in the FRG and GDR were at the same time shaped by the tug-of-war between the two Germanys for hegemony. East and West German politicians relied on contrasts to the other Germany to support their arguments for and against the new family laws. The GDR finally implemented its new FGB in 1965. The FRG proceeded in two steps. The Equal Rights Act (*Gesetz über die Gleichberechtigung von Mann und Frau auf dem Gebiet des bürgerlichen Rechts*) of 1957 repealed the so-called

Stichentscheid in the BGB, which gave the husband the final decision in all marriage and family matters. The First Law for the Reform of the Marriage and Family (*Erstes Gesetz zur Reform des Ehe- und Familienrechts*) of 1976 ended the legal norm of the "housewife marriage."[37] As in other Western countries, women won legal equality in marriage and family, i.e. "civil citizenship," decades after their access to equal political-citizenship rights, which proves the importance of civil laws for the maintaining of a patriarchal social order.[38]

One intentional result of the family policies pursued by the two German states was the extreme difference in the female employment rate, especially among mothers. In 1964, the proportion of employed women among all women of working age (15–65 years) was already 69 percent in the GDR, but only 50 percent in the FRG. In the GDR, it increased to 78 percent by 1989 and in the FRG to only 56 percent, one of the lowest rates in Western Europe.[39] In addition, as the chapter by Treber shows, the GDR tried much earlier than the FRG to facilitate female work in sectors of its economy and professions that were traditionally perceived as "male," and encouraged young women to pursue professional training or a degree in subjects traditionally chosen only by men, such as engineering. Although the SED touted this policy as evidence of the equalizing effects of its socialist gender ideology, two of its major motivations were pragmatic: the greater "surplus" of women in the postwar population of the GDR than the FRG, and East Germany's dramatic and increasing labor shortage.[40] A paradigmatic shift in the FRG's official family and labor policy occurred only slowly. The first step toward a modernized family ideal was made in the 1960s when the model of the male breadwinner and female homemaker and part-time earner took hold. This model dominated state policies in the West until the first decade of the twenty-first century.[41]

Gender, Health Policy, and Control of the Female Body

Women and gender historians have also shown the impact of gender images on policies related to health, the female body, and reproduction. Most of the relevant laws and institutions in both the FRG and GDR originated in the Weimar Republic or even the Wilhelmine Empire. Only in the GDR can we observe a partial break with these traditions, as demonstrated in the chapter by Donna Harsch on "Gendering Health Politics: East and West German Healthcare Systems in Comparison, 1950–70." She discusses the parallels between East and West German policies toward contagious and chronic diseases that were conditioned both by long-standing medical norms and by the epidemics of the immediate postwar period.

Depending on the disease, biases about femininity and masculinity came more or less to the fore—very much in the cases of venereal disease and heart disease, less so when confronting tuberculosis or cancer. One major contrast in health policy was the GDR's strong and the FRG's weak emphasis on preventive care, which was most pronounced in policies related to women's reproductive health, including reproductive cancers and, above all, pregnancy and childbirth. From the late 1960s on, though, the FRG increasingly adopted the East German orientation toward preventive healthcare. Rising concern about the health of women (and infants) motivated this shift in the West German healthcare system, just as it had always undergirded the GDR's consistent focus on prevention.[42]

Other important areas in which the policy of both German states pursued a pronatalist policy were birth control and abortion. The latter is an especially underexplored subject of research for the two post-1945 Germanys. Passed in 1871, Paragraphs 218 and 219 of the German Penal Code (*Reichsstrafgesetzbuch*, StGB) banned every form of abortion by a woman, any type of assistance in obtaining an abortion, and any advertising of it.[43] Women who aborted their pregnancy faced punishment of six months to five years imprisonment. After 1926, medically indicated and approved abortions were allowed. A growing nonpartisan and extraparliamentary movement of liberals, social democrats, socialists and communists, men and women, and experts and laymen fought for the legalization of abortion and birth control in Weimar Germany. Even with millions of supporters, the effort did not succeed.[44] In 1933, the Nazis legalized abortion for "racial hygiene" reasons to prevent "hereditary diseases." After 1945, except for two years of partial legalization in some regions of the Soviet zone of occupation, the pre-1933 version of Paragraphs 218 and 219 was revalidated in both German states.[45] In 1965, the GDR eased the ban and allowed some socially indicated abortions. Only in 1972 did the GDR change the law and legalize abortion in the first trimester of a pregnancy (a policy known as the *Fristenregelung*). GDR health services began to provide birth control, including contraceptive pills, free of charge.[46] In the FRG, the new women's movement took up the struggle for abortion reform with great vigor. In the same year that the GDR legalized abortion, political pressure from women's organizations reached a crescendo. In response, the SPD/FDP-controlled Bundestag implemented a *Fristenregelung* too, but in 1975 the Federal Constitutional Court (Bundesverfassungsgericht) declared this regulation unconstitutional. Subsequently, the social-liberal government introduced a law that allowed abortion only for a limited number of circumstances, including "eugenic," "medical," and "social" reasons (*Indikationsregelung*). Thus, the feminist struggle for the right of women to control their own body succeeded, although only in a limited way.[47]

Gendered Activism in West Germany

The reform of Paragraphs 218 and 219 was one important aim of the new women's movement in West Germany in the early 1970s. This movement emerged in the context of the extraparliamentary opposition (*Außerparlamentarische Opposition,* APO), especially the student movement, in the late 1960s. Feminist research on the new movement started in the 1980s and radically changed and extended the understanding of politics in academia and civil society. Most of the early works focused on autonomous feminism, but in the last two decades this narrow construction of feminism has been increasingly challenged.[48] The chapters in this volume on women's activism in the FRG, too, revise the conventional interpretation of this movement, broaden our view of its origins and composition, and/or explore a neglected aspect of the movement.

In "Finding Feminism: Rethinking Activism in the West German New Women's Movement of the 1970s and 1980s," Sarah Summers argues that the feminist movement was not coterminous with the ideology and separatist organization of autonomous feminism. A broad movement with various programmatic strands and strategies that sprang from a variety of sources and organizations, the feminist movement included women's associations with roots in the postwar years and even the Weimar Republic, female trade-union officials, and women in the major political parties (the CDU, SPD, and FDP). Working within as well as outside male-dominated organizations such as unions, parties, and the press, progressive women called for reform of family and social policy and employment equality. Furthermore, Summers, like other authors in this volume, argues that the competitive context of the Cold War shaped West German insistence on a gender division of labor in which the husband/father earned wages and the wife/mother stayed home.

In "Redefining the Political: The Gender of Activism in Grassroots Movements of the 1960s to 1980s," Belinda Davis explores the entanglement between the extraparliamentary opposition and its female members who presented an increasingly vocal and ever more radical challenge to its male leaders and their doctrinaire theories about revolution and social change. She traces women's bumpy path toward self-representation within the APO and the ways in which women learned from their own mistakes and, in the process, created a new kind of radical feminist politics that criticized the silencing of individual women by patriarchal society, male left-wing leaders, and even other feminists who presumed to speak for "women."[49]

Tiffany Florvil's chapter, "Connected Differences: Black German Feminists and Their Transnational Connections in the 1980s and 1990s," looks at the feminist movement from yet another angle of investigation. She traces the emergence of the organization Afro-German Women (Afrodeutsche Frauen, ADEFRA), which, she argues, stimulated Black German consciousness and activism by encouraging heterosexual and lesbian Women of Color to form a community to help them break out of social isolation and insist on their equal citizenship with white Germans and with men. She credits the Caribbean-American poet Audre Lorde with inspiring the formation of ADEFRA and with encouraging Afro-German women to see themselves as part of transnational feminism and as active in the politics of the African diaspora. ADEFRA was self-consciously international but also intent on forming ties to other women's groups in Germany.[50]

All three chapters call for more research on the West German feminist movement broadly defined to include women from different social, political, racial, and ethnic backgrounds.[51] The chapters by Summers, Davis, and Florvil in part three, but also the chapters on gender relations and sexuality by Jane Freeland, Clayton Whisnant, and Friederike Brühöfener in part four, demonstrate that future research needs to combine the study of feminism with the exploration of other movements like the student, peace, gay and lesbian rights, and environmental movements, as well as with women's engagement in mainstream political parties, trade unions, other organizations, and the media. Feminist activists were often involved in civil society far beyond the women's movement. They brought their knowledge and experiences in this movement to other spaces of their civic and political engagement.[52]

A theme highlighted especially in the chapters by Ruble and Summers is the long tradition of the new women's movement—often overlooked in studies of both post-1945 Germanys.[53] Scholars ignored both the history of women's activism from the mid-1940s to the late 1960s and the influence of the women's movement of the Weimar Republic on this post-1945 activism. Many of the women who founded women's associations and groups after 1945 had gained their first political experiences in the 1920s and 1930s. They carried into both postwar states the traditions of the strong and politically diverse German women's movement that the Nazis had crushed.[54] Weimar-era conflicts between Christian-conservative, liberal, social democratic, and communist women resurfaced after 1945 inside each state and across the Iron Curtain. In the context of the Cold War, three dominant dividing lines emerged in arguments among feminists. In both German states, Christian-conservative women disagreed with social democratic and communist women about women's right to employment, their social rights as workers and working mothers, and their right to control their own body. In the FRG, burgeoning anticommunism forced female SPD members to constantly distance themselves from women who sympathized with the KPD and its women's policy, even if they shared similar aims. The Cold War did not leave any space in West Germany for a strong leftist women's movement. In the GDR, former SPD and KPD women inside and outside the SED fought over the relationship of the women's movement to the socialist state and the interpretation of gender quality.

Resistance, Protest, and Opposition in East Germany

The history of resistance, protest, and opposition against the GDR regime has been unevenly studied. The intense repression of the early years by the SED and Soviet occupiers of the political opposition, especially by former Social Democrats as well as members of the CDU and the Liberal Democratic Party of Germany (Liberal-Demokratische Partei Deutschlands, LDPD) in the East, is well researched.[55] The uprising of June 1953 that started with a strike by East Berlin construction workers and turned into a widespread revolt against the GDR government has generated much interest for decades.[56] Also well covered are the peace and environmental movements of the 1980s in which pastors and members of the Protestant Church played a crucial role.[57] Less explored is church opposition to GDR policy in the 1950s. As Alexandria Ruble demonstrates in her chapter, both churches tried to use their influence on the East German population to shape SED policy, especially the reform of family law aimed at gender equality. In the early 1950s, some 92 percent of the population belonged to a church; 80 percent were Protestants and 12 percent Catholics.[58]

Even less attention has been paid to Christian women's resistance to SED policies. Yet such resistance was significant not only toward the end of the GDR, with the well-known opposition emanating from Protestant parishes, but also at its beginning. Kathryn Julian's chapter, "Under the Habit: Resistance of Catholic Sisters against East German State Authority in the 1950s," makes an important contribution to this unexplored topic by reconstructing a successful case of women's resistance to religious policy of the political elite in the GDR. The 1950s were the period of the most unyielding religious repression in the GDR. Yet, as Julian shows, Catholic nuns, neglected in studies of East German religious history, exercised remarkable agency in their interactions with the SED. They successfully protected their cloister, its charitable activities, and its property rights from state efforts to restrict its autonomy and end its good works. The chapter explores how and why apparently weak female orders were more effective than male religious leaders in their challenges to these plans. Ironically, the nuns and sisters benefited from gendered assumptions about the relative harmlessness of women's orders, while emphasizing their active contribution to social welfare. They exploited ties to their order in West

Germany to publicize their cause and, thus, turned Cold War rivalries over women and religion to their advantage.

East German nuns' resistance in the 1950s was surprisingly effective, although it could not be presented publicly, much less as a political challenge to the SED or socialism. A public and organized women's protest movement that aimed, self-consciously, at the destabilization of the whole political system did not emerge in postwar Germany until the 1960s and only in the FRG, with its constitutional protections of speech and assembly. As Summers, Davis, and Florvil show, this movement challenged women's exclusion from politics—whether from the leadership of political parties and organizations or the leadership of the extraparliamentary opposition movements. Feminist activists demanded reproductive rights, an end to patriarchal privilege in family and marriage, childcare provision, equal wages, and so forth. Although this activist destabilization of traditional politics occurred only in the West, there are signs of entanglement between the student movement in the FRG and politics in the GDR: the SED moved to rein in a rebellious youth culture in the 1960s and, arguably, legalized first-trimester abortion partly to showcase the GDR's reproductive rights as the feminist movement called for abortion reform in the FRG.[59] Furthermore, the new feminist movement in the West inspired not only independent feminist activism in the last years of the GDR but also the engagement of these feminists in the antistate opposition of the East German peace and environmental movement.[60]

Conclusion

This overview of the development of the research on the entanglements of gender and politics in post-1945 German history demonstrates that although women were excluded from political power in the Cold War era, they were both a major object of state policies and a major subject of efforts to bring excluded groups into politics as policy makers. Gendered assumptions about family, work, and consumption as well as health, welfare, and education infused Cold War ideology about the alleged superiority of one system over the other. Cold War competition often intensified the gendering of political decision-making, typically but not always reinforcing the ideology of the dominant political constellation rather than fostering pragmatism or accommodation. Two examples in this volume demonstrate this: In the Western zones of occupation, fixed ideas about the gender of work trumped the need for laborers to clear the rubble. In dealing with Catholic nuns who challenged specific antireligious measures, the SED accommodated the cloisters, in part because they were *women's* religious organizations.

From the late 1960s onward, in the European context of a policy of détente (*Entspannungspolitik*) with the East, the gendered rhetoric and policies of West Germany became more adaptive and less driven by the Cold War imperative to distinguish itself along gendered lines of comparison. One reason for this change was surely a shift of power in the federal government of the FRG. The conservative coalition of CDU/CSU and FDP was replaced first by the Grand Coalition of CDU/CSU and SPD (1966–69) and later by the social-liberal coalition of SPD and FDP (1969–82). This changing political landscape in the FRG informed not only international relations and the German East-West politics but also gendered rhetoric and policies.

Almost certainly the relationship between the two German states was overdetermined. In the 1950s, the GDR showed much more interest in West German policies and outcomes than vice versa. The imbalance in attention did not signify West German indifference but a feeling of superiority and disdain for developments in "the Zone." In the context of generational transition around 1960, this attitude started to change. The younger generation was more willing to consider the value of some East German policies, for example in the health sector and child welfare. Convergence was also furthered by the organized public activism of West German women. From the late 1960s through the 1990s, these women fought for a wide variety of social and political reforms, radically challenged the private and public silencing of women, and reminded West German women and men that theirs was, in fact, a multiracial and multiethnic society. With these actions and arguments, women pushed and, arguably, tore open the envelope of "politics" by fighting for an ever-greater expansion of the right to a place of power on the political stage and, thus, an expansion of the stage itself to include the parliamentary hall, the extraparliamentary street, and even the feminist room.

Karen Hagemann is the James G. Kenan Distinguished Professor of History at the University of North Carolina at Chapel Hill. She has published widely in Modern German and European history, combining the fields of the social, political, cultural, military and gender history. Her recent English books relevant for the theme of the volume include: *Gendering Modern German History: Rewriting Historiography* (ed. with Jean H. Quataert, Berghahn Books, 2007/2010, in German 2008); *Children, Families and States: Time Policies of Child Care, Preschool and Primary Schooling in Europe* (ed. with Konrad H. Jarausch and Cristina Allemann-Ghionda, Berghahn Books, 2011, in German 2015); *Gender and the long Postwar: Reconsiderations of the United States and the Two Germanys, 1945–1989* (ed. with Sonya Michel, Johns Hopkins University Press, 2014); *Oxford Handbook on Gender, War and the Western World since 1600* (ed. with Stefan Dudink and Sonya o. Rose, Oxford University

Press, 2018) and started a new monograph entitled *Forgotten Soldiers: Gender, the Military and War in European History, 1600-2000*. She has started the work on a new monograph titled *Forgotten Soldiers: Women, the Military, and War*.

Donna Harsch is professor of history at Carnegie Mellon University, Pittsburgh. She is a social and political historian of twentieth-century Germany. Her recent publications include: *Revenge of the Domestic: Women, the Family, and Communism in the German Democratic Republic* (Princeton University Press, 2007); and "Women in Communist Societies," in *The Oxford Handbook of the History of Communism* (ed. by S. A. Smith, Oxford University Press, 2013). Currently she is researching the history of health and medicine in the Cold War Germanys. She is working on a book-length comparative study of infant mortality and efforts to reduce it in the German Democratic Republic and Federal Republic of Germany from 1945 to 1990.

Notes

1. Joan W. Scott, "Gender: A Useful Category of Historical Analysis," in *American Historical Review* 98, no. 4 (1986): 1070, and *Gender and the Politics of History* (New York, 1999); for a recent critical reassessment, see AHR Forum: Revisiting "Gender: A Useful Category of Historical Analysis," *American Historical Review* 113, no. 5 (2008): 1344–430, esp. Joan W. Scott, "Unanswered Questions," 1422–30.
2. Scott, "Gender," 1067.
3. Ibid., 1070.
4. An overview of the development of the interdisciplinary debate and state of research provides, Georgina Waylen et al., eds., *The Oxford Handbook of Gender and Politics* (Oxford, 2013); and with a focus on civil society, Karen Hagemann et al., eds., *Civil Society and Gender Justice: Historical and Comparative Perspectives* (New York, 2008).
5. See Waylen et al., eds., *Oxford Handbook*; for an overview of the gendered research in the field of German political history, see Thomas Kühne, "Staatspolitik, Frauenpolitik, Männerpolitik: Politikgeschichte als Geschlechtergeschichte," in *Geschlechtergeschichte und Allgemeine Geschichte: Herausforderungen und Perspektiven*, ed. Hans Medick and Anne-Charlott Trepp (Göttingen, 1998), 171–232; Belinda Davis, "The Personal Is Political: Gender, Politics, and Political Activism in Modern German History," in *Gendering Modern German History: Rewriting Historiography*, ed. Karen Hagemann and Jean H. Quataert (New York, 2007), 107–27; and Robert G. Moeller, "The Elephant in the Living Room or Why the History of Twentieth-Century Germany Should Be a Family Affair," in ibid., 228–49.
6. See Davis, "Personal Is Political"; and Hagemann et al., eds., *Civil Society*.
7. For a critique of the conventional "*Politikgeschichte*," see Ute Frevert, "Neue Politikgeschichte: Konzepte und Herausforderungen," in *Neue Politikgeschichte: Perspektiven Einer historischen Politikforschung*, ed. Ute Frevert and Heinz Gerhard

Haupt (Frankfurt/M., 2005), 7–26; and Heinz Gerhard Haupt, "Historische Politikforschung, Praxis und Problem," in ibid., 304–13. One example for a "modernized" approach to the old *Politikgeschichte* of post-1945 German history is Eckart Conze, "Sicherheit als Kultur: Überlegungen zu einer 'modernen Politikgeschichte' der Bundesrepublik Deutschland," *Vierteljahrshefte für Zeitgeschichte* 53, no. 3 (2005): 357–80.

8. See Gabriele Bremme, *Die Politische Rolle Der Frau in Deutschland: Eine Untersuchung über den Einfluß der Frauen bei Wahlen und ihre Teilnahme in Partei und Parlament* (Göttingen, 1956); Mechthild Fülles, *Frauen in Partei und Parlament* (Cologne, 1969); Gabrielle Gast, *Die politische Rolle der Frau in der DDR* (Cologne, 1974); and Gisela Helwig, *Frau und Familie in beiden deutschen Staaten* (Cologne, 1982).

9. Florence Hervé, ed., *Geschichte der deutschen Frauenbewegung* (Cologne, 1982); Gaby Swiderski, *Die westdeutsche Frauenfriedensbewegung in den 50er Jahren* (Hamburg, 1983); Gesine Obertreis, *Familienpolitik in der DDR 1945–1980* (Opladen, 1986); Beate Hoecker, *Frauen in der Politik: Eine soziologische Studie* (Opladen 1987); Eva Kolinsky, *Women in West Germany: Life, Work and Politics* (Oxford, 1989); Ute Gerhard, "Westdeutsche Frauenbewegung: Zwischen Autonomie und dem Recht auf Gleichheit," *Feministische Studien* 10, no. 2 (1992): 35–55; Dorothy Rosenberg, "Women's Issues, Women's Politics and Women's Studies in the Former German Democratic Republic," *Radical History Review*, no. 54 (1992): 110–26; and Gisela Helwig and Maria Nickel, eds., *Frauen in Deutschland 1945–1992* (Berlin, 1993).

10. See the introduction of this volume on "Gendering Post-1945 German History" by Karen Hagemann, Donna Harsch, and Friederike Brühöfener.

11. For recent overviews of the development of the research, see Julia Paulus et al., eds., *Zeitgeschichte als Geschlechtergeschichte: Neue Perspektiven auf die Bundesrepublik* (Frankfurt/M., 2012); and Karen Hagemann and Sonya Michel, eds., *Gender and the Long Postwar: The United States and the Two Germanys, 1945–1989* (Baltimore, MD, 2014).

12. Especially Bremme, *Die Politische Rolle*; Fülles, *Frauen in Partei*; Gast, *Die politische Rolle*; and Helwig, *Frau und Familie*.

13. Ute Gerhard, "Die Staatlich institutionalisierte 'Lösung' der Frauenfrage: Zur Geschichte der Geschlechterverhältnisse in der DDR," in *Sozialgeschichte der DDR*, ed. Hartmut Kaelble et al. (Stuttgart, 1994), 392–96.

14. Cornelia Hippmann, "Gleichberechtigung in der Politik? Über Karrierechancen und schwierigkeiten ostdeutscher Frauen," *Gender . . . Politik . . . Online* (November 2012): 4, at: www.fu-berlin.de/sites/gpo/pol_sys/partiziption/Gleichberechtigung_in_der_Politik/hippmann-Politikerinnen-Ost.pdf (19 August 2017); and Andrea Malycha and Peter Jochen Winters, *Die SED: Geschichte einer Partei* (Munich, 2009), 414.

15. Anne Hample, "'Arbeite mit, plane mit, regiere mit': Zur politischen Partizipation von Frauen in der DDR," in Helwig and Nickel, *Frauen in Deutschland*, 281–320; later also, Donna Harsch, "Approach / Avoidance: Communists and Women in East Germany, 1945–9," *Social History* 25, no. 2 (2000): 156–82, and *Revenge of the Domestic: Women, the Family, and Communism in the German Democratic Republic* (Princeton, NJ, 2007), 61–86 and 243–45; Maria-Barbara Watson-Franke, "Germany, 1949–1990 (German Democratic Republic [GDR])," in *Women's Studies Encyclopedia*, ed. Helen Tierney (Westport, CT, 1999), vol. G–P: 590–92;

and Susanne Kranz, "Women's Role in the German Democratic Republic and the State's Policy towards Women," *Journal of International Women's Studies* 7, no. 1 (1005): 69–83.

16. Grit Bühler, *Mythos Gleichberechtigung in der DDR: Politische Partizipation von Frauen am Beispiel des Demokratischen Frauenbunds Deutschland* (Frankfurt/M., 1997).

17. Oskar Niedermeyer, "Die soziale Zusammensetzung der Parteimitgliederschaften," *Bundeszentrale für politische Bildung*, 12 July 2017, www.bpb.de/politik/grundfragen/parteien-in-deutschland/zahlen-und-fakten/140358/soziale-zusammensetzung (accessed 7 August 2017).

18. See "Women in National Parliaments," Inter-parliamentary Union, www.ipu.org/wmn-e/arc/classif251297.htm (accessed 7 August 2017).

19. Waltraud Cornelissen, "Politische Partizipation von Frauen in der alten Bundesrepublik und im vereinten Deutschland," in Helwig and Nickel, *Frauen in Deutschland*, 321–50; and Beate Hoecker, "50 Jahre Frauen in der Politik: Späte Erfolge, aber nicht am Ziel," *Aus Politik und Zeitgeschichte* B 24–25 (2008): 10–18.

20. Tom Burghause, "Die 'Mitgliederkrise im Deutschen Gewerkschaftsbund" (master's thesis, Universität Trier), 80; see also Renate Wiggershaus, *Geschichte der Frauen und der Frauenbewegung in der Bundesrepublik Deutschland und in der DDR nach 1945* (Wuppertal, 1979), 23–154.

21. See for example Barbara Böttger, *Das Recht auf Gleichheit und Differenz: Elisabeth Selbert und der Kampf der Frauen um Artikel 2.3 des Grundgesetzes* (Münster, 1990); Heike Trappe, *Emanzipation oder Zwang? Frauen in der DDR 1945–1980* (Berlin, 1995); Bühler, *Mythos Gleichberechtigung*; Heide-Marie Lauterer, *Parlamentarierinnen in Deutschland 1918/19–1949* (Sulzbach/Ts., 2002); Gisela Notz, *Frauen in der Mannschaft: Sozialdemokratinnen im Parlamentarischen Rat und im Deutschen Bundestag 1948/49 bis 1957* (Bonn, 2003), and *Mehr als bunte Tupfen im Bonner Männerclub: Sozialdemokratinnen im Deutschen Bundestag 1957–1969* (Bonn, 2007); Petra Holz, *Zwischen Tradition und Emanzipation: CDU-Politikerinnen in der Zeit von 1946 bis 1960* (Sulzbach/Ts., 2004); Marianne Zepp, *Redefining Germany: Reeducation, Staatsbürgerschaft und Frauenpolitik im US-amerikanisch besetzten Nachkriegsdeutschland* (Göttingen, 2007); Sarah Elise Wiliarty, *The CDU and the Politics of Gender in Germany: Bringing Women to the Party* (New York, 2010); and Sylvia Heinemann, *Frauenfragen sind Menschheitsfragen: Die Frauenpolitik der Freien Demokratinnen von 1945 bis 1963* (Sulzbach/Ts., 2012). See for comparative mainstream studies Peter Bender, *Deutschlands Wiederkehr: Eine ungeteilte Nachkriegsgeschichte 1945–1990* (Stuttgart, 2007); Konrad H. Jarausch, *After Hitler: Recivilizing Germans, 1945–1995* (Oxford, 2006); and Frank Bösch, ed., *Geteilte Geschichte: Ost- und Westdeutschland 1970–2000* (Göttingen, 2015).

22. Volumes that include at least one or two chapters on women/gender are: Richard Bessel and Ralph Jessen, eds., *Die Grenzen der Diktatur: Staat und Gesellschaft in der SBZ/DDR* (Göttingen, 1996); Thomas Lindenberger, ed., *Herrschaft und Eigen-Sinn in der Diktatur: Studien zur Gesellschaftsgeschichte der DDR* (Berlin, 1999); Mary Fulbrook, *The People's State: East German Society from Hitler to Honecker* (New Haven, CT, 2005), and Mary Fulbrook, ed., *Power and Society in the GDR, 1961–1979: The "Normalization of Rule"?* (New York, 2009); and Hans-Ulrich Wehler, *Deutsche Gesellschaftsgeschichte, Bundesrepubilk und DDR 1949–1990* (Munich, 2008). Gender is included systematically in Jeannette Madarász-Lebenhagen, *Conflict and Compromise in East Germany, 1971–1989* (New York, 2003).

23. See for example Robert G. Moeller, ed., *West Germany under Construction: Politics, Society and Culture in the Adenauer Era* (Ann Arbor, MI, 1997); Konrad H. Jarausch, ed., *Dictatorship as Experience: Towards a Socio-Cultural History of the GDR* (New York, 1999); Hanna Schissler, ed., *The Miracle Years: A Cultural History of West Germany, 1949–1968* (Princeton, NJ, 2001); David Crew, ed., *Consuming Germany in the Cold War* (Oxford, 2003); Katherine Pence and Paul Betts, eds., *Socialist Modern: East German Everyday Culture and Politics* (Ann Arbor, MI, 2008); and Mary Fulbrook and Andrew I. Port, eds., *Becoming East German: Socialist Structures and Sensibilities after Hitler* (New York, 2013).
24. See for example Bessel and Jessen, eds., *Die Grenzen der Diktatur*; Lindenberger, ed., *Herrschaft und Eigen-Sinn*; Jürgen Kocka, "The GDR: A Special Kind of Modern Dictatorship," in Jarausch, *Dictatorship as Experience*, 47–69; Mark Allinson, *Politics and Popular Opinion in East Germany, 1945–1968* (Manchester, 2000); Madarász-Lebenhagen, *Conflict and Compromise*; and Fulbrook, *People's State*.
25. Sandrine Kott, *Communism Day-to-Day: State Enterprises in East German Society* (Ann Arbor, MI, 2014), ix.
26. See for example Uta Poiger, *Jazz, Rock, and Rebels: Cold War Politics and American Culture in a Divided Germany* (Berkeley, CA, 2000); Dagmar Herzog, *Sex after Fascism: Memory and Morality in Twentieth-Century Germany* (Princeton, NJ, 2005); Harsch, *Revenge*; Josie McLellan, *Love in the Time of Communism: Intimacy and Sexuality in the GDR* (Cambridge, 2011); Elizabeth Heineman, *Before Porn Was Legal: The Erotica Empire of Beate Uhse* (Chicago, 2011); Sybille Steinbacher, *Wie der Sex nach Deutschland kam: Der Kampf um Sittlichkeit und Anstand in der frühen Bundesrepublik* (Munich, 2011); Jennifer V. Evans, *Life among the Ruins: Cityscape and Sexuality in Cold War Berlin* (London, 2011); and Paul Steege, *Black Market, Cold War: Everyday Life in Berlin, 1946–1949* (Cambridge, 2007).
27. Axel Schildt and Arnold Sywottek, eds., *Modernisierung im Wiederaufbau: Die westdeutsche Gesellschaft der 50er Jahre* (Bonn, 1993); Katrin Schäfgen, *Die Verdoppelung der Ungleichheit: Sozialstruktur und Geschlechterverhältnisse in der Bundesrepublik und der DDR* (Opladen, 2000); Rainer Geißler, *Die Sozialstruktur Deutschlands: Die gesellschaftliche Entwicklung vor und nach der Vereinigung*, 3rd ed. (Wiesbaden, 2002); Jarausch, *After Hitler*; Josef Mooser, *Die Sozialgeschichte der Bundesrepublik Deutschland bis 1989/90* (Munich, 2007); Wehler, *Deutsche Gesellschaftsgeschichte*; and Donna Harsch, "Industrialization, Mass Consumption, Post-Industrial Society," in *The Oxford Handbook of Modern German History*, ed. Helmut Walser Smith (Oxford, 2011), 663–88.
28. Paul Betts, *Within Walls: Private Life in the German Democratic Republic* (New York, 2010); and Inga Markovits, *Justice in Lüritz: Experiencing Socialist Law in East Germany* (Princeton, NJ, 2010).
29. A partial exception was a reference to the emphasis on family policy in West German political campaigning in Christoph Kleßmann, *Zwei Staaten, eine Nation: Deutsche Geschichte 1955–1970* (Göttingen, 1988), 56.
30. See Karen Hagemann, "Between Ideology and Economy: The 'Time Politics' of Child Care and Public Education in the Two Germanys," *Social Politics* 13, no. 2 (2006): 217–60.
31. See for the importance of the family and the household as a marker of difference already, Robert G. Moeller, *Protecting Motherhood: Women and the Family in the Politics of Postwar West Germany* (Berkeley, CA, 1993); later Hagemann, "Between

Ideology," and Karen Hagemann et al., eds., *Children, Families and States: Time Policies of Childcare, Preschool and Primary Education in Europe* (New York, 2010); and Ruth Oldenziel and Karin Zachmann, eds., *Cold War Kitchen: Americanization, Technology, and European Users* (Cambridge, MA, 2009).

32. Moeller, *Protecting Motherhood*.
33. See Elizabeth D. Heineman, *What Difference Does a Husband Make? Women and Marital Status in Nazi and Postwar Germany* (Berkeley, CA, 1999); Michael Schwartz, "1972: 'Liberaler als bei uns'? Zwei Fristenregelungen und die Folgen; Reformen des Abtreibungsstrafrechts in Deutschland," in Udo Wengst and Hermann Wentker, eds., *Das doppelte Deutschland: 40 Jahre Systemkonkurrenz* (Berlin, 2008); and Annette F. Timm, *The Politics of Fertility in Twentieth-Century Berlin* (Cambridge, 2010). See also, recently, James Chappel, "Nuclear Families in a Nuclear Age: Theorising the Family in 1950s West Germany," *Contemporary European History* 26, no. 1 (2017): 85–109.
34. See Moeller, *Protecting Motherhood*; Erica Carter, *How German Is She? Postwar West German Reconstruction and the Consuming Woman* (Ann Arbor, MI, 1997); Merith Niehuss, *Familie, Frau und Gesellschaft: Studien zur Strukturgeschichte der Familie in Westdeutschland 1945–1960* (Göttingen, 2001); Greg Castillo, "Domesticating the Cold War: Household Consumption as Propaganda in Marshall Plan Germany," *Journal of Contemporary History* 40, no. 2 (2005): 267–70; and Karin Zachmann, "Küchendebatten in Berlin? Die Küche als Kampfplatz im Kalten Krieg," in *Konfrontation und Wettbewerb: Wissenschaft, Technik und Kultur im geteilten Berliner Alltag 1948–1968*, ed. Michael Lemke (Berlin, 2008), 181–205.
35. See Leonie Treber, *Mythos Trümmerfrauen: Von der Trümmerbeseitigung in der Kriegs- und Nachkriegszeit und der Entstehung eines deutschen Erinnerungsortes* (Essen, 2014).
36. See also Ines Reich-Hilweg, *Männer und Frauen sind gleichberechtigt: Der Gleichberechtigungsgrundsatz (Art. 3 Abs. 2 GG) in der parlamentarischen Auseinandersetzung 1948–1957 und in der Rechtsprechung des Bundesverfassungsgerichts 1953–1957* (Frankfurt/M., 1979).
37. See also Christiane Kuller, *Familienpolitik im föderativen Sozialstaat: Die Formierung eines Politikfeldes in der Bundesrepublik 1949–1975* (Munich, 2004); and Obertreis, *Familienpolitik*.
38. See Ruth Lister, *Citizenship: Feminist Perspectives* (New York, 2003); and Ute Gerhard, "Family Law and Gender Equality: Comparing Family Policies in Postwar Western Europe," in Hagemann et al., *Children, Families and States*, 75–93.
39. For the statistics, see Karen Hagemann, "A West German 'Sonderweg'? Family, Work and the Half-Day Time Policy of Childcare and Schooling," in Hagemann et al., *Children, Families and States*, 286; Monika Mattes, "Economy and Politics: The Time Policy of the East German Childcare and Primary School System," in ibid., 355; Hildegard Maria Nickel, "'Mitgestalterinnen des Sozialismus': Frauenarbeit in der DDR," in Helwig and Nickel, *Frauen in Deutschland*, 233–56; and Friederike Maier, "Zwischen Arbeitsmarkt und Familie: Frauenarbeit in den alten Bundesländern," in ibid., 257–80. For an overview, see Klaus-Jörg Ruhl, *Verordnete Unterordnung: Berufstätige Frauen zwischen Wirtschaftswachstum und konservativer Ideologie in der Nachkriegszeit 1945–1963* (Munich, 1994); Gunilla-Friederike Budde, ed., *Frauen arbeiten: Weibliche Erwerbstätigkeit in Ost- und Westdeutschland nach 1945* (Göttingen, 1997); Carola Sachse, *Der Hausarbeitstag: Gerechtigkeit und Gleichberechtigung in Ost und West 1939–1994* (Göttingen, 2002);

Christine von Oertzen, *The Pleasure of a Surplus Income: Part-Time Work, Gender Politics, and Social Change in West Germany, 1955–1969* (New York, 2007): and Harsch, *Revenge*.

40. See Gunilla-Friederike Budde, *Frauen der Intelligenz: Akademikerinnen in der DDR 1945 bis 1975* (Göttingen, 2003); and Karin Zachmann, *Mobilisierung der Frauen: Technik, Geschlecht und Kalter Krieg in der DDR* (Frankfurt/M., 2004).
41. Hagemann, "West German 'Sonderweg.'"
42. Winfried Süß, "Gesundheitspolitik," in *Drei Wege deutscher Sozialstaatlichkeit: NS-Diktatur, Bundesrepublik und DDR im Vergleich*, ed. Hans Günter Hockerts (Munich, 1998), 55–100. Recently also, Pierre Pfütsch, *Das Geschlecht des "präventiven Selbst" Prävention und Gesundheitsförderung in der Bundesrepublik Deutschland aus geschlechterspezifischer Perspektive (1949–2010)* (Stuttgart, 2017).
43. "Gesetz, betreffend die Redaktion des Strafgesetzbuches für den Norddeutschen Bund als Strafgesetzbuch für das Deutsche Reich," *Deutsches Reichsgesetzblatt*, vol. 1871, no. 24 (15 May 1871): 127–205; see https://de.wikisource.org/wiki/Strafgesetzbuch_f%C3%BCr_das_Deutsche_Reich_(1871)#%C2%A7._218.
44. Atina Grossmann, *Reforming Sex: The German Movement for Birth Control and Abortion Reform, 1920–1950* (New York, 1995).
45. Ibid., 189–212.
46. See Kirsten Poutrus, "Von den Massenvergewaltigungen zum Mutterschutzgesetz: Abtreibungspolitik und Abtreibungspraxis in Ostdeutschland 1945–1950," in *Die Grenzen der Diktatur*, ed. Bessel and Jessen, 170–98; Donna Harsch, "Society, the State, and Abortion in East Germany, 1950–1972," *American Historical Review* 102, no. 1 (1997): 53–84; and Annette Leo and Christian König, *Die "Wunschkindpille": Weibliche Erfahrung und staatliche Geburtenpolitik in der DDR* (Göttingen, 2015).
47. See Hermann Tallen, *Die Auseinandersetzung über § 218 StGB: Zu einem Konflikt zwischen SPD und Katholischer Kirche* (Paderborn, 1977); and Simone Mantei, *Nein und Ja zur Abtreibung: Die evangelische Kirche in der Reformdebatte um Paragraph 218 StGB 1970–1976* (Göttingen, 2004).
48. See Ute Kätzel, ed., *Die 68erinnen: Porträt einer rebellischen Frauengeneration* (Berlin 2002); Kristina Schulz, *Der lange Atem der Provokation: Die Frauenbewegung in der Bundesrepublik und in Frankreich 1968–1976* (Frankfurt/M., 2002); Gisela Notz, "Die autonomen Frauenbewegungen der Siebzigerjahre: Entstehungsgeschichte—Organisationsformen—politische Konzepte," *Archiv für Sozialgeschichte* 44 (2004): 123–48, and Gisela Notz, ed., *Als die Frauenbewegung noch Courage hatte: Die "Berliner Frauenzeitung Courage" und die autonomen Frauenbewegungen der 1970er und 1980er Jahre* (Bonn, 2007); Elisabeth Zellmer, *Töchter der Revolte? Frauenbewegung und Feminismus in den 1970er Jahren in München* (Munich, 2011); Kristina Schulz, ed., *The Women's Liberation Movement: Impacts and Outcomes* (New York, 2017); and Katharina Karcher, *Sisters in Arms: Militant Feminisms in the Federal Republic of Germany since 1968* (New York, 2017).
49. See Belinda Davis, *The Internal Life of Politics: Extraparliamentary Opposition in West Germany, 1962–1983* (Cambridge, 2018); Kristina Schulz, "Macht und Mythos von 1968: Zur Bedeutung der 68er Protestbewegung für die Formierung der neue Frauenbewegung in Frankreich und Deutschland," in *1968—Vom Ereignis zum Gegenstand der Geschichtswissenschaft*, ed. Ingrid Gilcher-Holtey (Göttingen, 1998), 256–72; and Christina von Hodenberg, *Das andere Achtundsechzig: Gesellschaftsgeschichte einer Revolte* (Munich, 2018).

50. See Sara Lennox, "Divided Feminism: Women, Racism, and German National Identity." *German Studies Review* 18, no. 3 (1995): 481–502; and Peggy Piesche, "Rückblenden und Vorschauen: 20 Jahre Schwarze Frauenbewegung," in *Euer Schweigen schützt Euch nicht: Audre Lorde und die Schwarze Frauenbewegung in Deutschland*, ed. Peggy Piesche (Berlin, 2012), 17–40.
51. See Elizabeth Lapovsky-Kennedy, "Socialist Feminism: What Difference Did It Make to the History of Women's Studies?," *Feminist Studies* 34, no. 3 (2008): 497–525; Myra Marx Ferree, *Varieties of Feminism: German Gender Politics in a Global Perspective* (Stanford, CA, 2012); Frigga Haug, "Rückblick auf die westdeutsche Frauenbewegung," in *Linkssozialismus in Deutschland: Jenseits von Sozialdemokratie und Kommunismus?*, ed. Christoph Jünke (Hamburg, 2010), 221–41.
52. Belinda Davis, "Civil Society in a New Key? Feminist and Alternative Groups in 1970s West Germany," in Hagemann, et al., *Civil Society,* 208–23; Belinda Davis, "'Women's Strength against Crazy Male Power': Gendered Language in the West German Peace Movement of the 1980s," in *Frieden—Gewalt—Geschlecht: Friedens- und Konfliktforschung als Geschlechterforschung*, ed. Jennifer Davy et al. (Essen, 2005), 244–65.
53. See Belinda Davis, "Transnation und Transkultur: Gender und Politisierung von den fünfziger bis in die siebziger Jahre," in *Das Alternative Milieu: Antibürgerlicher Lebensstil und linke Politik in der Bundesrepublik Deutschland und Europa 1968–1983,* ed. Detlef Siegfried and Sven Reichardt (Göttingen, 2010), 313–34.
54. See Angelika Schaser, *Frauenbewegung in Deutschland 1848–1933* (Darmstadt, 2006), part X; and Gisela Bock, *Women in European History* (Oxford, 2002), 174–205.
55. See for example Ehrhart Neubert, *Geschichte der Opposition in der DDR 1949–1989* (Bonn, 1997), 35–79. For an overview of opposition and protest in the GDR, see also Ulrike Poppe et al., eds., *Zwischen Selbstbehauptung und Anpassung: Formen des Widerstands und der Opposition in der DDR* (Berlin, 1995); Detlef Pollack and Dieter Rink eds., *Zwischen Verweigerung und Opposition: Politischer Protest in der DDR 1970–1989* (Frankfurt/M. 1997); and Klaus-Dietmar Henke et al., eds., *Widerstand und Opposition in der DDR* (Cologne, 1999).
56. Two recent studies include, Jonathan Sperber, "17 June 1953: Revisiting a German Revolution," *German History* 22, no. 4 (2004): 619–43; and Ilko-Sascha Kowalczuk, *17. Juni 1953: Geschichte eines Aufstands* (Munich, 2013).
57. See for example Thomas Klein, *"Frieden und Gerechtigkeit": Die Politisierung der unabhängigen Friedensbewegung in Ost-Berlin während der 80er Jahre* (Cologne, 2007); and Neubert, *Geschichte der Opposition,* 335–498.
58. See Bernd Schäfer, *The East German State and the Catholic Church, 1945–1989* (New York, 2010), 32.
59. Uta G. Poiger, "Generations: The 'Revolutions' of the 1960s," in *The Oxford Handbook of Modern German History,* ed. Helmut Walser Smith (Oxford, 2011): 640–62.
60. Lynn Kamenitsa, "East German Feminists in the New German Democracy: Opportunities, Obstacles, and Adaptation," *Women in Politics* 17, no. 3 (1997): 41–68; Ingrid Miethe, *Frauen in der DDR-Opposition: Lebens- und kollektivgeschichtliche Verläufe in einer Frauenfriedensgruppe* (Opladen 1999); and Myra Marx Ferree, "'The Time of Chaos was the Best': Feminist Mobilization and Demobilization in East Germany," *Gender and Society* 8, no. 4 (1994): 597–623.

Selected Bibliography

Bühler, Grit. *Mythos Gleichberechtigung in der DDR: Politische Partizipation von Frauen am Beispiel des Demokratischen Frauenbunds Deutschlands*. Frankfurt/M., 1997.
Davis, Belinda. "The Personal Is Political: Gender, Politics, and Political Activism in Modern German History." In *Gendering Modern German History: Rewriting Historiography*, ed. Karen Hagemann and Jean H. Quataert, 107–27. New York, 2007.
Ferree, Myra Marx. *Varieties of Feminism: German Gender Politics in a Global Perspective*. Stanford, CA, 2012.
Frevert, Ute, and Heinz Gerhard Haupt, eds. *Neue Politikgeschichte: Perspektiven einer historischen Politikforschung*. Frankfurt/M., 2005.
Georgina, Waylen, Karen Celis, Johanna Kantola, and S. Laurel Weldon, eds. *The Oxford Handbook of Gender and Politics*. Oxford, 2013.
Hagemann, Karen. "Between Ideology and Economy: The 'Time Politics' of Child Care and Public Education in the Two Germanys." *Social Politics* 13, no. 2 (2006): 217–60.
Hagemann, Karen, and Sonya Michel, eds. *Gender and the Long Postwar: The United States and the Two Germanys, 1945–1989*. Baltimore, MD, 2014.
Harsch, Donna. "Approach / Avoidance: Communists and Women in East Germany, 1945–9." *Social History* 25, no. 2 (2000): 156–82.
———. *Revenge of the Domestic: Women, the Family, and Communism in the German Democratic Republic*. Princeton, NJ, 2007.
Heineman, Elizabeth D. *What Difference Does a Husband Make? Women and Marital Status in Nazi and Postwar Germany*. Berkeley, CA, 1999.
Heinemann, Sylvia. *Frauenfragen sind Menschheitsfragen: Die Frauenpolitik der Freien Demokratinnen von 1945 bis 1963*. Sulzbach/Ts., 2012.
Helwig, Gisela, and Hildegard Maria Nickel, eds. *Frauen in Deutschland 1945–1992*. Berlin, 1993.
Holz, Petra. *Zwischen Tradition und Emanzipation: CDU-Politikerinnen in der Zeit von 1946 bis 1960*. Sulzbach/Ts., 2004.
Karcher, Katharina. *Sisters in Arms: Militant Feminisms in the Federal Republic of Germany since 1968*. New York, 2017.
Kühne, Thomas. "Staatspolitik, Frauenpolitik, Männerpolitik: Politikgeschichte als Geschlechtergeschichte." In *Geschlechtergeschichte und Allgemeine Geschichte: Herausforderungen und Perspektiven*, ed. Hans Medick and Anne-Charlott Trepp, 171–232. Göttingen, 1998.
Miethe, Ingrid. *Frauen in der DDR-Opposition: Lebens- und kollektivgeschichtliche Verläufe in einer Frauenfriedensgruppe*. Opladen, 1999.
Moeller, Robert G. *Protecting Motherhood: Women and the Family in the Politics of Postwar West Germany*. Berkeley, CA, 1993.
———. "The Elephant in the Living Room or Why the History of Twentieth-Century Germany Should Be a Family Affair." In *Gendering Modern German History: Rewriting Historiography*, ed. Karen Hagemann and Jean H. Quataert, 228–49. New York, 2007.
Notz, Gisela. *Frauen in der Mannschaft: Sozialdemokratinnen im Parlamentarischen Rat und im Deutschen Bundestag 1948/49 bis 1957*. Bonn, 2003.
Notz, Gisela. *Mehr als bunte Tupfen im Bonner Männerclub: Sozialdemokratinnen im Deutschen Bundestag 1957–1969*. Bonn, 2007.

Paulus, Julia, Eva-Maria Silies, and Kerstin Wolff, eds. *Zeitgeschichte als Geschlechtergeschichte: Neue Perspektiven auf die Bundesrepublik*. Frankfurt/M., 2012.

Rosenberg, Dorothy. "Women's Issues, Women's Politics, and Women's Studies in the Former German Democratic Republic." *Radical History Review* no. 54 (1992): 110–26.

Sachse, Carola. *Der Hausarbeitstag: Gerechtigkeit und Gleichberechtigung in Ost und West 1939–1994*. Göttingen, 2002.

Schäfgen, Katrin. *Die Verdoppelung der Ungleichheit: Sozialstruktur und Geschlechterverhältnisse in der Bundesrepublik und der DDR*. Opladen, 2000.

Schulz, Kristina. *Der lange Atem der Provokation: Die Frauenbewegung in der Bundesrepublik und in Frankreich 1968–1976*. Frankfurt/M., 2002.

Trappe, Heike. *Emanzipation oder Zwang? Frauen in der DDR, 1945–1980*. Berlin, 1995.

Treber, Leonie. *Mythos Trümmerfrauen: von der Trümmerbeseitigung in der Kriegs- und Nachkriegszeit und der Entstehung eines deutschen Erinnerungsortes*. Essen, 2014.

Wiliarty, Sarah Elise. *The CDU and the Politics of Gender in Germany: Bringing Women to the Party*. New York, 2010.

CHAPTER 2

Entangled Gender Relations and Sexuality in the Historiography on the Two Post-1945 Germanys

Jennifer Evans

Scholarship on the history of sexuality in postwar Germany has built on the objectives of the feminist and gay rights movements to rethink essentialist norms and gender practices within contemporary society. Emerging in the 1970s out of radical student politics and influenced by social history and the turn toward discourse analysis and cultural history, it has evolved into a vibrant platform for thinking about how societies shape and are shaped by sexual fantasies, desires, norms, and identities.[1] Scholars study the links between the intimate world of the gendered self and the wage economy, household structures, social welfare, and state politics, and investigate the construction and regulation of sexual subjectivities through the prism of gender—but they still analyze these themes by focusing on *either* straight or queer life worlds. They tend to study the construction of heterosexual institutions and their impact on normative gender expression *or* same-sex desire and the price (or lure) of transgression. The history of sexuality, in other words, is compartmentalized into studies of heterosexuality or homosexuality despite the fact that both subjects have always been entangled with gendered forms of comportment and behavior. In part, this is the result of the different state policies and mechanisms of regulation and control in respect to hetero- and homosexuality; in part, this is the result of the different political agendas of the researchers and the movements that informed their approach to the sexuality: the student movement, the new women's movement, and the gay and lesbian rights movement.[2] Another tendency in scholarship on the history of sexuality is its entanglement of theoretical frameworks with other disciplines, among them gay, lesbian, and queer studies, women's and gender studies, and sociology. More recently critical race and trans studies have also influenced the field. In addition, the historiography reflects regional and national differences in the study of sexuality and gender.

The history of sexuality in the two postwar Germanys is informed by three factors. First, there are differences between Anglo-American historians and those trained at continental European institutions in their approaches and interpretations. Second, of influence are the distinctions between the approaches of university-based scholars and those outside the academy. Third, and most importantly, the long shadow of the Third Reich and the Holocaust influences the approaches to and themes of the history of postwar sexuality in both Germanys. This shadow has tended to occlude the continued experience of homophobia and racism after the Second World War. In general, one can neither understand the complex, nonlinear history of gender and sexuality in the post-1945 period without reckoning with previous periods in German history nor make sense of political pivots and change over time in postwar Germany without integrating the histories of sexuality into its broader evolution.

This chapter addresses these tensions and entanglements. First, it briefly outlines the origins of the field of the history of sexuality. Then it discusses how the scholarship on gender relations and sexuality in modern German history dealt with the legacies of the Nazi past and the challenges of the first postwar years. Subsequently, the chapter discusses ways in which the misremembering of the Third Reich as a sexually repressive regime structured how West Germans understood sexual policy and practice surrounding family structure, personal pleasure, and sexual self-determination. It further explores how this dynamic functioned differently in East Germany. The chapter concludes with an examination of the history and memory of homosexual persecution in both Germanys.

The Origins of the Field

The history of sexuality is a vast and complex field encompassing studies of prostitution, fertility control, reproduction, abortion, sexual violence, disease transmission, hetero- and homosexuality, deviance, and transsexuality among other themes. The literature has focused variously on how people understood and experienced their bodies, how states regulated social norms, and how the churches and other cultural and social organizations shaped public mores. The origins of the field are informed on the one hand by the sexual research conducted by early twentieth-century scholars, including physicians, sexologists, and psychiatrists. In Germany, the work by the Scientific-Humanitarian Committee (Wissenschaftlich-humanitäres Komitee, WhK), founded in Berlin in 1897 by the Jewish physician and sexologist Magnus Hirschfeld, and from 1919 to 1933 his Institute of Sexual Research (Institut für Sexualwissenschaft) in Berlin, which was shut down by the Nazis, became particularly influential.[3]

On the other hand, the modern history of sexuality has its roots in the social and cultural historiographical turns of the 1970s and 1980s.[4] The *History of Sexuality* by the philosopher Michel Foucault published in French in 1976, English in 1978, and German in 1983 has proven especially influential. Foucault shifted attention away from sexual practices to how sexuality surfaced as a site of social, legal, and medical control and state intervention.[5] He convinced historians of sexuality to think about the roles of medicine, psychiatry, policing, and the law in liberal democracies in shaping discourses around social norms and deviation that hardened into constructs of self-understanding for hetero- and homosexual people. Foucault argued that law and discipline were not simply repressive mechanisms—they helped to shape what behaviors might be countenanced as desirable and normal. As translations became available, Foucauldian analysis spread from France to the English-speaking world and, later, Germany and Austria.[6]

The Legacies of the Nazi Past and the Challenges of the First Postwar Years

Whatever the questions and the theoretical and methodological frameworks, the history of sexuality in both post-1945 Germanys cannot be studied without taking into account the legacy of the sexual, gender, and racial policies of the Nazi regime or German women's immediate postwar experiences, especially the mass rapes by Allied soldiers. The interpretation of both was fundamentally changed by the so-called *Historikerinnenstreit* (quarrel between female historians) that started in the late 1980s as a transatlantic conflict. The dispute focused on German women's role in National Socialism. It began as a disagreement between the German historian Gisela Bock and the American historian Claudia Koonz over whether National Socialism's sexual, eugenic, and racist policies victimized German women as women or benefitted them as Germans.[7] Their contrasting interpretations brought to light differences of method and interpretation in considering women's agency in supporting Nazi population and family policy. On both sides of the Atlantic, the *Historikerinnenstreit* soon developed into a discussion of the spectrum of roles played by German women in the Third Reich, from perpetrators to bystanders, victims, and resisters. The debate affected historiography far beyond women's and gender history. In calling attention to female agency, it opened up new realms of historical scrutiny including the broad variety and often ambiguity of female experiences.[8] Scholars came to accept that the intimate sphere and sexual relations were sites of both political opposition to and support for the Nazi regime; that reproduction and the home front were linked to genocide and war—and vice versa. Rigid divisions between different formulations of female agency that previously categorized victims, adherents, fellow travelers, and oppressors as mutually exclusive were questioned. Furthermore, the debate complicated the idea of collective responsibility for the normalization of the regime's repressive and murderous policies.[9]

The *Historikerinnenstreit* shaped the conceptualization of the postwar period too. Important was here in particular the historical understanding of the mass rape of German women by, primarily, Soviet occupation forces but also, as new research demonstrates, soldiers of the other allied militaries.[10] The first scholarship by the German feminist scholars Ingrid Schmidt-Harzbach, Annemarie Tröger, and Helke Sander, published in the 1980s and early 1990s, still emphasized that women were doubly victimized by Nazi policies and Soviet aggression and that the story of postwar victimization was buried in Cold War Germany.[11] One widely discussed example for this interpretation is the 1992 film *BeFreier und BeFreite: Krieg, Vergewaltigung, Kinder* (released in English as *Liberators Take Liberties: War, Rape, and Children*) by Helke Sander, who aimed to "break the silence" around the violation of women in 1945. After an initially positive reception inside Germany, art scholar and film critic Gertrud Koch penned an influential negative review, asking whether Sander oversimplified the issue of women's culpability given that many German women had benefitted from their unique class and racial status in a regime built on racial hierarchy and genocide. More provocatively, Koch suggested that the film teetered toward the same kind of exculpatory narratives about the origins and impact of National Socialism that some right-leaning historians had put forward during the *Historikerstreit* (quarrel among historians) in the 1980s.[12] Subsequently Sander's film faced similar criticisms from feminist US film critics and historians. One influential example for the intensive transatlantic debate is the special issue of the journal *October* published in 1995 under the title "Berlin 1945: War and Rape; 'Liberators Take Liberties.'"[13] Regardless of these reservations, most critics agreed that Sander's film, despite the uneasy collapsing of differences between and among victim groups, shed light on a variety of experiences at the war's end, including mass rape, venereal disease, prostitution, rape as a weapon of war, fraternization, occupation children, and abortion. Since the 1990s, women and gender historians who worked on postwar Germany increasingly took up these topics.[14]

The most recent historical studies of gender relations and sexuality in the German postwar periods provide a more nuanced understanding of women's sexual choices and subjectivities. Elizabeth Heineman explored in her 2003 book *What Difference Does a Husband Make? Women and Marital Status in Nazi and Postwar Germany* how women's varied and fluctuating legal, social, and sexual situations as single, married, widowed, or "standing alone" indelibly shaped their sense of loss and suffering. These multifaceted and complex experiences at war's end served, she concluded, as foundational myths in West German national memory.[15] Annette Timm's 2010 study *The Politics of Fertility in 20th Century Berlin* examined the changing policies and experiences of marriage counseling and venereal disease control in the city in a long-term perspective. It portrayed women as resourceful in navigating the conflicting health policies. Timm also brought men into the equation, treating them as gendered sexual agents, both as offenders who spread disease and as partners or life mates eager to build tangible relationships amid the destruction.[16] Writing about postwar Berlin, Jennifer Evans in her 2011 book *Life among the Ruins: Cityscape and Sexuality in Cold War Berlin* reconstructed a complex web of relations woven from strands of victimization and resilience. She argued that the destroyed city with its administrative chaos provided opportunities for residents to subvert confining gender and sexual norms.[17] These works and others prompted historians to continue to blur the 1945 boundary by looking at ways in which memories of the Nazi era continued to influence postwar experience and state policy as officials and ordinary people linked sexuality and gender norms to matters of national memory, citizenship, and statecraft.

When the archival collections in East Germany opened up after the fall of the wall and also more West German collections became available for the post-1945 period, historians could evaluate previously inaccessible documents. The access to massive amounts of new primary sources led women and gender historians on both sides of the Atlantic to move away from discussions of victimhood, guilt, and complicity to consider, instead, the ways in which ordinary people's attitudes and behaviors—nonmarital sex, illicit love, same-sex desire, prostitution, and efforts to purchase contraceptives and sex aids—challenged family, population, and social policies of both German states in the 1950s.[18] These policies focused, above all, on the family and its gender relations. Broken familial bonds, war-caused separation, estrangements between spouses after their respective war experiences, and the privations of the first postwar decade made it hard to reestablish intimacy, leaving the nascent East and West German states to believe that policy must buttress the family, which both governments perceived as a pillar of state and society.[19] As historian Robert Moeller argued in his pathbreaking 1996 study *Protecting Motherhood: Women and the Family in the Politics of Postwar West Germany,* the Christian-conservative government of the newly founded Federal Republic of Germany (FRG) pursued in its legislation and family and social policies a reinvigoration of the male-breadwinner/female-homemaker family. The aim, he contended, was to remasculinize state and society while also discursively repackaging male physical and sexual aggression to symbolize democratic values rather than authoritarian ones.[20] In East Germany, too, moral conservatism dominated social policy as the Socialist Unity Party of Germany (Sozialistische Einheitspartei Deutschlands, SED) and its leader Walter Ulbricht instructed citizens in the *Ten Commandments for Socialist Personhood* in 1958 to "live cleanly and decently with respect for family." And yet, despite these strictures, as the historians Ina Merkel, Donna Harsch, and Josie McLellan argued in their monographs on East German gender relations and policies, the 1950s was not a time of unrelieved repression in East Germany, even if the state nurtured reproductive heterosexuality. Albeit with mixed success, women staked claims to ameliorate difficulties in their personal lives, whether in addressing unfair work/life conditions, seeking ways to limit family size, or finding entertainment and release in the pages of the monthly *Das Magazin,* which was salacious by reputation but tame in content.[21] In youth cultural and education policy on both sides of the Iron Curtain, the preoccupation with healthy, heterosexual mores undergirded efforts to limit the influence of consumer capitalism, mass culture, and American music, linking what one read, listened to, watched, or consumed to whether one was being an upstanding citizen. Here, heterosexual norms extended to visions of preferential male and female gender roles.[22] Just as much as femininity and mothering, healthful manliness devoted to labor and fatherhood was a concern, and both were deemed essential to the recovery and strength of the postwar economy. As the historians Paul Betts and Dorothee Wierling showed, people managed to circumvent the ever-watchful eye of the East German state. They created personal spaces for themselves, continued to seek out nonconventional sexual liaisons, and consumed prohibited cultural productions, such as underground print literature and West German television.[23]

Nazi Sexual Repression and the Sexual Revolution

Even as the historiography pushed the temporal focus of study of the history of sexuality into the 1960s and 1970s, the Nazi period and to a lesser extent the Weimar years continued to dominate how historians of sexuality engaged with their subjects. Dagmar Herzog's groundbreaking 2005 book *Sex after Fascism: Memory and Morality in Twentieth-Century Germany* fundamentally changed how scholars conceptualize the sexual revolution, particularly in West Germany. Herzog argued that in the service of advancing their own counterpolitics of sexual liberation, the postwar generation of New Left activists and "1968ers" misremembered the Nazi period as one of sexual repression. Eager to challenge the Catholic and Protestant Churches' hold over state policy, many New Left activists tied West German policy to a Nazi-style regulation of social and sexual mores. They claimed that the Third Reich had repressed individual sexual pleasure. Adopting the theories of Sigmund Freud, the Austrian founder of psychoanalysis, and Herbert Marcuse, the German-American philosopher, sociologist, and political theorist associated with the Frankfurt School and critical theory, they charged that sexual repressiveness led to the sublimation and redirection of desire and, thus, motivated and drove Nazi crimes. Based on Marcuse, Reimut Reiche, one of the national leaders of the Socialist German Student Union (Sozialistischer Deutscher Studentenbund, SDS), linked sexual repression and Nazi crimes in his 1970 book *Sexualität, Moral und Gesellschaft* (Sexuality, Morality, and Society).[24] Herzog showed that in contrast to the New Left's assumptions in the 1960s and 1970s, Nazi sexual policies were more complex than the repression narrative suggested. Nazis repressed and denounced the sexuality of their racial and political enemies while encouraging sexual activity, including for pleasure, among eugenically "positive" Germans. The contradictions in policy allowed "fascist" sexuality to be politicized by both postwar moral conservatives and sixties radicals. According to Herzog, the perpetrator generation during the 1950s and the generation that came of age in the 1960s similarly used an essentialized version of Nazi sexuality to distance their generation and their politics from the crimes of National Socialism.

The New Left denounced not just fascist sex but all bourgeois sex. Nazi repression, they argued, fit into a long history of bourgeois sexual norms that continued after 1945. The 1968ers concluded that emancipation could only come via "nonrepressive desublimation," i.e. the willful transgression of reigning sexual-moral proscriptions. They aimed in theory and in practice to lead a sexual revolution that would democratize society by liberating its libido. And, indeed, one could argue that the FRG liberalized politically and socially as it also carried out major reforms in marriage, family, and "decency" laws between the late 1950s and the early 1980s. Women moved toward holding equal rights in family and marriage; divorce law was loosened; homosexuality was decriminalized; possession of pornography was decriminalized; marital rape was recognized as a crime.[25]

Given these important and dramatic legal changes, it is not surprising that both popular and academic opinion has long believed that the 1968ers ushered in a sexual revolution. Some historians nevertheless questioned received notions about the origins, terms, and timing of the sexual revolution. Others have maintained that it is still massively undertheorized, especially in understanding the relationship between national liberalizing trends and transnational processes.[26] Feminist scholars contributed to these debates by pointing to the gender differences in the so-called sexual revolution. They emphasized that the sexual politics of the student movement were, at least initially, much more liberating in practice and theory for men than for women.[27] Among much evidence for this claim is the cavalier use of rape imagery and pornography in the underground magazines, flyers, and pamphlets produced by individuals and groups on the radical left.[28] Furthermore, historians of sexuality have extended the timeframe of the sexual revolution for West Germany and other Western societies by pushing its origins back to the 1950s and arguing that shifts in discourses of privacy, intimacy, and sexual selfhood occurred more gradually than abruptly.[29] Sybille Steinbacher and Elizabeth Heineman, for example, argued that the first postwar decade bears reconsideration as a time of sexual change in West Germany. Like Josie McLellan, who focused on East Germany, they emphasized the rising demands by ordinary people, both women and men, for information and aids to enhance sexual pleasure in and outside marriage. They also documented the gradually accelerating circulation of knowledge regarding alternative sexual practices not sanctioned by state and society.[30]

In her 2011 book *Wie der Sex nach Deutschland kam: Der Kampf um Sittlichkeit und Anstand in der frühen Bundesrepublik* (How Sex Came to Germany: The Fight over Morality and Decency in the Early Federal Republic), Steinbacher looked at the transatlantic circuits of knowledge that connected the United States to West Germany in the 1950s. The mainstream discourse in both countries promoted a postwar society built on a clear division between the sexes and a family-based morality, but the belief in these ideals was increasingly challenged by findings of sexual research that shook up conventional understandings of sexuality. *The Kinsey Reports on Sexual Behavior in the Human Male* (1948) and *Sexual Behavior in the Human Female* (1953), published by Alfred Kinsey and his team, were especially influential on both sides of the Atlantic. These two reports, Steinbacher showed, stirred up huge interest among West Germans and changed the direction of discourses on sexuality. As pulp magazines and films broached sexual subjects, letters to the editor and opinion surveys referenced a person's right to sexual happiness. This "sex-boom" ran against moral campaigns and decency laws pushed by state authorities, many of whom were former Nazis working in the West German Ministry of Justice (Bundesjustizministerium), police, and youth-welfare services. The back and forth had the paradoxical effect of creating a more open, if still fraught, public sphere for debates over matters previously deemed intimate and personal. People became more vocal about their desire for advice to augment sexual pleasure and, eventually, for "the Pill," which became available in the 1960s, as others continued to insist on sexual propriety. Over time, a chorus of voices in pursuit of sexual freedom and choice effectively modernized West Germany in matters of sexual knowledge and eventually policy.[31] In her 2011 book *Before Porn Was Legal: The Erotica Empire of Beate Uhse,* Elizabeth Heineman too saw Nazi-era connections to the democratization of social mores in matters of sex.[32] Heineman characterized this push and pull between state and society on matters of sexual prohibition and choice as an arena in which Germans "learned liberalism," politically as well as socially.[33] Uhse, a former stunt pilot who flew supply missions during World War II and later founded the largest sex-shop business in the FRG, changed the playing field for how people talked about marriage and sex by appealing to women's desires. Targeting the "woman next door" who remembered the privations of war and rebuilding, Uhse ingratiated herself and her products to a clientele interested in sexual aids and erotica. Whether through the media, commodities, or cultural production, the market for sex slowly normalized previously hidden knowledge and emboldened citizens to become ever more vocal agents of their own sexual desires.

The situation in the GDR was both similar to and different from the FRG. In the West, democratization drove the relaxation of sexual mores and the laws and strictures governing them. Could liberalization happen in the absence of vocal opposition movement and free press, a reformist judiciary, and an open society? Both Herzog and McLellan argued that it could—and did. In her chapter on the GDR in *Sex after Fascism*, Herzog contended that liberalization occurred but at a much different pace and under unique conditions. She dubbed it a sexual evolution rather than a revolution. In her 2011 study *Love in the Time of Communism: Intimacy and Sexuality in the GDR*, McLellan argued even more strongly for the comparability of changes in the intimate and public spheres on matters of desire and sex, owing to parallel processes of urbanization, secularization, and mobility in East and West Germany. Echoing historians like Hera Cook who have stressed the importance of ordinary women's century-long quest for control over their own fertility, McLellan contended that East Germany witnessed a profound change in popular attitudes from one generation to another, and this shift help drive reform from above.[34] A shortened workweek, increased leisure time, and better access to housing in the 1960s and 1970s also contributed to the changing role of sex in people's lives. Still, she was careful to point out the unevenness of change in the East.[35]

Rethinking the origins, causes, and impact of the sexual revolution is essential if we are to better understand the history of democratization and reform in both postwar Germanys. Two of the chapters in this volume directly take up this issue. Clayton Whisnant in his chapter on "Searching for Identity: 1950s Homophile Politics in West Germany and Its Roots in the Weimar Homosexual Movement" presents a twist on the question of periodization. He emphasizes the importance of the Weimar era for our understanding of the sexual revolution and the liberation of gays and lesbians. How gay and lesbian activists in the 1960s and 1970s remembered the activist movements before them—in Cold War West Germany of the 1950s and the Weimar German state—influenced their aims and forms of struggle. The accommodationist politics of homophile activism in the 1950s became their legitimation for their direct-action politics in the 1970s. The blooming alternative urban subculture of gay men and lesbian women in Weimar Germany became a model of inspiration. Here too we see an important and perhaps overlooked continuity in the role of Weimar- and Nazi-era physicians, psychiatrists, and sexologists, who in the postwar period lobbied for a more humane understanding of gay male sexuality. But this was not the concern of 1970s radicals. They focused their attention on a politics of respectability pursued by homophile groups in the 1950s that sought to change from within by blending in with the dominant society. By casting his gaze back to the 1950s to show how reformists' actions created a scaffolding upon which, later, more radical groups built their politics, Whisnant underlines the importance of using a wider lens to capture the long march toward sexual liberalization.

While Whisnant asks readers to reconsider the origins of the sexual revolution, Jane Freeland examines assumptions surrounding its impact in women's actual lives in her chapter "Domestic Abuse and Women's Lives: East and West Policies during the 1960s and 1970s." As the scholars discussed here have shown, socially conscious policies on both sides of the German-German border during the era of the sexual revolution demonstrate that both governments recognized that the emotional lives of their citizens mattered to the political economy of the state.[36] Freeland shows, though, that this hard-won attention to the principles of sexual autonomy and protection did not necessarily mean the state actually listened to women's voices when it formulated policy. The response to domestic violence sharply reveals the ways in which ideology can make health and welfare authorities deaf to women's claims and concerns. In East Germany, officials assumed that women had attained social equality, so they treated women's claims of violence as the vestige of bourgeois mores or a sign of mental instability or depression. In West Germany, officials in some states established homes and shelters, but they generally rebuffed feminist attempts to improve policy and practice to protect women from violent partners. Thus, in both East and West, despite different political and socioeconomic conditions, women's sexual self-determination remained circumscribed by unrealistic and/or outmoded attitudes toward gender and sexuality. The sexual revolution, in other words, might also be judged by its limited impact on women's right to sexual safety.

The Gender of the Persecution of Queer Sexuality

As we have seen, the history of heterosexuality in the post-1945 period was dominated in interesting ways by the Nazi era and Weimar Germany. It structured the scholarly interpretation of women's sexual agency and victimhood and provided the foil in generational battles over the relationship between sexual mores and postfascist politics. The postwar history of queer sexuality and the persecution of lesbian, gay, bisexual, trans, queer, and intersex people (LGBTQI) likewise demonstrates the centrality of the Nazi past as well as that of Weimar-era sex reform to what unfolded after 1945.

The first studies of queer sexuality in postwar Germany have mainly been written by West German activist scholars who typically have loose professional affiliations to German universities and cultural centers.[37] Starting in the early 1970s and initially concerned with Nazi-era persecution of homosexuality, they were among the first to mine police and court records, read law-commission findings, and research the various gay and lesbian literary, activist, and social scenes in both Germanys.[38] The first academic studies of postwar homosexuality in West Germany emerged in the late 1970s. One example is the 1977 volume edited by sociologist Rüdiger Lautmann and published by Suhrkamp under the title *Gesellschaft und Homosexualität* (Society and Homosexuality) that explored different themes of the past and present of homosexuality.[39] The first study on homosexuality in the GDR was published by the West German sociologist Gudrun von Kowalski in 1987. In East Germany, the philosopher Bert Thinius, cofounder of the interdisciplinary working group "Homosexuality" at the Humboldt University in Berlin (HUB) in 1984, discussed the subject in his well-attended lectures at the HUB, but he published his research only after the wall fell, and in nonacademic presses.[40]

Transnational collaboration played a pivotal part in how the history of queer sexuality unfolded in the GDR. Gay rights activists made important connections to two visiting American university students and junior scholars, James Steakley and John Bornemann, both of whom later published ethnographically informed accounts of the scene they encountered in the 1970s and 1980s. Indeed, both had a hand in securing an English translator and publisher for Jürgen Lemke's series of interviews with gay men in East Germany.[41] These earlier collaborations continued to be part of the outreach work of two important West Berlin initiatives, the Magnus Hirschfeld Gesellschaft, an association reconstituted in West Berlin in 1981 as a research group committed to keeping the legacy of the famed 1920s sexologist alive. Some activist historians even held contracts with the West Berlin state government to process archival files in the Berlin *Landesarchiv* (state archive) and the Schwules Museum, a museum exhibiting LGBT life in Berlin that opened in 1984. With the publication of volumes from a yearly conference retreat at the Waldschlösschen facility outside the Lower Saxon city of Göttingen, their work continues to make an impact on the field.[42] And yet, their peripheral position in the university system underscores that, with very few exceptions, German academe remains reluctant to take seriously the study of homosexuality.[43]

The situation is different in the United States, where this field of study is more represented at universities. American scholars of West and East German queer history demonstrated that law and labor codes along with health and welfare provisions defined the ideal citizen on both sides of the Cold War boundary as someone engaged in healthy, reproductive, family-based heterosexual sex. They applied a gendered lens to crisis of parental and patriarchal authority unleashed by defeat in World War II and addressed by state efforts to prop up normative masculinity.[44] Here, Foucauldian-infused analyses of self-governance and the regulation of comportment proved useful for interpreting the politicization of same-sex sexuality in the era of the Cold War. Jennifer Evans showed in her work on homosexuality in the GDR that even in isolated regions of the East, state concern with homosexual liaisons among, for example, uranium miners had less to do with youth welfare than with longstanding fears connecting homosexuality to sedition. The SED shared this worry with Western governments that underwent and produced a so-called lavender scare in the 1950s driven by anxiety about the untrustworthiness of queer citizens. Although East Germany stopped prosecuting men for same-sex relations well before the Federal Republic did, there were other forms of discrimination against gay men, such as surveillance and the denial of opportunities for work, education, and military service. This sort of discrimination remained a feature of life in the GDR until the dismantling of the Berlin Wall.[45] Despite efforts to circumscribe gay life in East Germany, queer subcultures flourished in underground salons, with cross-dressing and themed party nights captured in private photography.[46]

The newly liberalized law codes of 1968 (East Germany) and 1969 (West Germany), which sanctioned homosexuality among consenting adult men, gave rise to new fears that the total decriminalization of homosexuality might harm pubescent men. Both states increased the policing of masculinity and the age barrier, with different ages of consent for homosexual and heterosexual sex.[47] This primarily affected young men, because historically only sex between men was illegal, unlike sex between women. The perceived link between homosexuality and effeminacy in addition to ongoing fears surrounding seduction meant that therapeutic and psychological interventions emerged as preferred ways to shore up healthy masculine social and sexual roles. Social and mental health services thus took over the policing of male sexual subjectivity and legal personhood, meaning that across the Iron Curtain, a more medicalized—though no less invasive—treatment plan was put in place to tackle the supposed problem of sexual deviance.[48]

In liberal democracies as well as under communist dictatorship, the ideal sexual self and citizen remained straight and male with a robust, though suitably contained, heterosexually oriented desire. In her chapter on "Contested Masculinities: Debates about Homosexuality in the West German Bundeswehr in the 1960s and 1970s," Friederike Brühöfener discusses the treatment of gay men in the West German military in the years following the decriminalization of same-sex sexuality. She shows that in the FRG, as in other countries, the tension between hegemonic masculinity and homosexuality is particularly vexed in homosocial, military contexts, where the lines around normativity are drawn more sharply and the stakes for belonging are higher. Her chapter unearths competing notions of masculinity for the men serving and for wider society that came to the surface as gay rights activists, members of the Federal Ministry of Defense (Bundesministerium der Verteidigung), and servicemen themselves became embroiled in this struggle to negotiate the meaning of decriminalization for the West German military. In examining this process, a host of assumptions about hegemonic masculinity and its place in the armed forces comes into view. Considered alongside the East German emphasis on proper gender and sexual psychosocialization, the tensions surrounding gay rights in the Bundeswehr confirm that the heteronormative civic ideal remained a cornerstone of West and East German political culture well after the 1960s. As Brühöfener's chapter illustrates, the history of post-1945 gay and lesbian sexuality is often periodized around legal persecution and the decriminalization of same-sex sexuality in 1968/69.

Another approach is more influenced by queer theory and challenges the seemingly natural construction of a gender binary and the related assumption that men possess masculinities and women femininities. This approach did not become influential until the 1990s and 2000s. Only then did scholars begin to think more carefully about the ways in which so-called cisgendered men (those who pass as straight with normative masculine gender expression) experienced regulation as opposed to more soft-mannered, effeminate men.[49] For inspiration in interpreting the different ways in which gender and race function in the making of hegemonic and minoritarian queer selves, they turned to a variety of disciplines and approaches. Albeit in different ways, Jin Haritaworn, Fatima El-Tayeb, Clayton Whisnant, Benno Gammerl, Jennifer Evans, and most recently Josie McLellan looked to subcultural studies, the history of emotions, human geography, photography theory, and antiracist queer and trans theory to explore how gender normativity and mainstreaming work in contemporary German history.[50] Haritaworn and El-Tayeb provided salient analysis of the questions of how to think about the increasing acceptance of queers by mainstream society in Western Europe after 1989. They complicated this narrative of progress by pointing to the parallel reinforcement of new lines of demarcations between queer citizens, frequently according to race and ethnicity. Both argued that the enlarged public sphere, now including anti-hate legislation and gay marriage, still constructs belonging around a vision of white, middle-class respectability. In essence, normalization in the Western European neoliberal framework hinges on the creation of new Others against which to define inclusion. The "respectable" queer citizenship has come about on the backs of Muslims and migrants, who are presumed to be hostile to same-sex sexuality. At the same time, trans persons and sexual dissidents like street workers, sex radicals, and addicts are still othered because their lives do not fit the frame of the monogamous, family-based, gender-conformist citizens—gay or straight—who want to marry. Haritaworn and El-Tayeb asked how truly forward and progressive the hard-won rights and privileges of the gays and lesbians are if they too rest on stereotypes and exclusion.[51]

Conclusion

Despite scholarly efforts to expand our understanding of the inner workings of the various LGBTQI scenes—urban and rural, gay, lesbian, nonbinary, and trans—there remains much work to be done in making visible the diversity of past and present experiences along with their specific gender encodings. Viewed from the perspective of mainstream acceptance, we have made great strides in writing queer lives back into history. However, as Dagmar Herzog argued, the modern history of German sexuality and gender suggests the need to resist a progressive teleology when thinking about how liberalism and democracy function in the sexual arena, because this teleology fails to account for continued moments of exclusion amid an otherwise forward-thinking agenda.[52]

This observation forces us to consider the uncomfortable truth that what often stands in for progressive politics can also contain elements of social conservativism. As Laura Duggan argued, that what passes as radical and transformative politics actually can de facto represent a quite conservative, assimilationist vision of the "queer citizen." Such a vision confirms and reproduces heteronormative gender norms, practices, and institutions instead of critiquing them.[53] The chapter by Jane Freeland on domestic violence shelters, for example, includes this sort of critique in her cautionary tale about the West German state's belief that protecting women from violence was evidence of its own pro-feminist, liberal moorings. This official policy failed to involve women as stakeholders in their own protection. Despite the rhetoric of equality, the state perpetuated a highly gendered, paternalistic form of intervention in the name of the protection and promotion of individual rights without respect for women's knowledge about the subject.

Such reflections point to the ways in which new histories of gender relations and sexuality and their particular entanglements can challenge traditional historical periodization in terms of both general twentieth-century historical progression and in the field itself. However, they also serve as a reminder of the need to take seriously the categories and assumptions at the heart of historical analysis. More importantly, they make us realize the usefulness of viewing the history of sexuality over the *longue durée* in order to recognize the inheritances and assumptions carried over into the twenty-first century. A possible way forward might be to draw more explicitly on queer and feminist methodological frameworks. After all, strands within both have long been preoccupied with seeing human relationships as expressions of dissimilarity and difference, of skepticism about norms and norm building, and of performance over essentialism. In emphasizing complexity instead of consensus, we might see more clearly the problematic reassertion of norms in moments when we think we have successfully exposed the ambiguousness of identity construction. Similarly, it seems important to plead for more intersectional analyses while we also recognize the distinctiveness of individual struggles. Homophobia affected men, women, and trans persons differently, but at the same time the misogynistic thinking behind the homophobia links the experience of these diverse communities in important ways. Homonormativity can be just as damaging as heteronormativity, if we fail to take seriously the normativizing impulses at work in most claims to representation.

Jennifer Evans is professor of history at Carleton University in Ottawa, Canada, where she teaches courses in the history of Europe, sexuality, and visual culture. Her publications include: *Life among the Ruins: Cityscape and Sexuality in Cold War Berlin* (Palgrave Macmillan, 2011); *Queer Cities, Queer Cultures: Europe since 1945* (ed. with Matt Cook, Continuum Press, 2014); *Was ist Homosexualität?* (ed. with Florian Mildenberger, Jakob Pastoetter, and Rüdiger Lautmann, Männerschwarm, 2014); and *The Ethics of Seeing: 20th Century German Photography* (ed. with Paul Betts and Stefan-Ludwig Hoffmann, Berghahn Books, 2017). In addition, she edited the special issue "Queering German History" of *German History* 34, no. 3 (2016). Her collaborative monograph *Holocaust Memory in the Digital Mediascape* will be published in 2019 with Bloomsbury.

Notes

1. Jeffrey Weeks, *What Is Sexual History?* (Hoboken, NJ, 2016).
2. On the historiography of sexuality in the twentieth century, see Victoria Harris, "Something a Bit Peculiar? Sex, the Germans, and the History of Sexuality," *Central European History* 23, no. 2 (2014): 283–93 and "Sex on the Margins:

New Directions in the Historiography of Sexuality and Gender," *Historical Journal* 53, no. 4 (2010): 1085–104; Jennifer Evans and Jane Freeland, "Rethinking Sexual Modernity in 20th Century Germany," *Social History* 37, no. 3 (2012): 314–27; Mark Fenemore, "The Recent Historiography of Sexuality in Twentieth-Century Germany," *Historical Journal* 52, no. 3 (2009): 763–79; and Donna Harsch, "Eroticism, Love and Sexuality in the Two Postwar Germanys," *German Studies Review* 35, no. 3 (2012): 627–36.

3. See Laurie Marhoefer, *Sex and the Weimar Republic: German Homosexual Emancipation and the Rise of the Nazis* (Toronto, 2015); Kirsten Leng, *Sexual Politics and Feminist Science: Women Sexologists in Germany, 1900–1933* (Ithaca, NY, 2017); and Harry Oosterhuis, *Stepchildren of Nature: Krafft-Ebing, Psychiatry, and the Making of Sexual Identity* (Chicago, 2000).

4. John Boswell, *Christianity, Social Tolerance, and Homosexuality* (London, 1980); and Natalie Zemon Davis, *Society and Culture in Early Modern France: Eight Essays* (Stanford, CA, 1975).

5. Laura Doan, *Disturbing Practices: History, Sexuality, and Women's Experience of Modern War* (Chicago, 2013).

6. See Jan Goldstein, *Foucault and the Writing of History* (London, 1994); Jan Goldstein, "Framing Discipline with the Law: Problems and Promises of the Liberal State," *American Historical Review* 98, no. 2 (1993): 364–75; and Rudy Koshar, "Foucault and Social History: Comments on 'Combined Underdevelopment,'" *American Historical Review* 98, no. 2 (1993): 354–63.

7. Gisela Bock, "Die Frauen und der Nationalsozialismus: Bemerkungen zu einem Buch von Claudia Koonz," *Geschichte und Gesellschaft* 15, no. 4 (1989): 563–79; Claudia Koonz, "Erwiderung auf Gisela Bock's Rezension von Mothers in the Fatherland," *Geschichte und Gesellschaft* 18, no. 3 (1992): 394–99; and Gisela Bock, "Ein Historikerinnenstreit?," *Geschichte und Gesellschaft* 18, no. 3 (1992): 400–404. The major studies of both scholars on which they based their arguments are: Gisela Bock, *Zwangssterilization und im Nationalsozialismus: Studien zur Rassenpolitik und Frauenpolitik* (Opladen, 1986); and Claudia Koonz, *Mothers in the Fatherland: Women, the Family and Nazi Politics* (New York, 1987).

8. Atina Grossmann, "Feminist Debate about Women and National Socialism," *Gender and History* 3, no 2 (1991): 350–58. For an overview of the debate see for example Claudia Koonz, "A Tributary and a Mainstream: Gender, Public Memory and the Historiography of Nazi Germany," in *Gendering Modern German History: Rewriting Historiography*, ed. Karen Hagemann and Jean H. Quataert (Oxford, 2007), 147–68.

9. See Adelheid von Saldern, "Victims or Perpetrators? Controversies about the Role of Women in the Nazi State," in *Nazism and German Society, 1933–1945*, ed. David F. Crew (New York, 1994), 141–65; Lerke Gravenhorst, "Nehmen wir Eigentum in Anspruch? Zu Problemen im feministisch-sozialwissenschaftlichen Diskurs der BRD," in *Töchter Fragen NS Frauengeschichte*, ed. Lerke Gravenhorst and Carmen Tatschmurat (Freiburg/Br., 1990), 17–37; and Mary Nolan, "Work, Gender, and Everyday Life in Twentieth Century Germany," in *Stalinism and Nazism: Dictatorships in Comparison*, ed. Ian Kershaw and Moshe Lewin (Cambridge, MA, 1997), 333–34.

10. The most important studies on the subject are: Norman Naimark, *The Russians in Berlin* (Cambridge, MA, 1995); Miriam Gebhardt, *Crimes Unspoken: The Rape of German Women at the End of the Second World War* (Oxford, 2017); and Marie

Louise Roberts, *What Soldiers Do: Sex and the American GI in World War II France* (Chicago, 2014). See also, Kirsten Poutrus, "Von den *Mothers,* Massenvergewaltigungen zum Mutterschutzgesetz. Abtreibungspolitik und Abtreibungspraxis in Ostdeutschland 1945–1950," in *Die Grenzen der Diktatur: Staat und Gesellschaft in der DDR,* ed. Richard Bessel and Ralph Jessen (Göttingen, 1996), 170–98.
11. See Ingrid Schmidt-Harzbach, "Eine Woche im April: Berlin 1945-Vergewaltigung als Massenschicksal," *Feministische Studien* 2 (1984): 51–65; Annemarie Tröger, "Between Rape and Prostitution," in *Women in Culture and Politics,* ed. J. Friendlander et al. (Bloomginton, IN, 1986), 97–117; and Helke Sander and Stuart Lieberman, "Remembering/Forgetting," in "Berlin 1945: War and Rape; 'Liberators Take Liberties,'" special issue, *October* 72 (spring 1995), 15–26.
12. See Gertrud Koch, "Kurzschluß der Perspektiven," *Frankfurter Rundschau,* 17–18 November 1992. For an overview of the so-called *Historikerstreit,* see Geoff Eley, "Nazism, Politics and the Image of the Past: Thoughts on the West German Historikerstreit 1986–1987," *Past and Present* 121 (1988): 171–208; and Charles S. Maier, *The Unmasterable Past: History, Holocaust and German National Identity* (Cambridge, MA, 1988).
13. See "Berlin 1945: War and Rape"; interesting also are Gertrud Koch and Stuart Lieberman, "Blood, Sperm and Tears," 27–41, Atina Grossmann, "A Question of Silence? The Rape of German Women by Occupation Soldiers," 43–63, and Andreas Huyssen, Silvia Kolbowski, Stuart Liebman, Annette Michelson, and Eric Santner, "Round Table: Further Thoughts on Helke Sander's Project," 89–113. Furthermore, see Marie-Louise Gättens, "Helke Sander's *Liberators Take Liberties* and the Politics of History," in *Triangulated Visions: Women in Recent German Cinema,* ed. Ingeborg Majer O'Sickey and Ingeborg von Zadow (Albany, NY, 1998), 261–71; Barbara Kosta, "Rape, Nation and Remembering History: Helke Sander's *Liberators Take Liberties,*" in *Gender and Germanness: Cultural Productions of Nationhood,* ed. Patricia Herminghouse and Magda Mueller (Providence, RI, 1997), 217–31; Richard W. McCormick, "Rape and War, Gender and Nation, Victims and Victimizers: Helke Sander's BeFreier und BeFreite" *Camera Obscura* 46, no. 1 (2001): 99–141; and Atina Grossmann, "Question of Silence," 43–65.
14. See for example, Petra Goedde, *GIs and Germans: Culture, Gender, and Foreign Relations, 1945–1949* (New Haven, CT, 2003); and Maria Höhn, *GIs and Fräuleins: The German-American Encounter in 1950s West Germany* (Durham, NC, 2002).
15. Elizabeth Heineman, "The Hour of the Woman: Memories of Germany's 'Crisis Years' and West German National Memory," *American Historical Review* 101, no. 2 (1996): 354–95, and *What Difference Does a Husband Make? Women and Marital Status in Nazi and Postwar Germany* (Berkeley, CA, 2003).
16. Annette F. Timm, *The Politics of Fertility in Twentieth-Century Berlin* (Cambridge, MA, 2010).
17. Jennifer V. Evans, *Life among the Ruins: Cityscape and Sexuality in Cold War Berlin* (Basingstoke, 2011).
18. Uta Falck, *VEB Bordell: Geschichte der Prostitution in der DDR* (Berlin, 1996); Atina Grossmann, *Jews, Germans, and Allies: Close Encounters in Occupied Germany* (Princeton, NJ, 2007); Heineman, *What Difference?*; Dagmar Herzog, *Sex after Fascism: Memory and Morality in Twentieth-Century Germany* (Princeton, NJ, 2005); Evans, *Life among the Ruins.*
19. See also chapter 1 by Karen Hagemann and Donna Harsch in this volume.

20. Robert G. Moeller, "Reconstructing the Family in Reconstruction Germany: Women and Social Policy in the Federal Republic, 1949–1955," *Feminist Studies* 15, no. 1 (1989): 137–69, and *Protecting Motherhood: Women and the Family in the Politics of Postwar West Germany* (Berkeley, CA, 1996). See also Frank Biess, *Homecomings: Returning POWs and the Legacies of Defeat in Postwar Germany* (Princeton, NJ, 2006); Svenja Goltermann, *Die Gesellschaft des Uberlebenden: Deutsche Kriegsheimkehrer und ihre Gewalterfahrungen im Zweiten Weltkrieg* (Munich, 2009); and Elizabeth Heineman, "Gender, Sexuality, and Coming to Terms with the Nazi Past," *Central European History* 38, no. 1 (2005), 47.
21. Ina Merkel, . . . *Und du Frau an der Werkbank: Die DDR in den 1950er Jahren* (Berlin, 1990); Donna Harsch, *Revenge of the Domestic: Women, the Family, and Communism in the German Democratic Republic* (Princeton, NJ, 2007); and Josie McLellan, *Love in the Time of Communism: Intimacy and Sexuality in the GDR* (Oxford, 2011).
22. Mark Fenemore, "The Growing Pains of Sex Education in the German Democratic Republic," in *Shaping Sexual Knowledge: A Cultural History of Sexuality in Twentieth Century Europe*, ed. Lutz D. H. Sauertig and Roger Davidson (London, 2009), 71–90, and *Sex, Thugs, and Rock 'n' Roll: Teenage Rebels in Cold-War East Germany* (New York, 2007); and Uta Poiger, *Jazz, Rock, and Rebels: Cold War Politics and American Culture in Divided Germany* (Berkeley, CA, 2000).
23. Paul Betts, *Within Walls: Private Life in the German Democratic Republic* (Oxford, 2010); and Dorothee Wierling, "How do the 1929ers and the 1949ers differ?," in *Power and Society in the GDR, 1961–1979: The Normalization of Rule*, ed. Mary Fulbrook (New York, 2013), 204–19, 212.
24. Reimut Reiche, *Sexualität, Moral, und Gesellschaft* (Frankfurt/M., 1970).
25. Franz X. Eder, "The Long History of the Sexual Revolution," in *Sexual Revolutions*, ed. Gert Hekma (Basingstoke, 2014), 99–112.
26. Margot Canaday, ed., "AHR Forum: Transnational Sexualities," *American Historical Review* 114, no. 5 (2009): 1250–353.
27. Ulrike Kätzel, *Die 68erinnen: Porträt einer rebellischen Frauengeneration* (Berlin, 2002), 151; Franz X. Eder, "Die Lange Geschichte der Sexuellen Revolution in Westdeutschland," in *Sexuelle Revolution? Zur Geschichte der Sexualität im deutschsprachigem Raum seit den 1960er Jahren*, ed. Peter-Paul Bänziger et al. (Bielefeld, 2015), 25–61.
28. Massimo Perinelli, "Longing, Lust, Violence and Liberation: Discourses on Sexuality on the Radical Left in West Germany 1969–1972," in *After* The History of Sexuality: *German Genealogies with and beyond Foucault*, ed. Scott Spector et al. (New York, 2012), 248–81; and Kristina Schulz, "1968—Lesarten der 'sexuellen Revolution,'" in *Demokratisierung und gesellschaftlicher Aufbruch: Die sechziger Jahre als Wendezeit der Bundesrepublik*, ed. Matthias Frese et al. (Paderborn, 2003), 121–33.
29. See for example the international comparative volume, Heike Bauer and Matt Cook, eds., *The Queer 1950s: Rethinking Sexuality in the Postwar Years* (Basingstoke, 2012).
30. Sybille Steinbacher, *Wie der Sex nach Deutschland kam: Der Kampf um Sittlichkeit und Anstand in der frühen Bundesrepublik* (Munich, 2011); Elizabeth Heineman, *Before Porn Was Legal: The Erotica Empire of Beate Uhse* (Chicago, 2011); and McLellan, *Love in the Time of Communism*.

31. Steinbacher, *Wie der Sex nach Deutschland kam*, 355; see also Fenemore, "Recent Historiography," 763–79.
32. Heineman, *Before Porn Was Legal*.
33. Here she is drawing on the work of Ulrich Hebert, specifically his chapter "Liberalisierung als Lernprozess: Die Bundesrepublik in der deutschen Geschichte— eine Skizze," in *Wandlungsprozesse in West Deutschland: Belastung, Integration, Liberalisierung, 1945–80*, ed. Ulrich Hebert (Göttingen, 2002), 7–52.
34. McLellan, *Love in the Time of Communism*; and Hera Cook, *The Long Sexual Revolution: English Women, Sex, and Contraception, 1800–1975* (Oxford, 2004).
35. McLellan, *Love in the Time of Communism*, 11.
36. Heineman, *Before Porn was Legal*.
37. For a selection, see Gudrun v. Kowalski, *Homosexualität in der DDR* (Marburg, 1987); Jürgen Lemke, *Ganz normal anders: Auskünfte schwuler Männer* (Berlin, 1990); Jean Jacques Soukup, ed., *Die DDR: Die Schwulen. Der Aufbruch. Versuch einer Bestandsaufnahme* (Stuttgart, 1990); Kurt Starke, *Schwuler Osten: Homosexuelle Männer in der DDR* (Berlin, 1994); Eduard Stapel, *Warme Brüder gegen Kalte Krieger: Schwulenbewegung in der DDR im Visier der Staatssicherheit*, Landesbeauftragte für die Unterlagen des Staatssicherheitsdienstes der ehemaligen DDR (Sachsen-Anhalt, 1999); Günter Grau, "Return of the Past: The Policy of the SED and the Laws against Homosexuality in Eastern Germany Between 1946 and 1968," *Journal of Homosexuality* 37, no. 4 (1999): 1–21; Andreas Pretzel, *Berlin—"Vorposten im Kampf für die Gleichberechtigung der Homoeroten": Die Geschichte der Gesellschaft für Reform des Sexualrechts e.V. 1948–1960* (Berlin, 2001), and *Homosexuellenpolitik in der frühen Bundesrepublik* (Hamburg, 2010); and Wolfram Setz, *Homosexualität in der DDR: Materialien und Meinungen* (Hamburg, 2006).
38. Heinz Heger, *Die Männer mit dem Rosen Winkel: Der Bericht eines Homosexuellen* (Gifkendorf-Vastorf, 1972).
39. Rüdiger Lautmann, ed., *Gesellschaft und Homosexualität* (Frankfurt/M., 1977).
40. Kowalski, *Homosexualität*; Bert Thinius, *Aufbruch aus dem grauen Versteck, Ankunft im bunten Ghetto? Randglossen zu Erfahrungen schwuler Männer in der DDR und in Deutschland Ost* (Berlin, 1994). The first dissertation on the subject at the HUB was: Gerhard Fehr, "Zu einigen Aspekten der Entwicklung der Risikogruppe der männlichen Homosexuellen und der Risikogruppe der kriminellgefährdetetn, nicht lesbischen, weiblichen Jugendlichen und Jungenerwachsenen in der Hauptstadt Berlin" (DPhil diss., Humboldt Universität zu Berlin, 1983). See also Dennis M. Sweet, "Bodies for Germany, Bodies for Socialism: The German Democratic Republic Devises a Gay (Male) Body," in *Gender and Germans: Cultural Productions of the Nation*, ed. Patricia Herminghause and Magda Mueller (New York, 1997), 248–61, 259.
41. John Borneman, *Belonging in the Two Berlins: Kin, State, Nation* (Cambridge, 1992); Jürgen Lemke, *Gay Voices from East Germany* (Bloomington, 1989); and Jim Steakley, "Gays under Socialism: Male Homosexuality in the GDR," *Body Politic*, no. 29 (1976/77): 15–18.
42. The most recent book in the Waldschlösschen series is Rainer Marbach and Volker Weiss *Konformitäten und Konfrontationen. Homosexuelle in der DDR*, Edition Waldschlösschen: Geschichte der Homosexuellen in Deutschland nach 1945 (Hamburg, 2017).

43. Jennifer V. Evans, "Introduction: Why Queer German History," *German History* 34, no. 3 (2016): 1–11.
44. Robert G. Moeller, "Private Acts, Public Anxieties, and the Fight to Decriminalize Male Homosexuality," *Feminist Studies* 36, no. 3 (2010): 528–52; Jennifer V. Evans, "Decriminalization, Seduction, and 'Unnatural Desire' in East Germany," *Feminist Studies* 36, no. 3 (2010): 553–77, and "The Moral State: Men, Mining, and Masculinity in the Early GDR," *German History* 23, no. 3 (2005): 355–70.
45. Evans, *Life among the Ruins*; and Jens Richard Giersdorf, "Why Does Charlotte von Mahldorf Curtsy? Representations of National Queerness in a Transvestite Hero," *GLQ: A Journal of Lesbian and Gay Studies* 12, no. 2 (2006), 171–96, 174.
46. Josie McLellan, "From Private Photography to Mass Circulation: The Queering of East German Visual Culture," *Central European History* 48, no. 3 (2015): 405–23.
47. Matthew Waite, *The Age of Consent: Young People, Sexuality, and Citizenship* (Basingstoke, 2002).
48. Greg Egighian, "The Psychologization of the Socialist Self: East German Forensic Psychology and Its Deviants, 1945–1975," *German History* 22, no. 2 (2004): 181–205.
49. Clayton Whisnant, "Styles of Masculinity in the West German Gay Scene, 1950–1965," *Central European History* 39, no. 3 (2006): 359–93.
50. Jin Haritaworn, "Queer Injuries: The Racial Politics of 'Homophobic Hate Crime' in Germany," *Social Justice* 37, no. 1 (2011): 69–89; Fatima El-Tayeb, "'Gays Who Cannot Properly Be Gay': Queer Muslims in the Neoliberal European City," *European Journal of Women's Studies* 19, no. 1 (2012): 79–95; Clayton Whisnant, *Male Homosexuality in West Germany: Between Persecution and Freedom, 1945–69* (Basingstoke, 2012); Benno Gammerl, "Queer Romance? Romantische Liebe in den biographischen Erzählungen von westdeutschen Lesben und Schwulen," *L'Homme* 24, no. 1 (2013): 15–34; Jennifer V. Evans, "Seeing Subjectivity: Erotic Photography and the Optics of Desire," *American Historical Review* 118, no. 2 (2013): 430–62; and Josie McLellan, "Lesbians, Gay Men, and the Production of Scale in East Germany," *Cultural and Social History* 14, no. 1 (2017): 85–105.
51. Fatima El-Tayeb, *Europe's Others: Queering Ethnicity in Postnational Europe* (Minneapolis, MN, 2011), and "Gays Who Cannot Properly Be Gay," 79–95; Jin Haritaworn, "Women's Rights, Gay Rights and Anti-Muslim Racism in Europe," *European Journal of Women's Studies* 19, no. 1 (2012): 73–80, and, *Queer Lovers and Hateful Others: Regenerating Violent Times and Places* (London, 2016).
52. Dagmar Herzog, "Syncopated Sex: Transforming European Sexual Cultures," *American Historical Review* 114, no. 5 (2009): 1287–308.
53. Lisa Duggan, "The New Homonormativity: The Sexual Politics of Neoliberalism," in *Materializing Democracy: Toward a Revitalized Cultural Politics*, ed. Dana D. Nelson and Russ Castronovo (Durham, NC, 2002), 175–94, 179.

Selected Bibliography

Bänziger, Peter-Paul, Magdalena Beljan, Franz X. Eder, and Pascale Eitler. *Sexuelle Revolution? Zur Geschichte der Sexualität im deutschsprachigem Raum seit dem 1960er Jahren*. Bielefeld, 2015.

El-Tayeb, Fatima. *Europe's Others: Queering Ethnicity in Postnational Europe*. Minneapolis, MN, 2011.

Evans, Jennifer V. *Life among the Ruins: Cityscape and Sexuality in Cold War Berlin*. Basingstoke, 2011.

Falck, Uta. *VEB Bordell: Geschichte der Prostitution in der DDR*. Berlin, 1996.

Fenemore, Mark. *Sex, Thugs, and Rock 'n' Roll: Teenage Rebels in Cold-War East Germany*. New York, 2007.

Grau, Günter. "Return of the Past: The Policy of the SED and the Laws against Homosexuality in Eastern Germany Between 1946 and 1968." *Journal of Homosexuality* 37, no. 4 (1999): 1–21.

Grossmann, Atina. "A Question of Silence? The Rape of German Women by Occupation Soldiers." *October* 72 (1995): 43–63.

———. *Jews, Germans, and Allies: Close Encounters in Occupied Germany*. Princeton, NJ, 2007.

Harsch, Donna. *Revenge of the Domestic: Women, the Family, and Communism in the German Democratic Republic*. Princeton, NJ, 2007.

Heger, Heinz. *Die Männer mit dem Rosen Winkel: Der Bericht eines Homosexuellen*. Gifkendorf-Vastorf, 1972.

Heineman, Elizabeth. "The Hour of the Woman: Memories of Germany's 'Crisis Years' and West German National Memory." *American Historical Review* 101, no. 2 (1996): 354–95.

———. *What Difference Does a Husband Make? Women and Marital Status in Nazi and Postwar Germany*. Berkeley, CA, 1999.

———. *Before Porn Was Legal: The Erotica Empire of Beate Uhse*. Chicago, 2011.

Herzog, Dagmar. *Sex after Fascism: Memory and Morality in Twentieth-Century Germany*. Princeton, NJ, 2005.

Lemke, Jürgen. *Gay Voices from East Germany*. Bloomington, IN, 1989.

McLellan, Josie. *Love in the Age of Communism: Intimacy and Sexuality in the GDR*. Cambridge, 2011.

Perinelli, Massimo. "Longing, Lust, Violence and Liberation: Discourses on Sexuality on the Radical Left in West Germany 1969–1972." In *After* The History of Sexuality: *German Genealogies with and beyond Foucault*, ed. Scott Spector, Helmut Puff, and Dagmar Herzog, 248–81. New York, 2012.

Poiger, Uta. *Jazz, Rock, and Rebels: Cold War Politics and American Culture in Divided Germany*. Berkeley, CA, 2000.

Poutrus, Kirsten. "Von den *Mothers*, Massenvergewaltigungen zum Mutterschutzgesetz: Abtreibungspolitik und Abtreibungspraxis in Ostdeutschland, 1945–1950." In *Die Grenzen der Diktatur: Staat und Gesellschaft in der DDR*, ed. Richard Bessel and Ralph Jessen, 170–98. Göttingen, 1996.

Pretzel, Andreas. *Berlin—"Vorposten im Kampf für die Gleichberechtigung der Homoeroten": Die Geschichte der Gesellschaft für Reform des Sexualrechts e.V. 1948–1960*. Berlin, 2001.

———. *Homosexuellenpolitik in der frühen Bundesrepublik*. Hamburg, 2010.

Reiche, Reimut. *Sexualiät, Moral, und Gesellschaft*. Frankfurt/M., 1970.
Schmidt-Harzbach, Ingrid. "Eine Woche im April: Berlin 1945—Vergewaltigung als Massenschicksal." *Feministische Studien* 2 (1984): 51–65
Setz, Wolfram. *Homosexualität in der DDR: Materialien und Meinungen*. Hamburg, 2006.
Soukup, Jean Jacques, ed. *Die DDR. Die Schwulen. Der Aufbruch: Versuch einer Bestandsaufnahme*. Stuttgart, 1990.
Starke, Kurt. *Schwuler Osten: Homosexuelle Männer in der DDR*. Berlin, 1994.
Steinbacher, Sybille. *Wie der Sex nach Deutschland kam: Der Kampf um Sittlichkeit und Anstand in der frühen Bundesrepublik*. Munich, 2011.
Thinius, Bert. *Aufbruch aus dem grauen Versteck: Ankunft im bunten Ghetto? Randglossen zu Erfahrungen schwuler Männer in der DDR und in Deutschland Ost*. Berlin, 1994.
Timm, Annette F. *The Politics of Fertility in Twentieth-Century Berlin*. Cambridge, MA, 2010.
Whisnant, Clayton, *Male Homosexuality in West Germany: Between Persecution and Freedom, 1945–69*. Basingstoke, 2012.

CHAPTER 3

Contact Zones and Boundary Objects

The Media and Entangled Representations of Gender

Erica Carter

The important goal of this volume is to add a gendered perspective to the growing body of research that seeks a new understanding of the histories of East and West Germany as both divided and entwined—or in Christoph Kleßmann's terms, as marked by "*Abgrenzung und Verflechtung*" (demarcation and integration) across, within, and between the two German states.[1] This chapter offers some reflections on how these divided yet also integrated gendered histories might be understood in the context of media entanglements. It emphasizes the interconnections and resonances across the two postwar German media systems. Those connections were generated through the positioning of both states within a longer history of European modernity in which media texts have been central to the shaping of popular consciousness, political legitimacy, and ideological consent.

The question of gender is central to that history in the sense that modernity's promise has regularly been articulated not only through notions of gender equality, but also gendered fantasies of social futures, including those of the post-1949 German Democratic Republic (GDR) and the Federal Republic of Germany (FRG). Yet despite these connections of *longue durée* within a German history of gendered modernity, it is clear that political and ideological efforts were directed on both sides on the inner German border to drawing lines of demarcation between the media systems of East and West Germany. Demarcation occurred in the first instance on the level of institutional structure and economic organization. The cultural policies of the four occupying powers—the United States, Britain, France, and the Soviet Union—had between 1945 and 1949 already laid the foundations for a bifurcated media system in the three western zones and, later, the FRG. Indebted to liberal capitalist models of economic organization, Western Allied media policy created the framework for a West German hybrid public-private media economy organized (initially at least) around public funding for broadcast media via the federal *Länder* (states) of the FRG, commercial income for a decartelized and privatized press and film industry, and systems of constitutional law and regional state oversight designed to enshrine universal freedom of expression as the media norm.[2] In the Soviet zone, media systems were designed in accordance with the three functions of propaganda, agitation, and organization assigned to the mass media under Marxism-Leninism. In East Germany after 1949, this meant state control of all branches of the print and audiovisual media, with broadcasting systems centralized in state hands and control exercised via government committees and the Central Committee (Zentralkomitee, ZK) of the leading Socialist Unity Party of Germany (Sozialistische Einheitspartei Deutschlands, SED). Press organs were similarly subject to government licensing and state censorship, while film was produced by a handful of studios under state monopoly control, by far the most significant of those entities being the German Film Company (Deutsche Film Aktiengesellschaft, DEFA), the first German film studio to be licensed by the occupying authorities in 1946 and the main production house for feature films and documentaries throughout the GDR's forty-year existence.

The institutional history of media systems in the two Germanys is thus one of a structural *disentanglement* that began soon after the end of World War II and persisted until unification in 1990. This situation led to the prevailing emphasis in media history on separation and division between the two postwar states. The difficulty of grasping the ambivalence of an infrastructural division that went hand in hand with forms of symbolic or lived interconnectivity is evidenced by the distinctions emphasized in standard histories of media institutions across the binational divide.[3] Many studies draw lines of demarcation, offering nuanced views of West and East German public spheres while arguably neglecting the zones of contact in which divisions were blurred or shared historical experiences articulated.[4] If cross-border porosity surfaces at all in the scholarship, then it does so most often in accounts of media reception.[5]

Contributions in part five of this volume on the "The Media and Representations of Gender" by Deborah Barton, Jennifer Lynn, and Brittany Lehman take a different approach to entangled representations of gender as well as gendered media networks. They demonstrate how infrastructural division was undercut by intermittent moments of interconnectivity, which in some cases—as Lynn and Lehman show—occurred only virtually, through forms of symbolic mirroring and othering, but that in others assumed embodied form in the trajectories of images, sounds, objects, and (as in the case of Barton's peripatetic journalists) bodies traveling through rare but nonetheless significant channels of cross-border exchange.[6] For the mass-mediated gendered subjectivities explored in part five, cross-border entanglement occurred across three arenas of contestation of a shared gender history: the spaces of modernity, the nation, and transnational experience. The modes of entanglement visible in this triply located media history include the cross-border circulations of texts, artifacts, and bodies; the mobilization of media images and texts as German-German "boundary objects" located in the "contact zones" between the two Germanys;[7] the configuring of aesthetic form and experience in ways that produce common perspectives across borders; and a gendered labor of cultural production that similarly generated correspondences but also cultural differences and dissimultaneities across two distinct media systems.

In the following I draw on work by Lynn, Barton, and Lehman to examine these different arenas and modes. As a counterpoint to these three contributions, I introduce the missing medium of film by comparing the work of several important East and West German directors, and I end the chapter with a focus on the transnational dimensions of the representational regimes discussed in part five.

Negotiating Gendered Modernity: Media Texts as Boundary Objects

In feminist histories of twentieth-century modernity, the role of media technologies and forms in the production of gendered subjects is regularly emphasized. Numerous studies of the "New Woman" of early to mid-century stress the significance of mass-cultural forms, including photography, design, film, radio, or the popular press, both in forging symbolic equivalences between modernity itself and the image of the emancipated woman—such icons of Weimar New Womanhood as film stars Brigitte Helm or Marlene Dietrich come to mind—and in furnishing female audiences and readers with figures of identification embodied by images of fashion models, sports personalities, musical divas, and so on.[8]

The two postwar Germanys shared this common history of an early twentieth-century female modernity shaped by liberal-democratic ideals of equality and liberty (expressed, for instance, in the Weimar constitution's stated commitment to gender equality) but filtered through politically ambivalent media presentations of an image-driven femininity. Yet the two postfascist states, and their respective media systems, responded quite differently to the challenge of a recuperation of the gender legacies of Weimar Germany. Jennifer Lynn's chapter on representations of women in the East and West German illustrated press of the 1950s identifies a common, albeit ideologically bifurcated, German-German representational strategy that involved mobilizing images of women to articulate competing conceptions of postwar modernity. Lynn's essay marks an important development of feminist scholarship on the "new woman international" and the "modern girl." An illuminating comparative study of modernities in the postwar GDR and FRG,[9] the essay shows how global processes of social, political, technological, and economic modernization from the late nineteenth century on helped forge new social identities for the putatively emancipated New Woman.[10] From her account of the postwar illustrated press across the inner German border emerges an understanding of media images as explicitly (GDR) or implicitly (FRG) addressing each other across the German-German divide. Media analysts have begun in recent years to explore intermedial practices in which the image itself "calls out," refigures, translates, or hybridizes its counterparts in other mass media regimes.[11] Lynn's account of this mode of dialogic intermediality as a form of media entanglement is as convincing as her location of femininity as a key figure for the articulation of opposing but also ambivalently interconnected ideas of the postwar modern.

Three core insights emerge from Lynn's analysis. The first is a sense of the intense ideological pressure to which representations of femininity were subjected in the immediate postwar era. After 1949, both states laid claim to a status as the political home of gender equality. Equality before the law, as is well known, was constitutionally guaranteed in both states; equally familiar is the differential interpretation of constitutional law that saw sexual equality realized in the GDR in women's active participation in all fields of waged work and in the FRG in the cultural value accorded to women's unpaid domestic labor.[12] We see very clearly in Lynn's analysis how German-German struggles over the legitimacy of the two states' competing claims to gender equality were fought on the terrain of the female body in media representations. In the West, it would not be until the advent of second-wave feminism that an effective oppositional voice emerged to challenge this functionalizing of the female body as an ideologically freighted media icon. Striking in Lynn's account, by contrast, are the ways in which East German critiques in the 1950s magazine *Die Frau von heute* of West German media representations parallels the post-1968 criticism by West German feminists of both the hypersexualization of femininity and the denigration of women's waged work in media representations of the FRG during the 1950s and 1960s.[13]

These rhetorical similarities remind us that media entanglements must be conceived, secondly, not as necessarily simultaneous across the inner German border but as caught in long-term processes of emergence, consolidation, and cultural lag. If, in other words, the two media systems were in dialogue across the German-German border, then the game of call-and-response occasionally took decades to unfold. This intermedial dialogue was also fraught with ambivalence. In the introduction to their 2004 volume *Across the Blocs: Cold War Cultural and Social History,* Rana Mitter and Patrick Major coined the suggestive term "mirror opposites" to encapsulate the complex process of mutual recognition and disavowal that characterized postwar cultural interchange.[14] Exactly this fluctuation between repudiation and mimetic reenactment occurs—and this is Lynn's third key insight—in the images she discusses from the postwar illustrated press.

Most arresting in *Die Frau von heute*'s images of GDR female workers are the minute but nonetheless perceptible fluctuations in aesthetic convention they register: shifts in visual idiom that signal a profound ambivalence in their relation to the very West German images the magazine so roundly condemns. Photographs from feature articles, for instance, adopt an agitprop aesthetic of gritty realism, evidenced in their grainy image quality and the apparent spontaneity of gesture in their subjects. Their snapshot mode locates the primary source of the image's modernity in the rhythms and movements of the laboring body in motion, not in the female body as icon or symbol. The magazine's April 1953 cover image, with its close-up of a young and beautiful woman in her overalls working at a machine (see figure 15.1 in the chapter by Jennifer Lynn in this volume), catches the reader's attention, by contrast, by employing obviously Western representational codes. The image deploys a self-consciously artful composition that is more characteristic of 1950s advertising and fashion photography in the West than of socialist worker iconography: hence its disposition of bodies and objects in ways that foreground the beauty of the female form as well as its rather too-studied posing of the photograph's female models.

We see at work in these images practices of appropriation, mimicry, repudiation, and remediation that the film theorist and historian Malte Hagener has identified as common to the media artifact as "boundary object."[15] The term refers to objects that may be "abstract" (such as a social space or institution) or "concrete" (such as a cultural artifact, image, or embodied social actor), but which share the capacity to simultaneously "inhabit several intersecting social worlds" while also exhibiting a structure that is "common enough to more than one world to make them recognizable, a means of translation."[16] Media texts are arguably ontologically predestined to function as boundary objects; their core function as mass-cultural artifacts is, after all, precisely to circulate among diverse readerships and audiences. Media texts thus inhabit those "intersecting social worlds" described by the term "boundary object" while at the same time mediating (or "translating") across boundaries of language, culture, and meaning.[17] Media practitioners also have a function in this context as networked social actors who assist in the process of translation, carrying texts and images with them as they move through professional, social, and industrial networks, and decoding and remediating media forms for new communities or audience groups.

In the postwar German context, there were of course multiple barriers—physical (walls, checkpoints, border patrols), institutional (censorship bodies in particular), and ideological—to such fluid circulation and dialogic interaction both of cultural practitioners and of media messages. Recent research on East-West cultural interactions (not least the research underpinning chapters in this volume) may have begun to shed light on breaks and fissures in the cultural borders between the two German states. Deborah Barton's chapter in this volume develops precisely this perspective by tracing the trajectories of women journalists through institutional channels and professional networks that, initially at least, spanned the four zones of occupation and persisted briefly in the two postwar German states. The fluid East-West connections identified by Barton across the occupation zones in the immediate postwar period are exemplified in the activities of the Association of the German Press (Verband der Deutschen Presse, VDP), which was based in the East but boasted an interzonal working group that Barton cites as a particularly important site of cross-border networking in the aftermath of war. After 1949, East-West journalistic contacts were significantly restricted. Personal connections and shared intellectual interests did allow some sustaining of contact across German-German boundaries. As Barton demonstrates, however, the dangers of such contacts were considerable, with sanctions stretching from public censure to professional demotion or, in one case, disappearance during a six-year prison term.

Attempts to stem the flow of media texts and images across the inner German border proved less successful. Certainly, in West Germany in particular, engagement with media images of the other Germany was held in check by forms of Cold War ideological regulation—censorship and anticommunist agitation—as well as a far-reaching consumerization and Americanization that diminished popular affiliations to a Soviet-style socialist imaginary. That GDR publics, by contrast, remained decidedly receptive to media images from the capitalist West is evidenced by historical studies of popular music, light-entertainment film, radio, and, centrally, television that show audiences regularly favoring Western media forms. Media historians have shown that cultural artifacts from television broadcasts to popular film musicals, pop music, and radio functioned as boundary objects in Hagener's sense, providing, on the one hand, a focus for the articulation of common East-West narratives and shared desires and, on the other, a source of differentiation between socialist utopias and capitalist dreams.[18]

Film as Boundary Object:
Die Legende von Paul und Paula (1973)

One example from 1970s cinema illustrates in greater detail this boundary function of media texts while also highlighting the significance of questions of gender. One of the most prominent films of the DEFA canon is Heiner Carow's *Die Legende von Paul und Paula* (The Legend of Paul and Paula, 1973). Scripted by Ulrich Plenzdorf and starring the GDR-audience darling Angelica Domröse as the eponymous Paula, the film, though not well received by some East German critics, nor indeed by the SED regime, was a runaway success among GDR audiences on its March 1973 release.[19] Imaginations were fired, apparently, by the boldness of a narrative that brought fantasies of a better everyday life within reach. Set in an unforgiving urban landscape—an unfinished construction site for prefabricated residential tower blocks—the film centers on Paula's life as a single mother of two who meets Paul (played by Winfried Glatzeder) when she is on the brink of a loveless marriage to an older admirer. Paula falls in lustful love with Paul, helps him overcome bourgeois misgivings over leaving his (unfaithful) wife, and embarks with him on a new romantic partnership. Though the narrative ends on a hopeful note—Paula is carrying Paul's child—it acquires a whiff of tragedy when the voice-over informs viewers that she will subsequently die in childbirth.

While the everyday trials that dog this tragicomic love story lend to *Paul und Paula* the ordinary authenticity required of entertainment in the socialist East, the film gains a flavor of fantasy through zany fairy-tale interludes, coupled with a music track from the GDR's much-loved rock band, the Puhdys, and a mise-en-scène peppered with signs of 1970s consumer modernity: glossy interior décor in Paul's diplomat milieu; miniskirts, kinky boots, and feathered hairstyles, sported variously by Paula, her love rival Ines, and sundry friends on a fairground trip at the beginning of the film. This colorful backdrop, alongside the film's intermittent shots of tenement buildings dynamited to make way for modern tower blocks, signals a socialist consumer modernity that was fully in line with the SED regime's post-1971 commitment to consumer-oriented economic reform.[20]

Yet the film's utopia of a fully realized romantic passion was less easily accommodated to regime norms. As the GDR film critic Fred Gehler noted in a 1973 review, East German audiences were gripped by the film's "intensely emotional and subjective" attitude and its "longing" for a life that was not "frittered away in monotony" but lived to the full by a new generation hungry for experiences of change and renewal.[21] That this longing for intensity was a social, not an individual, fantasy is suggested by one much-discussed seduction sequence in Paula's flat. Summoning an initially reluctant Paul away from evening family duties, Paula greets him on a bed bestrewn with a bacchanalian feast of food and flowers. As their lovemaking begins, the film cuts to a fantasy montage of a barge trip, the boat populated by admiring onlookers from previous generations of Paula's canal-worker family, the lovers' bed floating amidships under a blanket of blossoms thrown onto their two bodies by the assembled crowd. The montage echoes a later sequence when an embrace between Paul und Paula is witnessed by, and meets general acclamation from, the assembled inhabitants of her crumbling but convivial tenement block. The presence of an appreciative crowd in both sequences locates Paul and Paula's romance within a social fantasy of community that is fully in line with socialist norms. Paula's love for Paul, by contrast, is wilder, driven by a female zest for sex that breaks the bounds of social convention and its attendant gender codes. The boundlessness of Paula's desire is evident for instance in a further fantasy sequence when her eyes appear to undress Paul publicly, stripping him naked in the inappropriate setting of an open-air classical concert. Paula's desire also drives the early stages of the romance narrative; it is she who arranges nightly assignations with Paul or appears in wig and sunglasses at a private drinks reception, longing for a glimpse of the man whom she has chosen but who still refuses to embark on a new life as her partner and lover.

Let us now consider *Die Legende von Paul und Paula* as a (gendered) boundary object in Hagener's sense. Certainly, this was a film that traveled across "intersecting social worlds" between East and West. Though in West Germany it never attracted the three-million-plus audience it had drawn in the GDR, the film ran for several weeks in West Berlin and, albeit for shorter runs, across the Federal Republic. Despite harsh words from some West German critics (the left-liberal *Frankfurter Rundschau* called it "unspeakable kitsch"), *Paul und Paula* garnered popular success and has passed into film history as a cult film on both sides of the inner German border.[22] Critics have attributed the film's cross-border success to its treatment of shared gender dilemmas between East and West. Cultural historian Stephen Brockmann discerns a feminist resonance "across the socialist and capitalist worlds" in Paula's efforts "to combine individual happiness with responsible life as a citizen, a parent, and a worker."[23] The West German feminist activist and filmmaker Helke Sander has similarly identified *Paul und Paula* as an emblem of women's common experiences across East-West blocs.[24] Sander's response to *Paul and Paula* is, however, unequivocally critical. Already on the film's release, Sander cowrote with Renate Schlesier an excoriating critique in the feminist journal *frauen und film* that decried *Paul und Paula*'s "misogynist" celebration of a new image of female compliance. "It is no longer the monogamous and prudish woman who is the ideal," argue Schlesier and Sander, "but the sexually liberated woman who takes the Pill, and commits herself voluntarily to loving that one and only man whose children she also bears."[25]

Thirty-five years later, Sander came together with the East German filmmaker Iris Gusner to publish in 2008, under the title *Fantasie und Arbeit: Biografische Zwiegespräche* (Fantasy and Labor: Biographical Dialogues), a series of conversations on their personally shared but divided history as women cineastes working in East and West Germany respectively in the two states' latter years. Musing retrospectively on *Paul und Paula*'s enduring success, Sander remains withering in her assessment of Carow's film. "The acceptance of the film across both Germanys," she writes, "shocked me because in some sense it presented you with the futility of your own personal and political struggles. You've spent time considering the origins of the global oppression of women, you've worked to . . . 'throw off your own chains'—and then millions (of men) celebrate this woman who wants to die for her man for no reason other than for the propagation of his sperm."[26]

Sander's interlocutor Gusner makes no specific reply to these comments on *Paul und Paula*. But in a later discussion in *Fantasie und Arbeit* on the broader question of feminist filmmaking, she highlights how neither women nor men under the coercions of state socialism looked to the women's movement for "gestures of political solidarity across the gender divide." Instead, she suggests, they sought out niche communities of practice, including like-minded colleagues, for instance, who shared women filmmakers' critical perspectives on the regime.[27] For Sander and Gusner, then, shared memories of films and filmmaking across the border become a focus for precisely that "translation" of different but related experiences—here, the experience both of women's filmmaking and film reception, and of feminist politics—that is a feature of boundary objects straddling symbolic, geographical, and social borders between East and West. For Sander, Carow's *Paul und Paula* becomes an especially significant boundary object in the sense outlined above and in that context a trigger for the practice of what one might term—as an extension of the translational model offered by Hagener—feminist cultural translation across the German-German divide. The film takes center stage both in Sander's 1974 *frauen und film* review and in her later statements on films for women in *Fantasie und Arbeit*. In both contexts, *Paul und Paula* provides on the one hand a symbolic object through which shared feminist concerns are articulated across the East-West border: concerns with combining work and family, for instance, or with the autonomous articulation of female desire. On the other hand, the film provokes Sander to name with especial clarity the distinctions she perceives between feminisms across the political systems the two states represent. Sander's controversial comments on *Paul und Paula* as a misogynist text that harnesses women's emancipation to the sexual gratification of men reposition the film within Western feminist discourse. In so doing, she also highlights larger splits between an East German discourse of women's emancipation grounded in notions of socialist equality within a putatively ungendered public sphere and a West German feminist politics of difference that worked at the level of private life, intimate relations, and subjectivity to challenge entrenched gender identities and norms.

Audiovisual Media in the Contact Zone

I have so far drawn on the work of Barton and Lynn, as well as a brief discussion of Sander and Carow, for evidence of the processes whereby traveling media artifacts, embodied social actors, and gendered images came to act as vessels for a negotiation of gendered meanings across the cultural boundaries between the two postwar Germanys. I move now to reflect on a further aspect of gender entanglement that becomes visible in studies of media forms. I refer in the following to both an emergent historiography of German-German film relations and the research on what Mary Louise Pratt famously termed "contact zones" in the interstices of film culture across the East-West border.[28]

Studies by film scholars have begun in recent years to explore a postwar history in which cultural exchange through film is seen not simply as constrained by Cold War enmities, ideological prejudice, or politically motivated censorship on both sides of the inner German border.[29] The fissures in Cold War boundaries, these studies contend, were numerous enough to warrant further investigation of the "porosity of the [German-German] border, both on the analytical and discursive level, and temporally and geographically."[30] Studies of the import, export, and distribution of media have revealed, for instance, the particular interest of the GDR industry in West German genre film and charted the release and reception of selected titles in East German cinema and on television.[31] The West German reception of DEFA film was less extensive, in part due to the activities of the Federal Republic's special censorship office for films from the GDR, which, despite a constitutional prohibition on censorship, is said to have outlawed an estimated 130 GDR films between 1953 and 1967 alone. Film-industry professionals did enjoy privileged access to films across the border, with regional festivals in Leipzig, Mannheim, and Oberhausen providing important fora for cross-border engagement. The (West) Berlin Film Festival, by contrast, outlawed screenings of GDR films until the early 1970s, when a period of limited film-industrial détente began in the context of a general East-West thaw under Willy Brandt, the social democratic chancellor of West Germany from 1969 to 1974.[32] The East German interest in Western genre film as a model for light entertainment in the GDR also prompted clandestine forms of cross-border exchange, with administrators at the Central Film Administration, as well as many film directors, accessing "almost any film they wanted" from the West, and *Reisekader* (officials with travel permits) traveling westward to research films for potential purchase and GDR distribution and exhibition.[33]

The extent of GDR-FRG cinematic exchange should on the one hand not be overemphasized; in terms of film reception alone, contact was limited, with censorship and ideological regulation on both sides of the German-German divide ensuring that only a handful of films were seen by cross-border audiences in any given year. On the other hand, film culture did provide opportunities for the emergence of East-West "contact zones": cultural spaces enabling limited, sporadic, and disconnected, but nonetheless significant, forms of connection, negotiation, appropriation, and, occasionally, East-West convergence. Mary Louise Pratt has defined the contact zone as a social space "where cultures meet, clash and grapple with each other, often in contexts of highly asymmetrical relations of power."[34] As indicated above, festivals, film archives, and the film-industrial marketplace, as well as cinemas themselves, were among the locations within film culture of the modes of engagement that Pratt names as characteristic of the contact zone, including often highly conflictual dialogue around representational modes; the appropriation nonetheless of representational idioms across borders; and the concomitant challenging of dominant conventions through parody, irony, and satire.[35]

Research on gender in the East-West German cinematic contact zone is not yet extensive. But Pratt's model is helpful as a starting point for future work. Claudia Lenssen and Bettina Schoeller-Bouju have helped lay the foundations with an important edited collection and double DVD bringing together films, interviews, critical perspectives, and personal reflections from successive generations of women filmmakers across the inner German divide.[36] The collection may at first glance seem to offer slim pickings for a history of cross-border exchange. As Lenssen and Schoeller-Bouju indicate in their introduction, the book shows generations of women directors, producers, editors, and critics engaging with significant others across the border in the first instance through relations of rivalry or mutual incomprehension. Some West German feminists (among them Helke Sander) remained critical of their East German counterparts' sustained commitment to male-female solidarity and socialist feminism, while some of their would-be DEFA sisters maintained stereotypes of Western feminists as misandrists or liberal individualists with little understanding of the lived experience of gender under the party dictatorship of the SED.

Yet the vehemence of some contributors' repudiation of cross-border feminism during the years of German division suggests that what is in play here may be in part a proto-Freudian disavowal: a more or less violent negation of the other woman across the border, precisely because she is a figure of psychic identification, the emblem of an identity across borders that cannot be fully recognized, since to do so would carry with it an admission of the pain of traumatic separation across East-West German political blocs. Certainly, Lenssen and Schoeller-Bouju's collection suggests elements of similarity and mirroring as well as separation or distinction, showing women filmmakers grappling with similarly gendered life situations in East and West, and finding cognate solutions, despite differences of politics or film-industrial context.[37] Gusner and Sander write for instance in *Fantasie und Arbeit* of shared experiences of conflicts and difficulties fueled by similarly restrictive gender hierarchies and norms.[38] If we return once more to Lynn, we see echoed in Gusner and Sander's discussion the identification in her chapter on women's magazines of a shared but contested gendered modernity: a historical state of being in which women on both sides of the border struggle to realize the utopia of equality and liberty that pertains in all domains—social, political, economic, and cultural—and in all cases regardless of gender difference.

Also evident in Gusner and Sander's remarks on German history is the legacy they share of state authoritarianism in its relation to subjective experience. Sander grapples with that history explicitly in films on women's experience of the Berlin Wall and German division—*REDUPERS: Die allseitig reduzierte Persönlichkeit* (The All-Round Reduced Personality) from 1978, shown for the first time one year later on West German public television (ZDF)—or on gendered violence and mass rape during and after World War II, as in her *Befreier und Befreite* (Liberators Take Liberties) from 1992. Iris Gusner's DEFA feature from 1973, *Die Taube auf dem Dach* (Dove on the Roof), dealt, if more obliquely, with similar questions of utopian dreams unrealized in the German-German political present. Centering on a young male worker who rejects the ideal type of the socialist worker hero and exploring the arguably more "feminine" possibilities of personal fulfilment in social relationships and love, the film was banned in the GDR in 1973 on grounds of its presumed anti–working class and petit-bourgeois, individualist sentiment. The fact that it was made in the same decade as Sander's film suggests a straining on both sides of the border against the social suppression of subjective longings, including the gendered longings of women. *REDUPERS* and *Taube auf dem Dach*, as well as Gusner and Sander's coauthored *Fantasie und Arbeit*, supply evidence, then, of shared concerns among filmmakers East and West with gender hierarchies and inequalities; with aesthetic forms and perspectives adequate to gendered experience; and with the place of gender in recent German history. These close encounters remind us that the contact zones for shared histories of gender and media emerge not only, or even primarily, between the bounded spaces of nation-states, but in dispersed localities, city regions, and international points of intersection.

Transnational Media Entanglements and Gender

This spatially stretched and dispersed aspect of gendered media entanglements is explored further in Brittany Lehman's contribution to part five, "Gendered Orientalism: Representations of 'the Turkish' in the West German Press of the 1970s and 1980s." Lehman's chapter examines these representations as an example of gendered Orientalist stereotypes. Her focus is on the pervasive media stereotypes of the victimized girl and her villainous father and brothers. She locates part five's discussion of post–World War II gender and media both within a longer history of Muslim-Christian gender discourse and within an Orientalist spatial imaginary. Lehman draws on cultural-studies approaches that, since Edward Said's seminal 1978 study, have understood "Orientalism" as a "style of thought" based upon an "ontological and epistemological distinction" that fosters and cements relations of power between Occident and Orient.[39] Her specific focus is on the reproduction in mainstream media representations from late twentieth-century West Germany of Said's Orientalist division between the "dangerous [. . .] backward and uncivilized" Muslim man and the "beautiful, veiled, and powerless" woman. But her chapter also highlights the larger importance of a focus in gendered media histories on the transnational and intersectional dimensions of media entanglements.[40]

Earlier in this chapter, I drew on writing by Malte Hagener to discuss the status of media texts as boundary objects that travel across cultural communities and mediate relations between them. In Lehman's examples, it is the body and image of a woman that functions as a boundary object in Hagener's sense. In the press texts she studies, the fantasized Muslim man or woman functions to mark the border between Occidental and Oriental cultures and to provide a site for the articulation of both common and opposing gender norms. A comparative example is provided by postwar German film. In films contemporaneous with Lehman's case study, the intersection she traces between a Cold War sociopolitical and spatial imaginary and a gendered transnational or indeed global discourse of cultural difference is also evident. A comparison, once again, between Carow's *Paul und Paula* and contemporaneous feminist filmmaking from the West illustrates further the function of the female body as boundary object. In a scene from *Paul und Paula* immediately following the protagonists' fantasy lovemaking sequence on a river barge, Paula, distressed by Paul's failure to return to her flat for further lovers' trysts, intrudes on an official reception Paul stages for visiting African dignitaries. She finds Paul watching from the sidelines as his sexually wayward wife Ines dances with an African man. Sporting a modish mix of European dress (a white T-shirt) and African dress (a colorful Kente cloth wrapper), Ines's dancing partner is one of a group of African men who lend the scene a racialized touch of Black exoticism and cosmopolitan flair.

The Africans who move in and out of shot during this sequence also stand metonymically, however, for a larger, and ambivalent, history of postwar GDR-African affiliation. The GDR's African engagements had, from the late 1950s, taken the initial form of diplomatic and material support for anticolonial liberation movements. But by the time of Carow's film, the GDR had come in its turn to depend on Africa as one source of hard currency to feed the new "consumer socialism" initiated by SED general secretary Erich Honecker in 1971.[41] In *Paul und Paula,* the complex interdependencies in play in this geopolitical relation are made explicit by Paul in a whispered aside to Paula.[42] Paul is moving to close a lucrative deal with the African visitors; he is busy chasing hard currency (*Devisen*), he says, and can devote no further time to their adulterous affair. Most telling in gender terms at this point is an editing style that cuts repeatedly from point-of-view shots of the Ines's gyrating body, to close-ups of both white and Black men whose admiring gaze is established as the source of the camera's eroticized look. The viewer's prior knowledge of Ines's sexual infractions (she has previously deceived Paul with a lover) strengthens the inference in this shot-countershot sequence of a connection between female sexual allure, interracial mixing (Ines's, with her Black dancing partner), class politics (fashionable dress and extravagant hair and make-up establish Ines as a figure in thrall to "bourgeois" consumerism), and a political ambivalence deriving (as Paul's comments indicate) from the GDR's newly subservient relation to a decolonized Africa.

Ines's dancing body, then, becomes the nodal point in this sequence for a network of male gazes whose intensity derives from the intersection of heterosexual lust with racialized and geopolitical anxieties and desires. Located at this meeting point of competing male gazes, Ines's body at one and the same time marks the meeting point of competing male desires and the boundary that divides those desires along racial and geopolitical lines. The sequence points then to an understanding of the female body in postwar German media images not only, as in Jennifer Lynn's account, as a site of contestation for competing East and West German ideological visions. The East German *Paul und Paula,* like the "Orientalist" West German press reportage analyzed by Lehman, moves us instead to consider the mediated body of woman as a figure in which a gendered and sexualized East-West spatial imaginary intersects with social fantasies of race, class, and geopolitics.

In *Paul und Paula,* this functionalizing of the female body as the site of competing gendered but also classed and racialized cultural-political affiliations remains unquestioned. The film's romance narrative instead confines the uncomfortably contradictory figure of Ines within the stereotype of love rival to Paula and manages the ambivalence she provokes through Paul's insouciant repudiation of her at the film's dénouement (he finds Ines's latest lover in the wardrobe, laughs, bids his wife farewell, and heads off for a lovers' reunion at Paula's flat). It is, then, not Carow but once again Helke Sander to whom I turn finally for a feminist refiguring of the gendered boundaries that define transnational and global relations.

This chapter has identified Sander as an important figure in discussions of postwar gender and media, in part because of her prominent position as woman filmmaker, feminist activist, and media critic (the latter in her capacity as founding editor of the influential feminist journal *frauen und film*). But she is significant too in the context of this volume as a West German feminist who concerned herself repeatedly with cross-border questions of gender, sexual politics, and media form. Already in REDUPERS, Sander explored the capacity of feminist media interventions to afford insight into commonalities as well as differences in media perceptions between East and West. The film follows the activities of a women's photography group in West Berlin. The group's creations include large-format photographs that reorient viewer perceptions toward a woman's urban eye-view, and a street performance staged on one of several West Berlin viewing platforms, offering a glimpse of what turns out to be the entirely recognizable daily round of mundane activities—working, walking, shopping, driving—on the wall's eastern side.

The inference is that a feminist look can retrain the eye to identify a mundane East-West sameness, even across the most heavily fortified cultural boundaries (here, the Berlin Wall). In Sander's later film *Der subjektive Faktor* (The Subjective Factor) from 1981, that insight develops into a full-blown critique of the gender dimensions both of a binary geopolitics and of its media articulation. Taking a semiautobiographical view of feminist organizing within (and against) a male-dominated West German student movement, the film is noteworthy for its recognition of student activism as a form of media-saturated event politics. The dependence of the movements of 1968 on experimental form and media intervention is evident in the omnipresence in Sander's film of media artifacts including posters, photographs, newspapers, pamphlets, leaflets, typescripts, television, and film. In the film's loosely episodic narrative, characters including the central protagonist Anni (Angelika Rommel) search in this forest of media texts for models of a postfascist political subjectivity. Important in the context of the film are the transnational dimensions of that political desire. For the male characters who populate Anni's West Berlin commune, the role models are revolutionary men, such as Vietnam's Ho Chi Minh and, centrally, the Argentinian-born Cuban revolutionary Che Guevara. Anni, too, looks initially to "Third World" heroines to give shape to her own revolutionary desires. One scene has her posing against a poster of a Vietcong female liberation fighter. The woman squats expectantly, gun in one hand, and in the other a baby cradled to shield him against unseen enemies beyond the frame. Anni mimics the woman's posture but finds herself shifting awkwardly, never settling her body into its desired position as mirror to a militant revolutionary motherhood.

Later in the film, the Vietcong poster sits upside down and abandoned by the desk. The shot's implied critique of what the film identifies as a masculine mimicry of Third World liberation fighters is reinforced when Anni questions an analysis by her flatmate Matthias (Dominik Bender) of the politics of housework. Matthias has been watching Vietnam actuality footage with Anni's young son, Andres (Kai Opitz). When Matthias urges Andres to use Vietcong militancy as a model for his own behavior around the household, Anni mocks this masculinist equation of the Vietnam liberation struggle with household chores. Andres is a child, she reminds Matthias, and masculine hero worship an inappropriate model for a young boy's integration into domestic relationships in their communal home.

Anni's own exemplars for her nascent version of feminist radicalism are quieter, culled certainly in part from socialist classics, including August Bebel's *Die Frau und der Sozialismus* (Woman and Socialism) from 1879, a text that sits among the apartment's kitchen cookbooks.[43] But Anni also finds more proximate models in her engagements with other women on the personal politics of daily life. In snatched conversations, first in kitchens, corridors, and hallways, later in meetings arranged hurriedly on the margins of Socialist German Student League (Sozialistischer Deutscher Studentenbund, SDS) events, the film's emergent feminists build on their experience of the student movement's masculine aggressions and blind spots to articulate a new politics of sexual liberation. For Anni, as for the *REDUPERS* photography group (and, indeed, for Sander herself), feminist interventions are certainly predicated on transnational media engagements that reach from West to East Germany (the Bebel text, for instance, is brought across the border from East Berlin by a woman flatmate) and stretch out also to global spaces, including the war zone inhabited by the Vietcong poster's guerilla mother. Crucially, however, as the activities of the feminist photo collective and Anni's work as typesetter and leaflet designer show, the labor of fashioning this new political subjectivity depends on more quotidian forms of media activism. Documentary inserts in *Der subjektive Faktor* include photographic, film, poster, and leaflet coverage of women's pro-abortion marches, demonstrations against sexual violence, and, in one memorable scene, a back figure of Sander herself in documentary footage of her famous speech to the 1968 SDS national conference announcing a new program of feminist activism by the feminist group she cofounded, the Aktionsrat zur Befreiung der Frauen (Action Council for the Liberation of Women, Aktionsrat).[44]

Conclusion

In *Der subjektive Faktor*, media practices from graphic art to photography, from filmmaking to pamphleteering, link western feminism to a transnational politics of race, class, sexuality, and (post)colonialism, not through mimicry of revolutionary heroes but through a creative refiguring, as well as a circulation through local, national, and transnational dissident networks, of media images of female collectivity and shared gendered experience across cultural and geopolitical divides. The film's utopia of a global feminism articulated through media images of shared experience has, of course, been multiply contested, not least through Black feminist calls for an intersectional "rethinking and recasting" of feminism in ways that pay due heed to the multiplicity of gendered, raced, classed, sexed, and embodied social experience.[45] This chapter's focus on the simultaneous divisions and entanglements that shaped gendered media images and experience across German-German as well as regional and transnational sociopolitical divides draws some of its inspiration from the intersectional feminist demand for multidimensional and multidirectional thinking in gender critique. It argues for a phenomenological understanding of media texts that considers not primarily what they represent but how they have functioned historically to delineate and, occasionally, also to dissolve cultural, spatial, and geopolitical boundaries between German-German territories as well as across the geopolitical spaces of the global East, West, North, and South. Alongside Mary Louise Pratt's thinking on the arts of the contact zone, Malte Hagener's notion of media texts and bodies as boundary objects has been offered as a conceptual tool for a spatialized and embodied media historiography oriented as much toward gendered media experience as toward representation and meaning.

There is certainly more work to be done on untangling this history of embodied media form and its relation to gendered experience during forty years of German division. Oral histories and biographical research on media practitioners have much to tell us about the migrations and transnational mobilities that shaped German-German encounters across political divides. Studies of German media texts circulating beyond the German-speaking countries—films, music, and photographs, for instance, that garnered a following elsewhere in Europe, or in the decolonizing nations—would show more clearly how German-German entanglements arose across circuits of transnational and global media distribution and exchange. A sustained focus on media distribution would be helpful here, with exemplary extant studies including Rosemary Stott's excellent book on Western film distribution in the GDR, as well as the expanding historiography of television images traveling across East-West borders during forty years of German division.[46] As a contribution to these cross-border studies, this chapter offers methodological insights, a small handful of film case studies, an overview of the extant literature on media entanglements, and an introduction to the chapters by Lynn, Barton, and Lehman to which part five of this volume will turn.

Erica Carter is professor of German and film at King's College London and chair of the UK German Screen Studies Network. She has researched and written widely on questions of gender and consumption in German history and film studies. Her publications include: *How German Is She? Postwar West German Reconstruction and the Consuming Woman* (University of Michigan Press, 1997); *The German Cinema Book* (ed. with Tim Bergfelder and Deniz Göktürk, British Film Institute, 2002); *Dietrich's Ghosts: The Sublime and the Beautiful in Third Reich Film* (British Film Institute, 2004); and with Béla Balázs, *Early Film Theory* (Berghahn Books, 2010). Current projects include a revised and updated edition of *The German Cinema Book*; a coedited collection on the everyday history of postwar Germany; and a monograph on film and the colonial sensibility.

Notes

1. Christoph Kleßmann, "Introduction," in *The Divided Past: Rewriting the Post-War German History,* ed. Christoph Kleßmann (New York, 2001), 1–9.
2. Jessica Gienow-Hecht, "American Cultural Policy in the Federal Republic of Germany 1945–1968," in *The United States and Germany in the Era of the Cold War, 1945–1968,* ed. Detlef Junker et al. (Cambridge, 2004), 401–8; Jessica Gienow-Hecht, *Transmission Impossible: American Journalism as Cultural Diplomacy in Postwar Germany, 1945–1955* (Baton Rouge, LA, 1999); and Uta G. Poiger, *Jazz, Rock, and Rebels: Cold War Politics and American Culture in a Divided Germany* (Berkeley, CA, 2000).
3. Karl Christian Führer and Corey Ross, eds., *Mass Media, Culture and Society in Twentieth-Century Germany* (Basingstoke, 2006), esp. Thomas Lindenberger, "Looking West: The Cold War and the Making of Two German Cinemas," 113–28, Knut Hickethier, "Television and Social Transformation in the Federal Republic of Germany," 129–45; and Heather L. Gumbert, "Split Screens? Television in East Germany, 1952–89," 146–64. See also Sabine Hake, *German National Cinema* (London, 2008), chapters 4–6; and Tim Bergfelder et al., eds., *The German Cinema Book* (London, 2010).

4. See for instance, Christina von Hodenberg, *Konsens und Krise: Eine Geschichte der westdeutschen Medienöffentlichkeit* (Göttingen, 2006); and Heinz Pürer and Johannes Raabe, *Presse in Deutschland*, 3rd edn. (Konstanz, 2007).
5. Heather L. Gumbert, *Envisioning Socialism: Television and the Cold War in the German Democratic Republic* (Ann Arbor, MI, 2014); Jürgen Wilke., ed., *Journalisten und Journalismus in der DDR: Berufsorganisation, Westkorrespondenten, "Der schwarze Kanal"* (Cologne, 2007); and Rosemary Stott, *Crossing the Wall: The Western Feature Film Import in East Germany* (Bern, 2011).
6. For literature with a gender perspective, see Erica Carter, *How German Is She? Postwar West German Reconstruction and the Consuming Woman* (Ann Arbor, MI, 1997); Gunilla-Friederike Budde, "Der Körper der 'sozialistischen Frauenpersönlichkeit': Weiblichkeits-Vorstellungen in der SBZ und der frühen DDR," *Geschichte und Gesellschaft* 26, no. 4 (2000): 602–28; Jennifer Evans, "Constructing Borders: Image and Identity in *Die Frau von heute*, 1945–49," in *Conquering Women: Women and War in the German Cultural Imagination*, ed. Hilary Collier Sy-Quia and Susanne Baackmann (Berkeley, CA, 2000), 40–61; Dora Horvath, *Bitte recht weiblich! Frauenleitbilder in der deutschen Zeitschrift "Brigitte" 1949–1982* (Zurich, 2000); Judd Stitziel, *Fashioning Socialism: Clothing, Politics and Consumer Culture in East Germany* (New York, 2005).
7. I am indebted for my understanding of boundary objects to Malte Hagener, "Different Films, Different Practices: Looking Into the 'Other Films' of the European Interwar Film Avant-Garde," unpublished paper delivered at the 2017 conference, "Sensibility and the Senses: Media, Bodies, Practices," NECS—European Network for Cinema and Media Studies Paris, 29 June—1 July 2017; see also Mary-Louise Pratt, "Arts of the Contact Zone," *Profession* (1991): 33–40.
8. On the New Women in Weimar Germany, see Marsha Meskimmon and Shearer West, eds., *Visions of the "Neue Frau": Women and the Visual Arts in Weimar Germany* (Brookfield, VT, 1995); Katharina von Ankum, ed., *Women in the Metropolis: Gender and Modernity in Weimar Culture* (Berkeley, CA, 1997); Vibeke Rützou Petersen, *Women and Modernity in Weimar Germany: Reality and Its Representation in Popular Fiction* (New York, 2001); Patrice Petro, *Aftershocks of the New: Feminism and Film History* (New Brunswick, NJ, 2002); and Mila Ganeva, *Women in Weimar Fashion: Discourses and Displays in German Culture, 1918–1933* (Rochester, NY, 2008).
9. See Katherine Pence and Paul Betts, eds., *Socialist Modern: East German Politics, Society and Culture* (Ann Arbor, MI, 2008).
10. See Alys Eve Weinbaum et al., *The Modern Girl around the World: Consumption, Modernity, and Globalization* (Durham, NC, 2008); and Elizabeth Otto and Vanessa Rocco, ed., *The New Woman International: Representations in Photography and Film from the 1870s through the 1960s* (Ann Arbor, MI, 2011).
11. See for example Lars Elleström, ed., *Media Borders, Multimodality and Intermediality* (New York, 2010); Ágnes Pethő, *Cinema and Intermediality: The Passion for the In-between* (Newcastle upon Tyne, 2011); and Dunja Brötz, Beate Eder-Jordan and Martin Fritz, eds., *Intermedialität in der Komparatistik: Eine Bestandsaufnahme* (Innsbruck, 2013).
12. For the literature, see also the chapter by Karen Hagemann and Donna Harsch on "Entanglements of Gender, Politics, and Protest in the Historiography on the Two Post-1945 Germanys" in this volume.

13. Indicative critical studies of sexism in media representations by 1970s and 1980s second-wave West German feminists include Demokratische Fraueninitiative, AK Medien, *Frauen-Filmbuch* (Munich, 1978); Marieluise Janssen-Jurreit, *Sexismus: Über die Abtreibung der Frauenfrage* (Berlin, 1978); Heide Simonis, "Nichts gegen einen nackten Po: Aber Frauen dürfen nicht länger als kaufluststeigernde Medien eingesetzt werden," *Sozialdemokratischer Pressedienst* 33, no. 123 (June 1978): 4; Christiane Schmerl, ed., *Frauenfeindliche Werbung: Sexismus als heimlicher Lehrplan* (Berlin, 1980); Barbara Scheffer-Hegel and Brigitte Wartmann, eds., *Mythos Frau: Projektionen und Inszenierungen im Patriarchat* (Berlin, 1984). The feminist film journal *frauen und film*, founded in 1974, contributed significantly to West German feminist debates on media sexism, as did the two most prominent feminist illustrated magazines of the period, *Emma* (launched in 1977), and *Courage* (1976–84). A useful bibliographical source for activist literature of the period is Jutta Röser (with Beate Illg and Susanne Keunecke), *Frauen-Medien-Forschung. Graue Literatur 1980–1992: Eine kommentierte Bibliographie* (Münster, 1993).
14. Patrick Major and Rana Mitter, "East Is East and West Is West? Towards a Comparative Socio-Cultural History of the Cold War," in *Across the Blocs: Cold War Cultural and Social History*, ed. Patrick Major and Rana Mitter (London, 2004), 1–22.
15. See Hagener, "Different Films, Different Practices," unpublished talk, n.p.
16. Quotes are from the *locus classicus* of conceptualizations of the boundary object, Susan Leigh Star and James R. Griesemer, "Institutional Ecology, 'Translations' and Boundary Objects: Amateurs and Professionals in Berkeley's Museum of Vertebrate Zoology, 1907–39," *Social Studies of Science* 19, no. 3 (1989): 393.
17. See Erika Balsom, *After Unique-Ness: A History of Film and Video Art in Circulation* (New York, 2017).
18. See for instance Andrea Rinke, "Eastside Stories: Singing and Dancing for Socialism," *Film History* 18, no. 1 (2006): 73–87; Gumbert, *Envisioning Socialism*; Kate Lacey, "The Invention of a Listening Public: Radio and Its Audiences," in Führer and Ross, *Mass Media, Culture and Society*, 61–79; and Konrad Dussel, "Radio Programming, Ideology and Cultural Change: Fascism, Communism and Liberal Democracy," in ibid., 80–94; Jan Palmowski, "Narrating the Everyday: Television, Memory and the Subjunctive in the GDR, 1969–89," in *Experiencing Postwar Germany: Everyday Life and Cultural Practice in East and West, 1960–2000*, ed. Erica Carter et al. (Oxford, 2019), n.p.; and Michael Schmidt, "The Fragmentation of Pop: Music, Media, and Perception in Germany during the 1950s," in ibid., n.p.
19. On the unenthusiastic responses of GDR critics, see Fred Gehler, "Die Legende von Paul und Paula," *Sonntag*, Berlin, DDR, no. 16, 1973. The nervousness of the authorities was evident in restrictions placed on the number of screenings, perhaps because it became clear that the film had unleashed popular desires for utopian transformation that the regime was unwilling or unable to meet. See Rosemary Stott, "The State-Owned Cinema Industry and Its Audience," in *Re-Imagining DEFA: East German Cinema in its National and Transnational Contexts*, ed. Seán Allan and Sebastian Heiduschke (Oxford, 2016), 19–40, 35; and Daniela Berghahn, *Hollywood behind the Wall: The Cinema of East Germany* (Manchester, 2005), 197–220.
20. On SED leader Erich Honecker's turn to a new consumerism, see Philipp Heldmann, "Negotiating Consumption in a Dictatorship: Consumer Politics in the

GDR in the 1950s and 1960s," in Martin Daunton and Matthew Hilton, eds., *The Politics of Consumption: Material Culture and Citizenship in Europe and America* (Oxford, 2001), 185–202. On *Paul und Paula* in the context of East German consumerism, see also Stephen Brockmann, *A Critical History of German Film* (Rochester, NY, 2010), 259–73.
21. Gehler, "Die Legende von Paul und Paula."
22. N.N., *Frankfurter Rundschau*, 7 November 1975.
23. Brockmann, *Critical History*, 273.
24. Iris Gusner and Helke Sander, *Fantasie und Arbeit: Biografische Zwiegespräche* (Marburg, 2009), 81.
25. Helke Sander and Renate Schlesier, "*Die Legende von Paul und Paula*: Eine frauenverachtende Schnulze aus der DDR," *frauen und film* no. 2 (September 1974): 11.
26. Gusner and Sander, *Fantasie und Arbeit*, 80.
27. Ibid., 136.
28. Pratt, "Arts of the Contact Zone."
29. Andreas Kötzing, "Blinde Flecken: Das Jahr 1966 und die deutsch-deutschen Filmbeziehungen," in *Deutschland 1966: Filmische Perspektiven in Ost und West*, ed. Connie Betz et al. (Berlin, 2016), 82–95, 83. See also Michael Wedel et al., eds., *DEFA International: Grenzüberschreitende Filmbeziehungen vor und nach dem Mauerbau* (Wiesbaden, 2013); Marc Silberman and Henning Wrage, eds., *DEFA at the Crossroads of East German and International Film Culture* (Berlin, 2014); Allan and Heiduschke, *Re-Imagining DEFA*; Sabine Hake and John Davidson, eds., *Framing the Fifties: Cinema in a Divided Germany* (Oxford, 2008); and Andrea Rinke, "Eastside Stories: Singing and Dancing for Socialism," *Film History* 18, no. 1 (2006): 73–87.
30. Michael Wedel et al., "Einleitung," in Wedel et al., *DEFA International*, 12.
31. Rosemary Stott, *Crossing the Wall: The West German Feature Film Import in West Germany* (Oxford, 2012); and Kötzing, "Blinde Flecken."
32. Ibid., 88–89.
33. Stott, "State-Owned Cinema Industry," 24.
34. Pratt, "Arts of the Contact Zone," 34.
35. Ibid., 35–36.
36. Claudia Lenssen and Bettina Schoeller-Bouju, *Wie haben Sie das gemacht? Aufzeichnungen zu Frauen und Film* (Marburg, 2014); Bettina Schoeller-Bouju and Claudia Lenssen, *Wie haben Sie das gemacht: Filme von Frauen aus fünf Jahrzehnten*, 2 vols.: 1. *Spielen und Dokumentieren*; 2. *Neue Formen*, DVD (Berlin, 2014). See also Claudia Lenssen, "Frauen-Rollen-Bilder 1966," in Betz at al., *Deutschland 1966: Filmische Perspektiven*, 150–63.
37. See for instance Christel Gräf, "Waren Ostfrauen wirklich anders? Zur Darstellung von Frauen im DEFA-Gegenwartsfilm," in *Der geteilte Himmel: Höhepunkte des DEFA-Kinos 1946–1992*, ed. Raimund Fritz, 2 vols. (Vienna, 2001), 2: 107–17; also Gusner and Sander, *Fantasie und Arbeit*.
38. Ibid., 8.
39. Edward W. Said, *Orientalism* (London and Henley, 1978), 10.
40. I use the term "intersectional" in the sense outlined by Kimberlé Crenshaw, whose writings on the intersections of gender and race as well as class and sexuality in cases of rape and domestic violence against Women of Color demonstrate from a Black feminist perspective "the need to account for multiple grounds of iden-

tity when considering how the social world is constructed." Kimberlé Crenshaw, "Mapping the Margins: Intersectionality, Identity Politics, and Violence against Women of Color," *Stanford Law Review* 43, no. 6 (1991): 1245.
41. See Mark Landsman, *Dictatorship and Demand: The Politics of Consumerism in East Germany* (Cambridge, MA, 2005): 214–22.
42. For further insight into East German socialist internationalism in relation to decolonizing African nations, see Quinn Slobodian, ed., *Comrades of Color: East Germany and the Cold War World* (New York, 2015).
43. August Bebel, *Die Frau und der Sozialismus* (Zürich-Hottingen, 1879); first published in English as *Woman and Socialism* (New York, 1910).
44. The full text of Sander's speech is available at http://www.1000dokumente.de/pdf/dok_0022_san_de.pdf (accessed 22 January 2018).
45. Kimberlé Crenshaw, "Demarginalizing the Intersection of Race and Sex: A Black Feminist Critique of Antidiscrimination Doctrine, Feminist Theory and Antiracist Politics," *University of Chicago Legal Forum* 140 (1989): 140.
46. Stott, *Crossing the Wall*; Gumbert, *Envisioning Socialism*; and Palmowski, "Narrating the Everyday."

Selected Bibliography

Allan, Seán, and Sebastian Heiduschke, eds. *Re-Imagining DEFA: East German Cinema in Its National and Transnational Contexts*. Oxford, 2016.
Bergfelder, Tim, Erica Carter, and Deniz Göktürk, eds. *The German Cinema Book*. London, 2010.
Berghahn, Daniela. *Hollywood behind the Wall: The Cinema of East Germany*. Manchester, 2005.
Bösch, Frank. *Mass Media and Historical Change: Germany in International Perspective, 1400 to the Present*. New York, 2015.
Brockmann, Stephen. *A Critical History of German Film*. Rochester, NY, 2010.
Carter, Erica. *How German Is She? Postwar West German Reconstruction and the Consuming Woman*. Ann Arbor, MI, 1997.
———, Katrin Schreiter, and Jan Palmowski, eds. *Experiencing Postwar Germany. Everyday Life and Cultural Practice in East and West, 1960–2000*. Oxford, 2019.
Chin, Rita. "Turkish Women, West German Feminists, and the Gendered Discourse on Muslim Cultural Difference." *Public Culture* 22, no. 3 (2010): 557–81.
Fiedler, Anke, and Michael Meyen. *Fiktionen für das Volk: DDR-Zeitungen als PR-Instrument; Fallstudien zu den Zentralorganen Neues Deutschland, Junge Welt, Neue Zeit und Der Morgen*. Berlin, 2011.
Fritz, Raimund, ed. *Der geteilte Himmel: Höhepunkte des DEFA-Kinos 1946–1992*. 2 vols. Vienna, 2001.
Führer, Karl Christian, and Corey Ross, eds. *Mass Media, Culture and Society in Twentieth Century Germany*. New York, 2006.
Gumbert, Heather L. *Envisioning Socialism: Television and the Cold War in the German Democratic Republic*. Ann Arbor, MI, 2014.
Gusner, Iris, and Helke Sander, *Fantasie und Arbeit: Biografische Zwiegespräche*. Marburg, 2009.
Hake, Sabine. *German National Cinema*. London, 2008.

———, and John Davidson. *Framing the Fifties: Cinema in a Divided Germany.* New York, 2008.
Hodenberg, Christina von. *Konsens und Krise: Eine Geschichte der westdeutschen Medienöffentlichkeit 1945–1973.* Göttingen, 2006.
Horvath, Dora. *Bitte recht weiblich! Frauenleitbilder in der deutschen Zeitschrift "Brigitte" 1949–1982.* Zurich, 2000.
Korteweg, Anna, and Gökçe Yurdakul. *The Headscarf Debates: Conflicts of National Belonging.* Stanford, CA, 2014.
Laurien, Ingrid. *Politisch-Kulturelle Zeitschriften in den Westzonen 1945–1949: Ein Beitrag zur politischen Kultur der Nachkriegszeit.* Frankfurt/M., 1991.
Leeder, Karen, ed. *Rereading East Germany: The Literature and Film of the GDR.* Cambridge, 2015.
Lenssen, Claudia, and Bettina Schoeller-Bouju. *Wie haben Sie das gemacht? Aufzeichnungen zu Frauen und Film.* Marburg, 2014.
Major, Patrick, and Rana Mitter, eds. *Across the Blocs: Cold War Cultural and Social History.* London, 2004
Pence, Katherine, and Paul Betts, eds. *Socialist Modern: East German Politics, Society and Culture.* Ann Arbor, MI, 2008.
Poiger, Uta G. *Jazz, Rock, and Rebels: Cold War Politics and American Culture in a Divided Germany.* Berkeley, CA, 2000.
Ross, Cory. *Media and the Making of Modern Germany: Mass Communications, Society, and Politics from the Empire to the Third Reich.* Oxford, 2008.
Schlosser, Nicholas J. *Cold War on the Airwaves: The Radio Propaganda War against East Germany.* Urbana-Champaign, IL, 2015.
Silberman, Marc, and Henning Wrage, eds. *DEFA at the Crossroads of East German and International Film Culture.* Berlin, 2014.
Slobodian, Quinn, ed. *Comrades of Color: East Germany and the Cold War World.* New York, 2015.
Stitziel, Judd. *Fashioning Socialism: Clothing, Politics and Consumer Culture in East Germany.* New York, 2005.
Stott, Rosemary. *Crossing the Wall: The West German Feature Film Import in West Germany.* Oxford, 2012.

PART II
GENDER, POLITICS, AND POLICIES

CHAPTER 4

The Big Cleanup
Men, Women, and Rubble Clearance in Postwar East and West Germany

Leonie Treber

Since the 1980s, the so-called rubble woman (*Trümmerfrau*) has belonged to the inventory of collective memory in West Germany.[1] The rubble woman has come to represent not only the altruistic woman who cleared the ruins of the Second World War but also the forerunner of the German "economic miracle" (*Wirtschaftswunder*). Virtually every historical presentation of the postwar era incorporates this heroic narrative, regardless of whether the account appears on television or in print media, schoolbooks, or exhibitions by historical museums, such as at the German Historical Museum in Berlin.[2] The images of the rubble woman are conspicuously stereotypical and present her everywhere with a foreknotted headcloth and a hammer in her hand or at work in a bucket chain.[3] The related texts are no less standardized. One of many examples is an article in the left-liberal West German newspaper *Frankfurter Rundschau* that appeared on the occasion of the sixtieth anniversary of the founding of the Federal Republic of Germany (FRG) in May 1949. It cited a rubble woman from Berlin who reportedly said, "Removing rubble was always self-evident for me. The men were missing in war or came back as cripples. So we all had to get to work. Otherwise we would still be sitting in ashes and ruins today."[4]

For decades, the historiography did not question this clichéd public image of the rubble woman but instead perpetuated it. The West German historian Eckart Conze, for example, writes in his 2009 history of the Federal Republic of Germany from 1949 to the present, "Above all the 'rubble women' have found their place in the collective memory of the Germans. Because the men returned only gradually from confinement as prisoners of wars, many only years later, it was left to women, children and the elderly to remove the ruins."[5] This stereotypical narrative of the rubble woman, and with it the whole process of rubble clearance after World War II, is remarkable. After all, when the war finally had ended in May 1945, there were 400 million cubic meters of ruins and ashes in Germany. Piled in a single heap, they would have built an alpine mountain 4,000 meters high.[6]

Were German women with their bucket chains and hammers in hand really in a position to remove such a mass of rubble? In fact, they were not. Only in the Soviet Occupation Zone (SBZ) in the eastern half of Germany and in Berlin, which was divided too into four sectors controlled by the allies, were women recruited for rubble clearance in great numbers. In the three Western occupation zones administered by the United States, Great Britain, and France, the rubble clearance was mainly done by men. Furthermore, most of the women in East Germany and Berlin who indeed helped to clean the rubble did not volunteer for the job. They were obligated. Thus, little remains of the much-invoked altruistic motivation of the rubble women to help with Germany's reconstruction.[7] Nonetheless, the myth of the rubble women who labored to remove piles of rubble during Germany's "zero hour" and carried the burden of reconstruction has increasingly made its way into collective memory since the 1980s.

This chapter seeks to shed light on the collective myth of the rubble women who rebuilt postwar Germany. From a comparative gender perspective, it investigates the East and West German history of rubble removal during and after the Second World War. It asks what enabled and caused the rise of the rubble-women myth and its dominance in collective memory. The chapter unfolds in four sections. The first briefly traces the beginnings of rubble clearance during the Second World War and under the National Socialist regime. The second turns to the organization and main actors of rubble removal in the postwar period. The third compares and contrasts the role of women in rubble clearance in the three Western zones and the SBZ. The last addresses the origin and significance of the rubble-women myth.

The Tradition of the "Third Reich": Rubble Clearance during the Air War

Before the Allied air war against the German Reich even began, the National Socialists founded the Security and Aid Service (Sicherheits- und Hilfsdienst, SHD), later renamed Air Protection Police (Luftschutzpolizei), in the spring of 1940. This aid system aimed to suggest to the German population a certain measure of security in case Allied bombing was to occur. The Repair Service (Instandsetzungsdienst) of the SHD was to carry out the removal of rubble as well as the repair of streets and buildings after a bombing attack. And, in fact, these troops hurried to sites of damage and began rubble removal after the first air attacks on German cities occurred.[8]

In addition, in September 1940, the 18th Decree of the General Commissioner for Regulation of Building Construction (*Anordnung des Generalbevollmächtigten für die Regelung der Bauwirtschaft*) was issued. This decree integrated the construction trades into procedures for removing air-raid damage. It also gave city mayors the power to direct immediate efforts. Mayors in turn entrusted directors of building offices with coordination and implementation.[9] The armed forces of the Nazi state, the Wehrmacht, became another important actor in clearing rubble in the cities.[10] Soldiers of the Armed Forces Auxiliary Command (Wehrmachtshilfskommandos) took part as unskilled laborers. The Hitler Youth (Hitlerjugend, HJ), the mandatory youth organization of the National Socialist German Workers' Party (Nationalsozialistische Deutsche Arbeiterpartei, NSDAP) in Germany for boys, was also engaged in the removal of rubble, at least in the case of immediate need: if there were not enough assigned laborers available, members of the HJ were recruited for this work. From 1942 onward there was also the formal possibility of recruiting additional workers through the Reich Labor Service (Reichsarbeitsdienst, RAD) if there was immediate demand. The RAD, the major organization established in Nazi Germany in 1935 as an agency to help mitigate the effects of unemployment on German economy and to militarize the young men in the workforce between the ages of eighteen and twenty-five, however, played a subordinate role in rubble clearance during the air war.

As early as 1940, the National Socialists began to use forced laborers to clear rubble, a system that grew as the bombing damage steadily rose. After the first bombing attacks on Berlin, Chancellor Adolf Hitler ordered the formation of the first prisoners-of-war (POW) construction battalion, which consisted of glaziers and window carpenters standing ready to remove glass damage in the city.[11] By June 1941 three additional battalions, each consisting of 600 glaziers and window carpenters drawn from French POWs, were formed to work, respectively, in Duisburg, Frankfurt am Main, and Hamburg. The POWs of the glazier, roofer, construction, and labor battalions worked as skilled laborers in support of German construction craftsmen as they repaired buildings. From the end of 1942, foreign forced laborers in addition to the POWs were ordered to remove debris. Because the mounds of rubble grew larger as the war went on, the National Socialists finally also included concentration camp inmates in rubble-clearance measures. Under the direction of Albert Speer, Reich minister for armaments and munitions since February 1942, a concept was developed for these tasks to be carried out by mobile construction brigades under the control of the SS, the so-called Protection Squadron (Schutzstaffel), the major paramilitary organization of the Nazis.[12] By mid-October 1942, a total of 3,000 prisoners had been selected in the concentration camps of Buchenwald near Weimar, Neuengamme near Hamburg, and Sachsenhausen near Berlin for Construction Brigades I, II, and III. A fourth construction brigade of camp inmates was formed in 1943. They were deployed in Berlin, Cologne, Bremen, Duisburg, Düsseldorf, Osnabrück, and other cities. These first SS Construction Brigades consisted of non-Jewish male inmates, mainly from Eastern Europe, and were supervised by German inmates. The concentration camp inmates were used, above all, for heavy and dangerous work in rubble clearance; fatalities resulting from this work were looked upon with approval. The work of removing rubble during the air war was therefore forced labor to a high degree and, hence, was perceived by the German public as penal labor.

In addition, rubble clearance during the war was firmly in male hands. This was also true for POW battalions and SS Construction Brigades, for which only male inmates were recruited. Only toward the end of the Second Word War did the recruitment of forced laborers for rubble clearance become ever more chaotic and difficult, leading authorities to bring in female forced laborers from Eastern Europe.[13]

Postwar Rubble Clearance: Penal Labor, Professionalization, and Labor Recruitment

The use of male and female forced laborers for rubble clearance lasted until the end of the Second World War. They were deployed all the way up to surrender, especially in cities that were still being bombarded. Halberstadt, a town in Saxony-Anhalt, for example, experienced a devastating attack that destroyed 80 percent of the city on 8 April 1945. Before inmates of the nearby concentration camp were forced onto death marches, they were sent into the city for clearance work. Three days later the war was over for Halberstadt.[14] But there was only a short interruption in rubble clearing.

Early postwar measures for rubble removal were connected directly to those of the war years: rubble clearance remained penal labor. Self-appointed or newly installed municipal administrations and the Allied military authorities quickly decided to use former members and functionaries of the NSDAP and German POWs to deal with the piles of rubble.[15] Those whom the Allies and Allied-appointed administrators held responsible for the terror, horror, and death perpetrated by the Third Reich were to atone for their deeds. Without distinction of gender, NSDAP members were assigned to rubble clearance as "atonement measures." The policy was initiated by the Allied military governments as part of their denazification and demilitarization objectives. They demanded the use of former Nazi supporters and detained Wehrmacht soldiers for rubble clearance. Both groups were made available to city administrations by the relevant military government. The deployment, though, was carried out by Germans on their own authority, whether by the Anti-Fascist Committees that emerged everywhere in 1945–46 or by the representatives of city administrations legitimated by the military governments.

The use of former Nazis and German POWs for the removal of rubble was a widespread phenomenon in the immediate postwar period, but from the beginning military-government and city administrations were aware that the sheer and seemingly endless mountains of rubble could not be cleared through such measures alone. They lacked, however, the concepts and means for complete rubble clearance.[16] Consequently, the professionalization of rubble removal developed as a two-track process. The conceptual foundations were laid by representatives of municipal administrations and by contractors who owned construction companies. Despite the lack of a master plan, they did not have to begin from scratch. Thanks to continuities to the Third Reich in personnel and institutions, construction officials and contractors could fall back on wartime experience with rubble removal or comparable work. It nevertheless took a while until the concepts were even halfway matured and their execution could begin. For this reason, most municipal administrations initially concentrated on getting a handle on the most pressing problems: the clearance of main traffic arteries as well as the repair of damaged streets and only slightly damaged residential areas. To carry out these measures, a great variety of skilled workers were pulled in, so the professionalization of rubble clearance began early on and encompassed ever-wider circles. With the progressive stabilization of political and economic conditions, ever more professional actors were included, above all construction contractors located in the relevant cities and regions. More than any other groups, medium and large construction contractors played an increasingly important role in rubble clearance. During the National Socialist period, they had been involved less than the smaller and middling craft firms in repairing damage in the Third Reich but had concentrated on "war-related construction tasks in all parts of Europe."[17] For a rapid "new beginning" after the war, they now were depending to a high degree on the Allies who had confiscated what was left of their businesses, including machines and vehicle parks. For this and other reasons, the Allied military governments owned some of the better technical equipment, which they had to make available to municipal administrations.[18]

Municipal construction officials on their own authority assigned construction firms to clear main streets, destroyed residential areas, and whole quarters. Excavators, trucks, and rubble trains were used whenever possible, transfer and unloading dumps were set up in the cities, and procedures to dispose of or reuse rubble were developed. This process was planned and implemented with especial effectiveness in those cities with a corporation founded for that purpose. The most prominent example of this was Frankfurt am Main, in the American Occupation Zone, where the municipal administration together with the firms Philipp Holzmann AG, Metallgesellschaft AG, and Wayss & Freytag AG founded the Rubble Recycling Corporation (Trümmerverwertungsgesellschaft) in October 1945.[19]

Even if rubble removal was borne to a high degree by corporations and contractors, these organizations needed people to carry out the appropriate work. After the war, however, there was a lack of skilled labor. German municipal administrations, thus, set upon two measures for recruiting workers: the establishment of "citizen assignments" and the use of the unemployed. Citizen assignments for rubble clearance were called into life by municipal administrations in almost every large German city. Typically, they called up all employable "citizens" of a city to perform these assignments in their free time.[20] The scope of the hours to be worked differed from city to city. In the Saxon city of Dresden in the SBZ, for example, male and female citizens were urged over several years to participate in a four-hour weekend shift once per month. In Frankfurt am Main, on the other hand, they had to clear rubble for only two eight-hour days in total and thereby fulfilled their "citizenly duty." Not just the scope differed, but also the form of mobilization: in several cities, especially in the East, the municipal administrations operated with enormous moral pressure to urge the citizens to participate, while other cities required it from their citizens. Because these assignments were anything but popular, several cities like the Franconian town of Nuremberg in the American Occupation Zone later changed a voluntary commitment into an obligation, after winning the participation of only 610 of the 50,000 citizens envisaged by the mayor. Other cities like Stuttgart, Württemberg, also located in the in the American zone, completely ended the "citizen assignments" after citizens refused to take part. An important reason for the refusal was that rubble clearance continued to be seen by many as penal or atonement labor.

Things went differently with the use of the unemployed, who were easier to mobilize with appropriate sanctioning measures, but they were recruited on a grand scale only in Berlin and the SBZ.[21] Officials in all four zones required the jobless to register at the public employment offices (*Arbeitsämter*). In the American, British, and French zones, however, this measure had the character of a census and did not automatically convey unskilled workers into work assignments. The authorities limited themselves as a rule to identifying skilled workers among the unemployed and forwarding them to construction firms. In the Soviet zone, on the other hand, there was direct placement in tasks classified as "vital," mostly for available unemployed who were registered as unskilled or outside their traditional profession. These tasks included rubble clearance. In the first postwar weeks, the assignments for the unemployed were carried out by labor offices acting on their own, but later the unemployed were used by the new public construction offices (*Bauämter*) or turned over to construction firms.

The main reason why the unemployed were used at a much higher rate in the SBZ was its much worse economic starting position. In comparison to the three Western zones, the Soviet zone's industry was weakened much more severely by the consequences of war, which in addition to destruction by air raids especially included industrial dismantling and reparation payments to the Soviet Union.[22] In rubble removal, as in the economy in general, the lower level of mechanization was compensated for by a corresponding increase and management of laborers, spurred on by Soviet labor-assignment policy, which aimed at "total mobilization of workers."[23]

Because the Nazi regime used forced labor for rubble clearance and because postwar administrators compelled former members of the Nazi Party as well as German POWs to remove rubble as a form of atonement, the public in both East and West Germany viewed rubble clearance as penal labor. Simultaneously, though, the West German municipal administration in cooperation with construction contractors implemented professional, mechanized procedures that enabled a productive rubble clearance and allowed for the debris's reuse. In East Germany, on the other hand, the unemployed were deployed for rubble clearance in large numbers because of the worse overall economic situation.

Women in Rubble Clearance: A Question of the System

What was the role of women in rubble clearing in the four occupation zones of postwar Germany, and how did recruiting practices differ in the four zones? On the one hand, women who were known as NSDAP members were, like male party members and functionaries, assigned to rubble clearance after the war in all four occupation zones as an "atonement measure." On the other hand, unemployed women as potential workers moved quickly into the line of sight of labor offices, above all in the SBZ and in all four sectors of Berlin. Because of the labor shortage, the labor policy of the Soviet Military Administration was to mobilize *all* laborers, including women, who constituted the biggest reservoir of potential labor. The war had caused a general "surplus" of women, but the gender imbalance in the population was far more developed in Berlin and the

SBZ. Although women's deployment in rubble clearance transgressed the traditional gendered division of labor of the prewar economy, the mobilization of women for such work had been made thinkable by the employment of women in men's occupations during "total war." For the Soviet Military Administration, the extensive use of women in all sectors of the economy was not unusual either, because during the Second World War women in the Soviet Union too had replaced men in not only the workforce but also the armed forces in large numbers. The new officeholders in the municipal administrations of the SBZ, most of them members of the Socialist Unity Party of Germany (Sozialistische Einheitspartei Deutschlands, SED) founded in April 1946, supported this labor-market policy. Many of the former Communists or Social Democrats that united in the SED supported the old socialist idea of female "emancipation" through paid work and the ideal of the dual-earner family.[24]

In Berlin, which was completely controlled by the Soviets until July 1945, guidelines for labor assignments adopted in June 1945 stated that labor duty in clearance and construction work applied to "all able men from 15 to 55 years old" and to "all able women from 15 to 50 years old." There were exceptions only for "women with children under age of 3 [or] two or more children under age of 14," for the war injured and ill who had a physician's certification, as well as for otherwise fully employed workers with a corresponding work permit.[25] Accordingly, labor duty applied to unemployed women and men who were correspondingly registered at labor offices and obligated to carry out clearance and construction work. At the beginning of the postwar period, however, there were simply no male laborers available to assign to rubble clearance. A report of District Labor Office Tiergarten, South Post, from February 1946 explained:

> Of 21,000 inhabitants some 6,000 were still in residence [at the end of the war], whose number by now has increased to 8,000. Those remaining are composed for the most part of the overaged, children, and women. Only about 60 usable men fit for service were available to join in the work of reconstruction. Huge labor actions must be undertaken to make the streets and sidewalks drivable and passable again, barricades must be removed, rubble from bridge demolitions removed from the Landwehr Canal to enable the flow of water, corpses and cadavers retrieved and buried. [. . .] To solve all these enormous tasks only women are available to us.[26]

As the report illustrates, the work of rubble removal in Berlin began almost exclusively with women. Only at the end of August 1945—the first month of statistics on work assignments—did the number of male workers approach one thousand, while early in the month 2,500 and by month's end more than 5,000 female workers were engaged. And this trend continued: at the end of November 1945, among 30,000 laborers committed to rubble removal, 23,000 women stood alongside only

7,000 men, and in May 1946, when the final peak of 35,000 workers was reached, 26,000 women and 9,000 men worked in the ruins. Only as the number of laborers in the district of the Labor Office Tiergarten declined from summer 1946, settling in early 1947 at the relatively constant figure of around 5,000 workers, did the number of men and women more or less balance out, although somewhat more women than men were always drawn into these assignments.[27]

Although jobless women made up the majority of rubble clearers for a relatively short period of time, the rubble-removing women were not a mass phenomenon in Berlin even in the first postwar years. In a population of about 500,00 female Berliners aged twenty to thirty-nine, 6,000 women—or 5 percent of women of that age group—were engaged in rubble disposal. In fact, given that women from fifteen to fifty years old were considered fit for labor, the percentage of rubble-clearing women among all eligible women must surely have been still lower.[28] And this is true not only for Berlin but also for cities of the SBZ. In Magdeburg and Dresden, for example, women were initially the majority of unemployed assignees, but the gender ratio among rubble clearers had already reversed by 1946, reflecting the fact that ever more released male POWs returned and were available to the labor market.[29] In addition, the professionalization of rubble clearance had progressed also in the East, and relatively inefficient manual labor by unskilled workers was increasingly replaced by the use of large machinery and skilled personnel.

Even if it was not a mass phenomenon, the assignment of unemployed women to rubble clearance in Berlin and the other cities of the Soviet Occupation Zone remained in practice until the beginning of the 1950s. For the women engaged in such labor it was a hard, daily reality. As a rule these "auxiliary construction workers" did not report voluntarily for rubble clearance. Typically, the labor offices assigned the work to them. Two major groups of women forced to accept this assignment were, first, widows who had lost their husbands in war and, second, married women who awaited the return of their husbands held as POWs. These women were the sole breadwinners for their families and as such were dependent either on paid work and ration cards or on welfare services. Their number rose by leaps and bounds after the German surrender because the Soviets froze all private accounts and stopped all support payments, including pensions.[30] "War widows and soldiers' wives who had received comparatively high [pensions] during the war saw themselves suddenly downgraded to welfare status. Even after the payment of support benefits had begun again, war widows only received a pension if they were unfit to work or had reached the age of sixty."[31]

Even among putative volunteers, altruism was less a motivator than were necessity and food insecurity. When it came to food provisioning, not every rations card was equal: consumers were allotted rations based on the physical exertion of the labor they performed. Housewives were slotted into the lowest consumer group and therefore obtained a card that on its own hardly allowed for survival and was, thus, popularly dubbed the "hunger card."[32] Yet this classification was a calculated decision to entice women to take up paid work. The deputy mayor of Berlin defended the rationing scale: "If housewives and domestics are classified unfavorably, then they should 'leave their cooking pots and help with building.'"[33] And that is precisely what women did if they could not otherwise ensure their survival. If they reported "voluntarily" for rubble disposal at their local labor office, they were bestowed not only a salary, however modest (in Berlin female auxiliary construction workers received an hourly wage of 0.72 Reichsmarks) but, more importantly, a food card with the second-highest ration.[34]

In the SBZ, women were assigned to rubble clearance not only as "unemployed" but also through the "citizen assignments" discussed earlier. In the case of rubble clearing, the term "citizen" typically referred to both men and women. Again, because women were in the majority at war's end, as in the case of deployment of the unemployed, they also accounted for the majority of "citizen assignments" and, thus, cleared away ruins alongside men.[35]

The situation was wholly different in the three Western occupation zones. Here women and men very rarely worked together in rubble clearance. The disposal of rubble remained a "man's business," as it already was during the Second World War. The recruitment of workers in the Western zones followed a different logic due to the lower scarcity of labor, the higher degree of mechanization in the construction business, and an entirely different occupation policy compared to the SBZ. The public labor offices in the West focused on conveying unemployed skilled workers to appropriate construction firms. In addition, the assignment of unskilled workers, still less that of women, for the rubble clearance took a much lower priority. There is virtually no evidence that women were drawn into rubble clearance by labor offices in cities of the French and American occupation zones.[36] The major aim of the labor market policy in the Western zones was to put men back to work, demobilize women who had replaced conscripted men during the war, and restabilize in this way the male-breadwinner/female-homemaker family. Especially in the American zone this policy was also supported by the occupying power.[37]

The British occupational authorities followed a policy somewhat different from that of their American and French counterparts. At the beginning of 1946, the British military government issued an order to German labor administrations in their zone to engage women in the construction trades to carry out clearance and construction work and to make up for the lack of male laborers.[38] This intervention, however, did not lead to the desired result. The population census of October 1946 counted only 7,427 women as employed in main and subsidiary construction trades overall and only 2,931 of them as engaged in rubble disposal. Accordingly, only 0.27 percent of all working women were employed in main and subsidiary construction trades, of whom not even half worked in rubble clearance.[39]

The main reason for these low figures in the British zone was the resistance of German authorities. The assignment of women to men's work fundamentally contradicted their agenda for the postwar labor market and family policy, which aimed for the restabilization of the male-breadwinner/female-homemaker family. As discussed, they regarded this family model as an important means for the reconstruction of postwar society and the integration of returning soldiers. Their first priority was to procure gainful employment for veterans. The presidents of the state employment offices (*Landesarbeitsämter*) of North Rhine-Westphalia and Westphalia-Lippe found a way to fulfill the injunctions of the British authorities and at the same time to avoid the mass assignment of women to rubble removal. Both state administrations lifted the 1938 labor ban against women in construction, yet at the same time they hemmed in women's employment in construction through many labor-protection regulations, thereby sharply restricting such employment. The motivation behind this effort is revealed in the opening lines of the circular that informed the local labor offices about the new regulations. This circular argued against women's work in "men's occupations" even as an "emergency measure." The declared aim was to "normalize" gender relations in the labor market after the demands placed on it by "total war," when women had to replace men in the war industries. The following statement by the president of the North Rhine Province Labor Office on 27 February 1946 makes this clear:

> In the immediate future, clearance and construction work in the building industry will take place on a more intense scale. The relevant tasks are so urgent and so extensive that all available workers, among others even female laborers, must be made available for this. The use of German women in building construction is completely novel and does not correspond to the existing tradition of German women's work. The typically male work in the construction industry, foreign to the women's essence, not only poses physically high demands on the woman, it also brings her in danger of psychic brutalization, which has spread widely under the difficult living conditions of recent years. To prevent damaging effects from the outset, women's work in construction must be carried out with the greatest care. Construction work for women will occur on order of the military government; it is an *emergency measure* which momentary conditions compellingly require.[40]

To ensure that the use of women in clearance work remained an "emergency measure" and, even in that context, an absolute exception, it was determined that women would be called up only if all available male workers were already engaged. The circle of women who would be considered at all was circumscribed: no expectant or nursing mothers, no mothers with a child under ten years old in the household, and no sick mothers. These restrictive stipulations prevented the use of unemployed women for rubble disposal from becoming a normal state of affairs. Among the women who did work in rubble clearance, probably a disproportionate share consisted of displaced refugees from former German territories in Eastern Europe who needed to earn an income and in addition constituted a socially marginal group.[41]

A similar approach toward female work was pursued by the German administration in the three Western zones in the case of "citizen assignments." Here too women were drawn in only as an exception. In many cities, including Duisburg and Saarbrücken in the French occupation zone, the summons was directed to the "male population" or "all men fit for work." In Frankfurt am Main, "all males 18–60 years old able to work who live or have their workplaces" in the city were asked to participate.[42] Here, the representatives of the building administration had decided explicitly against asking women to participate in the "citizen deployment for rubble clearance": "Any use of women should, whenever possible, be avoided. First, their work performance would naturally remain within moderate limits. Besides that, however, one must reckon with so many justified excuses or unverifiable excuses that the administrative effort would stand in no satisfactory relationship to any useful effect."[43] This argumentation not only denied women the ability to make a reasonable contribution to rubble removal, it also insinuated that they would have no interest at all in this kind of work and would, in fact, use any plausible possibility to withdraw from participating in this citizen assignment. Yet, women did participate in "citizen assignment to rubble removal." Their participation was, however, interpreted by the town council of Frankfurt am Main as a "patriotic" exception: "All circles of the population, even women and elderly men, have through active assistance declared their true love of homeland."[44] All women who volunteered to participate were perceived and presented as a female exception.

To sum up, women's involvement in the rubble clearance in the early postwar period shows a pronounced imbalance between the Western and Eastern occupation zones. In the American, French, and British zones women played only a subordinate role in rubble clearance. It never came to a forced assignment of women to rubble clearance—neither in the context of unemployed or citizen assignments. The use of women on a larger scale remained limited to the SBZ and Berlin as a whole, where in the months after the end of World War II labor offices compulsorily enlisted, above all, unemployed women as well as men. The reasons for this striking difference were manifold. The Eastern zone and the three Western zones differed in their initial economic and demographic situations and the degree of mechanization in the construction business. The policies of the occupying authorities diverged in the East and the West ever more as the Cold War emerged. In addition, the dominant ideals of the gender order played an important role. Neither for the American nor French occupation authorities, less for the British, and still less for the German men controlling most municipal administrations in the West, was the deployment of women for rubble clearance thinkable because of their traditional image of women and family. In the context of the Cold War, this attitude was strengthened by the repeatedly drawn contrast to the SBZ. The mayor of Frankfurt am Main explained, for example, in a speech given in 1949 that the municipal administration of the city had refused to follow the Berlin model of assigning respectable citizens and, even worse, Frankfurt women to slave away in the ruins.[45] Quite similarly the director of the Hamburg building administration had argued already for years before according to a report:

> All Hamburg citizens—explicitly only the men—were called upon in 1946 to voluntarily collect a hundred stones a month at prepared places. The majority of Hamburg citizenry was proud that this work in Hamburg—for men and women—was voluntary. This voluntariness was already [one year after the end of the war] used to draw an ideological demarcation against the Soviet zone. The director of the building administration commented on this summons that it would be very welcome if women would also sometime join this call. "It is certainly not the same as when this stone-heaping takes place compulsorily in the Russian zone . . ." He asked the women to do it as a "voluntary sacrifice for the general public."[46]

Already in the first postwar year, the rapidly intensifying Cold War with its competition over the best economic, social, and political system between the SBZ oriented toward socialism and a planned economy, which became the German Democratic Republic (GDR) in 1949, and the three Western zones oriented toward democracy and a market economy, which became the Federal Republic of Germany (FRG) in 1949, made the role of women an important marker of difference between the systems. This included the participation of women in rubble clearance. If in the Soviet Occupation Zone the (mandatory) enlistment of women for rubble clearance was pushed ahead under the slogan of equal inclusion of women in economy and society, then this "Communist" option could hardly be established in the three Western zones. This contrast continued after the founding of the GDR and FRG. While in the FRG the gainful employment of married women and above all of mothers was rejected into the 1960s by the official policy of the Christian-conservative-dominated federal government, which at best promoted part-time work for mothers, the

GDR pursued all-day employment for all women, even mothers, as a path to "women's emancipation."

The Origin of a German-German Myth: The Rubble Woman as Commemorative Icon

Given that women played a subordinate role in rubble clearance, especially in the West, and their participation was typically rejected in the Western zones, how did the myth of the rubble woman develop since the 1980s? Moreover, how did the narrative of women's contribution to reconstruction become a firm component of all-German collective memory? The historical core of the myth of the rubble women is the female auxiliary construction workers engaged in rubble clearing in Berlin and the SBZ. At the very moment that daily newspapers and women's magazines were authorized in the Soviet zone and Berlin in 1945–46, the rubble-clearing women became a media hit. The Berlin press painted a picture of the "heroic women" who selflessly began to clean up the city. It coined the term "rubble women" for them and assigned them many of the stereotypes still associated with the term today. The illustrated magazine *Die Frau von heute*, approved by the Soviet administration in 1946 and produced in Berlin, for example, wrote, "Women saw this chaos in their daily goings-about. But not for long, for they were stirred by the will to pitch in and clean up. And the will became the deed, without an order from above . . ."[47] This article, like many others that followed, emphasized that the women *volunteered* to clean up the rubble and rebuild the destroyed city. With the help of women's magazines like *Die Frau von heute* and other print media, this narrative spread quickly from Berlin to the whole SBZ, not without calculation. Women initially constituted a substantial part of the labor reserve in the Soviet zone. Only an uplifting story could turn rubble clearance—coded as male and penal labor—into work unemployed women might be willing to do.

The media coverage in the SBZ aimed for more than refurbishing the image of the rubble woman in order to recruit more women for the work of rubble disposal. It had a political agenda. The rubble woman was built up as a positive female identification figure for the emerging socialist state: she became a forerunner of gender equality, a prototype of the new socialist woman. Her allegedly voluntary initiative in rubble removal was interpreted as emancipatory deed awakened by her passion for equal wage-work opportunities with men, including construction work. Furthermore, the reporting suggested that the unskilled female auxiliary construction worker would be trained to become a full-fledged construction craft worker.[48] The icon of the rubble woman thus served the goal of integrating women into all areas of the labor force, including occupations traditionally done by men, to balance out the labor scarcity in the economy.[49]

This image of the rubble woman was less helpful for women's policy in the young FRG, for there the aim was not to integrate the woman into the occupational world but rather to restore her role as mother and housewife.[50] Researchers agree that the FRG and GDR formulated women's policy as a conscious countermodel to the other German state—women's policy guidelines were therefore also always interpreted as evidence of the superiority of one's own system. This held also for the image of the rubble woman, which in the 1950s was decisively shaped by the competition between the two systems. Thus, the memory of the rubble woman was taken in different directions.

Unlike the GDR, the collective memory of the rubble woman in the FRG was split into two; from West Berlin the figure of the rubble woman could not be ignored.[51] Women had removed rubble in all sectors of Berlin and were familiar to all via media reports. West Berlin memory built upon this. In 1955, the West Berlin Senate commissioned a memorial to the rubble woman. In addition, at the suggestion of the city's mayor Ernst Reuter, a member of the Social Democratic Party of Germany (Sozialdemokratische Partei Deutschlands, SPD), and Federal President Theodor Heuss, who belonged to the Free Democratic Party (Freie Demokratische Partei, FDP), bestowed the Federal Cross of Merit (*Bundesverdienstkreuz*) upon several rubble women from West Berlin. These commemorative acts were reported by the West Berlin media. Yet their news stories did not associate the rubble woman with equal rights for women, but rather made her a symbol for the reconstruction of the city. As such, the illuminating power of the rubble woman was very limited.

To be sure, between 1948 and 1955 one finds scattered reports in the transregional West German press that sing the praises of the Berlin rubble women[52]—but only of women in Berlin. Moreover, the stories had little effect because the rubble woman became a negative counterimage in West Germany in the 1950s, one projected onto the GDR and its policy on women.[53] In controversies over the future social role of women in the FRG, opponents of legal equality declared the rubble woman to be the poor Eastern sister who had to perform men's work. A 1951 publication of the Federal Ministry of All-German Affairs (Bundesministerium für gesamtdeutsche Fragen), for example, condemned very sharply the Law for the Protection of Motherhood and Children and Rights of Women (*Gesetz über den Mutter- und Kinderschutz und die Rechte der Frau*), issued the previous year in the GDR. The supposed "pressure" on women, even mothers, to work in the SBZ was demonized and documented with the images of the rubble women. The FRG used pictures of rubble-clearing women to illustrate the hardships to which women were subjected in the

GDR. As a result, the image of the "rubble woman," which in the GDR represented the prototype of the socialist ideal of the working woman and mother, became in West Germany a counterimage to its own ideal of the woman as a mother and housewife.

In the GDR, the authorities further embellished the image of the rubble woman in the 1960s as a "builder of socialism," and so she had her firm and steady place in the GDR's collective memory. In the FRG, it took until the 1980s for the rubble woman to arrive as a positive commemorative icon in the collective memory. Key to this were two social developments. The more specific catalyst was the pension debate instigated by the Christian-conservative government of Chancellor Helmut Kohl. In 1986 his coalition of the Christian Democratic Union (Christlich Demokratische Union, CDU), Christian Social Union (Christlich-Soziale Union, CSU), and FDP introduced the "baby year" following years of controversy over a reform of the pension system.[54] Since then, the first year of a child's life was counted toward its mother's pension—or, if so wished, toward its father's. However, women born before 1921 were excluded from this regulation, which provoked opposition. Leading the opposition was the senior-rights league Gray Panthers (Graue Panther), which was joined by representatives of the Green Party (Die Grünen) and SPD. Together they fought for an expansion of the reform to include the older generation of female pensioners born before 1921. To emphasize this demand, they appropriated the image and concept of the "rubble woman." A whole generation was declared to be rubble women who, having rebuilt Germany after 1945, were now denied the chance to profit from a pension increase.

This demand was also supported by many in the new women's movement in West Germany, which had emerged in the late 1960s. Since the 1970s, female historians who were part of this movement had started to write women's history for a broader female readership. A main aim of these first publications was the search for the history of the generations of the mothers and grandmothers and their experiences during the time of National Socialism, the Second World War, and postwar. In several of these early publications intended to give women an identity-generating past, the German woman is presented as a victim of National Socialism and war but also as a heroine of postwar reconstruction.[55] The woman of the "zero hour" was frequently presented as strong woman who never despaired and whom later generations had to thank for the quick postwar recovery and economic upturn. This narrative was underscored mainly with illustrations and stories of Berlin rubble women. The act of rubble clearance was presented along with the struggle for housing, food, and family survival as the lived reality of most postwar women. As a result, the icon of the rubble woman became more and more a synonym for the postwar woman in general.[56] In this way, not only was the experience of the rubble woman generalized, but she was belatedly elevated to an iconic figure of West German postwar memories who represented a counterimage not to the GDR but to National Socialism. As a reaction to this ahistorical narrative, an intensive debate between women and gender historians started in the second half of the 1980s, labeled the *Historikerinnenstreit* (quarrel between women historians). In this quarrel a younger generation challenged these dominant narratives. They intensively discussed the broad variety of roles that women held in the period of National Socialism and postwar, from victims to bystanders, from protestors to perpetrators. But this debate did not influence the construction of public memory, which reflects the marginal role of women's and gender history in the academia of the FRG.[57]

Thus, if via different routes, a very compatible public image of rubble women had emerged in the FRG and GDR before the turning point of 1989–90. This rubble woman could finally become part of an all-German collective memory that has, however—and this must be emphasized—a much stronger East than West German tradition and imprint.

Conclusion

The image of a destroyed Germany cleaned up by rubble women working in bucket chains and with hammer in hand belongs to the realm of legend, or at least in the West at any rate. Outside of Berlin and Soviet Occupation Zone cities, female workers accounted for only a minority of those recruited by labor offices. Women took up this activity out of social distress; their engagement in rubble clearance had little to do with voluntary work. Interwoven with the myth of the "rubble woman," the narrative of voluntary engagement emerged out of a media campaign in Berlin and the SBZ that created the ideal of a rubble woman in order to bolster the labor morale of potential female workers. This media campaign aimed to refurbish the image of rubble clearance. Until then, rubble work was closely associated with penal labor through the Nazis' wartime use of forced laborers and the Allies' use of POWs and former NSDAP members after the war. Moreover, construction work was classically male labor and was formally forbidden to German women after 1938. Thus, a suitable role model had to be found for female auxiliary construction workers in Berlin and the Soviet zone. That model was the "rubble woman." She also fit women's policy in the GDR, and so the rubble woman was turned into a positive commemorative icon that prevailed as the forerunner of women's equal rights and builder of socialism in the GDR.

In the young FRG, however, outside of West Berlin the rubble woman was rather negatively freighted and was projected onto the GDR's objectionable women's policy as a counterimage to the feminine ideal of the FRG. The image of the rubble woman underwent a positive turn in the FRG only in the 1980s, when it emerged as a generational concept during the pension debates and through publications about women's history. Thus, the rubble woman also became a commemorative icon for the FRG. So embellished, the rubble woman has ever since enjoyed an assured seat in the collective memory of reunited Germany.

Leonie Treber works as the managing director for the German Historical Association (*Verband der Historiker und Historikerinnen Deutschlands e.V.*), Germany. She received her doctorate from the University of Duisburg-Essen in 2013. Her dissertation *Mythos Trümmerfrauen: Von der Trümmerbeseitigung in der Kriegs- und Nachkriegszeit und der Entstehung eines deutschen Erinnerungsortes* was published by Klartext Verlag in 2014. She has published several German book chapters and articles on the subject of her dissertation.

Notes

1. I would like to thank John Weigel as well as the editors for their help with the translation from German into English.
2. See Marita Krauss, "Trümmerfrauen: Visuelles Konstrukt und Realität," in *Das Jahrhundert der Bilder,* ed. Gerhard Paul, 2 vols., vol. 1: *1900 bis 1949* (Göttingen, 2009), 738.
3. Ibid., 740.
4. "Wir sind Deutschland," *Frankfurter Rundschau,* 22 May 2009.
5. Eckart Conze, *Die Suche nach Sicherheit: Eine Geschichte der Bundesrepublik Deutschland von 1949 bis in die Gegenwart* (Munich, 2009), 25.
6. See *Statistisches Jahrbuch deutscher Gemeinden* (Berlin, 1949), 362; and "Mit Großbagger und Kleinbahn," *Nürnberger Nachrichten,* 30 July 1947.
7. See Leonie Treber, *Mythos Trümmerfrauen: Von der Trümmerbeseitigung in der Kriegs- und Nachkriegszeit und der Entstehung eines Erinnerungsortes* (Essen, 2014).
8. Ibid., 29–34.
9. See "Schreiben des OB an das Bauamt, 8. Oktober 1940," Institut für Stadtgeschichte Frankfurt am Main, Magistratsakten (ISFM), 3.808; and "Schreiben v. Städt. Oberbaurat an das Stadtamt, 4. Dezember 1941," Stadtarchiv Duisburg, 600/1845.
10. Treber, *Mythos Trümmerfrauen,* 34–39.
11. See Hans Pfahlmann, *Fremdarbeiter und Kriegsgefangene in der deutschen Kriegswirtschaft 1939–1945* (Darmstadt, 1968), 117–18; and Treber, *Mythos Trümmerfrauen,* 44–51.
12. See Karola Fings, *Krieg, Gesellschaft und KZ: Himmlers SS-Baubrigaden* (Paderborn, 2005), 55, 84–86, 112, 120–21, 130, and "Sklaven für die 'Heimatfront': Kriegsgesellschaft und Konzentrationslager," in *Die deutsche Kriegsgesellschaft 1939 bis 1945,* ed. Jörg Echternkamp, 2 vols., vol. 1: *Politisierung, Vernichtung, Überleben* (Munich, 2004), 219.

13. See Marc Buggeln, *Arbeit & Gewalt: Das Außenlagersystem des KZ Neuengamme* (Göttingen, 2009), 57–58; and Treber, *Mythos Trümmerfrauen*, 201.
14. See Klaus Neumann, "Lange Wege der Trauer: Erinnerungen an die Zerstörung Halberstadts am 8. April 1945," in *Luftkrieg: Erinnerungen in Deutschland und Europa*, ed. Jörg Arnold et al. (Göttingen, 2009), 212–13.
15. See Treber, *Mythos Trümmerfrauen*, 84–99.
16. Ibid., 102, 105–11.
17. Manfred Pohl, *Philipp Holzmann: Geschichte eines Bauunternehmens 1849–1999* (Munich, 1999), 245.
18. See "Abschlußbericht für die Trümmerbeseitigung in Saarbrücken von 1945 bis 1966, 30. Dezember 1966," Stadtarchiv Saarbrücken, Dezernat G 60, Nr. 69.
19. See Pohl, *Philipp Holzmann*, 303–6.
20. See Treber, *Mythos Trümmerfrauen*, 157–72.
21. Ibid., 139–57.
22. See Rainer Karlsch, "Umfang und Struktur der Reparationsentnahmen aus der SBZ/DDR 1945–1953: Stand und Probleme der Forschung," in *Wirtschaftliche Folgelasten des Krieges in der SBZ/DDR*, ed. Christoph Buchheim (Baden-Baden, 1995), 46, and "Die Reparationsleistungen der SBZ/DDR im Spiegel deutscher und russischer Quellen," in *Die Wirtschaft im geteilten und vereinten Deutschland*, ed. Karl Eckart (Berlin, 1999), 9–30.
23. See Treber, *Mythos Trümmerfrauen*, 137; Karlsch, *Reparationsentnahmen*, 58; and Marcel Boldorf, *Sozialfürsorge in der SBZ/DDR 1945–1953: Ursachen, Ausmaß und Bewältigung der Nachkriegsarmut* (Stuttgart, 1998), 39.
24. See, for example, for Berlin, Dieter Hanauske, *Die Sitzungsprotokolle des Magistrats der Stadt Berlin 1945/46*, vol. 2.1 (Berlin, 1995), 31–56.
25. "Bestimmungen über den Arbeitseinsatz, 11. Juni 1945," Landesarchiv Berlin (LAB), F Rep. 280 LAZ-Sammlung, Nr. 2666.
26. "Bericht vom Arbeitsamt Tiergarten Ortsstelle Süd, 21. Februar 1946," LAB, C Rep. 103 Nr. 80.
27. See "Entwicklung des Arbeitseinsatzes, [Ende 1947]," LAB, C Rep. 110 Nr. 56.
28. See Wolfgang Zank, *Wirtschaft und Arbeit in Ostdeutschland 1945–1949: Probleme des Wiederaufbaus in der Sowjetischen Besatzungszone Deutschlands* (Munich, 1987), 41.
29. See Thomas Widera, *Dresden 1945–1948: Politik und Gesellschaft unter sowjetischer Besatzungsherrschaft* (Göttingen, 2004), 299.
30. See Günther Schmid et al., "Arbeitsmarktpolitik und Arbeitslosenversicherung (Westzonen) und Arbeitskräftegewinnung und Arbeitskräftelenkung (SBZ)," in *Geschichte der Sozialpolitik in Deutschland seit 1945*, 11 vols., vol. 2.1: *Die Zeit der Besatzungszonen 1945–1949: Sozialpolitik zwischen Kriegsende und der Gründung zweier deutscher Staaten*, ed. Udo Wengst (Baden-Baden, 2001), 321–23.
31. Zank, *Wirtschaft und Arbeit*, 133.
32. See Irmgard Weyrather, "'Was Männer zerstören, bauen Frauen wieder auf': Frauenarbeit am Bau in den Trümmerjahren," in *Hand in Hand: Bauarbeit und Gewerkschaften—Eine Sozialgeschichte*, ed. Arno Klönne and Olaf Bartels (Frankfurt/M., 1989), 285.
33. Hans Joachim Reichhardt, "… raus aus den Trümmern": *Vom Beginn des Wiederaufbaus 1945 in Berlin* (Berlin, 1987), 82.
34. See Weyrather, "Was Männer zerstören," 285.
35. See Treber, *Mythos Trümmerfrauen*, 225–30.

36. Ibid., 219.
37. See Karen Hagemann and Sonya Michel, eds., *Gender and the Long Postwar: The United States and the Two Germanys, 1945–1989* (Baltimore, MD, 2014).
38. See "Schreiben des Präsidenten des Landesarbeitsamtes Nord-Rheinprovinz an die Herren Vorsitzenden der Arbeitsämter, 27. Februar 1946," Stadtarchiv Jülich, IV-740; and "Rundverfügung Nr. 118/1946 des Präsidenten des Landesarbeitsamtes Westfalen-Lippe an die Arbeitsämter, 5. Juni 1946," Landesarchiv Nordrhein-Westfalen Düsseldorf, NW 37 Nr. 647.
39. See Klaus-Jörg Ruhl, *Verordnete Unterordnung: Berufstätige Frauen zwischen Wirtschaftswachstum und konservativer Ideologie in der Nachkriegszeit 1945–1963* (Munich, 1994), 35–36.
40. "Schreiben des Präsidenten des Landesarbeitsamtes, 27. Februar 1946." Emphasis in original.
41. See Treber, *Mythos Trümmerfrauen*, 222.
42. "Ausschnitt aus Duisburger Mitteilungen, 1. Dezember 1945," Stadtarchiv Duisburg, 600/2910; "Aufruf zur Gemeinschaftsarbeit, [1946]," Stadtarchiv Saarbrücken, StASb PL 517; and "Schreiben von Allgemeine Bauverwaltung an den Magistrat, 4. September 1946," ISFM, 6.553.
43. "Schreiben von Allgemeine Bauverwaltung an den Magistrat, 4. September 1946."
44. "Protokoll-Auszug der Stadtverordneten-Versammlung der Stadt Frankfurt am Main, Abschrift des mündlichen Berichtes von Stadtverordneten-Vorsteher Miersch, 6. Februar 1947," ISFM, 6.553.
45. See "Erklärung des Herrn Oberbürgermeisters in der Stadtverordnetenversammlung am 10. März 1949 zu den Unglücksfällen am 1. März 1949, 10. März 1949," ISFM, 6.552.
46. Quoted in Weyrather, "Was Männer zerstören," 291.
47. "Unsere Schipperinnen feiern ein Fest," *Die Frau von heute*, no. 1, 1 February 1946, 16.
48. See Weyrather, "Was Männer zerstören," 288; and Gunilla-Friedericke Budde, "Der Körper der 'sozialistischen Frauenpersönlichkeit': Weiblichkeitsvorstellungen in der SBZ und frühen DDR," *Geschichte und Gesellschaft* 26, no. 4 (2000): 610.
49. See Michael Schwartz, "Emanzipation zur sozialen Nützlichkeit: Bedingungen und Grenzen von Frauenpolitik in der DDR," in *Sozialstaatlichkeit in der DDR: Sozialpolitische Entwicklungen im Spannungsfeld von Diktatur und Gesellschaft 1945/49–1989*, ed. Dierk Hoffmann (Munich, 2005), 47–87; Beatrix Bouvier, *Die DDR: Ein Sozialstaat? Sozialpolitik in der Ära Honecker* (Bonn, 2002), 244–97; and Treber, *Mythos Trümmerfrauen*, 291–97.
50. On the role of West German women in the 1950s, see Merith Niehuss, *Familie, Frau und Gesellschaft: Studien zur Strukturgeschichte der Familie in Westdeutschland 1945–1960* (Göttingen, 2001).
51. See Treber, *Mythos Trümmerfrauen*, 318–25; and Nicole Kramer, "Ikone des Wiederaufbaus: Die 'Trümmerfrau' in der bundesdeutschen Erinnerungskultur," in *Luftkrieg: Erinnerungen in Deutschland und Europa*, ed. Jörg Arnold et al. (Göttingen, 2009), 261–64.
52. See "Hut ab vor unseren Frauen," *Constanze* 2 (1948): 4–5; and "Ein Denkmal für 26000 Frauen," *Constanze* 10 (1955): 20–21, 52–53.
53. See Treber, *Mythos Trümmerfrauen*, 335–39.
54. Ibid., 408–15; and Kramer, "Ikone des Wiederaufbaus," 266–70.

55. See Klaus-Jörg Ruhl, *Unsere verlorenen Jahre: Frauenalltag in Kriegs- und Nachkriegszeit 1939–1949 in Berichten, Dokumenten und Bildern* (Darmstadt, 1985); Sibylle Meyer and Eva Schulze, *Wie wir das alles geschafft haben: Alleinstehende Frauen berichten über ihr Leben nach 1945* (Munich, 1985); and Birgit Bolognese-Leuchtenmüller, *Frauen der ersten Stunde 1945–1955* (Vienna, 1985).
56. See Treber, *Mythos Trümmerfrauen*, 397–98.
57. See Susanne Landwerd and Irene Stoehr, "Frauen- und Geschlechterforschung zum Nationalsozialismus seit den 1970er Jahren: Forschungsstand, Veränderungen, Perspektiven," in *Frauen- und Geschlechtergeschichte des Nationalsozialismus: Fragestellungen, Perspektiven, neue Forschungen*, ed. Johanna Gehmacher and Gabriella Hauch (Innsbruck, 2007), 22–68; Christina Herkommer, *Frauen im Nationalsozialismus: Opfer oder Täterinnen? Eine Kontroverse der Frauenforschung im Spiegel feministischer Theoriebildung und der allgemeinen historischen Aufarbeitung der NS-Vergangenheit* (Munich, 2005); and Atina Grosmann, "Feminist Debates about Women and National Socialism," *Gender & History* 3, no. 3 (1991): 350–58.

Selected Bibliography

Bouvier, Beatrix. *Die DDR: Ein Sozialstaat? Sozialpolitik in der Ära Honecker.* Bonn, 2002.
Budde, Gunilla-Friedericke. "Der Körper der 'sozialistischen Frauenpersönlichkeit': Weiblichkeitsvorstellungen in der SBZ und frühen DDR." *Geschichte und Gesellschaft* 26, no. 4 (2000): 602–28.
Fings, Karola. *Krieg, Gesellschaft und KZ: Himmlers SS-Baubrigaden.* Paderborn, 2005.
Hagemann, Karen, and Sonya Michel, eds. *Gender and the Long Postwar: The United States and the Two Germanys, 1945–1989.* Baltimore, MD, 2014.
Heineman, Elizabeth. "The Hour of the Woman: Memories of Germany's 'Crisis Years' and West German National Identity." In *The Miracle Years: A Cultural History of West Germany, 1949–1968*, ed. Hanna Schissler, 21–56. Oxford, 2001.
Kramer, Nicole. "Ikone des Wiederaufbaus: Die 'Trümmerfrau' in der bundesdeutschen Erinnerungskultur." In *Luftkrieg: Erinnerungen in Deutschland und Europa*, ed. Jörg Arnold, Dietmar Süß, and Malte Thiessen, 259–76. Göttingen, 2009.
———. "Die 'Trümmerfrau' und ihre Schwestern: Die Erinnerung an Frauen im Zweiten Weltkrieg in Westdeutschland, Großbritannien und Italien." *Ariadne: Forum für Frauen- und Geschlechtergeschichte*, no. 59 (2011): 24–31.
———. *Volksgenossinnen an der Heimatfront: Mobilisierung, Verhalten, Erinnerung.* Göttingen, 2011.
Krauss, Marita. "Trümmerfrauen: Visuelles Konstrukt und Realität." In *Das Jahrhundert der Bilder*, ed. Gerhard Paul, 2 vols. Vol. 1: *1900 bis 1949*, 738–45. Göttingen, 2009.
McAdams, Kay L. "'Ersatzmänner': Trümmerfrauen and Women in 'Men's Work' in Berlin and in the Soviet Zone, 1945–1950." In *Arbeiter in der SBZ –DDR*, ed. Peter Hübner and Klaus Tenfelde, 151–67. Essen, 1999.
Merkel, Ina. *... und Du, Frau an der Werkbank.* Berlin, 1990.
Niehuss, Merith. *Familie, Frau und Gesellschaft: Studien zur Strukturgeschichte der Familie in Westdeutschland 1945–1960.* Göttingen, 2001.

Pappai, Anna-Sophia. "'Trümmerfrauen' und 'Trümmermänner': Symbolische und reale Wiederaufbauarbeit in Dresden und Warschau nach 1945." In *Geschlechterbeziehungen in Ostmitteleuropa nach dem Zweiten Weltkrieg: Soziale Praxis und Konstruktionen von Geschlechterbildern,* ed. Claudia Kraft, 43–57. Munich, 2008.

Schwartz, Michael. "Emanzipation zur sozialen Nützlichkeit: Bedingungen und Grenzen von Frauenpolitik in der DDR," In *Sozialstaatlichkeit in der DDR: Sozialpolitische Entwicklungen im Spannungsfeld von Diktatur und Gesellschaft 1945/49–1989,* ed. Dierk Hoffmann, 47–87. Munich, 2005.

Treber, Leonie. "Die 'Trümmerfrau' im Blitzlichtgewitter: Bilder eines deutsch-deutschen Erinnerungsortes." In *Erinnerungskulturen in transnationaler Perspektive: Memory Cultures in Transnational Perspective,* ed. Ulf Engel, Matthias Middell, and Stefan Troebst, 95–114. Leipzig, 2012.

———. "Die Geburtsstunde der 'Trümmerfrau' in den Presseerzeugnissen der deutschen Nachkriegszeit." In *Geschlecht und Geschichte in populären Medien,* ed. Elisabeth Cheauré, Sylvia Paletschek, and Nina Reusch, 189–207. Bielefeld, 2013.

———. *Mythos Trümmerfrauen: Von der Trümmerbeseitigung in der Kriegs- und Nachkriegszeit und der Entstehung eines Erinnerungsortes.* Essen, 2014.

———. "Mythos 'Trümmerfrau': Deutsch-deutsche Erinnerungen." *Aus Politik und Zeitgeschichte* 65, nos. 16–17 (2015): 28–34, www.bpb.de/apuz/204282/mythos-truemmerfrau (accessed 25 May 2017).

Weyrather, Irmgard. "'Was Männer zerstören, bauen Frauen wieder auf': Frauenarbeit am Bau in den Trümmerjahren." In *Hand in Hand: Bauarbeit und Gewerkschaften—Eine Sozialgeschichte,* ed. Arno Klönne and Olaf Bartels. 280–95. Frankfurt/M., 1989.

CHAPTER 5

Children, Church, and Rights
East and West German Protests against Family Law Reforms in the 1950s

Alexandria Ruble

After 1945, Germans inherited a Civil Code (*Bürgerliches Gesetzbuch*, BGB) that dated back to 1900 and designated women as second-class citizens in spousal relations, marital property, and parental authority. The liberal and socialist women's movements had fought against the BGB since the early years of the Wilhelmine Empire, demanding the legal equality of women in marriage and family law. After the end of the Second World War, liberal, social democratic, and communist women continued the old struggle for women's equal civil citizenship. In the context of the founding of the East and West German states in 1949 and the rising Cold War, female activists reinforced their push for the reform of the family law sections of the Civil Code in both German states—the German Democratic Republic (GDR), ruled by the Socialist Unity Party of Germany (Sozialistische Einheitspartei Deutschlands, SED), and the Federal Republic of Germany (FRG), governed by a coalition led by the Christian Democratic Union of Germany (Christlich Demokratische Union Deutschlands, CDU). But in both states, the supporters of reform faced fierce resistance mainly from Christian-conservative organizations, including the CDU and also in the West her Bavarian sister party, the Christian Social Union (Christlich-Soziale Union, CSU), Christian women's and welfare associations, and the Protestant and Catholic Churches.

This chapter focuses on the responses of the Protestant and Catholic Churches to family law reforms in the divided Germanys in the context of the early Cold War. The two major churches reemerged as spiritual, political, and social institutions in 1945 after years of persecution under and/or support of the Third Reich.[1] Christian belief and church, some scholars have argued, offered Germans comfort and stability in the early postwar years.² Christians also enjoyed political representation via the interconfessional CDU, which was active in both states, and protection under both constitutions. At the same time, the churches faced radically different situations in the two states. In the East, the SED actively sought to undermine the Protestant and Catholic Churches and maintained ambiguous relations with them that ranged from acquiescent to antagonistic, depending on the context. Here, in 1949, 92 percent of the population belonged to a church; 80 percent were Protestant and 12 percent Catholic.³ In the West, both of the major churches, but Catholics especially, enjoyed a privileged relationship with the leading Christian Democrats. Here, even more people belonged to a Christian church, with 51 percent Protestant and 43 percent Catholic.⁴

After 1949, church leaders and politicians on each side homed in on the Civil Code, which was still in effect and yet no longer applied in the context of the vast demographic changes, postwar "crisis" of the family, and the diverging political, social, and economic developments in each state. Using *histoire croisée,* or the "history of entanglements," this chapter examines how a shared legal history created a dialogue between the two states that ultimately set them on different paths regarding women's rights in marriage and the family in the early years of the Cold War.⁵ This chapter shows that when church leaders perceived the new family laws as threatening to Christian autonomy, they tried negotiating the terms of the new legislation with their respective governments but met with different outcomes because of systemic differences between the two states. In the East, the churches appropriated the SED regime's own rhetoric about German unity and argued that a new socialist Family Code (*Familiengesetzbuch*, FGB) would further divide the two states. In the West, the churches stuck to dogmatic arguments and avoided much discussion of unity in their opposition to the discussed Equal Rights Act (*Gleichberechtigungsgesetz*). The results were paradoxical. Although East German Christians had a testy relationship with the SED dictatorship, they prevailed and prevented the regime from passing reforms in 1954. Meanwhile, the efforts of West German Catholics and Protestants, despite holding the favor of the ruling Christian conservatives, floundered, and the Bundestag did not adhere to their demands to the extent they had hoped for.

The first section of this chapter examines the background of family law and its stakes in the postwar Germanys. The second section explores how and why the Protestant Church in East Germany successfully halted the SED's reforms. The third section explores why the West German churches did not gain more leverage in their negotiations with the government. The conclusion compares and contrasts the different strategies employed by both sides and argues that this case provides a lens into "entangled" history.

The Failure of the Family Code in the GDR, 1949–55

In 1896, the Reichstag of the German Empire ratified the Civil Code, which then went into effect on 1 January 1900. The family law sections of the BGB limited married women's legal personhood in several areas of spousal relations, parental authority, and marital property. For example, provisions such as the *Stichentscheid*, which gave men the legal authority of a final decision in all matters related to their marriage and family, restricted married women's rights. Furthermore, married men had the right to control their wives' property. Through the German Empire (1871–1918) and the Weimar Republic (1919–33), different branches of the German women's movement, social democrats, and some liberals campaigned to change the BGB, but met little success.[6] In 1939, a Nazi legal commission began revising the Civil Code to fit its racist and misogynist agenda but stopped when World War II began, intending to complete it upon victory.[7] After their victory over Nazi Germany, the Western and Soviet occupiers passed the Allied Control Council Law No. 16 on 20 February 1946, a new marriage law that largely reinstituted the patriarchal provisions of the old BGB.[8] This law remained in effect for the next decade in both states.

In 1949, following the establishment of two separate German states, the SED-controlled government in the East immediately pursued reforms of the Civil Code. The ruling SED moved quickly for several reasons. It had to fill an urgent legal gap, as its new constitution had technically undone all laws opposing equal rights for women. Furthermore, the intensifying Cold War competition urged the SED to beat the West to the reforms. There was a pragmatic side to the issue as well: they feared that continuing to deny women equal civil rights would have dire electoral effects.[9] More broadly, the SED had an ideological imperative to make good on the longstanding communist and socialist goals for "women's emancipation" and more egalitarian family structures.[10] Thus, by early 1950, under the guidance of communist lawyer Hans Nathan, the GDR's Justice Ministry (Ministerium der Justiz) produced a new legislative draft, the "Bill for the Reordering of Family Law." Although the ministry aimed to pass it by the end of the year, the regime failed to hit its target. Instead, the government incorporated some key reforms, such as the removal of the *Stichentscheid*, into the 1950 "Law for the Protection of Motherhood and Children and Rights of Women," a separate piece of legislation aimed at expanding women's rights in the workplace, and postponed the reforms of family law multiple times between 1950 and 1953.[11]

Only in late 1953 did family law come to the fore. That year, Hilde Benjamin—a longtime communist women's rights activist, lawyer, and vice president of the Supreme Court of the GDR—took over as the minister of justice after a purge of party officials in the wake of the 17 June

1953 uprisings.[12] Within a year, on 30 June 1954, the Justice Ministry published the draft of the new socialist Family Code, designed to replace the 1900 Civil Code. The new law would have changed the age of majority, eliminated the guilt principle in divorce, given women greater independence to work or live away from their spouses, and allowed partners to choose which surname they preferred.[13] More broadly, the new law emphasized the necessity of equality for women in marriage and society as a whole. It would also govern relationships between spouses, parents, children, and other relatives "for the development and stabilization of the family and upbringing of children in the spirit of democracy, socialism, patriotism, and friendship between nations."[14] Finally, it asserted that raising children was the duty not only of parents but of the state (represented by youth organizations and schools).[15] The introduction to the new Family Code (FGB) demonstrated the SED's dual commitment to fostering equal rights and building strong, properly socialist families, albeit with a greater degree of state intervention.

Eager to court citizen support and publicize the legislation's merits, the SED conducted public forums in the summer of 1954. The Ministry of Justice set up hundreds of "Justice Conversation Evenings," where the public could pose questions to ministry functionaries and comment on the law. By October 1954, the ministry had held 6,117 "Justice Conversation Evenings" in which 313,538 GDR citizens participated.[16] In a typical session, SED representatives guided the participants through each part of the law. Additionally, the presenters often underscored the "pan-German [*gesamtdeutsch*] meaning of the legislative draft."[17] There were both ideological and practical reasons for employing this argument. First, the SED repeatedly proclaimed itself the protector of German unity, in contrast to the West. Second, the border between East and West Germany was not entirely closed until 1961, and many Germans harbored fantasies of reunification. Third, the 1946 Allied Control Council's marriage law still governed both Germanys. On the one hand, highlighting the pan-German implications of the law allowed the SED to portray itself as the German state that would keep German families united in opposition to its Western counterpart. On the other hand, the pan-German argument demonstrated that the SED was fully aware of the looming consequences of the law's imminent approval and sought to head off accusations that the GDR aimed to divide Germany permanently.

Beyond persuading the citizens of the GDR of the SED's good intentions, stressing the pan-German nature of the law was also a way to provoke the West to act. Well aware of the ongoing controversies over family law reforms in the West, Minister of Justice Hilde Benjamin in August 1954 sent a copy of the GDR's Family Code to the West German minister of justice, Fritz Neumayer, a member of the liberal Free Democratic Party (Freie Demokratische Partei, FDP), the coalition partner of the governing CDU/CSU, hoping to engage him in a public conversation about the parallel laws. Neumayer never responded directly to Benjamin's letter. Instead, he issued a press release condemning Benjamin and the FGB for only deepening the divide between West and East through its thorough societal restructuring.[18] The SED, in turn, declared Neumayer the divisive one in the pages of its newspapers.[19] The West's rejection of the SED's Family Code signified more than just ideological disagreements over the status of women and the family. It represented the fact that the West would not legitimize the East's existence by engaging with its political leaders and foremost legal experts on the topic of family law.

The issue of German unity became a rallying cry for opposition to the draft law by the Protestant and Catholic Churches. In the early 1950s, the SED had a contradictory relationship with the Christian churches. It had alienated them and their parishioners with various "de-Christianizing" measures. Yet it also recognized the popular influence of the churches and their many ties to the West. In preparing the ground for the publication of the draft FGB, the SED and Ministry of Justice tried to forestall opposition from the churches by courting and attaining the Protestant leadership's favorable opinion on the new family law in March 1954. This effort seemed to have paid off in the case of the Protestant Church, only to come to naught after the skirmish between Hilde Benjamin and Fritz Neumayer in August. Rather than oppose the law, the church's synod initially resolved only vaguely that in Christianity, "marriage and parenthood are endowed by God."[20]

SED leaders were presumably quite surprised when Christians on the local level started to protest the law. As historian Donna Harsch has convincingly shown, their petitions and discussions labeled "the law as anti-Christian and as forcing women to work and abandon their children."[21] Interestingly, Christians also often underscored their assertions about gender, the family, and religious rights with arguments about German reunification. On 24 August 1954, for example, a district court in Karl-Marx-Stadt joined forces with the local CDU chapter in Reichenbach to conduct a "Justice Conversation Evening" about the Family Code. Attendees objected to the notion "that caring for children is the law, rather this is the *natural* right of parents"—a classical Catholic stance.[22] They cited Article 6 of West German Basic Law, which guaranteed that caring for children was a natural right, and argued that "this formulation has a meaningful pan-German character."[23] They invoked the West to undermine the SED's position that the state could intervene before the parents in the nurturing and education of children.

Then, on 1 September 1954, the governing body of the Protestant Church in East Germany, the Ecclesiastical Eastern Conference of the

Protestant Church in Germany (Kirchliche Ostkonferenz der Evangelischen Kirche in Deutschland, KO-EKD), issued an official opinion to the Ministry of Justice on the GDR's draft FGB. No longer employing just vague Lutheran dogma, the new statement was distinctly political and oppositional.[24] Their petition cited the separation of church and state and the right to educate and raise children in Christian, rather than socialist, beliefs. Furthermore, the KO-EKD argued that the parallel developments in the West were cause for concern. They called for the SED to halt the passage of the law on the basis that it was creating "an artificial cleft in cultural cohesion."[25] The law, they asserted, must be considered for and by all Germans, especially in the case of future reconciliation. With such arguments, the conference simultaneously appropriated the SED's own rhetoric about desiring a unified Germany while criticizing the East German government's efforts to keep their nation divided on the basis of marriage, family, and culture.

The KO-EKD disseminated its message that the new FGB endangered both Christian beliefs and all-German unity in its weekly newsletter *Die Kirche* (published primarily in the Berlin-Brandenburg region). An unsigned article from 26 September 1954 titled "About Marriage and Family" noted the similarities between the equality and family protection clauses of the East German constitution and West German Basic Law. Furthermore, the author argued that "divergent developments in this area in the still separated parts of Germany would only lead to deep regret."[26] The article encouraged readers to follow the petition issued a few weeks before, which said to avoid anything that created "an artificial rift in unified German cultural relations."[27] The author then went on to explain the dogmatic reasons why the Protestant churches did not support the FGB: the legislation opposed the Christian idea that marriage came from God and that parents had the right to raise the children in the church (not under socialist indoctrination). The article ended by stating that "the overwhelming majority of the German population in East and West belong to a Christian church," reminding readers that their strength lay in numbers and that they belonged to a unified Christian community in spite of the Iron Curtain.[28]

Capitalizing on the idea of strength in numbers, several local parishes petitioned the East German government, opposing state intervention in childrearing and employing the language of all-German unity.[29] Perhaps the most telling example is the case of a Protestant congregation in the Eastern Saxon town of Bautzen in November 1954. At an illegal meeting, the pastor spoke to approximately 450 participants about the issue of "legal unity [*Rechtseinheit*] between East and West."[30] He observed that both states had made a mutual commitment to equal rights in 1949, yet neither side had passed new legislation, though the GDR was close to doing so. He then stated that "the church must reject it, that separate laws will be made and that only family relations will be regulated in the GDR."[31] Finally, he asserted, "Legal unity and legal security are holy and where they are split, there the Bible and belief in God are much holier than the law."[32] He condemned the East German government for deepening the rift between East and West not only on a legal basis but a spiritual one. He suggested that the regime's legislation governing women's legal status and the family was not only divisive on a human level, it would also separate Germans from God.

Although the majority of the petitions came from Protestant ministers and their parishes, the Catholic Church formally opposed the new FGB as well. On 28 August 1954, the Catholic bishop of Berlin, Wilhelm Weskamm, wrote to Otto Grotewohl, the minister-president of the GDR, on behalf of the other Catholic bishops in the East.[33] Weskamm did not mention the developments in West Germany, but he was nevertheless highly critical of the FGB's intervention in family life, calling it "very radical and momentous."[34] He also stated that the law had "only an economic-social function," and as such it "abused the natural order that basically assigns married women and mothers their places within the family."[35] Moreover, he asserted, it moved family life "into the state's sphere of power without allowing human figures space in their peculiarities."[36] Although Weskamm avoided any mention of the West, other Catholics alluded to its specter in their petitions. In January 1955, for example, the Catholic Church in the Saxon town Limbach-Oberfrohna wrote to the GDR's deputy prime minister and chief of the Church Office, the East CDU member Otto Nuschke, to express concern that "this legislative draft poses a new obstacle for all of us who have longed for a reunified Germany."[37]

Despite the staunch opposition of the Catholic Church on the basis of dogma and reunification, the church leadership's impact on the SED was largely inconsequential. Historian Konrad H. Jarausch suggests that in the GDR "there were too few Catholics to have any political impact."[38] Additionally, according to Donna Harsch, the Catholic Church never mobilized at the grassroots level like the Protestant parishes.[39] Both factors contributed to the church's relatively minor role and the SED's general negligence of the Catholic Church.[40] The SED recognized this imbalance and had not sought out the Catholic leadership for an opinion on the law the way it had the Protestant churches. In one letter responding to the KO-EKD and Catholic opinion pieces, Benjamin appeared distraught that the Protestant Church leadership had abruptly changed its earlier positive position. She only added in Catholics as an afterthought.[41] Although the Catholic Church had little impact on Benjamin and the Ministry of Justice, it is still significant that its leaders thought they had power to wield.

The SED knew that it was facing formidable opponents. Within a few days of the issuance of the KO-EKD's petition, the SED drew up a report that lamented that church leaders had many possibilities to critique the law's provisions or offer proposals. In all likelihood, the ruling party was also upset that the petition had gone public. The SED indicated that it might have been open to these suggestions, because "one can make do with a short explanation."[42] Instead, the author expressed indignation that the churches chose to point out the consequences for reunification. He or she stated, "The church should realize that everything [in the law] is omitted that can deepen the cleft between both parts of Germany. We strongly see this hazard as a given."[43] The dogmatic rifts between communism and Christianity—namely the aforementioned issue of state intervention in the family and childrearing—did not appear to cause the writer much concern. Despite his or her clear annoyance with the KO-EKD, the author conferred a certain amount of respect on the church leadership for pointing out the issue of a divided Germany, stating, "In conclusion it is indeed not unimportant, but also does not come directly in the central question."[44] The best way that the SED could momentarily brush off the criticism of the churches was to claim that reunification was not much of an issue.

Perceived developments in the West further compounded the regime's anxieties. On 5 October 1954, Hilde Benjamin wrote to the SED Central Committee to express some apprehension that the West German Bundestag would pass its own family law reforms before East and West German jurists had a chance to meet to discuss the laws.[45] The press release that accompanied her letter portrayed the West as uncooperative and preventing its own citizens from discussing the laws, stating,

> Neither the refusal of the Bonn Minister of Justice Neumeier [sic] to meet with the Justice Minister of the GDR, Dr. Benjamin, nor the lies and attempts at destruction can detract from [the fact] that numerous citizens and jurists in West Germany recognize the meaning of the draft and were prepared [to join] the pan-German conversation in the area of law in the manifestation of its different forms.[46]

The language of the press release relied on the image of West Germans, willing and eager to discuss the East German FGB, to depict the West German government as the problem. The letter, however, demonstrated that Benjamin saw herself in a bind. If the West went forward with its reforms and completely ignored the East, then the GDR would appear as a failure.

The rejection by the Western government and the protests of East German churches shook the SED. In November 1954, the SED closed discussion of the FGB. In January and again in April 1955, Benjamin forwarded petitions from the churches to Erich Mielke, then lieutenant-general (second in command) of the Ministry for State Security (Ministerium für Staatssicherheit, MfS).[47] Her letters did not explicitly ask the secret police to watch and inform on church members, but it might be inferred that this was her intent. While it is not clear exactly which routes the MfS pursued to observe the leaders and members of the protesting churches, it is more evident what conclusions they drew. In 1956, the MfS produced an internal report chronicling its activities between 1 September 1954 (the same date the KO-EKD issued its opinion piece) and 1 September 1955. The report labeled the churches' work as representative of "the policy of aggression" of the West.[48] In particular, the author singled out the Western Protestant bishop Otto Dibelius for "opposing the democratic institutions of our republic [. . .] against the regulations of our government, for example against the Law of Equal Rights of Women, against the youth confirmation, against the family law, etc."[49] The MfS's inflammatory rhetoric placed the blame for the churches' rebellion over women's legal rights and the family on the West. As a stopgap measure, the Ministry of Justice released the "Decree on Marriage and Dissolution of Marriage" on 24 November 1955, but otherwise did not return to the matter of family law for another decade, finally passing the Family Code on 20 December 1965.[50]

The Western Struggles to Change Family Law, 1949–57

Like in the East, the West German Federal Ministry of Justice (Bundesjustizministerium) began to pursue reforms of the family law in 1950, albeit at a much slower pace. Unlike the SED, the Christian-conservative administration of CDU chancellor Konrad Adenauer was in no immediate hurry to pass the law. For one thing, the Basic Law, the new provisional West German constitution from 1949, gave the Bundestag until 31 March 1953 to make changes to the old Civil Code, meaning there was no urgent legal vacuum to fill. Additionally, the CDU/CSU, in a coalition with the FDP and the conservative German Party (Deutsche Partei), had control of the legislature and government. Its major opponents were the Social Democratic Party of Germany (Sozialdemokratische Partei Deutschlands, SPD) and the Communist Party of Germany (Kommunistische Partei Deutschlands, KPD).[51] Furthermore, the CDU/CSU-dominated government saw traditional gender roles, as prescribed by the old Civil Code, as a restabilizing force for West Germany in the catastrophic postwar "crisis" years. Finally, Adenauer's anticommunism made him reticent to openly engage with the East, even though it was by default an implicit presence in West German politics. His regime therefore shied away from mentioning the East German family law reforms as an explicit point of comparison.

Thus, Thomas Dehler, the FDP minister of justice, debuted the new legislation only in March 1952. Over the preceding year, the Federal Ministry of Justice had solicited opinions from leaders of independent women's associations, trade unions, churches, and professional organizations.[52] The resulting reforms were decidedly liberalizing in certain regards. According to Dehler, the ministry's goal was "to adapt the current law to the principle of equal rights of the sexes."[53] The legislative draft therefore no longer allowed men to make all decisions for their wives and families, overturned old marital property schemes, and permitted women to hyphenate their married names, among other provisions. Furthermore, he stated that the FRG wished to "restore legal unity in the area of family law."[54] Unlike the SED, however, West German politicians did not explicitly focus on the legal unity with the East, but rather the "entire federal territory [*Bundesgebiet*]," meaning all of the Western sectors.[55]

Although the ministry's draft legislation met the approval of secular women's associations, trade unions, and some professional federations, it never sat well with Protestants and Catholics. In formal opinions issued to the federal government, Otto Dibelius together with the Catholic archbishop Josef Frings outlined several reasons not to adopt a more expansive law. First, they proclaimed that the law could not "mechanically" erase sexual difference.[56] Second, they pointed to the relationship of church to state. As Dibelius put it, mainstream Protestant leaders felt any marriage law reforms had to leave space for the practice of Christian marriage as God or the Bible prescribed it.[57] Finally, each church leader alluded to other legal traditions to point out the superiority of German law and the dangers of liberalizing reforms. For example, Frings criticized the "seemingly unscrupulous envisaged approximation of our forthcoming law to Nordic and Eastern laws."[58] Meanwhile, Dibelius defended the retention of the male family name, for example, because "in Soviet Russian law, that always means an anonymization [. . .] and finally the dissolution of human existence."[59] Both leaders constructed an image of the Federal Ministry's law as endangering to Christians. According to them, the law stood poised to eliminate sexual difference and prevent Christians from following biblical or papal prescriptions for home life. They found support from numerous Protestant and Catholic regional church leaders, religious organizations, and public figures who wrote to the Federal Ministry of Justice to express their opinions as well, echoing the arguments of their respective leaders that religious freedom should trump individual rights.[60]

Cognizant of the controversial nature of the legislation, Dehler negotiated with Protestant and Catholic Church leaders in April and May 1952. Above all, the Catholics present at the meeting wanted to preserve the *Stichentscheid* that allowed men to make all decisions in marriage and the family; the Protestants, though reticent to continue allowing men to make all decisions for their wives, still saw value in paternal authority over children.[61] Dehler had several options before him. He could ignore the church leaders and rile up many Christians. He could give in to the churches and risk angering secular women's associations, trade unions, and other vital professional organizations that supported his version of the law. In the end, he chose compromise, dismissing the husband's right to decide in marital relations but preserving it in parental authority.[62]

Compromise, as Dehler soon discovered, was not the correct solution in the eyes of the Adenauer administration. In July 1952, under duress from the chancellor and other ministers, Dehler reinstated provisions that he had so fervently opposed, such as the *Stichentscheid*. Furthermore, he agreed to change another clause to read, "A wife is permitted to be employed as long as it is reconcilable with her duties in marriage and the family."[63] Now, Dehler had compromised on two of the key issues he had set out to change. His decision to acquiesce to Adenauer's demands resulted in numerous letters from women's organizations, trade unionists, and professional organization leaders who opposed the more conservative version of the law.[64] The Adenauer administration, however, did not bend to their requests.

Despite Adenauer's stubbornness and a Christian-conservative majority in the Bundestag, the law never came to pass. The opposition, namely the SPD and KPD, and some members of the liberal FDP, banded together and refused to approve the legislation.[65] The Bundestag elected instead to send the law to a special parliamentary committee for revisions. Its work, however, resulted in a political stalemate. Neither the churches and Christian conservatives nor the Social Democrats and Free Democrats achieved the legislative reforms that they wanted by the constitutionally mandated 31 March 1953 deadline.

Christians, who enjoyed governmental and popular support, had not anticipated this outcome. Several factors help explain why Christian conservatives lost this time. One consideration is that the West German churches never really presented a unified front, a fact upon which the SPD and its coalition partners in the Bundestag seized. Protestants and Catholics did not see eye to eye on several matters in marriage and family law. Dehler's consultation with church leaders, for example, exposed these divisions. While Catholics sought to strengthen patriarchal authority by keeping provisions such as the *Stichentscheid* intact, Protestants were more willing to grant women equal rights in marriage. For the ruling CDU/CSU—a party designed to overcome confessional difference—these discrepancies presented a challenge.

Furthermore, gender divided the churches, another factor that the SPD and its allies exploited. There were divisions not only between male and female religious leaders but also among different factions of religious women. Some Catholic women, namely the chairwomen of the Catholic German Women's Union (Katholischer Deutscher Frauenbund), supported Archbishop Frings and other Catholic Church leaders.[66] Others opposed church leaders, choosing to side with the Social Democrats and Free Democrats.[67] Meanwhile, Protestant women navigated the waters between Otto Dibelius, with whom they disagreed, and the Social Democratic and Free Democratic proposals for the law.[68] When the Christian-conservative alliance in the Bundestag claimed that Catholics and Protestants were on their side, the SPD and a female CDU member, Elisabeth Schwarzhaupt, cited the responses of the religious women's associations as evidence that not all Christians, especially women, agreed.[69]

The eventual failure of the churches also suggests deficiencies in their rhetorical strategy. With the exception of two brief allusions to the GDR and Soviet law, church leaders largely shied away from any references to the volatile political situation of the Cold War. This strategy differed significantly from their Eastern counterparts, who relied on rhetoric of legal unity to undermine the communist dictatorship. Rather, Western church leaders—and by extension, the CDU/CSU—tended to focus on dogmatic reasons to retain the Civil Code. As they discovered, Christian arguments for biblical adherence did not hold up in a legal setting. After all, under the SPD/FDP's formulations, Christian men and women could continue to structure their partnerships as they pleased; it was simply no longer legally applicable to all. But this approach reflected the broader political culture of the West as well. Adenauer's administration did not officially recognize the East or bring up legal unity in any matter. It is therefore unsurprising, in some regards, that the issue of legal unity remained an "elephant in the room" and that politicians and church leaders employed other language in their arguments.

The weeks immediately following the 31 March 1953 deadline offered the risk of *Rechtschaos,* or legal chaos—meaning that without a law, judges would be responsible for all adjudication—but it also meant that West Germans, especially married women and mothers, could finally claim their constitutional right to equality in court cases concerning marriage and family law. When it became clear that judicial review could not resolve marital or familial matters forever, the Federal Constitutional Court urged the CDU/CSU-led government to reopen the debate over family law in January 1954. A Bundestag committee then discussed and formulated the law for about two years. On 18 June 1957, the Bundestag finally approved legislation to reform the parts of the old Civil Code on marriage and the family: the Equal Rights Act, or *Gleichberechtigungsgesetz,* which went into effect a year later, on 1 July 1958.

As this section has shown, the Catholic and Protestant Churches initially enjoyed privileged status with the Christian-conservative Adenauer administration, which seemed poised in 1952 to uphold the patriarchal provisions of the old Civil Code. Yet this version of the law never passed, and the Bundestag instead expanded women's rights in certain areas such as marital decision-making and marital property. Reform-oriented members of the Bundestag were able to achieve liberalizing changes of the family law because they exploited certain rifts and rhetorical inconsistencies to undermine the powerful position of Protestant and Catholic Church leaders and their parliamentary allies. As a result, women's rights in West Germany witnessed a small step forward in the 1950s.

Conclusion

This chapter has employed *histoire croisée* to illuminate the different political, social, and cultural factors that shaped the entangled contours of Protestant and Catholic protests against family law reforms in East and West Germany in the early 1950s. First, the new German states inherited several laws and institutions, such as the Civil Code, that opposed the East and West German governments' commitments to equal rights of men and women after 1945. This strong resistance was especially evident in West Germany, where, in the context of postwar reconstruction of liberal democracy in the wake of Nazism's destruction and the burgeoning Cold War, Christian-conservative politicians were willing to leave the Civil Code intact indefinitely. In the East, the SED and the Soviets, in the context of founding an antifascist and socialist Germany, were eager to abandon the Civil Code.

Second, political factors, in particular different political cultures, played significant roles in shaping politicians' decisions on family law reforms on each side as well. The SED and the Soviets fought to maintain political dominance, and yet still yearned for their population's approval. The ruling party halted in its tracks because it was reticent to impose the Family Code on a public that clearly opposed the legislation—a phenomenon that happened elsewhere in the GDR, such as in the debates over the *Hausarbeitstag* (a day of paid leave for addressing family and household issues), as Carola Sachse has shown.[70] In Sachse's case of the *Hausarbeitstag*, the SED wanted to overhaul the legislation but refused to alienate female workers, who were quick to petition the government when it threatened to remove the "housework day." In my own study, the ruling party feared isolating Christians. The SED's responses thus allow us to rethink the concept of dictatorship. Although hardly democratic, the ruling party's surrender reminds us that, at times, even dictatorships work actively to keep their citizens happy, exemplifying historian Jürgen Kocka's assertion that "the dictatorship's rule was more limited than assumed by theories of totalitarianism."[71] Meanwhile, in the West, the tug-of-war between the CDU/CSU and the SPD for political control delayed approval of the Equal Rights Act. The Christian-conservative coalition in the Bundestag, supported by Protestant and Catholic leaders, fought to keep the old Civil Code, which they believed would maintain the "natural order" of the sexes as they rebuilt the West. They opposed the Social Democrats' efforts—supported by women's associations, trade unions, and professional organizations—to overhaul the Civil Code. In the FRG, this struggle displays that postwar democratization efforts were working. Despite the Adenauer administration's willingness to bow to the demands of the Protestant and Catholic Churches, the Bundestag proved more resistant, and it rejected the measures that clergymen supported in favor of expanding women's rights in marriage (and later parental authority).

Third, social and cultural factors mattered. Both German regimes recognized the influence of the churches on the general population and therefore sought out their guidance on the forthcoming family laws. Both German governments believed that they had attained the blessing of the church leaders to go forward with the reforms. In the case of the East, the churches wielded enough influence to delay the SED's plans. In the case of the West, the churches' dogmatic arguments resonated with the Christian-conservative government, but failed to sway other parties in the Bundestag. These paradoxical results point to the power of longstanding social and cultural norms in both Germanys. Many Germans were reluctant to radically overhaul marriage and family law because it did not fit their long-held ideas, shaped by Christian teaching, about gender, women, and the family.

Finally, the context of the Cold War shaped the parallel debates in each state. Both governments presented their new family laws as essential to all-German unity. On the one hand, the SED in the East wanted to beat the West to the reforms. On the other hand, leading party members noted that legal disunity could result from moving too fast. Church leaders then used this rhetoric against SED leaders, who were vulnerable in the context of the Cold War to any criticism that they were pursuing divisive policies. In comparison, West German politicians and church leaders made fewer overt references to the East but still took the Cold War context into account, at times expressing reservations about resembling the GDR or creating legal confusion between the two Germanys.

The story of the parallel reforms of family law in the postwar Germanys offers historians new insights into several aspects of the two states. In addition to highlighting the centrality of gender, women's status, and the family to governmental discourse on both sides of the Iron Curtain, the parallel developments illuminate how entangled these debates were.[72] The

Civil Code offered a somewhat unique instance of a common denominator shared by the two states that otherwise followed divergent paths in the 1950s. At different points, politicians on both sides of the Iron Curtain considered family law a potential obstacle to German reunification, which is important because it displays how deeply entwined these two states were in the early years of the Cold War. The Cold War conflict between the two Germanys was not a distant, looming specter; it was present in every decision both states made regarding the formulation and propagation of the new Family Code in the East and the Equal Rights Act in the West.

Alexandria Ruble is assistant professor of European history at Spring Hill College, Mobile, Alabama, United States. She earned her Ph.D. in 2017 University of North Carolina at Chapel Hill. Her research interests include modern German and European history; women's and gender history; global history; and comparative/entanglement history. Her publications include a chapter in the volume *A History of the Family in Modern Germany* (ed. by Lisa Pine, Bloomsbury Academic, 2018); and an article titled "Creating Post-Fascist Families: Reforming the Civil Code in East and West Germany in the 1950s," in the special issue *Burdens and Beginnings: Rebuilding East and West Germany after Nazism and War—Comparative and Entangled Perspectives of Central European History* (ed. by Karen Hagemann, Tobias Hof and Konrad H. Jarausch, vol. 53, no. 2).

Notes

1. For more on churches under the Third Reich, see Doris Bergen, *Twisted Cross: The German Christian Movement in the Third Reich* (Chapel Hill, NC, 1996); and Hubert Wolf, *Pope and Devil: The Vatican's Archives and the Third Reich* (Cambridge, MA, 2010).
2. Robert G. Moeller, "The Homosexual Man Is a 'Man,' the Homosexual Woman Is a 'Woman': Sex, Society, and the Law in Postwar West Germany," in *West Germany under Construction: Politics, Society, and Culture in the Adenauer Era*, ed. Robert G. Moeller (Ann Arbor, MI, 1997), 275. See also Rudolf Uertz, *Christentum und Sozialismus in der frühen CDU: Grundlagen und Wirkungen der Christlich-Sozialen Ideen in der Union, 1945–1949* (Stuttgart, 1981).
3. Bernd Schäfer, *The East German State and the Catholic Church, 1945–1989* (New York, 2010), 32.
4. "Decline in Religious Observance among Catholics and Protestants (1960–1989)," *Datenreport 1992: Zahlen und Fakten über die Bundesrepublik Deutschland,*

ed. Federal Office of Statistics [Statistisches Bundesamt] (Bonn, 1992), 190–11, germanhistorydocs.ghi-dc.org/sub_document.cfm?document_id=846 (accessed 7 August 2017).

5. Christoph Kleßmann, "Verflechtung und Abgrenzung: Aspekte der geteilten und zusammengehörigen deutschen Nachkriegsgeschichte," *Aus Politik und Zeitgeschichte* B 29–30 (1993), 30–41; see also Heinz-Gerhard Haupt and Jürgen Kocka, "Comparative History: Methods, Aims, Problems," in *Comparison and History: Europe in Cross-National Perspective*, eds. Deborah Cohen and Maura O'Connor (New York, 2004), 33. For path dependency, see Paul Pierson, "Increasing Returns, Path Dependence, and the Study of Politics," *American Political Science Review* 94, no. 2 (2000): 253; and Karen Hagemann, "Halbtags oder Ganztags? Zeitpolitiken von Kinderbetreuung und Schule in Europa im historischen Vergleich," in *Halbtags oder Ganztags? Familie, Frauenarbeit und Zeitpolitik von Kinderbetreuung und Schule in Europa im historischen Vergleich*, ed. Karen Hagemann and Konrad H. Jarausch (Weinheim, 2014), 20–83. Path dependency theories acknowledge that major political and social changes have costs that often determine their outcomes. In particular, systems and institutions are extremely difficult to change and changes to these structures come at a great cost. For this case, this helps illuminate why the churches and German cultural norms about marriage and the family posed problems for the SED.

6. For more on the nineteenth-century women's movement, see Angelika Schaser, *Frauenbewegung in Deutschland 1848–1933* (Darmstadt, 2006); Barbara Greven-Aschoff, *Die Bürgerliche Frauenbewegung in Deutschland 1894–1933* (Göttingen, 1981); Irene Stoehr, *Emanzipation zum Staat? Der Allgemeine Deutsche Frauenverein-Deutscher Staatsbürgerinnenverband (1893–1933)* (Pfaffenweiler, 1990); and Karen Offen, *European Feminisms, 1700–1950: A Political History* (Stanford, CA, 2000).

7. Justus Wilhelm Hedemann et al., *Volksgesetzbuch*, Arbeitsberichte der Akademie für Deutsches Recht, vol. 22 (Munich, 1942).

8. Kontrollratsgesetz Nr. 16 (Ehegesetz) (20 February 1946).

9. Donna Harsch, *Revenge of the Domestic: Women, the Family, and Communism in the German Democratic Republic* (Princeton, NJ, 2007), 29.

10. See Catherine Dollard, "Socialism and Singleness: Clara Zetkin," in *The Surplus Woman: Unmarried in Imperial Germany, 1871–1918* (New York, 2009), 164–75; Jean Quataert, *Reluctant Feminists in German Social Democracy, 1885–1917* (Princeton, NJ, 1979), 5–17; Karen Hagemann, *Frauenalltag und Männerpolitik: Alltagsleben und gesellschaftliches Handeln von Arbeiterfrauen in der Weimarer Republik* (Bonn, 1990), 516–51; and Karen Offen, *European Feminisms, 1700–1950: A Political History* (Stanford, CA, 2000), 200–212.

11. *Gesetz über den Mutter- und Kinderschutz und die Rechte der Frau vom 27. September 1950*, www.verfassungen.de/de/ddr/mutterkindgesetz50.htm (accessed 25 May 2017).

12. For the biography of Hilde Benjamin, see Andrea Feth, *Hilde Benjamin: Eine Biographie* (Berlin, 1997).

13. Harsch, *Revenge*, 205.

14. "Entwurf eines Familiengesetzbuches der Deutschen Demokratischen Republik," *Neue Justiz*, 8, no. 12 (30 June 1954): 377.

15. Ibid.

16. "Bericht über die Ergebnisse der Diskussion zum Entwurf des Familiengesetzbuches auf der Arbeitstagung im Ministerium der Justiz vom 19.10.1954," 1, Bundesarchiv Berlin (BArch-B), DO 1/14398; Harsch, *Revenge*, 205.
17. "Protokoll über eine Justizaussprache, 24.8.54," Stiftung Archiv der Parteien und Massenorganisationen der DDR im Bundesarchiv Berlin (SAPMO), DY30/IV2/14/35, Bl. 61.
18. Maria Hagemeyer, *Der Entwurf des Familiengesetzbuches der "Deutschen Demokratischen Republik,"* ed. Bundesministerium für gesamtdeutsche Fragen, 3rd ed. (Bonn, 1955).
19. "Ein Nein? Das wackelt," *Berliner Zeitung*, 7 August 1954, 2; "Gedankenaustausch über Familiengesetz von Bonn abgelehnt," *Neues Deutschland*, 7 August 1954, 2; "Bonn wünscht keine Verständigung," *Neue Zeit*, 7 August 1954, 2.
20. "Entschließung der Synode der Evangelischen Kirche in Deutschland zu Fragen der Ehe und Familie, 19. März 1954," Evangelisches Zentralarchiv Berlin (EZA), 99/639.
21. Harsch, *Revenge*, 206.
22. "Protokoll über eine Justizaussprache, 24.08.54," SAPMO, DY30/IV2/14/35, Bl. 62. Emphasis in original.
23. Ibid.
24. Ibid.
25. "Stellungnahme der Kirchlichen Ostkonferenz zu dem Entwurf eines Familiengesetzbuches der Deutschen Demokratischen Republik, 1. September 1954," 1, EZA, 99/639.
26. "Um Ehe und Familie," *Die Kirche*, 26 September 1954, SAPMO, DY 30/IV2/14/35, Bl. 75.
27. Ibid.
28. "Um Ehe und Familie," Bl. 77.
29. See several petitions in BArch-B, DO 4/1555. The SED received petitions from parishes around the GDR simply stating that they and their fellow parishioners opposed the law. Others, such as the Protestant churches of Berlin-Brandenburg, Rüdersdorf, Lichterfelde, Rehfelde, a women's group in Magdeburg, and a parish in Langensalza, wrote to express agreement with the KO-EKD's statement from 1 September 1954.
30. "Bericht über die Versammlung der evangelischen Kirchengemeinde Bautzen, November 8," SAPMO, DY30/IV2/14/35, Bl. 107. According to this document, 450 people attended. Another document on the same meeting from DO 4/1555 states that 500 people attended. This document also indicates that the pastor was informed ahead of time that his meeting was not to be held, but he chose to have it anyway.
31. Ibid.
32. Ibid.
33. For the biography of Weskamm, see "Bishop Wilhelm Weskamm Dies at 65: Led Roman Catholics in East Germany," *New York Times*, 22 August 1956; for the biography of Otto Grotewohl, see Dierk Hoffmann, *Otto Grotewohl (1894–1964): Eine Politische Biographie* (Munich, 2009).
34. "Wilhelm Weskamm an Otto Grotewohl, August 28, 1954," SAPMO, DY30/IV2/14/35, Bl. 1.
35. Ibid., Bl. 2.

36. Ibid., Bl. 1.
37. "Limbach-Frohna an den Stellvertreter des Ministerpräsidenten, Volkskammerabgeordneten und Vorsitzenden der Christlich-Demokratischen Union Deutschlands, Herrn Otto Nuschke in Berlin, 2. Januar 1955," BArch-B, DO 4/1555.
38. Konrad H. Jarausch, *After Hitler: Recivilizing Germans, 1945–1995* (Oxford, 2006), 193.
39. Harsch, *Revenge*, 205–6.
40. Schäfer, *East German State*, 32.
41. "Benjamin an Plenikowski," SAPMO, DY30/IV2/14/35, Bl. 46.
42. "Aufzeichnung, 6. September 1954," BArch-B, DO 4/2095.
43. Ibid.
44. Ibid.
45. "Benjamin an Plenikowski, 5. Oktober 1954," SAPMO, DY30/IV2/14/35, Bl. 70. Either her intelligence was faulty or the Bundestag's plans changed, because the law did not go up for a vote until 1957.
46. Ibid., Bl. 71.
47. "Benjamin an Mielke, 15. April 1955," BArch-B, DP 1/243; and "Benjamin an Mielke, 21. Januar 1955," BArch-B, DP 1/243. For the biography of Erich Mielke, see www.hdg.de/lemo/biografie/erich-mielke.html.
48. "Auskunftsbericht Nr. 3 über die Situation und Tätigkeit der evangelischen Kirchen in Deutschland vom 1.9.1954 bis 1.9.1955," Der Bundesbeauftragte für die Unterlagen des Staatssicherheitsdienstes der ehemaligen Deutschen Demokratischen Republik, MfS JHS 001 Z 9/56, 0003.
49. Ibid.
50. "Verordnung über Eheschließung und Eheauflösung: Vom 24. November 1955," *Gesetzblatt der Deutschen Demokratischen Republik*, Teil I, Nr. 102 vom 29. November 1955, 849–51.
51. Robert G. Moeller, *Protecting Motherhood: Women and the Family in the Politics of Postwar West Germany* (Berkeley, CA, 1993), 81.
52. "Vermerk über die Tagung über Frauenfragen im Bundesministerium des Innern, 28. Februar," Bundesarchiv Koblenz (BArch-K), 1951, B141/2055/63.
53. "Begründung zu dem Entwurf eines Gesetzes über die Gleichberechtigung von Mann und Frau auf dem Gebiete des bürgerlichen Rechts und über die Wiederherstellung der Rechtseinheit auf dem Gebiete des Familienrechts, 21. April 1952," BArch-K, B106/43313.
54. Ibid.
55. Ibid.
56. "Dibelius an Dehler, 22. März 1952," and "Frings an Dehler, 12. Januar 1952," BArch-K, B106/43313.
57. "Dibelius an Dehler, 22. März 1952."
58. "Frings an Dehler, 12. Januar 1952."
59. "Dibelius an Dehler, 22. März 1952."
60. "Katholiken-Ausschuß der Stadt M.-Gladbach an den Herrn Bundeskanzler, 1 August 1952," BArch-K, B136/540/262-264; "Vorschläge zur Reform des Familienrechts, 1. April 1952," BArch-K, B136/539/204; "Stellungnahme zur Denkschrift, die Frau Oberlandesgerichtsrätin Dr. Hagemeyer im Auftrage des Bundesjustizministeriums verfaßte, über die durch Artikel 3 des Grundgesetzes gebotenen Gesetzesänderungen, 25. Januar 1952," BArch-K, B106/43313; "Bosch an Adenauer, 15. Februar 1952," BArch-K, B136/539/68.

61. "Aktenvermerk über eine Besprechung mit Vertretern der evangelischen und der katholischen Kirche, 4. April 1952," BArch-K, B141/2057/97.
62. Christine Franzius, *Bonner Grundgesetz und Familienrecht: Die Diskussion um die Gleichberechtigung von Mann und Frau in der westdeutschen Zivilrechtslehre der Nachkriegszeit 1945–1957* (Frankfurt/M., 2005), 61.
63. "Dehler an Adenauer, 10. Juli 1952," BArch-K, B136/540.
64. "Denkschrift des Deutschen Frauenrings zum Kabinettsentwurf eines Gesetzes über die Gleichberechtigung von Mann und Frau auf dem Gebiete des bürgerlichen Rechts und über die Wiederherstellung der Rechtseinheit auf dem Gebiete des Familienrechts, 23. Dezember 1952," DGB-Archiv, 2414450102, FES; see also "Else Ulich-Beil an den Herrn Bundeskanzler, 1. September 1952," BArch-K, B136/540/282; "Dora Hansen-Blancke an den Herrn Bundeskanzler, Frauenring Hamburg, 18. September 1952," BArch-K, B136/540/343; "Fränkischer Frauenarbeitskreis und Frauenring Südbayern an die Mitglieder des Deutschen Bundestages, 15. September 1952," BArch-K, B136/540/354; "Der DGB zur Familienrechtsreform, 26. November 1952," Archiv der Sozialen Demokratie, 5/DGAR000798 (24/4461).
65. "Erste Beratung des Entwurfs eines Gesetzes . . .," Deutscher Bundestag [1.], 239. Sitzung, 27. November 1952, 11052–72.
66. "Stellungnahme zur Denkschrift, . . ., 25, Januar 1952," BArch-K, B106/43313.
67. "Arbeitsgemeinschaft der katholischen deutschen Frauen an Adenauer, 7. Juli 1952," BArch-K, B136/540/186.
68. "Stellungnahme der Evangelischen Frauenarbeit in Deutschland zum Gutachten des Rates der Evangelischen Kirche in Deutschland zu den Fragen der Revision des Ehe- und Familienrechts, 2. Mai 1952," BArch-K, B 141/2030/136.
69. "Erste Beratung des Entwurfs eines Gesetzes über die Gleichberechtigung von Mann und Frau auf dem Gebiete des bürgerlichen Rechts," Deutscher Bundestag [2.], 15. Sitzung, 12. Februar 1954, 473–516, 483, 498, 499.
70. Carola Sachse, *Der Hausarbeitstag: Gerechtigkeit und Gleichberechtigung in Ost und West 1939–1994* (Göttingen, 2002), 148–49. See also Sachse, "Ein 'heißes Eisen': Ost- und westdeutsche Debatten um den Hausarbeitstag," in *Frauen arbeiten: Weibliche Erwerbstätigkeit in Ost- und Westdeutschland nach 1945*, ed. Gunilla-Friederike Budde (Göttingen, 1997), 262–63.
71. Jürgen Kocka, *Civil Society and Dictatorship in Modern German History* (Hanover, NH, 2010), 29.
72. For theoretical literature on the history of entanglements, see Haupt and Kocka, "Comparative History," 33; Michael Werner and Bénédicte Zimmermann, "Vergleich, Transfer, Verflechtung: Der Ansatz der *Histoire croisée* und die Herausforderung des Transnationalen," *Geschichte und Gesellschaft* 28, no. 4 (2002): 607–36. For examples of other studies that compare gender in both Germanys, see Sachse, *Der Hausarbeitstag*; Karen Hagemann, "Between Ideology and Economy: The 'Time Politics' of Child Care and Public Education in the Two Germanys," *Social Politics* 13, no. 2 (2006): 239–41, and "A West-German "*Sonderweg*"? Family, Work, and the Half-Day Time Policy of Childcare and Schooling," in *Children, Families, and States: Time Policies of Childcare, Preschool, and Primary Education in Europe*, ed. Karen Hagemann et al. (New York, 2011), 275–300; and Monika Mattes, "Economy and Politics: The Time Policy of the East German Childcare and Primary School System," in Hagemann et al., *Children, Families, and States*, 344–63. Leonie Treber's study *Mythos Trümmerfrauen: Von der Trüm-*

merbeseitigung in der Kriegs- und Nachkriegszeit und der Entstehung eines Deutschen Erinnerungsortes (Essen, 2014), although not on policy, nevertheless provides an interesting comparison of gender and memory in the two postwar states. See also Budde, *Frauen arbeiten,* an edited volume that compares women in the labor force in both Germanys.

Selected Bibliography

Budde, Gunilla-Friederike. *Frauen Arbeiten: Weibliche Erwerbstätigkeit in Ost- und Westdeutschland nach 1945.* Göttingen, 1997.
Franzius, Christine. *Bonner Grundgesetz und Familienrecht: die Diskussion um die Gleichberechtigung von Mann und Frau in der westdeutschen Zivilrechtslehre der Nachkriegszeit (1945–1957).* Frankfurt/M., 2005.
Gerhard, Ute. *Frauen in der Geschichte des Rechts: Von der frühen Neuzeit bis zur Gegenwart.* Munich, 1999.
———. "Family Law and Gender Equality: Comparing Family Policies in Postwar Western Europe." In *Children, Families, and States: Time Policies of Childcare, Preschool, and Primary Education in Europe,* ed. Karen Hagemann, Konrad H. Jarausch, and Cristina Allemann-Ghionda, 75–93. New York, 2011.
Hagemann, Karen, and Konrad Jarausch, eds. *Halbtags oder Ganztags? Familie, Frauenarbeit und Zeitpolitik von Kinderbetreuung und Schule in Europa im historischen Vergleich.* Weinheim, 2014.
Harsch, Donna. *Revenge of the Domestic: Women, the Family, and Communism in the German Democratic Republic.* Princeton, NJ, 2007.
Haupt, Heinz-Gerhard, and Jürgen Kocka. "Comparative History: Methods, Aims, Problems." In *Comparison and History: Europe in Cross-National Perspective,* ed. Deborah Cohen and Maura O'Connor, 23–40. London, 2004.
Heineman, Elizabeth. *What Difference Does a Husband Make? Women and Marital Status in Nazi and Postwar Germany.* Berkeley, CA, 2003.
Jarausch, Konrad H. *After Hitler: Recivilizing Germans, 1945–1995.* Oxford, 2006.
Kleßmann, Christoph. "Verflechtung und Abgrenzung: Aspekte der geteilten und zusammengehörigen deutschen Nachkriegsgeschichte." *Aus Politik und Zeitgeschichte* B 29–30 (1993): 30–41.
Kocka, Jürgen. *Civil Society and Dictatorship in Modern German History.* Hanover, NH, 2010.
Moeller, Robert G. *Protecting Motherhood: Women and the Family in the Politics of Postwar West Germany.* Berkeley, CA, 1993.
Niehuss, Merith. *Familie, Frau und Gesellschaft: Studien Zur Strukturgeschichte der Familie in Westdeutschland 1945–1960.* Göttingen, 2001.
Obertreis, Gesine. *Familienpolitik in der DDR 1945–1980.* Opladen, 1986.
Oertzen, Christine von. *Teilzeitarbeit und die Lust am Zuverdienen: Geschlechterpolitik und gesellschaftlicher Wandel in Westdeutschland 1948–1969.* Göttingen, 1999.
Pierson, Paul. "Increasing Returns, Path Dependence, and the Study of Politics." *American Political Science Review* 94, no. 2 (2000): 251–67.
Poiger, Uta. *Jazz, Rock, and Rebels: Cold War Politics and American Culture in a Divided Germany.* Berkeley, CA, 2000.

Reich-Hilweg, Ines. *Männer und Frauen sind gleichberechtigt: Der Gleichberechtigungsgrundsatz (Art. 3, Abs. 2 GG) in der parlamentarischen Auseinandersetzung 1948–1957 und in der Rechtsprechung des Bundesverfassungsgerichts 1953–1975.* Frankfurt/M., 1979.

Sachse, Carola. "Ein 'heißes Eisen': Ost- und westdeutsche Debatten um den Hausarbeitstag." In *Frauen arbeiten: Weibliche Erwerbstätigkeit in Ost- und Westdeutschland nach 1945,* ed. Gunilla-Friederike Budde, 252–85. Göttingen, 1997.

———. *Der Hausarbeitstag: Gerechtigkeit und Gleichberechtigung in Ost und West, 1939–1994.* Göttingen, 2002.

Treber, Leonie. *Mythos Trümmerfrauen: Von der Trümmerbeseitigung in der Kriegs- und Nachkriegszeit und der Entstehung eines deutschen Erinnerungsortes.* Essen, 2014.

CHAPTER 6

Gendering Health Politics
East and West German Healthcare Systems in Comparison, 1950–70

Donna Harsch

Divided by the Cold War and connected by their common past, the two Germanys (re)constructed gendered health cultures that were as entangled as other aspects of these postwar societies. This applies to all three important areas of health policy after 1945: postwar epidemics, chronic disease, and pregnancy and childbirth. Responses to surges in tuberculosis and venereal disease illuminate the interaction between early Cold War health policies and the gendered understanding of contagious disease. Discourse about cancer and heart disease exemplifies the gendered interpretation of chronic disease as it emerged as the main health challenge facing both Germanys. Policies toward pregnancy and childbirth illustrate the rise in concern about women's health.

This chapter compares all three areas of health politics from the 1950s to the 1970s but focuses on the construction of women's health, reflecting the greater attention from contemporaries to women's health, especially after 1960. The available sources—medical literature, conference transcripts, official reports, and state correspondence—are full of explicitly gendered language about *female health* and provide direct evidence of attitudes about women and health. In contrast, contemporary commentators in the medical profession, media, and politics typically employed a gender-neutral language when talking about diseases that affected *men*. To reconstruct the narratives about the male body and its health, it is therefore often necessary to analyze them in the context of gendered cultural assumptions held by contemporaries about men and their health and refer to these assumptions as indirect evidence.

East and West models of the gender of health and illness, the chapter argues, shared basic resemblances forged by mutual tradition or experience: Western medicine, German medical and public-health customs before 1933, and the racist health policy of the Third Reich and the Second World War. Within broadly comparable gendered constructions of disease, however, discrepancies emerged in rhetoric, attention, and policy toward specific illnesses. Dissimilarity arose from Cold War rivalry and contrasting ideologies and social systems. Most significant was a partially divergent understanding of what endangered the female body. In the 1950s, for example, mainstream West German medical opinion portrayed employment as a health risk to women and assumed pregnancy and childbirth to be a normal biological process, while East German discourse described paid labor as natural for women but medicalized pregnancy and childbirth. During the 1960s, interpretations of dangers to women's health increasingly converged. In the context of a rising number of women, and especially mothers, joining the workforce in West Germany, its health discourse moved closer to the East German point of view on employment and pregnancy and childbirth.

The history of healthcare in the postwar Germanys is not well studied beyond research on the basic characteristics of healthcare structures and their medical orientation. After their founding in 1949, the Federal Republic of Germany (FRG) and the German Democratic Republic (GDR) created strikingly different systems. In power from 1949 until 1969, the West German Christian Democratic Union of Germany (Christlich Demokratische Union Deutschlands, CDU) forged a decentralized healthcare system that was almost completely administered by private doctors, many of whom opposed even the small public-health component of healthcare provision in the FRG. The East German system was highly centralized and organized around state care with an ever-smaller role for private providers. The Ministry of Health Care (Ministerium für Gesundheitswesen, MfG) in the GDR placed great rhetorical and considerable practical emphasis on prevention, while West German healthcare was oriented toward curative care and treatment. Only starting in the late 1960s did the system turn toward prevention. This turn was part of an era of reform that opened as political power shifted from the CDU to the Social Democratic Party of Germany (Sozialdemokratische Partei Deutschlands, SPD). Health policy in the FRG was influenced not just by politics but also by newspapers, magazines, and popular books that sometimes invented or sensationalized a health crisis. In the GDR, far fewer actors and interests competed to influence discourse and policy. In sum, the GDR's official healthcare culture was quite determined from above, communicated in a fairly unified voice, and aimed to be proactive about health problems. The FRG's healthcare culture was hostile to control from above, spoke in many different voices, and often responded passively to health issues.[1] The two healthcare systems also generated very different "paper trails." The archive of the centralized, interventionist MfG contains a much larger number and variety of documents related to health issues. The FRG's decentralized and weak health-political institutions produced less quantitative data and much less qualitative evidence, even after the formation of a Federal Ministry of Health Care (Bundesministerium für Gesundheitswesen) in 1961. With the exception of tuberculosis treatment and prevention, the degree of explicit attention to international developments, including in the other German state, was also lopsided. East German health officials saw health outcomes as major "social indicators" and, thus, continually evaluated data and "best practices" from the entire industrialized world, including West Germany. The vogue for international comparisons of social indicators took off in the FRG only around 1960. References to East German health data were few and almost always dismissive until the late 1960s, when maternal and infant mortality dropped lower in the GDR than the FRG. Many medical professionals in East and West shared an initially condescending attitude toward American medicine but gradually changed their view, again in tandem. Most striking was the early adoption by health officials and doctors in both states of "risk-factor analysis" of chronic disease.[2]

The history of gendered health culture in the two Germanys has barely been investigated. This chapter draws, therefore, on insights from studies of Western discourse about the gendered body. The long-held Western understanding of the male body as the biological norm and the female body as a special case shaped medicine into the modern era. Indeed, far into the twentieth century, popular and medical cultures pathologized the *average* female body but only the *deviant* male body. Extrapolating from the physical dangers associated with childbirth, women's bodies were constructed as weaker, more susceptible to illness, and likelier to succumb to sickness than men's self-reliant and robust bodies. Due in part to declining maternal mortality, women have lived longer than men in countries with modern healthcare systems since the early 1900s. Yet the idea of the frail female body dominated medical and public-health discourse in Europe and the United States into the 1960s (and beyond). Health propaganda targeted women much more than it did men. Women were urged to visit the doctor if they felt ill or suspected cancer. As a result, women went to the doctor more frequently and were more receptive than men to advice about disease prevention and early detection.[3] The few studies of the gender of preventive health in East and West Germany have shown that they too aimed preventive health rhetoric at women and directed preventive policies toward women's health, especially their reproductive health.[4]

The historical and sociological literature leaves us with a paradox that makes it difficult to interpret the meaning of gendered (over)attention to or, alternatively, neglect of an illness or bodily condition. Given that women's longevity has increased more than men's, even as women have remained less well off than men, we can conclude that women's health has, on average, benefited from the public-health and medical attention to women's bodies in the modern era. Yet a paternalistic understanding of female biology has often motivated the concern. This puzzle bedevils the interpretation of gendered healthcare in the two Germanys. Did biological patriarchalism, reinforced by natalism, motivate the enduring East German and rising West German attention to women's health? Or did the concerns about women's health reflect growing commitment to women's social equality and individual well-being?

Epidemics of the Postwar Era: Tuberculosis and Venereal Disease

In the immediate postwar years, every zone of occupation experienced the same war-related epidemics. Of major concern were tuberculosis (TB) and venereal disease (VD). The tuberculosis epidemic received extraordinary public, medical, and official attention in both East and West. The high anxiety is not surprising. TB is a deadly, easily communicable disease that can go undetected until the infected person is mortally ill. It is difficult to cure, even with antibiotics. Tuberculosis detection, vector identification, prevention, and treatment were central to the work of both public-health systems. At congresses in the GDR, West and East German doctors communicated with each other directly about TB treatments. Prevention of TB was, in contrast, a politically fraught issue. The GDR opted for (voluntary) mass vaccination of children with Bacillus Calmette-Guerin (BCG) in 1949. For years, West German doctors criticized the GDR for mass inoculations with what they saw as an ineffective vaccine.[5] The mutually intense focus on tuberculosis makes less sense when TB mortality is placed in comparative disease context. After 1945, tuberculosis was never the top cause of mortality in either state. With antibiotics, mortality declined, especially in comparison to deaths from cardiovascular disease and cancer. The absolute and relative magnitude of medical research devoted to tuberculosis by German-language researchers remained, however, very high. TB's postwar rise, contagiousness, and long history as a public-health scourge probably explain the outsized attention it received. Yet a gendered interpretation is not implausible. TB historically affected and killed more boys and men than girls and women in Germany. After 1945, the greater susceptibility of men (but not boys) was even more pronounced.[6] East and West German medical writers noted the gender imbalance but did not portray tuberculosis as a biologically conditioned "male" disease. They attributed male susceptibility to an exogenous cause beyond men's control: the deleterious effects of war and captivity on the immunity of soldiers and prisoners of war (POWs).[7] Public-health officials did not stigmatize men as TB transmitters. In both East and West, derogatory rhetoric about transmission by noncompliant patients did exist, but it did not defame "men" or "women"; instead it targeted "asocials"—people whose behavior allegedly showed contempt for the general welfare.[8] To fight the disease, mothers were addressed as guardians of family health. In the GDR, the Ministry of Health Care aimed intense propaganda in favor of its BCG vaccination program at mothers.[9]

Venereal disease is another contagious illness whose incidence shot up in all zones of occupation after 1945, alarming occupation authorities and German health officials. Although rates of sexually transmitted disease were historically higher among men, venereal diseases were gendered female in Germany as elsewhere. Popular and medical opinion pointed to promiscuous women and, especially, female prostitutes as primary sources of infection. This assumption initially dominated postwar discourse about VDs. To contain the epidemic, German authorities resorted to old means: they conducted raids searching for supposed "prostitutes," registered every woman who had sex with an Allied soldier, and relied on controls of women's behavior. Over time, several cross-zonal factors de-moralized public discourse about VD: commentators and the public sympathized with women whom Allied soldiers coerced into sexual relations; war, scarcity, and occupation relaxed sexual mores; last but not least, the curative power of penicillin made gonorrhea and syphilis less frightening than earlier. In part due to pressure from occupation authorities, the imagery of public-health posters about sexually transmitted diseases became gender-neutral and nonstigmatizing. VD control came to include education, counseling, and (in the West) voluntary testing and treatment.[10]

In the West, doctors and medical professors gradually adopted individualist arguments for treatment by private practitioners. Interest in sexually transmitted diseases remained lively as politicians debated the terms of a proposed VD law. The draft law emphasized welfare measures and a trusting patient-doctor relationship, while also including some police controls. It became law in 1954, despite opposition from conservatives and moral crusaders. Thereafter, interest in sexually transmitted diseases waned. Fearmongering no longer scapegoated female promiscuity as the source of venereal disease but, as historian Ulrike Lindner points out, women prostitutes were still seen as the main "transmitters" even though men, as before the war, suffered higher rates of infection.[11] In the East, the Soviet occupiers supported police measures, including compulsory treatment, public naming of patients, and imprisonment of anyone who knowingly infected a Soviet soldier. The police arrested German men as well as women and enforced treatment of all infected people. Simultaneously, the press and posters educated people about VD and urged them to get treated at health centers.[12] After 1949, the GDR reverted to examining and treating female prostitutes but not their clients. Rhetoric remained, however, gender neutral.[13] In sum, the social consequences of war, political context of occupation, and the medicalization of treatment vitiated the gendered meanings long assigned to VD. East and West German discourse about venereal disease became less gender biased. That happened earlier and more thoroughly in East Germany. Policy reform, however, was more substantial in the FRG, where treatment became private and voluntary. In East Germany, public-health measures and police controls still targeted female prostitutes.

Chronic Disease: Cancer and Cardiovascular Disease

The gendering of the two most significant postwar chronic diseases in East and West Germany matched the pattern of discourse and policy in other European states and the United States in the Cold War era. Heart disease, or cardiovascular disease (CVD), was gendered male, although a substantial minority of CVD sufferers were female. Cancer tended to be gendered female, although it was distributed fairly equally between the sexes historically and with the rise of lung cancer affected more men.[14] Public-health education about early detection focused on female reproductive cancers. Popular interest in cancer ran high before the Second World War and surged again after 1945. In both German states, the press publicized the fact that cancer killed many more people than did tuberculosis.[15] German medical research did not reflect the popular interest in cancer. The outpouring of money for American and British cancer research dwarfed the resources spent on cancer research in either German state through the 1960s.[16] The GDR Health Ministry created a cancer research institute, but there is no evidence that major funds flowed to it. The contrast between East and West was not in treatment or research but in East Germany's attention to early detection. From 1947 through the 1960s, the East German Hygiene Museum in Dresden (Deutsches Hygiene-Museum Dresden, DHMD) devoted numerous exhibitions to cancer. As in the United States, public-health propaganda and the press made much of the benefits of bodily self-awareness and early detection, and, similarly, this message was heavily aimed at women.[17] A traveling cancer exhibition of 1948 included a poster on the lifesaving importance of breast self-examinations that explained what to look for and featured a drawing of a woman performing a self-exam.[18] No poster highlighted an early detection method for a male cancer, although several posters discussed occupational cancers and depicted men working with carcinogenic materials. The DHMD exhibitions defined woman's cancer as reproductive, i.e. originating in her private life, but men's as occupational and, thus, arising from public activity.

The focus here is on discourses and policies in East and West Germany toward cervical cancer and lung cancer. Judging by the number of articles in medical journals, interest in cervical cancer ran high relative to interest in prostate cancer, a comparable male reproductive cancer in both states.[19] The higher rate of attention did not, however, match the sixfold higher incidence of all genital cancers among women than men.[20] Interest in cervical cancer was spread quite evenly between East and West German doctors/researchers. Authors expressed no clear opinion on the etiology of cervical cancer; some assumed its cause was endogenous, others believed it was exogenous.[21]

The East/West difference in discourse and policy lay, again, in attention to early detection. Health exhibitions urged East German women to see a doctor if they experienced irregular menses or other abnormalities.[22] The state also took on responsibility for early detection exams. In the early 1950s, the GDR Ministry of Health Care introduced a protocol for mass examinations of women employees while at work. The aim was to produce colposcope machines and train doctors to carry out an annual colposcopy on every woman over thirty years of age. (Colposcopy is an optical magnification system that can detect (pre)malignant neoplasms on the cervix.[23]) Public propaganda touted the wonders of early detection through colposcopy.[24] Internal documents suggest that the plan for mass colposcopy was meant in earnest.[25] The gap between intent and practice was, however, wide. Although thousands of women were examined in the early 1950s, the campaign soon lost steam as did so many campaigns in the GDR. Mass exams created extra work for an extremely shorthanded medical workforce. The Zeiss optics firm produced too few colposcopes, and the health system struggled to train enough doctors to use the instrument.[26]

West German medical writers too peddled the value of early detection of cervical cancer, but their discourse was less unified, slightly more moralistic, and largely confined to scholarly publications. Some authors questioned whether a minimally improved rate of cure due to a colposcopy justified the expenditure on early detection. Others faulted diffident or indifferent women who did not visit their doctor when they had a suspicious symptom.[27] Articles did not mention that West Germany's nonprofit, regulated insurance funds did not cover the cost of colposcopy (or most other prophylactic exams). Only in the mid-1960s did powerful physicians' organizations take up the banner for insurance overage of preventive exams.[28] In the 1960s, West and East Germany began to shift toward the less expensive and more easily interpreted Pap smear exam, but for unclear reasons, most likely the cost, neither state approached mass coverage before 1970.

Lung cancer was the deadliest cancer for men in East and West Germany as early as 1950. Men were seven times likelier to die of lung cancer than were women. Historian Robert Proctor's research revealed the Third Reich's support of pathbreaking research on the causal link between cigarette smoking and lung cancer. Proctor assumed incorrectly that Nazi-era research was forgotten or even smothered after 1945.[29] Postwar medical writers cited Nazi-era antismoking research. West German doctors showed no more and, arguably, less resistance than British and American physicians to statistical evidence linking smoking to lung cancer. In the GDR, there was virtually no medical or official opposition to this explanation. Authors in East and West always noted the heavily lopsided male incidence and mortality of lung cancer.[30] In sum, awareness of the rise in and demography of lung cancer, on the one hand, and openness to cigarette smoking as the causal explanation, on the other, were quite widespread in the Germanys. Yet German-language medical publications about lung cancer were few in number. German research interest in lung cancer was much lower than interest in TB and much, much lower than interest in lung cancer in the Anglo-American research world.

Official and/or medical discourse on the health risks of smoking also lagged. The US Surgeon General's Report and the report of the Royal College of Physicians came out to huge fanfare in the early 1960s. No antismoking report of even remotely equal standing appeared in the FRG or, more surprisingly, the GDR. The GDR did produce a considerable amount of antismoking propaganda but, to the dismay of its nonsmoking citizens, the state did not ban smoking (mainly by men) in offices or (nonhazardous) workshops.[31] Factors other than gender conspired against research and policy attention to smoking and lung cancer. War-related epidemics captured research resources; both states had inherited medical-research paths that focused on TB over cancer; lung-cancer mortality climbed more slowly in Germany than in the UK and US; both states depended on tax revenues from cigarette sales. Gender bias may also have played a role. The Germanys shared a concept of masculine bodily autonomy and strength that may have had the ironic effect of belittling the deadly effects of a habit that was overwhelmingly male. Both West and East German health authorities and doctors tended to deny that tobacco was addictive and that state policy could change smoking behavior. Instead, they argued, smokers could and, indeed, only would give up smoking when they decided to do so on their own. The state, it was suggested, should not curtail smokers' freedom of choice.[32]

If discourse in both Germanys (and elsewhere) concentrated on the reproductive cancers of women and, thus, contributed to a perception of cancer as a female disease, rhetoric about heart disease ignored women and highlighted men. Cardiovascular disease was the number-one cause of death in both German states after 1945. Men, certainly, were three times likelier than women to suffer a first heart attack over the age of fifty (and the imbalance was more lopsided at younger ages). Still, women's five-year survival rate was considerably lower than men's. Medical treatises ascribed differential mortality rates not to biological difference but, instead, to women's tendency to return to work (in the family) as opposed to men's "protected" convalescence.[33] The press paid much attention to CVD but not to women's higher rate of mortality after a heart attack, much less the gendered reason for it. Advice about the causes and prevention of cardiovascular disease, historian Jeannette Madarász-Lebenhagen argues, was doubly gendered. As in other countries, medical and daily press articles not only assumed that men were at risk and needed to follow the advice to lower their risk of CVD—eat less fat, get more exercise, suffer less stress—but directed this advice at their wives.[34] Thus, both health cultures assigned to women the responsibility to protect and monitor health—their own health in the case of cancer and their husband's in the case of cardiovascular disease.

In the FRG, the reigning concept of heart disease was in addition class biased. A statistical study allegedly showed that "the mortality of leading men in the economy, free professions and politics between the ages of 50 and 65 is eight to nine times higher than in other occupational groups."[35] *Managerkrankheit* (managers' illness) became the buzzword in discussions of CVD and stress, although actuarial statisticians pointed out that the study's flawed methodology did not, in fact, prove that managers died at a higher rate than other men.[36] Cardiovascular disease was, of course, a real disease, but discourse about *Managerkrankheit* fabricated a nonexistent risk profile for CVD: supervisory occupations performed by upper-class men. No one suggested that biology predisposed men to stress-related sickness, much less implied that they were unfit for employment.

West German discourse, meanwhile, invented a disease complex related to women and employment. Medical writers argued that women's weak constitution was damaged by the stress and strain of *paid* labor. The symptoms were exhaustion, nervousness, and paleness so extreme that "even the husband notices it." Serious illness could follow.[37] Publications by doctors claimed that maternal employment was as "unhealthy" for mother and child, as was child labor.[38] Fearmongering attributed the harmful association between women and employment to female biology. Like anxiety about *Managerkrankheit,* this discourse was exclusively West German. East German social hygienists advertised employment as good for women. Only in the 1960s did they acknowledge the psychological and physical toll on women of *their double burden*. A realistic medical discourse about women's employment gradually spread in the West—partly imported from the East, partly fostered by a steady increase of the employment of married women and mothers. In 1958, the Munich publisher Lehmann issued a massive tome entitled *Geschlecht und Krankheit* (Gender and Illness) written by Dr. Max Bürger, a former member of the NSDAP and medical professor at the University of Leipzig until 1957, who believed that women and men had fundamentally different biological systems and that women's main life task was to bear and raise children. He emphasized, however, that statistical data did not show that employment had a negative impact on women's health.[39]

With the exception of West German warnings about the debilitating effects of waged work on women, the gendering of chronic disease was less obviously politicized than that of infectious disease. East Germany's Health Ministry devoted more attention and resources to the early detection of cervical cancer than did West Germany's fragmented health system. Still, both states devoted more attention to female reproductive cancers than to prostate cancer or lung cancer. Gendered male in East and West, heart disease garnered much interest in both states.

The Medicalization of Pregnancy and Childbirth

Historically, the "special" case of female reproduction underpinned misogynistic assumptions about women's weaker constitution. From the mid-1800s onward, public-health advocates, social hygienists, and women's rightists reinterpreted the risks of pregnancy and childbirth as contingent, not inherent, dangers that society could reduce with safer, antiseptic delivery methods. Whether driven by male obstetrician-gynecologists as in the United States or by social democratic and communist governments in Europe, the medicalization of pregnancy and childbirth accelerated after 1945. Before the 1970s, socialists, feminists, and health reformers promoted pregnancy counseling and clinic birth as evidence of public commitment to women's well-being. Postmodern theoretical perspectives, on the one hand, and women's negative experiences with medicalized delivery, on the other, have complicated that interpretation. Foucauldian and second-wave feminist scholarship often criticizes pregnancy monitoring as another case of biomedical interventionism and liberal governance through expert opinion and bodily self-discipline.[40] Sociologist Ann Oakley, for example, critiques "antenatal care as both an exemplar and a facilitator of the wider *social* control of women."[41] The feminist critique of clinic birth equates its rise with the "pathologizing" of pregnancy and delivery and the demise of a woman-centered culture of home birth.[42]

The pace and extent of the medicalization of pregnancy and childbirth were very different in the GDR and FRG. It occurred quickly in the GDR where the notion of "pathologization" was alien to East German social hygiene. The Ministry of Health Care heavily propagated the benefits of prenatal exams and clinic delivery, as had the SPD in the Weimar Republic (with considerable success in cities such as Hamburg).[43] The GDR's Mother and Child Law (1950) included strict prohibitions on abortion while also creating the framework for woman and young-child healthcare: registration of pregnant women; pregnancy counseling including medical care, explication of social and legal rights, and hygiene education; medical care for nursing mothers; medical observation of children. Women workers received (a short) paid maternity leave.[44] The Department of Mother and Child in the Ministry of Health Care set up pregnancy-counseling centers, worked to identify pregnant women, sent out guidelines for prenatal exams, and used monetary rewards to entice women to show up. Here too it adopted the model developed by the Weimar SPD.[45] East German health authorities also doggedly pursued the transition to clinic birth. They never doubted that clinic delivery reduced maternal mortality, birth trauma, and perinatal mortality.[46] Health officials faced resistance to the campaign for clinic births from rural communities and from midwives. In some large cities, clinic births had already been common in the early 1930s. By the mid-1950s, opposition was overcome; by the early 1960s, birth was fully hospitalized.[47] Clinic birth in the FRG advanced slowly, especially in rural areas. As in the East, city dwellers were the first fans of clinic birth. As early as 1953, 70–80 percent of urban deliveries in the West took place in clinics. In contrast to East Germany, pregnant women, not health authorities, propelled the shift. In 1957, a survey of 10,000 women found that 81 percent in Cologne and 73 percent in Aachen favored a clinic birth for medical and social reasons. Antibiotics had taken away their fear of dying from childbed fever. Their infant would be safer, they believed, delivered in a clinic. As a social impetus, they pointed to the cramped conditions of postwar housing and lack of extended family to help in the household.[48]

From 1949 onward, articles in East German medical journals compared East German infant and maternal mortality to rates in Western and Eastern Bloc countries. The Ministry of Health Care showed especially strong interest in the West German situation and made much of the fact that by 1955 maternal mortality and "early" (first-month) infant mortality had fallen lower than West German rates. German-German rivalry did not create East Germany's commitment to fight infant and maternal mortality, but Cold War competition certainly helped to motivate the effort.

In contrast to East German social hygienists, West German medical opinion, public discourse, and insurance policies tended to treat pregnancy and childbirth as a natural condition that required medical intervention only in exceptional instances. West Germany certainly exercised paternalistic control over reproductive decision-making through its continuation of Germany's antiabortion Paragraph 218 in the Penal Code (*Strafgesetzbuch*, StGB). However, before the late 1960s it did not seriously monitor pregnancy or encourage women in general to give birth in a clinic.[49] Neither infant nor maternal mortality rose to the status of a major public-health issue until after 1960. No press or doctors' campaign called for either prenatal care or clinic birth, and neither one increased by much, if only because the insurance funds did not pay for routine prenatal care for nonemployed women and did not cover clinic birth without a doctor's prescription. The FRG passed a Law for the Protection of Mothers at Work, in Training and Studies (*Gesetz zum Schutz von Müttern bei der Arbeit, in der Ausbildung und im Studium*) in 1952, but this law did not apply to all women. It protected pregnant workers from dismissal and provided (a short) paid maternity leave to them. Few of the federal states extended and most, in fact, partially dismantled the system of prenatal and infant counseling that had emerged in the Weimar Republic and continued, within the framework of racial hygiene, in the Third Reich. After 1945, only in cities did public-health clinics continue to provide some pregnancy counseling.[50] There were, certainly, advocates of pregnancy care. Public-health physicians, medical professors, and doctors at public hospitals tried to raise the alarm about West Germany's levels of infant and maternal mortality. They recommended cooperation between public-health and private doctors in implementing routine prenatal care.[51] At the end of the fifties, articles in medical journals and the daily press began to underline the relatively poor international standing of the FRG in levels of infant and maternal mortality. The comparative standards were other Western countries (and, occasionally, Czechoslovakia). Commentators resolutely ignored health data from the GDR. In 1964–65, East German (full-year) infant mortality fell slightly below the FRG's. Only then did West German advocates of prenatal counseling begin to note the East German comparative achievement.

The Federal Health Agency (Bundesgesundheitsamt), founded in 1952, created a committee in 1960 to discuss measures to promote preventive healthcare; it included a subcommittee on maternal and infant care.[52] In the mid-1960s, Bundestag deputies from the SPD and CDU put "queries" (*Anfragen*) about infant and maternal mortality to the Federal Ministry of Health Care (Bundesministerium für Gesundheitswesen), founded in 1961. They elicited answers that placed a glaring light on infant and maternal mortality in the FRG.[53] Abruptly, physicians' organizations called for the insurance funds to cover regular pregnancy counseling—provided by private doctors. In 1965, for the first time since the war, the annual meeting of the Physicians Chamber devoted a session to preventive healthcare. Many discussants touted the value of pregnancy and infant prophylactic examinations.[54] The government, insurance funds, and physicians' associations negotiated the terms of an amended Protection of Motherhood Law. Passed by the Bundestag in 1966, it guaranteed nonemployed women the right to a certain number of pregnancy examinations/tests.[55] These exams were to be conducted by private doctors. As had occurred earlier in the GDR, "maternal guidelines" increasingly medicalized pregnancy care to include tests to determine blood group, antibodies, measles immunity, etc.[56]

Once pregnancy counseling was on the agenda, in other words, private practitioners moved to assert control over its provision. They also insisted on controlling the medical information generated by the tests. Already in 1960, the federal state (*Bundesland*) North Rhine-Westphalia, governed by the SPD, had introduced an experimental program called the *Mütterpaß*: pregnant women who went to public-health or private medical exams received a "passport," kept by the woman, which listed her visits and the results of her tests. A woman who held on to the record of her results would, it was hypothesized, go to more exams. The experiment confirmed the thesis. More federal states introduced the *Mütterpaß*. In Bavaria, however, the physicians' association warned that knowledge of negative results might dangerously unsettle pregnant women; they might inadvertently allow their medical information to become public. Bavaria introduced the pass system with a major change: doctors kept the cards. The Protection of Motherhood Law of 1966 gave physicians throughout the FRG control over the *Mütterpaß* system.[57]

In both East and West, public-health rhetoric and medical articles about pregnancy and childbirth always emphasized their benefits for infant health. Authors only sometimes argued for them as methods to reduce maternal mortality. The emphasis on infant mortality reflected, in part, the fact that maternal mortality declined much faster than infant mortality after 1945. Public concern about maternal mortality, however, rose again in the 1960s when international comparisons revealed that both German states suffered from proportionally high maternal mortality.[58] Fundamentally, though, the vaunted measures for "mother protection" in both states were about infant protection. One sees the fusion of woman's well-being with maternity and infant health in a booklet published by the Dresden Hygiene Museum. Although titled *Die Frau*, the pamphlet devoted more pages to teaching mothers to care for their infants than for themselves.[59]

The diligent registration and tracking of pregnancies in the GDR aimed, among its other natalist goals, to reduce recourse to illegal abortion, although one finds only oblique references to this incentive. An explicit motivation was to reduce the lopsidedly high mortality of infants born to unmarried women. East German law prohibited legal discrimination against children born out of wedlock and worked to improve the social standing of single mothers. Nonetheless, single mothers remained poorer than married mothers and faced popular prejudice. A single woman was likelier to try to end a pregnancy through neglect or abortion. If a pregnant woman was socially isolated, fourteen to sixteen years old, and/or assumed to be in danger of aborting spontaneously or intentionally, the East German Department of Mother and Child placed her in a home. Quite a few overburdened pregnant wives spent a few weeks in a "rest home," but the *Hausschwangere* (in-home pregnant women) were all single and stayed in the home through delivery. Many young women surely resented being put in such a home. Reports, though, emphasized the low mortality among births to *Hausschwangeren*.[60] There were homes for single pregnant women in the FRG too.[61] If only because the policy toward all pregnancies was quite laissez-faire in the 1950s, however, attention to the pregnancies of single women was much lower than in the GDR.

Despite their different practices of pregnancy care and childbirth in the 1950s, the GDR and FRG shared similar population-political frameworks. Both were natalist and exercised control over women's bodies through legal restrictions on reproductive choice. Natalism became more pronounced as fertility rates fell in the late 1960s and was certainly a motivation of East Germany's continual and West Germany's rising emphasis on pregnancy care and clinic birth. The effort to exercise control over women's bodies, however, diminished, and, thus, a social-control interpretation applies less well as one approaches the 1970s. East Germany began to relax abortion regulation in the mid-1960s, legalized abortion in the first three months of a pregnancy in 1972, and allowed doctors to prescribe the Pill at no cost, while significantly extending maternity leave and raising child allowances. It, thus, transitioned to a system that encouraged but did not control biological reproduction. Although West Germany did not legalize abortion, it reformed Paragraph 218. While maintaining the unlawfulness of an abortion, the reform of 1976 allowed a woman's right to an abortion in case of one of four indications: medical, eugenic, social, and in case of a rape. It allowed wide access to the contraceptive pill to women of full age from the 1960s on and, if less generously, lengthened maternity leave and increased child allowances.[62] If driven by domestic considerations, in East and West these decisions were also motivated by Cold War rivalry over birth rates *and* women's social situation.

Both states shifted, one could argue, toward a regime of liberal governance that used biomedical discourse and scientific expertise to encourage bodily self-discipline by women toward the goal of producing healthy babies. From the 1970s onward, in East and West, sociologists and public-health officials studied the demography of prenatal visits. They concluded that the more educated the woman, the more likely she would go early and frequently to pregnancy counseling. In both the FRG and the GDR, investigators attributed this behavior to educated women's high level of autonomy and self-control accompanied by a strong motivation to seek medical advice.[63]

Ironically, paternalistic interest in mothers and children became intertwined with a growing conviction that educated and "independent" women were the best protectors of themselves and their infants-to-be. The GDR's Ministry of Health Care had always held to a version of this paradoxical combination of commitments. In the FRG, received opinion about gender relations did not jibe with evidence that education, more than marital status, determined whether a mother made "healthy" decisions for her children. Such evidence was, in fact, only one straw on top of the many developments that simultaneously reflected and contributed to an expanding appreciation of women's rights and roles in West Germany. In 1957, the Bundestag finally reformed the family and marriage law of the old Civil Code from 1900 and struck down the sole power of the husband to make familial decisions. In the 1960s, a parliamentary committee debated whether to allow single mothers guardianship over their children.[64] The new women's movement pushed for a further reform of the marriage and family law in 1976. The employment of married women rose, if not dramatically.[65] And, of course, the Pill provided women with effective and self-administered contraception.

Conclusion

The gendering of East and West German health cultures and politics was entangled due to national history, Western traditions, Cold War competition, and international postwar trends in medicine, healthcare, and women's rights and roles. Cold War rivalry could produce a dynamic entanglement as one German state used health discourse or policy as a propaganda weapon and the other dug in its heals in response. Notably, however, in neither West nor East did popular, medical, or official discourse stigmatize men *as men* or blame normative masculinity for a behavior or social role dominated by men and presumed to increase susceptibility to a disease. In both states, concern about men's health fixated on occupational dangers, whereas worries about women's health centered on reproductive illnesses.

East German health interventionism was not gender neutral. The Ministry of Health Care expressed no qualms about channeling and, later, enticing women to follow the prescribed prophylactic solutions to detect cervical cancer or protect pregnant women (and infants). In contrast, it adopted a relatively passive approach toward smoking. This disparity had several sources but, I would argue, gender played a part. Communist health culture shared the Western assumption that the self-sufficient male, given accurate information, would behave rationally, obviating the need for intrusions on his autonomy. West German health culture was not initially interventionist or preventively oriented in general or toward women's health in particular. As it pivoted toward prevention, however, the shift was especially notable in rhetoric and policy about pregnancy and childbirth. This shift expressed a complicated evolution in attitudes toward women's bodies, reproductive health, and social roles. The resulting composite entwined state paternalism with a gradually declining commitment to private patriarchy and rising awareness of the social benefits of women's greater equality. In consequence, the gendered contradictions of West German health discourse and policy became more similar to those in the GDR. Convergence became more pronounced in the 1970s and 1980s, as both healthcare systems devoted ever-increasing attention to pregnancy, birth, and infant care. The rise of preventive healthcare and growing concern about women's health are examples of intertwined cultural and policy trends that the GDR inaugurated and the FRG emulated—and which united Germany has consistently reinforced.

Donna Harsch is professor of history at Carnegie Mellon University, Pittsburgh. She is a social and political historian of twentieth-century Germany. Her recent publications include: *Revenge of the Domestic: Women, the Family, and Communism in the German Democratic Republic* (Princeton University Press, 2007); and "Women in Communist Societies," in *The Oxford Handbook of the History of Communism* (ed. by S. A. Smith, Oxford University Press, 2013). Currently she is researching the history of health and medicine in the Cold War Germanys. She is working on a book-length comparative study of infant mortality and efforts to reduce it in the German Democratic Republic and Federal Republic of Germany from 1945 to 1990.

Notes

1. Winfried Süß, "Gesundheitspolitik," in *Drei Wege deutscher Sozialstaatlichkeit: NS-Diktatur, Bundesrepublik und DDR im Vergleich*, ed. Hans Günter Hockerts (Munich, 1998), 55–100; Thomas Elkeles et al., eds., *Prävention und Prophylaxe: Theorie und Praxis eines gesundheitspolitischen Grundmotivs in zwei deutschen Staaten 1949–1990* (Berlin, 1991); Ulrike Lindner, *Gesundheitspolitik in der Nachkriegszeit: Großbritannien und die Bundesrepublik Deutschland im Vergleich* (Munich, 2004); and Sabine Schleiermacher, "Contested Spaces: Models of Public Health in Postwar Germany," in *Shifting Boundaries of Public Health: Europe in the Twentieth Century*, ed. Susan Gross Solomon et al. (Rochester, NY, 2008), 175–204.

2. Carsten Timmermann, "Appropriating Risk Factors: The Reception of an American Approach to Chronic Disease in the Two German States, c. 1950–1990," *Social History of Medicine*, 25, no. 1 (2012): 157–74, eScholarID:120211, doi:10.1093/shm/hkr051.
3. Will H. Courtenay, "Constructions of Masculinity and their Influence on Men's Well-Being: A Theory of Gender and Health," *Social Science and Medicine* 50 (2000): 1385–401; Monika Sieverding, "Geschlecht und Gesundheit," in *Gesundheitspsychologie*, ed. Ralf Schwarzer (Göttingen, 2005), 55–70; Dagmar Ellerbrock, "Geschlecht, Gesundheit und Krankheit in historischer Perspektive," in *Handbuch Gesundheitswissenschaften: Geschlecht, Gesundheit und Krankheit: Männer und Frauen im Vergleich*, ed. Klaus Hurrelmann and Petra Kolip (Bern, 2002), 118–41; and Jenny Linek, "'Männer gibt es doch auch!': Geschlechterspezifische Gesundheitserziehung und Prävention in der DDR in den 1950er bis 1970er Jahren," *Medizinhistorisches Journal* 50, nos. 1–2 (2015): 200–222.
4. Linek, "Männer"; Lindner, *Gesundheitspolitik*; and Jeannette Madarász-Lebenhagen, "Medico-politics of Gendered Health: The Case of Cardiovascular Prevention in East and West Germany, 1949–1990," *Social History of Medicine* 28, no. 4 (2015): 1–20.
5. Lindner, *Gesundheitspolitik*, 144–59; Donna Harsch, "Medicalized Social Hygiene? Tuberculosis Policy in the German Democratic Republic," *Bulletin of the History of Medicine* 8, no. 3 (2012): 394–423; Sylvelyn Hähner-Rombach, *Sozialgeschichte der Tuberkulose: Vom Kaiserreich bis zum Ende des Zweiten Weltkriegs unter besonderer Berücksichtigung Württembergs* (Stuttgart, 2000); and Melanie Arndt, *Gesundheitspolitik im geteilten Berlin 1948 bis 1961* (Cologne, 2009).
6. Alfred Beyer and Kurt Winter, *Lehrbuch der Sozialhygiene* (Berlin, 1953), 433–34.
7. Max Bürger, *Geschlecht und Krankheit* (Munich, 1958), 317–35; and Beyer and Winter, *Lehrbuch*, 433–34.
8. Harsch, "Social Hygiene"; Lindner, *Gesundheitspolitik*, 153; "Tuberkulosekongreß in Leipzig 14.–16.12 1951," Bundesarchiv Berlin (BArch-B), DQ1/4756.
9. Harsch, "Social Hygiene"; and "Rat des Bezirkes Rostock an MfG, 17.4.59, Betr: Maßnahmen zur Tuberkulosebekämpfung," BArch-B, DQ 1/1928.
10. Annette F. Timm, *The Politics of Fertility in Twentieth-Century Berlin* (Cambridge, MA, 2010), 205–09, 213–16, 219, 225, 270–71; and Lindner, *Gesundheitspolitik*, 301, 318–20, 324–26, 395.
11. Timm, *Politics of Fertility*, 195–97, 295–99; and Lindner, *Gesundheitspolitik*, 301, 316–17, 320–29, 395–96.
12. "Geschlechtskrankheiten (1958)," Deutsches Hygiene Museum Dresden (DHMD), KA2 14; and "Geschlechtskrankheit (early 1960s)," DHMD, KA2/1 Lep. 15.
13. Timm, *Politics of Fertility*, 257–58, 270–71; Uta Falck, *VEB Bordell: Geschichte der Prostitution in der DDR* (Berlin, 1998), 37–40, 51–57, 60–61.
14. Bürger, *Geschlecht und Krankheit*, 234–36.
15. "Krebsforschung 1950–1955, Geschwulstkrankheiten (Krebs), Organisation und Richtungen der Krebsforschung," BArch-B, DQ 1 4848.
16. Gabriele Moser, *Deutsche Forschungsgemeinschaft und Krebsforschung 1920–1970* (Stuttgart, 2011), 245–59, 262–64, 270–71; and "Krebs: Die letzte Seuche," *Der Spiegel*, no. 7, 8 February 1965, 75.
17. "Krebsforschung 1950–1955"; "Geschwulstkrankheiten Problemkommission 1963–1968, Bl. 18, Die Organisation der Geschwulstbekämpfung in der DDR," BArch-B, DQ 1 2386; "Wanderausstellung Volkskrankheiten (1947)," DHMD,

WA- F 1177; C. J. Ruck, "Wesen und Wirkungen staatlich organisierter Krebsbekämpfung," *Der Krebsarzt* 13, no. 8 (1958): 373–79; and Adolf Keil, "Krebs—eine Volkskrankheit" (1957), DHMD, 2001 284. Also see Susanne Hahn, "'Der moderne Mensch will wissen und handeln . . .': Ein kritischer Blick auf die 85jährige Geschichte der Krebsaufklärung durch das Deutsche Hygiene-Museum in Dresden," *Zeitschrift für Medizinische Psychologie* 4, no. 5 (1996): 186–91; Leslie J. Reagan, "Engendering the Dread Disease: Women, Men and Cancer," *American Journal of Public Health* 87, no. 11 (1997): 1179–87; and Kirsten E. Gardner, *Early Detection: Women, Cancer, and Awareness Campaigns in the Twentieth-Century United States* (Chapel Hill, NC, 2006), 128.
18. "Krebs (1948)," DHMD, A1 2/14 B45; "Hygiene der Frau (1966)," DHMD, KA 17 Lep. 40.
19. A keyword search of the WorldCat database turns up three times as many German-language articles on cervical cancer (310) than on prostate cancer (92) from 1950 through 1969.
20. Bürger, *Geschlecht und Krankheit*, 235.
21. In 1983, Harald zur Hausen, a West German virologist, identified human papilloma virus as the main cause of cervical cancer.
22. "Hygiene der Frau (1966)."
23. Hans Hinselmann invented the colposcope in1925. During World War II, Hinselmann supervised forced sterilizations of prisoners with cervical cancer. He was convicted in 1946 and released in 1949. Banned from working in state/university clinics, he had a private practice in West Germany and Latin America. See Ilana Löwy, *A Woman's Disease: The History of Cervical Cancer* (Oxford, 2011).
24. "Hygiene der Frau (1966)."
25. "Krebsbeirat 1946–1957, HA Heilwesen, Lagebericht über das Arbeitsgebiet Bekämpfung der Geschwulstkrankheiten, 31.7.52," BArch-B, DQ 1 6503.
26. "Professor Ganse, Betr: Problemkommission Geschwulstbekämpfung 19.9.67," BArch-B, DQ 1/2386 Bl. 130, and "Dr. Jahr an Professor Ganse, Dresden Frauenklinik, Betr: Produktion von transportablen Kolposkopen, 10.9.68," Bl. 59. Also see Linek, "Männer," 214.
27. E. Philipp, "Wirksame Krebsbekämpfung: Erfahrungen und Vorschläge," *Strahlentherapie*, 129, nos. 3–10 (1953): 4; W. Gitschmann, "Über die Ergebnisse von Vorsichtsuntersuchungen sowie von Beratungsstellen zur Verbesserung der Krebsfrüherfassung," *Gesundheitsfürsorge—Gesundheitspolitik: Zeitschrift für die gesundheitlichen Aufgaben im Rahmen der Familienfürsorge* (Gesundheitsfürsorge) 8, no. 2 (1958/59): 25–26.
28. Wortbericht des 68. Deutschen Ärztetages . . . Mai 1965 in Berlin, ed. Bundesärztekammer (Cologne and Berlin, 1965), 111.
29. Robert N. Proctor, *The Nazi War on Cancer* (Princeton, NJ, 2000), 47.
30. Donna Harsch, "Translating Smoke Signals: West German Medicine and Tobacco Research, 1950–70," *Social History of Medicine* 28, no. 2 (2015): 369–91; Rosemary Elliot, "From Youth Protection to Individual Responsibility: Addressing Smoking among Young People in Postwar West Germany," *Medizinhistorisches Journal* 45, no. 1 (2010): 1–36, and "Smoking for Taxes: the Triumph of Fiscal Policy over Health in Postwar West Germany, 1945–55," *Economic History Review* 65, no. 4 (2012): 1450–74.
31. On the FRG: Elliot, "Youth Protection," and "Smoking for Taxes." On the GDR: Young-Sun Hong, "Cigarette Butts and the Building of Socialism in East Ger-

many," *Central European History* 35, no. 3 (2002): 327–44; and Linek, "Männer," 210.
32. Harsch, "Smoke Signals"; Hong, "Cigarette Butts"; and Elliot, "Smoking for Taxes."
33. Bürger, *Geschlecht und Krankheit,* 367–68, 372–74.
34. Madarász-Lebenhagen, "Medico-politics."
35. Quoted in "Manager-Krankheit: Wen die Götter lieben," *Der Spiegel,* no. 16, 14 April 1954, 34.
36. Dr. Herbert von Denffer, "Gedanken zur Managersterblichkeit," *Versicherungswirtschaft* 9, 15.2.1954, 80, Bundesarchiv Koblenz (BArch-K), NW 945, Nr. 95; and Bürger, *Geschlecht und Krankheit,* 375.
37. Otto Speck, *Kinder erwerbstätiger Mütter: Ein soziologisch-pädagogisches Gegenwartsproblem* (Stuttgart, 1956), 64–67.
38. Madarász-Lebenhagen, "Medico-Politics," 6; Rudolf Meinert, "Kind und berufstätige Mutter," *Gesundheitsfürsorge* 3, no. 2 (1953/54): 30–32; and Georg Meinecke and Theodor Wolters, "Die berufstätige Mutter—ein schwieriges Problem der Gesundheitserziehung," *Gesundheitsfürsorge* 5, no. 7 (1955/56), 134–35.
39. Bürger, *Geschlecht und Krankheit,* 140–41, 221, 247–48.
40. K. K. Barker, "A Ship upon a Stormy Sea: The Medicalization of Pregnancy," *Social Science & Medicine* 47, no. 8 (1998): 1067–76; and Lealle Ruhl, "Liberal Governance and Prenatal Care," *Economy and Society* 8, no. 1 (1999): 95–117.
41. Ann Oakley, *The Captured Womb: A History of the Medical Care of Pregnant Women* (Oxford, 1984), 2. Emphasis in original.
42. Marion Schumann, *Vom Dienst an Mutter und Kind zum Dienst nach Plan: Hebammen in der Bundesrepublik 1950–1975* (Göttingen, 2009); and Tania McIntosh, *A Social History of Maternity and Childbirth: Key Themes in Maternity Care* (London, 2012).
43. "Entschließung der Kinderärzte—Tagung in Leipzig 1953," BArch-B, DQ1 4496; and Ruth Schnürer, "Ergebnisse der Schwangerenberatung an der Landesfrauenklinik zu Magdeburg in den Jahren 1951 und 1952" (MD diss., Medizinische Akademie Magdeburg, 1955).
44. Donna Harsch, *Revenge of the Domestic: Women, the Family, and Communism in the German Democratic Republic* (Princeton, NJ, 2007), 62, 133; and Sabine Major, "Zur Geschichte der außerklinischen Geburtshilfe in der DDR" (MD diss., Humboldt-Universität zu Berlin, 2003), 21–25.
45. "Richtlinien für die Tätigkeit der Schwangerenberatungsstellen 7.9.1953," BArch-B, DQ1 2512.
46. Major, "Geburtshilfe," 35–43; "MfG Hauptabteilung Mutter und Kind, Dr. Re. Kl., Berlin, den 12.11.1952, Auswertung über die Tagung der perinatalen Sterblichkeit," BArch-B, DQ1/21533.
47. Harsch, *Revenge,* 136, 139–43; "Entwurf Merkblatt zur Senkung der Säuglingssterblichkeit in der DDR, 13.10.1952," BArch-B, DQ1/ 21533; Lynne Falwell, *Modern German Midwifery, 1885–1960* (London, 2013), 124–36; and Major, "Geburtshilfe," 45–54.
48. Josef Fitzek, "Über die Einstellung der Frau zur klinischen und häuslichen Geburtshilfe" (MD diss., Universität zu Köln, 1957), 7–20. On midwifery, see Falwell, *Midwifery,* 124–36; Rosalie Linner, *Tagebuch einer Landhebamme 1943–1980* (Rosenheim, 1989); and Schumann, *Hebammen.*
49. Susan L. Erikson, "Maternity Care Policies and Maternity Care Practices: A Tale of Two Germanys," in *Birth by Design: Pregnancy, Maternity Care, and Midwifery*

in North America and Europe, ed. Raymond DeVries et al. (New York, 2001), 203–17.
50. Lindner, *Gesundheitspolitik*, 422–25; and "Hamburger Gesundheitsbehörde an das Bundesministerium des Innern, 16.7.54," BArch-K, B 142/369 Bl. 128–29.
51. See, for example, Prof. Dr. W. Hagen, "Aktuelle Aufgaben der praktischen Ärzte und des öffentlichen Gesundheitsdienstes in der Volksgesundheitspflege," Landesarchiv NRW, Akademie für Staatsmedizin Generalia, NW 945, Nr. 114, 7. Juni 1958; and M. Maneke, "Die Säuglings- und Kleinkinderfürsorge im Lichte der modernen Pädiatrie," *Der öffentliche Gesundheitsdienst* 27 (1965): 406–16.
52. "Bundesgesundheitsrat, Ausschuß 3: Gesundheitsvor- und -fürsorge, Niederschrift über den Verlauf der Sitzung . . . am 11. März 1960," BArch-K, 142/3528, Bl. 563, 567–68.
53. "Schriftlicher Bericht des Ausschusses für Arbeit über den von der Fraktion der SPD eingebrachten Entwurf eines Zweiten Gesetzes zur Änderung und Ergänzung des Mutterschutzgesetzes—Drucksache IV/562, 23. Juni 1965," Deutscher Bundestag [4.], zu Drucksache IV/3652, and "Fragen des Abg. Schmidt, Mutterschutzgesetz, Schwangerenfürsorge . . .," Deutscher Bundestag [5.], 142. Sitzung, 8. Dezember 1967, 7277.
54. *Wortbericht des 68. Deutschen Ärztetages . . . Mai 1965 in Berlin*, ed. Bundesärztekammer (Cologne and Berlin), 111.
55. Schumann, *Hebammen*, 254.
56. Heinrich-Adolf Krone, "Gegenwärtige Situation der Schwangerenvorsorge und Vorschläge zur Verbesserung," in *Fortschritte der perinatalen Medizin: 2. Deutscher Kongreß für Perinatale Medizin, Berlin, 26.—28. Juni 1969*, ed. Erich Saling and Karl Arno Hüter (Stuttgart, 1971), 6–14, 13.
57. K. P. Färber, "Vorsorgeuntersuchungen in der Schwangerschaft," *Der Öffentliche Gesundheitsdienst* 28 (1966): 359; "Mütterpass," *Der Spiegel*, no. 48, 21 November 1966, 70–71; Thomas Gerst, "Neuaufbau und Konsolidierung: Ärztliche Selbstverwaltung und Interessenvertretung in den drei Westzonen und der Bundesrepublik Deutschland 1945–1995," in *Geschichte der deutschen Ärzteschaft*, ed. Robert Jütte (Cologne, 1997), 232; and H. Arnold, "Die Malaise der Schwangerenfürsorge," *Das Deutsche Gesundheitswesen*, 31 November 1969, 436–42.
58. FRG: Prof. Dr. W. Hagen, "Die Fürsorge für Mutter und Kind in 9 Europäischen Staaten" (1954?), BArch-K, B 142/369; and Prof. Dr. Gaethgens, "Herabsetzung der Mütter- und Neugeborenensterblichkeit durch präventive Schwangerenfürsorge und Frühbehandlung," *Gesundheitsfürsorge* 6 (1956/1957): 5–9. GDR: "Müttersterblichkeit Fachkommission 1963/1965," BArch-B, DQ1 4182.
59. DHMD, ed., "Die Frau" (Berlin, 1955), DHMD, 2010 157.
60. Harsch, *Revenge*, 137–39; "Schmidt-Kolmer/Sch Landesregierung Magdeburg MfG Abteilung Mutter und Kind, An die DDR Regierung MfG HA M und K Dr. Neumann 1. Juli 1952. Betreffend: Bekämpfung der Frühsterblichkeit," BArch-B, DQ1 21533; and H. Enke and K. Werner, "Soziologische Aspekte der Säuglingssterblichkeit unter besonderer Berücksichtigung der Legitimität der Geburt des Säuglings," *Zeitschrift für die gesamte Hygiene und ihre Grenzgebiete* 13, no. 4 (1967): 291–97.
61. Bodo Kester, *Heime für Mutter und Kind in der Bundesrepublik Deutschland* (Lauterbach, 1979).
62. Christiane Kuller, *Familienpolitik im föderativen Sozialstaat: Die Formierung eines Politikfeldes in der Bundesrepublik 1949–1975* (Munich, 2004), 239.

63. GDR: Elisabeth Wolk, "Zusammenhang zwischen sozialen Merkmalen der Mutter und der Rate der untergewichtig Lebendgeborenen sowie der Säuglingssterblichkeit: DDR-Analyse" (MD diss., Akademie für Ärztliche Fortbildung der DDR, 1987), 51, 104. FRG: Bundeszentrale für gesundheitliche Aufklärung, "Die Situation der werdenden Mütter: Bericht über eine Repräsentativstudie in der Bundesrepublik Deutschland, durchgeführt im Auftrag des Bundesministers für Jugend, Familie und Gesundheit von der Gesellschaft für Grundlagenforschung mbH" (Munich, 1970); and Helge Prinz, *Zur Bedeutung der sozialen Schicht für die Schwangeren- und Kleinkindervorsorge* (Marburg, 1973).
64. Sybille Buske, "'Fräulein Mutter' vor dem Richterstuhl: Der Wandel der öffentlichen Wahrnehmung und rechtlichen Stellung lediger Mütter in der Bundesrepublik 1948 bis 1970," *WerkstattGeschichte* 27 (2000): 48–67.
65. Christine von Oertzen, *Teilzeitarbeit und die Lust am Zuverdienen: Geschlechterpolitik und gesellschaftlicher Wandel in Westdeutschland 1948–1969* (Göttingen, 1999).

Selected Bibliography

Buske, Sybille. "'Fräulein Mutter' vor dem Richterstuhl: Der Wandel der öffentlichen Wahrnehmung und rechtlichen Stellung lediger Mütter in der Bundesrepublik 1948 bis 1970." *WerkstattGeschichte* 27 (2000): 48–67.

Elkeles, Thomas, Jens-Uwe Niehoff, Rolf Rosenbrock, and Frank Schneider, eds. *Prävention und Prophylaxe: Theorie und Praxis eines gesundheitspolitischen Grundmotivs in zwei deutschen Staaten 1949–1990*. Berlin, 1991.

Ellerbrock, Dagmar. "Geschlecht, Gesundheit und Krankheit in historischer Perspektive." In *Handbuch Gesundheitswissenschaften: Geschlecht, Gesundheit und Krankheit; Männer und Frauen im Vergleich,* ed. Klaus Hurrelmann and Petra Kolip, 118–41. Bern, 2002.

Erikson, Susan L. "Maternity Care Policies and Maternity Care Practices: A Tale of Two Germanys." In *Birth by Design: Pregnancy, Maternity Care, and Midwifery in North America and Europe,* ed. Raymond De Vries, Cecilia Benoit, and Edwin van Teijlingen, 203–17. New York, 2001.

Falwell, Lynne. *Modern German Midwifery, 1885–1960*. London, 2013.

Hahn, Susanne. "'Der moderne Mensch will wissen und handeln . . .': Ein kritischer Blick auf die 85jährige Geschichte der Krebsaufkläung durch das Deutsche Hygiene-Museum in Dresden." *Zeitschrift für Medizinische Psychologie* 4, no. 5 (1996): 186–91.

Harsch, Donna. *Revenge of the Domestic: Women, the Family, and Communism in the German Democratic Republic*. Princeton, NJ, 2007.

———. "Medicalized Social Hygiene? Tuberculosis Policy in the German Democratic Republic." *Bulletin of the History of Medicine* 8, no. 3 (2012): 394–423.

Kuller, Christiane. *Familienpolitik im föderativen Sozialstaat: Die Formierung eines Politikfeldes in der Bundesrepublik 1949–1975*. Munich, 2004.

Lindner, Ulrike. *Gesundheitspolitik in der Nachkriegszeit: Großbritannien und die Bundesrepublik Deutschland im Vergleich*. Munich, 2004.

Linek, Jenny. "'Männer gibt es doch auch!': Geschlechterspezifische Gesundheitserziehung und Prävention in der DDR in den 1950er bis 1970er Jahren." *Medizinhistorisches Journal* 50, nos. 1–2 (2015): 200–222.

Madarász-Lebenhagen, Jeannette. "Medico-politics of Gendered Health: The Case of Cardiovascular Prevention in East and West Germany, 1949–1990." *Social History of Medicine* 28, no. 4 (2015): 1–20.

McIntosh, Tania. *A Social History of Maternity and Childbirth: Key Themes in Maternity Care*. London, 2012.

Oertzen, Christine von. *Teilzeitarbeit und die Lust am Zuverdienen: Geschlechterpolitik und gesellschaftlicher Wandel in Westdeutschland 1948–1969*. Göttingen, 1999.

Schleiermacher, Sabine. "Contested Spaces: Models of Public Health in Postwar Germany." In *Shifting Boundaries of Public Health: Europe in the Twentieth Century*, ed. Susan Gross Solomon, Lion Murard, and Patrick Zylberman, 175–204. Rochester, 2008.

Schumann, Marion. *Vom Dienst an Mutter und Kind zum Dienst nach Plan: Hebammen in der Bundesrepublik 1950–1975*. Göttingen, 2009.

Sieverding, Monika. "Geschlecht und Gesundheit." In *Gesundheitspsychologie*, ed. Ralf Schwarzer, 55–70. Göttingen, 2005.

Süß, Winfried. "Gesundheitspolitik." In *Drei Wege deutscher Sozialstaatlichkeit: NS-Diktatur, Bundesrepublik und DDR im Vergleich*, ed. Hans Günter Hockerts, 55–100. Munich, 1998.

Timm, Annette F. *The Politics of Fertility in Twentieth-Century Berlin*. Cambridge, MA, 2010.

PART III
GENDERED RESISTANCE, PROTEST, AND SOCIAL MOVEMENTS

CHAPTER 7

Under the Habit

Resistance of Catholic Sisters against East German State Authority in the 1950s

Kathryn C. Julian

In the spring of 1945, the Red Army occupied large sections of East Germany, including the area surrounding the Benedictine priory of St. Gertrud in Brandenburg. The Soviet army established its command in Wünsdorf, just twelve kilometers from the village of Alexanderdorf where the priory was located. Sisters watched as Soviet soldiers marched through their fields and to the convent gate. These early encounters were unexpectedly positive. The Soviet soldiers expressed genuine curiosity toward the nuns and wanted to see the bakery where the sisters baked sacramental bread. The nuns and the resident priest were surprised when some of the soldiers defied their own superiors by requesting rosaries. Later, in a particularly bold act, the Benedictines gifted soldiers illegal Russian Bibles that had been smuggled from Belgium. The Soviet troops, who were forbidden from fraternizing with the general German population, much less religious organizations, thanked them for the gifts and promised to keep them secret from their superiors.[1]

This early instance of subversion by Catholic sisters against Soviet authority presaged further everyday acts of resistance against both the Soviet Military Administration and the Socialist Unity Party of Germany (Sozialistische Einheitspartei Deutschlands, SED), the governing political party of the German Democratic Republic (GDR) founded in 1949. The soldiers' enthusiasm and curiosity validated the traditional Benedictine mission to offer hospitality. Such moments of affirmation inspired Catholic orders to contest state authority when it threatened their continued survival. Consequently, the interactions between Catholic orders and secular citizens in East Germany created a tenuous relationship between the GDR regime and the Catholic Church. While religion and state power seemed fundamentally opposed in East Germany, the two were in fact quietly entangled. This domestic entanglement between religious communities and GDR officials often went unacknowledged and was unequal, given the political power of the East German state. It involved both explicit repression and resistance, but sometimes state toleration and even encouragement of certain forms of religious life. These dynamics were also deeply dependent on contemporary understanding of gender.

The following chapter investigates how women in Catholic orders in East Germany challenged the state from the Soviet occupation in 1945 to the building of the Berlin Wall in 1961—a period usually marked by scholars as the height of religious repression. It traces how Cold War politics, tradition, and social gender roles shaped the relationship of religious communities to the GDR state from the largely unexplored perspective of Catholic sisters in a socialist state. Much of the scholarship addressing the topic of religion in the GDR explores the negotiation of religious leaders with the state, often in a teleological narrative linked to the fall of communism in the 1980s. These studies focus on institutions and gloss over gender as a category of analysis for the state's treatment of religious communities, and few scholars have included the role of Roman Catholic orders in East German society.[2] The agency of religious women has also been absent from discourses on gender, resistance, and power. In his study of peasants in Southeast Asia, historian James Scott suggested that everyday acts of the seemingly powerless should be considered forms of resistance. Whether songs to mock authority figures or slowdowns in production, the oppressed rely on whatever cultural or economic resources are at their disposal to ensure their survival.[3] Though he did not closely examine gender or religion, Scott's analysis of resistance provides a framework through which to understand how Catholic practice in the early years of the GDR could constitute resistance—not only in explicit acts like giving Soviet soldiers Bibles but also in helping the poor or maintaining the integrity of a cloister. Even actions within the legal parameters of the GDR regime, like negotiating property rights, challenged the secular state by strengthening an alternative form of identity opposed to socialism and preserving physical spaces where that identity could be cultivated.

The way these dynamics intertwined with gender reveals other elements of power resistance and questions how activism can be redefined. Women and other marginalized elements of society frequently sought creative forms of agency in challenging the conservative GDR state, from domestic consumerism to private jokes in the home and workplace.[4] Religious women in particular retained a certain freedom to act in East Germany specifically because of assumptions regarding the apolitical and passive nature of their gender. The involvement of orders in an organization that transcended national boundaries provided them with important resources, but at the same time created some institutional constraints and brought them under closer state scrutiny.

Given the contentious history of the Catholic Church in the GDR, the story of the SED's relationship with sisters in several orders in the 1950s and early 1960s is surprising whether observed from above or below. The regime's lenient policies toward female orders allowed sisters to circumvent, negotiate, and even challenge religious restrictions and prohibitions, precisely because the SED left them more space than what historians have assumed based on how the state dealt with male orders. This chapter provides first an overview of the regime's policies toward religious orders, especially female communities. It then presents evidence of religious sisters' quiet, but effective, acts of resistance. Finally, the chapter argues that by preserving their institutions, sisters created spaces that allowed for an insular semipublic sphere for Catholic practice and discourse. Through their tenacity and adaptability, this small minority of women laid the foundations for a distinct East German Catholic identity.

State Policy and Catholic Orders

In 1949, the year of the founding of the GDR, 92 percent of its population belonged to a church. Eighty percent were Protestants and 12 percent Catholics; around 2.7 million East Germans identified as Catholic. As a result of the Second World War, the number of Catholics had grown significantly in the East German territory, where 1.5 million German refugees of Catholic faith from Eastern Europe settled.[5] In 1988, still 40 percent of the GDR population were members of a church; 5.4 million belonged to the Protestant Church, and 1 million to the Catholic Church.[6] These numbers indicate that religion continued to play a relatively important role in the GDR in both the Protestant and the Catholic milieu, despite attempts to secularize society. Religious spaces, such as churches but also monasteries, shrines, confessional hospitals, and cemeteries, remained vital for religious and secular communities. Unlike the Protestant Church, which integrated itself into socialist society and developed an organizational structure independent from West German Protestantism by forming in 1969 the Federation of Protestant Churches in the GDR (Bund der Evangelischen Kirchen in der DDR), the Catholic Church, represented by the Vatican, never recognized the GDR as a state and never gave up its pre-1945 ecclesiastical jurisdictions, which straddled East and West Germany. The Catholic Church in the GDR was situated in what historians refer to as a "dual diaspora": at once a minority vis-à-vis the majority Protestant Church in the region and in opposition to state authorities.[7] The Catholic hierarchy in East Germany established a kind of political abstinence, refusing paths of assimilation and overt opposition to socialist society.[8] These policies established an insular Catholic presence in East Germany, but one that did not preclude religious congregations, sisters, priests, and laypeople from interacting with secular communities and making a life for themselves in East German society.

The end of the Second World War and the Soviet occupation brought a great deal of political uncertainty for religious communities, because the Marxist-Leninist rejection of religion had led in the Soviet Union to the oppression of the Russian Orthodox Church in the 1930s. Unlike in many Eastern Bloc countries in the postwar era, churches in East Germany maintained a degree of freedom from the state. Even under Soviet occupation, churches and religious congregations could work without much interference by the Soviet and local administrations in the East. The constitution of the newly founded GDR from October 1949 confirmed the individual freedom of religion and ostensibly gave churches the right to advocate on behalf of the people. Officially, this right was only abrogated in the revised constitution of April 1968. In the early 1950s, the GDR changed its *Kirchenpolitik* (church policy) under pressure from Moscow. The new policy reflected the Marxist-Leninist view of religious institutions as "obsolete" and "archaic." It was informed by hope that religion would inevitably fade into obscurity under communism with the help of administrative procedures and propaganda campaigns. The primary aim of the new church policy was to control and monitor "negative Christian elements" in society. For this purpose, it combined two seemingly contradictory strategies: repression and alliance, including negotiation with church officials.[9] What the SED's new church policy underestimated was the power of religious devotion as a lived experience, the extent to which communities relied on religious institutions, and in respect of the Catholic Church, the resilience of orders, which were at the heart of the Catholic community within the GDR.

The number of novices entering Catholic orders grew in the first decade of the GDR, despite the SED's increasingly anticlerical policy. Authorities expressed concern not only with the slightly higher number of people taking holy vows but also with their influence over communities and youth. For example, the Congregation of the Sisters of St. Elizabeth, commonly called the Gray Sisters, who ran St. Elisabeth's Hospital in Halle, Saxony-Anhalt, reported having fourteen novices and eighteen new candidates in 1953.[10] The increase of the Catholic population in East Germany, caused by the displacement of German men and women from Eastern Europe, contributed to the rise in the number of novices who entered monastic or clerical life. In postwar Berlin alone there were 177 Catholic cloisters and more than 3,000 members of religious institutes in the GDR, over half of whom were women.[11] Of these institutes, most were secular and had community ministries, like homes for the elderly or disabled. The cloistered monasteries included the Benedictines in Alexanderdorf; the Ursuline nuns in Neustadt, Brandenburg, and Erfurt, Thuringia; and the Cistercians near Dresden, Saxony. The SED tracked the growth of orders, noting seemingly unusual events, like the 1953 investiture of a sister of the Holy Name of Mary congregation in Mecklenburg—the first since the sixteenth century.[12] Observation reports by the Ministry for State Security (Ministerium für Staatssicherheit, MfS) from the 1950s complained about the profusion of Catholic institutions and their negative effects on young people, though there were rarely clear prescriptions for curtailing the proliferation of orders.[13]

Indeed, the SED regime enacted, despite its anticlerical rhetoric, relatively mild policies toward the churches in the East. Government documents in the 1950s even emphasized the need for cooperation with religious communities. Party functionaries frequently referred to Article 41 of the GDR's constitution that declared every citizen would be guaranteed full protection under the law for practice of their religious beliefs.[14] The regime's strategy was to gradually weaken religious influence by setting standards that had to be met for their continued existence and to ensure that the Catholic Church would not establish new institutions within East Germany. In a lengthy and tedious 1949 report, state officials, working with the Catholic bishop of Berlin, outlined legal requirements that church institutions would have to meet in order to remain in public service, including verifying property contracts and being subject to taxes and tariffs on trade.[15]

Despite legal dictates, central policies and regional practice often diverged. Many towns still relied on the services of confessional institutions. A few reports from local cadres, especially in rural areas, went so far as to state that religious involvement in society was positive, particularly peace activism and work in hospitals. In large part, this early tolerance could be attributed to the practical needs of a society rebuilding from the devastation of war. The state needed functional hospitals and orphanages, irrespective of the fact that many, like St. Joseph's Hospital in Dresden or St. Barbara's in Halle, were run by Catholic sisters. Unlike many of their Eastern Bloc counterparts, the SED state did not ban religious orders, though these countries provided precedents and justifications for religious oppression. The Soviet Union served as a model through its 1929 passing of a statute that forbade Orthodox priests and monastics from wearing religious garb in public.[16] Bulgaria confiscated the property of the Catholic Church in a 1953 centralization of land and forbade religious orders to live as communities.[17] The Czechoslovakian authorities waged an especially stringent campaign against Catholic communities and took actions to terminate male and female orders beginning in 1949. Police and military forces seized monasteries and sent their members to detention centers to undergo reeducation.[18] Yet these actions were sometimes more limited than they appeared. Even under the oppressive conditions, the Czechoslovakian state, like most communist nations, took into account regional needs and allowed many sisters to continue in health and social services, industries that were difficult to staff in the postwar period.[19] Poland's strong institutional Catholicism, which was intertwined with Polish nationalism and grassroots opposition, complicated attempts by party elites to uproot religious orders in that country.[20]

In the case of East Germany, an additional factor was at work. Despite the desire to create a secular state, the East German government sought to distance themselves from Nazism, which had waged a war on monasticism and Catholic orders, including liquidating monasteries and repurposing land belonging to cloisters.[21] GDR officials at times even supported institutions that ran counter to the official policy of secularization. The regime relied on the work of Caritas, an international Roman Catholic relief and social service network. SED reports from the early 1950s acknowledged the presence of Caritas in every region in the GDR, including more than 42 hospitals, 100 nursing homes, and 154 kindergartens.[22] As a result of the state's tacit support, both cloistered and noncloistered sisters established a strong presence in Catholic and secular communities alike and demonstrated their belief publicly in perhaps the most tangible symbol of religious vestment. These factors contributed to the East German government's tolerance of female orders.

State Policy and Female Catholic Orders

The East German regime was considerably less hostile toward Catholic female orders than toward male orders, a reality that allowed women more maneuverability around state dictates than was enjoyed by their male counterparts, whom SED officials perceived as a threat to the socialist state. Despite the public rhetoric of gender equality and the promise that socialism would transform gender roles toward more equality, the male leadership of the SED maintained traditional views on the role of women in society and praised domestic work and motherhood.[23] While these traditional ideas of women might have put more pressure on many women in East German society, they had the potential to allow Catholic sisters, who were not perceived as threatening by the SED, more agency. Not only did the GDR permit female orders to carry out various social services, it even praised them at times for these services. Religious communities, like the Sisters of St. Elizabeth, which since its founding in 1842 had dedicated its work to nursing, therefore played a central role in local life and participated in continual de facto negotiation with the state.

This importance of the role of religious sisters in social services was often recognized by the state. One example is a report from the GDR Ministry of Culture (Kultusministerium) from 1954 that praised the work of female orders in retirement homes and hospitals. According to the report, these institutions mainly run by the Gray Sisters contributed to East German society in a positive way. The report even used quasi-religious language in its praise: "In this case, Christian charity has yielded considerable, earthly fruits."[24] In general, direct commendation from officials was rare. More often the SED availed itself of the services provided by these female communities while practicing a sort of benign neglect. The existence of such establishments should have been problematic to the state, as people in a socialist system should not have been reliant on charity, yet numerous secular people and even party functionaries were patients in Catholic hospitals. In the late 1950s, the Ministry of Health Care (Ministerium für Gesundheitswesen) supported the educational advancement of sisters in health services and sometimes hired religious sisters to work in state-run hospitals and subsidized the income they received from charities.[25] Because of sisters' important services to the wider community, officials had trouble putting a stop to masses, last rites, and liturgical celebrations within the walls of institutions run by orders. The State Secretariat for Church Affairs (Staatsekretär für Kirchenfragen), the head of the Secretariat for Church Affairs established in 1957, which was responsible for the government's relationship toward churches and religious groups, cautioned in 1959 that Catholic orders used social services, youth education, church presses, literature, and processions to influence the lives of East Germans within and outside of the Catholic Church.[26]

Reacting against the continued influence of religious communities, the SED pursued more aggressive strategies against clergy in the late 1950s through the newly formed Secretariat for Church Affairs and the MfS. In 1959, SED member Werner Eggerath, the first state secretary for church affairs, wrote, "The orders are elite troops of political Catholicism."[27] He further implicated orders as bearers of militaristic and economic-imperialist NATO policies. Their duty, he claimed, was to be "bases of political Catholicism," to build up "reactionary centers" through their institutions, and to organize political campaigns to implement and guarantee Vatican policies. His report accused clerics, especially male priests, of being responsible for the Hungarian uprising of 1956. Even their daily activities, Eggerath claimed, revealed profound counterrevolutionary tendencies. The reports by the Secretariat for Church Affairs during the 1950s noted that numerous orders had swelled in size since the end of the war, including the Jesuits in Leipzig in Saxony, the Schönstätt Sisters of Mary in

Erfurt, the Franciscans in the Eichsfeld region of Thuringia, and the Gray Sisters of St. Elizabeth, which was the largest female congregation in East Germany.

Although officials noted the growth of women's orders, the new policies against religious communities targeted male orders rather than their female counterparts, who, interestingly, often interacted more with the secular community. Because of the church's patriarchal hierarchy, only ordained men could administer sacraments, and order priests and brothers were often occupied with their ministries to the dispersed East German Catholic community. The nature of women's ministry was more inclusive, as it involved social services in which both secular and religious communities could partake. Regional cadres rarely commented on the negative effects of female charity and indeed sometimes arranged for the transfer of Western currency to cover the costs of the sisters' charity.[28] The same tacit policies of noninterference were not afforded to priests and brothers. A 1955 report from Erfurt that praised the work of female orders also cautioned against the proselytizing activities of the Jesuits and Redemptorists, a Roman Catholic missionary congregation. The official expressed specific concerns about the Redemptorists' desire to lead pilgrimages and erect wayside crosses in the region. Although he noted that there were only 59 monks compared to more than 650 sisters, he characterized order priests and brothers as the threatening elements, due to their authority in Catholic congregations and because they were believed to be more political.[29]

The state's continued gendered treatment of Catholic religious organizations was further evidenced by its tolerance of activities led by female congregations. In 1952, the Catholic Church requested permission to hold a seminar for children, which would include short pilgrimages to the medieval monasteries of St. Marienstern and St. Marienthal near Dresden.[30] Bishops emphasized the involvement of female clerics and educators as well as the historic nature of the two Cistercian monasteries. The Ministry of the Interior (Innenministerium) reluctantly approved the "children's week." Later, an official in the Secretariat for Church Affairs dismissed concerns over the growing participation in the annual children's pilgrimage to a church in Halberstadt, Saxony-Anhalt, since most of the participants "were only women."[31] The secretariat's emphasis on sisters as maternal and gentle enabled female orders to maintain institutions like the kindergarten that were often the targets of secularization.

Female orders were therefore rarely subjected to the scrutiny directed toward their male counterparts, which is precisely how kindergartens and children's homes such as St. Martinsheim in Berlin kept their doors open, while the Franciscan brothers in Berlin-Pankow could not open their soup kitchen as a social service until after 1990.[32] Communist officials often characterized the day-to-day practices—from sermons to the sacrament of confession—of male orders as overtly political and aggressive, a concern indicated by the increased surveillance on Jesuits and Franciscans by the MfS.[33] The state's fears of religious men's influence over East German Catholics was rooted in the knowledge that they could join the church hierarchy and were intimately tied to international networks of men like Cardinal József Mindszenty in Hungary who openly opposed communism. To SED officials, male orders represented the martial arm of Western imperialism. The Secretariat for Church Affairs accordingly cautioned that the Jesuits appeared to be "normal citizens" and could thus act as political spies.[34]

Perhaps the most poignant example of the state's new stringent policies against Catholic religious organizations was the so-called Biesdorf Trial, in which the MfS arrested four Jesuit priests in Berlin-Biesdorf in 1958, charging them with espionage. The interrogation of the four priests and members of their parish communities concluded that the Jesuits had subverted the socialist state by counseling parishioners to move to the West, by possessing religious tracts, and by owning Western mopeds.[35] In other contexts, these actions might seem benign, but in the GDR they were considered explicit forms of resistance. The connection to the West and the privileged position of being able to receive gifts and religious educational tracts were certainly troubling, but perhaps most threatening to the state was the reputation of Jesuits for their unconventional methods of educating and proselytizing. The admitted purpose of this trial against the Jesuits was an attempt to silence the Catholic Church and limit the role and visibility of orders in society.

News of the Jesuit arrests was a source of discomfort in the East German Catholic community, though there is little evidence that it discouraged religious men and women from their ministries. Instead they learned how to subtly adapt within the confines of the system. The regime's highly gendered politicization of religious communities in fact provided women more opportunity for action than was available to priests and brothers. Nuns and sisters successfully maintained a degree of autonomy and pushed back against the political pressures of the SED state.

Resistance from Catholic Sisters

As physical representations of the Catholic Church, women in religious vocations were familiar with opposition to secular authority—from the Protestant Reformation to Bismarck's *Kulturkampf,* or culture war, to the Nazi seizure of cloisters and landholdings. This history of persecution provided Catholic orders the resourcefulness to survive in the post-1945 political order. Acts of resistance created a narrative of identity for women who had chosen a consecrated life and inspired those in religious communities living under a regime that was inconsistent and often unpredictable in its treatment of religious congregations. The Catholic Church and members of orders continuously negotiated state ordinances to maintain a Catholic community within socialism. The church hierarchy envisioned orders as a loyal base for the East German church, especially as so many devout laypeople streamed to the West during the 1950s. To ensure their continued existence and ministries, church officials, lay organizations, and orders had to adapt to new legalities enforced by an often hostile regime.

The disconnect between the state's ideology and practice in addition to the highly gendered official interpretations of religious women's activities provided opportunities for sisters to engage in open discourse with the state. The often conciliatory rhetoric in bureaucratic reports regarding women suggested a sense that nuns embodied female morality and appropriate modesty in a way that seemed to affirm the state's own conservative view of women. Sisters often took advantage of the regime's benign view of their practices. Whether consciously or not, gender became a tool of political resistance for female orders. Womanhood defined much of their work, but East German sisters did not imagine their gender as something limiting or demeaning. Instead, it was liberating.[36]

Because of the state's preconceptions, women in religious vocations asserted themselves by manipulating official rhetoric to negotiate property rights and continue ministries antithetical to the regime's materialist agenda. The church's belief system, rooted in sacred texts and religious symbolization, transcended material realities and put orders in confrontation with civil authorities. Transnational networks that connected religious communities to their Western counterparts posed an even more tangible and immediate problem for the party. Religious communities in the East established their institutions with the support of the German Caritas Association and church officials who held diplomatic status. Bishops intervened on behalf of seemingly minor establishments. The bishop of Berlin, for example, joined forces with a motherhouse in West Germany to petition the Secretariat for Church Affairs to help maintain a home for children run by nuns in Stralsund on the Baltic Sea.[37] These applications were sometimes rejected, but they usually resulted in correspondence and negotiation between church and state officials as well as members of orders and local priests who operated on the ground.

While female orders relied in part on the support of religious authorities, sisters were also resourceful in promoting their own interests. Travel provides a particularly interesting case. Religious women were creative when applying for permission to travel. Every sister who worked at St. Barbara's Hospital in Halle was permitted four weeks of vacation, and most visited relatives in other parts of the GDR, West Germany, or Poland or went on contemplative retreats. In a letter to the Gray Sisters' mother superior in West Germany, one sister explained that she would use the opportunity of visiting her family in Hanover to extend her stay at their motherhouse in the West.[38] Brothers and priests were often not as successful with their travel plans and encountered problems for movement even within East German borders. In April 1953, the police took two Franciscans into custody during a trip to visit the sick and to preach. According to Brother Wigbert, who reported the incident to the Erfurt diocese, the police confiscated their travel documents, demanded they change out of their habits, and accompanied them on their return trip.[39] The relative success of sisters' travel approvals compared to those submitted by members of male orders can be attributed to religious women's capability to act within an authoritarian system and the official inclination to hold men and women to different standards.

Because of the state's politicization of religion and its reliance on religious communities for some social services, the party obscured the contradictions between its ideology and its acceptance of private philanthropy. Rather, by praising the work of sisters, the SED attempted to make Catholic charity commensurate with state policies and to mold charity to existing socialism. This ambivalence gave sisters space to assert themselves outside of state authority. In their chronicles, which were private annual histories, the Gray Sisters emphasized the practicality of continuing their work as nurses and teachers.[40] The sisters justified the continued existence of their institutions by drawing on their history and by appealing to Western congregations. Like other religious organizations in the 1950s, the congregation fought to maintain its property and establish legality in the face of new statutes that appropriated some church holdings.[41]

The churches in the GDR, both Protestant and Catholic, had to legitimate their existence by pointing to a long history and the cultural value of their buildings. In order to ensure that their sacred spaces—places of worship, cloisters, secular institutes, cemeteries, and shrines—would not be destroyed or appropriated, churches learned to "speak the language of the state."[42] The East German faithful adapted their practices according to state dictates and even coopted official language, not as a result of ideological control but to maintain their own cultures and practices, a process historian Xin Liu termed "creative accommodation," or the ability for people to use the language of the state when it allowed them to circumvent a government's ideological hegemony.[43]

In practice, "speaking the language of the state" often took the form of legal contracts and official letters. For religious institutes that had survived the German Empire and the National Socialist regime, this often meant drawing on their experiences of managing modern bureaucracies. Documents from the 1950s expressed a great deal of uncertainty about the future of Catholic institutions, churches, and residences. The spirituality of orders like the Gray Sisters was rooted in their ability to care for people through hospitals and schools, and that depended on a certain degree of self-sufficiency and property ownership. The Gray Sisters in Brandenburg and Halle wrote a lengthy letter to their mother superior pleading with her to intervene on behalf of their congregations. There was no guarantee that they would be able to keep their landholdings or even their charitable establishments. The letter expressed fear that their institutes would be severely taxed and that they would lose their communities, directly citing state interference with the property of other orders.[44]

The difficulty of establishing property rights and procuring materials to rebuild made East German orders all the more reliant on creative diplomacy and help from their international networks. It was far easier to obtain state approval for structures the state often classified as having cultural worth, like Erfurt's medieval St. Mary's Cathedral, the centerpiece of the city. These historical spaces were protected under cultural-heritage management, or *Denkmalschutz*, and often received state funding for repairs and upkeep.[45] The Ursuline nuns attempted to claim *Denkmalschutz* status for their institution in Erfurt. The sisters and church officials in Erfurt petitioned state authorities beginning in the early 1950s. In 1957, Sister Gregoria successfully applied to the city for permission to begin construction on the cloister's church, but the local government could not fund the project, which was estimated to cost around 30,000 East German marks.[46] The bishop in Erfurt and the Ursuline mother superior negotiated with Otto Nuschke, who at that time was minister of cultural affairs, and West German church officials to fund the project. This long and arduous negotiation process of securing state approval and procuring funds from internal and external sources was typical for church-related projects. Like other citizens in socialism, members of orders learned to practice patience, though they certainly benefited from their international connections. Catholic relief organizations and bishoprics in the West allowed communities in the East more flexibility and ensured that members of orders would have at least basic commodities.

In addition to funds allocated to rebuild structures, orders received international aid for the restoration of relics and other objects of devotion. Arranging for the shipments of religious objects usually meant cooperating with the Ministry of Exports and Imports. Even before their church was rebuilt, the Ursuline convent in Erfurt requested the return of a golden ciborium (a small shrine used for housing the Eucharist), a silver reliquary, and a chalice to administer Holy Communion.[47] These sacred items had been sent to a sister convent in Bad Tölz, Bavaria, during the war for safekeeping, but as the Ursuline sisters settled back into their ministries in Erfurt, it was important for them to have their possessions of ritual significance returned. It is perhaps surprising that officials approved the shipment, despite any hesitancy they might have had about items that had little secular value and promoted "superstitious practices."

The Gray Sisters proved particularly adept at navigating the GDR's laws in order to retain autonomy. Their letters from the 1950s are full of petitions to officials from the church hierarchy, their mother superior, and even local cadres advocating on the sisters' behalf. Included with the letters were often copies of land purchases, contracts, lawyers' letters, and notary signatures. The Gray Sisters were able to accept land bequeathed to them by a man in Gernrode in 1948 after filing paperwork and legal contracts with civil authorities.[48] Because they acted within the legal code set forth by the East German state, nuns in the GDR successfully maintained possession of the majority of their institutes, if not their landholdings, and were able to continue ministries for the community. The sisters' protest of the state's claims to their property also ensured their own legal protection and revealed their ability to manipulate the socialist bureaucracy, though their everyday practices were rooted in established Catholic rituals.

Charity, like the Gray Sisters' soup kitchen that fed nearly 50,000 people after the war, was largely possible because of ties to West Germany and Rome.[49] Throughout the 1950s, the Gray Sisters in Halle welcomed goods from their motherhouse in West Germany. Mother Theresia Visarius, the provincial head and hospital matron, ensured that her sisters were provided for in their work with the ill and poor in Halle. They were able to first repair the roof of their residence as well as the foyer of the hospital with financing from the Paderborn Diocese. In 1956, the Gray Sisters received a new washing machine, and in 1958 a renovated kitchen with an electric oven, which made the job of cooking for the 450 patients, sisters, and other hospital staff much easier. The donations and collections were so generous that the Gray Sisters at St. Barbara's Hospital had extra building material, which they shared with city tradespeople, an action that surely endeared them to the larger community.[50]

Because of community support and modern technology sent from Caritas and motherhouses in the West, Catholic hospitals in the GDR remained stable. More important in the context of the SED regime, the sisters had the foresight to define themselves and their schools for nurses under the Ministry of Health Care instead of the Ministry of Education (Volksbildungsministerium).[51] As a result, confessional schools for nurses remained the only church-directed education that survived the duration of the GDR, and it was often the sisters themselves who fought for these schools to be accredited for training medical professionals.

Educational and charitable activities ensured that members of orders, especially those who served in public roles as nurses or educators, acted in visible roles in their communities. Whether perceived as strange and anachronistic or admired for their social services and piety, sisters were well known for their charity. Their visual distinctiveness in a society that was primarily secular and Protestant gave them an air of exoticism. Sister Modesta in Halle, for instance, became a semicelebrity in the postwar era for her charitable work but also because she was a curiosity. Nearly every day she carried two large bags full of provisions for the needy through the city, and by the 1960s she became known as the "sister with the two bags." Citizens of Halle assigned a more honorable nickname to her in the late 1970s: "Mother Teresa of Halle" for her work with the homeless.[52] When Sister Modesta died in the early 1990s, a crowd of religious and secular citizens alike joined her funeral procession through Halle, attesting to her local celebrity status. Therein was perhaps the unspoken problem for the state: these women were active and visible and wore their true loyalties in the form of a habit in the East German streets instead of remaining hidden behind cloister walls.

Creating a Catholic Public Sphere

Yet cloisters could also be provocative as they, along with secular institutions, created spaces for Catholics to exercise their faith and discuss subjects that were taboo within socialism. Historians Bernd Schaefer and David Doellinger posited that by the 1980s East German churches developed an alternative public sphere nurtured by church authorities and grassroots initiatives.[53] Individual religious communities carved out spaces for political discourse and religious practices, though it was religious women who were integral in managing a Catholic religious sphere that existed apart from political power apparatuses. The development of a semiautonomous space was more pluralistic than the scholarship suggests and began much earlier in the 1950s, when female orders resisted state encroachment and provided room for the Catholic faithful to exercise everyday devotion.

The church used these religious spaces to perform public Christian rites as well as private devotion, especially the observance of holidays and masses within hospitals, kindergarten, and on the stairs of churches. The Gray Sisters in Halle regularly included the poor and children in their Christmas celebrations, even giving gifts and money and endearing themselves to the local community.[54] The way nuns recorded these events revealed a certain degree of intentionality in their flouting of state ideology. One chronicler of the Gray Sisters included some rare criticism of the state's care for its people. She wrote that Sister Odilia had been caring for the "poorest of the poor," those forgotten by society. This was scathing criticism of a state that was supposed to ensure equality among its citizens, but because these chronicles were typically for the purpose of recording an order's private history, they allowed sisters more freedom of expression. Annual histories afforded a sense of private space secure from political scrutiny, evidenced by the fact that the Gray Sisters in Halle penned Sister Odilia's charitable service in contrast with the state's failings not long after the interrogation of Jesuit priests in the late 1950s.[55]

The traditional cloister could likewise become a site of subversion. For women in a publicly male-dominated society, the convent was liberating as a space free from political rhetoric and the pressures of secular and church hierarchies. Historian Patricia Ranft details the various advantages monastic life afforded women in premodern Europe: The cloister provided an escape from the pressures of familial control and offered opportunities for education and creativity. Women also used the convent as a means to gain political power.[56] Nuns from both Christian and non-Christian traditions have written about the relation of personal freedom and the convent. For Buddhist nuns in nineteenth-century China, for instance, the monastery was a refuge from civil unrest, poverty, and the pressures of wife- and motherhood.[57] It was for this sense of autonomy that Red Cross Sisters moved from Berlin to Alexanderdorf, where they established the priory of St. Gertrud in the early 1930s. The cloistered Benedictine nuns played a vital role in the villages in remote Brandenburg after the Second World War. For a time the priory even served as a place of respite for wounded soldiers. The willingness of orders like the Benedictines to interact with and aid a diversity of people helped them survive and negotiate a difficult and often unpredictable political landscape in the GDR regime.

After the Second World War, the Benedictine priory resumed small agricultural work and opened their doors for guests. They provided poor villagers with food and farmed the land surrounding their convent.[58] The nuns even took advantage of collectivization in 1960. The Agricultural Production Cooperatives (Landwirtschaftliche Produktionsgenossenschaften, LPGs) merged the leased land near the cloister, a process that made farming more manageable for the sisters. The priory was also able to purchase small-scale farm machinery from local farmers, since the LPGs used primarily large-scale tractors.[59] The Ministry of Agriculture exercised authority over smaller plots of land as well, requiring convents and monasteries to report to state authorities. The auxiliary bishop in Erfurt signed a contract with the LPG and the city of Erfurt on behalf of the Ursuline cloister every year to certify their use of garden plots and cloister land.[60] The unremitting negotiation centered on private property involved a variety of actors, including nuns from the West and East, church dignitaries, and secular authorities. The perseverance of sisters and their motherhouses ensured that orders kept ownership of many of the establishments that enabled them to continue their work.

Cloistered nuns provided other important services, such as hospice care and work opportunities for builders and farmhands in the surrounding villages, and in return they received the support of local families. In the late 1940s and 1950s, young people often stayed in the priory's barn for special holidays and festivals. The Benedictine sisters opened their chapel for ecumenical services and prayer, as there were few places in the postwar era to hold church-related events. Devout women, in particular, spent time at the cloister for retreat and prayer, while Catholic families from Berlin and Erfurt visited for long weekends and Christmas festivities. The isolated medieval Cistercian monasteries Marienthal and Marienstern were likewise centers of pilgrimage that drew not only annual East German pilgrims but also Polish Catholics and international church dignitaries.[61] The Cistercian nuns emphasized their historical and cultural heritage—a poignant line of reasoning for a regime that sought to legitimate itself as the inheritor of positive German culture. These spaces brought together East Germans from different regions and connected the broader Eastern Bloc Catholic community.

In the early 1960s, young people traveled to the Benedictine priory in Alexanderdorf for youth retreats and camps. Polish nuns and sisters from a neighboring Protestant order visited the cloister. Two Bulgarian nuns also sojourned at St. Gertrud for the opportunity to observe cloistered life, a meaningful experience for women from a society that forbade Catholic religious congregations. According to state regulations, the sisters had to register all guests with local officials. West Germans could only visit if they were family members, and so the sisters continually registered visiting nuns, priests, and monks from the West as their cousins.[62]

Activities like this in the early years of the GDR established social networks centered on experiences at the convent and ensured that it remained a focal point for poor villages in Brandenburg. In 1974, the Catholic Church officially consecrated the convent as an abbey, an act of spiritual and political significance. The Benedictine nuns also began construction on a church building on the abbey's grounds during this time, a project made possible with money from the Catholic Church in West Germany. The sisters again demonstrated that they had earned learned their lessons in the early years of the GDR and reported the money as inheritance, which was one way to circumvent the laws that limited gifts from the West.[63] Though isolated from much of everyday life and politics in the GDR, the cloister maintained connections with villagers, West Germans, and Eastern Bloc neighbors. They also carved out their own identity by refusing to move their cloister and observing aspects of the Rules of St. Benedict intended for autonomous, contemplative communities. In particular, their ability to circumvent the East German system in this way reflected their continued independence.

Female orders remained vital to East German communities and to religious life for Catholics in the GDR because of their persistence in maintaining devotional spaces set apart from the politically and ideologically charged Cold War atmosphere. Cloistered women, too, learned to adapt their practices to state regulations in order to preserve ones that ran counter to scientific materialism. Activism in the case of regular canonical orders like Benedictines or Cistercians could be centered on daily work and prayer as forms of resistance. The very survival of these religious communities in the GDR was a testament to their ingenuity and their ability to alter spirituality and communal living to their political realities.

Conclusion

The theoretical perspective of entanglement between church and state not only reveals negotiations from the top down but also highlights the importance of the experiences and interactions taking place at the grassroots levels, especially from often marginalized actors like Catholic sisters. It moves the researcher beyond a narrow approach focused only on resistance, which obscures the reason the state would tolerate and endorse the work of female orders. It also challenges the bifurcated notion of church and state by highlighting the complex relations between different actors and their own complicated entanglement with political and ideological structures. Local functionaries, for instance, shared concerns with Catholic orders regarding the poor in their towns and sometimes disregarded central authorities who attempted to establish ideological coherency and placate Soviet allies. Bishops often acted on behalf of nuns but were equally concerned with the church's international standing. Members of orders made the deliberate choice to stay in the East after the war and minister to the existing minority Catholic community and those displaced from Silesia and the Sudetenland. Because of their opposition within the political landscape of the Eastern Bloc, East German orders learned when to negotiate with, resist, or adapt to state authority. The existence of Catholic orders created possibilities for alternative identity and discourse, and they functioned as a means through which women in vocational life could persist in postwar social conditions.

East German Catholics retained a strong identity arguably because of their marginalized position in a secular society. Catholic identity in socialism was cultivated by the actions of an even smaller minority of nuns and sisters. It was the implicit subversion by these women that ensured spaces for religious discourse and ritual. Sisters took advantage of the fact that traditional notions of gender directly influenced state policy toward religion and redefined political action. Intense negotiation and diplomatic intervention, coupled with the state's conservative views on women, allowed many religious institutes to preserve their roles as teachers, nurses, and caregivers. The ability of these women to work around systematic restrictions, like the SED's ban on religiously based education, revealed their ingenuity. Their identity was tied to the spiritual experience of a regimented schedule centered on the church year, prayer, liturgy, and work. Direct activism was likely not their aim as they tended to the sick or taught children, but because they were a visible minority in opposition to a secular worldview, their continued presence carried political meaning within socialism. Even the central creed of religious institutes—leading a life consecrated to the church and the devotion to God through charity—ran counter to the socialist mission of establishing Marxism-Leninism. East German officials continued to view religious orders as threatening to their authority, and with good reason. After all, the foundational act for a person joining an order was to take a vow of obedience to laws and to a hierarchy that existed outside of the state.

Perhaps unintentionally, the cloister became a symbol of quiet resistance within socialism. That sisters not only continued their devotional practices but also maintained external ministries within two traditionally patriarchal spheres—the state and the church—revealed a level of resourcefulness often overlooked in the narrative of church and state relations in the GDR. Because of the inviolable nature of religious establishments and the regime's unspoken gendered policies, the monasteries and convents provided a venue for religious, female expression. More important, sisters' actions highlighted that religious life could be dynamic and evolving, even while firmly rooted in tradition. It was this juxtaposition that led to the conflicts and negotiations between religious women and the East German state in the 1950s and illustrated how truly intertwined religion, gender, and geopolitics were in postwar socialist society.

A cloister might conjure images of complete isolation—an institution entirely separated from secular state power. In a self-avowed secular state within the Eastern Bloc, the cloister might seem to represent one of the least "entangled" sites, but these religious institutions were in fact deeply entangled with domestic political structures and with the global monastic and religious communities in a myriad of practical ways. Sisters had to constantly negotiate with the state to secure or defend funding, to establish property rights, and to maintain their traditional ministries. The state, in turn, had to negotiate with individual female orders and with the larger Catholic Church in an attempt to downplay the church's ideological validity while making use of their charitable services. Sisters used the tools of both the church and the GDR state to achieve their goals, especially the language of the law regarding property and ideology. Religious sisters were also adept at turning general assumptions about the apolitical nature of women directly to their advantage. Though perhaps not intentional acts of subversion, their ability to negotiate laws and share devotional practices like prayer and pilgrimage with an international community was a direct challenge to secular authority and laid the foundation for a third space that was neither East nor West and a semipublic sphere that would nurture a distinct East German Catholic identity.

Kathryn C. Julian is assistant professor of history at Westminster College, Salt Lake City, United States. She defended her dissertation titled "The Socialist Devout: Religious Orders and the Making of an East German Catholic Community" in Modern European History at the University of Massachusetts Amherst in 2017. Her research focuses on sacred space, the natural environment, and communities of the devout within socialism. She is particularly interested in comparisons between East Germany, Hungary, and the People's Republic of China. She is currently revising the dissertation for a manuscript that considers transnational relations of religious communities during the postwar era.

Notes

My thanks to Jennifer Heuer and Jon Olsen for their comments on earlier versions of this chapter. Special thanks to the Benedictine nuns at the Abbey of St. Gertrud and the Sisters of St. Elisabeth in Berlin Schlachtensee.

1. Karl-Heinz Schulisch, *Das Kloster St. Gertrud in Alexanderdorf 1949–1989: Wie Benediktinerinnen die DDR erlebten*, ed. Sisters of the Cloister (Töpchin, 2001), 63–64.
2. See John P. Burgess, *The East German Church and the End of Communism* (New York, 1997); and Bernd Schaefer, *The East German State and the Catholic Church, 1945–1989* (New York, 2010).
3. James Scott, *Weapons of the Weak: Everyday Forms of Peasant Resistance* (New Haven, CT, 1986).
4. See Donna Harsch, *Women, the Family, and Communism in the German Democratic Republic* (Princeton, NJ, 2007); and Kathleen Riley, *From Joking to Revolting: Everyday Subversion in the German Democratic Republic* (East Lansing, MI, 2008).
5. "Kirche und Staat in der Deutschen Demokratischen Republik," *Deutscher Wochendienst*, 3 November 1952, Stiftung Archiv der Parteien und Massenorganisationen der DDR im Bundesarchiv Berlin (SAPMO), DY 30/ IV/ 2/ 14/ 23; and Bernd Schaefer, *The East German State and the Catholic Church, 1945–1989* (New York, 2010), 32.
6. Peter Maser, *Glauben im Sozialismus: Kirchen und Religionsgemeinschaften in der DDR* (Berlin, 1989), 13–20.
7. Josef Pilvousek, "Die katholische Kirche in der DDR," in *Die Rolle der Kirchen in der DDR: Eine erste Bilanz*, ed. Horst Dähn (Munich, 1993): 56–72; and Christoph Kösters and Wolfgang Tischner, "Die katholische Kirche in der DDR-Gesellschaft: Ergebnisse, Thesen und Perspektiven," in *Katholische Kirche in SBZ und DDR*, ed. Christoph Kösters and Wolfgang Tischner (Paderborn, 2005), 13.

8. Barbara Thériault, *"Conservative Revolutionaries": Protestant and Catholic Churches in Germany after Radical Political Change in the 1990s* (New York, 2004), 30.
9. Schaefer, *East German State*, 1–3.
10. "St. Elisabeth Krankenhaus, Provinzhaus, Tätigkeitsbericht 1953," Provinzarchiv der Kongregation der Schwestern von der heiligen Elisabeth, Provinz Deutschland, Berlin (PAB), HAL 140/1 1948–1971.
11. "Ordensstatistik, Bistum Berlin. Orden und Kongregationen, Ordensreferat, Ordensschwestern," Diözesanarchiv, Berlin (DAB), Ia 4-3-1.
12. "Katholisches Ordensleben in der DDR," SAPMO, DY 30/ IV/ 2/ 14/ 237.
13. "Klöster und Ordensniederlassungen im Bezirk Erfurt, 1955," SAPMO, DY 30/ IV/ 2/ 14/ 241.
14. "Kirchenfragen des ZK," SAPMO, DY 30/ IV/ 2/ 14/ 23.
15. "Rechtsgutachten und Beschwerden der Kirchen, 1949–1956," SAPMO, DO 4/ 2286.
16. Jennifer Wynot, "Monasteries without Walls: Secret Monasticism in the Soviet Union, 1928–39," *Church History* 71, no. 1 (2002): 64.
17. Daniela Kalkandjieva, "The Bulgarian Eastern Catholic Church," in *Eastern Christianity and Politics in the Twenty-First Century*, ed. Lucian N. Leustean (New York, 2014), 697.
18. Milan J. Reban, "The Catholic Church in Czechoslovakia," in *Catholicism and Politics in Communist Societies*, ed. Perdo Ramet (Durham, NC, 1990), 142–55.
19. Ibid., 149.
20. Sabrina Ramet, *Nihil Obstat: Religion, Politics, and Social Change in East-Central Europe and Russia* (Durham, NC, 1998), 91–92.
21. See Annette Mertens, *Himmlers Klostersturm: Der Angriff auf katholische Einrichtungen im Zweiten Weltkrieg und die Wiedergutmachung nach 1945* (Paderborn, 2006).
22. "Katholisches Ordensleben in der DDR," SAPMO, DY 30/ IV/ 2/ 14/ 237.
23. Carola Sachse, *Der Hausarbeitstag: Gerechtigkeit und Gleichberechtigung in Ost und West 1939–1994* (Göttingen, 2002), 400; see also Dagmar Herzog, *Sex after Fascism: Memory and Morality in Twentieth-Century Germany* (Princeton, NJ, 2005), 219.
24. "Klöster und Ordensniederlassungen im Bezirk Erfurt, 1955," SAPMO, DY 30/ IV/ 2/ 14/ 241.
25. "Bistum Berlin, Orden und Kongregationen," DAB, Ia 4-5-5.
26. "Bericht, 18. Juni 1959," SAPMO, DY 30/ IV/ 2/ 14/ 249.
27. "Katholische Orden in der DDR, 1959," SAPMO, DO 4/ 1918.
28. "Caritas in der DDR, 1951–1990," SAPMO, DO 4/ 1311.
29. "Klöster und Ordensniederlassungen im Bezirk Erfurt, 1955," SAPMO, DY 30/ IV/ 2/ 14/ 241.
30. "Katholische Kirche im Bistum Meißen, 1952," SAPMO, DO 4/ 237.
31. "Information über Frauenwallfahrt der katholischen Kirche nach dem Kerbschen Berg bei Dingelstädt (Kreis Worbis)," SAPMO, DO 4/ 669.
32. "Ordensstatistik, Bistum Berlin. Orden und Kongregationen, Ordensreferat, Ordensschwestern," DAB, Ia 4-3-1.
33. "Gerichtsakte des Beschuldigten, 1958," Der Bundesbeauftragte für die Unterlagen des Staatssicherheitsdienstes der ehemaligen Deutschen Demokratischen Republik, Zentralarchiv und Außenstellen, Berlin (BStU), 100/ 59.

34. "Klöster und Ordensniederlassungen im Bezirk Erfurt, 1955," SAPMO, DY 30/ IV/ 2/ 14/ 241.
35. "Gerichtsakte des Beschuldigten, 1958," BStU, 100/ 59.
36. Jo Ann Kay McNamara, *Sisters in Arms: Catholic Nuns through Two Millennia* (Cambridge, MA, 1996).
37. "Katholische Kirche, 1957–1959," SAPMO, DO 4/ 2480.
38. "Chronik St. Barbara-Krankenhaus und St. Elisabethheim, Halle," PAB, PD 237.
39. "Franziskanerkloster Kerbscher Berg, 1948–1971, Abbruch der Mission in Herzberg, 1953," Bistumsarchiv Erfurt, Regionalarchiv Ost (BAE), 66 A VIII b 3. There were no cases in church or state archives of sisters in the GDR arrested for travel.
40. "Chronik des St. Barbara-Krankenhauses, Halle," PAB, PD 966. The sister who authored the year's report took heart in the fact that the Gray Sisters institutions and services had always been valued in the city despite the political milieu.
41. "Provinz Halle-KWA 1944–1976, Chronik 1953," PAB, MH 1110.
42. Stephen Kotkin refers to the manipulation of state language as "speaking Bolshevism." See Stephen Kotkin, *Magnetic Mountain: Stalinism as a Civilization* (Berkeley, CA, 1995).
43. Xin Liu, *The Otherness of Self: A Genealogy of the Self in Contemporary China* (Ann Arbor, MI, 2001), 104.
44. "Vikarie für den Ostteil der Provinz Brandenburg, Bericht April 1951," PAB, MH 1109.
45. "Beschwerde über Bautätigkeit der Kirchen, May 1957," SAPMO, DO 4/ 2377.
46. "Ursulinenkloster Erfurt, Berichte 1948–1963," BAE, 70/ A VIII c1.
47. Ibid.
48. "Chronik Provinz Halle-KWA 1944–1976," PAB, MH 1110.
49. "Chronik des St. Elisabeth-Krankenhauses, 1950," PAB, HAL 140/ 1.
50. "Chronik des St. Barbara-Krankenhauses, Halle," PAB, PD 966.
51. Cornelia Ropers, "Katholische Krankenpflegeausbildung in der SBZ/DDR und im Transformationsprozess" (PhD diss. Universität Erfurt, 2009), 36.
52. "Interview zum 90. Geburstag, 2. Dezember 1992, 152/2, and Interview zum 90. Geburstag, 3. Dezember 1992. Schwester M. Modesta Dudkowiak," PAB, HAL 799.
53. Schaefer, *East German State*, 280; and David Doellinger, *Turning Prayers into Protests: Religious-Based Activism and Its Challenge to State Power in Socialist Slovakia and East Germany* (Budapest, 2013), 116–17.
54. "Chronik des St. Elisabeth-Krankenhauses, 1950," PAB, HAL 140/1.
55. "Chronik Halle, Mauerstraße, Chronik nach 1946," PAB, HAL 953/ 2.
56. Patricia Ranft, *Women and Religious Life in Premodern Europe* (New York, 1996).
57. Elizabeth Abbot, *A History of Celibacy: From Athena to Elizabeth I, Leonardo da Vinci, Florence Nightingale, Ghandi, and Cher* (Cambridge, MA, 2001), 177.
58. Schulisch, *Kloster St. Gertrud*, 41.
59. Ibid., 24.
60. "Ursulinenkloster Erfurt, Berichte 1948–1963," BAE, 70/ A VIII c1.
61. "Wallfahrtsorte in der DDR," *Neue Zeit*, 14. April 1977, SAPMO, DO 4/ 5000.
62. Schulisch, *Kloster St. Gertrud*, 36.
63. Ibid.

Selected Bibliography

Abu-Lughod, Lila. "The Romance of Resistance: Tracing Transformations of Power through Bedouin Women." In *Beyond the Second Sex: New Directions in the Anthropology of Gender*, ed. Peggy Reeves Sanday and Ruth Gallagher Goodenough, 311–37. Philadelphia, PA, 1990.

Brennan, Sean. *The Politics of Religion in Soviet Occupied Germany: The Case of Berlin-Brandenburg, 1945–1949.* Lanham, MD, 2011.

Cox, Terry, ed. *Challenging Communism in Eastern Europe: 1956 and Its Legacy.* New York, 2008.

Doellinger, David. *Turning Prayers into Protests: Religious-Based Activism and Its Challenge to State Power in Socialist Slovakia and East Germany.* Budapest, 2013.

Donert, Celia. "Women's Rights in Cold War Europe: Disentangling Feminist Histories," *Past and Present* 218, no. 8 (2013): 178–202.

Ewald, Björn, and Carlos F. Norena, eds. *The Emperor and Rome: Space, Representation, and Ritual.* Cambridge, 2010.

Ford, Caroline. *Divided Houses: Religion and Gender in Modern France.* Ithaca, NY, 2005.

Formes, Malia. "Beyond Complicity versus Resistance: Recent Work on Gender and Imperialism." *Journal of Social History* 28, no. 3 (1995): 629–42.

Harsch, Donna. *Revenge of the Domestic: Women, Family, and Communism in the German Democratic Republic.* Princeton, NJ, 2007.

Herzog, Dagmar. "East Germany's Sexual Evolution." In *Socialist Modern: East German Everyday Culture and Politics*, ed. Katherine Pence and Paul Betts, 71–95. Ann Arbor, MI, 2008.

Jeffery, Patricia, and Amrita Basu, eds. *Appropriating Gender: Women's Activism and Politicized Religion in South Asia.* New York, 1998.

Kenney, Padraic. "The Gender of Resistance in Communist Poland." *American Historical Review* 104, no. 2 (1999): 399–425.

Kösters, Christoph. *Staatsicherheit und Caritas 1950–1989: Zur politischen Geschichte der katholischen Kirche in der DDR.* Paderborn, 2001.

Marsh, Christopher. *Religion and the State in Russia and China: Suppression, Survival, and Revival.* New York, 2011.

McNamara, Jo Ann Kay. *Sisters in Arms: Catholic Nuns through Two Millennia.* Cambridge, MA, 1996.

Mecham, June L. "Cooperative Piety among Monastic and Secular Women in Late Medieval Germany." *Church History and Religious Culture* 88, no. 4 (2008): 581–611.

Mikula, Maja, ed. *Women, Activism and Social Change.* London, 2005.

Morcillo, Aurora. *True Catholic Womanhood: Gender and Ideology in Franco's Spain.* DeKalb, IL, 2000.

Morin, Karen M., and Jeanne Kay Guelke, eds. *Women, Religion, and Space: Global Perspectives on Gender and Faith.* Syracuse, NJ, 2007.

Pence, Katherine. "'You as a Woman Will Understand': Consumption, Gender and the Relationship between State and Citizenry in the GDR's Crisis of 17 June 1953." *German History* 19, no. 2 (2001): 218–53.

Peperkamp, Ester, ed. *Religion and the Secular in Eastern Germany, 1945 to the Present.* Leiden, 2010.

Riley, Kerry Kathleen. *Everyday Subversion: From Joking to Revolting in the German Democratic Republic.* East Lansing, MI, 2008.

Rosenberger, Siegelinde, and Birgit Sauer, eds. *Politics, Religion and Gender: Framing and Regulating the Veil.* London, 2012.

Schaefer, Bernd. *The East German State and the Catholic Church, 1945–1989.* New York, 2010.

Scott, James. *Weapons of the Weak: Everyday Forms of Peasant Resistance.* New Haven, CT, 1986.

Wynot, Jennifer. "Monasteries without Walls: Secret Monasticism in the Soviet Union, 1928–39." *Church History* 71, no. 1 (2002): 63–79.

Zatlin, Jonathan R. *The Currency of Socialism: Money and Political Culture in East Germany.* Cambridge, 2007.

CHAPTER 8

Finding Feminism

Rethinking Activism in the West German New Women's Movement of the 1970s and 1980s

Sarah E. Summers

A women's movement, diverse in strategy, ideology, and spaces of activism, emerged in the Federal Republic of Germany (FRG) beginning in the late 1960s. Skeptical of the effectiveness of traditional forms of activism as represented by political parties and trade unions, young women organized into local activist groups on university campuses and in the kitchens of their shared apartments (*Wohngemeinschaften*, WGs). Professional feminist journalists informed the reading public about feminist debates and the women's question in both feminist and mainstream publications. These women joined an established women's movement in participating in political parties, trade unions, and women's associations (re)founded after the Second World War, such as the German Women's Circle (Deutscher Frauenring), the German Women's Council (Deutscher Frauenrat), and the Information Service for Women (Informationsdienst für die Frau) to name a few. During the 1970s, these groups consolidated their resources to lobby for women's issues in the federal government and in the workforce. Within these varied spaces of activism, women of different generations and social and political backgrounds discussed and supported a variety of concepts of feminism, approaches to gender equality, and feminist issues, such as reproductive rights, patriarchy, the reconciliation of family and work through family policy, cultural images of women, and equal employment and wages.

Despite the broad variety of forms of feminist activism in the 1970s, the majority of scholarship on West German feminism and the women's movement focuses on autonomous feminism, also termed the new women's movement.[1] Many of those who study autonomous feminism also participated in it. As scholars and activists, they have defined autonomous feminism in two ways. The first was through political actions, where autonomous feminism refers to a distinct form of political organization—autonomy—defined by the sociologist Ute Gerhard as "an individual self-determination and institutional independence from previous forms of political organization" that also included a rigid gender segregation from men.² Autonomous feminists rejected participation in political parties, trade unions, and other such forms of political alliances with men. They concentrated instead on local self-help groups, an independent press, and the cultivation of a gender-segregated, women-only subculture consisting of consciousness-raising groups, women's centers, homes for battered women, bookstores, cafes, and artistic production.³ Second, these scholar-activists defined the movement ideologically, arguing that autonomous feminists believed patriarchal gender oppression was foundational to the structure of modern society. Therefore, their feminist program focused on ending the criminalization of abortion, combating violence against women, challenging cultural stereotypes of women, and debating the homemaker role for women.⁴

Autonomous feminism played a pivotal part in altering gender roles in West Germany, but it did not act alone.⁵ In this chapter I argue for a wider interpretative framework that broadly defines both the organizational strategies and the feminist program of West German feminist activists. I include as part of the feminist movement autonomous feminists, women active in political parties and trade unions, journalists at mainstream publications, and female activists in the emerging citizen initiative movement. With this approach I highlight the variety of feminist strategies, including autonomous, individual, relational, and socialist feminism,⁶ and a broader feminist program that advocated family policy and workplace equality. This wider perspective reveals the history of a quite diverse feminist political activism in West Germany, beginning in the late 1960s and with roots reaching back to the 1950s, the Weimar Republic, and even the Wilhelmine Empire. A handful of scholars have reconsidered the dominant scholarly narratives about the West German new women's movement. In her case study of the autonomous women's movement in Munich, for example, historian Elisabeth Zellmer extends the understanding of "autonomous feminism," arguing that autonomy had different meanings for different activists.⁷ Within the concept of "state feminism," the political scientists Amy Mazur and Dorothy E. McBride include female politicians and bureaucratic institutions that works toward improvement of the status of women.⁸ However, their focus on the Women's Affairs Offices (Büros der Frauenbeauftragten) in the West German federal government created in the 1980s skips over the significant work of female politicians in the 1970s that led to the creation of these institutions.⁹ The sociologist Ingela Naumann has put forward a more general challenge to the conventional understanding of feminism. She argues that "any collective activity or organization of women is feminist to the extent that it aims at improving the status of women as a group."[10]

This chapter combines and applies these interventions. It acknowledges diverse meanings of autonomy within the autonomous movement and uses the broad definition of feminism suggested by the sociologists Myra Marx Ferree and Carol McClurg Mueller. Feminism is for them the articulation of the "goal of challenging and changing women's subordination to men." Accordingly, the term "women's movement" refers to "mobilizations based on appeals to women as a constituency and thus an organizational strategy . . . [to] bring women into political activities."[11] This broadened understanding of feminism and the women's movement allows me to include women in West Germany's trade unions and in its two major political parties, the left-wing Social Democratic Party of Germany (Sozialdemokratische Partei Deutschlands, SPD) and the conservative Christian Democratic Union of Germany (Christlich Demokratische Union Deutschlands, CDU) in my study. The chapter demonstrates that their participation resulted in stronger lobbies for women's issues and in small but significant changes in family policy. In the West German context, it argues, similar feminist beliefs produced a wide range of feminist strategies. Finally, a broadened understanding of the new women's movement lets us discern within it multiple feminisms that stretch back well into the nineteenth century and include the traditions of individual, relational, and socialist feminism. In the Wilhelmine Empire and Weimar Germany, the German middle-class and socialist women's movements were the strongest in Europe, which the National Socialist takeover in January 1933 abruptly ended.[12] Female activism in political parties, trade unions, and reestablished women's associations was one way this tradition continued in West Germany after 1945.

While this chapter highlights the significance of these continuities, it also analyzes the importance of the Cold War context in shaping the postwar women's movement by focusing on debates over reconciling family and employment and over family policy. The Cold War reinforced the political, social, and cultural importance of the male-breadwinner/female-homemaker family model in West Germany in discourses, policies, and everyday practices. Since the early postwar years, the CDU supported this family model as West Germany's bulwark against communism and as a new form of "civilized" domestic masculinity to replace the militarized masculinity of the Third Reich.[13] In the 1960s, politicians, trade unions, and industry officials "modernized" the dominant family model by including the part-time employment of mothers in a response to labor force needs.[14] But the ideal of the male-breadwinner family persisted in West Germany, reinforced by Cold War rhetoric and scientists who argued that mothers were the best caregivers for children under the age of three and that they should care for their children after the prevailing half-day school.[15] At the same time, however, the 1970s marked the beginning of family policy reform that at least rhetorically acknowledged working mothers, culminating in a paid maternal leave policy in 1979. Very few scholars of the West German welfare state have acknowledged the role of the women's movement in these debates.[16] Analysis of the debates in and actions of the women's movement reveals an interesting interaction of the different wings of the women's movement in West Germany: while the autonomous women's movement pressured the public to recognize the "women's question," the legislative outcomes mainly reflected the agenda of women active in the two largest political parties and the trade unions, and the limits of female influence in these male-dominated organizations.

The following will extend the understanding of the West German women's movement not only by broadening the perspective but also by analyzing the multiple entanglements among different actors in this movement. The first section examines the autonomous movement and its press, and groups that bridged grassroots and institutional political participation. It argues that feminists defined and practiced autonomy in wide-ranging ways. The next section focuses on women in the two major political parties, the SPD and CDU. It demonstrates that powerful leadership and increased membership of women, on the one hand, and the challenge of the autonomous women's movement, on the other, not only instigated a new era of organizing in these long-standing political party movements but also led to increased activities in the field of family policy. The chapter concludes by analyzing women's activism in the major trade-union organization, the German Trade Union Confederation (Deutscher Gewerkschaftsbund, DGB), and their debates over family and employment.

Autonomous Feminism

Forms of activism and feminist ideology varied widely among the women who self-identified as autonomous feminists. These forms also changed over time. Founded in 1968 in West Berlin as one of the first autonomous feminist groups in West Germany, the Action Council for the Liberation of Women (Aktionsrat zur Befreiung der Frauen), for example, engaged in the self-help activism commonly associated with the movement. The more open Women's Forum Munich (Frauenforum München e.V.), founded in 1971, and the socialist feminist Democratic Women's Initiative (Demokratische Fraueninitiative, DFI), established in 1975–76 as a national organization, intentionally cultivated relationships with mixed-gender organizations and institutions. The media of the new women's movement was similarly diverse. The feminist magazine *Courage*, founded in 1976 in West Berlin, mainly addressed autonomous feminist activists and never exceeded a circulation of 70,000 copies. The bimonthly journal *Emma,* founded by the well-known journalist Alice Schwarzer in Cologne in 1977, aimed for a broader audience and started with a run of 200,000 copies. Other feminist journalists wrote for mainstream publications like the popular liberal illustrated weekly *Stern*. As diverse as the spectrum of autonomous groups and projects was, their approaches to feminism likewise varied, as demonstrated by debates over the gendered division of labor, the call for salary for housework, and the role of socialist feminism in the autonomous movement. Overall, these examples establish a narrative of a much more strategically and ideologically diverse movement than that commonly found in the historiography.[17]

This diversity was a result of the development of the new women's movement in West Germany. Many early feminists in this movement were politicized while participating in the antiauthoritarian student protest movements of the 1960s. By far the most significant was the Socialist German Student League (Sozialistischer Deutscher Studentenbund, SDS), founded in 1946. The emerging student protest movement of the 1960s led by the SDS took up issues of university reform, the Vietnam War, state violence, the Grand Coalition of all of West Germany's major political parties, and the conservative Springer press. A very strong countercultural component included commune experiments in WGs, the politicization of arts and popular culture, and the growth of alternative media.[18] However, the small number of female SDS members began to criticize the conventional gender relations in the SDS. They condemned the lack of discussion of sexism and gender inequality, both in the student movement and in West German society. Beginning in 1968, female activists began meeting separately in discussion groups that focused on their experiences as women, such as the Women's Council (Weiberrat) in Frankfurt am Main and the Aktionsrat in West Berlin.[19]

Autonomy, then, grew out of women's political experiences in the left-wing student movements of the time. It was based on the antiauthoritarian approach of the student movement itself. Movement activists wanted to develop their politics independently from traditional political institutions and organizations like the main political parties because, they argued, former supporters of National Socialism in these organizations poisoned them with authoritarianism. Women's activists took this antiauthoritarian approach even further and turned it against the men in their own movement. For the early feminists, the term "autonomy" had a double meaning. It included independence from traditional institutions and organizations dominated by a male leadership and from men in the antiauthoritarian student movement itself because they tended to neglect women's issues.[20]

However, only some of the early feminists practiced a rigid autonomy. The storefront daycare movement (*Kinderladenbewegung*) exemplifies early engagement with the question of reconciling family and work within an autonomous framework.[21] In 1967, the first storefront daycare collective (*Kinderladen*) was organized in Frankfurt am Main. One year later, a similar initiative started in West Berlin led by Helke Sander, a single mother and film student. During a meeting of eighty to one hundred women and some men at the Free University of Berlin, the Aktionsrat was created and started to organize five daycare centers in cheap, vacant storefronts in West Berlin. With little money for professional early childhood educators, they took turns minding the children, providing mostly half-day care so that mothers could attend classes or seek part-time employment.[22] The *Kinderläden* offered another childcare option outside of the perceived "authoritarian" state-run system (that encompassed only 1.3 percent of children under the age of three but provided more space for children aged three to six) and an emancipatory space for activists to reflect on not only their positions as women and mothers but also their approach to education.[23] The movement quickly spread to many other university towns in West Germany. Eventually it became engrossed in creating a new form of antiauthoritarian childcare that attracted many fathers to the movement, demonstrating that the exclusion of men was not always strictly enforced.[24]

This self-help culture is the organizational strategy most associated with the autonomous women's movement. However, other groups that considered themselves part of the autonomous movement cultivated their own relationships with political parties and trade unions, maintaining their autonomy by meeting separately to set their own agenda. Both the Women's Forum Munich and the DFI employed this strategy. The 1971 Women's Forum, cofounded by the journalist Hannelore Mabry, viewed itself partly as a lobbying organization. The activists in the Women's Forum believed that women's emancipation involved the participation of men and maintained a male membership of about 10 percent. They tried to influence policy by hosting forums on feminist issues with local and regional politicians and penned countless letters to politicians to criticize their policies and suggest new courses of action.[25] The female members of the DFI, formed in 1975–76 with branches in many West German cities, took this strategy further by joining citizen-initiative groups, the environmentalist movement, and even trade unions and political parties in order "to bring our demands as emphatically as possible to the established organizations, parties, and parliaments through versatile activities."[26] DFI members felt that the existing strategies of the autonomous movement limited its influence and the range of issues addressed, but they too maintained some autonomy by meeting separately to formulate their agendas.[27]

The feminist press and feminist journalists also exercised autonomy in various ways. The feminist magazines *Courage* and *Emma* provided national forums for debates over issues such as reproductive rights, employment for women, government policy, and the reconciliation of family and work.[28] The editorial collective of *Courage*, based in West Berlin, claimed to practice strict autonomy and to reflect the values of the autonomous movement. Their editorial staff was nonhierarchical, and it equally distributed tasks such as determining the themes for each issue and selecting its articles. Rather than solicit articles, they chose articles that reflected general trends in the topics submitted from articles and letters.[29] *Emma*, in contrast, had an editor-in-chief, journalist Alice Schwarzer, and aspired to become *the* mainstream feminist magazine written by professional female journalists. *Emma*'s higher circulation confirmed this strategy. Other autonomous feminists, however, criticized *Emma* for its commercial appearance and association with the mainstream publisher Gruner & Jahr, even though the magazine maintained its editorial independence through self-financing via magazine sales, loans from coworkers, and Schwarzer's profits from her popular books.[30]

The examples up to this point have focused on various nuanced interpretations of autonomy as praxis. Yet, feminist ideologies and issues were just as varied across the autonomous movement. This becomes apparent through not only a heated debate in the feminist press over the question of reconciling family and work but also the seldom-discussed arguments about socialist feminism. *Emma* and *Courage* were often at odds over the politics of managing their respective publications. These magazines also regularly landed on opposing sides of feminist debates over issues of family and work, which we can see in their respective positions during the wages-for-housework debate.

The International Women's Collective (a group of women from Britain, France, and Italy) founded the Wages for Housework movement in Padua, Italy, in 1972.[31] Its activists questioned the socialist feminist belief that paid labor outside the home and competition between women for low-paying, menial jobs ensured women's emancipation. *Courage* became a sounding board for their movement. In January 1976, the young feminist historian Gisela Bock published an article in the magazine wherein she contended that monetary compensation for housework through a government-subsidized wage would provide women's work in the home with similar political, social, and economic power as men's paid employment.[32] She based her argument in a feminist critique of Marxism that contended that society should recognize the societal benefits of women's reproductive roles in childbearing and housework rather than favoring productive labor, i.e. paid labor.[33] She further argued that the wage was a solution to dejection over "receiving lower wages and being blocked from better jobs [. . .] despite often being better qualified than men in the same position."[34] Many employers and government officials, in West Germany and elsewhere, had long considered women—particularly married women and mothers—a "reserve army" of the workforce.[35] During the oil-shock recession of the 1970s, this perception justified firing married women and mothers first. In West Germany, much like other hard-hit countries, these groups constituted just 31 percent of the workforce in 1980 but made up 50 percent of West Germany's unemployed.[36]

Alice Schwarzer responded in *Emma* in May 1977 with an article titled "Wage for Housewives?" Here Schwarzer argued that the major aim of the women's movement, a change in the gender order, required a *renegotiation* of the gendered division of labor in the home—men performing half of the housework and childcare duties, for example—as well as an expansion of state-funded full-day childcare, instead of a salary for housework.[37] The supporters of the Wages for Housework movement responded in *Courage* that same year with a critical "Open Letter to Alice," in which they accused her of reinforcing the "recipe of the male-dominated left" that called for women to "go forth into production," creating both unpaid and underpaid work for women both inside and outside the home.[38]

The theme of women's discrimination in the labor market, especially the challenges working mothers faced because of the lack of public childcare, also resonated among feminist journalists writing for mainstream publications like the illustrated weekly *Stern*. Some autonomous feminists condemned *Stern* for its oversexualized use of the naked female form.[39] Others, however, recognized that *Stern* was the only mainstream media outlet that actively engaged in contemporary feminist discourse. In regard to employment and the family, its articles emphasized women's emancipation through economic independence and employment along with social policies to support full-day employment of mothers. In 1971, *Stern* ran a series of articles under the title "Young, Beautiful, and Successful" that featured women who were leaders in their field as role models, such as an interior designer, a successful film director, and the manager of a department-store chain.[40] *Stern* also highlighted women's efforts to overcome discrimination in the workforce, such as the story of the aspiring commercial-airline pilot Rita Maiburg. With the support of politicians and the pilot's union, she legally challenged German Air's policy of only hiring male pilots.[41] One of the feminist journalists who wrote for the *Stern* was Christine Heide, who wrote about the difficulty of balancing family and employment for mothers in West Germany. In 1972, for example, *Stern* published a series of articles by Heide criticizing both the West German government and the DGB for ignoring the scarcity of daycare spots available at both federally and business-funded daycares.[42] In this way, Heide and her colleagues supported and publicized the new women's movement's demands and their critique of male-dominated politics.

The untenable generalizations about autonomous feminist positions on work and the family are partly a result of the absence of socialist feminism in the historiography of the West German new women's movement. As a result of its inherent anticommunism and its focus on the dominant approaches of autonomous feminism, this scholarship limits the spectrum of feminist groups included in its narrative of the history of the movement. Early groups like the Aktionsrat were included in the narrative, even though it supported elements of socialist feminism, because they were perceived as the "founding mothers." But feminist socialist organizations like the DFI, which were founded later, had no place in this narrative. For women in the Aktionsrat or the DFI, capitalism created a double burden of low-paying jobs and household obligations for women, thus straining relationships between men and women.[43] As much as other areas of politics and society, the Cold War also informed discourses and practices of feminism in the 1970s.

Socialist feminism influenced the early ideology of the new women's movement and also led to the formation of socialist feminist groups. The Socialist Women's Union West Berlin (Sozialistischer Frauenbund Westberlin, SFBW), for example, developed from the Aktionsrat and carried the socialist feminist tradition forward into the 1970s. More interested in trade-union organizing than working in *Kinderläden,* this group rejected the classical socialist assertion that only socialist revolution would bring about emancipation. Instead, they declared, "the struggle to change the societal relations of production must be waged in tandem with the fight for women's equality."[44] To achieve these aims, many members participated in trade unions and the SPD, meeting separately in the SFBW to ensure that their positions were developed independently from the larger organizations.[45] Thus, initially, socialist feminists challenged stringent definitions of autonomy, both in their ideology and through participation in mixed-gender institutions.

Socialist feminism was, however, soon rejected by many autonomous feminists due to a resurgent Cold War and a shift in the strategic focus of the West German autonomous movement. Having come to power in 1969 under the slogan "Let us dare more democracy!" the SPD-led federal government was put on the defensive in the early 1970s by accusations from conservatives impugning the SPD's alleged communist associations. In response, social democratic Chancellor Willy Brandt and the prime ministers of the federal states instituted the so-called Anti-Radical Decree (*Radikalenerlaß*) in January 1972. Under this law, anybody who was considered to have "radical views," especially if they were members of a "radical party," could be forbidden to work in the civil service, which includes a variety of public-sector occupations such as teaching. In practice, the law was directed mainly against the new and old left, especially members and "sympathizers" of the West German Communist Party (Deutsche Kommunistische Partei, DKP), refounded in 1968.[46]

The intensifying anticommunist atmosphere of the political culture affected the women's movement, and autonomous feminists began disengaging from even the New Left. Frigga Haug, a founding member of the SFBW, recalled, "We were not given any space in the women's centers [...] founded after 1972." She concluded, "This polarization of the women's movement was probably a phenomenon peculiar to West Germany and can only be explained in terms of the virulent all-purpose anti-communism of our country."[47] Around the same time, many participants of the new women's movement shifted focus from discussion groups like the Aktionsrat to a feminist subculture and an emphasis on patriarchy as the basis of women's oppression.[48] Thus, the split between autonomous and socialist feminism affected how one experienced feminist politics at the time and led to the exclusion of socialist feminists from the historical narrative.

The examples analyzed above emphasize the need to reconsider rigid definitions of autonomy in studying the West German autonomous women's movement. We find common mentalities, such as distrust of traditional political organizations, yet the willingness of autonomous groups to engage with these institutions was a matter of degree rather than kind. Furthermore, many different visions for West Germany's gender order coexisted. The autonomous movement intensively engaged with West German political and employment organizations and participated in civil society.

Women in Political Parties

While scholars have focused attention on the autonomous women's movement, the varieties of feminist activity in West Germany extended well beyond these individuals and groups. Multiple generations of women joined the ranks of West Germany's two dominant political parties, the Social Democratic Party and the Christian Democratic Union, which together received around 85 percent of the vote in federal elections in the 1970s.[49] The rise in their female membership outpaced overall party growth and reflected the politicization of women in this decade. Between 1970 and 1980, female membership as a percentage of total membership increased from 18.7 to 23 percent in the SPD and from 13 to 18 percent in the CDU.[50] In the SPD, female membership grew 156 percent, while the party grew 12 percent.[51] In the CDU, the women's membership grew

266 percent, while the party grew 13 percent.[52] The women of both parties utilized this noticeable increase and the public discussion of women's issues to strengthen their voice within their respective party. This new strength bore fruit in influencing family policy during the 1970s and 1980s. Yet, with the exception of the younger generation of women in the SPD, women in positions of power within the women's organizations promoted a comparatively more moderate, or even conservative, ideology regarding family policy. Often such ideology was not based on individual feminism, i.e. the assumption that individuals have equal rights and these rights are human rights, but on the traditional relational feminist belief that women as mothers and caregivers have an important but distinctive role to play in society and in politics and as such need special policies that take care of them. This older generation of female politicians in the SPD and CDU acknowledged the significance of employed mothers but were strongly influenced by the dominant cultural perspective from which mothers were viewed as the best caregivers for children as well as by Cold War family policy rhetoric that supported the male-breadwinner/female-homemaker and part-time worker family model.[53]

Elfriede Eilers was the woman most responsible for strengthening the women's lobby in the SPD. Eilers entered the West German parliament, the Bundestag, in 1957 and quickly gained a reputation for women's activism while serving on several of the SPD's special women's committees. She was an early proponent of abortion reform and collaborated on a family-planning campaign with SPD parliamentarian Käte Strobel, who served as minister of health from 1969 to 1972.[54] Born in 1921, Eilers was situated between an older and a younger generation of SPD party members. Her involvement in the SPD's women's politics during the 1950s is one example of female political activism that predates the rise of the autonomous women's movement. Like many other older feminists of her generation, Eilers recognized that the young autonomous feminists engendered an environment within which her activities finally could lead to concrete change. Eilers credited the autonomous women's movement with the 1970 reformulation of the SPD women's issues platform, which aimed to attract this "agitated generation of young women."[55] Along with other female party functionaries, including Annemarie Renger, who served as the first woman president of the Bundestag from 1972 to 1976, Eilers instituted organizational changes to strengthen the women's lobby and to alter the public image of the SPD as a men's party. The result was the foundation of the Working Group of Social Democratic Women (Arbeitsgemeinschaft Sozialdemokratischer Frauen, ASF) in 1973. Elfriede Eilers became the first leader of the ASF and held this position until 1977.

The majority of the female SPD leadership shared the CDU's position that mothers provided the best care for young children, but SPD women eventually distinguished themselves by supporting programs to aid mothers in holding full-time employment in cases of economic necessity. For instance, they had long advocated a maternal, and later parental, employment leave policy.[56] The older generation of female SPD functionaries especially hesitated to advocate for more radical feminist positions, not in the least because they feared the resistance of the male majority in the party. Historian Gisela Notz argues that they understood the plight of working mothers because of their own experiences of discrimination as women with political careers (although most entered politics after raising their children). However, they also struggled against the perception by their male colleagues that their sole interests lay in "token" women's platform issues, such as youth and family. These women intentionally distanced themselves from labels of feminism so as not to jeopardize their working relationships with their male colleagues.[57]

The feminist positions of the older ASF leadership often clashed with those of the younger generation of female SPD members who flooded into the party in the early 1970s. This new generation was connected to both the ideology and activities of the New Left and autonomous women's movement, and had worked within the ASF and the Working Group of Young Socialists in the SPD (Arbeitsgemeinschaft der Jungsozialisten in der SPD, Jusos), the youth wing of the party that tended to promote more radical positions.[58] The older generation grew concerned that the younger generation often advocated ideas and strategies considered "too radical" or even "communist" because they promoted a dual-earning household out of desire rather than necessity.[59] These tensions played out in the discussion over the SPD's family policy statement for the 1975 party congress in Mannheim. A group of female Jusos formed a separate working group to draft more radical suggestions, such as the expansion of full-day childcare.[60] The suggestions worried the older, more conservative leaders in the ASF who excoriated the women for "bring[ing] Marxist approaches to our family politics."[61]

Despite these conflicts, the ASF was nonetheless a force of change in family policy. The ASF was instrumental in lobbying for a Maternal Leave Law (*Mutterschaftsurlaubsgesetz*), passed in 1979 by the SPD and their liberal Free Democratic Party (Freie Demokratische Partei, FDP) coalition partners. The law provided an employed mother six months of paid leave after the birth of her child and an employment guarantee.[62] On the one hand, the policy did little to dismantle the male-breadwinner family model in West Germany. The maternal leave was only available to mothers. Female members of the trade unions criticized the amount of the stipend, 750 German marks (Deutsche Mark, DM), as it did not a sufficiently replace women's average monthly salary in 1979, which was 1,750 DM for industrial workers and 2,170 DM for white-collar positions. On the other hand, it did mark an important transition toward recognizing employed mothers in West German family policy.

The political position of the majority of female members and functionaries in the CDU was far more conservative than that of the SPD. Since its formation after 1945, the CDU developed a Christian-conservative and strict anticommunist rhetoric that presented the gender and family policy of the GDR as the negative counterimage.[63] The CDU Federal Women's Committee (CDU Bundesfrauenausschuß) represented women's issues in the CDU beginning in 1951 until the founding of the CDU Women's Union (CDU Frauenvereinigung) in 1956. Aenne Brauksiepe led the Women's Union from 1958 until 1969, followed by Helga Wex. The Women's Union capitalized on the significant collapse in the female vote for the CDU in the federal elections of 1972. With the argument that the CDU needed to develop a more women-friendly policy to win more female votes, the Women's Union pushed its party in this direction. This seems to have led indeed to an increase in female party membership in the 1970s.[64] In the heightened public debate over the women's question, Brauksiepe, Wex, and other leading Christian Democratic female functionaries represented a conservative counterimage to the autonomous women's movement and social democratic women's activists.[65]

The CDU Women's Union was firmly grounded in relational feminism, and it promoted separate but equal roles for women and men in society, a position that Wex, for example, propounded in a 1973 article in the CDU-affiliated journal *Die Neue Ordnung*.[66] It supported the stance of its party and the Catholic and Protestant Churches on the importance of children being cared for in the home by their mothers.[67] Even CDU women, though, had to adjust to the debates of the time and acknowledge in the 1970s the "modern" dilemma of West German women caught between their families, their child-rearing obligations, and their right to seek individual fulfillment through employment. Accordingly, they requested the equal treatment of employed mothers and housewives.[68] In practice, however, the policy of the CDU Women's Union focused mostly on middle-class housewives, the main female voter clientele, through policy suggestions such as a retirement pension for housework and a child-rearing allowance (*Erziehungsgeld*), a stipend paid to all new mothers regardless of their employment status before the birth of their newborns.[69]

The subtle shifts in CDU perceptions of "modern" women became more pronounced in 1982 after the CDU and her Bavarian sister party the Christian Social Union (Christlich-Soziale Union, CSU) regained a parliamentary majority in coalition with the FDP. From the beginning of the CDU/CSU/FDP's tenure as a parliamentary majority, the CDU Frauenvereinigung pushed for the implementation of *Erziehungsgeld*. This child-rearing allowance would expand benefits from the 1979 Maternal

Leave Law to child caregivers and fathers. The party's 1985 conference in Essen provided a venue for convincing the party as a whole to support the family policy initiative. The conference was unique in that it was devoted entirely to women's issues and ended with the adoption of new party guidelines on "The New Partnership between Men and Women." To justify the continuation of an employment guarantee for the reintroduction of parents into the workforce, conference organizers arranged panels devoted to topics such as "Women in Employment and Family" and "Women in Professional Life."[70] Delegates asserted both the necessity and the value of women and mothers working outside the home, and the conversation was almost completely devoid of concerns over the socialization of one's children, likely due to the fact that they were funding stay-at-home care for children.[71]

The Law for Child-Rearing Allowance and Parental Leave (*Gesetz zum Erziehungsgeld und zur Elternzeit*) was implemented in November 1985, after the Essen party conference successfully convinced the CDU of its importance. It offered a monthly stipend of 600 DM to *either* parent, regardless of employment status before the birth of the child, for six months. It also provided job security if the parent was employed before the birth. By offering paid leave to either parent, the law opened up the possibility for fathers to take a more active role in the care of their newborn children.[72] Critics nevertheless argued that the 600 DM per month stipend was too low to entice men to stay home.[73] The policy also acknowledged the importance of employment to mothers by offering job security but still reinforced the male-breadwinner view of the gender order and the party's commitment to the middle class by offering the stipend to all parents regardless of employment status.

The family policies enacted by the SPD and CDU between 1979 and 1985 reinforced many aspects of West Germany's male-breadwinner welfare state. However, for the women who were instrumental in lobbying for these measures in their respective political parties, these policies represented both their positions on reconciling family and employment and a significant step toward recognizing the significance of employment as both financially necessary and individually fulfilling for women.

Trade Union Activism

Another organization that receives little attention in the scholarship on the West German women's movement is the Women's Division of the German Trade Union Confederation (DGB Frauenabteilung), organized by the Federal Women's Committee (Bundesfrauenausschuß) of the trade unions. The DGB itself was an umbrella organization of trade unions, founded in October 1949 to eliminate feuding between suddenly reestablished unions. While it did not negotiate collective agreements, it represented its members in discussions with government authorities, political parties, and employer's organizations. In this capacity, it played an important role in the formulation of employment policy in West Germany.[74] The DGB Women's Division was founded along with the organization in 1949 to represent the interests of employed women and to implement the DGB's directives regarding employed women. As happened in the political parties, female membership increased in the 1970s, from 15.3 percent of total membership to 20.2 percent in 1980. This was due to the expansion of women's employment since the 1950s and a new trade union activism in the 1970s inspired by the reform policy of the 1960s and 1970s.[75] The DGB Women's Division engaged in feminist activism on work and family policy, even if political divisions split the organization's positions since members represented the whole political spectrum of political parties in the Bundestag.

Unlike the SPD and the CDU, the women activists in the DGB envisioned women first and foremost as employees in the West German workforce. These female trade unionists were on the front line in fighting for women's equal employment rights in an organization that represented millions of West German employees.[76] Equal wages for equal work, better education, and job training remained cornerstones of the political agenda of the DGB Women's Division.[77] However, like in the CDU and SPD, the issue of reconciling family and work was a highly contested one within the trade unions due to the structure of the DGB. When the trade unions of the three Western zones were united in October 1949, the resulting DGB included seven regional organizations that represented the members of seventeen unions of different segments of the workforce, who had varying political and religious affiliations. The ability to set an agenda was further complicated by a similar generational conflict to that found in the SPD. The flood of young feminists into the trade unions in the 1970s, in particular into the Trade Union of the Metal Industry (Industriegewerkschaft Metal), resulted in frequent clashes between them and women with more moderate or conservative political stances toward the family, and who tended to hold federal leadership positions within the Federal Women's Committee, the Women's Division, and the DGB at large.[78]

The DGB Women's Division finalized its program to "reconcile employment, family, and society" at the 1974 Federal Women's Conference of the trade unions. Much like women in the SPD, the DGB Women's Division first and foremost advocated paid parental leave "for either mothers or fathers" to last the first eighteen months after childbirth. They also demanded an increase in childcare places for children aged three to six along with more full-day options (most childcare offerings were only half day in

West Germany).[79] Finally, they called for more flexible working hours for parents, as well as for services to aid in care work. The DGB Women's Division did not solely endorse full-time employment, however. Like their colleagues in the political parties, they promoted part-time employment as an option for mothers to balance family and paid work.[80]

The DGB Women's Division was an important ally to the ASF in the push for a maternal-leave policy in the late 1970s, even when the policy did not fulfill all of their demands. The Women's Division initially reacted with criticism. For its members, the proposal only delayed the difficult question of what to do with children while mothers worked, since it was not matched by increased full-day childcare options. Furthermore, they criticized the proposal for its insufficient income replacement, which would make it very difficult for working-class women to take advantage of the policy, and for the exclusion of fathers. Nonetheless, the DGB Women's Division and its executive, the Federal Women's Committee, decided to support the measure and to only "*quietly* demand the inclusion of fathers."[81] The conclusion of the DGB executive represents the compromises that most women active in institutions were willing to make in order to advance family policy that helped reconcile family and work for mothers.

Conclusion

The broader reconstruction of the West German women's movement reveals a movement entangled with the Federal Republic's public, political, and economic spheres in the final decades of the Cold War. The autonomous movement not only redefined the political by politicizing private and women's-only spheres through consciousness-raising and political discussion, it also challenged the practice of institutional politics by bridging grassroots organizing with traditional membership in political parties and trade unions. The effects of this strategy could be felt in the heated debates between the younger and older generations of SPD and DGB women. While Cold War family policy and cultural conceptions of parenting prevented more radical positions from taking hold, it is clear that the approach of autonomous feminism prompted women in institutional politics to reconsider their organizing strategies. These new forms of advocacy empowered them to pursue and win acknowledgment of women's role in the workforce and compensation for their labor at home. Finally, feminists engaged in the public sphere of the press, beyond just the feminist press. Journalists such as Christine Heide raised awareness of feminist issues and debates in mainstream publications. To understand the political, social, and economic effects and significance of West German feminism in the 1960s, historians must move beyond a rigid definition of the autonomous movement. If we want to demonstrate the impact of the women's movement on West Germany's politics, society, economy, and culture by empirical means, we have to be open to finding feminism in spaces not previously considered feminist.

Sarah E. Summers is instructor of global and European history at Wilfrid Laurier University in Ontario, Canada. She received her PhD in modern European and women's and gender history from the University of North Carolina at Chapel Hill in 2012. Currently, she is completing a book manuscript tentatively titled "Reconciling Family and Work: Women's Emancipation and the West German Gendered Division of Labor, 1960s–1990s." Her publications include: "Mehr Wahlfreiheit für Mütter? Die westdeutsche Erziehungsgelddiskussion, die Emanzipation der Frau und die Arbeitsteilung nach Geschlecht in den 1970er und 1980er Jahren," in *Zeitgeschichte als Geschlechtergeschichte: Neue Perspektiven auf die Bundesrepublik* (ed. by Julia Paulus, Eva-Maria Silies and Kerstin Wolff, Campus Verlag, 2012). Furthermore, she recently published an article titled "'Thinking Green!' (and Feminist): Female Activism and the Greens from Wyhl to Bonn," in *German Politics and Society* 36, no. 4 (2018), and she has a forthcoming chapter in the volume *A History of the Family in Modern Germany* edited by Lisa Pine (Bloomsbury, 2019).

Notes

1. Renate Wiggershaus, *Geschichte der Frauen und der Frauenbewegung in der Bundesrepublik Deutschland und in der Deutschen Demokratischen Republik nach 1945* (Wuppertal, 1979); Myra Marx Ferree, "Equality and Autonomy: Feminist Politics in the United States and West Germany," in *The Women's Movements of the United States and Western Europe: Consciousness, Political Opportunity, and Public Policy*, ed. Mary Fainsod Katzenstein and Carol McClurg Mueller (Philadelphia, PA, 1987), 172–95; Florence Hervé, ed., *Geschichte der deutschen Frauenbewegung*, 3rd ed. (Cologne, 1987); Ute Gerhard, *Unerhört: Die Geschichte der deutschen Frauenbewegung* (Reinbek, 1990), and "Westdeutsche Frauenbewegung: Zwischen Autonomie und dem Recht auf Gleichheit," *Feministische Studien* 10, no. 2 (1992): 35–55, and *Atempause: Feminismus als demokratisches Projekt* (Frankfurt/M., 1999); Kristina Schulz, "Macht und Mythos von '1968': Zur Bedeutung der 68er Protestbewegungen für die Formierung der neuen Frauenbewegung in Frankreich und Deutschland," in *1968—Vom Ereignis zum Gegenstand der Geschichtswissenschaft*, ed. Ingrid Gilcher-Holtey (Göttingen, 1998), 256–72, and *Der lange Atem der Provokation: Die Frauenbewegung in der Bundesrepublik und in Frankreich 1968–1976* (Frankfurt/M., 2002); Gisela Notz, "Die Auswirkung der Studentenbewegung auf die Frauenbewegung," *Metis* 8, no. 16 (1999): 105–30;

and Myra Marx Ferree, *Varieties of Feminism: German Gender Politics in a Global Perspective* (Stanford, CA, 2012).
2. Gerhard, "Westdeutsche Frauenbewegung," 42.
3. Schulz, *Der lange Atem*, 79–96; Gisela Notz, "Die autonomen Frauenbewegungen der Siebzigerjahre: Entstehungsgeschichte—Organisationsformen—politische Konzepte," *Archiv für Sozialgeschichte* 44, (2004): 131–33; and Ferree, *Varieties of Feminism*, 83–110.
4. Lottemi Doormann, "Die neue Frauenbewegung: Zur Entwicklung seit 1968," in *Geschichte der deutschen Frauenbewegung*, ed. Hervé, 255–89; Schulz, *Der lange Atem*, 143–75; and Ferree, *Varieties*, 53–82.
5. The following histories of the Federal Republic acknowledge the transformative role of the New Women's Movement: Heinrich August Winkler, *Der Lange Weg nach Westen* (Munich, 2000); Konrad H. Jarausch, *After Hitler: Recivilizing Germany, 1945–1995* (New York, 2006); and Edgar Wolfrum, *Die geglückte Demokratie: Geschichte der Bundesrepublik Deutschland von ihren Anfängen bis zu Gegenwart* (Stuttgart, 2006).
6. Individualist or liberal feminists believe that individuals regardless of gender have equal rights, including an equal claim under the law to their own persons and property. Relational or maternal feminists believe that women as mothers and caregivers have an important, but distinctive role to play in society and in politics. They believe in women's autonomy as individuals, but always as women. See Karen Offen, *European Feminisms, 1700–1950: A Political History* (Stanford, CA, 2000), 20–23. Socialist feminists believe that the emancipation of women can only be achieved by ending both the economic and cultural oppression of women. See Elizabeth Lapovsky Kennedy, "Socialist Feminism: What Difference Did It Make to the History of Women's Studies?," *Feminist Studies* 34, no. 3 (2008): 497–525.
7. Elisabeth Zellmer, *Töchter der Revolte? Frauenbewegung und Feminismus in den 1970er Jahren in München* (Munich, 2011).
8. See Dorothy McBride Stetson and Amy Mazur, eds., *Comparative State Feminism* (Thousand Oaks, CA, 1995); and Dorothy E. McBride and Amy Mazur, eds., *The Politics of State Feminism: Innovation in Comparative Research* (Philadelphia, PA, 2010). Mazur and McBride are part of the *Research Network on Gender Politics and the State* (RNGS). See pppa.wsu.edu/research-network-on-gender-politics-and-the-state/ (10 May 2017).
9. Myra Marx Ferree, "Making Equality: The Women's Affair Offices in the Federal Republic of Germany," in *Comparative State Feminism*, ed. McBride Stetson and Mazur, 95–113; and Lynn Kamenitsa and Brigitte Geissel, "WPAs and Political Representation in Germany," in *State Feminism and Political Representation*, ed. Joni Lovenduski (Cambridge, 2005), 106–29. This concept of state feminism also informs Ingela K. Naumann, "Child Care and Feminism in West Germany and Sweden in the 1960s and 1970s," *Journal of European Social Policy* 15, no. 1 (2005): 47–63.
10. Naumann, "Child Care and Feminism," 48.
11. Myra Marx Ferree and Carol McClurg Mueller, "Feminism and the Women's Movement: A Global Perspective," in *The Blackwell Companion to Social Movements*, ed. David Snow, Sarah A. Soule, and Hanspeter Kriesi (New York, 2004), 576–607, 577.

12. See, for an overview, Angelika Schaser, *Frauenbewegung in Deutschland 1848–1933* (Darmstadt, 2006); on different movements, Ann Taylor Allen, *Feminism and Motherhood in Germany, 1800–1914* (New Brunswick, NJ, 1991); Jean H. Quataert, *Staging Philanthropy: Patriotic Women and the National Imagination in Dynastic Germany, 1813–1916* (Ann Arbor, MI, 2001); Nancy R. Reagin, *A German Women's Movement: Class and Gender in Hanover, 1880–1933* (Chapel Hill, NC, 1995); Gisela Breuer, *Frauenbewegung im Katholizismus: der Katholische Frauenbund 1903–1918* (Frankfurt/M., 1998); Jean H. Quataert, *Reluctant Feminists in German Social Democracy, 1885–1917* (Princeton, NJ, 1979); and Karen Hagemann, *Frauenalltag und Männerpolitik: Alltagsleben und gesellschaftliches Handeln von Arbeiterfrauen in der Weimarer Republik* (Bonn, 1990).
13. Frank Biess, *Homecomings: Returning POWs and the Legacies of Defeat in Postwar Germany* (Princeton, NJ, 2006), 97–125.
14. Christel Eckart, "Halbtags durch das Wirtschaftswunder: Die Entwicklung der Teilzeitarbeit in den sechziger Jahren," in *Grenzen der Frauenlohnarbeit: Frauenstrategien in Lohn- und Hausarbeit seit der Jahrhundertwende*, ed. Helgard Kramer, Christel Eckart and Ilka Riemann (Frankfurt/M., 1986), 183–249; Christine von Oertzen, *Teilzeitarbeit und die Lust am Zuverdienen: Geschlechterpolitik und gesellschaftlicher Wandel in Westdeutschland 1948–1969* (Göttingen, 1999); Monika Mattes, *"Gastarbeiterinnen" in der Bundesrepublik: Anwerbepolitik, Migration und Geschlecht in den 50er bis 70er Jahren* (Frankfurt/M., 2005).
15. Wiebke Kolbe, *Elternschaft im Wohlfahrtsstaat: Schweden und die Bundesrepublik im Vergleich 1945–2000* (Frankfurt/M., 2002), and "Kindeswohl und Müttererwerbstätigkeit: Expertenwissen in der schwedischen und bundesdeutschen Kinderbetreuungspolitik der 1960er- und 1970er-Jahre," *Traverse: Zeitschrift für Geschichte*, no. 2 (2001): 124–35; and Karen Hagemann, "A West German 'Sonderweg'? Family, Work, and the Half-Day Time Policy of Childcare and Schooling," in *Children, Families, and States: Time Policies of Childcare, Preschool, and Primary Education in Europe*, ed. Karen Hagemann, Konrad H. Jarausch and Cristina Allemann-Ghionda (New York, 2011), 275–301.
16. See, for example, Ursula Münch, *Familienpolitik in der Bundesrepublik Deutschland: Maßnahmen, Defizite, Organisation familienpolitischer Staatstätigkeit* (Freiburg/Br., 1990); Robert G. Moeller, *Protecting Motherhood: Women and the Family in the Politics of Postwar West Germany* (Berkeley, CA, 1993); Christiane Kuller, *Familienpolitik im föderativen Sozialstaat: die Formierung eines Politikfeldes in der Bundesrepublik 1949–1975* (Munich, 2004); and Kolbe, *Elternschaft*. The exception: Naumann, "Child Care and Feminism." For an overview from the nineteenth century to the present, see Karen Hagemann, Konrad H. Jarausch and Cristina Allemann-Ghionda, "Children, Families and States: Time Policies of Childcare and Education in a Comparative Historical Perspective," in ed. Hagemann et al., *Children, Families and States*, 3–50, 15–42.
17. See, for example, Gerhard, *Unerhört*; Schulz, *Der lange Atem*; and Ferree, *Varieties*.
18. Timothy Scott Brown, "1968 in West Germany: The Anti-Authoritarian Revolt," *The Sixties* 7, no. 2 (2014): 99–116, 100; and Wolfgang Kraushaar, *1968 als Mythos, Chiffre und Zäsur* (Hamburg, 2000).
19. Notz, "Auswirkung," 108–10; and Schulz, "Macht und Mythos."
20. Notz, "Auswirkung," 107–8.
21. See Hagemann, "A West German 'Sonderweg'?," 280.

22. "Bericht der Kindergarten-Gruppe Schöneberg," Frauenforschungs-, -bildungs- und informationszentrum, Berlin (FFBIZ), A/Rep. 400/20. Aktionsrat(2)/Berlin/Folder Handapp. Träger I, 2.
23. Ibid., 30
24. Zentralrat der sozialistischen Kinderläden, *Kinder im Kollektiv*, (Berlin, 1969), 2–3; Dagmar Herzog, *Sex after Fascism: Memory and Morality in Twentieth-Century Germany* (Princeton, NJ, 2005), 162–74; and Meike S. Baader, "Childhood and Happiness in German Romanticism, Progressive Education and in the West German Anti-Authoritarian Kinderläden Movement in the Context of 1968," *Paedagogica Historica: International Journal of the History of Education* 48, no. 3 (2012): 485–99.
25. "Bericht über die 1. große Veranstaltung des Frauenforums, München," *Information des Frauenforums*, no. 1 (1972), 2–7; Elisabeth Zellmer, "Danke für die Blumen, Rechte wären uns lieber! Das Frauenforum München e.V. 1971 bis 1975," in *Lieschen Müller wird politisch: Geschlecht, Staat und Partizipation im 20. Jahrhundert*, ed. Christine Hikel et al. (Munich, 2009), 115–26.
26. Lottemi Doormann, "Die neue Frauenbewegung in der Bundesrepublik: Geschichte—Tendenzen—Perspektiven," in *Keiner schiebt uns weg: Zwischenbilanz der Frauenbewegung in der Bundesrepublik*, ed. Lottemi Doormann (Weinheim, 1979), 64.
27. Ibid.
28. Frauenzeitschrift *Courage*, "Eine Selbstdarstellung der *Courage*-Frauen," in Doormann, *Keiner schiebt uns weg*, 261; and Bascha Mika, *Alice Schwarzer: Eine kritische Biographie* (Reinbek/Hamburg, 1998), 171–80.
29. Frauenzeitschrift *Courage*, "Eine Selbstdarstellung," 361.
30. "Im Januar 1977 sollen 200 000 Frauen penetriert werden," *Die Schwarze Botin*, no. 1 (1976): 36–37; and Mika, *Alice Schwarzer*, 171–80.
31. Hannelore Schröder, "Unbezahlte Hausarbeit, Leichtlohnarbeit, Doppelarbeit: Zusammenhänge und Folgen," in *Frauen als bezahlte und unbezahlte Arbeitskräfte: Beiträge zur Berliner Sommeruniversität für Frauen, Oktober 1977*, ed. Dokumentationsgruppe der Sommeruniversität für Frauen (Berlin, 1978), 108.
32. Gisela Bock, "Lohn für Hausarbeit und die Macht der Frauen: oder Feminismus und Geld" *Courage*, no. 1 (1976): 27–28.
33. Ibid.
34. Ibid., 28.
35. Karin Hausen, "Frauenerwerbstätigkeit und erwerbstätige Frauen: Anmerkung zur historischen Forschung," in *Frauen arbeiten: Weibliche Erwerbstätigkeit in Ost- und Westdeutschland nach 1945*, ed. Gunilla-Friederike Budde (Göttingen, 1997), 19–45; Oertzen, *Teilzeitarbeit*.
36. Statistisches Bundesamt Wiesbaden, *Statistisches Jahrbuch 1981 für die Bundesrepublik Deutschland* (Stuttgart, 1981), 105–7.
37. Alice Schwarzer, "Hausfrauenlohn?," *Emma*, no. 5 (1977): 3.
38. Gruppe "Lohn für Hausarbeit," Berlin, "Lohn für Hausarbeit: Offener Brief an Alice," *Courage*, no. 8 (1977): 38.
39. "Stern erniedrigt Frauen: Wir klagen an!," *Emma*, no. 7 (1978): 13.
40. Hannelore von der Leyen, "Fast über Nacht kam der Erfolg," *Stern*, no. 33, 1971, 58–64, and "Heidi Munte: Firmenchefin aus Passion," *Stern*, no. 34, 1971, 50–56, and "Aus dem Hobby machte Petra eine Karriere," *Stern*, no. 35, 1971,

58–65; and Ute Nauman, "Nach der Meisterprüfung wurde sie gleich Geschäftsführerin," *Brigitte*, no. 6, 1975, 76–78.
41. Heide Weidle and Michael Seuert, "Sind die Frauen zu blöd zum Fliegen?," *Stern*, no. 15, 1973, 80–84.
42. Christine Heide, "Notstand im deutschen Kindergarten," *Stern*, no. 41, 1972, 96–108, and "Mit dem Kind zur Arbeit," *Stern*, no. 42, 1972, 133–42, and "Eltern helfen Eltern," *Stern*, no. 43, 1972, 68–78.
43. "Selbstverständnis der Aktionsrats zur Befreiung der Frauen," FFBIZ, A/Rep. 400/20. Aktionsrat(1)/Berlin/Folder 1/; for an explanation of Marxist Feminism in the early autonomous women's movement, see Doormann, "Die neue Frauenbewegung," 43–49.
44. Anonymous, "Sozialistischer Frauenbund Westberlin (SFBW)," in *Wohin geht die Frauenbewegung? 22 Protokolle*, ed. Gisela Gassen (Frankfurt/M., 1981), 176.
45. "Jutta Menschik," *Pelagea: Materialien zur Frauenemanzipation*, no. 7/8 (1978): 6.
46. Karrin Hanshew, *Terror and Democracy in West Germany* (New York, 2012), 132–33.
47. Frigga Haug, "The Women's Movement in West Germany," *New Left Review*, no. 155 (1986): 58.
48. Schulz, *Der lange Atem*; Notz, "Frauenbewegungen"; and Ferree, *Varieties*.
49. "Election to the 7th German Bundestag on 19 November 1972," *The Federal Returning Officer*, www.bundeswahlleiter.de/en/bundestagswahlen/1972.html; and "Election to the 8th German Bundestag on 3 October 1976," *The Federal Returning Officer*, www.bundeswahlleiter.de/en/bundestagswahlen/1976.html (13 February 2017).
50. For SPD statistics, see Wolfgang Pausch, *Die Entwicklung der sozialdemokratischen Frauenorganisationen: Anspruch und Wirklichkeit innerparteilicher Gleichberechtigungsstrategien in der Sozialdemokratischen Partei Deutschlands, aufgezeigt am Beispiel der Arbeitsgemeinschaft sozialdemokratischer Frauen* (Frankfurt/M., 1985), 118, 142, 166. For CDU statistics, see Eva Kolinsky, *Women in West Germany: Life, Work, and Politics* (Oxford, 1989), 210.
51. Pausch, *Die Entwicklung*, 118, 142, and 166.
52. Sarah Elise Wiliarty, *The CDU and the Politics of Gender in Germany: Bringing Women to the Party* (New York, 2010), 85.
53. In the SPD, the shift of the majority from individual and socialist to relational feminism already happened in the 1920s; see Hagemann, *Frauenalltag und Männerpolitik*, 519–20.
54. Interview with Elfriede Eilers, in Renate Lepsius, *Frauenpolitik als Beruf: Gespräche mit SPD-Parlamentarierinnen* (Hamburg, 1987), 87–89.
55. Jürgen Reyer and Heidrun Kleine, *Die Kinderkrippe in Deutschland: Sozialgeschichte einer umstrittenen Einrichtung* (Freiburg/Br., 1997); Karen Hagemann, "Die Ganztagsschule als Politikum," *Zeitschrift für Pädagogik*, Beiheft 54 (2009): 209–29, and "A West German 'Sonderweg'?"
56. "Ergebnis der Familienpolitischen Konferenz" (1976), Archiv der sozialen Demokratie (Adsd), SPD-Parteivorstand (PV)/Referat Frauen/10322/.
57. Gisela Notz, *Mehr als bunte Tupfen im Bonner Männerclub: Sozialdemokratinnen im Deutschen Bundestag 1957–1969 mit 12 Biographien* (Bonn, 2007), 342–46.

58. While it is difficult to find gender-specific numbers, 65 percent of the 156,000 new SPD party members in 1972 were under the age of thirty-five; see Dietmar Süß, "Die Enkel auf den Barrikaden: Jungsozialisten in der SPD in den Siebzigerjahren," *Archiv für Sozialgeschichte* 44, (2004): 68.
59. Interview with Elfriede Eilers, 96; Pausch, *Die Entwicklung,* 172.
60. Pausch, *Die Entwicklung,* 172.
61. "Brief von Anni Jensen an Holger Börner-Vermerk," 1, AdsD, SPD-PV/Referat Frauen/10322.
62. "Gesetz zur Einführung eines Mutterschaftsurlaubs. Vom 25. Juni 1979," *Bundesgesetzblatt,* Teil I, Nr. 32, 798–802.
63. Moeller, *Protecting Motherhood.*
64. Wiliarty, *CDU and the Politics of Gender,* 89.
65. "Reden der Vorsitzenden der Frauenvereinigung der CDU zur Vorlage des Rechenschaftsberichts von Dr. Helga Wex," 9, Archiv für Christlich-Demokratische Politik, IV-003-069/2/.
66. Ibid., 274.
67. For the SPD, see "Ergebnis der Familienpolitischen Konferenz" (1976), Adsd, SPD-PV/Referat Frauen/10322/; for the CDU, see Helga Wex, "Politik für die Frau. Politische Aspekte zur Situation der Frau Heute," *Die Neue Ordnung* 27 (1973): 271.
68. Wex, "Politik für die Frau," 269.
69. Ibid.
70. *Protokoll 33. CDU-Bundesparteitag 20./22. März, Essen* (Bonn, 1985), 321–98.
71. Ibid., 328, 339.
72. "Gesetz über die Gewährung von Erziehungsgeld und Erziehungsurlaub (Bundeserziehungsgeldgesetz-BErzGG) vom 6. Dezember 1985," *Bundesgesetzblatt,* Teil I, Nr. 58, 2154–63.
73. Claudia Pinl, "Erziehungsgeld—ja oder nein?," *Emma,* no. 8 (1977): 23; and Helga Tölle, "Erziehungsgeld = Mutterschaftsurlaubgesetz?," *Frau und Arbeit,* no. 4/5 (1985): 1.
74. Michael Schneider, *A Brief History of the German Trade Unions* (Bonn, 1991).
75. Angelika Lippe, *Gewerkschaftliche Frauenarbeit: Parallelität ihrer Probleme in Frankreich und in der Bundesrepublik Deutschland 1949–1979* (Frankfurt/M., 1983), 119–20; and Deutscher Gewerkschaftsbund, *Da haben wir uns alle schrecklich geirrt: Die Geschichte der gewerkschaftlichen Frauenarbeit im Deutschen Gewerkschaftsbund von 1945 bis 1960* (Pfaffenweiler, 1993), 87.
76. Lippe, *Gewerkschaftliche Frauenarbeit,* 51–52.
77. "Antrag Nr. 44: Vereinbarkeit von Arbeitswelt, Familie und Gesellschaft," in *8. Bundesfrauenkonferenz des Deutschen Gewerkschaftsbundes am 9. und 10. Mai 1974 in Karlsruhe: Protokoll,* ed. DGB (Bochum, 1974), 328–29.
78. See for instance the debate over a federally funded nanny project, in "Protokoll Manuskript 8. Bundesfrauenkonferenz," 228–40, AdsD, DGB Bundesvorstand/Referat Frauen/4047/.
79. See Hagemann, "A West German 'Sonderweg'?"
80. "Antrag Nr. 44."
81. "Mutterschaftsurlaub Diskussion," 1–4, AdsD, DGB Bundesvorstand/Referat Frauen/4021/Transkript. Emphasis in original.

Selected Bibliography

Doormann, Lottemi, ed. *Keiner schiebt uns weg: Zwischenbilanz der Frauenbewegung in der Bundesrepublik.* Weinheim, 1979.
Ferree, Myra Marx. *Varieties of Feminism: German Gender Politics in a Global Perspective.* Stanford, CA, 2012.
Ferree, Myra Marx, and Carol McClurg Mueller. "Feminism and the Women's Movement: A Global Perspective." In *The Blackwell Companion to Social Movements,* ed. David Snow, Sarah A. Soule, and Hanspeter Kriesi, 576–607. New York, 2004.
Gerhard, Ute. *Unerhört: Die Geschichte der deutschen Frauenbewegung.* Reinbek, 1990.
———. "Westdeutsche Frauenbewegung: Zwischen Autonomie und dem Recht auf Gleichheit." *Feministische Studien* 10, no. 2 (1992): 35–55.
———. *Atempause: Feminismus als Demokratisches Projekt.* Frankfurt/M., 1999.
Hagemann, Karen. "Between Ideology and Economy: The 'Time Politics' of Child Care and Public Education in the Two Germanys." *Social Politics* 13, no. 2 (2006): 217–60.
Hervé, Florence, ed. *Geschichte der deutschen Frauenbewegung.* 3rd ed. Cologne, 1987.
Kolbe, Wiebke. *Elternschaft im Wohlfahrtsstaat: Schweden und die Bundesrepublik im Vergleich 1945–2000.* Frankfurt/M., 2002.
Lapovsky Kennedy, Elizabeth. "Socialist Feminism: What Difference Did It Make to the History of Women's Studies?" *Feminist Studies* 34, no. 3 (2008): 497–525.
Mazur, Amy, and Dorothy E. McBride. *Comparative State Feminism.* Thousand Oaks, CA, 1995.
McBride, Dorothy E., Joni Lovenduski, and Amy Mazur. *The Politics of State Feminism: Innovation in Comparative Research.* Philadelphia, PA, 2010.
Naumann, Ingela K. "Child Care and Feminism in West Germany and Sweden in the 1960s and 1970s." *Journal of European Social Policy* 15, no. 1 (2005): 47–63.
Notz, Gisela. "Die autonomen Frauenbewegungen der Siebzigerjahre: Entstehungsgeschichte—Organisationsformen—politische Konzepte." *Archiv für Sozialgeschichte* 44 (2004): 123–48.
———. *Mehr als bunte Tupfen im Bonner Männerclub: Sozialdemokratinnen im Deutschen Bundestag 1957–1969.* Bonn, 2007.
Offen, Karen. *European Feminisms, 1700–1950: A Political History.* Stanford, CA, 2000.
Schaser, Angelika. *Frauenbewegung in Deutschland 1848–1933.* Darmstadt, 2006.
Schulz, Kristina. "Macht und Mythos von '1968': Zur Bedeutung der 68er Protestbewegungen für die Formierung der neuen Frauenbewegung in Frankreich und Deutschland." In *1968—Vom Ereignis zum Gegenstand der Geschichtswissenschaft,* ed. Ingrid Gilcher-Holtey, 256–72. Göttingen, 1998.
———. *Der lange Atem der Provokation: Die Frauenbewegung in der Bundesrepublik und in Frankreich 1968–1976.* Frankfurt/M., 2002.
Wiggershaus, Renate. *Geschichte der Frauen und der Frauenbewegung in der Bundesrepublik Deutschland und in der Deutschen Demokratischen Republik nach 1945.* Wuppertal, 1979.
Wiliarty, Sarah Elise. *The CDU and the Politics of Gender in Germany: Bringing Women to the Party.* New York, 2010.
Zellmer, Elisabeth. *Töchter der Revolte? Frauenbewegung und Feminismus in den 1970er Jahren in München.* Munich, 2011.

CHAPTER 9

Redefining the Political

The Gender of Activism in Grassroots Movements of the 1960s to 1980s

Belinda Davis

What was the West German women's movement, and how should we position it relative to the larger extraparliamentary and alternative political movement? Was it defined by the fierce—and partially successful—demand for reproductive choice that coalesced in the early 1970s? Does its essence lie in women's frustration with men's dominating habits in the "student movement" of the late 1960s? Was it about the pragmatic need for childcare? Is it best represented by separatist groupings of the 1970s: women's centers, "self-discovery" groups, lesbian living communities, even the constitution of lives lived entirely among women only? By readers of feminist magazines *Emma*, or *Courage*? All of these constitute pieces of the movement but only limited parts thereof. Moreover, for all its concrete, specific achievements for women—indeed because of its larger achievements—"the" West German women's movement is deserving of attention too for its significant role in the broader contemporary extraparliamentary opposition (Außerparlamentarische Opposition, APO). Like that umbrella movement, in turn, the women's movement is worth thinking about as a process taking place over the course of many years, across a great breadth of experience, and through a wide diversity of action. This chapter argues that the West German women's movement—and its antecedents in actions prior to this designation from 1968—were deeply entangled with the APO from the early 1960s to the early 1980s. This entangled character is critical to understanding the women's movement, its influences, and its impact. The idea that the women's movement arose out of, and in part in protest against, the student movement and broader APO is hardly new. Likewise, there has been attention to the importance of the women's movement within the sphere of alternative politics in the 1970s. This chapter highlights the entanglements and examines their particular character. The city of West Berlin was a bastion of alternative politics from early on, though only one of innumerable loci of activity and action. However, within this chapter, it provides a site of especial focus.[1]

Scholarship on the new women's movement in West Germany has been penned mostly by social scientists and contemporary participants.[2] Historians have only recently taken up the subject, as they have the social movements of the 1970s more broadly.[3] There is little historical attention to date on the relationship between the women's movement, however defined, and broader oppositional politics. Yet attention to these relations helps uncover their generative if often tense character. It strengthens our understanding of the lack of hard boundaries between and among these movements. This intended permeability of any organizational boundaries both attracted feminists and was further developed by them in influential ways.

The chapter proceeds in four sections. The first section addresses the difficulty for activists, and particularly women activists, to speak out for themselves in a group, and of their discomfort with another, usually a man, speaking for them. The second examines many women's focus on themselves, and the relationships they forged, as both the object and subject of activism, and their insistent claims that this was itself politics: an important and effective politics. The third section considers sources of political knowledge and expertise, tracing how women in particular challenged not only the authority of individual political leaders but also the privileging of particular theories, especially totalizing theories, over their own experience and attendant transformations in thinking. In each case, I explore how some women responded, *as* women (by their own characterization), to remedy the perceived problem—being able to speak for themselves, to protest on their own behalf, to value their own experience and perceptions—in a fashion with broad implications for the practice of popular politics. These remedies were influential and worth understanding. But contemporaries themselves found their solutions no panaceas; their experiments often reflected rehearsal of the same or even new problems. This in turn suggests the lessons of the concluding section, which examine how the very contradictions, missteps, and even failures of women's activism and others' represented a key "learning process" for activists, for their own time and beyond.

Speaking Out, Speaking for Oneself

It is conventional wisdom that the West German women's movement emerged as protest against the student movement and APO. Many women found their male activist counterparts far too willing to step on their words, even to ignore them entirely. Women often saw the (usually male) leaders of oppositional groups as dominating, imposing a hierarchical structure. "The men were as bad as their fathers," former activist Teresa B. observed of the Socialist German Student League (Sozialistischer Deutscher Studentenbund, SDS) in Marburg, "in ignoring women, in cutting off other speakers, in posturing as authorities."[4] Women also unwillingly found their views represented by "spokesmen" (*Wortführer*), often self-identified, or even identified from the outside. Thus, women began to organize among themselves by the late 1960s, represented in iconic founding moments of "the women's movement" in West Germany: for example, the formation of the Action Council for the Liberation of Women (Aktionsrat zur Befreiung der Frauen, Aktionsrat) in January 1968, and of the Women's Council (Weiberrat) Frankfurt am Main.[5] Yet the move represented no abandonment of the APO or even specifically the student movement. These women (many of them nonstudents) drew heavily on what they thought worked well in their mixed-gender activist experience. They also contributed significantly, through their ideas as well as their activism, to the broader, ongoing movement.

Women first expressed their concerns to their male counterparts within these groups. Yet activist men—and even some women—were dismissive of these concerns, particularly throughout the 1960s. Rainer Langhans, former executive board member of the SDS chapter at the Free University of Berlin (FU Berlin), declared in retrospect that the men in the SDS were "already the most enlightened and the best there were in the [Federal] Republic, [. . .] because they were the least authoritarian. And, despite that, it was too little for the women." Katharina Rutschky, Langhans's contemporary in the SDS and later critic of the new women's movement, agreed with him. The problem for her, rather, was women who "let themselves be intimidated," she claimed. "I always told them, '*You* have to do something against it.'" If women felt they were being silenced, if they felt relegated to only typing up the words of men, it was their own issue. "*I* didn't let myself be pressured into 'women's roles' [. . .], and the friends I had were likewise not so fixated on such roles." This was a problem young women themselves brought to political groupings, and needed to address for themselves.

Indeed many activist men had also experienced difficulties with speech and self-expression. Rainer Langhans, long identified as a "leader" of the student movement, had spent years in virtual silence. He grew up feeling he was "the milkman's son" (*Kuckuckskind*): "very alone and very alienated," he "found no way there to myself." When he determined to attend university, his speechlessness followed. "For a year and a half I practically didn't speak at all." Yet Langhans claimed to see this as his own problem to solve. He began a "self-training" in the FU SDS. "I only listened, I only wrote, I let myself be taught." He voraciously worked through the SDS reading list, to make himself an "expert." "And there, for the first time [. . .], [I] eliminated my speechlessness, learned there to speak before many people, with the *greatest effort*." This self-training in speech was the basis for "doing something"; it was a step in the direction of making political change. Langhans believed that the task of bringing himself to speak, interact with others, and share opinions with them lay entirely within himself.

Activist women acknowledged, or came to acknowledge, the tendencies they also brought with them. Marianne Herzog, one of the founders of the Aktionsrat, noted that in the war and postwar period, girls especially had "learned early to shut up."[6] Jeanne T. offered a notable case in point. "As a child in school in the first years [. . .] I virtually never spoke [. . .] I also had a speech impediment. I couldn't say 'I,' *I couldn't say 'I.'*" Her pained efforts over years to use her voice thus provoked in her a particularly strong reaction when, as a traveling sidewalk artist, she dropped in on a reading group of the SDS in Munich in 1967. As she finally screwed up her courage to join the discussion, a man jumped forward to speak, and she withdrew. "I was completely furious" at the dominating voice that had seemed to step on her own. She regarded as "fucked up" those who simply "overpowered the discussion [. . .]. I wanted nothing to do with them." She and other women recognized their difficulties. But simply working on their own ability to speak out was not the whole answer. The much-touted "solidarity" that activists called for was also about listening to others; it was also about transforming *relationships,* young women insisted, which necessitated a broader effort.

This was the discovery of activist women in Frankfurt am Main who in autumn 1968 formed the Weiberrat, dedicated both to providing space for women's voices and to pointing up inequities in gender relations within "mixed" alternative political settings. Susanne T. found in the Weiberrat an unleashing of energies, a means of realizing her own activist potential through the relations she developed with the others. "I really do well only in groups of women," she concluded, "and as long as men are around, it's just crap." Members' own "self-training" also came in the form of adopting male "aggressiveness" that, some observed with ambivalence, was turned back on fellow activist men.[7] This was most notable in the group's notorious November 1968 "statement of accounts," which they mimeographed and widely distributed. The Weiberrat began their rhyming statement by claiming "we don't open our traps"—and ending it with a call for "the socialist eminences" to be "liberated from their bourgeois dicks."[8] Weiberrat participants claimed this "provo" (provocative) act was a mark of their frustration and a means of making themselves heard. But it "could have been predicted" that male fellow activists reacted only with their own "fury, chaotically and in aggressive-authoritarian fashion." The initial result was that "the women" felt "obligated to silence" anew.

Yet, participants in the Weiberrat argued in 1970, the "statement of accounts" was only an initial gesture, mirroring men's own practices. They insisted—or came to insist—that their ends were improved forms of group communications with men, in order to be able to work with them politically. "Back at home, we worked on it further," developing their own skills, aiding one another, listening to one another, and later sharing their "report" on this work with others.[9] Then they returned to the SDS in a public show of this "solidarity" among themselves.

> For the first time, all the female "comrades" [*die Genossinnen*] sat together in a corner at the SDS member assembly, and one could observe that the male "comrades" [*die Genossen*] quickly perceived this as a demonstration of power. When a woman made a contribution, she was listened to. In addition, she was much more secure herself, because she knew she had the other women behind her, and because she knew that another would help her in a pinch.[10]

In the coming years, however, in hundreds of iterations daily, women activists insisted there had to be more. They pushed to rework the terms of gendered interaction—and of group interaction generally—challenging power relations in group dynamics. They took the matter further still. Women's unfavorable position within activist groups was not just a hindrance to carrying out politics, they argued. It was itself a political question, a challenge to the adequacy of even such alternative forms as the SDS and other extraparliamentary groupings claimed to represent, to accommodate the political right to self-expression. It was not only women who raised such challenges, but, as a group, they presented the most formidable and effective force over time for the rethinking of alternative politics in West Germany. This effect is evident in increasingly commonplace experiments in forming and developing "equitable and compassionate" bonds—as a politics of personal life—and communal work as a central means to "revolutionize the bourgeois individual."[11]

The challenge concerned not only interpersonal relations in political groupings. It also encompassed conventional forms of political "leadership" and "representation," also hierarchical organization. Women argued this point through words and action, in and out of contexts that came to be defined as "the new women's movement" even before the concept existed. Eva Quistorp, who visited the FU SDS while a nurse's aide in West Berlin in 1965, found herself unable to break her silence among what she perceived as the intimidating men in the SDS. Yet she felt inspired by the example of other women there, such as leading student activists Sigrid Fronius, Sigrid Rüger, and Ines Lehmann. These women did not themselves start out as outspoken, seemingly confident participants. Fronius had faced her own explicit challenge in "autonomy training from the parental house," to free herself from debilitating "inhibitions."[12] By the time Quistorp saw them in action, these women exemplified models of leadership often different from the men in the SDS. Quistorp found it "totally important for me" to see these women "publicly advocating" in the group. They led with "precisely none of the airs of those throwing their weight around" but rather with "expert knowledge," she insisted. They did not commandeer meetings but rather "mediated," facilitating discussions through careful attention to different voices. Soon, Quistorp challenged conventional forms of political organization and leadership altogether. She determined to "avoid being seduced by a narrow pressure toward the group." "I didn't belong to SDS—and to its leaders—and didn't have to liberate myself from the feeling of having to be an insider." By eschewing "membership" in conventional political groupings, she was neither a "leader" nor a "mute, conformist lemming" (*Mitläufervieh*). Such characterizations were among the many uttered by contemporaries that referenced a transcendence of the Nazi past that underlay many activists' debates. Quistorp experimented with other means of political engagement, seeking a new balance between "solidarity" and maintaining her own voice. Evolving understanding of forms of political engagement, emerging from often-gendered experience and solutions, contributed ultimately to a radical unraveling of typical patterns of popular politics in the era and the creation of new models.

In successfully transforming themselves and simultaneously demanding more of others, these activist women, as women, contributed to reworking notions of politics and to opening to question the forms and practices of politics. Their impact is visible across the alternative politics of the late 1960s and the 1970s, in the "network" practices of political belonging, in the politics of everyday life in shared apartments (*Wohngemeinschaften*, WGs) and elsewhere. But was this work a definitive success? The Weiberrat "report" from 1970 adopts a triumphant tone, depicting the group's demonstrable effects in precipitating a transformation of their participation in mixed-gender groups.[13] Was the secret sauce for rectifying inequitable relations within mixed-gender groups simply a "demonstration of power" among women as well as men, as the report writer seemed to assert? Had they remade the status quo or simply successfully accommodated themselves to it?

Eva Quistorp's ongoing political career poses similar questions. Based on her experiences in the SDS, she preferred an antihierarchical leadership style, which she also tried to practice as the cofounder and leader of a number of political groupings throughout the 1970s and 1980s, from Women for Peace (Frauen für den Frieden) and the antinuclear Women of Gorleben (Gorleben Frauen) to several other such initiatives. Quistorp insisted that in these initiatives she and other participants defied conventional structures. Her co-"coordinat[ed]" 1980 petition drive, titled "Incitement of Women to Peace" (*Anstiftung der Frauen zum Frieden*), offers an example of such efforts, on paper, at least. The incitement "announced [. . .] that we want to practice civil disobedience." It ended with the call, "We women incite for freedom!/We will not organize ourselves in rank and file,/We dance out of line!"[14] The reference to rank and file referred directly to an unwillingness to serve in the military (for which some women advocated) but also unwillingness to join any such organization. Yet what of her own leadership practices? What of the practice of women-only groups? Were these groupings all successful examples of these developing political ideas?

Working on Oneself/Working for Oneself

In her speech to the 1968 SDS convention in Frankfurt am Main, Helke Sander talked about women's frequent sense of feeling "lesser"—and being treated as lesser—in groups with men.[15] Patriarchy's power within even alternative political groupings sometimes drove women out of such groups. Women's desire to congregate just among themselves was, however, spurred not only by deep frustration in groups with men. It also originated in actively positive impulses, interests that too came to define the women's movement. At the same time, women-only settings were rarely feminists' sole outlets for political activity and expression even at any single moment, not to mention over the course of the 1970s.[16] Still, no matter how typical they were, such settings offered women the opportunity to work closely together—and develop relationships—with others who shared powerful gender-specific life experiences, through WGs and "communes," cooperative childcare, and women's health centers. They founded women's centers that brought together study groups and theme-related action groups; magazine editorial collectives and presses; film clubs, cafes, and cabarets. In work that was pragmatic and drawn from their own experience—and inspired indeed by ideas of a New Left—many activist women set themselves as both the agents and subjects of change. As a group, they constituted a formidable force against creeping theoretical orthodoxies within alternative activism in 1970s West Germany. The work women accomplished in these settings specifically brought about deep, even radical changes in political thinking that profoundly influenced the larger alternative movement.

These ventures frequently began with common, often concrete circumstances that might prevent women from devoting their attention, for example, to the peasants of Vietnam: circumstances such as caring for their families; addressing an unwanted pregnancy; even grappling with the psychological burden of unwanted sexual advances or comments on their bodies. Many feminists proudly identified political pragmatism as a hallmark of the new women's movement. Helke Sander depicted this in stark relief in her fictionalized filmic account of the origins of the women's movement in West Berlin, the 1981 film *Der subjektive Faktor* (The Subjective Factor). The title itself works as a double entendre suggesting both that the film comes from her own perspective, as a woman, and that the self, the individual subject, is a critical site of change. In a key scene, protagonist Anni is pushed into the role of making coffee during a political meeting in her WG living room.[17] The other women present join her. Together in the kitchen, the women turn their effective ghettoization into a second political meeting. They address the fact that childcare leaves them no time for politics or any other pieces of their lives. They draw up an initial solution, both practical and politically significant, while the men in the living room continue their unproductive discussion about how to advance the interests of the Viet Cong in West Berlin and thereby "make revolution" in the West. The women-only meeting hints too at a critical characteristic of the range of relationships, actions, and manifestations of what got called the women's movement. That is, they started with themselves as the "revolutionary subject," the focus of their own efforts. Drawing on New Left thinking threatened with extinction by a reemerging traditional left focus on the working class by the end of the 1960s, these feminists in turn acted on these ideas, which began to take off throughout the alternative movement.

Their experiments, like those focused on relations, contributed to rethinking the content of politics by defining the personal as political. They further worked to redefine the political subject as a piece of an integrated subjectivity. It was in the context of individual self-discovery, through and with the help of other women, that Sabine M., cofounder of the feminist magazine *Courage*, claimed that she came to "the women's movement" as much as anything for "this activity (*Regsamkeit*) for one's own life feeling (*Lebensgefühl*), through friendship with other women." The appeal of the movement's more conventionally understood political content, such as the fight for reproductive choice, "was actually much less" a draw for her, notwithstanding her active work in more conventional political arenas. "One didn't access [the movement] through the articulation of 'political' goals"—in any conventional sense, at least. "Perhaps this was adequate, but it doesn't satisfactorily contain it all, I think. Yes, because this 'politicization' was also a bodily thing, and precisely not just cognitive, and not just against [. . .] §218, or whatever, it seems to me." Yet this was no less "pragmatic," no less concrete, for its highly emotional nature. Sabine found this a "beautiful awakening" to self-transformation and even self-integration.

> [T]his affection toward [. . .] other women [. . .] that one got, and this, this discovery for oneself that was possible through discussion with the other women, that was one of the greatest gifts that we had in our generation [. . .] a fire for the feeling of being alive [*Lebensgefühl*] [. . .] [I]t had something almost corporeal about it. [. . .] [T]his *enjoyment,* [. . .] that one is independent from men and one can just send them away, feeling at once both forms of independence and voluntary dependency.[18]

This focus on the self may sound more like a psychological palliative for a still-damaged society than a recipe for political action. To be sure, that is what many activist men especially thought, especially early on.[19] Yet these women came to claim that such experiments not only cleared the path to politics for some but also constituted in themselves a piece of political practice. Examining and even transforming the self (well beyond working to be able to speak in public) as a method to creating a revolution had a long history by then, stretching back at least to the French Revolution and through the early Soviet Union. In 1966 West Germany, future members of Kommune 1 and Kommune 2 congregated in a Bavarian farmhouse to work out how to transform themselves into a revolutionary vanguard that would help other peoples in the world by casting off "bourgeois" needs and desires.[20] Maoist groups (*K-Gruppen*) took up the charge of creating a vanguard in the 1970s. Many explicitly feminist efforts also drew on such examples and likewise foregrounded self-transformation, but in a form that rather embraced their own needs and desires as a piece of the revolution itself. Such women sought above all to integrate alienated parts of the self: mind and body, reason and emotion, political interests and the rest of life. This, along with the concomitant rebuilding of interpersonal relationships, went beyond even protests for reproductive rights in entirely redefining politics.

These experiments were useful too for questioning newly hardening ideologies that bore little relation to everyday realities. At the beginning of the 1970s, most male activists did not accept that they possessed structural and cultural privilege over women as a group. Yet, those who were active and former university students in particular felt deeply conflicted over their position vis-à-vis "the working class." Internalizing the charges of mainstream media and broad public attitudes that ridiculed "privileged students" and their protests, many found the notion of looking within themselves as a form of politics to be uncomfortable, self-indulgent, and absurd. From the end of the 1960s through the mid-1970s, swaths of the activist community increasingly focused their attention on recruiting workers to the cause of revolution, as well as to anti-imperialist campaigns. For many women activists particularly, however, introspection and acting politically on behalf of oneself felt like a growing imperative in the late 1960s and early 1970s. It was a means of connecting widespread feelings of "unworthiness" with the threat of violence in a range of forms, from legal controls enacted over women's bodies to customary behavior that likewise challenged women's control, to rape and physical violence (and the perceived threat thereof). The extraordinary reception of *Häutungen* (Moltings), Verena Stefan's 1975 bestselling volume of personal writings, suggests that Stefan's own experiences of fighting off unwanted male attention, and her concomitant sense of alienation from her body and from her own feelings, resonated widely with women.[21] As earlier, most feminists accepted that long-term sources of psychological "deformations" contributed to their perceptions and even to their self-presentation within alternative political groupings.[22] This was all the more reason to constitute themselves, among others, as subjects of their own political action.

Many activist men rejected this conclusion, however. In their view, the claim and exploration of the West German female self as a subject of oppression was suspicious, even "counterrevolutionary." Thus Verena Stefan courted opprobrium in her provocative assertion that she was, as a woman, "a colonized person in the city of the first world." Stefan acknowledged that her living and working conditions may have generally been better than, for example, the two men, both foreigners, who surrounded her one day in Berlin's Wittenberg Place. "But any German or foreign man can daily and hourly somehow abuse [women], regardless of his living and work circumstances. Do I have better living conditions because in particular circumstances I have a nicer apartment than my rapist?" Why, then, was it important to work in a factory or to protest on behalf of the Vietnamese but not to work on oneself, indeed, act for oneself? This latter was just what was necessary in order to refuse to men the right to render definitive judgment on the question.[23]

Yet, already in her speech at the 1968 SDS convention, Helke Sander emphasized that the issue was not just about women but, for all, about making one's own life the starting point of politics and recognizing the possibility of profound change through this means. It was a question of concreteness, of specificity. And it was about addressing one's own humanness, refusing to subjugate it to some magical theory or abstract orthodoxy. Addressing the men in the sea of SDS delegates, Sander asked in September 1968,

> Why don't you all finally just say that you're completely done in by this last year, that you don't know how much longer you can handle the stress of exerting yourself, body and mind, without even the gain of any pleasure to attach to it? Why don't you actually discuss before your next campaigns how exactly you might carry them out? Why do you even bother to buy [work by Wilhelm] Reich? And why do you speak here, then, of the class struggle—and at home of your trouble with your orgasms?[24]

These men could not see how mired they were in these thought processes, she argued, commingled with their unreflected "competitiveness," saturation in particular power relations, and a sadly misguided mission of "productivity," all arising out of the hegemonic ideology they sought to expose, criticize, and transcend. These insensitivities left them all but ineffectual, she claimed: just a combination of "helplessness and arrogance" that was indeed "no especial fun." Men's big ideas with no basis in practical, meaningful action, Sander averred, their very inability to listen and learn from such arguments as hers, rendered them, in her memorable locution, "inflated counterrevolutionary yeast dough," puffed up with air but no content.[25] Sander insisted that what she proposed was conversely a truly "radical" politics.

Sander kept up her broader critique of activism that grew out of abstract ideas with little material basis in the present, blinding men especially to knowledge born of their own experience. In 1968, she and other members of the Aktionsrat began their own work setting up storefront daycare collectives (*Kinderläden*), initially intended to provide mothers with a meaningful, regularized break from childcare. The idea was, however, also to aid in rearing children without the deforming problems of their parents and, ultimately, to provide parents too with a setting through which to pursue understanding of and change within themselves.[26] The idea spread quickly within the city, and soon mothers set up a council linking West Berlin *Kinderläden* all together, through which they could share ideas and other resources. Sander then remonstrated that, in this instance, far from keeping their distance from this concrete "women's" project, men barged their way into *Kinderläden* council meetings and tried to take over at the citywide level. Among other things, men tried to insist that the collectives push local immigrant parents to send their children to *Kinderläden*. Sander asked why it was not enough for participants to work on their own children—and on themselves. And could they not see how counterproductive and even harmful it could be for Turkish and (other) working-class toddlers to join the *Kinderläden,* "where they would learn behavior for which they would be punished in their own homes"?[27] These men's very response, Sander and other feminists intimated, was a product of their entrapment in modernist political thinking. The men privileged particular forms of knowledge—for example, theoretical models of how things were supposed to happen, how revolutionary change would come about—and then applied them without knowing a situation, without even knowing themselves.[28] Working for oneself, often on concrete and even personal problems, was politics, these women argued. It was, here once more, politics of the sort that could actually produce radical change within a foreseeable future, in contrast to imagined apocalyptic revolutions of the proletariat.[29]

At the same time, the range of women-only experiments remained as instructive for what did not work as for what did—and, unsurprisingly, there was much that did not. Wiebke S., who shared in Sabine M.'s all-woman WG, waxed rhapsodic at its early successes; she concluded with a laugh, "The disappointments that were to come—I didn't know about those yet!" As intense and thrilling as Wiebke S. found the experience of living in a WG with only women, and in working with the *Courage* magazine collective, she quickly came to challenge any imagined "women's" character and ability to work together. The women's WG was no utopian paradise. Housemates frequently came into conflict, "though more about the structure [. . .] not about politics. More about a bass line that was too loud, or the soap that was somehow lying wrong," Wiebke S. laughed. Of course, as the women's movement demonstrated, the perception of soap lying "wrong" was itself worthy of political consideration. Within the *Courage* collective too, Wiebke S. "was twice in some kind of *enormous* conflict. On the side [. . .] of the minority, and I felt very attacked." Despite the "women's connectedness" (*Frauenzusammenhang*, another movement neologism), there was "no real prescription against" even this "informal hierarchy formation."

Just how unifying was the category of "woman"? Some observed bitterly that motherhood was the litmus test for "women's issues." Battles broke out between lesbian and straight women. There were corrosive conflicts over feminism, its goals, and its forms between the *Courage* collective and "*Emma* feminists," as the former dismissively described the editors and readers of a rival magazine with a different understanding of feminism. As feminist activist Ursula Nienhaus wrote, "*one* women's center could not speak for all women."[30] West Germans were among early cohorts of feminist activists to grapple with the limits of what the category of woman could offer—and to think through the anti-utopian implications of those limits.

Working from Oneself: "Theory," Knowledge, Expertise, and Experience

As for many self-identified feminists, issues of knowledge and expertise continued to preoccupy Helke Sander into the 1970s. This is manifest in Sander's codirected 1972 documentary *Macht die Pille frei?* (Does the Pill Make One Free?), based on a group interview with young women of diverse backgrounds and ages.[31] One might have thought that the oral contraceptives introduced into West Germany in 1961 would have represented an unmitigated good for women, in just the personal and concrete ways many activist women sought: freeing them from the fear of unwanted pregnancy, putting them in control of their own bodies. And yet the women in Sanders's documentary paint a far more ambivalent portrait depending on one's relation to knowledge, or what counted as knowledge, and to expertise.

The documentary's interview subjects spoke freely and plainly, surprisingly confident in broaching this sensitive topic among themselves, despite the rolling camera. Yet they addressed their difficulty in communicating about the subject with others: their sexual partners, their parents, and their doctors (most often men). They too felt "unworthy" when asking their doctors—these "demigods," sources of expertise and authority—for what they needed. Many worried about the safety of the Pill yet saw their questions summarily dismissed. They commiserated in their frustration of trying to "explain over and again" to doctors their concerns about the side effects of the Pill, such as migraines, cramps, and circulation disorders. Doctors responded only by "shov[ing] prescriptions" at them and waving them out. Women described doctors' treatment of their bodies as equally unengaged, as if their bodies were somehow embarrassing. These women had no access to their doctors' knowledge. Conversely, their own knowledge, of their bodies' symptoms, of what they read on their own, seemed to count for nothing.

Many feminists considered unacceptable that others cast them as unable to understand or as unworthy of comprehending "expert" knowledge, and as not bearing valuable expertise of their own. They claimed for themselves the ability and right to their own knowledge and to critically assess that of others.[32] Informative "self-help" books about women's health issues became increasingly popular in the early 1970s. One of the most widespread was the 1972 *Frauenhandbuch Nr. 1: Abtreibung und Verhütungsmittel* (Women's Handbook No. 1: Abortion and Contraceptives), published by the West Berlin based women's group *Brot und Rosen* (Bread and Roses).[33] One year later, Dagmar Schultz cofounded the first Feminist Women's Health Center in West Berlin. She brought back with her from the United States the practice of examining one's own sexual organs, inside and out, using mirrors and cheap plastic specula to learn more about one's own body. At first, she met with resistance. Yet this experiment contributed to an ongoing change in the thinking among feminists about their bodies.[34] By the time that *Courage* featured Monika M. Schmid on the cover in 1977, simply holding a speculum, the practice was widely known in feminist circles, even if the magazine cover remained "shocking" for outsiders.[35] This fit with the proclaimed mission of the magazine, which aimed to provide information not easily found elsewhere. It offered the material through the words of women, to validate "women's knowledge," in all its forms, and to legitimize their ability to make themselves their own experts. That women became their own experts, able to control their "own affairs," defined their "radical perspective."[36]

Such enterprises in pursuit of change, multiplied throughout the women's movement, had a number of effects. First, they continued and deepened the paths New Left activists had begun to forge already by the early 1960s, in challenging the irrefragable knowledge of experts in government, the churches, the media, and otherwise: not only authorities' possession of the correct answers but their hold over what should be known at all. They questioned all the more the "common sense" of how things were to be done in West German society: how soap needed to lie in a soap dish. Secondly, they opened up to rethinking hardening forms of even "alternative" knowledge, in the form of left ideologies, and the "political education" (*Schulung*) that activists in many groups were required to undertake under watchful eyes. Such hardening had spread from many chapters of the SDS, through its dissolution in 1970, into the new political parties—among them the East German–oriented German Communist Party (Deutsche Kommunistische Partei, DKP), refounded in 1968, and the plethora of Maoist groups—that captured tens of thousands of activists especially in the first half of the 1970s. Yet dogmatic thinking and practice were hardly limited to these venues. In 1969, members of Kommune 2 wrote of how their collective self-exploration, and the very effort to find the self as expert, had led at times to a questionably "inquisitorial atmosphere."[37] Charges of dogmatism flew thick and fast within the broad women's movement itself. Anna F., who had left the DKP student organization because of increasingly oppressive dogmatism, initially found more of the same within the "radical feminist movement" (despite her dutiful donning of self-dyed purple overalls, the feminist sartorial symbol). Though counting herself a feminist, she determined that the movement somehow "didn't correspond to [her] own life situation."[38]

Was this a sign of the failure of the women's movement—and of the alternative movement more broadly—to ultimately transcend the practices and structures they criticized in society and politics at large? Contemporary youth psychologist Jörg Bopp did not see it this way. He found that this shift in thinking in the era both informed and represented the success of the extraparliamentary movement broadly. These activists, he wrote, refused to follow the routes on the societal map that their elders set them on and, indeed, resisted efforts "to drive them back to those correct paths, with strength and pitiless severity." They went even further, he argued, redrawing the very maps themselves, insisting on the legitimacy of their own experience and what it taught them, asserting their own forms of "expert" knowledge, as well as claiming for themselves other, more accepted forms of knowledge.[39] This was notable in Dagmar Schultz's introduction in West Germany of the newly developed practice of "menstrual extraction," through which women as nonmedical professionals could easily learn to safely induce early term abortions by using a manually operated vacuum aspiration apparatus to empty the uterus. This became a significant means to get an abortion when abortions were still illegal in the early 1970s.[40]

This variety of forms of "expert" knowledge was essential moreover in protestors' successive political wins against the erection of a nuclear power plant in tiny, rural Wyhl, a municipality in Baden-Württemberg, beginning in 1975. An impressive coalition of longtime movement activists and others gathered knowledge from consultation with nuclear scientists and with local farmers concerning their own crops. With this knowledge, activists stood toe-to-toe against officials, corporate builders, and their team of experts, ultimately winning in the court of public opinion. These activists also inspired protest at other facilities.[41] Feminists contributed heavily to the antinuclear movement, not only as activists but also through their challenges to ownership of knowledge and the legitimation of limited forms thereof. *Courage* collective member Monika Schmid claimed that women activists were mainstays (*Hauptträgerinnen*) of the movement, one reason why in 1979 *Courage* devoted a whole issue to concerns regarding nuclear power plants.[42] Women played a key role despite the continued need for them to prove to fellow protestors their ability to understand technical information.[43]

Yet, even within the women's movement, knowledge, expertise, theory, and other truth claims could still be deployed, as Anna F. felt, as a source of bullying and the assertion of power. Sabine M. remembered in addition to her feelings of rapture also "forms of orthodoxy" within the *Courage* collective, "so that you considered three times whether you should say something or not. Intimidating [. . .]. These, these hierarchies between women. And silences." Intimidation and silence were some of the very experiences that the women activists had sought to escape by forming women-only groups.

Conclusion

The inability of women in these experiments to entirely stamp out such individual claims of superior knowledge and insistence on their primacy relates, finally, to one more characteristic of the women's movement, women's participation in the broader extraparliamentary movement, and the tight entanglement of the two. The conflicts and tensions within the movement were part of the learning process for participants and fellow activists. Women drew lessons from Eva Quistorp's difficulties in negotiating her position as a nonhierarchical leader in the groups she helped found; from the ways that members of the Weiberrat deployed power in larger SDS meetings; and from the disappointments as well as delights

Sabine M. and Wiebke S. felt within the *Courage* collective. The constant learning (to learn) from one another was critical to the successes of the women's movement and larger alternative movements in West Germany in the 1970s and early 1980s. The importance of nontotal yet often profound changes in thinking and acting, and the need for their continuation, is too often lost in retrospective characterizations of the successes and failures of "the new women's movement" as well as other protest movements of the era. Experiments of the time provided no finished models to emulate. They were exemplary in contributing to the emerging understanding that there were no utopian end points; there was no end of history. The ongoing experiments were neither failures nor perceived successes easily subsumed under "reform." Activists generally came to learn much from these different kinds of efforts. Indeed, these experiments all contributed to radical rethinking in how change itself works, at what sites, at what speed, and so on. They moved ahead with experimentation informed by this new thinking, and influenced others' thinking.

Over time, activist men came to appreciate how women as a group within the larger movement, and how the new women's movement itself, came to transform their own political understanding: how entangled their own politics were with the women's movement, broadly speaking. Christian Semler, one of the SDS leaders, was suspicious when he first confronted SDS women at the FU Berlin. The SDS at Munich in the late 1950s and early 1960s, where he was active before coming to West Berlin, had been made up only of men. For him, it was originally a conflict that these women, "on the one hand, [. . .] loved the SDS, but, on the other, they were naturally against the authoritarian structures"—as he now willingly characterized the latter over which he presided. He claimed to have feared that these women might split the emerging movement, and he thought their concerns were "unpolitical." It was years before he could "acknowledge what the women [had] said. Later," he admitted, "I took it all more seriously. [. . .] Because I also read a little bit of it from them, and realized that it was all totally interesting." He still found the women's movement as such to have been unsuccessful in its own goals. "Indeed," he claimed, "the whole women's movement was fundamentally like the K Group movement." He spoke from experience: it was the result of his own very active efforts that many women's groups worked closely with and were even intermixed with the Maoist party that Semler himself had cofounded in 1970.[44] Rainer Langhans also retrospectively attacked the women's movement for its failures *tout court,* measuring its results against particular goals. He claimed, "The women's movement brought *only* slogans." By his assessment, feminists "didn't *live* it." And yet, he allowed, "We need[ed] these experiments from them [. . .], we can thank them for it [. . .], that we see that it doesn't work this way."[45]

To be sure, many contemporary women activists shared Semler's and Langhans's disappointments with what did not work. But the lesson of viewing change through the lens of constant, ongoing effort, sharing what works and what does not, moving away from apocalyptic models without sacrificing the possibilities for radical transformation: this all was one of the great successes of the new women's movement. Consider Langhans's still ongoing reworking of the self, including a discovery and privileging of "the feminine" within himself, and his retrospective insistence that he never wanted to be a leader, or spokesperson, but rather came to see his role differently.[46] Publications like the 1972 *Women's Handbook* and hundreds of similar projects sought to share knowledge, including precisely via the self-perceived failures as well as successes of the hundreds of experiments, especially in changes in everyday life, that feminists—and soon others—took on.[47] Like the innumerable experiments that inspired them, publications such as the *Women's Handbook* reflected on changing society through transforming the self and reworking relations; rethinking the sites and even the nature of usable knowledge; a reimagination of political goals and practice; even a rethinking of "movement" itself. These changes in thinking, which flowed between a broad women's movement and a larger, transforming alternative political movement, offer lessons still well worth considering.

Belinda Davis is professor of history at Rutgers University. Her publications include *Changing the World, Changing Oneself: Political Protest and Transnational Identities in 1960s/70s, West Germany and the US* (ed. with Wilfried Mausbach, Martin Klimke, and Carla MacDougall, Berghahn Books, 2010); *Alltag—Erfahrung—Eigensinn. Historisch-anthropologische Erkundungen* (ed. with Thomas Lindenberger and Michael Wildt, Campus, 2008); and *Home Fires Burning: Food, Politics, and Everyday Life in World War I Berlin* (University of North Carolina Press, 2000). She is currently completing the book project *The Internal Life of Politics: Extraparliamentary Opposition in West Germany, 1962–1983*.

Notes

1. West Berlin was a separate political entity from the Federal Republic of Germany. However, in this piece, reference to West Germany includes West Berlin unless otherwise noted. I argue against an overweaning focus on West Berlin—and on the SDS and "students"—in Belinda Davis, *The Internal Life of Politics: Extraparliamentary Opposition in West Germany, 1962–1983* (Cambridge, 2019).

2. See, for example, Ute Gerhard, "Westdeutsche Frauenbewegung: Zwischen Autonomie und dem Recht auf Gleichheit," *Feministische Studien* 10, no. 2 (1992): 35–55, and *Atempause: Feminismus als demokratisches Projekt* (Frankfurt/M., 1999), and "Frauenbewegung," in *Die sozialen Bewegungen in Deutschland seit 1945: Ein Handbuch,* eds. Roland Roth and Dieter Rucht (Frankfurt/M., 2008), 187–218; Myra Marx Ferree et al., *Shaping Abortion Discourse: Democracy and the Public Sphere in Germany and the United States* (New York, 2002), and *Varieties of Feminism: German Gender Politics in Global Perspective* (Stanford, CA, 2012); Ute Kätzel, *Die 68erinnen: Porträt einer rebellischen Frauengeneration* (Berlin, 2002); Ursula G. T. Müller, *Die Wahrheit über die lila Latzhosen: Höhen und Tiefen in 15 Jahren Frauenbewegung* (Frankfurt/M., 2004); and Michaela Karl, *Die Geschichte der Frauenbewegung* (Stuttgart, 2011). Compare Belinda Davis, "The Personal Is Political: Gender, Politics, and Political Activism in Modern German History," in *Gendering Modern German History: Rewriting Historiography,* ed. Karen Hagemann and Jean Quataert (New York, 2007), 107–27. Much of this work examines the West German women's movement in some larger context.

3. See Kristina Schulz, *Der lange Atem der Provokation: Die Frauenbewegung in der Bundesrepublik und in Frankreich* (Frankfurt/M., 2002); Katharina Karcher, *Sisters in Arms: Militant Feminisms in the Federal Republic of Germany since 1968* (New York, 2017); Elisabeth Zollmer, *Töchter der Revolte? Frauenbewegung und Feminismus der 1970er Jahre in München* (Munich, 2011); also Dagmar Herzog, *Sex after Fascism: Memory and Morality in Twentieth-Century Germany* (Princeton, NJ, 2005); Belinda Davis et al., eds., *Changing the World, Changing Oneself: Political Protest and Transnational Identities in West Germany and the U.S. in the 1960s and 1970s* (New York, 2010); Detlef Siegfried and Sven Reichardt, eds., *Das Alternative Milieu: Antibürgerlicher Lebensstil und linke Politik in der Bundesrepublik Deutschland und Europa 1968–1983* (Göttingen, 2010); Sven Reichardt, *Authentizität und Gemeinschaft: Linksalternatives Leben in den siebziger und frühen achtziger Jahren* (Frankfurt/M., 2014); also useful is Ilse Lenz, ed., *Die Neue Frauenbewegung in Deutschland: Abschied vom Kleinen Unterschied; Ausgewählte Quellen* (Wiesbaden, 2009).

4. Teresa B. is one of some fifty-five contemporary activists I interviewed for this project. Outside of the best-known interview subjects, I identify subjects by pseudonym.

5. Also Helke Sander's speech at the September 1968 SDS convention: Helke Sander, "Rede des Aktionsrates zur Befreiung der Frauen, gehalten auf der 23. Delegiertenkonferenz des Sozialistischen Deutschen Studentenbundes (SDS) im September 1968 in Frankfurt," in *Mein Kopf gehört mir: Zwanzig Jahre Frauenbewegung,* ed. Hilke Schlaeger (Munich, 1988), 12–22; and the Alice Schwarzer-organized statement, "Wir haben abgetrieben" (We've had abortions), *Stern,* no. 24 (6 June 1971), 16–23.

6. Marianne Herzog, *Nicht den Hunger verlieren* (Berlin, 1981), 21. Compare Nina Verheyen, *Diskussionslust: Eine Kulturgeschichte des "besseren Arguments" in Westdeutschland* (Göttingen, 2010).

7. "Bericht für den Weiberrat," reproduced in "Die Anfänge der Frauenbewegung," in *Frauen: Frauenjahrbuch* 1 (Frankfurt/M.,1975), 18.

8. Reproduced in "Die Anfänge der Frauenbewegung," 16.

9. "Bericht für den Weiberrat," 18.

10. Ibid. "Geschichte des Frankfurter Weiberrats," in *Frauen: Frauenjahrbuch* 1, 19–48; and Sibylle Flügge, "Der Weiberrat im SDS," in *Frauen: Frauenjahrbuch* 1, 15–18; also, *Glasnost-archiv*: www.glasnost.de/hist/apo/weiber4.html (accessed 8 September 2015).
11. Kommune 2, *Versuch der Revolutionierung des bürgerlichen Individuums: Kollektives Leben mit politischer Arbeit verbinden* (Cologne, 1971).
12. "Nachlaß Sigrid Fronius, 1965–66 #1, Studiumreform," Archiv "APO und soziale Bewegungen." Fronius drew on Theodor Adorno, *Erziehung zur Mündigkeit: Vorträge und Gespräche mit Hellmut Becker 1959 bis 1969* (Frankfurt/M., 1971); see also Halina Bendkowski and Heinrich-Böll-Stiftung, eds., *Wie weit flog die Tomate? Eine 68erinnen-Gala der Reflexion* (Berlin, 1999); and Dagmar Przytulla [Seehuber], "'Niemand ahnte, dass wir ein ziemlich verklemmter Haufen waren,'" in *Die 68erinnen: Porträt einer rebellischen Frauengeneration*, ed. Ute Kätzel (Berlin, 2002), 201–20.
13. "Bericht für den Weiberrat."
14. Eva-Maria Quistorp et al., "Anstiftung der Frauen zum Frieden," in *Frauen für den Frieden: Analysen, Dokumente und Aktionen aus der Frauenfriedensbewegung*, ed. Eva Quistorp (Frankfurt/M., 1982), 20–21.
15. Sander, "Rede des Aktionsrates," 13.
16. I use "feminist" in this context to mean women activists who identified with the women's movement.
17. *Der subjektive Faktor* (film), director Helke Sander, FRG 1981. See also Annette Schwarzenau, "Nicht diese theoretischen Dinger, etwas Praktisches unternehmen," in Kätzel, *Die 68erinnen*, 41–59. The title refers as well to the theoretical concept of the same time, thereby playing with the role of theory.
18. Sabine M., interview with author, 16 June 2006. Compare Luce Irigaray, "When Our Lips Speak Together," *Signs* 6, no. 1 (1980): 69–79.
19. Compare Klaus Hartung, "Die Psychologie der Küchenarbeit: Selbstbefreiung, Wohngemeinschaft und Kommune," in *CheShahShit: Die Sechziger Jahre zwischen Cocktail und Molotow*, ed. Eckhard Siepmann et al. (Berlin, 1984), 103.
20. Kommune 2, *Versuch*, 17–18.
21. Verena Stefan, *Häutungen: Biografische Aufzeichnungen. Gedichte. Träume. Analysen* (Munich, 1975), sold over two hundred thousand copies within five years. See also Sarah Nelson, "Das Verbrechen, über das niemand spricht," in *Emma* (1 April 1978): 20–26; "Zur Walpurgisnacht," *Frankfurter Frauenblatt* 7 (June 1981); *Die Macht der Männer ist die Geduld der Frauen* (film), director Cristina Perincioli, FRG 1978; and *Unter den Pflaster ist der Strand* (film), director Helke Sanders-Brahms, FRG 1975; items in Frauenforschungs-, -bildungs- und informationszentrum, Berlin (FFBIZ), GM, ZD / Gewalt, Repression Berlin 1976–1987.
22. Compare Inga Buhmann, *Ich habe mir eine Geschichte geschrieben* (Frankfurt/M., 1987).
23. Stefan, *Häutungen*, 21.
24. Sander, "Rede des Aktionsrates," 22. She referenced and resituated the question, attributed to the provocative Dieter Kunzelmann, of how he could worry about the war in Vietnam when he had trouble with his orgasm.
25. Ibid.
26. See Peter Appelbaum and Belinda Davis, "Curriculum as Disobedience: Raising Children to Transform Adults," *Journal of Curriculum Theorizing* 29, no. 1

(2013): 134–73; and Dagmar Herzog, *Sex after Fascism: Memory and Morality in Twentieth-Century Germany* (Princeton, NJ, 2005), 162–75.
27. Sander, "Rede des Aktionsrates," 20; and Gerhard Bott, "Vorwort des Herausgebers," in *Erziehung zum Ungehorsam: Antiautoritäre Kinderläden,* ed. Gerhard Bott (Frankfurt/M., 1970), 7–13, 11. That Turkish and working-class toddlers would experience particular contradictions between home and *Kinderladen* reflected Sander's own presumptions.
28. Sander, "Rede des Aktionsrates," 20.
29. Compare Sanders-Brahms, *Unter dem Pflaster.*
30. Ursula Nienhaus, "Wie die Frauenbewegung zu Courage kam: Eine Chronologie," in *Als die Frauenbewegung noch Courage hatte: Die "Berliner Frauenzeitung Courage" und die autonomen Frauenbewegungen der 1970er und 1980er Jahre,* ed. Gisela Notz (Bonn, 2007), 16.
31. *Macht die Pille frei?* (film), director Helke Sander and Sarah Schumann, FRG 1972.
32. For example, "Wir sind doch nicht blöd!" in *Hexenschuß. Berufsschulzeitung für Mädchen* 1, no. 3 (1971): 3.
33. Brot and Rosen, eds., *Frauenhandbuch Nr. 1: Abtreibung und Verhütungsmittel* (Berlin, 1972); see also Frankfurter Frauen, *Frauen: Frauenjahrbuch 75* (Frankfurt/M., 1975); and *frau* (Berlin, 1978).
34. Compare with the contemporary psychological-philosophical exploration, Luce Irigaray, *Speculum of the Other Woman* (Ithaca, NY, 1985 [orig. 1974]), and the relation to "embodiment."
35. Jutta Lauterbach et al., "Erstes Frauen-Gesundheits-Zentrum," *Courage* 2, no. 11 (1977): cover, 13–18.
36. Quoted in Gisela Notz, "Courage—Wie es begann, was daraus wurde und was geblieben ist," in Notz, *Courage,* 28; see also Nienhaus, "Frauenbewegung," 15.
37. Kommune 2, *Versuch,* 18.
38. Anna F., interview with author, 11 July 2008, Berlin.
39. Jörg Bopp, *Jugend: Umworben und doch unverstanden* (Frankfurt/M, 1985).
40. Feminist and founding member of the American Self-Help Clinic movement Lorraine Rothman developed the euphemistically named "menstrual extraction" technique, which Schultz brought from the United States. Compare Sandra Morgen, *Into Our Own Hands: The Women's Health Movement in the U.S.* (New Brunswick, NJ, 2002), 101. Abortion rights in the Federal Republic have had a rocky path. See Frauenaktion Dortmund, *Schwangerschaft und der neue Paragraph 218. Abtreibung in der BRD: Praxis und Möglichkeiten; Handbuch für Frauen* (Cologne, 1988).
41. Andrew S. Tompkins, *Better Active than Radioactive! Anti-nuclear Protest in 1970s France and West Germany* (Oxford, 2016); and Stephen Milder, *Greening Democracy: The Anti-nuclear Movement and Political Environmentalism in West Germany and Beyond, 1968–1983* (Cambridge, 2017).
42. *Courage* 4, no. 4 (1979); conversation (not formal interview) with Monika Meta Schmid, 14 October 2016. *Courage* also routinely featured pieces on the anti-nuclear movement.
43. Tompkins, *Better Active,* 62–63.
44. Christian Semler, interview with author, 7 July 2006, Berlin.
45. Rainer Langhans, interview with author, 24 July 2005, Munich.

46. Ibid.; see also Jutta Winkelmann, *Das Harem-Experiment: Begnungen mit Rainer Langhans, dem letzten APOnauten* (Munich, 1999), 107–10; also Rainer Langhans, *Ich bin's: Die ersten 68 Jahre* (Munich, 2008), 157–61.
47. Aside from regular columns and articles in the innumerable alternative serial publications (for women and otherwise), compare: Brot und Rosen, *Frauenhandbuch*; Frankfurter Frauen, *Frauen: Frauenjahrbuch75*; *frau*; Kommune 2, *Versuch*; Frank Böckelmann, *Befreiung des Alltags: Modelle eines Zusammenlebens ohne Leistungsdruck, Frustration und Angst* (Munich, 1970); Häuserrat Frankfurt, *Wohnungskampf in Frankfurt* (Munich, 1974); Albert Herrenknecht et al., *Träume, Hoffnungen, Kämpfe: Ein Lesebuch zur Jugendzentrumsbewegung* (Frankfurt/M., 1977); Klaus Jarchow, *Dörfer wachsen in der Stadt: Beiträge zur städtischen Gegenkultur* (Rheinsberg, 1980); and Herrad Schenk, *Wir leben zusammen nicht allein: Wohngemeinschaften heute* (Cologne, 1984).

Selected Bibliography

Bendkowski, Halina, and Helke Sander, eds. *Wie weit flog die Tomate? Eine 68erinnen-Gala der Reflexion.* Berlin, 1999.
Davis, Belinda. "The Personal Is Political: Gender, Politics, and Political Activism in Modern German History." In *Gendering Modern German History: Rewriting Historiography,* ed. Karen Hagemann and Jean Quataert. 107–27. New York, 2007.
———. "Transnation und Transkultur: Gender und Politisierung von den fünziger bis in die siebziger Jahre." In *Das Alternative Milieu: Antibürgerlicher Lebensstil und linke Politik in der Bundesrepublik Deutschland und Europa 1968–1983,* ed. Detlef Siegfried and Sven Reichardt, 313–34. Göttingen, 2010.
———. *The Internal Life of Politics: Extraparliamentary Opposition in West Germany, 1962–1983.* Cambridge, 2019.
Davis, Belinda, Wilfried Mausbach, Martin Klimke, and Carla MacDougall, eds. *Changing the World, Changing Oneself: Political Protest and Transnational Identities in West Germany and the U.S. in the 1960s and 1970s.* New York, 2010.
Ferree, Myra Marx, William Anthony Gamson, Jürgen Gerhards, and Dieter Rucht. *Shaping Abortion Discourse: Democracy and the Public Sphere in Germany and the United States.* New York, 2002.
———. *Varieties of Feminism: German Gender Politics in Global Perspective.* Stanford, CA, 2012.
———, and Silke Roth. "Gender, Class, and the Interaction among Social Movements: A Strike of West Berlin Daycare Workers." *Gender & Society* 12, no. 6 (1998): 626–48.
Gerhard, Ute. "Westdeutsche Frauenbewegung: Zwischen Autonomie und dem Recht auf Gleichheit." *Feministische Studien* 10, no. 2 (1992): 35–55.
———. *Atempause: Feminismus als demokratisches Projekt.* Frankfurt/M., 1999.
Karcher, Katharina. *Sisters in Arms: Militant Feminisms in the Federal Republic of Germany since 1968.* New York, 2017.
Karl, Michaela. *Die Geschichte der Frauenbewegung.* Stuttgart, 2011.
Kätzel, Ute. *Die 68erinnen: Porträt einer rebellischen Frauengeneration.* Berlin, 2002.
Lenz, Ilse, ed. *Die Neue Frauenbewegung in Deutschland: Abschied vom Kleinen Unterschied Ausgewählte Quellen.* Wiesbaden, 2009.

Müller, Ursula G. T. *Die Wahrheit über die lila Latzhosen: Höhen und Tiefen in 15 Jahren Frauenbewegung* (Frankfurt/M., 2004).
Nave-Herz, Rosemarie. *Die Geschichte der Frauenbewegung in Deutschland.* Opladen, 1994.
Notz, Gisela, ed. *Als die Frauenbewegung noch Courage hatte: Die "Berliner Frauenzeitung Courage" und die autonomen Frauenbewegungen der 1970er und 1980er Jahre.* Bonn, 2007.
Roth, Roland, and Dieter Rucht, eds. *Die Sozialen Bewegungen in Deutschland seit 1945: Ein Handbuch.* Frankfurt/M., 2008.
Schulz, Kristina. *Der lange Atem der Provokation: Die Frauenbewegung in der Bundesrepublik und in Frankreich.* Frankfurt/M., 2002.
Wiggershaus, Renate. *Geschichte der Frauen und der Frauenbewegung in der Bundesrepublik und in der Deutschen Demokratischen Republik nach 1945.* Wuppertal, 1979.
Zollmer, Elisabeth. *Töchter der Revolte? Frauenbewegung und Feminismus der 1970er Jahre in München.* Munich, 2011.

CHAPTER 10

Connected Differences

Black German Feminists and Their Transnational Connections in the 1980s and 1990s

Tiffany N. Florvil

In a 2012 interview, Black German feminist Katja Kinder explained, "For me the Black German women's movement was above all a feeling of belonging. To be a part of this was important and to experience a feeling of recognition."[1] She acknowledged the critical role that the Black German women's movement played in her life, helping her, along with other women, gain a sense of community with their Afro-German compatriots in Germany.[2] Kinder cofounded Afro-German Women (Afrodeutsche Frauen, ADEFRA), a Black German women's organization, which together with the Initiative of Black Germans (Initiative Schwarze Deutsche, ISD), another Black German organization, ushered in a new stage of Afro-German activism in the 1980s and 1990s.[3] Her comment underscores the value placed on creating new kinships and achieving acceptance among Black Germans, particularly in a white German society that often understood itself to be monocultural and monoracial and that ignored the existence of hyphenated German citizens. It was against this backdrop that Black Germans, particularly women, mobilized to challenge those understandings of Germanness, reimagine their identities, and reclaim their place as full citizens in the national polity in West Germany. These women also used ADEFRA, and the movement more broadly, to escape their isolation in majority-white settings, to pursue feminist and antiracist projects, and to cultivate connections to one another as well as others in Germany and beyond.

This chapter argues that Black German feminists and lesbians founded ADEFRA, which helped them normalize blackness and by extension Black Germanness in West Germany, and these women did this due in part to the encouragement of Caribbean American lesbian poet Audre Lorde (1934–92). They linked their Black Germanness to spaces near and far, in which Black German women became agents attempting to spur social change. ADEFRA activists also opened up possibilities for Black German feminism in German society, enabling them to privilege an intersectional approach that fused together transnational feminist and African-diasporic politics. As an organization that engaged in antiracist, African-diasporic, and feminist solidarity, ADEFRA also afforded its activists opportunities to consciously practice Lorde's concept of "connected differences."[4] In doing so, they formed ties with their German compatriots and other women through their organization of grassroots events in Germany and participation in international conferences. Black German women, I maintain, also practiced Black women's internationalism, in which they promoted transnational feminism, shared affinities and strategies with other women on how to challenge different forms of discrimination, and achieved recognition both at home and abroad.[5] Connecting across their own differences and stressing empowerment, the women of ADEFRA used the organization not only as an activist platform but also as a practical form of community, resistance, and survival.

The first section of the chapter provides a brief overview of the Black German movement, including the formation of the Initiative of Black Germans. It also explores Black German women's connection to Lorde and their community-based organizing in the early stages. Section two traces the development of ADEFRA and its feminist, diasporic, and queer underpinnings. It underscores the cultural and political significance of Black German feminists—several of whom were lesbians—and how they produced spaces for themselves in society. The final section analyzes ADEFRA activists' transnational engagements. These feminists linked up with women across the globe, created new customs, and stressed the importance of kinship and belonging. ADEFRA activists helped to publicize both their Black Germanness and Black feminism within and beyond the German nation.

The Black German Movement

As Black German activist and historian Katharina Oguntoye, cofounder of the Initiative of Black Germans and ADEFRA in West Berlin, wrote in an essay, "At the beginning of the Black German Movement [were] the Black German women."[6] Similarly, Ria Cheatom, a member of both ISD and ADEFRA in Munich, claimed, "Right from the beginning of the black movement in Germany one can clearly say, that without us women very little would have developed."[7] According to scholar of diversity studies and activist Maisha-Maureen Auma (formerly Maureen Maisha Eggers), Black feminists played a significant role in defining the movement's message through the production and spreading of Black German histories.[8] As the aforementioned quotations reveal, Black German women were instrumental figures during the early stages of the movement, and they remained active in it (even in the present day). Yet, much of this development was due to their connections to and inspiration drawn from the prominent writer-activist Audre Lorde. After several invitations in the 1980s from white West German feminist Dagmar Schultz, who taught women's studies and cultural issues at the Free University of Berlin (FU Berlin) from 1973 to 1986, Lorde became a visiting professor at the John F. Kennedy Institute for North American Studies at the FU Berlin, where she taught several courses on creative writing in the summer semester of 1984.[9]

Personal exchanges with Lorde proved crucial for Afro-German women. Lorde, along with her partner, Caribbean feminist professor Gloria Joseph, spent six months in West Berlin. Their presence "was of tremendous importance" personally and collectively to Black German women. For Oguntoye, "Both women demonstrated, in that there were two of them, that there are Black feminists around who are beautiful, strong and talented."[10] For several Afro-German women, Lorde represented Black women's internationalism with her connections to and investment in women globally. Lorde also served as a mentor and a model for intellectualism and political activism through her publications and her willingness to support antiracist and feminist causes.

On top of that Lorde was also well known by some Afro-Germans due to the 1983 publication of *Macht und Sinnlichkeit* (*Power and Sensuality*).[11] The volume was a compilation of Lorde's and American feminist poet Adrienne Rich's essays. Dagmar Schultz published the volume, which was the first German-language version of Lorde's work, with the independent Orlanda Women's Press (formerly Sub Rosa). Later, Schultz, who co-owned Orlanda, became the German publisher for much of Lorde's translated literature. In comparison to other well-known African American activists and writers such as Angela Davis, Alice Walker, or Toni Morrison, Lorde did not receive much major media coverage in West Germany. Instead, Lorde's work appeared in independent presses, alternative women's magazines, feminist and lesbian journals, and Afro-German publications.[12]

Lorde was keen on meeting and interacting with Black German women in West Berlin. Several of them, including Katharina Oguntoye and May Opitz (later Ayim), attended some of her seminars at the FU.[13] In her classroom discussions, which were taught in English, Lorde had a commanding yet open presence, and she pushed her West German students (white and black) to understand the substance of poetry and to tackle uncomfortable topics such as discrimination.[14] At a guest lecture in Schultz's "Racism and Sexism" seminar at the FU Berlin, Lorde stated,

> I was very interested in doing this reading and having some opening of discussion because I feel we cannot separate the causes or the motivations, the overall structure within which sexism *and* racism *and* classism *and* homophobia *and* heterosexism occur, that they basically are forms of dehumanization and as such have their roots in the same intolerance of difference that of course makes us very useful kogs [*sic*] in whatever machine we happen to be functioning. This one is West Berlin, I come from one kog [*sic*] in the United States of America. In any case, they are machineries.[15]

She continued,

> I'm very interested in finding how do we break step with the machine or how do we even ask the questions that might help us break step with the machine. I'm interested in that in my life, and I'm interested in encouraging each one of you to [ask] those questions in your life [. . .] Where do all of the oppressions that we recognize intersect, and they do [. . .][16]

Here, she conveyed the persistent inability of individuals to accept differences and the necessity of recognizing that systems of oppression were rooted in similar power structures that linked individuals throughout the world.

Throughout West Germany and Europe, Lorde also gave public readings and participated in conferences in the 1980s. Whether it was teaching her seminars at the FU, performing her poetry, or attending gatherings in West Germany, Lorde shaped Black German women and pushed them to interrogate their social positions and grasp the value of writing as a creative and political act. In "The Dream of Europe" speech, for instance, Lorde declared, "I am an African-American poet and believe in the power of poetry. Poetry, like all art, has a function: to bring us closer to who we wish to be: to help us vision a future which has not yet been: and to help us survive the lack of that future."[17] Moreover, Afro-German women's exchanges with Lorde led to their creation of the terms "Afro-German" and "Black German," analogous to "Afro-American."[18] These empowering self-designations helped to counter offensive terms that remained pervasive in West German society after the Second World War. Some Afro-Germans even forged emotional attachments to her, in which she became the Black elder, sister, and friend for whom they had longed. In this way, they chose familial dynamics that did not adhere to normative filial bonds, identities, or practices. Lorde continued traveling to Germany until a few months before her death on 17 November 1992. Black German and other Afro-European women wrote to Lorde from the mid-1980s until her death.[19] Interactions with Lorde and each other inside and outside the university classroom helped Black German women accept that West Germany, too, represented a site for the African diaspora and that they constituted a community because of their racialized experiences and "connected differences."

The Black German community that Lorde met was composed of individuals with diverse backgrounds.[20] By one estimate, Black Germans today consist of anywhere between 500,000 to 800,000 individuals.[21] The post-1945 generation of Black Germans grew up in isolation from other individuals of African descent and had rare or sporadic contact with their relatives of African descent. Afro-Germans were often raised by their white family members or sent to live in orphanages or in foster homes in predominantly white areas across West Germany. Therefore, the movement enabled them to gain emotional recognition, escape their social isolation, and unify to establish a dynamic community.

Besides her interactions with Black German women, Lorde also bonded with white West German feminists and guided them through difficult discussions about race. Lorde's time in West Germany also helped to shift attention toward the existence of racism within the women's movement. Prior to Lorde's arrival, a few Afro-German women actively participated in the women's movement. But they often were dismissed when they broached the topic of racism, and they also had a hard time finding acceptance and visibility as Black women in the movement.[22] Moreover, some white West German feminists claimed there were no Blacks in Germany and that there were no "Black feminist theorists," which caused the few active Black German feminists, especially Katharina Oguntoye, to feel further erased and excluded.[23] Shifting away from this ignorance, white West German feminists attended Lorde's public readings and learned about themselves in relation to racially or ethnically diverse minority women. At a reading, Lorde persuaded white German feminists to "accept antiracism and work against anti-[S]emitism as central to the women's movement or it will die." She asserted, "Not because racism and anti-[S]emitism are outside altruistic concerns, but because they are central, central to any kind of movement."[24] Due to these experiences, some of these feminists became involved in discussions about racism that they had long avoided, although change within the movement remained slow.[25] Lorde was in fact an early proponent of what one of the leading scholars of critical race theory and feminist Kimberlé Crenshaw in the early 1990s termed "intersectionality."[26] Indeed, white German feminists' relationships with Lorde were perhaps the single most important means by which some of them gained exposure to intersectional critiques that tied together race, class, sexuality, and gender.

Lorde encouraged Black German women to see themselves as constituting a part of the African diaspora, and emboldened them to use writing as a tool for knowledge production, self-expression, and coalition building. Her impression is visible in the 1986 Afro-German volume *Farbe bekennen: Afro-deutsche Frauen auf den Spuren ihrer Geschichte,* which was later published in English as *Showing Our Colors: Afro-German Women Speak*

Out in 1991.[27] The anthology, edited by Katharina Oguntoye, May Ayim, and Dagmar Schultz, included autobiographical texts, historical essays, poetry, interviews, and Ayim's master's thesis.[28] In many ways, *Farbe bekennen* followed the tradition of works by other Women of Color on both sides of the Atlantic, including Cherríe Moraga and Gloria Anzaldúa's *This Bridge Called My Back: By Radical Women of Color* published in 1981; Barbara Smith's *Home Girls* in 1983; Beverly Bryan, Stella Dadzie, and Suzanne Scafe's *The Heart of the Race: Black Women's Lives in Britain* in 1985; and three years later Shabnam Grewal, Jackie Kay, Liliane Landor, Gail Lewis, and Pratibha Parmar's *Charting the Journey: Writings by Black and Third World Women*. Written by activists who were involved in political movements in Britain and the United States, all these volumes centered lesbian and/or feminist-of-color narratives, privileged their agential voices, and demonstrated their intellectualism. The planning of and narratives in *Farbe bekennen* pushed Black Germans to connect to one another, cultivating new friendships in the process.[29] Their relationships with Lorde, moreover, served as a motivation to write about their experiences, impart their knowledge, promote their own Black German herstories, and maintain a political presence.

With Lorde's support, Oguntoye, Ayim, and other Black German activists created a pronounced feminist and African diasporic influence in their movement with the establishment of two grassroots associations: ISD and ADEFRA. This impulse gave rise to a new stage in Afro-German activism, with previous mobilizations having occurred in the German colonies and in the metropole during the nineteenth and twentieth centuries.[30] The first national Black German event of the modern movement took place in Wiesbaden in November 1985, and was a defining moment.[31] This initial meeting began the tradition of ISD's annual *Bundestreffen*—national meetings that occurred in different German cities and catered to Black Germans as well as other People of Color.[32] ISD activists, including some ADEFRA feminists, organized a variety of workshops and panels at the *Bundestreffen* that addressed national and international themes like Black German history before 1945, South African Apartheid, and the US Civil Rights Movement. After this meeting, regional ISD groups also sprung up in West German cities such as Frankfurt am Main and Munich, and in former East German cities such as Leipzig and Dresden after the fall of the Berlin Wall. In West Berlin, individuals like Oguntoye and Ayim had already started meeting before the event in Wiesbaden.[33] In 1988, the Berlin chapter of ISD had about ninety-five members recorded on their roster and additional individuals who expressed interest, attending events across the city.[34] While Afro-German feminists initiated the movement, its organization, evolution, and growth included the efforts of both men and women.

ADEFRA and Black German Feminism

Black German women borrowed and adapted some of Lorde's Black feminist ideas as demonstrated through ADEFRA. Prior to attending a conference in the Dutch city of Utrecht, several Black German women met and discussed forming their own organization in December 1986. At this initial meeting with Jasmin Eding, Katja Kinder, Katharina Oguntoye, and others, ADEFRA was born, giving Black German feminism a public face and rendering Black German women visible.[35] ADEFRA, which means "the woman who shows courage" in Amharic, the official language in Ethiopia, paid homage to African culture.[36] Lorde had long integrated African mythology in her work. In Lorde, Black German women also saw the embodiment of Black lesbian, feminist activism. In fact, "Black women, particularly lesbians, were the ones who set off the Black movement in Germany."[37] Some Black German women navigated the double bind of oppression of being both Black and lesbian. According to Ekpenyong Ani, a former president of ADEFRA, there were always concerns about sexual orientation. Ani stated,

> The theme of sexual orientation especially whether ADEFRA was a women's or lesbian association, remained a huge question at all times. I can only say, that the lesbians at ADEFRA were always more mobilized, because in a certain way the focus was clear: if you concentrate on women and want to work together with them, then of course, you will find a lot of lesbians.[38]

At the beginning, Black German women even contemplated naming the organization *Afrodeutsche Lesben,* or ADELE (Afro-German Lesbians). While Afro-German women worked together, this did not absolve them from also harboring some homophobic attitudes within ADEFRA or dealing with sexist attitudes in ISD.

Black German feminists recognized the necessity of establishing their own liberating and inclusive spaces in a majority white West German society that simultaneously othered and ignored them. Several of these women were involved in feminist and lesbian circles and brought that experience with them to the Black German movement. Katja Kinder observed that in the early 1980s "Black female activists were nonexistent in mainstream German society and it is exactly this fact that provided an opportunity to occupy a new space and break down the often quoted symbolic order piece by piece."[39] Dealing with the tensions of sexism and racism, Black German women engaged in new forms of politics in ADEFRA. Some of the lesbian founders of ADEFRA were Katja Kinder, Katharina Oguntoye, Judy Gummich, Jasmin Eding, Eva von Pirch, and Ja-El (Elke Jank). In addition, May Ayim, Helga Emde, Ika Hügel-Marshall, Ria Cheatom, Marion Kraft, Eleonore Wiedenroth-Coulibaly, and others helped with early efforts. Some but not all of them were lesbians, and some were already active in their local ISD chapters. Similar to ISD, local ADEFRA chapters sprang up in cafes or in the homes of activists in Bremen and Munich—to name a few.[40] Taken together, the establishment of these grassroots groups continued to broaden Afro-Germans' sense of community and spread ideas about Black feminist and diasporic practices.

Using writing to forge community, ADEFRA activists also created a short-lived journal titled *Afrekete: Zeitung für afro-deutsche und schwarze Frauen,* spearheaded by activists in the Bremen chapter. Published from 1988 to 1990, it featured essays, poetry, artwork, and conference reports about local, national, and international events from Black German contributors and maintained Black internationalist and feminist perspectives. Afro-German women continued to solidify their ties to Africa, especially since the title *Afrekete* was drawn from West African mythology; Afrekete was a trickster figure. In choosing this name, these women also sought ties to a culture of radical African women, past and present. Lorde also used the figure of Afrekete in diverse forms of writing and considered her a traditional source of women's power in Africa and the diaspora.

Stressing the critical significance of diasporic politics, one of the six published issues of *Afrekete* explicitly focused on the topic of Black feminism and featured diverse articles, reports about feminist conferences in Montreal and New York, and poetry that dealt with the themes of recognition, sisterhood, and Black identity.[41] Eva von Pirch, one of the editors of *Afrekete,* wrote an article titled "Black Feminism," in which she helped to define it in relation to Black German and Black women in Germany. She opined, "Black feminism is the national and international attempt by Black women to jointly analyze their social and individual conditions against the background of their national culture and identity."[42] Pirch continued to write about its importance for Black German women. Moreover, all of the issues of *Afrekete* centered on a particular theme and included pieces that engaged those themes. While it remains difficult to determine the circulation of the journal in West Germany given the limited records, *Afrekete* garnered some attention from individuals in the United States and Africa as evidenced by the letters to the editor. ADEFRA enabled Black German women to invent new cultural practices that acknowledged the power of women of the African diaspora, in which they reimagined themselves as a part of it.

From the outset, ADEFRA also constituted a feminist and queer African diasporic project. It allowed different Afro-German women to participate and articulate their identities, blending their feminist, queer, and diasporic politics. Here, ADEFRA activists were similar to other women across the diaspora, especially as they embraced the concept of being queer as a destabilizing act that altered static notions of identity and served as a tool for empowerment. Cultural theorist and ethnic studies scholar Fatima El-Tayeb maintains that queer signifies a verb, "describing a practice of identity (de)construction that results in a new type of diasporic consciousness neither grounded in ethnic identifications nor referencing a however mythical homeland, instead using the tension of living supposedly exclusive identities and transforming it into a creative potential, building a community based on the shared experience of multiple, contradictory positionalities."[43] El-Tayeb recognizes queer as an active practice of affiliation and connection, and ADEFRA exemplified this. Black German lesbians and feminists used ADEFRA to stress how the intertwining of the diaspora, feminism, and queerness would "strengthen and encourage self-awareness, self-determination, and self-organisation of Black women."[44]

Black German feminists and lesbians were not unlike their Black British counterparts who also organized and engaged in Black women's internationalism that focused on multiple forms of oppression. Some Black British feminists, such as Olive Morris, started mobilizing in the late 1960s and early 1970s with the British Black Panthers. But in 1970 some of these activists decided to establish a community-based women's collective called the Black Women's Group (later known as the Brixton Black Women's Group, BBWG) in London that covered women's issues.[45] Morris was a founding member of the BBWG and also helped to launch the Organization of Women of Asian and African Descent (OWAAD) in 1978 in London. OWAAD supported an Afro-Asian unity that drew attention to the legacy of British colonialism, racism, and sexism in the lives of Caribbean, African, and Asian women. Through these organizations, Morris theorized and promoted feminist causes, but she also shared a "commitment to global struggles in other parts of the world."[46] For Morris and other Black British feminists, the global and the local intersected in their lives and activism. Aside from these associations, Black British women remained active in other groups in Britain. As these examples indicate, Black British activism illustrated the contours of their intersectional approach and how they sought to forge political communities and advocate for social change—not unlike Black German women a few years later.

ADEFRA helped Afro-German women engender a space for activism, in which they formed kinships with their fellow compatriots. According to Eding, her involvement with ADEFRA made it possible for her to "[find] a home, or rather we created a home for ourselves."[47] For the most part, the organization provided Black German women with a safe space that offered them acceptance and recognition as Blacks, feminists, and, for many, lesbians. Given their experiences in other social movements in postwar West Germany, where there was rarely a full engagement with intersectional approaches, this was particularly compelling. For instance, some feminists in the West German movement shot down activist Ika Hügel-Marshall, especially when she referenced race and racial discrimination at women's meetings.[48] Ayim also described feeling marginalized as an Afro-German woman at a 1984 feminist congress in West Germany.[49] At ADEFRA, Black German activists actively acknowledged intersectional identities and promoted inclusivity and openness, although gendered tensions did exist among their members at times.

ADEFRA Activists' Transnational Activism

Black German women cultivated solidarity with individuals throughout Germany and the world. In this way, they were not unlike many of their West German counterparts who also created networks with others in the post-1945 period. West German students sponsored and arranged visits for feminists, Black Power activists, American activists, and civil rights movement leaders, and they also learned new political tactics through their relationships with foreign students at West German universities.[50] There was also the expression of Afro-Americanophilia that permeated the left and liberal postwar youth political culture of West Germany and the international politics of the German Democratic Republic in the East. This Afro-Americanophilia often exoticized, reified, and celebrated blackness and African American culture, but it entailed a different set of transatlantic connections and cultural exchanges and practices than those cultivated by Afro-Germans.[51] Afro-Germans continued African-diasporic traditions that sought transnational ties with diverse individuals who tried to combat discrimination, resist global white supremacy, and agitate for civil rights.[52] Black German women not only acknowledged the utility in cultivating connections to others at a variety of events but also continued to participate in activities that reflected their interests in feminism and antiracism.

Indeed, ADEFRA activists saw their efforts as a way of building additional communities, sharing knowledge, and engaging in direct action at international events in West Germany. Ayim and Nivedita Prasad, a German-based activist of Indian descent, brought together the Korean Women's Group, the Group of Feminist Migrant Mothers (FeMigra), and other such women's organizations in the "Paths to Alliances" conference held in Bremen in June 1990.[53] In addition to the variety of organizations, the conference is notable because its participants tackled many themes, some of which included exclusion within the women's movement, Jewish identity, Eurocentrism, and the difficulties that migrant women experienced in Germany. Discussions about using "Black" as a political designation for all minority women arose, but there was some reluctance based on the participants' own differences and privileges.[54] While some of these conversations were challenging, these minority women welcomed the opportunity to openly engage and offer solutions. ADEFRA and ISD activists were present, including Oguntoye, Hügel-Marshall, and Regina Stein. Both Ayim and Prasad also organized the second national congress for immigrant, Jewish, and Black German women held in October of 1991 in Berlin.[55] ADEFRA feminists' and lesbians' participation in these events showed their agency and their willingness to shed light on their plight. More importantly, their participation highlights their efforts to establish connections with women who were outside of the Black German community but who also faced discrimination and exclusion in Germany.

ADEFRA activist Helga Emde, for instance, was invited to participate on a panel at an International Women's Congress that took place in Frankfurt am Main in October 1989 to commemorate the 200th anniversary of the French Revolution with the aim to explore in an international comparative perspective the history and presence of the gendered laws, regulations, and practices of human rights. One of the main organizers of the conference, titled "Human Rights Have (No) Sex" (*Menschenrechte haben (k)ein Geschlecht*), was Ute Gerhardt, a professor of sociology and women's and gender studies at the Goethe University Frankfurt am Main since 1987.[56] The feminist conference organizers also extended invitations to several organizations, including the Interest Group for Women Married to Foreigners (Interessengemeinschaft der mit Ausländern verheirateten Frauen, IAF) and Amnesty for Women. Emde reported in the magazine *Afrekete* that she was the only Black woman on a panel that was supposed to debate the experiences of asylum seekers and foreign women in Germany as well as the treatment and lives of Afro-German women. Given this dynamic, Emde found "the white, academic, intellectual middle class women" organizers to be arrogant and the congress disappointing. In many ways, Emde echoed Oguntoye's earlier sentiments, especially as Emde felt excluded from this form of feminism. She also was struck by the fact that while the organizers had invited Angela Davis, who could not attend, they failed to invite additional Black women. Their invitation to Davis also entailed a type of Afro-Americanophilia that seemed to affirm American blackness and minimize German blackness. Again, the conference revealed for her the limitations of the West German feminist movement in its inability to critically engage with Black German and other Women of Color.[57]

Furthermore, activists such as Katharina Oguntoye sought to change dynamics specifically in the lesbian movement. She organized presentations at the first annual West Berlin Lesbian Weeks (*Berliner Lesbenwochen*) in 1985 and subsequent ones from 1986 to 1993.[58] Located in a cosmopolitan city with a particularly vibrant lesbian political culture, these *Berliner Lesbenwochen* drew participants from across Germany and elsewhere. While focusing on community and belonging, these events were not devoid of confrontation. At a session on the origins of the Black German movement, a few white West German women failed to understand that whiteness was normalized in society and that Black German women chose the designations of "Afro-German" or "Black German" to affirm their identities and agency. At this and other panel sessions, the organizers of the *Berliner Lesbenwochen* helped to lead discussions on lesbians and AIDS, lesbians under National Socialism, and also everyday racism in the lesbian movement and German society as a whole, addressing pressing issues in the community.[59] In this way, Black Germans fostered critical dialogues and disseminated knowledge to change the lesbian and feminist movements. Yet, they also did not shy away from centering Black Germanness by drawing attention to their social realities in Germany.

As ADEFRA members organized events that exemplified a feminist and queer African diasporic outlook, they also remained committed to forging solidarities and "connected differences" at home. Indeed, the ADEFRA-Munich chapter's international meeting of women in November 1990 represented those efforts. The three-day symposium titled "Risk Your Life and Leave Your House" (*"Wage dein Leben und verlasse dein Haus"*)—a title derived from an African proverb—was open to white and Black Germans as well as other international women. Supporting the diversity of women's experiences, the conference enabled Women of Color activists to network, share feelings, and exchange ideas. At the symposium, Black German women sponsored art exhibitions and seminars that addressed the themes of racism, sexism, Afro-German history, and Black women's literature. Some of the presentations for the general participants included "White Mother, Black Child" and "Differences among Women: A Critical Look at How to Deal with Others."[60] The organizers also coordinated Black-only events, where Black women could work through their specific concerns and issues, and some of these workshops revolved around topics such as "Reunification and United Racism," "Lesbian Politics—Women's Politics," and "The History of Slavery and Its Contemporary Meaning."[61]

It is against this backdrop that ADEFRA valued building alliances with other Black movements and a variety of women's groups that focused on solidarity and antiracist activism in Germany and beyond. Their commitment to coalition building and collaborative work remained a significant point that these activists continued to raise in several ADEFRA brochures.[62] Activists recognized that "we as black women have a responsibility to unite and initiate change in the family, in close surroundings, regionally and globally. We have the responsibility to survive politically, culturally, and economically. As women, we cannot only think about our immediate space, but we must look after our global community. Our commitment must be 100 percent [. . .]"[63]

The symposium, which took place at the Kommunikationszentrum für Frauen zur Arbeits- und Lebenssituation (Kofra), a feminist center in Munich, offered an opportunity for ADEFRA activists and participants to connect with women, particularly from the former East as well as other European countries and to learn more about diverse women's situations and survival strategies. Through the 1990 conference, Black East Germans, including Peggy Piesche, Carmen Oliver-Stanley, and Ina Röder, to name a few, forged ties and cultivated kinships to Black Germans from West Germany; it also prompted their involvement in the Afro-German movement. Underscoring the appeal of the conference, Cheatom, Eding, and Mary Powell—all three ADEFRA-Munich feminists—mentioned,

> For most of the black women (many came from the former East and other European countries), this was the first time that they took part in a meeting exclusively for women. Despite our different ways of life and also partly our different self-image (for example, the label Afro-German was met with confusion and even a lack of acceptance by our black African, Arabic, French, and Dutch [. . .] sisters [. . .]) the response to the meeting was very positive.[64]

In linking up with Afro-German women from the East along with women from abroad, conference participants and activists acknowledged themselves and their new friendships as a source of empowerment and community; they also learned and produced knowledge about women's rights and identities. Demonstrating strength in numbers, the conference afforded these women opportunities to become visible as Afro-German, lesbian, and feminist, and to engage in meaningful political activism in a major German city.

This international event in 1990 Munich was possible because Black German women had forged connections by previously attending similar conferences abroad. For example, ADEFRA activists Emde, Kraft, and Oguntoye had attended the Third International Feminist Book Fair in Montreal, Canada, in June 1988, where they presented on panels that examined writing, discrimination, and the African diaspora.[65] There, they connected with Lorde, African American poet Sonia Sanchez, South African feminist Ellen Kuzwayo, and others. Lorde actually alerted the organizers about *Farbe bekennen*. Activists such as Oguntoye and Ayim also had participated in the Second Cross-Cultural Black Women's Summer Institute in New York City in July 1988.[66] These Black German women met with members from feminist organizations in Angola, Trinidad and Tobago, the West Bank, and the Netherlands and engaged in grassroots activism at the conference.

In the same year as the Munich conference, Ayim and Oguntoye practiced Black women's internationalism by attending the "I Am Your Sister: Forging Global Connections across Differences" conference, which took place in Boston in October 1990. Organized by Women of Color feminists, over a thousand participants from twenty-two countries came to honor Lorde's life; this was Lorde's last major conference.[67] There, they imparted antiracist strategies and vocabularies and networked with feminists from across the globe. ADEFRA activists such as Kraft, Emde, Oguntoye, Ayim, and others continued to attend international events after 1990, including several of the international Cross-Cultural Institutes, which were organized annually from 1987 to 1991 and then every two to three years from 1993 to 1998. Black German women also organized the Fifth Cross-Cultural Institute in reunified Germany in August 1991 under the theme of "Black People and the European Community." Occurring in Frankfurt am Main, Bielefeld, and Berlin, the three-week institute was the first time that an entire international conference in Germany was dedicated to the theme of Blacks in Europe. At this event, they emphasized the plight of Afro-Germans in the context of neo-Nazis' resurgent ethno-nationalism.[68] Again, ADEFRA activists used these settings to validate their experiences, impart knowledge, and garner recognition for the Afro-German community.

In addition, Ayim, along with Turkish German writer Emine Sevgi Özdamar and German writer and activist Hilke Schlaeger, attended the Fifth International Feminist Book Fair in Amsterdam in June 1992, signaling their commitment to sustain feminist discussions, share theories, and practice coalitional politics.[69] Black German women also reached out to other Afro-Europeans and traveled to Amsterdam to meet Gloria Wekker, who cofounded the Afro-Dutch lesbian group Sister Outsider in 1984; Sister Outsider also pursued collaborative projects with ADEFRA, recognizing their "connected differences." Attending these events certainly helped ADEFRA activists negotiate their identities, perform their feminist and diasporic work, cultivate relationships with diverse women, and publicize the experiences of Afro-Germans more broadly.

Conclusion

Feminists and lesbians, inspired by Lorde, pioneered the modern Afro-German movement of the 1980s and 1990s, including the Initiative Schwarze Deutsche and especially Afrodeutsche Frauen. Embracing transnational feminism, Black German women established ADEFRA to explicitly engage in intersectional politics that did not elide their experiences of sexism, homophobia, and racism. As a result, they opened up more possibilities for themselves and others in which they sought recognition in society and internationally. They also used the diverse conferences and workshops to show how Germany constituted a part of the African diaspora by offering contextualization of Black Germans' experiences and histories, producing knowledge in the process. ADEFRA activists not only attended to intersectional themes but also stressed the interplay of the global and local in their activism. Imbibing Lorde's mantra of "connected differences" and practicing their Black women's internationalism, ADEFRA activists forged connections and solidarity with one another and other individuals, including feminists and activists, in and beyond Germany, who also attempted to confront diverse forms of discrimination. In doing so, they cultivated a sense of community that offered them a degree of acceptance, belonging, and recognition.

Moreover, Black German women created ADEFRA to represent an explicitly feminist and queer African diasporic project that did not preclude ties to other excluded minorities. Black German feminists and lesbians even organized their own events, including international conferences. Events like their 1990 Munich conference afforded them opportunities to network and connect with fellow feminists from other countries, including their counterparts from the former East. This conference, much like their participation in other events, symbolized their Black women's internationalism in practice. In essence, Afro-German women used their activism in ADEFRA to "see each other when we dare to see ourselves," especially "without arrogance, belittlement or rejection, but with patience and understanding [. . .]"[70]

Tiffany N. Florvil is associate professor in the department of history at the University of New Mexico, Albuquerque. Her field of research is modern and late-modern European history, social movements, gender and sexuality, emotions, and the African diaspora. Her publications include: "Distant Ties: May Ayim's Transnational Solidarity and Activism," published in *To Turn this Whole World Over: Black Women's Internationalism during the Twentieth Century* (ed. by Keisha Blain and Tiffany M. Gill, University of Illinois Press 2019); *Rethinking Black German Studies: Approaches, Interventions, and Histories* (ed. with Vanessa Plumly, Peter Lang 2018); "Emotional Connections: Audre Lorde and Black German Women," in *Audre Lorde's Transnational Legacies* (ed. Stella Bolaki and Sabine Broeck, University of Massachusetts Press, 2015). Currently she is revising her manuscript tentatively entitled, *Making a Movement: A History of Black Germans, Gender, and Belonging*.

Notes

1. Peggy Piesche, "Rückblenden und Vorschauen: 20 Jahre Schwarze Frauenbewegung," in *Euer Schweigen schützt Euch nicht: Audre Lorde und die Schwarze Frauenbewegung in Deutschland*, ed. Peggy Piesche (Berlin, 2012), 22.
2. I will also use Afro-German and Black German interchangeably in this piece; both are used within the community.
3. ISD is now the Initiative of Black People in Germany, and ADEFRA is now Black Women in Germany. ADEFRA also includes Transwomen of Color and other Women of Color.
4. Alexis De Veaux, *Warrior Poet: A Biography of Audre Lorde* (New York, 2004), 330–32; and Marion Kraft, "The Creative Use of Difference," *EAST: Englisch Amerikanische Studien. Zeitschrift für Unterricht, Wissenschaft & Politik*, nos. 3–4 (1986): 549–56.
5. For more on black internationalism, see Tracy Fisher, "Transnational Black Diaspora Feminisms," in *What's Left of Blackness: Feminisms, Transracial Solidarities, and the Politics of Belonging in Britain* (New York, 2012), 65–92; Carol Boyce Davies, *Left of Karl Marx: The Political Life of Black Communist Claudia Jones* (Durham, NC, 2008); and Brent Hayes Edwards, *The Practice of Diaspora: Literature, Translation, and the Rise of Black Internationalism* (Cambridge, 2003).
6. Katharina Oguntoye, "The Black German Movement and the Women['s] Movement," March 1989, 8, The Audre Lorde Papers, Spelman College Archives (Lorde Papers), Box 24, Folder 104. The piece was eventually published in the Afro-German journal *Afrekete*.
7. Nicola Lauré al-Samarai, "'Es ist noch immer ein Aufbruch, aber mit neuer Startposition': Zwanzig Jahre ADEFRA und Schwarze Frauen/Bewegungen in Deutschland," in *re/visionen: Postkoloniale Perspektiven von People of Color auf Rassismus, Kulturpolitik und Widerstand in Deutschland*, ed. Kien Nghi Ha et al. (Münster, 2007), 353.
8. Maureen Maisha Eggers, "Knowledges of (Un-)Belonging: Epistemic Change as a Defining Mode for Black Women's Activism in Germany," in *Remapping Black Germany: New Perspectives on Afro-German History, Politics, and Culture*, ed. Sara Lennox (Amherst, MA, 2016), 34.
9. De Veaux, *Warrior Poet*, 295–96; Katharina Gerund, "Sisterly (Inter)Actions: Audre Lorde and the Development of Afro-German Women's Communities," in "Black Women's Writing Revisited," ed. Sabine Broeck, special issue, *Gender Forum: An Internet Journal for Gender Studies* 22 (2008): 56.
10. Oguntoye, "Black German Movement," 4. See also *Audre Lorde: The Berlin Years 1984–1992*, dir. Dagmar Schultz with Ika Hügel Marshall and Ria Cheatom (New York, 2012), DVD.
11. Audre Lorde and Adrienne Rich, *Macht und Sinnlichkeit: Ausgewählte Texte*, ed. Dagmar Schultz, 4th ed. (Berlin, 1993).
12. Katharina Gerund, "Visions of (Global) Sisterhood and Black Solidarity: Audre Lorde," in *Transatlantic Cultural Exchange: African American Women's Art and Activism in West Germany* (Bielefeld, 2013), 157–210, esp. 160, 175–91.
13. Rudolph Byrd et al., eds., *I Am Your Sister: Collected and Unpublished Writings of Audre Lorde* (Oxford, 2009), 81–149, esp. 87.
14. See Audre Lorde, "The Poetry as Outsider—Sitzung 6 (Audio)," Audre Lorde Archive, Free University of Berlin (Lorde Archive), Box 2.3–25.

15. "Reading and Discussion in Dagmar Schultz'[s] Seminar 'Racism and Sexism' at the JFK Institute of North American Studies at the Free University of Berlin, 7. Juli 1984," Lorde Archive, vol. 6, 7.
16. Ibid.
17. Handwritten draft remarks by Audre Lorde, "The Dream of Europe," Lorde Papers, Box 17, Folder 061; and "Ein Traum von Europa," *Kongress Zeitung*, 25–29 May 1988, Folder Lorde Lichtflut 1988, Orlanda Frauenverlag, Berlin Germany.
18. Starting in 2006, *afrodeutsch* began to appear in the German dictionary *Duden*.
19. Tiffany N. Florvil, "Emotional Connections: Audre Lorde and Black German Women," in *Audre Lorde's Transnational Legacies*, ed. Stella Bolaki and Sabine Broeck (Amherst, MA, 2015), 135–47.
20. See Doris Reiprich and Erika Ngambi Ul Kuo, "Unser Vater war Kameruner, unsere Mutter Ostpreußin, wir sind Mulattinnen," in *Farbe bekennen: Afro-deutsche Frauen auf den Spuren ihrer Geschichte*, ed. Katharina Oguntoye et al., 3rd ed. (Berlin, 2006), 73–92; and Fatima El-Tayeb, "'Colored Germans There Will Never Be': Colonialism and Citizenship in Modern Germany," in *Extending the Diaspora: New Histories of Black People*, ed. Dawne Curry et al. (Chicago, 2009), 225–44.
21. Marion Kraft, *Coming in from the Cold: The Black German Experience, Past and Present* (New York, 2014), 2.
22. Oguntoye, "Black German Movement," 4. Ika Hügel-Marshall also discussed a similar experience in her memoir. See Ika Hügel-Marshall, *Daheim unterwegs: Ein deutsches Leben* (Berlin, 1998).
23. Oguntoye, "Black German Movement," 5.
24. "Lesung in der Schoko Fabrik, 20. November 1987," Lorde Archive, vol. 12b, 8.
25. Oguntoye, "Black German Movement," 5; Fatima El-Tayeb, *European Others: Queering Ethnicity in Postnational Europe* (Minneapolis, 2011), 63; and Sara Lennox, "Divided Feminism: Women, Racism, and German National Identity," *German Studies Review* 18, no. 3 (1995): 482.
26. Kimberlé Williams Crenshaw, "Mapping the Margins: Intersectionality Identity Politics, and Violence against Women of Color," *Stanford Law Review* 43, no. 6 (1991): 1241–99.
27. For the importance of *Farbe bekennen*, see El-Tayeb, *European Others*, chapter 2; Leroy Hopkins, "Writing Diasporic Identity: Afro-German Literature since 1985," in *Not so Plain as Black and White: Afro-German Culture and History, 1890–2000*, ed. Patricia Mazón and Reinhild Steingröver (Rochester, NY, 2005), 183–208.
28. Oguntoye, et al., eds., *Farbe bekennen*. Ayim wrote a master's thesis titled "Afro-Deutsche: Ihre Kultur- und Sozialgeschichte auf dem Hintergrund gesellschaftlicher Veränderungen," at the University of Regensburg, where she studied psychology and education.
29. Piesche, "Rückblenden und Vorschauen," 25; Eleonore Wiedenroth-Coulibaly, "Die multiplen Anfänge der ISD," in *Spiegel Blicke: Perspektiven Schwarzer Bewegung in Deutschland*, ed. Denise Bergold-Caldwell et al. (Berlin, 2015), 28–32, esp. 30.
30. Katharina Oguntoye, *Eine afro-deutsche Geschichte: Zur Lebenssituation von Afrikanern und Afro-Deutschen in Deutschland von 1884 bis 1950* (Berlin, 1997); and Robbie Aitken and Eve Rosenhaft, *Black Germany: The Making and Unmaking of a Diaspora Community, 1884–1960* (Cambridge, 2013).

31. Christina Ampedu, Helga Emde, and Eleonore Wiedenroth, "Invitation letter," The May Ayim Archive, Free University of Berlin (Ayim Archive), Folder Projekt Afro-Deutsche/Zeitungsartikel über Afro-deutsche/Schwarze in den Medien.
32. Wiedenroth-Coulibaly, "Die multiplen Anfänge der ISD," 29; and Katharina Oguntoye, "Vorwort," in *Sisters and Souls: Inspirationen durch May Ayim*, ed. Natasha A. Kelly (Berlin, 2015), 23–42.
33. Wiedenroth-Coulibaly, "Die multiplen Anfänge der ISD," 29.
34. "I.S.D. Berlin e.V. Mitglieder/Interessenten (Stand: 12.09.88)," Ayim Archive, Box 6, Folder Dias Kontakte Afroscene. Sadly, there are limited sources that reveal the actual membership of other ISD chapters throughout Germany in the 1980s and 1990s.
35. Afrodeutsche Frauen (ADEFRA), *20 Jahre Schwarze Frauenbewegung in Deutschland / 20 Years of Black Women's Activism in Germany* (Berlin, 2006), 7; Denise Bergold-Caldwell, "Black to the Future: Ein Gespräch zwischen Katharina Oguntoye, Jasmin Eding und Abenaa Adomako," in Bergold-Caldwell et al., *Spiegel Blicke*, 34–35; and Piesche, "Rückblenden und Vorschauen," 19.
36. Al-Samarai, "Aufbruch," 347, 348; Ekpenyong Ani, "Die Frau, die Mut zeigt— der Verein ADEFRA Schwarze Deutsche Frauen / Schwarze Frauen in Deutschand," in *The BlackBook: Deutschlands Häutungen*, eds. AntiDiskrimierungs Büro (ADB) Köln and cyberNomads (Frankfurt/M., 2004), 145.
37. ADEFRA, *20 Jahre Schwarze Frauenbewegung*, 3.
38. Al-Samarai, "Aufbruch," 353.
39. ADEFRA, *20 Jahre Schwarze Frauenbewegung*, 5.
40. In my research, I have been unable to recover membership rolls for the regional ADEFRA chapters, although some of their events had anywhere from fifty to one hundred participants.
41. See *Afrekete: Zeitung von afro-deutschen und schwarzen Frauen (schwarzer Feminismus)* 2, no. 3 (1988): 1–45.
42. Eva von Pirch, "Schwarzer Feminismus," *Afrekete: Zeitung für afro-deutsche und schwarze Frauen* 2, no. 3 (1988): 34.
43. El-Tayeb, *European Others*, xxxvi.
44. ADEFRA, *20 Jahre Schwarze Frauenbewegung*, 5.
45. Fisher, "Transnational Black Diaspora Feminisms," 71–72.
46. Ibid., 77, 78. For more on Morris, see ibid., 74–78; Tanisha Ford, "We Were the People of Soul," in *Liberated Threads: Black Women, Style, and the Global Politics of Soul* (Chapel Hill, NC, 2015), 123–57.
47. ADEFRA, *20 Jahre Schwarze Frauenbewegung*, 7.
48. Ika Hügel-Marshall, *Invisible Woman: Growing Up Black in Germany* (New York, 2001), 98–99.
49. "May Opitz, Betrifft Frauenkongreß, 26. März 1984," Ayim Archive, Box 21, 3.
50. Martin Klimke, *The Other Alliance: Student Protest in West Germany and the United States in the Global Sixties* (Princeton, NJ, 2010); Belinda Davis, "A Whole World Opening Up: Transcultural Contact, Difference, and the Politicization of 'New Left' Activists," in *Changing the World, Changing Oneself: Political Protest and Collective Identities in West Germany and the U.S. in the 1960s and 1970s*, ed. Belinda Davis et al. (New York, 2010), 255–73; and Quinn Slobodian, *Foreign Front: Third World Politics in Sixties Germany* (Durham, NC, 2012).
51. Moritz Ege and Andrew Wright Hurley, "Periodizing and Historicizig German Afro-Americanophilia: From Antebellum to Postwar (1850–1967)," *Portal Jour-

nal of Multidisciplinary International Studies 12, no. 2 (2015): epress-dev.lib.uts.edu.au/journals/index.php/portal/article/view/4360/4997, and "Periodizing and Historicizing German Afro-Americanophilia: From Counterculture to Post-Soul (1968–2005)," ibid., epress.lib.uts.edu.au/journals/index.php/portal/article/view/4359/4996.

52. See, for example, Keisha Blain, "'For the Rights of Dark People in Every Part of the World': Pearl Sherrod, Black Internationalist Feminism, and Afro-Asian Politics during the 1930s," *Souls* 17, nos. 1–2 (2015): 90–112.
53. May Ayim and Nivedita Prasad, ed., *Dokumentation Wege zu Bündnissen* (Berlin, 1992).
54. Ibid., 1.
55. Ibid., 35–117.
56. Congress papers and comments are published in Ute Gerhard et al., eds., *Differenz und Gleichheit: Menschenrechte haben (k)ein Geschlecht* (Frankfurt/M.,1990). See also Dörthe Jung, "'Menschenrechte haben (k)ein Geschlecht'Bemerkungen zum Internationalen Frauenkongreß vom 5.–8. Oktober in der Frankfurter Universität," *Kritische Berichte*, no. 4 (1989): 122–25.
57. Helga Emde, "Internationaler Frauenkongreß in Frankfurt/Main vom 5.–8. 10.1989," *Afrekete: Zeitung für afro-deutsche und schwarze Frauen* 5, no. 4 (1989): 14–15, 14.
58. ADEFRA, "Black Is Beautiful ??," in *Dokumentation der 2. und 3. Berliner Lesbenwoche 1986 und 1987*, ed. Monika Brunnmüller et al. (Berlin, 1989), 171, Spinnboden Lesbenarchiv und Bibliothek Berlin (Spinnboden); and Katharina Oguntoye, "Afro-deutsche Lesben lesen aus *Farbe bekennen*," in *Dokumentation der 2. und 3. Berliner Lesbenwoche 1986 und 1987*, ed. Monika Brunnmüller et al. (Berlin, 1989), 32–34, Spinnboden.
59. Joliba—Lesbenwoche e.V, *Dokumentation 9. Berlin Lesbenwoche 1993: Die Herausforderung annehmen* (Berlin, 1993), The Private Collection of Katharina Oguntoye.
60. ADEFRA, in Kooperation mit FrauenAnstiftung und kofra, "Int. Treffen Schwarzer Frauen: 'Wage Dein Leben verlasse Dein Haus,'" 1.–4. November 1990, 1, The Private Collection of Ria Cheatom (Cheatom Collection).
61. Ibid., 2.
62. Ibid., 3. See ADEFRA-Munich brochure, "wir über uns," 1989, 3–5, Cheatom Collection.
63. Ria Cheatom et al., "Wage Dein Leben Verlasse Dein Haus!," *Kofra*, no. 10 (Feb./March 1991): 21, Cheatom Collection.
64. Ibid., 22.
65. Marion Kraft, "Impressionen von der 'Third International Feminist Book Fair' in Montreal," *Afrekete: Zeitung für afro-deutsche und schwarze Frauen* 2, no. 3 (1988): 5–8, Frauenforschungs-, -bildungs- und -informationszentrum, Berlin (FFBIZ); and 3rd International Feminist Book Fair 14–19 June 1988, Montreal Program, https://issuu.com/rimaathar/docs/3rd_international_feminist_book_fai.
66. See Anjuli Gupta, "Überlegungen zum 'Cross-Cultural Black Womans's [*sic*] Summer Institute," *Afrekete: Zeitung für afro-deutsche und schwarze Frauen* 2, no. 3 (1988): 12, FFBIZ.
67. "I Am Your Sister: Forging Global Connections across Differences," flyer, Cheatom Collection, and "I Am Your Sister: Forging Global Connections across Differences," letter, 12 May 1990, 1–2, Cheatom Collection; and Ayofemi Folayan

and Joanne Stato, "I Am Your Sister: A Tale of Two Conferences," *off our backs* 20, no. 11 (December 1990): 1–5, 9–11.
68. For more on the Cross-Cultural Institute, see Tiffany N. Florvil, "Transnational Feminist Solidarity, Black German Women, and the Politics of Belonging," in *Gendering Knowledge in Africa and the African Diaspora: Contesting History and Power*, ed. Toyin Falola and Olajumoke Yacob-Haliso (New York, 2018), 87–110.
69. "The Fifth International Feminist Book Fair Program, 24–28 June 1992, Amsterdam," Ayim Archive, Box 24, 30. See also Kristen Hogan, *The Feminist Bookstore Movement: Lesbian Antiracism and Feminist Accountability* (Durham, NC, 2016).
70. Ibid. The quotation is taken from Audre Lorde, *Lichtflut: Neue Texte* (Berlin, 1988).

Selected Bibliography

Afrodeutsche Frauen (ADEFRA). *20 Jahre Schwarze Frauenbewegung in Deutschland / 20 Years of Black Women's Activism in Germany*. Berlin, 2006.
Aitken, Robbie, and Eve Rosenhaft. *Black Germany: The Making and Unmaking of a Diaspora Community, 1884–1960*. Cambridge, 2013.
Al-Samarai, Nicola Lauré. "'Es ist noch immer ein Aufbruch, aber mit neuer Startposition': Zwanzig Jahre ADEFRA und Schwarze Frauen/Bewegungen in Deutschland." In *re/visionen: Postkoloniale Perspektiven von People of Color auf Rassismus, Kulturpolitik und Widerstand in Deutschland*, ed. Kien Nghi Ha, Nicola Lauré al-Samarai, and Sheila Mysorekar, 347–60. Münster, 2007.
Ayim, May, and Nivedita Prasad, eds. *Dokumentation Wege zu Bündnissen*. Berlin, 1992.
Blain, Keisha. "'For the Rights of Dark People in Every Part of the World': Pearl Sherrod, Black Internationalist Feminism, and Afro-Asian Politics during the 1930s." *Souls* 17, nos. 1–2 (2015): 90–112.
Byrd, Rudolph, Johnnetta Cole, and Beverly Guy-Sheftall, eds. *I Am Your Sister: Collected and Unpublished Writings of Audre Lorde*. Oxford, 2009.
Crenshaw, Kimberlé Williams. "Mapping the Margins: Intersectionality Identity Politics, and Violence against Women of Color." *Stanford Law Review* 43, no. 6 (1991): 1241–99.
Davies, Carol Boyce. *Left of Karl Marx: The Political Life of Black Communist Claudia Jones*. Durham, NC, 2008.
De Veaux, Alexis. *Warrior Poet: A Biography of Audre Lorde*. New York, 2004.
Edwards, Brent Hayes. *The Practice of Diaspora: Literature, Translation, and the Rise of Black Internationalism*. Cambridge, 2003.
Eggers, Maureen Maisha. "Knowledges of (Un-)Belonging: Epistemic Change as a Defining Mode for Black Women's Activism in Germany." In *Remapping Black Germany: New Perspectives on Afro-German History, Politics, and Culture*, ed. Sara Lennox, 33–45. Amherst, MA, 2016.
El-Tayeb, Fatima. "'Colored Germans There Will Never Be': Colonialism and Citizenship in Modern Germany." In *Extending the Diaspora: New Histories of Black People*, ed. Dawne Curry, Eric Duke, and Marshanda Smith, 225–44. Chicago, 2009.
———. *European Others: Queering Ethnicity in Postnational Europe*. Minneapolis, MN, 2011.

Fisher, Tracy. *What's Left of Blackness: Feminisms, Transracial Solidarities, and the Politics of Belonging in Britain*. New York, 2012.
Florvil, Tiffany. "Emotional Connections: Audre Lorde and Black German Women." In *Audre Lorde's Transnational Legacies*, ed. Stella Bolaki and Sabine Broeck, 135–47. Amherst, MA, 2015.
Ford, Tanisha. *Liberated Threads: Black Women, Style, and the Global Politics of Soul*. Chapel Hill, NC, 2015.
Gerund, Katharina. *Transatlantic Cultural Exchange: African American Women's Art and Activism in West Germany*. Bielefeld, 2013.
———. "Sisterly (Inter)Actions: Audre Lorde and the Development of Afro-German Women's Communities." In "Black Women's Writing Revisited," ed. Sabine Broeck, special issue, *Gender Forum: An Internet Journal for Gender Studies* 22 (2008): 56–72.
Hopkins, Leroy. "Writing Diasporic Identity: Afro-German Literature since 1985." In *Not so Plain as Black and White: Afro-German Culture and History, 1890–2000*, ed. Patricia Mazón and Reinhild Steingröver, 183–208. Rochester, NY, 2005.
Kraft, Marion. *Coming in from the Cold: The Black German Experience, Past and Present*. New York, 2014.
Lennox, Sara. "Divided Feminism: Women, Racism, and German National Identity." *German Studies Review* 18, no. 3 (1995): 481–502.
Lorde, Audre, and Adrienne Rich. *Macht und Sinnlichkeit: Ausgewählte Texte*, ed. Dagmar Schultz. 4th ed. Berlin, 1993.
Oguntoye, Katharina. *Eine afro-deutsche Geschichte: Zur Lebenssituation von Afrikanern und Afro-Deutschen in Deutschland von 1884 bis 1950*. Berlin, 1997.
———. "Vorwort." In *Sisters and Souls: Inspirationen durch May Ayim*, ed. Natasha A. Kelly, 23–42. Berlin, 2015.
Oguntoye, Katharina, May Ayim, and Dagmar Schultz, eds. *Farbe bekennen: Afro-deutsche Frauen auf den Spuren ihrer Geschichte*. 3rd edn. Berlin, 2006.
Piesche, Peggy. *Euer Schweigen schützt Euch nicht: Audre Lorde und die Schwarze Frauenbewegung in Deutschland*, ed. Peggy Piesche. Berlin, 2012.
Slobodian, Quinn. *Foreign Front: Third World Politics in Sixties Germany*. Durham, NC, 2012.

PART IV
GENDER RELATIONS AND SEXUALITY

CHAPTER 11

Domestic Abuse and Women's Lives
East and West Policies during the 1960s and 1970s

Jane Freeland

When Frau A. first reported her husband to the police in the East German city of Leipzig for assault in 1986, she "had the feeling that at least as far as the two police officers were concerned, whatever took place within a marriage, so long as it didn't disturb the peace in the building or anything, wasn't such a big deal."[1] When she attempted to divorce her husband, she was told she would need a doctor's certificate, which her doctor refused to give her, arguing that her injuries could have been sustained by falling down the stairs. At the divorce hearing her application was denied, and she was required to attend two reconciliation sessions with her husband.

Frau M. from West Berlin had similar experiences. After telling child services about her violent husband, she was accompanied home by a social worker. Once at the home, the social worker spoke to the husband, who "hammed it up, saying that he has to work very hard and do overtime," calling his wife "sick and unstable."[2] Frau M. reported, "Suddenly everything changed. She [the social worker] advised me to get some medication prescribed by the doctor, and told my husband that he shouldn't hit me or the children, which he promised to do."[3] Before the social worker left, she told Frau M. that if Frau M. were older, she would have thought she was going through menopause, dismissing her stories of abuse as hormonal.

Taking the first steps toward leaving a violent partner is not easy. Domestic violence is a reality experienced by all kinds of women, regardless of race, class, or sexuality. It creates mutually reinforcing patterns of shame, isolation, control, and dependence that impede women from trying to leave abuse, and this was no different in divided Germany.[4] Indeed, what the two examples highlight is just how similar the experiences of women across the Berlin Wall were as they attempted to cope with a violent home life. They were disbelieved, and their stories were dismissed as harmless private affairs by neighbors and family, the police, and social services. These attitudes hindered women's ability to access legal and social support mechanisms and to find safety.

This similarity in battered women's stories across the Berlin Wall is particularly striking given the profound differences between East and West Germany during the Cold War. Not only did the two states have divergent social, political, and legal systems but they also promulgated competing ideals of the family and gender roles. Since the 1950s, the male-breadwinner/female-homemaker model dominated in the West; in the East, it was the ideal of a dual-income family that informed state politics. In everyday life under socialism, however, women's role in the workforce was still combined with traditional gender relations in which the wife did most of the housework and childcare, despite her own employment. These differences and similarities shaped policies and attitudes toward domestic violence.

Drawing from legal cases, activist literature, and newspaper articles, this chapter compares and contrasts state and societal responses to domestic violence in East and West Germany from the 1960s to the 1980s. In doing so, it shows how, in the face of different economic, political, and social systems, women living with violence struggled to be heard on both sides of the Iron Curtain. The chapter begins by examining how the different attitudes toward gender shaped responses to domestic violence in the two German states. It argues that on both sides of the Berlin Wall, dealing with domestic violence meant challenging established patriarchal gender norms. In the West, this started from below as feminists politicized domestic abuse, drawing attention to the role gender inequality played in perpetuating and enabling violence against women. Women activists established grassroots services and shelters for battered women, many of which received public funding and political support. In East Germany, however, challenging patriarchy was a central part of constructing socialism. This made domestic violence an official concern that was primarily addressed in the courts and marriage-counseling centers.

The second half of this chapter focuses on the consequences of these approaches. Indeed, although there was support for dealing with domestic abuse and women's inequality, both states failed to confront the gendered power imbalances that enable male violence toward women. This failure allowed public attitudes and official initiatives in both Germanys to see domestic violence as a woman's problem, although this was expressed differently in the two states. In the German Democratic Republic (GDR), ideal notions of the socialist community assumed that women could rely on neighbors and family to deal with domestic violence. Meanwhile, in the Federal Republic of Germany (FRG) beliefs about individual rights underlay thinking about domestic violence and the protection of women. This meant that feminist activists and politicians expected women to be both responsible for leaving a violent relationship and for assisting battered women. Ultimately then, efforts to address domestic violence in divided Germany only contributed to the reification of conservative gender norms.

The "long 1970s" prove to be an important period for thinking about violence against women in divided Germany.[5] Since 1945, successive conservative governments controlled by the Christian Democratic Union of Germany (Christlich Demokratische Union Deutschlands, CDU) had entrenched traditional gender norms in West Germany. In September 1969, the election of Willy Brandt as the first Social Democratic chancellor heralded a more liberal reform era, and between October 1969 and October 1982, the Social Democratic Party of Germany (Sozialdemokratische Partei Deutschlands, SPD) formed the government together with the liberal Free Democratic Party (Freie Demokratische Partei, FDP). This spirit of reform was also reflected in the rise of the student movement and the new women's movement in the late 1960s. Indeed, it was out of this new women's movement that domestic violence finally gained widespread public and political attention in West Germany and internationally. In 1971, Chiswick Women's Aid, the world's first modern women's shelter, opened in the United Kingdom.[6] This refuge and its outspoken organizer, Erin Pizzey, a British family-care activist and author, acted as a model for women's projects throughout the West, and in 1976 the first domestic-violence shelter in Germany opened in West Berlin. Offering safe haven to battered women and their children, shelters spread throughout the Federal Republic in the late 1970s as activists brought increasing awareness to the issue of violence against women.

In the GDR, meanwhile, the 1970s heralded a period of liberalization following the forced change of leadership of the head of the Socialist Unity Party of Germany (Sozialistische Einheitspartei Deutschlands, SED). In May 1971, Walter Ulbricht, general secretary of the SED since 1951 was replaced by Erich Honecker, who stayed in power until 1989. Under Honecker, policies on women and the family emphasized the importance of sexual autonomy for women, with first-trimester abortions legalized in 1972. Reforms also pushed for greater equality between husband and wife in the private sphere and attempted to fulfill consumer desires.[7] Many of these developments had their origins in the mid-1960s.[8] In 1965, women in the GDR gained access to the oral contraceptive pill, known as the *Wunschkindpille* (literally the "much-wished-for-child pill").[9] In that same year, the new Family Code (*Familiengesetzbuch*) of the GDR was implemented, which guaranteed women more legal equality in the family and marriage. Alongside these reforms and the systematic support for women's education and career development, changes were also evident in everyday life in the GDR. Women became increasingly sexually assertive, common-law partnerships (a marriage-like relationship in which the couple is not legally married) became more widespread, and divorce rates soared, mainly initiated by women. Indeed, throughout the 1970s, no-fault divorce—introduced with the new Family Code—became increasingly straightforward, enabling women living with a violent husband to more easily obtain a divorce.[10]

Looking at domestic violence during this period of transformation in both Germanys provides a critical view into the extent and success of liberalization in an era known for social change. Domestic violence, while a topic of several sociological works, remains largely understudied in histories of Germany.[11] Recent literature on post-1945 German state-making, however, has shown how the private sphere, gender, and sexuality were mobilized by the state in the aftermath of World War II. Rehabilitating the family, reaffirming masculinity, and negotiating women's employment were key areas of postwar reconstruction in East and West Germany and played important roles in cementing Cold War tensions.[12] By highlighting the long-term effects of the postwar politicization of women's roles in the family, this chapter takes up historian Dagmar Herzog's call to critically examine assumptions of the "steady liberalization" of gender and sexuality by showing how developments in women's rights were contingent on the reassertion of traditional patriarchal gender roles.[13]

Furthermore, this study focuses on the entanglement of East and West Germany, engaging with recent work that encourages historians to think beyond political boundaries and instead look for interconnections between countries, nations, and states.[14] By looking for points of sharedness across the Berlin Wall—in this instance, the impact of responses to domestic violence—what emerges is a story of the similar ways in which the private sphere and civil citizenship were constructed and resisted in East and West Germany, and what this meant for women in the decades prior to German reunification in November 1989. Rather than reifying Cold War political and ideological divisions, this chapter shows the ways in which "the category of 'women' [. . .] is produced and restrained by the very structures of power through which emancipation is sought."[15]

Reconstructing Gender, Challenging Patriarchy, and Responding to Domestic Violence

The remaking of families and gender roles took on renewed importance following German defeat in May 1945.[16] Indeed, popular anxieties surrounded what many believed to be the breakdown of traditional gender roles resulting from the deleterious impact of the Second World War and Allied occupation. With millions of German men killed in the war, detained in prisoner-of-war camps, or slowly returning from the front, women constituted the majority of the population in occupied Germany in the first postwar year. This meant that they had to organize the survival of their families on their own and often were also subjected to the widespread lawlessness and sexual violence, including rape, of the early occupation. In addition, particularly in the Soviet Occupation Zone and in Berlin, women were responsible for much of the early physical reconstruction work, as the chapter by Leonie Treber in this volume demonstrates. At the same time, politicians and medical professionals were concerned with the physical and mental health of German men returning from war and their reintegration into society.[17]

In this way, redefining and reconstructing relationships between men and women became an important part of postwar reconstruction, as recent scholarship demonstrates.[18] The gender order of the postwar society became a focal point of the debate over liberal or socialist values. With respect to the Federal Republic, historians like Robert G. Moeller have highlighted the significance of the "return to the family" and "housewife marriages" to postwar state-building.[19] With this family model, Christian-conservative politicians, the Catholic and Protestant Churches, and related associations and welfare organizations encouraged women to be stay-at-home mothers while their husbands earned the main family income. Indeed, during the late 1940s and early 1950s, political and legal debates, as well as family and labor policy in the FRG aimed to enforce this family model, as the chapter by Alexandria Ruble in this volume shows. The discussion particularly focused on whether husbands and fathers could maintain legal control over property and children while still upholding the guarantee of equality between men and women, which was guaranteed in the West German Basic Law (*Grundgesetz*), the new provisional constitution from May 1949.[20] For conservative politicians, like Family Minister Franz-Josef Wuermeling (CDU), who influenced West German family policy between 1953 and 1962, reinforcing the gender hierarchy in the family by law was a way to reassert masculinity and male authority in the home and wider society, and in doing so entrench Western Christian values. Defining gender roles in this way was also a way to distance the Federal Republic from the politicization of women's roles as mothers and workers in the Third Reich and the GDR.[21]

In East Germany, women also played an important role in the reconstruction of the economy and society. Labor shortages and a predominantly female population meant that women were key to the rebuilding effort. Additionally, the ideology of "women's emancipation" from traditional gender roles has a long tradition in the socialist movement. For socialists like August Bebel, the leader of the social democratic movement in the German Empire, and Clara Zetkin, a prominent social democrat and, from 1919 to 1933, the leader of the communist women's movement, women's equality could only be reached by equal female participation in the workforce because economic independence was perceived as a precondition for individual autonomy. Indeed, August Bebel's book *Woman and Socialism*, first published in German in 1879, was still a classic text in the GDR. Consequently, in East Germany the ruling SED sought to bring women into the workplace and pursued measures that enabled women to combine full-time work and motherhood, such as establishing all-day childcare and giving women a day of paid leave every month to take care of housework. Furthermore, the narrative of equality between men and women in the GDR was particularly important for the SED, as it enabled them to underscore socialism's moral superiority over capitalism. Only under socialism could men and women—freed from the confines of gender roles and bourgeois values—find true love and fulfillment.[22]

These different valuations of women's roles and gender relations significantly affected domestic-violence intervention. In the 1950s and 1960s, there was very little discussion of domestic abuse. On both sides of the Berlin Wall, the popular attitude that spousal abuse was a private matter has resulted in very few traces of partner violence in the archive. Indeed, the people at the front line of dealing with violence—police officers and social workers—either dismissed abuse out of hand or were restricted in what they could do to help. In both halves of Germany, police rarely pursued criminal charges.[23] Social workers in the West, as evidenced in Frau M.'s story above, often ignored women's claims of abuse. Even if they wanted to help, there was no system of support for aiding women living with violence. Similarly, in the East, state-run marriage-counseling centers and workplace collectives were charged with maintaining socialist marriages and preventing divorce.[24] This meant that women living with a violent husband were instructed, both by the courts and at trade-union meetings, to keep working on their marriage. Furthermore, fault-based divorce laws in both Germanys meant that women seeking divorce on the basis of abuse had to prove it took place, requiring a doctor's evaluation or a criminal charge.[25] Again, this proof was difficult to obtain, as doctors and neighbors were often unwilling or reluctant to testify to abuse.[26] Indeed, West German women from this era reported doctors prescribing vitamins to help them deal with abuse.[27] This would only change following the introduction of no-fault divorce, which was legislated in the GDR in 1965, and in the FRG in 1976, when the SPD-FDP government finally enacted the new Marriage and Family Law.

As discussed above, this situation started to change in the 1970s, with the rise of women's activism against domestic violence. In 1971, British feminists opened Chiswick Women's Aid, the first modern battered-women's shelter. Not only did this refuge lead to a network of shelters throughout the United Kingdom, but the publication of Erin Pizzey's 1974 book *Scream Quietly or the Neighbours Will Hear* based on her experiences at Chiswick Women's Aid, provided a model for women's shelter movements globally.[28] In the United States, although women activists in St. Paul, Minnesota, and Milwaukee, Wisconsin, established helplines for women living with abuse in 1971 and 1973 respectively, it was not until the mid-1970s that crisis housing services for battered women opened. The first shelter in the United States was established in 1974 in St. Paul and was followed in 1976 by refuges in Cambridge, Massachusetts; Minneapolis, Minnesota; and Lawrence, Kansas.[29]

From there the movement spread to Western Europe, and in 1974 a group of feminists began meeting at the West Berlin Women's Center with the intention of opening a service for women living with violence. In addition to holding rallies and drawing attention to domestic violence, they attended the 1976 International Tribunal on Crimes against Women in Brussels, the first major international event of its kind. During that same year, the West Berlin group "Women Helping Women" finally procured funding to open the first women's shelter in Germany. This shelter was a model project for addressing domestic violence in the Federal Republic, and as such it received financial support from the Federal Ministry of Family Affairs, Senior Citizens, Women, and Youth (Bundesministerium für Familie, Senioren, Frauen und Jugend) and the Berlin Senate Office for Family, Youth, and Sport. Notwithstanding this *Staatsknete,* as some feminists disparagingly called the financial support by the state on the local and federal level, the shelter was staffed solely by women and was organized according to feminist principles of autonomy, antiauthoritarianism, and women's empowerment.[30]

For these activists, domestic violence was a manifestation of patriarchy. They believed that patriarchy was more than just inequality between men and women, that it was also a system that reproduced and maintained this inequality at both macro and micro levels of society and daily life. Not only did gendered power imbalances enable men to hit, rape, disrespect, and ignore women, but patriarchal norms that saw women as subordinate to men, as the property or responsibility of men, allowed this abuse to go unchallenged. For feminists, then, part of dealing with domestic violence was to contest this system—a process that started on the grassroots level. While relying on federal and local funding, West German activists created spaces and groups for women living with violence to come together and empower one another.[31]

There was nothing like the West German women's shelter movement in East Germany. Indeed, it was only in 1987 that the first crisis shelter opened in East Berlin. This refuge, run by the Catholic welfare organization Caritas, offered housing and support to anyone in need, including battered women, the homeless, and drug addicts. Prior to this, women living with an abusive partner turned to their workplace collectives, the legal and justice systems, and socialist marital-counseling services for assistance. The family court system, in particular, was a prime venue for the discussion of domestic violence. Although abuse could be used as a justification for divorce from as early as 1956 in the GDR, it became a much more common reason following the introduction of the new Family Code in 1965. This code outlined the principles of socialist marriage, highlighting that "[e]quality between men and women crucially defines the character of the family in socialist society," and introduced no-fault divorce. This meant that rather than apportioning blame and needing to prove the dissolution of the relationship, the court only had to be convinced that the marriage had lost its meaning "for the couple, the children, and also for society."[32] Subsequently, divorce rates increased, growing from 14 per 100 marriages in the early 1960s to 38 per 100 at the end of the 1980s.[33]

Much like in the West, addressing domestic violence in the GDR also involved challenging women's inequality and patriarchy. However, unlike West German feminists, SED officials understood patriarchy as a relic of capitalist, bourgeois gender relations that kept women at home. It was antithetical and anachronistic in socialism, and contesting patriarchy was an official issue. In cases of domestic abuse, judges typically made pronouncements denouncing violence in the family as alien to the principles of gender equality in socialism.[34] This was also echoed in the wider media. Following the opening of women's shelters in West Berlin in 1976 and 1979, the East Berlin press used the opportunity to highlight women's equality under socialism. In 1981, the *Berliner Zeitung* article "Ways of Life under Capitalism: Women's Shelters as a Last Refuge" discussed the creation of domestic violence shelters in West Germany.[35] The article emphasized that although the activists who had initiated these shelter projects were "keen and committed" to helping women leave abusive partners, their work was "restricted," not only by their inability to find apartments and employment for shelter residents but more generally because, limited by the fundamental inequality of men and women under capitalism, they were unable to "change the social roots of the women's misery." Similarly, a 1978 *Berliner Zeitung* article, after describing abusive men in the West as the "flotsam and jetsam of capitalist society," argued, "in socialist society, where the exploitation of people by people has been cast aside and the conditions for a humane existence are provided, women and mothers, as men's equals, have law, justice, and the welfare of the entire society at their side."[36]

However, as the following sections show, although the two German states created approaches that were meant to challenge patriarchy and affirm women's equality, in reality they maintained male authority in the private sphere and supported traditional gender roles. This meant that at the same time as they attempted to address domestic violence, inequalities between men and women nevertheless persisted. These were the very inequalities that enabled violence against women.

An Expectation of Equality: Addressing Domestic Violence in East Germany

The strong rhetoric of equality under socialism meant that women in the East did not have to fight to have domestic violence recognized as a problem. However, looking at the cases that appeared in the East German legal system from the 1960s and 1970s, it becomes apparent that the official assumption that socialism had created real equality between men and women shaped legal decisions in problematic ways. The court system—alongside the workplace collective and socialist marriage-counseling centers—was a venue for the construction and perfection of socialist citizenry.[37] This meant that women attempting to address domestic violence, either through divorce or criminal proceedings, were exposed to the state's vision of equality and marriage. Indeed, as legal-studies scholar Inga Markovits has argued, "The socialist process of conciliation, where plaintiff and defendant together are charged with the restoration of social harmony, also subjects both to the state's definition of what harmony should look like."[38] This meant that when instances of abuse were heard in the courtroom, the main issue for judges was not the violence itself but rather what it signified about the man's commitment to socialism.[39]

Legal cases would always begin by outlining the socialist credentials of the couple, and in cases involving allegations of abuse, the court would particularly focus on the life of the husband. Examining his work morale, childhood, education, how often he drank alcohol, and even whether he watched Western television, judges would draw connections between domestic violence and a failed socialist development. In doing so, the court presented domestic abuse as something that could be fixed with more stringent adherence to socialism. This resulted in pedagogical legal remedies aimed at improving socialist comportment. These included: couples being sent to attend marriage-counseling sessions; requiring the husband to maintain steady employment; or, as in a 1970 case heard by the Dispute Commission at VEB Transformer Plant "Karl-Liebknecht" in Berlin-Köpenick, a husband who stood accused of drunkenly beating his ex-wife with whom he still had to live because of the apartment shortage in the GDR was ordered to apologize and swear never to hit her again.[40] While these remedies may have improved the husband's socialist demeanor, they did little to protect the wife.

The second feature of legal cases involving domestic violence in East Germany was a clear expectation that women take advantage of official and informal social services and support networks. This had the effect of eliding the existence of gendered power imbalances, leaving women vulnerable to further violence.[41] In East Berlin in 1963, for example, a twenty-two-year-old woman, Frau S. faced criminal charges of grievous bodily harm with deadly outcome for the death of her husband.[42] According to the court, the couple's neighbors and family were not aware of the fighting, despite having seen the visible signs of abuse on her body. When asked directly by both her neighbor and her mother, Frau S. denied being beaten by her husband, feeling too ashamed to tell anyone. The marriage continued to deteriorate when, following a family event and after several bottles of wine and schnapps, the couple went to their neighbor's apartment to continue drinking. Herr S. soon became angry and demanded that they leave. In the stairwell on the way back to their apartment, he started to hit and threaten his wife. She then fled back to the neighbor's, grabbing a knife from the kitchen for protection. Her husband promptly followed her, and forcibly tried to make her leave. Once in the stairwell, he started strangling her. Still holding the knife, she lashed out at him blindly, the wound causing him to retreat to their apartment. Although an ambulance was called, Herr S. died from his injuries. It is clear from the court's reasoning there was an expectation that Frau S. should have sought outside support. After describing violence in marriage as "the grossest inconsistency with the morality of our workers," the court admonished Frau S. for not accessing any one of the various social mechanisms available to workers in the East, whether that be her collective, a counseling center, or even her mother or neighbors. The defense's argument that Frau S. was too ashamed to speak about her abuse was rejected by the court.[43]

On the surface this decision highlights a very advanced attitude toward violence in the family, acknowledging it as an issue of women's oppression. However, there were also serious limitations with this approach. First, the expectation that women access official networks of support exposed women to the state's pedagogically driven vision of marital harmony, which could result in women being sent back to live with an abusive husband. Second, at the very least women were expected to be able to turn to neighbors, coworkers, family, and friends when dealing with a violent partner. This reveals how the SED was more than willing to get citizens—primarily the women experiencing abuse, but also their coworkers, family, or friends—to compensate for the shortcomings of the system, in particular the failure to transform gender roles. The expectation of equality between men and women, and of a socially engaged citizenry willing to intervene in the private sphere, left women vulnerable not only to further violence but also to the machinations of the state.[44] Furthermore, the expectation leaves open the question of what a woman living with abuse could do if no one was willing to help. As the fate of Frau S. makes clear, it was often the case that neighbors and coworkers were more inclined to turn a blind eye than get involved in domestic affairs.

In addition, patriarchal attitudes shaped popular understanding of violence against women and, consequently, women's ability to leave abuse. For example, in 1987 the highly popular socialist youth magazine *Neues Leben* (New Life), published by the Free German Youth (Freie Deutsche Jugend, FDJ), the youth organization of the SED, printed an article on "unwanted sexuality" written by Dr. Hans-Joachim Ahrendt, a Magdeburg gynecologist and sexologist who specialized in young women's sexuality. Ahrendt encouraged girls to consider how their dress and behavior (flirting, smiles, wearing tight jeans or miniskirts) awakens the "passionate desire for sexual encounter" that drives young men to pressure or force girls into sex. He then compared this to rape, which he said is typically a violent attack committed by sick and unloved men in "dark parks."[45] These kinds of beliefs—that violent men were mentally unstable and that rape was typically committed by strangers—were widely held and were also reflected in attitudes toward domestic violence. Indeed, Frau A. recalls her neighbor telling her that, as a woman, she needed do more for her husband, essentially blaming her for her husband's violence.[46]

In the final years of the GDR there was some movement to address violence against women more critically. In the late 1970s and 1980s, filmmakers and novelists began to feature gender-based violence in their works, and in 1986 the High Court of East Germany requested a report on the topic of "Violence in the Family."[47] Furthermore, in 1987, as mentioned, Caritas opened a crisis shelter in Berlin-Hohenschönhausen that offered housing to women fleeing abuse. In spite of these moves in the direction of a more critical attitude toward domestic violence, attempts to address domestic abuse in the GDR were for the most part largely ad hoc, brought to the court's attention by women seeking a divorce. The latent patriarchal views that dismissed violence against women were never challenged, because as far as the SED was concerned, equality existed. Instances of violence were aberrations, attributable to individual, bad men, and stemmed from outdated, bourgeois gender relationships. Much like the image of rapists presented in *Neues Leben,* the man who hit his wife was alien to socialism. At the same time, this discourse of equality also created expectations that women behave as equals—able to work with their husband to improve their socialist commitment, access social services, and deal with violence in the home. In this way, while the SED might have crafted policies to enable women's formal equality, the work of creating day-to-day equality and of addressing gender violence in the workforce and in education was firmly on women's shoulders.

The Importance of Self-Help: Women's Equality and Domestic Violence in West Germany

In the West, it was the new women's movement that first broke the taboo against speaking about domestic violence. Feminist organizing in West Germany began in the late 1960s in response to the failure of the New Left and radical politics to address women's issues and needs. Leftist women, frustrated with being ignored by their male comrades, formed groups like the Action Council for the Liberation of Women (Aktionsrat zur Befreiung der Frauen) in West Berlin and the Women's Council (Weiberrat) in Frankfurt am Main. They began protesting the restrictive West German abortion law, opened women's centers and communal childcare services, and attempted to liberate women from the "tyranny of the private sphere."[48]

Women's activism against domestic violence grew out of this milieu in West Berlin during the early 1970s. The group Women Helping Women (Frauen helfen Frauen) based out of the West Berlin Women's Center was the first to draw attention to violence against women. They challenged assumptions that domestic violence was a private matter and lobbied politicians from the SPD and FDP in the federal government in Bonn and in the West Berlin Senate (the city government). In this era of reform, when the federal government was controlled by a social-liberal coalition, the FDP pursued a particularly progressive social policy, aimed at entrenching equal rights for citizens. Indeed, in cooperation with the West Berlin FDP Working Group on Emancipation, feminist activists first brought domestic violence to the attention of the West Berlin Senate when sitting FDP member Ulrich Roloff asked it to investigate how many women living in West Berlin experienced abuse.[49] This acted as a catalyst for opening the first women's shelter in the FRG in Berlin-Grunewald in 1976.

Following the British example, the Grunewald shelter was founded on the feminist principle of "self-help," a concept that encompassed values of women helping women, autonomy, equality, and antiauthoritarianism.[50] The importance of these beliefs is not only underscored in the use of the word *Frauenhaus* or "women's house" (as compared with the use of "shelter" in the United States and "refuge" in the United Kingdom), implying a modicum of communality between women, but also by the names of the women's projects themselves: the first two autonomous shelters in West Berlin were organized by Women Helping Women and Women's Self-Help—Women against Violence toward Women (Frauenselbsthilfe—Frauen gegen Gewalt an Frauen).[51]

Feminist activists believed these values were central to the fight against women's oppression and for the empowerment of women.[52] They found expression not only in the organization of the shelter, but also in its approach to rehabilitation and the way it engaged people in domestic-violence intervention and women's equality. First, the autonomous shelters in West Berlin were organized as nonhierarchical, women-only spaces—men were not permitted entry—and all the work in the shelter was to be built on the principle of teamwork, with no distinction to be made between residents and workers, or between workers themselves.[53] Second, the sharing of experiences of abuse and gender oppression between women was equally as important as the formal counseling services offered by the state. For feminists, discussing what were seen as shared experiences of womanhood was central to enabling women—both residents and shelter workers—to empower themselves, whether through the "relief" of hearing about other women's similar experiences or the confrontation with self-destructive habits.[54] Furthermore, allowing women to organize their own lives and share in household duties, such as cooking and cleaning, were also seen as ways of encouraging self-direction and self-worth.

In this manner, empowerment was forged as a defining feature of the feminist approach to domestic violence, and these practices were meant to radically privilege women's voices and their experiences as a way of addressing the control and violence exercised over them in their intimate relationships with men in particular and in society more generally. However, it also framed domestic violence as a women's issue, purposefully excluding men, which would filter through in problematic ways as the feminist shelter system entered mainstream political consciousness. In political discussions of domestic violence and violence against women more broadly, "self-help" and "empowerment" were interpreted simplistically, leading to a superficial understanding of the causes of violence against women. For example, in a 1978 meeting to discuss the creation of a second shelter in Berlin, the FDP's Working Group on Emancipation defined a shelter as "a group of women who through self-help overcome their problems, wherein the main emphasis lies on the self-initiative of the victim herself."[55] Similarly, after claiming that the primary goal of women's shelters was the maintenance of the family, Minister for the Family Katharina Focke (SPD), who held this position from 1972 to 1976, acknowledged that to fight the root causes of domestic violence, the state needed to "make women as a whole more self-sufficient—through better education, better job opportunities [. . .] so that women are not so dependent on their husbands."[56] A similar stance was taken by Heiner Geißler (CDU), the minister for the family following the collapse of the SPD-FDP coalition in 1982. At this time, the increasingly neoliberal FDP changed alliances to form a government with the conservative CDU/CSU. Geißler, who remained as minister until 1985, argued that it was the "role of the Federal Government and the entire Parliament to stand on the side of those who are weaker physically and socially, and to protect them from the strong."

In order to do this, women needed to be encouraged to confront domestic violence in their lives.[57] While Minister Focke framed empowerment and domestic violence as issues of women's financial independence, the FDP Working Group on Emancipation and CDU Family Minister Geißler underscored self-help as being about a woman's own responsibility for the violence she experienced. Both perspectives undermined the radical feminist project of using self-help to fight the structural gender inequalities that permit domestic violence. Not only did these statements misconstrue the work being done by shelters, but both emphasized women's own responsibility for creating gender inequality: in order for women to stop being victims of domestic violence, they first needed to stop being victims of the systemic gender imbalances that limited women's life choices. Despite advocating for women, the project of help as devised by government did not envision a change in masculinity because men were not expected to help or even to change their behavior. Rather, women were expected to maneuver around an unchanging masculinity.

Not unsurprisingly these conceptualizations of empowerment and self-help fit closely with the worldview of the FDP, as indicated by *Info-Blätter Frauen* (Women's Info-Sheets) published between 1972 and 1979.[58] This position had its roots in late nineteenth-century German liberalism. Liberal development in Germany had long been tied to a sexual moral order, in which paternal authority in the home was enshrined both socially and legally in the German Civil Code (*Bürgerliches Gesetzbuch,* BGB) of 1900.[59] While the subject of an ongoing discussion during the German Empire and the Weimar Republic, the tension between the maintenance of a heteropatriarchal family unit, in which women's abilities to enter into contracts and own property were circumscribed, and liberal values of equality became irreconcilable in the postwar era. Despite the guarantee of equality in the West German Basic Law, the Christian-conservative government under Konrad Adenauer (CDU), chancellor of coalition of the CDU/CSU and the FDP from 1949 to 1963, attempted to legislate patriarchal authority in the family. Because of the conflict with the Basic Law, the Adenauer government was forced to compromise on the Equal Rights Law (*Gleichberechtigungsgesetz*) of June 1957, which came into effect in July 1958.[60] Despite this *de jure* triumph of gender equality, as the attempt to forge domestic violence as a women's issue shows, patriarchy had become entwined within the West German liberal system.

Dealing with domestic violence, and gender equality more broadly, was framed as a woman's individual responsibility. Feminist activists and politicians charged women with helping others and themselves. In doing so, state responsibility for protecting its citizens was weakened, as the role of the state was framed not as an enactor of change or even as a protector of rights but rather as a catalyst for enabling people to create social change.

This approach reinscribed domestic violence as a women's issue, foreclosing a more thorough reckoning with the gender imbalances that make violence against women possible.

Conclusion

Addressing domestic violence in divided Germany meant challenging patriarchal gender norms and reflected the entangled nature of Cold War gender mobilization. Since the early postwar era, East and West Germany created competing visions of family life from which they drew legitimacy and stability. In East Germany, this happened from above, as ensuring women's equality was a part of constructing socialism. Indeed, equality was one of many weapons the SED used to legitimize its rule and distinguish itself from the West. Domestic violence was therefore an official concern, and socialist judges and journalists condemned violent men as anachronistic and highlighted East Germany's claimed moral superiority to capitalism. In the West, it was feminists who contested patriarchal norms that dismissed domestic violence as a private matter. Creating grassroots initiatives, which oftentimes received and accepted federal or local funding, West German feminists opened shelters for women living with abuse. In doing so, they challenged the reassertion of masculinity and male authority in the home that was entrenched in response to Nazism and socialism after 1945.

As a result of their postwar development, different approaches to addressing domestic violence were established in East and West Germany. Women in West Germany had access to shelters and emergency services, while in the East women sought assistance from the legal system. However, in both cases women were responsible for dealing with domestic violence, as the patriarchal roots of male violence were left largely unquestioned. Women under socialism were expected to turn to family and friends, and in spite of the importance of the rhetoric of equality, popular attitudes that blamed women for their own abuse went unchallenged. Meanwhile, in the West, "self-help" was interpreted simplistically. Violence against women could be addressed through greater female employment, and women were responsible for helping women living with violence. Consequently, few questioned the issue of violent masculinity.

By looking at gender and domestic violence in post-1945 Germany, we see how challenging the patriarchal structures present in postwar Germany was about more than just access to an open public sphere or a strong rhetoric of gender equality. Rather, it was also about contesting the legacy of postwar redevelopment. As women on either side of the Berlin Wall attempted to address or speak about gender inequality and domestic abuse, they confronted competing visions of women's roles that were a part of the fabric of divided German state-making. These visions, however, were structured on long-standing heteropatriarchal norms, and the responses to domestic violence only solidified this as women continued to be left vulnerable to violence. This shows how the process of creating a liberal German state, based on civil rights and the rule of law, was built on women's labor. Whether as activists working for equality or as women leaving an abusive husband, everyday German women on both sides of the Berlin Wall helped to create equality and bring social change.

Jane Freeland is research associate in modern German history at German Historical Institute London, United Kingdom. Her research interests focus on the histories of feminism in divided Germany, and historical and contemporary issues of gender violence, citizenship and legal reform. She completed her PhD in History in 2016 at Carleton University, Canada, where her dissertation "Behind Closed Doors: Domestic Violence, Citizenship and State-Making in Divided Berlin, 1969–1990" focused on approaches to domestic violence in divided Berlin, as a way of thinking about the role of women in German state-making after 1945.

Notes

Names have been changed to protect the women's identity.
1. Gabriela Eßbach and Vera Fünfstück, "Frauen mit Gewalterfahrung in der ehemaligen DDR: Wahrnehmungszugänge und Bewältigungsstrategien: Eine Untersuchung aus dem Blickwinkel autonomer Frauenhausarbeit in Sachsen," (Diplomarbeit, Evangelische Fachhochschule für Sozialarbeit, Dresden, 1997), III.
2. Carol Hagemann-White et al., *Hilfen für mißhandelte Frauen: Abschlußbericht der wissenschaftlichen Begleitung des Modellprojekts Frauenhaus Berlin* (Stuttgart, 1981), 109.
3. Ibid.
4. Hagemann-White et al., *Hilfen*; R. Emerson Dobash and Russell P. Dobash, *Violence against Wives: A Case against the Patriarchy* (New York, 1979), and *Women, Violence and Social Change* (New York, 1992).
5. The "long 1970s" is taken to mean a period stretching from the late 1960s to the early 1980s. On this concept, see Poul Villaume et al., eds., *The "Long 1970s": Human Rights, East-West Détente and Transnational Relations* (Oxford, 2016); Timothy Brown, *West Germany and the Global Sixties: The Anti-authoritarian Revolt, 1962–1978* (London, 2013); and Joachim C. Häberlen, "Feeling like a Child: Dreams and Practices of Sexuality in the West German Alternative Left during the Long 1970s," *Journal of the History of Sexuality* 25, no. 2 (2016): 219–45. On how 1970s activism was connected to previous social movements,

see Simon Hall, "Protest Movements in the 1970s: The Long 1960s," *Journal of Contemporary History* 43, no. 4 (2008): 655–72.
6. On the opening of this shelter, see Erin Pizzey, *Scream Quietly or the Neighbours Will Hear* (Harmondsworth, 1974).
7. Paul Betts, *Within Walls: Private Life in the German Democratic Republic* (New York, 2010); Josie McLellan, *Love in the Time of Communism: Intimacy and Sexuality in the GDR* (Cambridge, 2011); and Dagmar Herzog, *Sex after Fascism: Memory and Morality in Twentieth-Century Germany* (Princeton, NJ, 2005).
8. Donna Harsch, *Revenge of the Domestic: Women, the Family, and Communism in the German Democratic Republic* (Princeton, NJ, 2007).
9. Annette Leo and Christian König, *Die "Wunschkindpille": Weibliche Erfahrung und Staatliche Geburtenpolitik in der DDR* (Göttingen, 2015).
10. Lothar Mertens, *Wider die sozialistische Familiennorm: Ehescheidung in der DDR 1950–1989* (Opladen, 1998). On divorce in the early GDR, see Andrew I. Port, "Love, Lust, and Lies under Communism: Family Values and Adulterous Liaisons in the German Democratic Republic," *Central European History* 44, no. 3 (2011): 478–505.
11. Sociological works include: Hagemann-White et al., *Hilfen*; Monika Schröttle, *Politik und Gewalt im Geschlechterverhältnis: Eine empirische Untersuchung über Ausmaß, Ursache und Hintergründe von Gewalt gegen Frauen in ostdeutschen Paarbeziehungen vor und nach der deutsch-deutschen Vereinigung* (Bielefeld, 1999); Birgit Bütow, "Gewalt gegen Frauen im 'anderen Deutschland,'" in *Dokumentation Fachforum 2—Frauenhaus in Bewegung, 20.–22.11.1996* (Berlin, 1996), 27–37; and Eßbach and Fünfstück, "Frauen mit Gewalterfahrung." Those historical works containing a discussion of domestic violence include: Betts, *Within Walls*; Harsch, *Revenge*; and Karrin Hanshew, *Terror and Democracy in West Germany* (Cambridge, 2012).
12. Betts, *Within Walls*; Harsch, *Revenge*; McLellan, *Love*; Herzog, *Sex after Fascism*; Port, "Love, Lust and Lies"; Katherine Pence and Paul Betts, eds., *Socialist Modern: East German Everyday Culture and Politics* (Ann Arbor, MI, 2008); and Elizabeth Heineman, *What Difference Does a Husband Make? Women and Marital Status in Nazi and Postwar Germany* (Berkeley, CA, 1999)
13. Dagmar Herzog, "Syncopated Sex: Transforming European Sexual Cultures," *American Historical Review* 114 (2009): 1287–308.
14. In postcolonial history, see Frederic Cooper and Ann Laura Stoler, eds., *Tensions in Empire: Colonial Cultures in a Bourgeois World* (Berkeley, CA, 1997); Sebastian Conrad and Shalini Randeria, eds., *Jenseits des Eurozentrismus: Postkoloniale Perspektiven in den Geschichts- und Kulturwissenschaften* (Frankfurt/M., 2002); and Michael Werner and Bénédicte Zimmermann, "Beyond Comparison: *Histoire Croisée* and the Challenge of Reflexivity," *History and Theory* 45, no. 1 (2006): 30–50.
15. Judith Butler, *Gender Trouble: Feminism and the Subversion of Identity* (New York, 1999), 5.
16. Robert G. Moeller, *Protecting Motherhood: Women and the Family in the Politics of Postwar West Germany* (Berkeley, CA, 1993); Frank Biess, *Homecomings: Returning POWs and the Legacies of Defeat in Postwar Germany* (Princeton, NJ, 2006); Maria Höhn, *GIs and Fräuleins: The German-American Encounter in 1950s West Germany* (Chapel Hill, NC, 2002); McLellan, *Love*; Harsch, *Revenge*; Paul Betts, *Within Walls*; and Heineman, *What Difference*.

17. Biess, *Homecomings*.
18. See for example Karen Hagemann and Sonya Michel, eds., *Gender and the Long Postwar: The United States and the Two Germanys, 1945–1989* (Baltimore, MD, 2014).
19. Moeller, *Protecting Motherhood*; Heineman, *What Difference*; Biess, *Homecomings*; Herzog, *Sex after Fascism*; Elizabeth Heineman, "Complete Families, Half Families, No Families at All: Female-Headed Households and the Reconstruction of the Family in the Early Federal Republic," *Central European History* 29, no. 1 (1996): 19–60; Maria Höhn "Frau im Haus, Girl im Spiegel: Discourse on Women in the Interregnum Period of 1945–1949 and the Question of German Identity," *Central European History* 26, no. 1 (1993): 57–90; Robert G. Moeller, "'The Last Soldiers of the Great War' and Tales of Family Reunions in the Federal Republic of Germany," *Signs* 24, no. 1 (1998): 129–45; and Elizabeth Heineman, "Single Motherhood and Maternal Employment in Divided Germany: Ideology, Policy, and Social Pressures in the 1950s," *Journal of Women's History* 12, no. 3 (2000): 146–72.
20. Moeller, *Protecting Motherhood*.
21. Herzog, *Sex after Fascism*.
22. Harsch, *Revenge*; Heineman, *What Difference*; Carla Sachse, *Der Hausarbeitstag: Gerechtigkeit und Gleichberechtigung in Ost und West 1939–1994* (Göttingen, 2002); Karen Hagemann, "Between Ideology and Economy: The 'Time Politics' of Child Care and Public Education in the Two Germanys," *Social Politics* 13, no. 1 (2006): 217–60; McLellan, *Love*; and Jane Freeland, "Creating Good Socialist Women: Continuities, Desire and Degeneration in Slatan Dudow's *The Destinies of Women*," *Journal of Women's History* 29, no. 1 (2017): 87–110.
23. Ulla Terlinden, *Verbesserung der Wohnsituation von Frauen und ihren Kindern nach dem Verlassen des Frauenhauses* (Stuttgart, 1987); Eßbach and Fünfstück, *Frauen mit Gewalterfahrung*; Hagemann-White et al., *Hilfen*; and Schröttle, *Politik und Gewalt*.
24. McLellan, *Love*; and Annette Timm, *The Politics of Fertility in Twentieth-Century Berlin* (Cambridge, 2010).
25. Hagemann-White, *Hilfen*; and "Geschlagen-Getreten-Gedemütigt: Frauen werden von Männern mißhandelt! Wo finden sie Hilfe? Wir brauchen ein Frauenhaus," Landesarchiv Berlin (LAB), E Rep 300-96/9.
26. "Geschlagen-Getreten-Gedemütigt," LAB.
27. Sarah Haffner, ed., *Gewalt in der Ehe und was Frauen dagegen tun* (Berlin, 1976).
28. Carol Hagemann-White, "Die Frauenhausbewegung," in *Der große Unterschied: Die neue Frauenbewegung und die siebziger Jahre*, ed. Kristina von Soden (Berlin, 1988), 48–52; and Frauenzentrum Berlin, ed., *Gewalt gegen Frauen in Ehe, Psychiatrie, Gynäkologie, Vergewaltigung, Beruf, Film und was Frauen dagegen tun: Beiträge zum Internationalen Tribunal über Gewalt gegen Frauen, Brüssel März 1976* (Berlin, 1976).
29. Elizabeth B. A. Miller, "Moving to the Head of the River: The Early Years of the U.S. Battered Women's Movement" (PhD diss., University of Kansas, 2010).
30. Hagemann-White, *Hilfen*; Verein zur Förderung des Schutzes mißhandelter Frauen (e.V.), "Projektantrag zur Einrichtung eines Frauenhauses in Berlin (West) (1976)," LAB, B Rep 002/12504. For a feminist debate about the state funding of autonomous feminist projects, see for example Myra Marx Ferree, *Varieties of Feminism: German Gender Politics in Global Perspective* (Stanford, CA, 2012),

94–99; Gilla Dölle, "Weiberwirtschaft: Einblicke in die Finanzgeschäfte der Frauenbewegung des 20. Jahrhunderts," in *Geld und Geschlecht: Tabus, Paradoxien, Ideologien,* ed. Brigitta Wrede (Wiesbaden, 2003), 166–80.
31. Hagemann-White, *Hilfen*; Verein zur Förderung des Schutzes mißhandelter Frauen (e.V.), "Projektantrag zur Einrichtung eines Frauenhauses in Berlin (West) (1976)," LAB, B Rep 002/12504; Frauenzentrum Berlin, ed., *Gewalt gegen Frauen.*
32. *Familiengesetzbuch* 1965 (GDR), §2 and §24(1).
33. Mertens, *Wider die sozialistische Ehenorm*; Port, "Love, Lust and Lies"; and McLellan, *Love.*
34. See, for example, "Case 3BF 29.71, 10.5.1971, Stadtgericht Berlin," LAB, C Rep 301/3760, 1-49/71.
35. Birgit Walter, "Lebensweise im Kapitalismus: Frauenhäuser als letzte Zuflucht; Zunehmende Brutalität im Ehealltag in westeuropäischen Ländern," *Berliner Zeitung,* 21 November 1981, 4.
36. Susanne Statkowa, "Zuflucht ohne Recht," *Berliner Zeitung,* 5 August 1978.
37. Timm, *Politics of Fertility.*
38. Inga Markovits, as quoted in Peter W. Sperlich, *The East German Social Courts: Law and Justice in a Marxist-Leninist Society* (Westport, CT, 2007). See also the discussion of married harmony in Margarete Wolfram, "Die Gründung von Ehe und Familie erfordert hohe gesellschaftliche Verantwortung," *Der Schöffe* 22 (1975): ix–xiv.
39. Jane Freeland, "Morals on Trial: State-Making and Domestic Violence in the East German Courtroom," *Perspectives on Europe* 44, no. 1 (2014): 55–60.
40. "Konfliktkommission Beschluß, 4.11.1970, VEB Transformatorenwerk, 'Karl-Liebknecht,'" LAB, C Rep 411/1358.
41. On the assumed transformations of citizens under socialism, see Jan Palmowski, "Citizenship, Identity and Community in the German Democratic Republic," in *Citizenship and National Identity in Twentieth Century Germany,* ed. Geoff Eley and Jan Palmowski (Stanford, CA, 2008), 73–91.
42. "Case 910 S 113/63, 1–3 October, 1963, SBG Berlin-Weißensee," LAB, C Rep 301/3145 (1963). This case was also reported in: "Unser Gerichtsbericht: Aus Furcht getötet," [*sic*] *Berliner Zeitung,* 4 October 1963, 12.
43. Ibid.
44. "Bezirksverwaltung Potsdam, BV Pdm Abt II 244," Der Bundesbeauftragte für die Unterlagen des Staatssicherheitsdienstes der ehemaligen Deutschen Demokratischen Republik, Berlin.
45. "Ungewollte Sexualität," *Neues Leben* 9 (1987): 10–11.
46. Eßbach and Fünfstück, *Frauen mit Gewalterfahrung,* VI.
47. For artist portrayals of violence against women, see, for example, Brigitta Reimann, *Fransizka Linkerhand* (Berlin, 1998), and the films *Bis daß der Tod euch scheidet* (1979) by Heiner Carow, and *Solo Sunny* (1980) from directors Konrad Wolf and Wolfgang Kohlhaase.
48. "Selbstverständnis des Aktionsrats zur Befreiung der Frauen," Frauenforschungs-, -bildungs- und -informationszentrum, Berlin (FFBIZ), A Rep 400 17.20 0-4.
49. Verein zur Förderung des Schutzes misshandelter Frauen (e.V.), "Projektantrag zur Einrichtung eines Frauenhauses in Berlin (West) (1976)," LAB, B Rep 002/12504; "Protokoll der AKE-Sitzung am 10.2.1976, FDP LV Berlin, AK Emanzipation 16844," Archiv des Liberalismus (AdL); "Arbeitskreis-Emanzipation, Bibl/Druckschrift D1-592(1978)," AdL.

50. Ferree, *Varieties of Feminism*, 94–99.
51. Ibid.; Verein zur Förderung, "Projektantrag zur Einrichtung eines Frauenhauses"; and "Konzeption für das zweite Berliner Frauenhaus (1978)," LAB, B Rep 002/12504.
52. Hagemann-White, "Die Frauenhausbewegung"; and "Darum haben Männer im Frauenhaus nichts zu suchen," *EMMA* 6 (1978), 32–36. See also Ferree, *Varieties of Feminism*.
53. Verein zur Förderung, "Projektantrag zur Einrichtung eines Frauenhauses."
54. "Konzeption für das zweite Berliner Frauenhaus (1978)."
55. "Protokoll der Sitzung vom 20.12.1978, FDP LV Berlin, AK Emanzipation," AdL, 16850.
56. "Parlamentarisch-Politischer Pressedienst, *Das aktuelle PPP-Interview. Brutalität in der Ehe ist ein ernstes Problem*, 6. Mai 1976," FFBIZ, A Rep 400 BRD 22.5 (1970-78).
57. "Fachtagung zur 'Gewalt gegen Frauen'" held by the Bundesminister für Jugend, Familie, Gesundheit, Dr. Heiner Geißler, published 13 January 1984 by the Pressedienst des Bundesministeriums für Jugend, Familie und Gesundheit, LAB, B Rep 002/12505.
58. "FDP Info-Blätter-Frauen, 1978–79," AdL.
59. Moeller, *Protecting Motherhood*; Elizabeth Heineman, *Before Porn Was Legal: The Erotica Empire of Beate Uhse* (Chicago, 2011); Carole Pateman, *The Sexual Contract* (Cambridge, 1988); Isabel V. Hull, *Sexuality, State, and Civil Society in Germany 1700–1815* (Ithaca, NY, 1996); and Dieter Schwab, "Gleichberechtigung und Familienrecht im 20. Jahrhundert," in *Frauen in der Geschichte des Rechts*, ed. Ute Gerhard (Munich, 1997), 796–801.
60. Moeller, *Protecting Motherhood*.

Selected Bibliography

Betts, Paul. *Within Walls: Private Life in the German Democratic Republic*. New York, 2010.

Ferree, Myra Marx. *Varieties of Feminism: German Gender Politics in Global Perspective*. Stanford, CA, 2012.

Freeland, Jane. "Morals on Trial: State-Making and Domestic Violence in the East German Courtroom." *Perspectives on Europe* 44, no. 1 (2014): 55–60.

———. "Creating Good Socialist Women: Continuities, Desire and Degeneration in Slatan Dudow's *The Destinies of Women*." *Journal of Women's History* 29, no. 1 (2017): 87–110.

Hagemann-White, Carol. "Die Frauenhausbewegung." In *Der große Unterschied: Die neue Frauenbewegung und die siebziger Jahre*, ed. Kristina von Soden, 48–52. Berlin, 1988.

———, et al. *Hilfen für mißhandelte Frauen: Abschlußbericht der wissenschaftlichen Begleitung des Modellprojekts Frauenhaus Berlin*. Stuttgart, 1981.

Harsch, Donna. *Revenge of the Domestic: Women, the Family, and Communism in the German Democratic Republic*. Princeton, NJ, 2007.

Heineman, Elizabeth. *What Difference Does a Husband Make? Women and Marital Status in Nazi and Postwar Germany*. Berkeley, CA, 1999.

———. *Before Porn Was Legal: The Erotica Empire of Beate Uhse*. Chicago, 2011.
Herzog, Dagmar. *Sex after Fascism: Memory and Morality in Twentieth-Century Germany*. Princeton, NJ, 2005.
———. "Syncopated Sex: Transforming European Sexual Cultures." *The American Historical Review* 114 (2009): 1287–1308.
Höhn, Maria. *GIs and Fräuleins: The German-American Encounter in 1950s West Germany*. Chapel Hill, NC, 2002.
Lister, Ruth. *Citizenship: Feminist Perspectives*. London, 1997.
McLellan, Josie. *Love in the Time of Communism: Intimacy and Sexuality in the GDR*. Cambridge, 2011.
Moeller, Robert G. *Protecting Motherhood: Women and the Family in the Politics of Postwar West Germany*. Berkeley, CA, 1993.
Palmowski, Jan. "Citizenship, Identity and Community in the German Democratic Republic." In *Citizenship and National Identity in 20th Century Germany*, ed. Geoff Eley and Jan Palmowski., 73–91. Stanford, CA, 2008.
Pateman, Carole. *The Sexual Contract*. Cambridge, 1988.
Pence, Katherine, and Paul Betts, eds. *Socialist Modern: East German Everyday Culture and Politics*. Ann Arbor, MI, 2008.
Schröttle, Monika. *Politik und Gewalt im Geschlechterverhältnis: Eine empirische Untersuchung über Ausmaß, Ursache und Hintergründe von Gewalt gegen Frauen in ostdeutschen Paarbeziehungen vor und nach der deutsch-deutschen Vereinigung*. Bielefeld, 1999.
Weeks, Jeffrey. "The Sexual Citizen." *Theory, Culture and Society* 15, nos. 3–4 (1998): 35–52.

CHAPTER 12

Searching for Identity
1950s Homophile Politics in West Germany and Its Roots in the Weimar Homosexual Movement

Clayton J. Whisnant

When the Nazis took power in 1933, they began to reverse the astonishing advances the homosexual movement in Germany had made since the 1890s. The numerous gay magazines of the Weimar era were shut down by the police in March. The wide network of friendship clubs, as the local gay and lesbian social organizations of the 1920s are generally known, ceased operation in the course of the summer of 1933. Adolf Brand—founder of the world's first gay magazine, *Der Eigene*—had his house searched by the police five times in the first month after the takeover, losing all of his photographs, magazines, and books in the process.[1] Magnus Hirschfeld, who was recognized internationally as Germany's chief advocate for homosexual rights, had to watch from France as the institutions that he had spent years building were destroyed. His Institute of Sexual Research (Institut für Sexualwissenschaft) in Berlin was plundered by the Nazis on 6 May 1933. His Scientific-Humanitarian Committee (Wissenschaftlich-humanitäres Komitee, WhK) met for the last time in June. This organization had worked tirelessly since 1897 to convince the German public of the need to repeal Germany's sodomy law, Paragraph 175 of the Penal Code (*Reichsstrafgesetzbuch*, StGB). Now, they decided understandably to dissolve the organization rather than face the Nazi police state.

After 1945, a new generation of political activists tried to rebuild many of the institutions of the old gay movement in the three Western occupation zones. Unfortunately, hardly any of these organizations lasted more than a few years, and none of the magazines they promoted ever had the success of the 1920s-era periodicals. Between the old Paragraph 184 of the 1872 Penal Code that still prohibited pornography and the new 1953 Law against the Distribution of Written Material Endangering Youth (*Gesetz über die Verbreitung jugendgefährdender Schriften*), the new homosexual publishers in West Germany found it very challenging to get a toehold in the market.[2] Only *Der Weg zu Freundschaft und Toleranz* survived through the 1960s. In its final year, *Der Weg* had a print run of only about 400 copies per issue.

An overly narrow focus on the weakness of the West German movement, however, misses the international network of associations and publications that appeared after 1945. Much-needed leadership was provided by *Der Kreis,* a magazine published out of Switzerland beginning in 1943 that had an international readership, as well as the Amsterdam-based International Committee for Sexual Equality founded in 1951. It had taken some time, but Hirschfeld's dream of an international movement for sexual reform was finally taking root.

The homophile movement, as this international network of the 1950s and 1960s is generally called, is largely remembered for what gay activists and historians of international gay rights movements alike describe as a conservative strategy of achieving legal reform and social recognition by asserting the respectability of gay men and lesbians. For that generation of activists who came of age after the 1969 Stonewall riots in New York, whose goals were shaped by the radical aspirations of the 1960s and the countercultural efforts at building alternative social institutions during the 1970s, homophiles had failed to deal with the deeply grounded mechanisms of sexual repression and other kinds of social subjugation that underpinned prejudices against gay and lesbian relationships. This politics of respectability was really a kind of politics of the closet, they argued: like African Americans who played the "Uncle Tom," gay men who sought respectability on the terms of straight society were only engaging in a form of mimicry that made them implicit in their own repression. However, this difference between the 1950s homophiles and 1970s gay liberation activists was deeper than a tactical dispute. Whereas the homophiles sought social assimilation, gay liberation activists dreamed of a more thoroughgoing reorganization of society. Armed with Marxist-inspired theories of social revolution and the radical psychoanalysis of Wilhelm Reich, they imagined a day when sexual liberation could be linked with deeper forms of freedom in a postcapitalist, postimperialist, and postracist world.

Historians have also downplayed the significance of the homophile movement. Though they have certainly acknowledged the fact that in many cases these groups were taking the first steps in their respective countries toward organizing gay men and lesbians for political purposes, in general historians have described the efforts of homophile activists in this period as timid and restrained. The outlook and political strategy of the homophiles were reflective of the times, fitting neatly into the mentality of the crew-cut, gray-on-gray world of the 1950s and early 1960s.

Certainly the social and political context of the era cannot be ignored. In the case of 1950s West Germany, we need to keep in mind that this was a nation that had gone through decades of war, economic turbulence, and dictatorship. The whole country at some level was engaged in what historian Hanna Schissler aptly calls a "normalization project."[3] And like in the United States and elsewhere in the West during the Cold War, anxiety about communism in West Germany—a constant threat from just across the border and from within as evidenced by the 1955 ban of the Communist Party in West Germany—significantly shaped the young country's society and political culture.[4] So did Christianity, as both the Catholic and Lutheran Churches found themselves reinvigorated after the war and knew the vast majority of the population supported them. When it came to public attitudes toward sexuality, as historian Dagmar Herzog has demonstrated, such a restrictive atmosphere was certainly a product of a country working through its sordid past, trying to find an ethical foundation for itself in traditional Christianity, and also remaining wary of anything that might be deemed radical.[5] In an environment in which the media, religious authorities, and many political leaders united in emphasizing the rewards and joys of traditional marriage and the importance of family for rebuilding West German society, it is no surprise to find that homophile activists encountered significant obstacles in organizing and in fashioning a strategy to achieve their goals.

Does this mean that the movement of the 1950s was simply a disappointment? Was it at best a brief episode between the pioneering years of the 1920s and the revitalization of activism that came after 1969? Scholars are now reevaluating the importance of the homophile movement. Leila Rupp stresses the pathbreaking nature of the international connections made by the various organizations.[6] David Churchill demonstrates how these international connections nurtured a rich environment in which ideas could be shared and a discourse based on "humanist psychology, citizenship, and rights talk" could ultimately be developed.[7] Julian Jackson's analysis of France's homophile organization, *Arcadie*, emphasizes that given the cultural context of the time, this group was anything but timid.[8] Martin Meeker argues that, at least in the case of the Mattachine Society, founded in 1950 as one of the earliest homophile organizations in the United States, the "mask of respectability" put on by the organization was in fact a successful strategy of "dissimulation" that "disarmed some of the antigay sentiment in American society while it also enabled the homophiles to defend and nurture the gay world."[9] And in my book *Male Homosexuality in West Germany* I suggest that the division between a "conservative" homophile movement and a more "radical" gay liberation movement fails to acknowledge the ways that the homophiles paved the way for the activism of the 1970s.[10]

In this chapter I look backward instead of forward, focusing in particular on lines of continuities in the attitudes and political strategy between the Weimar-era movement and postwar homophile activism. I explore the role that memories of the institutions and strategies of an earlier period played in the movement as it reemerged after 1945. After a section that briefly reviews the major factions within the 1920s movement, focusing in particular on the friendship clubs and the magazines that were connected with them, I turn to Hans Giese, who became a prominent figure in the fight against Paragraph 175 of the Penal Code in the 1950s and 1960s, and then afterward to the friendship clubs and homophile magazines of the postwar era. Giese and other homophile writers, I argue, championed a politics of respectability that was remarkably similar to the strategy favored by the Weimar-era friendship clubs. This strategy suggested that the best way to achieve the decriminalization of homosexuality and to otherwise fight public prejudices about same-sex love was for gay men to demonstrate through their personal behavior and public presentation that they were well-behaved, law-abiding citizens who posed no threat to public order or the safety of their fellow citizens—and indeed that they had much in common with the straight majority.

The Politics of Respectability in the Weimar Movement

The German homosexual movement as it emerged in the early twentieth century was at first divided into two main wings: the WhK led by Magnus Hirschfeld, and the "masculinists" associated with intellectuals such as Benedict Friedlaender, John Henry Mackay, Hans Blüher, and Adolf Brand. Although some recent research has underlined some of the values and relationships that linked these two wings of the movement together, there is no doubt that an intense rivalry between Hirschfeld and Brand had developed by the time that the First World War broke out, a rivalry that was only papered over in 1922–23 when the wings were united briefly by the Operations Committee (Aktionausschuß), led by the writer Kurt Hiller, in the hope of achieving the reform of Paragraph 175.[11]

The WhK advocated above all a strategy based on scientific research into the nature of sexuality and public education that would gradually undermine people's prejudices toward homosexuality. Most members followed Magnus Hirschfeld's theory that homosexuality represented one version of a range of "sexual intermediaries" that manifest themselves in human life. Since humans all begin life as an embryo that only develops sexual characteristics as it matures, Hirschfeld reasoned, many adults ultimately exhibit a range of both masculine and feminine characteristics whether biologically, emotionally, psychologically, or sexually.[12] Homosexuality, therefore, was a completely natural psychic and behavioral variation that presented no threat to society and certainly should not be considered immoral or illegal. Politically, Hirschfeld and many of his colleagues were sympathetic with the goals of social democracy and by the 1920s had united with other sex reformers interested in the liberalization of marriage laws, easier access to contraception, and the modernization of public attitudes toward sexuality.[13]

The masculinists, on the other hand, resented the suggestion that homosexuality effectively represented a form of effeminacy. They did not deny the existence of effeminate homosexuals, but they insisted that a majority of men who loved other men were quite masculine. Friedlaender and Blüher called them "men's heroes" (*Männerhelden*)—individuals capable of making great spiritual and cultural contributions and who could demonstrate tremendous bravery and self-sacrifice. A misogynist language and an ardent antifeminist stance characterized these masculinists' ideology. Dependent as the masculinists were on German notions of *Kultur*, they were often skeptical of the way that Hirschfeld used the biological sciences for his arguments. They preferred instead a more anthropological or social-psychological understanding of homosexuality (sometimes borrowing ideas from Freud once psychoanalytic theories began to circulate). Sexual desire, both conscious and unconscious, played an important role in solidifying relationships between people and in inspiring men to accomplish great deeds. Though nearly all educated gay men and lesbians in Germany at the time developed ideas about their sexuality by looking back to ancient Greece, masculinists were especially insistent on the connection and were perhaps more likely than most to pursue relationships with adolescents or younger men in their search for love. Politically, the masculinists tended to be more diverse than their WhK counterparts. Like Brand, many were anarchists, although the racism, antifeminism, and Romantic nationalism espoused by key members of the group meant that they had something in common with right-wing parties. Indeed, Blüher found himself drawn into conservative circles shortly after the First World War, and his concept of the emotionally charged and homoerotically tinged *Männerbund* (male-bonding society) found some reception among Nazis during the 1920s, especially in the party's paramilitary wing, the Sturmabteilung (SA).[14]

So much of the literature on the Weimar homosexual movement has focused on the political infighting between Hirschfeld and the masculinists that only in the past decade or so have we started to uncover the independent position forged by the author and publisher Friedrich Radszuweit, the founder of the Federation for Human Rights (Bund für Menschenrecht) in 1923. In much of the early literature, Radszuweit was categorized with the masculinists because of his tendencies to spar with Hirschfeld and his opposition to Hirschfeld's scientific theory of intersexuality.[15] More recent scholarship, though, has started to appreciate that Radszuweit was really an entirely independent player—a third pole, and given the influence of his magazines and his many political connections, really a more important one than Brand by 1929.[16] If anyone was Hirschfeld's chief rival by the end of the Weimar era, it was Radszuweit.

Radszuweit emerged out of the milieu of the Weimar friendship clubs, that network of social organizations for gay men and lesbians that materialized surprisingly rapidly after the end of the First World War. At first organized into a large umbrella organization known as the German Friendship Alliance (Deutscher Freundschafts-Verband), these clubs initially looked to a newly founded magazine, *Die Freundschaft*, to disseminate information and publicity for their activities. Under the oversight of the founder and editor of the magazine, Karl Schultz, *Die Freundschaft* published short stories, poems, essays, and readers' letters. Although it experienced some difficult years legally and financially, it was still successful enough to inspire a host of imitators in the following decade.

Die Freundschaft and other titles of the Weimar-era homosexual press often included images of attractive young men alongside the other printed material. From today's point of view, the subjects were shockingly young—adolescents or even younger boys—given that they were generally portrayed nude or scantily clad. Sometimes the images were clear efforts to imitate or at least remind viewers of classical or Renaissance works, with the Hellenistic statues *Boy with Thorn* and *The Praying Boy* being noteworthy favorites. Photographers worked in a style pioneered in the 1870s and 1880s by Wilhelm von Plüschow and Wilhelm von Gloeden, who had specialized in classically posed photos of Italian boys taken in the rocky terrain of small Italian towns or along Mediterranean seashores.[17] The other common style portrayed athletic-looking men in natural settings, standing against a tree, wading in a river, or doing some light exercise in a field. This second category of images embodied a tradition of naturalism that was influential at the time. In both nudist publications and many Weimar-era homosexual magazines, healthy, fit physiques were intended as signs of bodies that had escaped the enfeebling constraints of civilization.[18]

The artistic pretensions of these images were part of a larger effort of the magazines to assert their respectability by borrowing the trappings of German *Kultur*. As such, it fit into the politics of respectability initiated by *Die Freundschaft* and soon adopted by most other titles in the homosexual press in the course of the decade. According to the historian Stefan Micheler, who has done the most work on these magazines, numerous writers across the entire industry focused on the importance of respectability (*Anständigkeit*) and inconspicuousness (*Unauffälligkeit*). They called on readers to "give their best at work and in their lives," to work hard, and to seek the respect of others through their service and achievements.[19] Such respectability also meant avoiding any activity that might connect homosexuality with public disorder or criminality. Many warned against looking for sexual opportunities around public urinals, parks, or similar locations. One author showed little sympathy for such behavior in his letter to *Die Freundschaft*, remarking that he found the "dirty" goings-on that took place in many bathrooms thoroughly disgusting.[20] Other authors attacked specifically male prostitution as a dangerous criminal activity that attracted violent, immoral young men into the gay scene and fostered negative stereotypes of homosexuality in the wider population.[21]

Calls for respectability in the homosexual press frequently had a significant gendered dimension. Gay men were advised to dress and act in masculine ways. Those who did not—*Tante* or *Tunte* (pansy), as effeminate homosexuals were sometimes called in the parlance of the early twentieth-century gay scene—were attacked for undermining the movement's efforts.[22] Especially in the first few years of the decade, there was an epidemic of "pansy baiting" (*Tantenhetze*) that broke out in the magazines. Numerous writers accused effeminate homosexuals of "playing at being women" (*Weiberspielen*). Others did not go so far but still insisted that homosexuals who felt an urge to act effeminately should do what they could to suppress or hide the tendency. One man took it as a personal challenge, insisting that we all need to "work hard on ourselves to discard every tendency toward effeminacy."[23]

By the mid-1920s, Friedrich Radszuweit had emerged as the most prominent champion of this politics of respectability. After taking control of the German Friendship Alliance in 1923, he established a more disciplined and centralized structure for the national organization and renamed the group as the Federation for Human Rights.[24] The individual chapters continued to focus on organizing social activities for its members, but at the national level Radszuweit sought to give his organization more public visibility and a political focus as well. Establishing his own press, he started a number of newspapers and magazines to target different male and female audiences: *Die Blätter für Menschenrechte, Das Freundschaftsblatt, Die Insel, Die Freundin,* and *Das dritte Geschlecht*. He printed pamphlets and other educational materials, and also nourished relationships with politicians and the mainstream press. He sponsored lectures, and over the Easter weekend of 1926 he even organized a series of public meetings in thirty-four locations. Politically, Radszuweit insisted that his Federation for Human Rights remain unaffiliated with any one specific party so that it could appeal to as many gay men and lesbians as possible. The group's members consequently represented every party within the broad spectrum of Weimar politics. A majority supported the socialists, communists, or the two liberal parties, but a not inconsiderable number voted for the more conservative Catholic Center Party, the right-wing German National People's Party, and even by 1930 the Nazi Party.[25]

In a move designed to establish his own position within the homosexual movement, Radszuweit distanced his Federation for Human Rights from Kurt Hiller, Magnus Hirschfeld, and other key leaders of the WhK in late 1923 and 1924.[26] It should be said that Radszuweit was certainly not opposed to scientific work on homosexuality. In fact, he relied on specialists connected with the WhK to provide summaries of some of the scientific research for his various publications. He also, we should note, basically agreed with Hirschfeld that homosexuality was an inborn trait.[27] However, Radszuweit and most of the other writers associated with his magazines were fundamentally opposed to the gender implications of Hirschfeld's theories. This tension with Hirschfeld did not mean that Radszuweit aligned himself with Adolf Brand or the other masculinists. Their so-called "Manly Culture," he wrote in an article for his *Blätter für Menschenrechte*, will "always remain a specter (*Schemen*), for one needs to create not simply a masculine culture but also a feminine culture as well."[28] He rejected as politically risky the masculinist tendency to associate homosexuality with pederasty as they imagined it practiced in ancient Greece. He also distrusted the masculinists' cultural snobbery. Although many of the men in Brand's circle were anarchists or otherwise vaguely leftist, they still betrayed an elitist attitude born of education and an immersion in the art world. Radszuweit made it clear that he represented the "everyday" homosexual—the gay men and women of the middle class who, armed with the legal rights that they deserved, could make an important contribution to an orderly society and a strong state. He hoped that his movement would raise the public visibility of the "respectable, law-abiding majority of homosexual citizens," demonstrating to the rest of German society that not all homosexuals were child predators, effeminate "pansies," and criminal prostitutes.[29]

Radszuweit was not necessarily hostile to cross-dressers or individuals whom we would label as transgender. In fact, his lesbian magazine *Freundin* was notable for simultaneously addressing a transvestite audience, and in the early 1930s he experimented briefly with establishing *Das Dritte Geschlecht* as a magazine dedicated specifically to transvestite issues. However, he did firmly believe that it was politically dangerous to equate male homosexuality with effeminacy. Radszuwiet insisted that Hirschfeld drew wrong conclusions by basing his research on a limited sample of "abnormal" men rather than on the "respectable homosexual."[30] "When will Hirschfeld realize," he once asked, "that by revealing his freak show to the public he does not help the homosexual struggle but only hurts it? [. . .] Why does Dr. Hirschfeld represent only these abnormalities that exist only in a few isolated cases and not any number of homosexual men and women as they look in reality?"[31]

Like later homophiles, Radszuweit would also search for another word that might serve as an alternative to "homosexual." As historian Stefan Micheler observes, many of the gay men who wrote for these periodicals clearly did not approve of the term. Some men complained that the term's emphasis on sexuality led it to be associated with something "dirty." Instead, they hoped that a new terminology could be found that emphasized love and relationships and consequently might make it easier to accept publicly. Quite a few used "homoerotic," "friend," or *gleichgeschlechtlich* (same-sex). They talked of *mann-männlicher Eros* (male-male Eros) or more obliquely of *Lieblingsminne* (favored love). "Invert" was borrowed from the sexological literature of the day and used fairly often. And then many of the magazines published by Friedrich Radszuweit's press tried to push the politicized concept of "comrades of a species" (*Artgenossen*).[32] "Comrade" was an especially resonant choice, as it was a word that had been used by German social democrats since the 1860s, and in the Weimar era the term would have reminded people of the revolutionary "comrades" of 1918–19.

Hans Giese and the "Authentic" Homosexual

Despite his growing importance in the gay scene by the end of the Weimar era, Radszuweit fell into oblivion quickly after his death in 1932. Hirschfeld's name and work, in contrast, continued to carry significance in the memory of postwar gay activists. For them, though, it was not specifically Hirschfeld's theories of intersexuality that were important; these theories were sometimes discussed in the gay press but were largely seen as outmoded in comparison with more recent psychological and sociological work into sexuality. Instead, it was his outstanding role in building a foundation for political activism and scientific research into sexuality that was held up as a model to be followed.

In April 1949, a twenty-eight-year-old doctor and aspiring sexologist from Frankfurt am Main named Hans Giese founded a new Institute of Sexual Research. Though clearly inspired by Hirschfeld's clinic and research facility, Giese's new institute was much more modest to say the least: no palatial mansion, no clinical staff, no medical facilities to conduct research, and certainly no museum to attract tourists. In fact, it really was just a small psychiatric practice housed in his parents' apartment building that Giese hoped to use as a springboard to do his own research.

Giese had completed his first study of homosexuality in 1946 with a dissertation in medicine titled *Die Formen männlicher Homosexualität* (The

Forms of Male Homosexuality).³³ It proved difficult to find a permanent academic position with this dissertation topic in postwar West Germany, but his father—who held a prominent chair in the law school of Frankfurt's Goethe University—had connections that allowed him to eke out a living for his son for the next few years. By 1949, Giese had clearly set his mind on trying to step into the big shoes left by Magnus Hirschfeld. He contacted *Der Kreis,* sending them a notice that he planned on refounding the Scientific-Humanitarian Committee. This effort was stillborn, but in 1950 he organized the first major postwar conference for sexology in West Germany, and soon afterward became the chair for a newly created German Society for Sexual Research (Deutsche Gesellschaft für Sexualforschung, DGfS). He established a new academic journal, *Die Zeitschrift für Sexualforschung,* and in 1953 also a new monograph series entitled *Beiträge zur Sexualforschung.* In 1958, he published his first major work, *Der homosexuelle Mann in der Welt.* Giese's habilitation at the University of Hamburg in the same year allowed him to find employment there of a more permanent nature. By the end of the 1960s, he had catapulted into the public eye as both a prominent professional voice in favor of liberal legal reform and a researcher documenting the changing sexual behaviors and attitudes of the decade.³⁴

Giese might have seen himself as inheriting the mantel of Hirschfeld, but he was a very different person. Struggling with depression much of his life, he was attracted early on to the angst-ridden German philosophy of Martin Heidegger, not the self-assured Enlightenment thinking exhibited by Hirschfeld's works. His own research, in fact, was derived not from biologically based psychiatry at all but instead from the phenomenological psychotherapy that Viktor von Gebsattel had pioneered during the 1920s. Giese did borrow heavily from the sociological methods being championed in the United States, frequently using extensive questionnaires that were circulated among the population that he was studying. However, in going through the results, he exhibited a phenomenological attention to language and an interest in letting his subjects "speak for themselves."

Surprisingly, Giese had been a member of the Nazi Party. The exact level of his engagement with the Nazis is not yet known, though his chief biographer Barbara Zeh does note that he was acquitted by the local tribunal (*Spruchkammer*) put in charge of the denazification process.³⁵ Still, what significance to place on this acquittal is unclear since many academics and scientists who were dangerously involved in Nazi political work and even with Nazi medical experiments somehow made it safely through denazification, keeping their academic standing and scientific reputations intact after 1945. Indeed, Giese would work closely with many of this older generation of academics in the 1950s—especially the phenomenological psychiatrist Hans Bürger-Prinz, who did more than anyone to help guide and promote Giese's early career.

Admittedly, Bürger-Prinz was mostly known at the University of Hamburg during the 1950s as a cheerful, supportive mentor whose good-naturedness and eloquence in front of the classroom did much to win many young students over to the study of psychiatry.[36] Unfortunately, largely forgotten for decades was Bürger-Prinz's involvement in some awful experiments on shell-shocked or otherwise disturbed soldiers during the Third Reich, and he probably also had some role in the Nazi euthanasia program.[37] When it came to homosexuality, Bürger-Prinz had suggested in some of his 1930s essays that it was essentially a failure of courage—a sign of immaturity that predisposed some men toward various kinds of addictive, self-destructive behavior. He certainly was a supporter of the Nazi government's homosexual policies, which he and many other psychiatrists at the time saw as a necessary safeguard preventing the further spread of homosexuality in society.

Giese's ideas about homosexuality betrayed some troubling similarities with Bürger-Prinz's, as suggested by the scholar Peter von Rönn's important work on the topic. Like his mentor, Giese portrayed homosexuality as a lifestyle built around the fear of venturing forth into the heterosexual world of adulthood. He drew parallels between homosexuality and narcissism, which also, Giese claimed, involved an absorption with the experience of one's own body. Moreover, he worried about the tendency of homosexuals to become addicted to sexual encounters, which he thought drove many to seek endless engagements in public bathrooms or among male prostitutes.[38] However, he did introduce an important novelty into Bürger-Prinz's framework for understanding sexual desire between members of the same sex. In *Der homosexuelle Mann in der Welt,* he insisted that, despite the psychic origin of the condition, homosexuals could still achieve an "authentic" version of sexuality that involved true love, understanding, and commitment. In this book, he documented several cases of men who lived and stayed together in long-lasting relationships without "the vicious circle of promiscuity, the increasing frequency, and so on" that could be found among unattached homosexuals.[39]

Giese drew two conclusions from his findings. First, society was committing a crime by hindering homosexuals from forming permanent, loving, ethical relationships with each other, and it should accept some of the blame for the sexual promiscuity of the male homosexual. Equally important, though, was the lesson for homosexual men themselves. Despite the obstacles, Giese insisted, gay men could form faithful relationships with each other if they put their minds to it. Turning to the street was no answer. In a later essay titled "The Role of Addiction," he warned that anonymous sexual encounters produced a "growing feeling of emptiness, a growing insecurity, disconnectedness, even extremity" which only leads to "more and more encounters of the same sort."[40]

We might speculate about the psychological roots of Giese's work. Were his concerns about sexual "addiction" rooted in his own conflicted feelings toward his sexuality? It is certainly easy to read his warnings about the danger of "the streets" as reflecting anxieties about his own sexual urges, which are known to have gotten him into some trouble during his school years.[41] Especially now as an adult who was trying to manage an increasingly public persona as both a respectable, authoritative scientific expert and also an advocate for the reform of the laws regarding sexuality, such anxieties must have been considerable.

However, placing his work into the context of the larger homophile movement suggests that other mechanics played a role as well. Like other homophile activists, he was no doubt trying to fashion a strategy that he believed might resonate with the political and cultural contours of the postwar world. And, though he was too young to have direct memories of Friedrich Radszuweit or the friendship clubs of the Weimar era, his contact with members of the homophile movement allowed him to adopt their political strategy that involved making claims toward respectability and work it into his own thinking.

A New Era of Friendship Clubs

It was possible for Giese to try to step into Hirschfeld's position because so many of the familiar faces of the Weimar-era homosexual movement were dead. Radszuweit was the first to pass away. Suffering from tuberculosis, he died in 1932; his life partner and heir, Martin Butzkow, had the sad experience of watching the Nazis shut down Radszuweit's lifework. Hirschfeld suffered a fatal heart attack in southern France in 1935. Adolf Brand died in the Allied bombing in Berlin. Of the major leaders of the Weimar-era movement, only Kurt Hiller was still alive. After a long period of exile, first in Czechoslovakia and later in Britain, Hiller did return to live in Germany, but only in 1955. He was peripherally involved with efforts to revive the WhK, but as an independent socialist he was much more concerned with the political future of a postfascist Germany.[42]

The efforts to rebuild the WhK might have led to nothing, but slightly more successful were those organizations modeled on the old friendship clubs of the 1920s. Social events, such as dances, festivities, and outings, filled much of their calendar. Most were also affiliated with a magazine that helped to promote events and attract members. Even as some tried to promote greater political consciousness through public talks or essays printed in the magazines, social activities continued to be vital to political organization. Giese had some contact with one of the earliest organizations, Frankfurt's Association for a Humane Way of Life (Verein für humanitäre Lebensgestaltung), established by Heinz Meininger in 1949. In West Berlin, the Society for the Reform of Sexual Law (Gesellschaft für Reform des Sexualrechts) registered with the city authorities in July 1951. Hamburg's Club of Friends (Club der Freunde) was organized by Johannes Dörrast, who simultaneously began to publish one of the first postwar homosexual magazines, *Die Freunde*. In Bremen, several anti-Nazi resistance activists established the International Friendship Lodge (Internationale Freundschaftsloge), which was connected with its own magazine, *Die Insel*—a name clearly designed to remind people of Friedrich Radszuweit's successful entertainment magazine of the same name. The largest of the organizations, though, was the Society for Human Rights (Gesellschaft für Menschenrechte), which by 1953 was led by Erwin Haarmann, the editor for *Humanitas,* another one of West Germany's gay magazines.[43]

Within this emerging movement, "homophile" gradually acquired currency as the preferred term to describe men and women who loved members of the same sex. Proposed as an alternative to "homosexual," "homophile" was thought by the activists of the movement to downplay the sexual aspects of the relationship between gay men and between lesbians. Although it had been coined by Karl Günter Heimsoth in the 1920s, the term entered regular use only now in the postwar era, most likely originally because of its use by Dutch activists involved with a homosexual friendship club known as the COC (Cultuur en Ontspanningscentrum, or Center for Culture and Recreation). After the Second World War, the COC became critical for establishing new international connections between the various homosexual organizations popping up on both sides of the Atlantic. Through the work of the COC's International Committee for Sexual Equality, but also through *Der Kreis,* which worked closely with the COC in these years, the term "homophile" became widespread in the 1950s and 1960s. It was especially popular among activists and those sympathetic to the cause, and so it consequently acquired the function of signaling that the person who used it sought wider public acceptance of same-sex love and was most likely in favor of decriminalization. By the early 1960s, the term was even being used by progressive-minded psychiatrists, doctors, theologians, and sexual-education writers.

There were many notable similarities between the homophile magazines of the 1950s and their Weimar-era predecessors. *Die Insel, Der Weg, Die Freunde, Die Gefährten, Der Ring,* and *Vox* also included a mix of essays, romantic stories, poems, pictures, and personal ads. Only *Humanitas* stood out as something different—more serious and political with very little fluff. Readers who were old enough to remember the 1920s would have found much to make them nostalgic. Even references to Thomas Mann, Stefan George, or other turn-of-the-century writers and artists admired by gay men were not unusual.

Moreover, many of the magazine's photographs were taken in a style very similar to that found in the homosexual and nudist publications of the early twentieth century. True, by 1952 the influence of American bodybuilding magazines and similar "beefcake" drawings and photographs was clearly making its mark. Still, a surprising number of the images were either reprints of pre-1945 photographs or were composed in either the classical or naturalist styles that had been so popular at the turn of the century. Nazi-era art had also been marked by classicism and naturalism, and so a casual observer of the postwar magazines could easily miss the surprising number of Nazi-era images that were reproduced in them (for example, photographs of Arno Brecker's statues and reproductions of Leni Riefenstahl's work).

Whether 1950s readers were disturbed by these images is harder to say. Certainly no letter was ever published by the magazines objecting to the use of Nazi-era art. When it came to the use of images of naked or partially clothed adolescents, there might have been at least some awareness that there was a problem with publishing them given the efforts to win social recognition. When in 1952 the editors of *Die Freunde* tried to evade the country's pornography laws by moving away from nude photos and replacing them with images of clothed men working or enjoying free time together, one man wrote in support of the decision, "The disappearance of nude photos from our magazines can only be welcomed. We do not want any sort of pornographic sheet, but an ethically upright magazine that defends our view of life."[44] Noticeable too in the images published in *Die Freunde* under the "new line," as the editors called it, was a shift toward slightly older models in their late teens or early twenties. Implicitly, this suggests some awareness that there was a real problem with publishing images of nude boys during an era in which homosexual men were widely stereotyped as sexual predators who preyed on vulnerable children.[45]

Whatever the style of the photography, the magazines of the 1950s clearly chose to emphasize the masculine quality of their subjects. Certainly these representations could be challenging and even potentially offensive for the heterosexual audience of the day since they offered the male body as an object of physical desire. This objectification of masculine bodies, so common today in media and advertising, was rare in the 1950s, notwithstanding Elvis and a few American films. Nevertheless, we should keep in mind the photographs that were absent. There were no images of cross-dressers such as those that could be found in some of Magnus Hirschfeld's books from the turn of the century. There were also no depictions of men otherwise acting or dressing effeminately, such as what might have been found in the art of the 1920s.

This absence is significant, especially given the ideological bent of the magazines. These magazines were quite diverse in terms of the essays, stories, and letters that they published, but taken together, all these voices suggested that homosexuals could be many people—lawyers, scientists, professors, artists, writers, and even husbands and fathers. They were knowledgeable, articulate people who played a range of important social roles. Moreover, there were also calls for gay men to present themselves as "respectable" citizens. Take for example *Der Kreis*: this leading gay magazine of the era has been analyzed by the historian Hubert Kennedy, who notes the tendency of *Der Kreis* to present male homosexuals (its primary audience) as both masculine and respectable.[46] Cautions against finding love in "the street" were plentiful, the pleasures of which were "the most fleeting thing in the world," since it is "awash with the flotsam of society and can slowly strangle even homosexual love in its monotony."[47] Other writers called on male homosexuals to live discreetly yet honestly. One author suggested, "Tact shows itself not only in knowing how to keep silent, but above all in the manner of behavior toward the outside world and toward the companions-in-destiny."[48] When it came to effeminate behavior, another author at least once called for some sympathy for those "pansies" who after all also had no choice in their fate. However, many other writers complained about such behavior that attracted negative attention. Physician and sexologist Rudolf Klimmer, the most prominent East German activist for legal reform, argued in a letter to the magazine in 1957 that the effeminate homosexual "has the duty to conduct himself in public as inconspicuously as possible, not indulge himself, and all the more not exaggerate his feminine behavior to the outside." He agreed with Hans Bürger-Prinz that effeminacy was "an extreme imitation that cloaks the kernel of vital weakness, empty experience and great desire to show off."[49]

A similar analysis can be made of much of the material presented in the magazines published in West Germany. Here as well were verbal attacks on men who acted too effeminately. F. F. Wesely, who wrote for *Die Insel*, asserted that it was "every homosexual's duty [. . .] to honorably and respectably hate all obsequiousness [*Muckertum*] and effeminacy to death, for it is [these characteristics] that make different sexual dispositions so laughable. After all it is a small step from laughable to contemptible, and from contemptible to persecuted."[50] He complained that people still identified homosexuals with "hordes of feeble and unmanly men that can only have a deleterious effect on male society." Just as they assumed that lesbian women were "masculine-hard," they dismissed gay men for their allegedly characteristic "walk, gestures, clothing, and so on," which were seen as signs of deeper "unmanliness and weakness." This conflation of homosexuality and femininity did an injustice to gay men who took "no part in femininity." It overlooked the many "manly homosexuals, who love their friends based on a masculine disposition."[51]

In 1952, several writers discussed the story of Christine Jorgensen, an American transwoman who received a tremendous amount of media attention for having undergone sex-reassignment surgery in Denmark. Though some of their essays expressed sympathy with the emotional turmoil that must have driven her to take such a radical step, they also expressed concern that her case would only reinforce stereotypes that the movement was trying to dispel. *Humanitas*'s editor Erwin Haarmann noted that there were many homosexual men who "in no way felt womanly," had no desire "to take on feminine mannerisms or to play the female role," and yet had no desire to be heterosexual. Some even found the female body "repulsive, not only sexually but also aesthetically." Such men were deeply disturbed by the Joergensen case, Haarmann reported.[52] Another writer for the same magazine suggested that her case should be chalked up as a failure of medicine rather than a success, because psychotherapy had not succeeded in allowing her to come to terms with her true self.[53]

Beside this emphasis on the masculinity of many homosexual men, there were also warnings about turning to the streets to seek love among male prostitutes. One reader of *Die Freunde* noted in a letter to the magazine,

> When these days I walk through certain streets and see the shy, dull glances from the living things that live like animals down there, nausea overcomes me—or is it a deeply felt sympathy?—and I realize how a man can shrink into nothing. At these moments, I feel as if I no longer have the right to walk through the green world.[54]

In *Humanitas*, the liberal-minded lawyer Botho Laserstein published an extended essay entitled "Hustler Karl: A Criminological Report" in serial form between June and August 1954. Laserstein described male prostitutes as "the most dangerous of criminals" who robbed, blackmailed, and even murdered homosexuals. In a language that implied class prejudices, Lasterstein portrayed the boys who hung around public toilettes looking for clients as often so "brutal, dirty, and ragged" (*brutal, verschmutzt, und zerlumpt*) that it was remarkable they could find any takers.[55] The fact that they could find men to whom they could sell sex acts was due ultimately to Paragraph 175, which drove otherwise harmless and respectable men to seek love and companionship in such circumstances.

Conclusion

Given the continuity between the attitudes of the homophile movement and the magazines of the 1950s, on the one hand, and the political line championed by the homosexual press and friendship clubs during the 1920s, on the other, it is remarkable that a more direct line between the two eras cannot be drawn. However, in my research, I have never seen Radszuweit mentioned by name in the postwar magazines or other published material, nor were the political tactics of the Federation for Human Rights discussed explicitly. Other factors would nevertheless suggest that memories left some imprint on the minds of the generation that took over after 1945. As we have seen, the social clubs that appeared after the war were very similar to those that had made up his Federation for Human Rights. Erwin Haarmann's Society for Human Rights was clearly named with Radszuweit's earlier organization in mind. Nearly all the magazines associated with the different West German homophile groups were plainly modeled on Weimar-era publications. And even figures as young as the sexologist Hans Giese adopted a strategy based on the politics of respectability that was remarkably similar to that promoted by the Weimar-era friendship clubs.

By drawing this connection between the 1920s and the 1950s, we can conclude that specific institutional forms and political strategies of the postwar era were at least as dependent on memories of an earlier era as they were reflective of contemporary culture and politics. However, I also want to go a little father by suggesting that the long-term picture actually forces us to change how we view the significance of homophile activism. From this point of view, it looks less like a short, unsuccessful period of conservative activism and more like a phase within a much longer homosexual engagement with a politics of respectability. Indeed, given the way that the gay- and lesbian-marriage debate has forcefully reemerged since the 1990s, it is really the radicalism of the 1970s and early 1980s that seems unusual. This is not to say that gay liberation's critique of the homophile movement was always wrong. Nevertheless, the dilemmas faced by the homophile movement have not been somehow bypassed by the forward march of history but are very much still with us today. How to seek acceptance and yet still maintain difference? How to shape a language that will effectively communicate with others what LGBTQ people want and convince them of the need for change? And how to make alliances that can generate real social change but without sacrificing what is truly important to the LGBTQ community? All are issues with which the homophile movement grappled, and they deserve consideration in our ongoing reevaluation of this period of activism.

Clayton J. Whisnant was recently named Chapman Professor of Humanities at Wofford College, Spartanburg, South Carolina. His research focus is on issues of masculinity and sexuality in Cold War West Germany.

His publications include: *Male Homosexuality in West Germany: Between Persecution and Freedom, 1945–1969* (Palgrave Macmillan, 2012); and *Queer Identities and Politics in Germany: A History, 1880–1945* (Harrington Park Press, 2016). He started a new research project on social democracy during the 1970s.

Notes

Parts of this chapter have been previously published in Clayton J. Whisnant, *Queer Identities and Politics in Germany: A History, 1880–1945* (New York: Harrington Park Press, 2016).

I wish to thank Friederike Brühöfener, Karen Hagemann, Donna Harsch, and Dagmar Herzog for their suggestions and insightful comments.

1. Manfred Herzer, "Die Zerschlagung der Schwulenbewegung," in *Goodbye to Berlin? 100 Jahre Schwulenbewegung*, ed. Schwules Museum (Berlin, 1997), 157–58.
2. Clayton J. Whisnant, *Male Homosexuality in West Germany: Between Persecution and Freedom, 1945–69* (Basingstoke, 2014), 105–8.
3. Hanna Schissler, "'Normalization' as Project: Some Thoughts on Gender Relations in West Germany during the 1950s," in *The Miracle Years: A Cultural History of West Germany, 1949–1968*, ed. Hanna Schissler (Princeton, NJ, 2001), 359–75.
4. Eric D. Weitz, "The Ever-Present Other: Communism in the Making of West Germany," in Schissler, *Miracle Years*, 219–32.
5. Dagmar Herzog, *Sex after Fascism: Memory and Morality in Twentieth-Century Germany* (Princeton, NJ, 2005), 101–22.
6. Leila J. Rupp, "The Persistence of Transnational Organizing: The Case of the Homophile Movement," *American Historical Review* 116, no. 4 (2011): 1034.
7. David S. Churchill, "Transnationalism and Homophile Political Culture in the Postwar Decades," *GLQ: A Journal of Lesbian and Gay Studies* 15, no. 1 (2008): 33.
8. Julian Jackson, *Living in Arcadia: Homosexuality, Politics, and Morality in France from the Liberation to AIDS* (Chicago, 2009).
9. Martin Meeker, "Behind the Mask of Respectability: Reconsidering the Mattachine Society and Male Homophile Practice, 1950s and 1960s," *Journal of the History of Sexuality* 10, no. 1 (2001): 81.
10. Whisnant, *Male Homosexuality*, 208.
11. For a recent effort to highlight some of the connections between the two factions of the movement, see Marita Keilson-Lauritz, "Tanten, Kerle und Skandale: Die Geburt des 'modernen Homosexuellen' aus den Flügelkämpfen der Emanzipation," in *Homosexualität und Staatsräson: Männlichkeit, Homophobie und Politik in Deutschland 1900–1945*, ed. Susanne zur Nieden (Frankfurt/M., 2005), 82–83.
12. A good recent biography is Elena Mancini, *Magnus Hirschfeld and the Quest for Sexual Freedom: A History of the First International Sexual Freedom Movement* (New York, 2010).
13. A good, very readable account of the work of Hirschfeld and his Scientific-Humanitarian Committee can be found in Robert Beachy's recent book *Gay Ber-*

lin: Birthplace of a Modern Identity* (New York, 2014). Other recent works include Laurie Marhoefer, *Sex and the Weimar Republic: German Homosexual Emancipation and the Rise of the Nazis* (Toronto, 2015), as well as my book *Queer Identities and Politics in Germany: A History, 1880–1945* (New York, 2016).

14. Whisnant, *Queer Identities,* 33–39, 74–78, 187–92. See also Claudia Bruns's work, especially "The Politics of Masculinity in the (Homo-)Sexual Discourse (1880–1920)," *German History* 23, no. 3 (2005): 306–20.
15. See, for example, Hans-Georg Stümke, *Homosexuelle in Deutschland: Eine politische Geschichte* (Munich, 1989), 58.
16. Stefan Micheler, *Selbstbilder und Fremdbilder der "Anderen": Männer begehrende Männer in der Weimar Republik und der NS-Zeit* (Konstanz, 2005); Glenn Ramsey, "The Rites of Artgenossen: Contesting Homosexual Political Culture in Weimar Germany," *Journal of the History of Sexuality* 17, no. 1 (2008): 85–109; and Marhoefer, *Sex and the Weimar Republic.*
17. Whisnant, *Queer Identities,* 139–44.
18. For more on naturalism as used in this sense, see Michael Hau, *The Cult of Health and Beauty in Germany: A Social History, 1890–1930* (Chicago, 2003). Also, for an in-depth consideration of the theme of youth as it developed in the Weimar homosexual movement, see Javier Semper Vendrell, "Youthful Perversity: Adolescence and Homosexuality in the Weimar Republic" (PhD diss., University of Wisconsin, 2015).
19. Micheler, *Selbstbilder und Fremdbilder,* 172.
20. Ibid., 178.
21. Ibid., 179–80, 226.
22. *Tunte* is a variation of *Tante,* which literally means "aunt." However, I generally translate the term as "pansy" or "fairy," since both give a better sense in English of what was meant.
23. Ibid., 184.
24. Though *Bund* can also be translated as "League," I normally translate it in this case as "Federation" to distinguish the group from the pacifist organization called the Liga für Menschenrechte to which many prominent Weimar intellectuals belonged.
25. Stefan Micheler, "Zeitschriften, Verbände und Lokale gleichgeschlechtlich begehrender Menschen in der Weimar Republik," 1 August 2008, www.stefanmicheler.de/wissenschaft/stm_zvlggbm.pdf (accessed 11 August 2017), 44.
26. Ibid., 45.
27. Micheler, *Selbstbilder und Fremdbilder,* 144.
28. Quoted in ibid.
29. Ramsey, "Rites of Artgenossen," 100.
30. Micheler, *Selbstbilder und Fremdbilder,* 144.
31. Quoted in Andreas Sternweiler, "Die Freundschaftsbünde–eine Massenbewegung," in Schwules Museum, *Goodbye to Berlin?,* 95.
32. Micheler, *Selbstbilder und Fremdbilder,* 163–66.
33. Hans Giese, "Die Formen männlicher Homosexualität: Untersuchungen an 130 Fällen" (PhD diss., Philipps-Universität Marburg, 1947).
34. Whisnant, *Male Homosexuality,* 70–78, 170–72.
35. Barbara Zeh, "Der Sexualforscher Hans Giese—Leben und Werk" (PhD diss., Johann Wolfgang Goethe-Universität Frankfurt am Main, 1988), 18–19.

36. Hans Hippius, "Nachkriegsdeutschland: Mein Weg zur Psychiatrie," in *Irgendwie kommt es anders: Psychiater erzählen*, ed. Frank Schneider (Berlin, 2012), 115.
37. Karl-Heinz Roth, "Großhungern und Gehorchen: Das Universitätskrankenhaus Eppendorf," in *Heilen und Vernichten im Mustergau Hamburg: Bevölkerungs- und Gesundheitspolitik im Dritten Reich*, ed. Angelika Ebbinghaus et al. (Hamburg, 1984), 130–34.
38. Peter von Rönn, "Die Homosexualitätsentwürfe von Hans Giese und der lange Schatten von Hans Bürger-Prinz," *Zeitschrift für Sexualforschung* 13 (2000): 277–310.
39. Hans Giese, *Der homosexuelle Mann in der Welt* (Stuttgart, 1958), 218–27.
40. Hans Giese, "Die Rolle der Sucht," in *Mensch, Geschlecht, Gesellschaft: Das Geschlechtsleben in unserer Zeit gemeinverständlich dargestellt*, vol. 2, ed. Hans Giese (Munich, 1969), 335.
41. Zeh, "Der Sexualforscher Hans Giese," 14.
42. For a recent discussion of Hiller's role in the postwar movement, which specifically treats his difficult relationship with Giese, see Raimund Wolfert, *Homosexuellenpolitik in der jungen Bundesrepublik: Kurt Hiller, Hans Giese und das Frankfurter Wissenschaftlich-humanitäre Komitee* (Göttingen, 2015).
43. Whisnant, *Male Homosexuality*, 70–91.
44. Quoted in a letter from a friend from Saarbrücken, *Die Freunde: Monatsschrift für ideale Freundschaft* 2 (January 1952): 32.
45. Whisnant, *Male Homosexuality*, 51–63.
46. Hubert Kennedy, *The Ideal Gay Man: The Story of "Der Kreis"* (London, 2000).
47. M. M. from Stuttgart, quoted in ibid., 168.
48. Quoted in ibid., 172.
49. Quoted in ibid., 172–73.
50. F. F. Wesely, "Homosexualität, Verbrechen und Öffentlichkeit," *Die Insel* 2 (February 1952), 4–5.
51. F. F. Wesely, "Homosexualität und Verweichlichung," *Die Insel* 2 (February 1952): 23.
52. Erwin Haarmann, "Die Würde der Menschennatur," *Humanitas* 2 (January 1954): 17–20.
53. Dr. med. W. Hagen, "Geschlechtsumwandlung," *Humanitas* 2 (January 1954): 15.
54. A. O., "Ethik der Freundschaft," *Die Freunde* 1 (September 1951): 26.
55. I cite the reprinted version: Botho Laserstein, *Strichjunge Karl: Ein kriminalistischer Tatsachenbericht*, 2nd ed. (Berlin, 1994), 18.

Selected Bibliography

Beachy, Robert. *Gay Berlin: Birthplace of a Modern Identity*. New York, 2014.
Bruns, Claudia. "The Politics of Masculinity in the (Homo-)Sexual Discourse (1880–1920)," *German History* 23, no. 3 (2005): 306–20.
Churchill, David S. "Transnationalism and Homophile Political Culture in the Postwar Decades." *GLQ: A Journal of Lesbian and Gay Studies* 15, no. 1 (2008): 31–65.
D'Emilio, John. *Sexual Politics, Sexual Communities: The Making of a Homosexual Minority in the United States, 1940–1970*. Chicago, 1983.

Giese, Hans. *Der homosexuelle Mann in der Welt.* Stuttgart, 1958.
———. "Die Rolle der Sucht." In *Mensch, Geschlecht, Gesellschaft: Das Geschlechtsleben in unserer Zeit gemeinverständlich dargestellt,* vol. 2, ed. Hans Giese, 330–35. Munich, 1969.
Hau, Michael. *The Cult of Health and Beauty in Germany: A Social History, 1890–1930.* Chicago, 2003.
Herzog, Dagmar. *Sex after Fascism: Memory and Morality in Twentieth-Century Germany.* Princeton, NJ, 2005.
Hippius, Hans. "Nachkriegsdeutschland: Mein Weg zur Psychiatrie." In *Irgendwie kommt es anders: Psychiater erzählen,* ed. Frank Schneider, 109–18. Berlin, 2012.
Jackson, Julian. *Living in Arcadia: Homosexuality, Politics, and Morality in France from the Liberation to AIDS.* Chicago, 2009.
Keilson-Lauritz, Marita. "Tanten, Kerle und Skandale: Die Geburt des 'modernen Homosexuellen' aus den Flügelkämpfen der Emanzipation." In *Homosexualität und Staatsräson: Männlichket, Homophobie und Politik in Deutschland 1900–1945,* ed. Susanne zur Nieden, 81–99. Frankfurt/M., 2005.
Kennedy, Hubert. *The Ideal Gay Man: The Story of Der Kreis.* London, 2000.
Laserstein, Botho. *Strichjunge Karl: Ein kriminalistischer Tatsachenbericht.* 2nd ed. Berlin, 1994.
Mancini, Elena. *Magnus Hirschfeld and the Quest for Sexual Freedom: A History of the First International Sexual Freedom Movement.* New York, 2010.
Marhoefer, Laurie. *Sex and the Weimar Republic: German Homosexual Emancipation and the Rise of the Nazis.* Toronto, 2015.
Meeker, Martin. "Behind the Mask of Respectability: Reconsidering the Mattachine Society and Male Homophile Practice, 1950s and 1960s." *Journal of the History of Sexuality* 10, no. 1 (2001): 78–116.
Micheler, Stefan. *Selbstbilder und Fremdbilder der "Anderen": Männer begehrende Männer in der Weimar Republik und der NS-Zeit.* Konstanz, 2005.
Ramsey, Glenn. "The Rites of Artgenossen: Contesting Homosexual Political Culture in Weimar Germany." *Journal of the History of Sexuality* 17, no. 1 (2008): 85–109.
Rönn, Peter von. "Die Homosexualitätsentwürfe von Hans Giese und der lange Schatten von Hans Bürger-Prinz." *Zeitschrift für Sexualforschung* 13 (2000): 277–310.
Rupp, Leila J. "The Persistence of Transnational Organizing: The Case of the Homophile Movement." *American Historical Review* 116, no. 4 (2011): 1014–39.
Schissler, Hanna, ed. *The Miracle Years: A Cultural History of West Germany, 1949–1968.* Princeton, NJ, 2001.
Sternweiler, Andreas. "Die Freundschaftsbünde—eine Massenbewegung." In *Goodbye to Berlin? 100 Jahre Schwulenbewegung,* ed. Schwules Museum, 95–104. Berlin, 1997.
Stümke, Hans-Georg. *Homosexuelle in Deutschland: Eine politische Geschichte.* Munich, 1989.
Whisnant, Clayton J. *Male Homosexuality in West Germany: Between Persecution and Freedom, 1945–69.* Basingstoke, 2014.
———. *Queer Identities and Politics in Germany: A History, 1880–1945.* New York, 2016.
Wolfert, Raimund. *Homosexuellenpolitik in der jungen Bundesrepublik: Kurt Hiller, Hans Giese und das Frankfurter Wissenschaftlich-humanitäre Komitee.* Göttingen, 2015.

CHAPTER 13

Contested Masculinities

Debates about Homosexuality in the West German Bundeswehr in the 1960s and 1970s

Friederike Brühöfener

In June 1972, the small, Hamburg-based publication *MIX: Zeitschrift für Sexuelle Emanzipation* published an article about the treatment of gay men in the West German armed forces, the Bundeswehr. The magazine maintained that military customs presented a threat to any young man, but especially to gay men. *MIX*'s basic argument was that even though the military considered them generally fit for military service, gay men were not welcomed in the Bundeswehr. Quoting Reimut Reiche of the Hamburg Institute for Sex Research (Institut für Sexualforschung), *MIX* reported that every young man who discovered that he was gay while serving in the Bundeswehr would face difficulties, because the military practiced "rituals of manhood" (*Männlichkeitsrituale*) that aimed to transform all recruits into "normal men."[1] Because heterosexuality was normative, young recruits had to carefully conceal their homosexuality and masquerade as "normal men." As a result, *MIX* argued, gay men would experience a "double deformation." In addition to becoming "emotionally crippled," like any man who served in the armed forces, gay recruits would suffer doubly from having to deny their true sexual identity.[2]

Because it offered a gendered analysis that closely linked military culture with ideals of masculinity and sexuality, the *MIX* article exemplifies one voice in the growing public debate in West Germany about gay Bundeswehr soldiers and their masculinity in the 1960s and 1970s, the theme of this chapter. Beginning in the 1960s, the relationship between sexuality, masculinity, and military practices became a topic of discussion for West German media outlets because of the reform of the Penal Code (*Reichsstrafgesetzbuch*, StGB), which had been originally implemented in 1871. This so-called Great Reform of the StGB (*Große Strafrechtsreform*) provided for the revision of the laws governing sexual offenses, including Paragraph 175, which criminalized sexual relations between men.[3] Although the *Große Strafrechtsreform* fell short of abolishing Paragraph 175 and its subclauses, the two-step revision of the law in 1969 and 1973 fundamentally altered the legal standing and rights of gay men.

Focusing on the prolonged revision of Paragraph 175 in the context of the *Große Strafrechtsreform,* this chapter analyzes the role that the Bundeswehr assumed in this process. Prompting diverse and nationwide arguments about law, morality, and sexuality, the *Große Strafrechtsreform* also brought the issue of gay men in military uniform to the forefront. As this chapter shows, the West German Federal Ministry of Defense (Bundesministerium der Verteidigung), federal parliamentarians in the Bundestag, other governmental leaders, and social, legal, and medical experts as well as extraparliamentary activists debated how the reform of Paragraph 175 would affect the West German armed forces. In addition to deliberating internally whether gay men were fit for military service and could therefore be recruited into the Bundeswehr, representatives of the Ministry of Defense were actively involved in the legal reform process. Following common procedures, the different commissions and committees responsible for revising the StGB conferred with a variety of legal, medical, and social experts, including officials working for the Ministry of Defense. Because of Paragraph 175's reform, the Ministry of Defense and related institutions had to furthermore reconsider the Bundeswehr's treatment of gay men. The changing legal situation led to more than intensive discussions within the Ministry of Defense and the revision of military guidelines and manuals. It also resulted in a number of court cases that focused on how gay men were treated in the military and what rights gay men had while serving in the armed forces.

Interestingly, references to the reform of Paragraph 175 in East Germany are strikingly absent from these discussions. Like the Federal Republic of Germany (FRG), the German Democratic Republic (GDR) reformed the StGB. Although homosexuality never ceased to be a sensitive topic east of the Iron Curtain, it was legalized much more quickly in the GDR than in West Germany. While the GDR returned to the pre-Nazi version of the law in 1950, Paragraph 175 was rarely enforced after the legal reform of 1957, and it was eventually struck from the Criminal Code in 1968. This 1968 reform introduced Paragraph 151, which penalized sexual acts carried out by an adult—man or woman—with a juvenile under 18 of the same sex. Yet, this law was repealed in 1988.[4] As the East German reforms preceded the changes in the FRG, the general silence of West German officials can be interpreted as a form of quiet demarcation; a conscious or unconscious choice to not acknowledge the "other" Germany.[5]

The ways in which the West German military participated in and reacted to the revision of Paragraph 175 was, however, not met by silence.

On the contrary, it attracted scrutiny from critical observers. Numerous gay rights and peace activists as well as mainstream journalists charged that the Bundeswehr continued to unjustly discriminate against and stigmatize gay men. In the context of the revived and expanding gay rights activism and flowering peace protests,[6] they advanced a critical assessment of the political and military apparatus that closely linked the oppression of gay men, masculine norms, and military customs.[7] In doing so, critics contributed to an understanding that military ideals of masculinity and sexuality were outdated and out of place.

When debating the reform of Paragraph 175 and whether gay men should be allowed to serve in the Bundeswehr, contemporaries used competing rhetorical strategies focusing on morality, child protection, gay rights (that is, human rights), equality before the law, and military effectiveness. This chapter argues that at the center of these negotiations stood contested and entangled notions of masculinity and sexuality. Gender, as the editors state in the introduction of this volume, "only works in connection with other 'categories of difference'" that include sexuality. As an intersectional and contingent category, it shapes ideas about gender and sexual relations.[8] Because West German law defined compulsory military service as a duty only male German citizens, who became liable to conscription at the age of eighteen, had to fulfill, contemporaries debated not only the ideal Bundeswehr soldier and officer but also what it meant to be a "normal" West German man (in military uniform). Military service in the Bundeswehr was for conscripts a rite of passage into adult manhood. Military training and service were supposed to reinforce hegemonic notions of masculinity.

As sociologist R. W. Connell has argued, societies produce through discourse and practices multiple concepts of masculinity that are related to each other in a hierarchy of power.[9] At the top of this hierarchy resides what Connell has termed a "hegemonic masculinity," against which other—competing or compliant—masculinities are measured. The value and position of any of these masculinities is, however, informed not only by gender but also by other categories of difference such as class, race, and sexuality. For instance, the "sexual nature" ascribed to and expected from the historical subject informs this hierarchy of power. As different social and cultural categories become entangled, they define differences and construct hierarchies within society, politics, and culture. When negotiating the reform of Paragraph 175, contemporaries measured "normal," "healthy" heterosexuality against "abnormal," "unhealthy" homosexuality.

By tracing this history, the chapter contributes to a growing field of research. Over the past few decades, scholars have begun to research extensively the history of sexuality in modern Germany. In addition to new studies on the German Empire, the Weimar Republic, and the Third Reich,[10] historians have also analyzed the post-1945 era.[11] This new academic interest led to more research into the lives of gay men and women as well as attention to the discourse on homosexuality in modern Germany.[12] Scholars working on the sexual history of the German military prior to 1945 have also shed light on the treatment of gay men in the armed forces during the era of the world wars.[13] Yet, in-depth studies that focus on homosexuality and the West German armed forces are still lacking. This chapter addresses this subject by first analyzing the disputes preceding and surrounding the 1969 and 1973 reforms of the StGB in West Germany. In a second step, the chapter turns to how the Ministry of Defense reconsidered its military customs and practices and how a critical public reacted to the ministry's resolution.

Contested Sexuality: The West German Reform of Paragraph 175 in the 1960s

Although arguments for a reform of the Penal Code and Paragraph 175 date back to 1871 when the German Empire implemented the StGB, the reform of the old Penal Code in West Germany was initiated in the early 1950s.[14] In 1953–54, the government of Chancellor Konrad Adenauer's conservative coalition of the Christian Democratic Union of Germany (Christlich Demokratische Union Deutschlands, CDU), its smaller Bavarian sister party the Christian Social Union (Christlich-Soziale Union, CSU), and the liberal-conservative Free Democratic Party (Freie Demokratische Partei, FDP)—charged the Great Penal Law Commission (Große Strafrechtskommission) with the drafting of a new version of the StGB. Since it was introduced with the Reich's Penal Code of 1871, Paragraph 175 had outlawed sexual relations between men, especially "coitus-like" acts. The StGB and with it Paragraph 175 retained its validity in Weimar Germany, but after their takeover the Nazis fundamentally tightened the persecution of gay men by "criminalizing a wider range of physical male homosexual acts" with a law in 1935.[15] Whereas the Penal Code of 1871 had stipulated imprisonment for "unnatural lewd acts" (*widernatürliche Unzucht*) between "persons of the male sex" or "committed with animals," the 1935 version of Paragraph 175 specified that "a man who actively or passively commits lewd acts [*Unzucht treiben*] with another man" was to be imprisoned.[16] As a result, previously unsuspicious behavior came under the purview of the law. According to contemporary interpretation, mutual masturbation, touching the clothed genitals of another person, and even a hug with allegedly lascivious intent could now fulfill the element of offense.[17] Even though the victorious allies in 1945 set out to repeal all legislation that the National Socialists had introduced, Paragraph 175 was not abolished. Therefore, the Nazi version of Paragraph 175 was still the law of the land at the time the commission went to work.

The *Große Strafrechtsreform* then raised the questions if and to what extent Paragraph 175 would be revised and, in this regard, male homosexuality decriminalized and persecuted. Following an initial proposal by the Great Penal Law Commission in 1959, a first draft of the Penal Code was discussed in 1960, and a revised draft was published in 1962. Referred to as *E 1962*, it was quickly approved by the cabinet of Adenauer's Christian Democratic government.[18] *E 1962* was, however, met with considerable opposition from legal experts and opposition-party politicians, especially the Social Democratic Party of Germany (Sozialdemokratische Partei Deutschlands, SPD). Even some church representatives raised concerns that the draft was reactionary. For instance, the commission continued to favor the criminalization of pornography, adultery, "lewdness" (*Unzucht*), and "severe lewdness" (*schwere Unzucht*) between men. According to *E 1962*, the term *Unzucht* referred to cases in which a man committed "coitus-like acts with another man," "a man over the age of 21 who actively or passively" committed "lewd acts with a man under the age of 21," or a man over the age of 18 committed "lewd acts with men who were under the age of 21." *Schwere Unzucht* referred to cases in which a man used his power as a superior in the workplace to force another man "to commit lewd acts," "a man over the age of 21 who seduce[d] a man under the age of 21 [. . .] to commit lewd acts," or cases in which a man committed "lewd acts professionally" (*gewerbsmäßig*).[19]

As historian Dagmar Herzog has pointed out, the commission's final report favored the continuing criminalization of male homosexuality because, it noted, "the overwhelming majority of the German population sees sexual relations between men as a contemptible aberration that is likely to subvert the character and destroy moral feelings."[20] Employing language fashioned and used during the Third Reich, conservative members of the commission maintained that gay men represented a "degradation of the *Volk*" (*die Entartung des Volkes*) and "a danger to our youth."[21] With such arguments they echoed the sentiments of Adenauer's Christian-conservative government, some of whose members worried that the decriminalization of male homosexuality would threaten the well-being of the young Federal Republic, which—in their view—rested on heterosexual masculinity. Members of the CDU/CSU cautioned that gay men were already "tightly organized" (*straff organisiert*) in "cliques" that could penetrate (*Eindringen*) "men's organizations such as the Bundeswehr, police, the state system, and the building industry [. . .]."[22] Gay men were seen as a threat not just to the West German armed forces but to the Federal Republic as a whole—its organization, its security system, and parts of its male-dominated economy. Thus, continuing the prosecution of gay men meant safeguarding the Federal Republic.

The commission's assessment of how West German society judged male homosexuality was both right and wrong. It was correct in stating that the majority of West Germans despised male homosexuality. To be sure, throughout the 1960s West Germans became more comfortable with different forms of family life as well as changing heterosexual roles and activities. Yet, the so-called sexual revolution did not benefit gay men. According to historian Robert G. Moeller, West Germans in 1969 still believed that male homosexuality was appalling and that gay men were more despicable than female prostitutes.[23] However, the commission missed the point in stating that this aversion translated into a general demand for the complete and utter penalization of male homosexuality.[24] In fact, *E 1962* and its version of Paragraph 175 received considerable criticism.[25] Most notable among the critiques was the anthology *Sexualität und Verbrechen* (Sexuality and Crime) edited by a well-known group of West German liberal intellectuals, including the legal scholar and Hessian attorney general Fritz Bauer (a German Jew who had fled to Sweden during the Third Reich), the much-younger legal expert Herbert Jäger, and the two well-known psychiatrists and sexologists Hans Bürger-Prinz and Hans Giese, both former Nazis.[26] They and other authors of the book vehemently challenged *E 1962*. One of these authors was the Frankfurt School philosopher and sociologist Theodor Adorno, who railed against the "repulsive homosexual paragraph."[27] Especially because of the ways that the commission justified the continuing criminalization of homosexuality, Adorno and the other authors argued that *E 1962* represented an unacceptable continuation of Nazi rhetoric, ideology, and law.

The initiation of the *Große Strafrechtsreform* and the proposed revision of Paragraph 175 led to lengthy and in-depth discussions—especially within the Ministry of Defense—between jurists, medical professionals, and military experts about the recruitment and military service of gay men. These initial deliberations, which followed on the heels of *E 1962*, focused on the broad question of whether gay men were generally fit to serve in the armed forces and could thus be conscripted for basic military service.[28] According to some legal advisors and medical professionals, the "mere declaration" by a recruit with "no previous convictions" that he was gay (*homosexuell veranlagt zu sein*) was not enough to spare him from military service. Only if the man's declaration was true and the doctor determined an "abnormal disposition" (*abartige Veranlagung*) or a "sexual perversion," meaning he had pursued or would pursue his sexual interests repeatedly while serving in the military, would a recruit be declared unfit for military service.[29] According to this assessment, homosexuality presented a deviation from normal heterosexuality and masculinity, which could endanger the effective functioning of the armed forces.

The immediate attention that the Ministry of Defense paid to the *Strafrechtsreform* and the revision of Paragraph 175 was further influenced by military recruitment practices. From the outset, the Bundeswehr was legally and in the imagination of contemporaries a "men's society." When the West German military was established in 1955–56, only male citizens could be recruited for armed military service. According to the Basic Law (*Grundgesetz*), women would not be compelled to serve in the Bundeswehr. Thus, the military represented an all-male, homosocial entity.[30] The Compulsory Military Service Act (*Wehrpflichtgesetz*) furthermore stipulated that all men who turned eighteen became liable to military service and would, if drafted, generally begin their basic military training when they turned twenty. Yet, the *Wehrpflichtgesetz* was amended over the course of the mid-1960s. In addition to setting new benchmarks to evaluate whether a recruit was fit for military service, the reform made it legally easier for young men to start their basic military training at an earlier age.[31] The *Große Strafrechtsreform* thus coincided with the reorganization of recruitment procedures and the possible, though limited, juvenescence of the armed forces, which troubled some ministerial officials.

Accordingly, the legal reform process triggered considerable interest and extensive communication between different departments within the Ministry of Defense as well as between the military, the Federal Ministry of Justice (Bundesjustizministerium), the Parliamentary Committee for Defense, and the Special Committee for the Reform of the Penal Code (Sonderausschuß für die Strafrechtsreform). In 1968, for instance, the Ministry of Justice requested various governmental authorities to suggest how the new Paragraph 175 should read. Faced with the request, the ministry's experts formulated several alternative drafts. Although all the alternative formulations proposed the prosecution of male homosexuality in the context of the armed forces, they also reflect that there was initially little consensus about how lenient or strict Paragraph 175 should be. For example, one proposal stipulated that a Bundeswehr soldier who committed "lewd acts with a soldier during active duty or within enclosed military bases" or who committed "lewd acts" with a subordinate could be punished with up to five years in prison.[32] Another, much more encompassing suggestion proposed imprisonment of up to three years for a "soldier of the Bundeswehr" who "actively or passively committed lewd acts." Based on these proposals, the Ministry of Defense officially proposed the continuing prosecution of "lewdness" committed by men between the ages of sixteen and twenty-one. In addition, it demanded a special subclause that addressed "lewdness" between military superiors and the lower ranks.[33]

However, the ministry soon learned that 1968 was not 1962 and that support for the comprehensive criminalization of male homosexuality was waning. Following the federal elections in 1965, criticism of the comprehensive criminalization of male homosexuality increased. While the elections resulted initially in the establishment of a coalition between the CDU/CSU and the FDP, political strife between the coalition partners led to the resignation of Chancellor Ludwig Erhard (CDU) and, under the aegis of Chancellor Kurt Georg Kiesinger (CDU), the formation of the Grand Coalition comprising the CDU/CSU and SPD, the opposition party since 1949. The Grand Coalition's newly appointed minister of justice, Gustav Heinemann (SPD), publicly argued against *E 1962*. In an interview with the left-wing magazine *Der Spiegel* in 1967, Heinemann pledged to decriminalize "homosexuality among adult men."[34] For the minister, the prosecution of adult men who voluntarily engaged in sexual acts was unjust, because—as he rightly pointed out—"same-sex intercourse between women" was not considered a crime.[35] Indeed, throughout the decades the German Penal Code had penalized male homosexuality, but not lesbianism. Heinemann's critique was in line with an alternative draft (*Alternativ-Entwurf*) of the Penal Code proposed by sixteen leading German and Swiss jurists that called "only" for the prosecution of adult men who engaged in sexual acts with a male minor who was between fourteen and eighteen years old.[36]

As the push for the thorough liberalization of Paragraph 175 continued, there was waning support for the addition of a subclause to specifically address the Bundeswehr. In February 1969, for example, the Committee of Defense of the Bundestag deliberated the ministry's proposal. Whereas all nine CDU politicians voted for the special restriction, arguing that "homosexuality would poison the climate," the eleven attending representatives of the SPD and the FDP voted against the provision.[37] Yet, according to the official records, neither the SPD nor the FDP opposed the provision because they thought that gay soldiers did not need to be prosecuted. On the contrary, they agreed with the CDU that homosexuality in the military had to be "confronted." They voted against it, because they feared that a special law addressing the Bundeswehr would "most likely stir public uproar. [. . .] The public might get the impression that they are many more homosexuals in the *Bundeswehr* than in the rest of society."[38] The FDP and SPD were thus concerned about the image of the armed forces if the Bundestag were to pass a special law. Second, the SPD politicians opposed the proposal because it could "defame a particular minority [. . .] and there is no evidence that gay soldiers achieve less that other soldiers."[39] According to the parliamentarians, gay men were generally fit for military service, but all sexual activities between men had to be prohibited. However, restrictions had to be put into place discreetly to not stir public discussion that could harm the military's reputation.

Given the growing consensus that homosexuality in the armed forces needed to be addressed, but that no special subclause should be included in the new West German Penal Code, the Ministry of Defense eventually refrained from pushing for such a provision. The First Law to Reform the Penal Code, which the Bundestag passed in June 1969, did not explicitly refer to men serving in the armed forces. Nevertheless, it stipulated up to five years imprisonment for "a man over the age of eighteen who—actively or passively—engages in lewd acts with a man under the age of twenty-one"; "a man who by abusing a dependency found in a service-, work-, or employment-based relationship coerces another man into lewdness—actively or passively—acts of fornication"; and "a man who professionally engages in acts of fornication."[40] This new version of Paragraph 175 drew immediate criticism and soon became known as Lex Bundeswehr.

Against a Lex Bundeswehr: The Continuing Reform of Paragraph 175

The reformed Paragraph 175 led to intense public debate. Whereas some contemporaries who supported the decriminalization of "simple homosexuality"—that is sexual acts between two consenting adult men—agreed that such a provision was necessary for barracked "men's societies," a number of activists as well as left-liberal newspapers and magazines were outraged. *Der Spiegel* was among the periodicals that energetically supported a more radical reform of Paragraph 175 in the Penal Code. Yet, in May 1969 it also observed an obvious fallacy of the suggested reform: according to its logic, gay men between eighteen and twenty-one years of age were old enough to serve in the armed forces but, unlike their heterosexual counterparts, somehow unqualified to determine their own sexual orientation.[41] For left-liberal magazines such as *Der Spiegel*, the ways in which the legislature distinguished between heterosexual and homosexual young men were unacceptable, for they violated any sense of equal treatment.

During the time *Der Spiegel* and other periodicals published articles on the reform of Paragraph 175, Klaus-Peter T., a young student, wrote several letters to the Ministry of Defense stating that the call for a Lex Bundeswehr was "a great injustice." For him, the continuing defamation and discrimination of gay men in the Bundeswehr was a "disgrace."[42] Arguing that in Germany "minorities such as Jews, gypsies, and homosexuals have always been tortured through psychological and physical terror," he emphasized that West German legislation represented a continuation of the antigay legislation that had dominated in the Imperial, Weimar, and Nazi German states. In writing to the Ministry of Defense, Klaus-Peter hoped to convince the minister and the entire social-liberal coalition "to put an end to the pogrom atmosphere" and special discriminatory laws.[43] His letter voiced the opinion of many young men and women in the New Left, especially the emerging student and homophile movements.

The criticism of the newly revised Paragraph 175 also extended to the world of jurists. In late 1969, for example, Helmut Ostermeyer, a left-liberal-leaning judge in the Bielefeld family court and who in 1979 became a founding member of the alternative Green Party (Die Grünen), published an article in the journal for legal policy, *Zeitschrift für Rechtspolitik*, titled "Is the New § 175 of the Penal Code Unconstitutional?"[44] The article showed Ostermeyer's irritation with the new version of Paragraph 175. He wrote, "Just imagine [. . .] two friends who are of the same age can maintain a same-sex relationship until they turn eighteen, then they have to pause for three years, and at the end of age 21 they can resume their relationship." He speculated that this strange age range was caused by the legislators' intent to "smuggle the highly controversial special right for the *Bundeswehr* [into the law] without causing much furor," and continued by bluntly exclaiming, "This is not acceptable!"[45]

This multilayered criticism influenced the continuing reform process fostered by the election of the Willy Brandt as the chancellor of an SPD-FDP government in October 1969. For the first time since 1949, the Federal Republic was headed by chancellor from the SPD. This change in political power reflected a change in the political culture of the whole West German society, which became more open to reform. In the wake of the elections, the Penal Code and Paragraph 175 once more fell under review. The subsequent negotiations were defined above all by the notion that Paragraph 175 created inequality between heterosexual and homosexual citizens, which could not be justified. Bidding farewell to the idea that the Penal Code had to preserve this particular heteronormative understanding of West Germany's decency and morality above all else, the members of the Special Reform Committee could not find a valid reason why homosexual men between the ages of eighteen and twenty-one had to be treated differently. As a result, Paragraph 175 of the Fourth Law to Reform the Penal Code, which the Bundestag passed in November 1973, stipulated that "a man over the age of 18 who engages—passively or actively—in sexual acts with another man under the age of 18 will be punished with imprisonment of up to five years."[46] The paragraph was renamed from "Crimes and Misdemeanors against Morality" into "Offenses against Sexual Self-Determination," and the word "lewdness" was replaced by the equivalent of the term "sexual acts." These changes indicate a new approach to homosexuality in politics and society.

Fit to Serve, but Not Fit to Command: Debates over Gay Men in the Bundeswehr

The two-step reform of Paragraph 175 intensified the discussions within the Ministry of Defense, because some of its employees continued to believe that "homosexual activities" were a perversion of normal masculinity and heterosexuality that could endanger the functioning of the Bundeswehr. Considering homosexuality to be "perverted" and "contemptuous," members of the general staff were concerned about servicemen whose homosexual activities were uncovered.[47] Whereas servicemen who did not "pursue their disposition" and did not engage in continuous "homosexual acts" (*homosexuell ausleben*) did not have to fear any repercussions or disciplinary punishment,[48] servicemen whose "disposition" became public knowledge would face a "grave loss of authority and trustworthiness."[49] This loss of authority was problematic, they argued, because it endangered the troops' cleanliness, order, and discipline.[50] Moreover, the ministry maintained that it had a "special responsibility toward the parents of young recruits" and had to do "everything to protect young men against perils" that derive from the military's "communal showers and sleeping arrangements."

Arguing that male homosexuality could pose a threat to the effective functioning of the armed forces and put young recruits at an unacceptable risk, the military's leadership and legal experts agreed that "soldiers' same sex activities" could still represent "malfeasance" (*Dienstvergehen*), even though it was not considered a crime outside of the Bundeswehr.[51] Although the revision of the Penal Code drastically reduced the threat of punishment for gay men, military officials agreed that this liberalization could not be fully extended to the Bundeswehr. This assessment derived from the relationship between the Military Discipline Code of the Bundeswehr and the Penal Code. Because of their special duties and their occupational loyalty and responsibility toward the state, soldiers' deeds or misdeeds were also regulated and prosecuted according to the Military Discipline Code. If a soldier violated his duties and responsibilities, he could be penalized even if his actions did not constitute a crime according to the Penal Code. As "homosexual activities" were considered a violation of soldiers' duties and responsibilities, gay servicemen could face punishment even if their actions or behavior did not fall under the purview of Paragraph 175.

This application of the disciplinary code against commanders was upheld throughout the 1970s. In October 1979, for instance, the First Military Affairs Division (1. Wehrdienstsenat) of the Federal Administrative Court (Bundesverwaltungsgericht) rendered a judgment regarding the treatment of gay soldiers and officers. The verdict resulted from a case in which the plaintiff, who wanted to promote the emancipation of gay men and did not accept that gay men could not be commanders, sought a ruling to overturn the restrictive interpretation of the disciplinary code.[52] The First Military Affairs Division maintained that "homosexual dispositions" would preclude the promotion of any commander, most notably officers. This decision was influenced by three considerations. First, the judges noted that gay men could not function as commanders because they would view their subordinates as possible sexual partners and their conduct would thus be "influenced by personal [*unsachlichen*], namely sexual motives."[53] Second, the First Military Affairs Division argued that "in men's societies" (*Männergesellschaften*) such as the Bundeswehr homosexuality was "predominantly not accepted." Consequently, if a commander's "homosexual tendencies" became known, "gossip," "suspicions," and the "rejection" of authority would ensue. Even behavior that was considered "normal" for heterosexual men, the verdict stated, would be perceived as "disruptive" if it involved gay men.[54] The judges saw no reason for the Bundeswehr to counteract such discriminatory attitudes, because any attempt to foster the emancipation of gay men in the armed forces would "weaken the combat strength of the troops and thus compromise their defense mission." Finally, the Wehrdienstsenat was displeased with the petitioner's decision to report his homosexual tendencies in what it viewed as an attempt to "publicly" promote the emancipation of gay men. The man's "blatant exhibition" of his homosexuality, the verdict stated, was unacceptable.[55]

Both the First Military Affairs Division and the leadership of the Bundeswehr held that it was necessary to treat gay officers differently than gay rank-and-file soldiers, especially the young men conscripted for basic military service. This becomes apparent in the judges' statement that soldiers who engaged in "same-sex relationships" privately and off duty (*außerdienstlich*) could still be considered "trustworthy" and allowed to serve in the Bundeswehr. The position of the military leadership is also reflected in the Central Service Regulation 46/1 (*ZDv 46/1*), which structured the medical examination that determined if recruits were fit for military service.[56] Over the course of *Große Strafrechtsreform*, the *ZDv 46/1* was amended several times, adding more detailed information for medical examiners to evaluate homosexuality. Section 5, "Assessment of Mental Capability," of the 1977 edition included a lengthy discussion of homosexuality. Although still associating homosexuality with "neurosis" and "psychopathy," the *ZDv 46/1* stated that homosexuality did not necessarily render a man unfit for service. It was not important, the *ZDv 46/1* noted, whether a soldier actually "suffered" from such conditions as long as he was "adaptable," "efficient," able to work in a team, and able to work under pressure and in stressful situations.[57] It "matters little if a man had on occasion same-sex contacts," the regulation specified. It was more important for the medical examiner to investigate if a man "is able to integrate himself into a men's society despite his sexual abnormality."[58] The medical examiner should assume a "sexual deviation" and declare a man unfit for service only if the patient was driven by his "abnormal sexuality" and not able to live among other men.[59] Accordingly, gay men could be declared fit for military service if they were able to integrate themselves into the "normal" heteronormative culture of the Bundeswehr and would suppress their "abnormal" identity and desires. However, being gay would preclude promotion or lead to removal from positions of command.

This particular treatment of gay men by the Bundeswehr and related institutions attracted attention and scrutiny from different media outlets, because the reform of the Penal Code in 1969 and 1973 turned the situation of gay men in the Federal Republic into a controversial public topic. This was especially due to the evolving gay rights movement during the 1970s. Although proponents of gay rights had demanded and fought for emancipation in earlier years, the far-reaching decriminalization of male homosexuality in the late 1960s and early 1970s opened new spaces for protest and demands.[60] In this context, newspapers and magazines associated with the gay rights movement as well as leftist and pacifist publications, not to mention mainstream newspapers, addressed the continuing prejudices and discrimination against gay men in the West German armed forces. Like in the 1972 *MIX* article cited at the beginning of this chapter, many authors offered a critical analysis of military standards and practices and connected them to a discussion of masculine and sexual ideals. In 1977, for instance, the newly founded magazine *Rosa* published an article titled "The Gay Officer," which argued that antigay sentiments were the result of a particular masculine culture that permeated the Bundeswehr. The author of the article asserted that "all the intolerances, all the mistakes, which also exist in the rest of society, surface much more" in the Bundeswehr, because it was a "mere men's society."[61] This line of argument was seconded by pacifist grassroots magazines such as the *graswurzelrevolution* because it viewed the armed forces' discrimination against gay men as evidence of militaristic tendencies. In 1980, the magazine maintained that the situation for gay men in the military was "very often insufferable."[62] In reaction to the 1979 verdict of the First Military Affairs Division's judgment that gay men were neither welcomed nor accepted by their heterosexual comrades, the magazine asserted that judge's verdict was indicative of the constant reprisals that gay men faced in this "supermen's world" (*Supermännerwelt*).[63] According to this assessment, the continuing criminalization of gay men in West Germany and, above all, the continuing discrimination against gay men in the Bundeswehr were the result of and symbolized misguided masculine ideals and customs. In contrast to the military, which continued to claim that heterosexual men epitomized the masculine norm and that gay men were the aberration of said norm, activists argued that the military's culture was actually deviant.

Conclusion

The *Große Strafrechtsreform* led to the gradual revision of Paragraph 175. While negotiating the reform, legal experts, parliamentarians, and military representatives paid close attention to the question of how the liberalization of the Penal Code would affect the Bundeswehr. Although the first revision in 1969 was still shaped by these considerations, the reform law passed in 1973 drastically limited the cases in which somebody could be prosecuted under Paragraph 175. As the reform proceeded, the Ministry of Defense had to reconsider its regulations and practices. Whereas occasional same-sex contacts outside of the barracks did not necessarily preclude the recruitment of young men, gay men were generally barred from promotion and commanding others. These judgments were based on the belief that male homosexuality not only was generally abnormal but also endangered the effective functioning of the Bundeswehr. Accordingly, gay men in military uniform could not expect to be like their heterosexual counterparts, because—in the Ministry of Defense's view—military needs trumped men's equal rights.

This unequal treatment led above all to a critical response by publications associated with the gay rights movement as well as the pacifist movement. Critics of the Bundeswehr maintained that gay men suffered because of the military's unacceptable heteronormative ideals of sexuality and masculinity. Criticizing the view that male homosexuality was unrestrained and deviant, they argued in turn that it was the military's norms and customs that were disturbing, abnormal, and problematic. Instead of allowing the Bundeswehr to continue this form of discrimination, laws and regulations needed to prevent the suffering of gay men in military uniform. The disputes surrounding the Bundeswehr and Paragraph 175 thus exemplify the contentious history of military masculinities. The two entangled categories of gender and sexuality created a contested societal hierarchy. The "sexual nature" and masculine qualities ascribed to gay men created a hierarchy of power that pitted heterosexual men against homosexual men.

The *Große Strafrechtsreform* is important beyond its immediate effects in the 1960s and 1970s. The critical arguments that were advanced in the wake of Paragraph 175's revision would also inform debates about women's military service and thus be carried into the 1980s.[64] These arguments testify to the military's decreased influence on how West German society defined ideals of masculinity and male sexuality.

Friederike Brühöfener is associate professor of modern European history at the University of Texas Rio Grande Valley. Her research interests include modern German and European history, cultural history, military history and gender with a special focus on the history of masculinities. She received her PhD in history from the University of North Carolina Chapel Hill in 2014. Currently she is transforming her dissertation to a book entitled *Forging States, Armies and Men: Military Masculinity, Politics and Society in East and West Germany, 1945–1989*. Her English publications include: "Sex and the Soldier: The Discourse about the Moral Conduct of Bundeswehr Soldiers and Officers during the Adenauer Era," *Central European History* 48, no. 4 (2015): 523–540; and "Politics of Emotions: Journalistic Reflections on the Emotionality of the West German Peace Movement, 1979–1984," *German Politics and Society* 33, no. 4 (2015): 97–111.

Notes

1. "Kein Platz für Homosexuelle in den Kasernen," *MIX: Zeitschrift für Sexuelle Emanzipation*, no. 2 (1972): 21, Schwules Museum Berlin, Akten Bundeswehr, Zeitungsausschnittsammlung.
2. Ibid., 22.
3. For the contested history of Paragraph 175, see Clayton Whisnant, *Queer Identities and Politics in Germany: A History, 1880–1945* (New York, 2016).
4. Mary Fulbrook, *The People's State: East German Society from Hitler to Honecker* (New Haven, 2005), 146–47. For a discussion focusing on Paragraph 175a and *Bahnhof Boys* in the divided city of Berlin, see Jennifer Evans, *Life among the Ruins: Cityscape and Sexuality in Cold War Berlin* (New York, 2011), 125–26.
5. For a similar observation that West German legal debates generally lacked overt references to East German practices, see the chapter by Alexandria Rubel in this volume.
6. For the postwar beginnings of the homophile movement, see Clayton Whisnant, *Male Homosexuality in West Germany: Between Persecution and Freedom, 1945–69* (New York, 2012), 64–111.
7. See Andrew Glenn Oppenheimer, "Conflicts of Solidarity: Nuclear Weapons, Liberation Movements, and the Politics of Peace in the Federal Republic of Germany, 1945–1975" (PhD diss., University of Chicago, 2010).
8. See the introduction by Karen Hagemann, Donna Harsch, and Friederike Brühöfener in this volume.
9. R. W. Connell, *Masculinities* (Berkeley, CA, 2005), 77. See also Jürgen Martschukat and Olaf Stieglitz, "Mannigfaltigkeit: Perspektiven einer historischen Männlichkeitsforschung," *Werkstatt Geschichte* 10, no. 29 (2001): 6.
10. See, for example, Michaela Freund-Widder, *Frauen unter Kontrolle: Prostitution und ihre staatliche Bekämpfung in Hamburg vom Ende des Kaiserreichs bis zu den*

Anfängen der Bundesrepublik (Munich, 2003); Victoria Harris, *Selling Sex in the Reich: Prostitutes in German Society, 1914–1945* (Oxford, 2010); and Annette Timm, *The Politics of Fertility in Twentieth-Century Berlin* (New York, 2010).

11. For the twentieth century and especially the post-1945 era, see, for example, Dagmar Herzog, *Sex after Fascism: Memory and Morality in Twentieth-Century Germany* (Princeton, NJ, 2007); Elizabeth Heineman, *Before Porn Was Legal: The Erotica Empire of Beate Uhse* (Chicago, 2011); Sybille Steinbacher, *Wie der Sex nach Deutschland kam: Der Kampf um Sittlichkeit und Anstand in der frühen Bundesrepublik* (Munich, 2011); Josie McLellan, *Love in the Time of Communism: Intimacy and Sexuality in the GDR* (Cambridge, 2011); Evans, *Life among the Ruins*, and "Repressive Rehabilitation: Sexual Delinquency, Youth Crime, and Retributive Justice in Berlin-Brandenburg," in *Crime and Criminal Justice in Modern Germany*, ed. Richard Wetzell (New York, 2014), 302–26.

12. Martin Lücke, *Männlichkeit in Unordnung: Homosexualität und männliche Prostitution in Kaiserreich und Weimarer Republik* (Frankfurt/M., 2008); Robert Beachy, *Gay Berlin: Birthplace of a Modern Identity* (New York, 2014); Laurie Marhoefer, *Sex and the Weimar Republic: German Homosexual Emancipation and the Rise of the Nazis* (Toronto, 2015). For West Germany, see Whisnant, *Male Homosexuality*; Robert G. Moeller, "The Homosexual Man Is a 'Man,' the Homosexual Woman Is a 'Woman': Sex, Society, and the Law in Postwar West Germany," in "Lesbian and Gay Histories," special issue, part 2, *Journal of the History of Sexuality* 4, no. 3 (1994): 395–429, and "The Regulation of Male Homosexuality in Postwar East and West Germany: An Introduction," in "Sex and Surveillance," special issue, *Feminist Studies* 36, no. 3 (2010): 521–27.

13. Jason Crouthamel, *An Intimate History of the Front: Masculinity, Sexuality, and German Soldiers in the First World War* (New York, 2014); Geoffrey Giles, "A Gray Zone among the Field Gray Men: Confusion in the Discrimination against Homosexuals in the Wehrmacht," in *Gray Zones: Ambiguity and Compromise in the Holocaust and Its Aftermath*, ed. Jonathan Petropoulos and John K. Roth (New York, 2005), 127–46, and "The Denial of Homosexuality: Same-Sex Incidents in Himmler's SS and Police," *Journal of the History of Sexuality* 11, no. 1/2 (2002): 256–90.

14. For early legal and academic discussions about the reform of the *Strafgesetzbuch*, see Petra Gödecke, "Criminal Law after National Socialism: The Renaissance of Natural Law and the Beginning of Penal Reform in West Germany," in *Crime and Criminal Justice in Modern Germany*, ed. Richard F. Wetzell (New York, 2014), 270–301.

15. Robert G. Moeller, "Private Acts, Public Anxieties: The Fight to Decriminalize Male Homosexuality in Postwar West Germany," in "Sex and Surveillance," special issue, *Feminist Studies* 36, no. 3 (2010): 528–52; and Geoffrey Giles, "The Institutionalization of Homosexual Panic in the Third Reich," in *Social Outsiders in Nazi Germany*, ed. Robert Gellately and Nathan Stolzfus (Princeton, NJ, 2001), 233–55.

16. With respect to modern German history, the terms *Unzucht* and *Unzucht treiben* have been translated in different ways, including fornication, lewdness, indecency, sex offense, illicit sexual acts, and immoral activity. In this chapter, I will use the term "lewdness" or "lewd acts" and provide the original German wording.

17. Moeller, "Homosexual Man," 402.

18. Christian Schäfer, *"Widernatürliche Unzucht": (§§ 175, 175a, 175b, 182 a.F. StGB): Reformdiskussion und Gesetzgebung seit 1945* (Berlin, 2006), 169–78; and "Entwurf eines Strafgesetzbuches (StGB), E 1962," Deutscher Bundestag [4.], Drucksache IV/650, 4. Oktober 1962.
19. Schäfer, *Widernatürliche Unzucht*, 324.
20. Quoted and translated in Herzog, *Sex after Fascism*, 129–30.
21. Quoted in Schäfer, *Widernatürliche Unzucht*, 173.
22. CDU/CSU Fraktion des Deutschen Bundestages, Arbeitskreis für Allgemeine und Rechtsfragen, "Niederschrift, Eichholzer Tagung, Strafrechtsreform, 4. Sitzung, 14.–29. September 1962," 8, Bundesarchiv Koblenz, B 141/82162. See also Schäfer, *Widernatürliche Unzucht*, 179–84.
23. Moeller, "Private Acts," 544.
24. Whisnant, *Male Homosexuality*, 197. See further Moeller, "Private Acts."
25. See Schäfer, *Widernatürliche Unzucht*, 179–84.
26. For a discussion of Giese and Bürger-Prinz, see the chapter by Clayton Whisnant in this volume.
27. Fritz Bauer et al., eds., *Sexualität und Verbrechen: Beiträge zur Strafrechtsreform* (Frankfurt/M., 1963). For a discussion of the book, see Herzog, *Sex after Fascism*, 132–34.
28. "Schreiben von VR III 7 an Pressereferat vom 3. Januar 1964, Az. 24-09-00, Betr. Einberufung von abartig veranlagten Wehrpflichtigen zur Bundeswehr," 1-2, BArch-F.
29. Ibid., 2.
30. See Friederike Brühöfener, "Sending Young Men to the Barracks: West Germany's Struggle over the Establishment of New Armed Forces in the 1950s", in *Gender and the Long Postwar: The United States and the Two Germanys, 1945–1989*, ed. Karen Hagemann and Sonya Michel (Baltimore, MD, 2014), 145–64, and "Sex and the Soldier: The Discourse about the Moral Conduct of Bundeswehr Soldiers and Officers during the Adenauer Era," *Central European History* 48, no. 4 (2015): 523–40.
31. "Schreiben des Leiters VR an den Stellvertretenden Inspekteur In San vom 22. September 1964," BArch-F, BW 1/60427. See Frank Nägler, *Der gewollte Soldat und sein Wandel: Personelle Rüstung und Innere Führung in den Aufbaujahren der Bundeswehr 1956 bis 1964/65* (Munich, 2011), 398–99.
32. "Schreiben des Hauptabteilungsleiter III an Herrn Minister vom 17. Januar 1969, betr. Strafrechtsreform: Neugestaltung des Sexualstrafrechts; hier: §175 StGB (Homosexualität)," 55–60, BArch-F, BW I/187212.
33. Schäfer, *Widernatürliche Unzucht*, 145.
34. See "Schuld ohne Strafe?," *Der Spiegel*, no. 16, 10 April 1967, 44–50.
35. Ibid. For Heinemann's position, see also Whisnant, *Male Homosexuality*, 198.
36. Schäfer, *Widernatürliche Unzucht*, 17–48; and Jürgen Baumann, *Alternativ-Entwurf eines Strafgesetzbuches* (Tübingen, 1966). Sexual acts with children younger than fourteen years old were addressed in a different paragraph, which focused generally on child abuse.
37. "VR II 7, Schreiben an den Herrn Staatssekretär betreff Sexualstrafrecht, hier Sprechzettel für die Sitzung des Verteidigungsausschusses, 14. März 1969," BArch-F, BW 1/187212.
38. Ibid.
39. Ibid.

40. Schäfer, *Widernatürliche Unzucht,* 325.
41. "Späte Milde," *Der Spiegel,* no. 20, 12 May 1969, 55–76. The article refers to the fact that the revised criminal code proposed a different age of consent for sexual acts between men than it did for sexual acts between men and women. The debated age of consent for young women and girls was fourteen or sixteen.
42. "Brief an Helmut Schmidt vom 16. Oktober 1970," Archiv der sozialen Demokratie, Helmut Schmidt Archiv, 1/HSAA005504.
43. Ibid.
44. Helmut Ostermeyer, "Ist der neue § 175 StGB verfassungswidrig?," *Zeitschrift für Rechtspolitik* 2, no. 7 (1969): 154.
45. Ibid.
46. Schäfer, *"Widernatürliche Unzucht,"* 324–26.
47. Ibid.
48. "Schreiben von VR IV 1 an IPZ vom 29. September 1970. Betr. Dokumentation der Zeitschrift 'Das Andere Magazin' über die Behandlung von Homophilen in der BW," 1-2, BArch-F, BW 1/73389.
49. "Fü S I 3, Schreiben an alle Kommandeure und Dienststellenleiter vom 7. August 1969," BArch-F, BW 1/131876.
50. Ibid.
51. "Schreiben von VR IV 1 an IPZ betreff Dokumentation der Zeitschrift 'Das andere Magazin' über die Behandlung der Homophilen in der BW, 29. September 1970," BArch-F, BW 1/13 18 74.
52. "Bundesverwaltungsgericht, 1. Wehrdienstsenat, Beschl. v. 25.10.1979, Az.: BVerwG 1 WB 113/78, Eignung und Verwendung eines Soldaten als Vorgesetzter; Ausschluss der weiteren Förderung eines Soldaten wegen dessen gleichgeschlechtlicher Veranlagung," www.jurion.de/urteile/bverwg/1979-10-25/bverwg-1-wb-113_78/ (accessed 11 August 2017).
53. Ibid.
54. Ibid.
55. Ibid.
56. "ZDv 46/1- Bestimmungen für die Durchführung der ärztlichen Untersuchung bei der Musterung von Wehrpflichtigen, Annahme, Einstellung und Entlassung von Soldaten (Tauglichkeitsbestimmungen), März 1977," BArch-F, BWD 3/251.
57. Ibid., 279/1.
58. Ibid.
59. Ibid.
60. Benno Gammerl, "Ist frei sein normal? Männliche Homosexualität seit den 1960er Jahren zwischen Emanzipation und Normalisierung," in *Sexuelle Revolution? Zur Geschichte der Sexualität im deutschsprachigen Raum seit den 1960er Jahren,* ed. Peter-Paul Bänziger et al. (Bielefeld, 2015), 223–43; and Hans-Georg Stümke and Rudi Finkler, *Rosa Winkel, Rosa Listen: Homosexuelle und "gesundes Volksempfinden" von Auschwitz bis heute* (Reinbek, 1981).
61. "Ein Schwuler Offizier," *Rosa,* no. 7 (January 1977): 20–22. For a development of gay magazines and newspapers, see also Dietmar Kreutzer, "Eine Chronik mit Ausblick: Die 1980er Jahre im Spiegel der Presse," in *Zwischen Autonomie und Integration: Schwule Politik und Schwulenbewegung in den 1980er und 1990er Jahren,* ed. Andreas Pretzel and Volker Weiß (Hamburg, 2013), 23–33.
62. "Schwule ins Militär? Therapie gefällig?," *graswurzelrevolution* (February/March 1980), 38.

63. Ibid.
64. See, for example, Belinda Davis, "'Women's Strength against Their Crazy Male Power': Gendered Language in the West German Peace Movement of the 1980s," in *Frieden—Gewalt—Geschlecht: Friedens- und Konfliktforschung als Geschlechterforschung*, ed. Jennifer. A. Davy et al. (Essen, 2005), 244–65. See further Richard L. Johnson, "The New West German Peace Movement: Male Dominance or Feminist Nonviolence," *Women in German Yearbook: Feminist Studies in German Literature & Culture* 1 (1985): 135–62.

Selected Bibliography

Beachy, Robert. *Gay Berlin: Birthplace of a Modern Identity*. New York, 2014.
Brühöfener, Friederike. "Sending Young Men to the Barracks: West Germany's Struggle over the Establishment of New Armed Forces in the 1950s." In *Gender and the Long Postwar: The United States and the Two Germanys, 1945–1989*, ed. Karen Hagemann and Sonya Michel, 145–64. Baltimore, MD, 2014.
Brühöfener, Friederike. "Sex and the Soldier: The Discourse about the Moral Conduct of Bundeswehr Soldiers and Officers during the Adenauer Era." *Central European History* 48, no. 4 (2015): 523–40.
Connell, R. W. *Masculinities*. Berkeley, CA, 2005.
Evans, Jennifer. *Life among the Ruins: Cityscape and Sexuality in Cold War Berlin*. New York, 2011.
———. "Repressive Rehabilitation: Sexual Delinquency, Youth Crime, and Retributive Justice in Berlin-Brandenburg." In *Crime and Criminal Justice in Modern Germany*, ed. Richard Wetzell, 302–26. New York, 2014.
Freund-Widder, Michaela. *Frauen unter Kontrolle: Prostitution und ihre staatliche Bekämpfung in Hamburg vom Ende des Kaiserreichs bis zu den Anfängen der Bundesrepublik*. Munich, 2003.
Gammerl, Benno. "Ist frei sein normal? Männliche Homosexualität seit den 1960er Jahren zwischen Emanzipation und Normalisierung." In *Sexuelle Revolution? Zur Geschichte der Sexualität im deutschsprachigen Raum seit den 1960er Jahren*, ed. Peter-Paul Bänziger, Magdalena Beljan, Franz X. Eder, and Pascal Eitler, 223–43. Bielefeld, 2015.
Giles, Geoffrey. "The Denial of Homosexuality: Same-Sex Incidents in Himmler's SS and Police." *Journal of the History of Sexuality* 11, no. 1/2 (2002): 256–90.
———. "A Gray Zone among the Field Gray Men: Confusion in the Discrimination against Homosexuals in the Wehrmacht." In *Gray Zones: Ambiguity and Compromise in the Holocaust and Its Aftermath*, ed. Jonathan Petropoulos and John K. Roth, 127–46. New York, 2005.
Gödecke, Petra. "Criminal Law after National Socialism: The Renaissance of Natural Law and the Beginning of Penal Reform in West Germany." In *Crime and Criminal Justice in Modern Germany*, ed. Richard F. Wetzell, 270–301. New York, 2014.
Harris, Victoria. *Selling Sex in the Reich: Prostitutes in German Society, 1914–1945*. Oxford, 2010.
Heineman, Elizabeth. *Before Porn was Legal: The Erotica Empire of Beate Uhse*. Chicago, 2011.

Herzog, Dagmar. *Sex after Fascism: Memory and Morality in Twentieth-Century Germany.* Princeton, NJ, 2007.

Kreutzer, Dietmar. "Eine Chronik mit Ausblick: Die 1980er Jahre im Spiegel der Presse." In *Zwischen Autonomie und Integration: Schwule Politik und Schwulenbewegung in den 1980er und 1990er Jahren,* ed. Andreas Pretzel and Volker Weiß, 23–33. Hamburg, 2013.

Lücke, Martin. *Männlichkeit in Unordnung: Homosexualität und männliche Prostitution in Kaiserreich und Weimarer Republik.* Frankfurt/M., 2008.

Marhoefer, Laurie. *Sex and the Weimar Republic: German Homosexual Emancipation and the Rise of the Nazis.* Toronto, 2015.

Moeller, Robert G. "The Homosexual Man Is a 'Man,' the Homosexual Woman Is a 'Woman': Sex, Society, and the Law in Postwar West Germany." In "Lesbian and Gay Histories," special issue, part 2, *Journal of the History of Sexuality* 4, no. 3 (1994): 395–429.

———. "The Regulation of Male Homosexuality in Postwar East and West Germany: An Introduction." In "Sex and Surveillance," special issue, *Feminist Studies* 36, no. 3, (2010): 521–27.

Schäfer, Christian. *"Widernatürliche Unzucht": (§§ 175, 175a, 175b, 182 a.F. StGB); Reformdiskussion und Gesetzgebung seit 1945.* Berlin, 2006.

Steinbacher, Sybille. *Wie der Sex nach Deutschland kam: Der Kampf um Sittlichkeit und Anstand in der frühen Bundesrepublik.* Munich, 2011.

Stümke, Hans-Georg, and Rudi Finkler. *Rosa Winkel, Rosa Listen: Homosexuelle und "gesundes Volksempfinden" von Auschwitz bis heute.* Reinbek, 1981.

Timm, Annette. *The Politics of Fertility in Twentieth-Century Berlin.* New York, 2010.

Whisnant, Clayton. *Male Homosexuality in West Germany: Between Persecution and Freedom, 1945–69.* New York, 2012.

———. *Queer Identities and Politics in Germany: A History, 1880–1945.* New York, 2016.

PART V
THE MEDIA AND REPRESENTATIONS OF GENDER

CHAPTER 14

In the Presence of the Past, in the Shadow of the "Other"

Women Journalists in Postwar Germany

Deborah Barton

On 21 January 1954, Ursula Rumin arrived home in West Berlin after sixteen months in Soviet captivity. A newspaper article titled "A Happy Homecoming from Forced Labor" told the story of how the young journalist and screenwriter disappeared on 25 September 1952 as she was on her way from her home in West Berlin to work in the Eastern part of the city. Arrested by the Soviet Ministry of State Security (MGB) and charged with espionage and conspiring with the enemy, Rumin was sentenced to fifteen years forced labor in Siberia. At the time of her arrest, Rumin was relatively new to journalism. After the postwar expulsion of ethnic Germans from Poland, she lost her childhood home in Silesia and eventually took up residence in Berlin.

Struggling in her dancing career, which she had started during the war, Rumin decided to try her hand at journalism in her new home city, where she soon established herself as a freelance journalist.

During the early stages of her career, Rumin focused primarily on film, celebrity gossip, and local "women's affairs," such as the opening of the first laundromat in West Berlin. Her work appeared in a range of West German publications, including the liberal illustrated news magazine *Stern*, the women's magazine *Constanze*, and various film publications. In 1950, she began to work as a journalist and screenwriter for the (East) German Film Company (Deutsche Film Aktiengesellschaft, DEFA). Rumin noted in her diary that she was concerned because her career and travel spanned East and West. She feared for her safety—a fear that turned out to be well founded.[1] Rumin's history, although not typical, demonstrates that in the first decade after the war, the division of Germany offered both opportunities and risks for women journalists.

While job opportunities initially expanded, women in all four occupation zones were relegated to the periphery of journalism, working in the areas of "soft" news, women's issues, and culture—all themes traditionally deemed appropriate for women journalists. The West labeled these areas apolitical and sought to position West German identity as based on the family and a return to traditional gender roles. In the East, the work of women journalists was more overtly political, both in terms of their writing and in the expectations placed upon them. Although the two Germanys attached different meanings to women's writing, female journalists in East and West became embroiled in political affairs and the growing Cold War in similar ways. At the same time, they were active in creating that politicized environment through their writing.

The historiography on the postwar German press has examined the continuity of journalists' careers between the Third Reich and after, the obstacles women faced in obtaining positions outside of soft-news areas, and the gendered nature of their writing.[2] Far less has been written about the entanglement of postwar East and West Germany with a focus on women journalists. This chapter will explore the ways in which the lives and careers of women journalists in East and West Berlin, the city at the epicenter of political turmoil, were entangled with and affected by the presence of the other Germany. Regardless of the seemingly harmless areas on which they typically reported, their profession exposed them to the risks—surveillance, discipline, and control—characteristic of the Cold War. Due to their visibility and activity in the public realm, these women became symbolic representatives of two competitive blocs seeking to position themselves as the legitimate successor to the collapsed National Socialist state.

First, this chapter explores the career prospects women found in the immediate aftermath of the war, irrespective of their connections to National Socialism. Next, it analyzes the opportunities and risks of negotiating a career in the changing politics of postwar Berlin. Finally, it examines the porous nature of journalism between East and West and how women's writing about the contested memory of the war and its ramifications—itself a factor in the growing Cold War—instrumentalized portrayals of the other as a means to promote the success of the journalists' own zone.

Women in the Postwar Press

National Socialist press authorities consigned women to a subordinate status within the field and endeavored to limit their roles. Although the number of women journalists increased from 1939 onward, women never accounted for more than 10 percent of accredited journalists throughout the Third Reich.³ Despite Nazi rhetoric and policy, which seemingly confined women to the private sphere, press authorities stressed that women journalists had an important institutional role: for the regime, they were to act as the connection between the Nazi state and German women. In a March 1936 speech to a gathering of Berlin-based female journalists, the head of the German Press Association (Reichsverband der Deutschen Presse), Wilhelm Weiss, declared that the role of a female journalist would be to write about topics and within areas that would primarily interest women: the women's supplements, features, and such "soft news" sections as travel and local events.⁴ Whether by choice or necessity, the majority of women journalists in Nazi Germany worked within the boundaries set by the German Press Association.⁵

In the immediate postwar period, the Allies perceived the majority of German women as apolitical and untainted by Nazism, certainly in comparison to men. As a result, the journalistic field in all four occupation zones seemed more accessible to women than it had in the past. In addition, women accounted for the majority of the population in war-torn Germany, and the Allies hoped to reach this audience through targeted publications. Already in April 1945, Soviet occupation authorities issued a license for the family-oriented magazine the *Neue Berliner Illustrierte* (*NBI*). In November 1945, the US Military Government's Information Control Branch approved journalist Ruth Andreas-Friedrich's application to publish a women's magazine entitled *Sie*.⁶ Women who had worked in Nazi Germany, those who had returned from emigration, and those new to journalism recalled stepping relatively seamlessly into positions at these and other publications. This was particularly true in divided Berlin, where women journalists constituted 18 percent of the field in 1946.⁷ Lore Walb, a young radio journalist and former supporter of Nazism, recalled the opportunities open to women after 1945:

> At that time women journalists stood under a lucky star. Journalists were rare and the Americans, mostly emigrants, instigated a very women friendly personnel policy. Never again did women have [. . .] such chances as they received in the radio and press in the American Occupation Zone shortly after the war.⁸

Writer Luise Rinser worked as a correspondent for the Munich-based, American-sponsored *Die Neue Zeitung* from 1945 to 1953. She recalled the opportunities open to her at the war's end: "What wasn't I offered back then. Control of women's affairs for Bavarian broadcasting, the job of chief editor of the literary supplement of a newly founded newspaper."⁹ Similarly, even journalist Ursula von Kardorff, who had achieved professional success under the Third Reich, found opportunities in the postwar era. Although American and Soviet press authorities critiqued Kardorff's Nazi-era articles for what they deemed excessive nationalism, she still managed to work for several West Berlin–based papers, including the *Kurier* and *Tagesspiegel* in the first year after the war.[10]

Despite these early opportunities for women, journalism in the three Western occupation zones remained male dominated, particularly after the Allies began to abandon their denazification efforts in 1947 and male journalists who had worked for the Nazi press returned to the field. After the founding of the Federal Republic of Germany (FRG) and the German Democratic Republic (GDR) in 1949, the attitude toward and opportunities open to women shifted to align with each state's political agenda. In addition, each state used gender as a marker of differentiation. West Germany, controlled by a Christian-conservative government under the leadership of Chancellor Konrad Adenauer, a member of the Christian Democratic Union of Germany (Christlich Demokratische Union Deutschlands, CDU), was characterized by conservatism in both the political and social spheres. The government, the Catholic and Protestant Churches, and their many associations led a concerted effort to reestablish the traditional family at the heart of West German society. Women's primary role was envisaged to be in the home as a wife and mother. Although in reality women worked outside the home, they were generally clustered in lower-skilled and lower-paid positions.[11] In contrast to the West, East Germany encouraged and expected women's participation in the workforce due in part to ideology. Socialist theory considered full-time labor as a precondition for women's economic autonomy, integration into the economy and society, and thus their ultimate emancipation.[12] More important, authorities viewed the full-time employment of women as a necessary means to alleviate the grave labor shortage.

In the East, the field of journalism too suffered from a labor deficiency. In 1946, press authorities in the Soviet Occupation Zone (Sowjetische Besatzungszone, SBZ), which later became the GDR, discussed a shortage of capable journalists. Like in other sectors of the workforce, popular dissatisfaction in the zone and the continuing loss of population to the West likely contributed to this shortfall. At the first membership meeting of the Allied-approved professional organization for journalists, the Association of the German Press (Verband der Deutschen Presse, VDP), in the SBZ in 1946, the elected chairman, writer Paul Ufermann, noted, "There has never been such a lack of journalists in [East] Germany as at this time. People come to us from everywhere [in the East] and say: 'We need journalists urgently.'"[13] But one year later, during a meeting in 1947, Ufermann could report that with membership steadily growing, he was pleased to see an increasing number of women entering the field.[14] Indeed, one group that contributed to this growth were women. Already in 1946, female journalists had accounted for 18 percent of the field in divided Berlin, up from 2.5 percent in 1925.[15] "It is an encouraging sign,"

Ufermann thus declared at the VDP meeting in 1946, "that in contrast to earlier periods, the press is dependent on women's inclusion, and, as a result, gives women a proper status in public life."[16]

Such statements aimed in part to promote the East, in contrast to the West, as committed to equality between the sexes and the economic emancipation of women. Yet reality did not fit the ideological imperative: many women suffered under the triple burden of home, work, and the demands that they participate in social and political life through organizations like the Free German Trade Union Association (Freier Deutscher Gewerkschaftsbund, FDGB) or the governing Socialist Unity Party of Germany (Sozialistische Einheitspartei Deutschlands, SED), founded in April 1946 by a union of the Social Democratic Party of Germany (Sozialdemokratische Partei Deutschlands, SPD) and the Communist Party of Germany (Kommunistische Partei Deutschlands, KPD) in the SBZ. Like their Western counterparts, women in the East largely worked in lower-skilled and lower-paid positions.[17] Still, they accounted for a greater percentage of the press cohort than their Western colleagues. By 1951, 16 percent of working journalists in the GDR were women.[18] In the FRG, the percentage of women journalists was much lower, as the example of the Ruhr and Rhineland-Palatinate areas demonstrates, where it languished at only 3 percent and 5 percent respectively.[19] Moreover, even with the field of journalism more accessible to women all over postwar Germany, it appeared easier for women to obtain positions and make progress in the East than it was in the West.

Hannelore Holtz, for instance, completed her journalistic training in 1944 at the *Kattowitzer Zeitung* in Silesia. She returned to her native Berlin shortly before the arrival of the Red Army in 1945. Living in West Berlin, Holtz applied to newspapers in all sectors of the city but only received offers from Soviet-licensed papers. With little experience, she began writing on culture and entertainment for East Berlin's *Nacht-Express*. "I was 22. One wouldn't get such an opportunity today," she recalled. "I had absolutely no experience to show for myself."[20] The News Agency of the Soviet Military (SND) sought and hired committed socialist Gerda Zorn, despite the fact that she had little prior experience.[21] She rose quickly to a position of responsibility. In the summer of 1946, author and journalist Elfriede Brüning easily repositioned her career in East Berlin. During the Third Reich, she was able to write for a range of publications despite her membership in the Weimar KPD and arrest on suspicion of communist activities. In 1943, the Nazi Ministry of Propaganda declared her work "indispensable" to the continuation of Germany's cultural life and exempted her from compulsory war work. Despite her Third Reich career and lack of editorial experience, Brüning became the features editor for *Sonntag*, the flagship publication of the SBZ's Cultural Union for the

Democratic Renewal of Germany (Kulturbund zur demokratischen Erneuerung Deutschlands).[22]

Positions in the postwar press appealed to an educated elite of women in occupied Germany for intellectual and practical reasons. Many cited their love of writing as the primary reason for pursuing a career in the press. In addition, for single mothers—not an uncommon phenomenon in the postwar decade—journalism allowed for flexible scheduling, which was valued by women in both East and West.[23] In the SBZ, artists and writers were placed in the highest ration-card category, making journalism an attractive career for material reasons too.[24] Finally, the profession in both regions often provided travel and privileged access to information. Whatever the personal or intellectual appeal of a career in journalism, the experiences of Rumin, Walb, Kardorff, Holtz, Zorn, Brüning, and other women journalists reveal that their different political stances and career trajectories during the Third Reich did not determine the nature of their postwar careers.

Obligation, Opportunities, and Entanglements

The Soviets and the Western Allies placed significant authority in the educational role of the press to help build an antifascist, antimilitaristic, and democratic (or socialist) Germany. Press authorities also considered individual journalists to be vital shapers of public opinion. The goal of the East German VDP in 1946 was "to help ensure that the German population emerge from the rubble to build a state that will be once again be respected by the world." According to its chairman Paul Ufermann:

> The VDP is a professional group that has a very special meaning in the life of a democratic state [. . .] Our numbers are small but our work has an impact like no other [. . .] Our task is the intellectual reeducation of the German people, without compromise, toward an antifascist and democratic foundation.[25]

As the Cold War intensified, the press increasingly became a vehicle through which the Soviet occupation administration and the SED hoped to curb Western influence while also legitimating and popularizing their own image.

The American, British, and French occupation regimes and German civil governments in the West assigned a similar role to the press. The US military occupation authority, for example, expressed its views about the power of the press in the 1947 *Fair Practice Guide for German Journalists*. The guide was designed to encourage a deeper understanding of the principles underlying "democratic journalism": "We believe that the success of democratic government depends upon sound public opinion, and that the newspaper should aid in creating and maintaining sound public opinion."[26] The importance the Allies placed on the press gave women journalists greater visibility and status in the public realm. As a result, their professional role connected them to the Cold War in a manner not experienced by most women.

In the first three postwar years, journalistic relations between East and West Germany were marked by a degree of sensitivity, fluidity, and communication. Ursula von Kardorff's experiences in the American Occupation Zone suggest that press authorities and newspaper editors in the West took Soviet sensibilities into consideration with regard to the employment of journalists. In the fall of 1946, the *Tagesspiegel*—founded in September 1945 in the American sector of occupied Berlin—rejected a submission by Kardorff due to concerns over the potential Soviet reaction to a wartime article she had written on Soviet women.[27] In 1948, *Die Neue Zeitung* reneged on its offer of employment to Kardorff due to the *Weltbühne*'s (a Soviet-zone paper) critique of her 1944 article on *Flakhelferinnen* (female flak auxiliaries) in the *Deutsche Allgemeine Zeitung*.[28] The editor-in-chief of the *Neue Zeitung* implied that, as a publication tied to the American military government, it had to take extra caution not to offend the other occupying powers with their choice of German employees.

East German press authorities sought and encouraged connections with Western journalists in the first postwar years, particularly in Berlin. The VDP was principally an East German organization, but it also included West Berlin–based journalists in its membership: "Although the association primarily represents the professional interests of journalists in the Eastern zone, the VDP also maintains an interzonal working group with journalist associations in the western and southern regions of Germany."[29] Even after the German Journalists Association (Deutscher Journalisten Verband, DJV) was founded in West Berlin in 1949, some journalists in the Western sectors retained their VDP membership.[30]

While the sources do not indicate with absolute clarity why East German press authorities sought linkages with their Western counterparts, a few reasons seem likely. Immediately after the war, the stated goal of both the United States and the USSR was to utilize the press as a means to eradicate National Socialist sentiments among the population. In this task, it seemed as if the press in the East and West was working toward similar goals. Press authorities in the East also viewed connections with the Western press as a way to influence politics and the representation of the Soviet zone in the West. Finally, the postwar press in all zones comprised people with commonalities and similar experiences, whether through having remained in Germany throughout the Third Reich and the destruction of the war or having returned from emigration after its downfall. Indeed, many journalists spoke of the camaraderie they felt with colleagues during and after the war.³¹ Finally, in the early years after the war, with the division of Germany not deemed permanent, physical and political barriers did not yet demarcate journalism in the East and West.

In the context of the escalating Cold War, the spirit and rhetoric of working together changed, and it mostly disappeared after the foundation of the two German states in 1949. The VDP still tried to connect to its Western counterparts, but this goal was primarily to track what they deemed the Western press's slanderous claims against the new East German state. Growing prosperity in the West also proved a visible challenge to the GDR's claims to supremacy. Adopting a defensive position, the GDR press focused on countering such narratives.³² The East German press also monitored the process of Westernization in the FRG in order to critique it in their own articles. It was within this context that in January 1950 the VDP's board of directors discussed various opportunities to ensure contact with its Western counterparts.³³ Suggestions included capitalizing on personal relationships, collecting addresses of Western journalists and circulating them to Eastern colleagues, creating a permanent committee responsible for establishing connections with West German journalists, and organizing ongoing correspondence with them. The board also discussed monitoring the work of West Berlin journalists and inviting West German colleagues to study improvements in the GDR. A board member of the VDP was tasked with traveling to the West to record meetings with journalists in order to prepare for interzonal discussions.³⁴

Gerda Zorn's experience demonstrates how these schemes to foster connections worked in practice and linked women journalists to the other German state. In 1950, Zorn began work in the SED's press office after she had finished her study of cultural politics (*Kulturpolitik*) in Leipzig. By 1950, the GDR press was centrally organized, yet media policies and methods of control were opaque, inconsistent, and often difficult to navigate.³⁵ Zorn's role was to provide "guidance" and suggest themes and articles for the cultural pages of GDR newspapers. Her position held a high level of responsibility. She was tasked with monitoring and evaluating the cultural pages of daily newspapers in the GDR and the Federal Republic, something she believed showed the trust communist press authorities placed in her.³⁶ As a dedicated socialist and party member, Zorn nevertheless claimed that she was not interested in the political pages of the West German press. Rather, her goal was to spot and critique the West's "lack of culture" while promoting the quality of Eastern cultural production.³⁷ In this way, she defined herself as apolitical, but her work was de facto quite political.

In the fall of 1951, Zorn was selected to look after Western journalists visiting the GDR. The visit was part of the SED's campaign "Germans at One Table" (*Deutsche an einen Tisch*), which aimed to lay the foundation for negotiating the unification of Germany. Zorn's task was to encourage Western journalists to write positive articles about the new social order that the GDR had built.[38] She escorted Western journalists through factories, organized discussions with women workers, and visited cultural events, the very subjects about which women journalists were expected to write. Zorn later recalled that the journalists she met believed it was important to "talk to one another" in order to establish closer relations between the two states.[39]

Contact between members of the press in the Eastern and Western regions of Germany was most pronounced in Berlin. In addition, the permeability of the city's zonal borders opened more professional opportunities for journalists than could be found in other regions. Journalists in the West journeyed back and forth between the zones when commuting to and from work. Journalists in the East and West communicated across the borders socially and intellectually through personal connections and by writing on themes relevant to all zones. Liselotte Thomas and Cläre Jung, for instance, were based in West Berlin but, beginning in 1946, wrote for *Sonntag* and the East German women's publication *Für Dich,* respectively. A number of Western-based journalists, including émigré Pauline Nardi, wrote for the resurrected leftist *Weltbühne* published in East Berlin. In the postwar years, the paper had many readers in the West, and the Soviets intended it to function as a bridge to Western intellectuals with the hope that it could influence these circles. Foreign correspondent Margret Boveri found freelance work at both Soviet- and US-licensed newspapers.

Journalists (and even newspaper companies) moved between zones for professional opportunities and due to political beliefs. Christa Rotzoll recalled the frequent movement of journalists between the East and West Berlin after the war: "Many of [my former] colleagues who came to East Berlin soon endeavored to gain a foothold in the Western sectors and most of them did so successfully."[40] Some moved in the opposite direction. Author and journalist Susanne Kerckhoff lived in the British sector of Berlin at the end of the war. She joined the newly formed SPD in the West sectors, but soon relocated to East Berlin and eventually joined the SED. Kerckhoff briefly wrote for the satirical magazine *Uhlenspiegel,* which had itself moved from the American to the Soviet sector after US authorities deemed it too left wing. In 1948, she became a reporter for the features section of the SBZ-based *Berliner Zeitung.*

However, women journalists working in the East and living in the West soon discovered unexpected professional threats. In West Berlin, Eva Siewert feared that writing under her own name for the East's *Weltbühne* would hinder her career at home in the West. After the war, Siewert worked as a freelance journalist for the *Weltbühne* and for Western publications, including *Der Spiegel* and the *Telegraph*. She wrote primarily about art, music, the ramifications of the war, and lingering antisemitism in Germany. Her work for the *Weltbühne*, however, brought Siewert unwanted attention at home in the West. In a July 1947 letter to the editor of the *Weltbühne*, Hans Leonard, Siewert complained that a "dark shadow" had fallen over her name in British-American military circles due to the fact that she wrote openly for the paper. "I am also aware that a number of journalists with similar intellectual or world outlooks to me [. . .] write for you under pseudonyms," she noted, "while I was courageous enough to use my own name, which has already sufficiently damaged my work on the other side of this, unfortunately prevailing, border."[41]

While the Western occupation powers could make life difficult for journalists, the real threat came from the Soviet and East German authorities. The vicissitudes of Soviet policy and actions toward unification and establishing connections with the West made it difficult for journalists to recognize and navigate the changing political landscape. In 1946, for instance, press authorities in the East sought closer relations with the Western press. But at the same time, police in the East were warning their citizens that subscribing to West Berlin–based newspapers could subject them to punishment.[42] Professional risks for journalists increased after the Stalinization of the SED and the foundation of the GDR in 1949. Hannelore Holtz, whose work focused largely on culture and entertainment, fled from East to West Berlin in 1950 after the GDR Ministry for State Security (Ministerium für Staatssicherheit, MfS) attempted to recruit her. As she began to establish a career at the US-licensed *Tagesspiegel*, Holtz faced accusations in the Western press that she was an East German spy. Having evaded the Soviet threat, Holtz unknowingly traded one risk for another.[43] Seeking to escape the Cold War atmosphere of Berlin, Holtz soon relocated to Hamburg, where she eventually became editor of the women's magazine *Brigitte*.

Journalist Christa Rotzoll, who lived and worked in West Berlin between 1946 and 1958, wrote primarily for Western publications about film and theatre productions in East Berlin. As she later recalled, "Not once in all of those years did I lose the unpleasant feeling that at any time I could be stopped and accused of stirring tensions or spying."[44] Rotzoll's fear of the ramifications of where her work in the East might lead her was not unfounded. Macropolitical events heightened the Cold War tensions, including the Communist takeover in Czechoslovakia in February 1948; the West's monetary reform in June 1948; the Soviet blockade of West Berlin in response, and the ensuing American and British Berlin Airlift (June 1948 and May 1949); the establishment of the North Atlantic Treaty Organization (NATO) in April 1949; and the end of the Greek Civil War in October 1949. The resulting tensions, particularly in Germany, elevated the risks for Germans who crossed Berlin's borders physically and intellectually. While women and men from any walk of life could find themselves inadvertently coming to the attention of Soviet and or East German authorities, journalism proved a particularly risky activity. According to Rumin, in the Soviet forced-labor camp Vorkuta, where she was interned in 1952, the plurality of "Western" German women belonged to the intelligentsia: mostly journalists, teachers, or artists. Rumin counted fifteen journalists in her circle in the Siberian camp.[45]

Brigitte Gerland was one such journalist. Abducted by the Soviet Ministry of State Security while traveling in the East in October 1946, she was tried by a Soviet "Special Committee" in Dresden. The committee found Gerland guilty of spying for England and sentenced her to ten years at Vorkuta. Immediately after the war, Gerland had joined the KPD and, like Zorn, initially was a reporter for the news agency of the Soviet military. She soon felt hampered by the limited intellectual freedom in her work. Gerland left the party and moved to West Berlin, where she worked as a freelance journalist for several West Berlin papers. Her reporting focused on the Eastern zone, drawing on her professional experience there and her relationships with, as she put it, "influential circles." Still a committed socialist, Gerland became a member of the West's SPD. At the time of her arrest, she was writing primarily for its paper *Sozialdemokrat: Organ der Sozialdemokratie Groß-Berlin*, which was licensed in the British sector. During her trial, Gerland was classified as a dangerous intelligence agent.[46]

Gerland's crossover from East to West and her writing for the SPD's flagship paper about life in the East in the wake of the forced merger between the KPD and SPD bore wider consequences in the emerging Cold War. Among other factors, it undoubtedly fueled ongoing Soviet and East German suspicions about nascent support for the SPD in the East. The Soviets increasingly viewed the Social Democrats as the primary obstacle to Soviet influence in the Eastern zone, particularly after the SPD set up an eastern bureau (*Ostbüro*) in April 1946 to gather information about and sustain contacts with Social Democrats in the East. The Soviet Union saw the bureau as a US endeavor to deprive it of its rightful place in shaping postwar Germany.[47] Gerland's case represents a precursor to the SED's repression of former Social Democrats beginning in 1947.[48] Her fate exemplifies the risks faced by politically minded journalists caught in the middle of the escalating Cold War and the question of German unity.

But it was not just political journalists who faced grave occupational hazards in early Cold War Germany. Even those journalists not aligned with political parties had difficulties. The young journalist Charlotte Fischer-Lamberg disappeared in June 1946 while on assignment in Brandenburg in the Soviet zone. Employed by the US-licensed *Weser-Kurier*, she had planned to cover a convention of the socialist youth organization

Free German Youth (Freie Deutsche Jugend, FDJ). After almost a year of inquiries, the US military's Information Control Division (ICD) discovered that Fischer-Lamberg had been arrested and sentenced to prison for traveling in the Soviet zone without the correct authorization. Although she had been carrying both an invitation from the FDJ and travel authorization from the American military authorities, these were insufficient protection. The director of the ICD wrote to the director of the Propaganda for the Soviet Military Administration, Colonel Sergei Tiulpanov, requesting Fischer-Lamberg's release. "I realize," he wrote, "that undoubtedly further Soviet approval probably should have been obtained but it is clear that Fräulein Fischer-Lamberg made the trip in good faith. I am sure you will agree with me that this is a case which deserves every consideration if a miscarriage of justice is to be avoided."[49] Fischer-Lamberg spent six years in prison in the East, eventually returning to the *Weser-Kurier* and continuing her journalistic career.[50]

It was not just women from West Germany who were at risk. The physical and ideological border was also dangerous for East German journalists. Gerda Zorn's successful career came to an abrupt end in 1951 due to her association with the Western journalists whom she was assigned to accompany in East Berlin. One evening, two of these journalists planned to travel to West Berlin for the evening and challenged Zorn to join them. Wishing to prove that the GDR was not a repressive state, and taking into account that she had never been forbidden to travel to the West, Zorn spent the evening in West Berlin watching an American film. Her intention, she recalled, had been to compare Western to Eastern culture with the goal of helping the GDR's cultural efforts gain traction in both regions of Germany. The deputy head of her department, a Russian woman, promptly told Zorn that she would face severe repercussions: "As a party member [. . . you] should have known better than to go to West Berlin."[51] According to the SED press office, Zorn had placed herself at risk of becoming unwittingly entangled in an American espionage network. "The Russians would have sent you to Siberia for 10 years," another colleague warned.[52] Zorn was called before a tribunal of 150 party members who debated her fate. Although not expelled from the party, Zorn lost her coveted position and was sent to work in a factory ostensibly to reconnect with the workers. Later, Zorn recalled that she was pressured to engage in the Stalinist exercise of self-criticism in front of her colleagues and fellow party members.[53]

Zorn's experience needs to be viewed against the backdrop of the relationship between East and West as both states sought legitimacy domestically and internationally. As the West became more prosperous and the East more insecure, the SED developed increasingly repressive policies aimed at intimidating alleged nonconformist forces within society. One method the party utilized to ensure its members' acquiescence was to humiliate and exclude them from particular social or professional circles, as was the case with Zorn.[54] As the SED used events and transformations of the FRG as a catalyst for its actions and reactions, the party led a campaign that was especially active in the cultural arena—Zorn's area of expertise—against the threatening influence of cosmopolitanism and Americanism.[55] The open border to West Berlin functioned as a doorway to Western culture and prosperity. Despite their vacillating rhetoric on the subject, party leaders became suspicious of any actions aimed at promoting closer links with the West. Zorn had crossed not only the GDR's physical border but also the SED's shifting boundary of what it considered ideologically acceptable behavior.

Porous Journalism: Writing the History of the War

The professional experiences of women journalists in the postwar period point to one set of entanglements between East and West; women's postwar writing indicates another. Articles focused on the war and its ramifications for Germany's women best exemplify these connections. Female journalists critiqued the other Germany's handling of those repercussions in a manner that sought to establish their own zone(s) as the rightful German state. In this way, they became part of the process that increasingly set East against West. In the first postwar years, journalists in both regions focused on the difficulties of everyday life and how best to cope. In addition, they addressed women's important roles in rebuilding Germany physically, socially, and, most important, morally, whether based on a democratic or socialist outlook.

In its September 1946 issue, the East German women's magazine *Für Dich* published an article titled "No Female Nuremberg?" The magazine critiqued a piece by Ursula von Kardorff that had appeared in the US-licensed women's magazine *Sie*. In her original article, Kardorff highlighted the fact that no women were on trial at Nuremberg in order to disassociate all German women from Nazism and its crimes. "Nuremberg is a male trial," she wrote, "Fortunately, women's names will not be burdened by associations with crime and murder."[56] According to Kardorff, even the leader of the National Socialist Women's League (*NS Frauenschaft*) Gertrud Scholtz-Klink was not among the defendants because the court believed that her role had had no political significance. *Für Dich's* rebuttal critiqued Kardoff's depiction of women as fundamentally unconnected with Nazism. According to the magazine, the population in the East had wished to see Scholtz-Klink and her department heads tried. It was not "elite" women such as Scholtz-Klink who paid the price for the war their husbands had waged, but rather the working-class women toiling to clear Germany's cities of rubble:

> We women who fought the hard fight against Nazism, who had to be on guard against denunciations from our neighbors or colleagues in the factories [. . .] cannot overlook the complicity of the women who stand behind the Nuremberg war criminals [. . .] It defies understanding, when one hears a German female journalist say: "there could never have been a female Nuremberg."[57]

Kardorff's article and *Für Dich*'s response embody both Western and Eastern postwar rhetoric about who bore responsibility—or not—for Nazism. In the West, women were viewed for decades after the war either as apolitical, and therefore not responsible for National Socialist crimes, or as primarily victims of Hitler's misogynist regime. *Für Dich* adopted the Soviet line that linked Nazism primarily to class rather than gender: the middle and upper classes were presumed to be supporters of National Socialism, while the working class was, at least theoretically, deemed antifascist.[58] In this way the original article and the response reflected each region's process of dealing with the past.

Women journalists in East and West addressed common themes about the repercussions of the war, including rubble women, refugees, POWs, and hunger. They did so, however, by focusing on the alleged suffering in the other Germany, a discourse meant to underscore the superiority of their own region. We can see these processes at work in the writing of Elfriede Brüning, who in the summer of 1946 worked for the East German publication *Sonntag*. Her articles focused primarily on so-called women's issues in relation to the effects of the war. In fact, the division of Germany had immediately impinged on her work, as the paper rejected her first article on East German refugees. Brüning had written of her trip to Berlin on the back of a truck with East German refugees, describing "the starving people who besieged our car, begging for a carrot." Her editor advised that if this article represented her approach to social issues in the East, she would be better off submitting it to the *Tagesspiegel* in the West. Naturally, he warned, she would no longer be welcome at *Sonntag* if she did so. Brüning keenly observed that the *Tagesspiegel* would have welcomed reports about misery in the East but that *Sonntag* required optimism about everyday life in the East.[59]

Brüning's next piece about refugees reflected this required optimism. In March 1948, she published an article titled "In Good Hands and Well Cared For" in *Neue Heimat*, a publication produced by the Central Administration for Resettlers (Zentralverwaltung für Umsiedler) in the Soviet zone. The purpose of *Neue Heimat* was to help settle Germans displaced or returning from Eastern territories. Brüning described the experiences of a group of East Prussian women returning from internment in Siberia. She wrote of the women's arrival at the resettlement camp in Pirna, Saxony, and the ways in which they had maintained their beauty and femininity under the duress of "intense" work. Although the women found the separation from family painful and the work strenuous, the article continued, they did not regret the experience. They rhapsodized over the beauty of the north: "the midnight sun," "blueberries as large as grapes and in lavish supply," "the colorful sky," "the northern lights," and "the multiple rainbows."[60] Brüning's words expressed the press's obligatory optimism about events in the East and the actions of the Soviet Union while keeping silent on the harsh reality of life in the Gulag.

The discourse in the West with regard to refugees and internees focused on German suffering. In her 1948 piece for the *Süddeutsche Zeitung,* based in Munich in the American Occupation Zone, titled "In Encircled Berlin: Notes from the Diary of Ursula von Kardorff," Kardorff wrote about the victimization of all Berliners in the wake of the war and particularly during the 1948–49 Soviet blockade. Referencing a series of documents about Germans deported to the Soviet Union that she had recently been shown, she described them as a "registry of horror." "This is the reality in Berlin," she wrote, "and this is the reality in the Eastern zone, in which the besieged [West] Berlin is a lighthouse. The window to freedom."[61] Kardorff's postwar writing championed the popular notion that Germany, and above all its women, were the primary victims first of Nazism and then of the Soviets—a narrative that provided a "usable" postwar identity for, and legitimated, the FRG.[62] This discourse suited the Western Allies in the Cold War contest for Germans' allegiance.[63]

Conclusion

West Berlin–based journalist Christa Rotzoll claimed that she had never been "political," nor had she ever considered her work political. Yet, according to Rotzoll, in the shadow of the Cold War all journalists became so whether they wished it or not.[64] Her comments were certainly self-serving—she claimed that as a female journalist during the Third Reich, who focused only on culture, she was never concerned or associated with politics. Yet, Rotzoll's words also illuminate how macropolitical changes after 1945 entangled women journalists in the Cold War. Because of their gender and their profession, female journalists in the two Germanys were both affected by and actors in the ever-changing social and political paradigms and processes of state-building in East and West. Moreover, their careers and writings reflect ruptures and continuities in gender relations between pre- and post-1945 Germany, and between East and West Germany.

Immediately after the war, it seemed that gender roles in both East and West were expanding and shifting. As the dogmas of the Cold War began to exert themselves in the political sphere, women's roles in the West quickly reverted to more traditionally defined functions. Positioned as apolitical, women there were to contribute to society primarily through their roles as wives and mothers. The East positioned itself on ideological terms, in contrast to the West, as committed to women's economic and political emancipation. The careers and writing of women journalists in the Eastern zone more clearly represented a break with traditional perspectives and rhetoric on gender. Yet in both halves of Germany, as they had been in the past, women were largely relegated to the areas of soft news, so-called women's issues, and culture. In the West, these areas—much like in the Third Reich—were constructed as apolitical, while in the East they were more overtly tied to politics. In this way, women journalists and their work came to symbolize the gender policies of two rival blocks. Through their profession and the visibility it entailed, they became vulnerable to the various risks associated with the Cold War, including surveillance and internment. Paradoxically, through their writing they were also actors in creating this context. Women's publications set East against West as they used the other's approach to the war and its repercussions to delegitimize the other Germany.

Deborah Barton is assistant professor of modern German history at the Université de Montréal, Canada. Her research interests focus on the two world wars, gender, and representations of violence in the media. She received her PhD from the University of Toronto in May 2015. Her dissertation titled "Writing for Dictatorship, Refashioning for Democracy: Women Journalists in the Nazis and Post-war Press," explores the role and influence of women journalists as political and cultural agents between 1933 and 1955.

Notes

1. See "Ursula Rumin, Nachlaß," Bundesarchiv Berlin, NY4620.
2. See Karl Christian Führer and Corey Ross, eds. *Mass Media, Culture and Society in Twentieth-Century Germany* (New York, 2006); Sigrun Schmid, *Journalisten der frühen Nachkriegszeit: Eine kollektive Biographie am Beispiel von Rheinland-Pfalz* (Cologne, 2000); and Carmen Sitter, *"Die eine Hälfte vergisst man(n) leicht!": Zur Situation von Journalistinnen in Deutschland unter besonderer Berücksichtigung des 20. Jahrhunderts* (Pfaffenweiler, 1998).
3. Sitter, *Die eine Hälfte*, 224.

4. Wilhelm Weiss, "Die Frau im Schriftleiter Beruf," *Deutsche Presse*, 7 March 1936, 118.
5. See Deborah Barton, "Writing for Dictatorship, Refashioning for Democracy: Women Journalists in the Nazis and Post-war Press" (PhD diss., University of Toronto, 2015).
6. "Michael Jobbelson, U.S. Civ. Chief of Research Section, Report, Office of Military Government, Information Control Branch, US Army, 2 June 1947," Bundesarchiv Berlin (BArch-B), Ruth Andreas-Friedrich File, RK I7.
7. "Mitglieder Liste, 1946," BArch-B, DY10/354.
8. As quoted in Sitter, *Die eine Hälfte*, 218.
9. Luise Rinser, *Den Wolf umarmen* (Frankfurt/M., 1981), 399.
10. "Brief von Kardorff an Frl. Rosenheim, 8. Oktober 1946," BArch-B, ED348/6; and "Brief von Kardorff an Peter Boyle, 20. September 1946," BArch-B, ED348/5.
11. Sitter, *Die eine Hälfte*, 267. See also Karen Hagemann and Sonya Michel, eds., *Gender and the Long Postwar: The United States and the Two Germanys, 1945–1989* (Baltimore, MD, 2014).
12. See Donna Harsch, "Sex, Divorce, and Women's Waged Work: Private Lives and State Policy in the Early German Democratic Republic," in *Gender and Everyday Life under State Socialism in East and Central Europe*, ed. Jill Massino and Shana Penn (Basingstoke, 2010), 97–113.
13. "Bericht über die 1. Mitglieder-Versammlung, 7. April 1946," BArch-B, DR2/1038. See Jürgen Wilke, ed., *Journalisten und Journalimus in der DDR: Berufsorganisation—Westkorrespondenten—"Der schwarze Kanal"* (Cologne, 2007).
14. "Verband der Deutschen Presse, 1947," BArch-B, DY10/3.
15. "Mitglieder Liste, 1946," BArch-B, DY10/354.
16. Ibid.
17. See Elizabeth Heineman, *What Difference Does a Husband Make? Women and Marital Status in Nazi and Postwar Germany* (Berkeley, CA, 1999); and Donna Harsch, *Revenge of the Domestic: Women, the Family, and Communism in the German Democratic Republic* (Princeton, NJ, 2007).
18. "Verband der Deutschen Presse, Mitgliederliste, 1. Januar 1951," BArch-B, DY10/862.
19. Sigrun Schmid, *Journalisten der frühen Nachkriegszeit: Eine kollektive Biographie am Beispiel von Rheinland-Pfalz* (Cologne, 2000), 208.
20. Hannelore Krollpfeiffer, *Wir lebten in Berlin: Eine Geschichte vom Ende des Krieges* (Berlin, 1947), 81.
21. Gerda Zorn, *Wiederkehr des Verdrängten: Autobiographische Erinnerungen* (Berlin, 2008), 159.
22. "Elfriede Brüning, Fragebogen für Mitglieder, Die Reichsschriftumskammer, 1. September 1937," BArch-B, R 9361-V/3909, "Betrifft: Freistellung vom Arbeitseinsatz, 1943," BArch-B, R 9361-V/3909; and Elfriede Brüning, *Und außerdem war es mein Leben* (Munich, 1998), 294. Brüning joined the KPD in 1930 and wrote for such left-wing publications as the *Rote Post* and *Berlin am Morgen*. During the Third Reich, she wrote for a range of publications, including the *Frankfurter Zeitung*, *B.Z. am Mittag*, *N.S. Funk*, *Fürs Haus*, and *Völkischer Beobachter*. The *Kulturbund zur demokratischen Erneuerung Deutschlands* was founded by the poet Johannes R. Becher in Berlin in July 1945.
23. See also personal interviews in Lissi Klaus, ed., *Medienfrauen der ersten Stunde: "Wir waren ja die Trümmerfrauen in diesem Beruf"* (Zurich, 1993).

24. Brüning, *Und außerdem*, 331. See also BArch-B, DY10
25. "Bericht über die 1. Mitglieder-Versammlung 7. April 1946," BArch-B, DR2/1038.
26. *The Fair Practice Guide for German Journalists: Wegweiser zum guten Journalismus*, Office of Military Government for Bavaria (Information Control Division / Press Control Branch) 1947, 10.
27. "Brief von Kardorff an Jürgen Schüddekopf, 7. November 1946," Institut für Zeitgeschichte, München (IfZ), ED348/6.
28. "Brief von Ursula von Kardorff an Herrn Fleischer," *Die Neue Zeitung*, 20. März 1948, IFZ, ED348/7.
29. "VDP Protokoll," undated, but likely 1948, BArch-B, DY 10/1.
30. It soon moved its head office to Bonn where it remained for decades.
31. See Christina von Hodenberg, *Konsens und Krise: Eine Geschichte der westdeutschen Medienöffentlichkeit 1945–1973* (Göttingen, 2006); and Helene Rahms, *Die Clique: Journalistenleben in der Nachkriegszeit* (Bern, 1999).
32. Simone Barck et al., "The Fettered Media: Controlling Public Debate" in *Dictatorship as Experience: Towards a Socio-Cultural History of the GDR*, ed. Konrad H. Jarausch (New York, 1999), 220.
33. "Vorstandssitzung des VDP, 21.–22. Januar, 1950," BArch-B, DY10/1.
34. Ibid.
35. Barck et al., "Fettered Media," 214.
36. Zorn, *Wiederkehr*, 211.
37. Ibid.
38. Ibid., 246.
39. Ibid., 247.
40. Christa Rotzoll, *Frauen und Zeiten: Porträts* (Berlin, 1991), 144.
41. "Breif von Eva Siewert an Hans Leonard, 8. Juli 1947," Landesarchiv Berlin, E. Rep. 200-63 Nr. 73.
42. Norman Naimark, *The Russians in Germany: A History of the Soviet Zone of Occupation* (Cambridge, MA, 1995), 364.
43. Erik Reger, "Editor's Letter," *Tagesspiegel*, 29 March 1951.
44. Rotzoll, *Frauen und Zeiten*, 145.
45. "Rumin Nachlaß," BArch-B, NY 4620/10.
46. See "Rumin Nachlaß," BArch-B, NY4620/12; and Brigitte Gerland, *Die Hölle ist Ganz Anders* (Stuttgart, 1954), 14.
47. Naimark, *Russians in Germany*, 387.
48. Michael Lemke, "Foreign Influences on the Dictatorial Development of the GDR, 1949–1955," in Jarausch, *Dictatorship as Experience*, 96. See also Beatrix Bouvier, *Ausgeschaltet! Sozialdemokraten in der Sowjetischen Besatzungszone und in der DDR 1945–1953* (Bonn, 1996).
49. "Gordon E. Textor, Top Secret Memo, 15 June 1947," IfZ, OMGUS, 5/260-1/15. In his letter, Textor misspelled Tiulpanov's name, referring to him as Tulpenov.
50. "Brief von Liselotte Weinsheimer an ihre Schwiegermutter, 15. Juli 1953," Weinsheimer Nachlaß, Staatsarchiv Bremen, 7202-1 vol. 5.
51. Zorn, *Wiederkehr*, 250.
52. Ibid., 251.
53. Ibid., 252.

54. See Phil Leask, "Humiliation as a Weapon within the Party: Fictional and Personal Accounts," in *Becoming East German: Socialist Structures and Sensibilities after Hitler*, ed. Mary Fulbrook and Andrew Port (New York, 2013), 237–56.
55. Lemke, "Foreign Influences," 98.
56. Ursula von Kardorff, "Weibliches Nürnberg," *Sie*, 24 August 1946, 2.
57. Ibid.
58. Naimark, *Russians in Germany*, 74.
59. Brüning, *Und außerdem*, 320.
60. Elfriede Brüning, "Gut aufgehoben, vorbildlich betreut," *Die neue Heimat*, 5 March 1948, 9.
61. "Ursula von Kardorff, 'Vom Reisen heutzutage,'" 1945/46. IfZ, Ed348/15.
62. See Robert G. Moeller, *War Stories: The Search for a Usable Past in the Federal Republic of Germany* (Berkeley, CA, 2003); and Elizabeth Heineman, "The Hour of the Woman: Memories of Germany's 'Crisis Years' and West German National Identity," *American Historical Review* 101, no. 2 (1996): 354–95.
63. See Petra Goedde, *GIs and Germans: Culture, Gender, and Foreign Relations, 1945–1949* (New Haven, CT, 2003).
64. Rotzoll, *Frauen und Zeiten*, 143.

Selected Bibliography

Bösch, Frank. *Mass Media and Historical Change: Germany in International Perspective, 1400 to the Present*. New York, 2015.

Conley, Patrick. *Der parteiliche Journalist*. Berlin, 2012.

Fiedler, Anke, and Michael Meyen. *Fiktionen für das Volk: DDR-Zeitungen als PR-Instrument; Fallstudien zu den Zentralorganen Neues Deutschland, Junge Welt, Neue Zeit und Der Morgen*. Berlin, 2011.

Führer, Karl Christian. *Medienmetropole Hamburg: Mediale Öffentlichkeiten 1930–1960*. Munich, 2008.

Führer, Karl Christian, and Corey Ross, eds. *Mass Media, Culture and Society in Twentieth-Century Germany*. New York, 2006.

Fulbrook, Mary, and Andrew Port, eds. *Becoming East German, Socialist Structures and Sensibilities after Hitler*. Oxford, 2013.

Gienow-Hecht, Jessica. *Transmission Impossible: American Journalism as Cultural Diplomacy in Postwar Germany, 1945–1955*. Baton Rouge, LA, 1999.

Harsch, Donna. *Revenge of the Domestic: Women, the Family, and Communism in the German Democratic Republic*. Princeton, NJ, 2007.

Hodenberg, Christina von. *Konsens und Krise: Eine Geschichte der westdeutschen Medienöffentlichkeit 1945–1973*. Göttingen, 2006.

Jarausch, Konrad H., ed. *Dictatorship as Experience: Towards a Socio-Cultural History of the GDR*. New York, 1999.

Laurien, Ingrid. *Politisch-Kulturelle Zeitschriften in den Westzonen 1945–1949: Ein Beitrag zur politischen Kultur der Nachkriegszeit*. Frankfurt/M., 1991.

Leeder, Karen, ed. *Rereading East Germany: The Literature and Film of the GDR*. Cambridge, 2015.

Massino, Jill, and Shana Penn, eds. *Gender and Everyday Life under State Socialism in East and Central Europe*. Basingstoke, 2010.

Moeller, Robert G. *War Stories: The Search for a Usable Past in the Federal Republic of Germany.* Berkeley, CA, 2001.
Mosebach, Bernd. *Alles bewältigt? Ehemalige Journalisten der DDR arbeiten ihre Vergangenheit auf.* Berlin, 1996.
Naimark, Norman. *The Russians in Germany: A History of the Soviet Zone of Occupation, 1945–1949.* Cambridge, MA, 1995.
Schmid, Sigrun. *Journalisten der frühen Nachkriegszeit: Eine kollektive Biographie am Beispiel von Rheinland-Pfalz.* Cologne, 2000.
Schlosser, Nicholas J. *Cold War on the Airwaves: The Radio Propaganda War against East Germany.* Urbana-Champaign, IL, 2015.
Schroeder, Steven M. *To Forget It All and Begin Anew: Reconciliation in Occupied Germany, 1944–1954.* Toronto, 2013.
Sitter, Carmen. *"Die eine Hälfte vergisst man(n) leicht!": Zur Situation von Journalistinnen in Deutschland unter besonderer Berücksichtigung des 20. Jahrhunderts.* Pfaffenweiler, 1998.
Sonntag, Christian. *Medienkarrieren: Biografische Studien über Hamburger Nachkriegsjournalisten 1946–1949.* Munich, 2006.
Steege, Paul. *Black Market, Cold War: Everyday Life in Berlin, 1946–1949.* Cambridge, 2007.
Wilke, Jürgen. *Journalisten und Journalismus in der DDR: Berufsorganisation –Westkorrespondenten—"Der schwarze Kanal."* Cologne, 2007.

CHAPTER 15

Entangled Femininities

Contested Representations of Women in the East and West German Illustrated Press of the 1950s

Jennifer Lynn

During the 1950s, the illustrated press in both Germanys attempted to define each state's and society's vision of modernity by using images of "the modern woman." Magazines in the Federal Republic of Germany (FRG) presented photographs of dutiful housewives, smiling female consumers, loving mothers, and good-looking young women in attractive jobs. The glossy publications were full of colorful advertisements for household products. Advice columns offered help for housework and marriage, which reinforced the dominant ideal of the male-breadwinner/female-homemaker family. In the German Democratic Republic (GDR), the magazines printed images of women at modern machinery doing "men's work," showcased the newest fashions from the Eastern Bloc, and attempted to convince their readers that the capitalist West exploited and degraded women. They praised the model of the dual-earner family for married women from all social backgrounds and propagated equal jobs and payment for men and women. In the West, like in the past, working-class wives and mothers were at best accepted, but only if the female income was really needed for the survival of the family. In both postwar Germanys, these images were not just meant for entertainment but were intended to promote specific economic and social orders and the related labor and family policies, consumer practices, and visions of modern femininity. Interestingly, the representation of the other state and society was quite uneven in the illustrated press. West German magazines rarely recognized the existence of the "other" Germany and its alternative to the capitalist gender order of the West. East German publications, in contrast, explicitly criticized the FRG (and the United States) as a capitalist system that exploited men and women and oppressed furthermore the female sex.

This chapter investigates the ideological and cultural significance of representations of women in the illustrated press of the two German states. How and why did gendered images implicitly or explicitly address "the other" Germany or ignore them? In the context of the Cold War, the chapter argues, the visual and textual images of femininity (and especially of images coded "modern") functioned within each German state as signs that differentiated "our" Germany from the other and defined "us" in relation to the *wrong* kind of femininity on the other side of the so-called Iron Curtain. Combining gender and media history, the chapter shows that the illustrated press reflected and fueled a relationship that, Christoph Kleßmann posits, was characterized by *Abgrenzung und Verflechtung* (demarcation and entanglement).[1] Yet, gender was not the only category of difference at work here. Rather, the magazines' depictions of femininity reflect the intersection of class and gender. The GDR's aim, in particular, to distinguish itself from the Federal Republic and portray itself as the "better" and more "socially just" Germany led to gendered images that were closely entangled with class distinctions and ideology.

My focus is on the East German magazines *Die Frau von heute* and *Neue Berliner Illustrierte* (*NBI*) and the West German women's magazines *Constanze* and *Brigitte*. The representation of women and gender in these magazines captures the (apparently) asymmetrical interest of the Germanys in each other. The magazines in the East articulated a counter-narrative to Western images of consumerism and prosperity. *Constanze* and *Brigitte*, in contrast, were silent about developments in the East. Their construction of femininity was presented as the (implied) universal standard. Thus, the chapter's analysis is somewhat inequivalent too. It examines representations of femininity in *Constanze* and *Brigitte* as an indirect rejection of the East German alternative. In the case of *Die Frau von heute* and *NBI*, the analysis is not only of positive representations of socialist femininity but also of negative images of the West and, in particular, of Eastern publications' appropriation of images of Western women from the FRG media.

Scholarship on postwar gender images in East and West Germany has demonstrated the important role that the illustrated magazines played in cultural and political constructions of gender, but it has focused on magazines in either the FRG or GDR and neglected their representations of the other state and, thus, missed their entanglement. In the FRG during the 1950s, the research shows, the emphasis was on the notion of the woman as a wife, mother, and consumer. This ideal was closely connected to the desire of the leading Christian-conservative political parties—the Christian Democratic Union of Germany (Christlich Demokratische

Union Deutschlands, CDU) and its Bavarian sister party, the Christian Social Union (Christlich Soziale Union, CSU)—as well as the Catholic and Protestant Churches and their organizations to establish a postwar gender order based on the conventional male-breadwinner/female-homemaker family that was perceived as a pillar of the state and society.[2] In the GDR, the political focus of the ruling Socialist Unity Party of Germany (Sozialistische Einheitspartei Deutschlands, SED) was on women's roles as workers and mothers. Its political aim was the dual-earner family, mainly because the socialist economy needed women in the workforce. This goal was supported by the ideal of socialist emancipation, which promoted women's paid work as a path to female equality. As scholarship on the GDR has shown, however, the visual narratives in its women's magazines rarely challenged the conventional gender division of labor in the household and the family.[3]

The scholarship on gendered representation has tended to neglect research by media historians. Scholars such as Simone Barck have argued that the FRG press, radio, and film industry "constituted a 'second' media that constantly influenced and subverted the 'first,' i.e. official GDR media."[4] As a result, "GDR media were increasingly forced into a defensive position vis-à-vis their challengers from the West that belied their public claims to superiority."[5] Moreover, the important role that magazines' gendered images have assumed in the German media landscape since the 1920s deserves more scholarly attention. With technological advances in printing and image reproduction, the illustrated press became a central part of Weimar political and popular culture.[6] During the Third Reich, the illustrated press was utilized as political propaganda as well as entertainment.[7] In 1945, the occupying powers quickly developed and founded new (and often long-lasting) illustrated magazines for women and general audiences.[8] The speed of the illustrated press's revival speaks to the central role assigned to it in formulating and propagating different versions of a postwar gender order.[9] Editors knew that photographs possessed an "evidential force" that demonstrated authenticity.[10]

Gender theory and the approach of intermediality allow me to analyze and interpret the entangled images of femininity in East and West German women's and family magazines.[11] The illustrated magazine is unique in its function to inform, entertain, persuade, and explain by using a combination of visual images and text. Unlike films, where images flicker across the screen, or novels, which construct a verbal image, illustrated magazines offer a distinctive forum that allows the reader to extrapolate meaning by both seeing and reading. Their photography seems to link illustrated magazines to the "scientific understanding" of the world, one that is "objective," where reality passes through a lens that editors present to the public. The camera's seemingly truthful picture of the world obscures the role of the photographer in framing the photograph and of the editor in placing it on the page.[12]

After a brief history of the featured magazines, the chapter explores images of female paid labor in East and West German women's magazines. Then, it examines how the GDR press appropriated images from Western media to prove that the FRG (and its American ally) exploited and degraded women in a capitalist system. The last section shows how the East used "overconsumption" to warn against the materialistic desires of the West while justifying the relative lack of consumer goods in the East.

Illustrated Magazines in Postwar East and West Germany

Die Frau von heute was one of the earliest East German magazines. It was approved by the Soviet administration in February 1946 as a newspaper of the local women's committees (*Kommunale Frauenausschüsse*) in Berlin. In March 1947, *Die Frau von heute* became the publication of the newly founded Democratic Women's League (Demokratischer Frauenbund Deutschlands, DFD). The thirty-two pages of images and text in the first issue from 1946 included photographs of a destroyed Berlin, offered practical advice for women coping in the aftermath of the war, and underlined women's roles in rebuilding Germany, specifically with an "antifascist" worldview.[13] The magazine enjoyed continued success in the postwar years and functioned as a general-interest woman's magazine. It reached a run of 300,000 to 600,000 copies per week before it was suspended in 1962 and reemerged as *Für Dich* in 1963.[14] The *Neue Berliner Illustrierte* began even earlier and lasted considerably longer. From April 1945 on, this popular weekly family magazine was published with approximately 730,000 copies per week until 1991. Women were a major target audience of the *NBI*. The magazine featured an eye-catching front-page photo, discussed political developments and progress in rebuilding the GDR, showcased technological advances, and presented human-interest stories. Initially, content aimed at women focused on popular tips for "making-do." Soon came articles that celebrated female paid work, "equal pay for equal work," and young women entering "male" professions.[15]

The first illustrated women's magazine in West Germany was the biweekly *Constanze*, which began publishing in February 1948 in the British zone. It appeared until 1969 and reached a run of 550,000 copies. *Constanze* became one of the most popular women's magazines in the FRG, second only to the biweekly illustrated women's magazine *Brigitte*. Launched in 1949 as *Brigitte: Das Blatt der Hausfrau* (The Housewife's Magazine), the magazine changed its subtitle in 1957 to *Die Zeitschrift für die Moderne Frau* (Journal for the Modern Woman). Increasing in both size and popularity during the 1950s and 1960s, *Brigitte* eventually swallowed up *Constanze* in 1969. Similar to other publications, the initial issues of both magazines focused on postwar deprivation, rationing, the lack of material goods, and advice for day-to-day cooking, cleaning, and mending clothes. However, by the early to mid-1950s, these glossy publications reflected social and economic change. No longer solely issuing practical tips for "housewives," the magazines emphasized ample consumer goods and summer vacations, featured larger fashion sections, and focused on relationships, romance, marriage, and motherhood. The magazines presented, by and large, a consistent and repetitive message of conventional gender roles and expectations.[16]

Images of Female Paid Labor in the Illustrated Magazines

One of the clearest differences between gendered images in East and West German illustrated magazines was their representations of female paid labor. The achievements of women were central to the East German construction of femininity and modernity, which magazines symbolized through the icon of the working woman. Photographs and accompanying texts attempted to convince readers about the importance and necessity of female labor. Reflecting the continuous shortage of the GDR labor market, which increased until 1961 with the growing number of refugees who left for the FRG, the East German government increasingly needed women, including mothers, in the workforce. Thus, the message in the SED propaganda as well as the illustrated women's magazines was directed at women of all classes and generations. The press strived to highlight women's roles in the building of a socialist society.[17]

In the FRG, images of working women presented in the illustrated women's magazines focused on modern, clean vocations for young, single women. They were the only group of women who were supposed to join the workforce in accordance with the dominant model of the male-breadwinner/female-homemaker family. This ideal type allowed for women's paid labor only as part of a three-phase life model for women: young women would leave the full-time labor market upon marrying and starting a family and only return when the children were grown up. The West German representations of employed women provide a counterpoint to the images of female paid labor in the GDR illustrated press. Interestingly, unlike many other West German images of women, the images of working women were neither reprinted nor explicitly addressed by the GDR media. One reason might be that there was little to criticize about young working women.

The most powerful icons of the East German working woman became the *Maschinistin* and the *Traktorfrau,* the female machine operator and tractor driver. Invoking the world of an industrialized, proletarian workforce, these representations were coded as profoundly "modern."[18] Scholars have debated the extent of a socialist "modernity" in the GDR. I argue that the plethora of images of the "socialist women" at work in a broad variety of modern, highly engineered workplaces strongly supports the argument of historians like Katherine Pence who assert that the GDR was modern. She contends, "The GDR state's assumption of responsibility for transforming the role of women was one way that the regime was radically modern, even if there were a myriad of ways that the ideal execution of these goals was only partially or not quite fulfilled," and concludes that, in fact, "the ongoing active engagement with the modern women's question in all its fraught manifestations was itself constitutive of GDR modernity."[19] Even in the first postwar years, women in the Soviet zone were presented in East German illustrated magazines as workers in modern, socialist industries who got equal opportunities and equal pay for equal work. This narrative dominated in the press throughout the 1950s.[20] Even though the magazines did not use the term *moderne Frau* (modern woman), they implicitly labeled working women as "modern." Their "modernity" resided in their paid work, which was often connected with modern technologies, new skills, and the rhetoric of equality. Similar to the social democratic press in the Wilhelmine Empire and the communist press during the Weimar Republic, the GDR magazines emphasized the emancipatory potential of female paid labor. Set in the style of socialist realism, articles and photo essays in the early 1950s emphasized women's ability and "right" to train and participate in former "men's work" or male professions.[21]

A photo essay in *Die Frau von heute* titled "Women and Girls of Our Day" from July 1950, for example, highlighted "capable women" behind machines. "This is Irma," noted one caption, "working with a modern high-pressure boiler."[22] Subsequent articles and photos made clear that women had not only a "right" to work but also an obligation to participate in the labor market, including holding jobs that were traditionally considered "masculine."[23] Accordingly, *Die Frau von heute* argued that women in the GDR "stand on equal footing" with men and had the "same responsibilities."[24] The magazine strongly encouraged the ambition of young women to study and master technical jobs that in the past were open only to men. The article "Her Goal—Technical University," for instance, printed in February 1952, proudly reported that the five-year plan allowed for more young people—men and women—to train at a *"Technische Hochschule"* (technical college) where students would learn the most "modern standards of the fields of hygiene and aesthetics."[25] The accompanying photos included young female students carefully listening to instructors and working on their own as they engaged in a variety of skills.

In an attempt to convince readers that women should participate in paid labor, *Die Frau von heute* praised women's contributions to the labor force, evidenced by photographs of happy and attractive women posed with tools and machines in the industrial workplace.[26] Already by the early 1950s, editors saw no need to interpret the image of women and machines for their readers. Photos could be printed on the cover page without captions (see figures 15.1 and 15.2). The women's smiling faces and

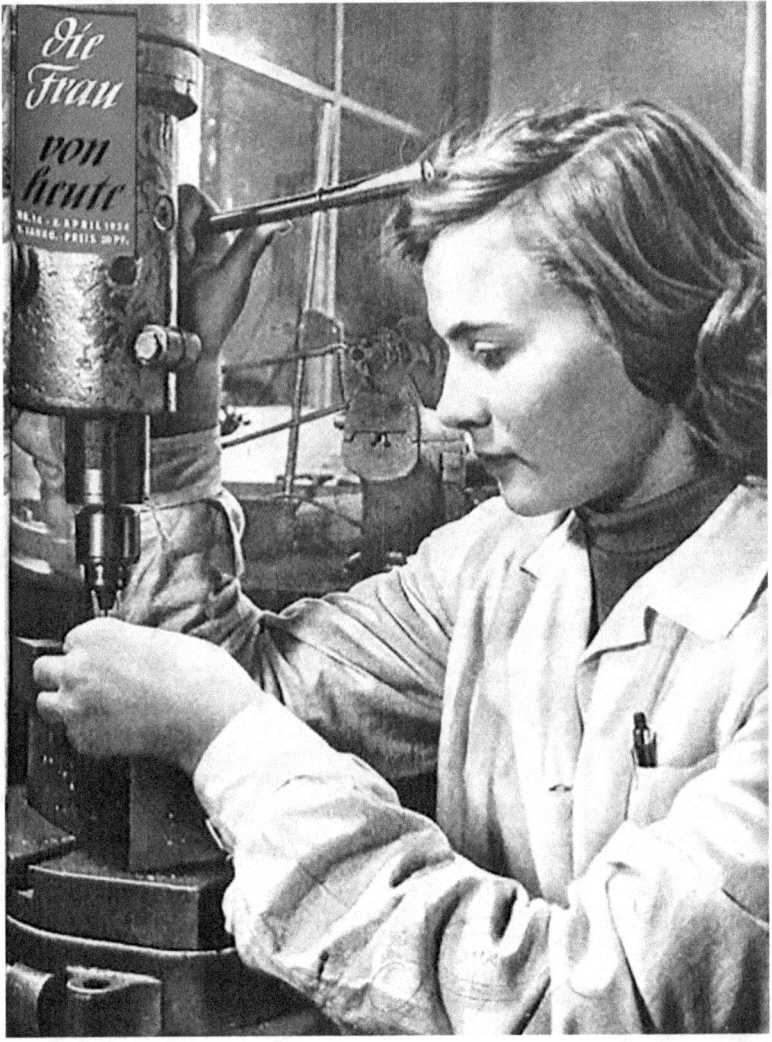

Figure 15.1. *Die Frau von heute,* no. 14, 1 April 1953. Staatsbibliothek zu Berlin, Preußischer Kulturbesitz.

Figure 15.2. *Die Frau von heute*, no. 25, 18 June 1954. Staatsbibliothek zu Berlin, Preußischer Kulturbesitz.

their concentration on their work were both a reminder and a celebration of women as equal members of the working class in modern industrial jobs.[27] Magazines in the GDR intentionally created such visual narratives, which served to accentuate an important modern aspect of the socialist state—the realm of female paid labor in new and exciting sectors of the labor market.

The magazines contrasted the positive image of the empowered working woman in the GDR with the counterimage of her exploited sister in the FRG. *Die Frau von heute* constantly reminded its readers about the economic and social problems women had to face in the capitalist West. One example is an article published in 1956 under the title "Illusion and Reality," supposedly written by a woman named Ruth, who described her chance to view a variety of magazines from West Germany. She critiqued the status of women in the FRG, linking their struggle to economic circumstances. For her, a photograph (somewhat faded and blurry) showing a woman in a bikini and men "fishing" was presented as a "characteristic image of the capitalist economic system."[28] The article argued that the wealth and "glitz" was a façade behind which "millions fight for their daily bread." Women, the article contended, often worked between thirteen and sixteen hours a day in a shoe factory or seventy hours a week in a textile factory while earning on average "20 to 40 percent" less than men. Furthermore, working mothers in the FRG lacked childcare; as a result, two million children were *Schlüsselkinder* (latchkey children).[29]

Prostitution was another social problem plaguing West German women, according to the same article, which painted a miserable picture of the lives of female prostitutes in West Germany. The author concluded, "There are thousands upon thousands of women and mothers, and there are more every day, who are struggling against the unscrupulous exploitation, against the decay of ethics and morality."[30] Using both images and text, *Die Frau von heute* reminded readers that luxury and privilege in the West only applied to a small fraction of society.[31] The magazine's visual narrative, repetitive and consistent, emphasized the clean, modern employment of the GDR—with ample opportunities for women—against the decay of the socially and economically stratified West.

West German media portrayals of working women were quite different. Since the mid-1950s the dominant image of the male-breadwinner/ female-homemaker family began to fracture, because an increasing number of married women and mothers did part-time work in the booming economy.[32] Women's magazines like *Constanze* provided a forum for the discussion of this phenomenon, where experts weighed in and readers responded. In contrast to the GDR, the West German media presented jobs of working women that not only were "typically feminine" but also adhered to middle-class ideals of fancy and fashionable female jobs for single women in a white-collar workforce, distinctly separated from working-class girls and women and their exhaustive and often dirty work in factories. Accordingly, flight attendants, models, and private secretaries were especially popular images. While models and secretaries were common tropes in publications since the 1920s, the flight attendant offered a glimpse of what *Constanze* called "chic and glamorous" female work in the postwar world. Merging the allure of mobility and adventure alongside stylish clothing, photo essays made clear that being a flight attendant was the perfect job for young women lucky enough to have the looks that were a crucial prerequisite for the job. This job, which embraced air travel, exotic locations, and futuristic adventure, was also decidedly modern.[33] In December 1958 under the headline "Every Third Will Be Married," an article in *Constanze* covered the most "modern stewardess school in the world," found in the United States.[34] The article included photographs of women in training as they learned "flight baby care," the daily schedule on board, and proper maintenance of hair and nails. It was the "dream job" for young women. And while "thousands" tried their hand, only "one percent" made it to employment, emphasizing the exclusivity of the profession. Photographs in a 1959 article in *Brigitte* echoed the sentiments of earlier profiles, stressing that young, single women with "good figures" were not in it for the money but instead wanted to "see the world."[35]

West German magazines also emphasized secretarial work as an excellent career option for young women, because it offered "practical and clean" white-collar work with the added benefit of the potential for marrying the boss. The image of office work in a stylish environment for young, single women was not new to the illustrated press. It populated the illustrated magazines of the 1920s and remained a prominent theme in publications during the Third Reich.[36] From the beginning, the image of the secretary proved to be flexible. She could be both an appealing example for female upward mobility and an object of desire for consumer fantasies. During the 1950s, the popular press presented the secretary as a realistic alternative to the dream jobs of becoming a model or flight attendant. A 1955 article series in *Constanze* titled "What Should You Be?" provided career guidance for young women and, especially, recommended office work. An accompanying fashion section underscored the desirability of such a career.[37] The photo essay "Blouses, Sweaters, Skirts!" from the same year focused exclusively on the suitable fashion for the office (see figure 15.3).[38] "Between the phone and the typewriter," the text noted, "blouses, sweaters, and skirts are still the most practical!" A photo depicted a young woman perched on the edge of a desk, heels kicked to the side, her typewriter abandoned as she files her nails. The tartan skirt and merino-wool sweater are punctuated by a thick leather belt. Other photos included a woman making coffee (presumably for her boss) and applying face powder. The photos emphasized female beauty—not work.

While East German magazines displayed and railed against capitalist exploitation of working women in the FRG, *Constanze* and *Brigitte* apparently saw no need to include a discussion (or images) of the East.

Figure 15.3. *Constanze,* no. 3, February 1955: "Blusen, Pullis, Röcke!" (Blouses, Sweaters, Skirts!). Staatsbibliothek zu Berlin, Preußischer Kulturbesitz.

Perhaps it seemed self-evident that images of luxurious fabrics, plentiful cosmetics, and trendy accessories effectively communicated a message of West German superiority.

Defining the East against the West

Throughout the 1950s, *Die Frau von heute* and the *Neue Berliner Illustrierte* used their pages as an opportunity to critique Western media and address the status of women in the West. In doing so, their publications sought to define the socialist alternative of a "modern woman."[39] The preoccupation with the West produced an uneven entanglement as, again, illustrated magazines in the FRG usually ignored its neighbor. In an attempt to build socialist legitimacy and undermine the West, East German magazines stressed its exploitation of women, the problems of mass culture, and Americanization. GDR media used the language of "decadence" and "degeneration," historian Uta Poiger argues, as a deliberate strategy to attack and present American culture as an "ideological tool" of both the United States and the West.[40]

Pursuing this strategy, illustrated magazines like the *Neue Berliner Illustrierte* cut, collaged, and commented on photos that had been printed in Western media. Often, the magazine would copy only the images, creating their own captions, headlines, and photo essays. This allowed editors to produce their own textual framework, (re)reading the images for their audience to guide their readers' interpretations. This practice of (re)contextualizing and collaging images had long been a tradition within the communist press, beginning with the *Arbeiter Illustrierte Zeitung* in Weimar Germany.[41]

Drawing on contemporary anxieties about Americanization, GDR magazines repeatedly asserted that the United States highly influenced the "debasement" of women in West Germany. These articles were especially important during the early 1950s when East Germany needed to establish an identity counter to the West—in the context of both Cold War politics and the recent Nazi past. These images encouraged readers to see for themselves the evidence of female exploitation in a capitalist society. The added benefit for publications was to present interesting and sometimes titillating images that might otherwise be forbidden.

For example, in December 1950 the *NBI* presented readers with images of female wrestlers in two-piece bathing suits next to photos of children quietly playing. Captioned "Nice Game—Ugly Game," it became clear that the "nice games" were played by children in the GDR, while "ugly games" were "imported" from the United States.[42] One photograph emphasized the violence between women during wrestling matches by showing a headlock "with strangulation." The caption informed readers that West German women must participate in such "American culture" like women's wrestling in order to receive their weekly wages. An issue of *Die Frau von heute* from June 1950 also included photos of women wrestlers from Minneapolis, Minnesota, with their legs in the air, presumably to emphasize their humiliation.[43]

Provocative and nude photos of exploited Western women became a common theme in the *NBI,* always published with a sense of outrage and with the purpose of unveiling the hypocrisy of capitalism. The images were ostensibly for edification, not titillation. While magazines justified printing the images by critiquing them via text, they nevertheless served voyeuristic tendencies. In April 1953, for instance, the *NBI* printed under the headline "Atombomb" an excerpt from an American erotic comic (initially printed in the popular West German magazine *Stern*) titled "What to Do in Case of an Atomic Attack." The magazine condemned the "pornographic pamphlet," which depicted a striptease and an "accidental" glimpse of panties and a garter belt. The caption noted the "shameless" use of this material and its "mocking of 100,000 citizens of Hiroshima who were the victims of the militarily unjustifiable American atomic bomb."[44] The outrage against the image should also be read within the larger context of the *NBI* protesting the development and potential use of nuclear weapons. The magazine included frequent articles warning against the proliferation of nuclear weapons, printed photographs of the impact of Hiroshima on the human body, and provided postapocalyptic scenarios for its readers.[45] The *NBI* intentionally situated the erotic comic and the outrage it demonstrated within their larger conversations about America's use of the atomic bomb and the arms race.

Hollywood films also became a recurrent target for the *NBI*, and photos of actresses with "sex appeal" served to condemn the film industry of the West. This included trashy films available in the FRG, which the magazine described as a "cesspool."[46] A story from November 1953, for instance, depicted the "Monroe Invasion" (see figure 15.4). The photo at the top of the page revealed images of thick, glossy magazine covers from the West (*Der Spiegel, Neue Illustrierte,* and *LIFE*) featuring the popular Hollywood star Marilyn Monroe. The text emphasized that these covers show the actress "strapless, with bedroom eyes." The "Western magazines" use "Marilyn's breasts" as a measure of the "Hollywood standard of beauty." What is worse, the "star maker" Joe Schenk (the manager of the "vamp"), profits from "enormous sums" when "the erotic atom bomb Marilyn strikes."[47]

The exploitation of women and unreasonable beauty standards in Hollywood were not the only critiques. The caption argued that this "Marilyn noise" attempts to cover why the soldiers "Joe and Tom must die in Korea" or why "living is getting more expensive." For the *NBI*, the links between Hollywood, the illustrated press, and global politics were clear. Three pinup photos of Marilyn and one photo of her manager are collaged against a backdrop of a battlefield; the caption explained that she is "the super blond offensive against culture." The language of war, within the context of the fear of remilitarization and American military maneuvers, was an attempt to deepen the disgust at the construct of the "blond hydrogen bomb," "Miss Flamethrower," and "Hollywood's alluring girl." Like Marilyn Monroe's nicknames, according to the *NBI*, American war films also use vocabulary with a "double dose of sex," which are popularized by the media. The "Monroe Invasion," proclaimed the paper, was "launched [. . .] at the height of the [1952] presidential election." This was a "maneuver" to "turn off the last minutes of a possible self-reflection of voters."

The images of Monroe, superimposed atop a battlefield, mimicked the language of war, thus visually and textually creating an argument for its readers that the FRG and the United States were an insidious threat. At the same time, the magazine's editors most likely understood that readers would pause to look at the photos of Marilyn in her classic swimsuit pose or wearing an off-the-shoulder blouse, shorts, and heels. In 1954, the *NBI* continued this argument by printing a photo of Marilyn Monroe in lin-

Figure 15.4. *Neue Berliner Illustrierte*, no. 46, November 1953: "Die Monroe-Invasion" (The Monroe Invasion). Staatsbibliothek zu Berlin, Preußischer Kulturbesitz.

gerie, perched cheekily on a dresser, high heels adorning her feet, posing as if talking into the phone. The "Sex-Bomb" is a "diversionary tactic" on the front page of newspapers, noted the *NBI,* while current events are ignored. The photographs may have been used to capture the reader's eye, but the publication's intent was to use Marilyn Monroe as a lesson of Western media's efforts to distract and manipulate its audience.[48]

East German publications condemned not only West Germany's allegedly Americanized society but also the West German media. "Showcase of Debasement," a March 1952 article in *Die Frau von heute,* scathingly analyzed the cover pages and content of West German magazines available at a kiosk at the Bahnhof Zoo in West Berlin (see figure 15.5).[49] The author denounced the lack of pictures of working women and the presentation instead of "the woman as a luxury female (*Luxusweibchen*) and object of purchase (*Kaufobjekt*)." Rather than German culture, the magazines "propagate the new order of Europe, the colonialism of the 'American Century.'"[50] To all of this, the author contrasted the newspaper stands of "the democratic sector" (East Germany), festooned with "more diverse, more colorful, and more interesting" images that demonstrated

Figure 15.5. *Die Frau von heute,* no. 21, 21 March 1952: "Schaufenster der Entwürdigung" (Showcase of Debasement). Staatsbibliothek zu Berlin, Preußischer Kulturbesitz.

"our brotherly hands are stretched out to the Germans in the West." The author also lauded the "great achievements" that "equal women" were making in the GDR.[51]

In the early 1950s, an era of intense Cold War antagonism, GDR publications used the West to define what socialism was *not* by reprinting photos from the West and instructing their readers on how to interpret them. The engagement with the illustrated media of the West suggests that East German editors believed that visual images of women mattered and that images revealed the true nature of (capitalist) democracy. For the GDR, the socialist woman represented a symbol of progress and modernity. Thus, in East German eyes the textual and photographic presentation of women functioned as a primary marker of difference between the West and East. In putting forth a visual narrative of distancing, East German editors clearly assumed that visual cues packed a big punch—and, therefore, had to be deconstructed for naïve readers of the West's illustrated magazines.

(Over)Consumption and Its Critics

While East German magazines often defined modernity in relation to paid labor, magazines in the FRG constructed the modern woman in relation to her domestic space and consumer goods. This representation became ever more visible as the West German "economic miracle" of the 1950s produced rising disposable income for millions of workers and higher spending by them and their families. Rather than "making do," women were able and encouraged to purchase consumer goods once considered luxuries. Ordinary people simultaneously felt the changes in wages, the availability of commodities, and economic stability and saw them reflected and interpreted in the visual landscape of advertisements, magazines, film, and television. The publications modeled themselves on the glossy pages of American and British magazines and offered abundant images of modern consumer goods and fashion spreads. West German magazines rarely referred to the Cold War, much less to women's policies in the GDR. Yet magazine features, advertisements, cover images, and photo essays transmitted a message about society and gender relations: they focused on (re)establishing the breadwinner/housewife family in their modern home complete with modern appliances and stylish furniture. They underscored the central role that women played in rebuilding their nation through spending. In *How German Is She? Postwar West German Reconstruction and the Consuming Woman,* Erica Carter argues that female consumption emerged, in fact, as crucial to national identity.[52] Following her, other scholars also see consumption as a primary marker of identity (and modernity) in the FRG. The rationalized housewife and consuming woman were also used, they conclude, to mark differences between East and West.[53]

Through a variety of channels, many East Germans had access to the West German press and saw the abundance depicted in its magazines. As the GDR fell relatively behind in the production of consumer goods, its press faced the difficult task of convincing East Germans that their situation was actually better than that of West Germans. One tactic was to tar West German consumption as excessive and then to link excessive consumption with health concerns and social problems. Another was to expose the false dreams of glamour incited by images of consumer abundance, a message that resurrected Weimar-era communists' criticism of the commercialized image of the *"Neue"* (new) or *"Moderne Frau"* (modern woman).[54]

In 1957, *Die Frau von heute* addressed an article titled "Pretty Girls—Expensive Clothing," which had originally appeared in the West German magazine *Brigitte*.[55] The story focused on young women who only had milk and crackers for dinner in order to afford expensive clothing and expansive wardrobes (see figure 15.6). The fact that this exposé was printed in the West only gave *Die Frau von heute* more ammunition to lambast the capitalist system that destroyed women's health. Perhaps the one-page article in *Brigitte* was an attempt to admonish women for overspending, but by and large the magazine was rarely critical of consumerism. The original article in *Brigitte* argued that the motto "clothes make the woman" is a "typical and glaring accompaniment to our highly acclaimed economic miracle" and is harmful to women's health. The photographs alongside the text reveal fashionable women, but the captions provide the appropriate interpretation. "Liselotte Stengle, 23 years old, secretary, has 20 dresses and 15 pair of shoes by eating sparingly. Her motto is: 'I can eat when I'm old!'" Another woman, Dagmar Kekule, was 19 and studying to be a kindergarten teacher. The caption notes, "She has 10 dresses and 9 pairs of shoes. Her evening meal: milk and crackers."[56] The photograph provided proof of this health risk. The young woman is sitting on her bed, her shoes and dresses on display, her meager dinner set before her.

Unable to compete with the visual display of wealth and the fantasy of buying, publications like *Die Frau von heute* and the *NBI* felt compelled to create a narrative that distanced socialism and socialists from consumer desires and replaced visions of abundance with praise of "quality."[57] Moreover, by linking economic and social problems with the capitalist system, the magazines argued that women themselves (while duped into overspending) were also objects to be bought and sold.

Figure 15.6. *Die Frau von heute*, no. 16, 19 April 1957: "Ihr Abendbrot? Milch und Kräcker" (Her Evening Meal? Milk and Crackers). Staatsbibliothek zu Berlin, Preußischer Kulturbesitz.

Conclusion

The articles and images discussed here show that the illustrated press in the FRG and GDR actively defined, constructed, and contested images of femininity and the modern woman. West and East German publications worked, however, in different ways. During the 1950s, publications linked the modern woman in the FRG with attractive images of paid work, consumer abundance, and domestic bliss. Magazines like *Constanze* and *Brigitte* saw no need to address the status of women in the GDR and focused instead on reinforcing conventional gender roles that fit with the larger social and economic goals of the FRG. The images of single working women and consumer abundance were appealing and alluring, and telegraphed a sense of social stability and a prosperous future.

In contrast, *Die Frau von heute* and *NBI* explicitly addressed both the standards and content of media in West Germany, defining East German publications within and against the West German media landscape of the 1950s. In doing so, they constructed and celebrated appropriate images of women in East Germany and expressed distress at the perception of capitalist exploitation in the West. One major theme of East German magazines was the working woman who, in the GDR, defined the modern, emancipated woman. In contrast to single women's fancy and "feminine" white-collar work that filled the pages of West German magazines, East German women were depicted in a broad variety of jobs, including "traditionally male" occupations, as an equal part of the proletarian workforce. Another important topic was "demeaning" images of women found in magazines in West Germany and the United States, underscoring the oppression of women and the false allure of beauty pageants, wealth, and luxury. These images, argued the East German magazines, were meant to create an illusion of prosperity and distract readers from the depredations of American imperialism and military conflicts. In contrast, the GDR press offered up alternative constructions of women and exalted the realm of modern workspaces and quality consumer goods.

The East German press explicitly defined the modern socialist woman and also directly contrasted her with the women presented in the Western press. *Die Frau von heute* and *NBI* used Western images to "prove" to their readers that the capitalist system was detrimental to women. The visual narratives of female labor in the GDR was strikingly similar to that in the communist press during Weimar Germany. The similarity demonstrates continuity across the deep political divides of both 1933 and 1945 in how the illustrated press presented a complicated visual image of the modern woman.[58] As during the Weimar Republic and the Third Reich, the legitimacy and "modernity" of both postwar Germanys were closely associated with the gendered images of the employment, domesticity, consumption, and body of the modern woman.

Jennifer Lynn is professor of history and the director of the Women's and Gender Studies Center at Montana State University Billings. Her interest in photography and media closely informs her teaching and research related to modern Germany, women's and gender history, and visual/cultural history. Currently she is transforming her dissertation, which she defended at the University of North Carolina at Chapel Hill in 2012, to a book with the draft title "Contested Femininities: Gendered Representations of Modern Women in the German Illustrated Press, 1920–1960." Her publications include: "Imagining the Neue Frau: Images of the Modern Women in the Weimar Germany Illustrated Press," *Latchkey: The Journal of New Woman Studies* (Spring 2016); and "The Reorientation of the Women of Germany: Constructing Ideal Femininities in the German Illustrated Press, 1945–1946," *Connections* 10 (Spring 2014).

Notes

1. Christoph Kleßmann, "Introduction," in *The Divided Past: Rewriting the Post-War German History,* ed. idem (New York, 2001), 1–9; Ina Merkel, "Sex and Gender in the Divided Germany: Approaches to History from a Cultural Point of View," in ibid., 91–103.
2. Erica Carter, *How German Is She? Postwar West German Reconstruction and the Consuming Woman* (Ann Arbor, MI, 1997); Christine von Oertzen, *The Pleasure of a Surplus Income: Part-Time Work, Gender Politics, and Social Change in West Germany, 1955–1969* (New York, 2007); Donna Horvath, *Bitte recht weiblich! Frauenleitbilder in der Deutschen Zeitschrift "Brigitte" 1949–1982* (Zurich, 2000); and Heide Fehrenbach and Uta G. Poiger, eds., *Transactions, Transgressions, Transformations: American Culture in Western Europe and Japan* (New York, 2000).
3. Ina Merkel, *. . . und Du, Frau an der Werkbank: Die DDR in den 50er Jahren* (Berlin, 1990); Gunilla-Friederike Budde, "Der Körper der 'sozialistischen Frauenpersönlichkeit': Weiblichkeits-Vorstellungen in der SBZ und der frühen DDR," *Geschichte und Gesellschaft* 26, no. 4 (2000): 602–28; Judd Stitziel, *Fashioning Socialism: Clothing, Politics and Consumer Culture in East Germany* (New York, 2005), 602–28; and Paulina Bren and Mary Neuburger, eds., *Communism Unwrapped: Consumption in Cold War Eastern Europe* (Oxford, 2012).
4. Simone Barck et al., "The Fettered Media: Controlling the Public Debate," in *Dictatorship as Experience: Towards a Socio-Cultural History of the GDR,* ed. Konrad H. Jarausch (New York, 1999), 220.
5. Ibid.
6. Cory Ross, *Media and the Making of Modern Germany: Mass Communications, Society, and Politics from the Empire to the Third Reich* (Oxford, 2008).

7. Karl Christian Führer, "Pleasure, Practicality and Propaganda: Popular Magazines in Nazi Germany, 1933–1939," in *Pleasure and Power in Nazi Germany*, ed. Corey Ross et al. (New York, 2011), 132–53; Habbo Knoch, "Living in Pictures: Photojournalism in Germany, 1900 to the 1930s," in *Mass Media, Culture and Society in Twentieth Century Germany*, ed. Karl Christian Führer and Corey Ross (New York, 2006), 217–33; and Rudolf Stöber, *Deutsche Pressegeschichte* (Konstanz, 2000).
8. Larry Hartenian, *Controlling Information in U.S. Occupied Germany, 1945–1949: Media Manipulation and Propaganda* (Lewiston, NY, 2003); James Rolleston, "After Zero Hour: The Visual Texts of Post-War Germany," *South Atlantic Review* 64, no. 2 (1999): 1–19; and Christina von Hodenberg, *Konsens und Krise: Eine Geschichte der westdeutschen Medienöffentlichkeit, 1945–1973* (Göttingen, 2006).
9. See Jennifer Lynn, "'The Reorientation of the Women of Germany': Constructing Ideal Femininities in the American and Soviet Zones of Occupation, 1945–1946," *Connections: European Studies Annual Review* 10 (2014): 8–17. See, for example, Robert G. Moeller, *Protecting Motherhood: Women and the Family in the Politics of Postwar West Germany* (Berkeley, CA, 1993); Elizabeth Heineman, *What Difference Does a Husband Make? Women and Marital Status in Nazi and Postwar Germany* (Berkeley, CA, 1999); and Donna Harsch, *Revenge of the Domestic: Women, the Family, and Communism in the German Democratic Republic* (Princeton, NJ, 2007).
10. Astrid Ihle, "Framing Socialist Reconstruction in the GDR: *Women under Socialism*—A Discussion of the Fragments of a Documentary Project by the Photographer Evelyn Richter," in *East Germany: Continuity and Change*, eds. Paul Cooke and Jonathan Grix (Amsterdam, 2000), 48. See also Elizabeth Harvey and Maiken Umbach, "Introduction: Photography and Twentieth Century German History," *Central European History* 48, no. 3 (2015): 287–99; and Frank Bösch, *Mass Media and Historical Change: Germany in International Perspective, 1400 to the Present* (New York, 2015).
11. For theories of intermediality, see W. J. T. Mitchell, *Picture Theory: Essays on Verbal and Visual Representation* (Chicago, 1994); Peter Wagner, ed., *Icons—Texts—Iconotexts: Essays on Ekphrasis and Intermediality* (Berlin, 1996); and Peter Burke, *Eyewitnessing: The Uses of Images as Historical Evidence* (Ithaca, NY, 2008). For a gendered approach to images, see Carolyn Korsmeyer, *Gender and Aesthetics: An Introduction* (London, 2004); and Patricia Hayes, ed., *Visual Genders, Visual Histories* (Oxford, 2006).
12. Hanno Hardt, "Negotiated Images: The Rise of Photojournalism in Weimar Germany," in *In the Company of Media: Cultural Constructions of Communication, 1920s–1930s* (Boulder, CO, 2000), 63.
13. "Liebe Berliner," *Die Frau von heute*, no. 1, 1 February 1946, 1.
14. See Merkel, . . . *und Du*; Jennifer Evans, "Constructing Borders: Image and Identity in *Die Frau von heute*, 1945–49," in *Conquering Women: Women and War in the German Cultural Imagination*, ed. Hilary Collier Sy-Quia and Susanne Baackmann (Berkeley, CA, 2000), 40–61, 55.
15. See Merkel, . . . *und Du*.
16. See Oertzen, *Pleasure*, 33, 42–45, 117; Horvath, *Bitte recht weiblich*, 19–24; and Hodenberg, *Konsens und Krise*, 185.
17. Harsch, *Revenge*, 88.
18. For example, see Merkel, . . . *und Du*; Harsch, *Revenge*; and Heineman, *What Difference*.

19. Katherine Pence, "Women on the Verge: Consumers between Private Desires and Public Crisis," in *Socialist Modern: East German Everyday Culture and Politics*, ed. Katherine Pence and Paul Betts (Ann Arbor, MI, 2008), 287, 292.
20. For example "Noch drei Wochen bis zum 8. März," *Die Frau von heute*, no. 7, 13 February 1953, 6–7; "Nicht nur mehr—sondern auch besser!," *Die Frau von heute*, no. 14, 8 April 1955, 4–5; and "Weißes Pulver + Flüssigkeit = Wolkrylon," *Die Frau von heute*, no. 49, 5 December 1958, 3–5.
21. See "Die Frau im Schiffsbau unserer Republik," *Die Frau von heute*, no. 40, 3 October 1952, 10–11; and "Hochöfen von Frauenhand regiert," *Die Frau von heute*, no. 47, 21 November 1952, 6–9.
22. "Frauen und Mädchen unserer Tage," *Die Frau von heute*, no. 2, January 1950, 8–9.
23. "Recht auf Arbeit—Recht auf Erholung," *Die Frau von heute*, no. 20, 7 July 1950, 4–5; an article in July explores female training and labor in "so-called men's jobs," including masonry, mechanics, and working with a boring machine. See also *Die Frau von heute*, no. 22, 21 July 1950, cover page and 4–5; and "Hauchdünn—und doch haltbar," *Die Frau von heute*, no. 13, 1 April 1955, 4–5.
24. "Die richtige Frau am richtigen Platz," *Die Frau von heute*, no. 22, 21 July 1950, 4–5; and Harsch, *Revenge*, 87–132.
25. "Ihr Ziel: Technische Hochschule," *Die Frau von heute*, no. 5, 1 February 1952, 4–5. See also "Inge, Ruth und Gisela haben keine Sorgen . . .," *Die Frau von heute*, no. 19, 30 June 1950, 4–5; and "Wir lassen uns unsere Gleichberechtigung nicht rauben," *Die Frau von heute*, no. 34, 21 August 1953, 4–5.
26. "Die Stalin-Allee: Das ist unsere Straße!," *Die Frau von heute*, no. 30, 25 July 1952, cover page and 8–9; "Ein Besuch bei den Technikerinnen von morgen," *Die Frau von heute*, no. 27, 10 July 1953, 4–5; and "Edith und Tupp, Gisela und Harold," *Die Frau von heute*, no. 24, 11 June 1954, 4–5.
27. *Die Frau von heute*, no. 14, 2 April 1954, cover page; and *Die Frau von heute*, no. 25, 18 June 1954, cover page. See also the following cover pages: *Die Frau von heute*, no. 2, 14 January 1955; *Die Frau von heute*, no. 26, 28 June 1956; and *Die Frau von heute*, no. 39, 27 September 1957.
28. "Illusion und Wirklichkeit," *Die Frau von heute*, no. 6, 10 February 1956, 14–15.
29. Ibid.
30. Ibid.
31. This was often a common tactic in the press; see Paul Betts, "Building Socialism at Home," in Pence and Betts, *Socialist Modern*, 100.
32. Oertzen, *Pleasure*, 15.
33. "Luftige Mädchen," *Constanze*, no. 4, February 1951, back cover. See also Guillaume de Syon, "Lufthansa Welcomes You: Air Transport and Tourism in the Adenauer Era," in *Selling Modernity: Advertising in Twentieth-Century Germany*, ed. Pamela E. Swett, S. Jonathan Wiesen, and Jonathan R. Zatlin (Durham, NC, 2007), 182–201.
34. "Jede dritte wird weggeheiratet," *Constanze*, no. 19, 17 September 1958, 6–9.
35. "So lebt eine Stewardeß," *Brigitte*, no. 25, 1 December 1959, 28–29. Another article from 1955 depicted similar themes. See "Das Glück liebt Stewardessen," *Brigitte*, no. 23, November 1955, 12–13.
36. See Karen Hagemann, *Frauenalltag und Männerpolitik: Alltagsleben und gesellschaftliches Handeln von Arbeiterfrauen in der Weimarer Republik* (Bonn, 1990); and Eric Weitz, *Creating German Communism: From Popular Protests to Socialist*

State (Princeton, NJ, 1997). Also see Jennifer Lynn, "Contested Femininities: Representations of Modern Women in the German Illustrated Press, 1920–1945" (PhD diss., University of North Carolina at Chapel Hill, 2012).
37. "Was wollen sie werden?," *Constanze,* no. 3, February 1955, 28–29.
38. "Blusen, Pullis, Röcke!," ibid., 36–37.
39. The framework of "multiple modernities" or "alternative modernities" is particularly helpful in analyzing different understandings of modernity. See for example Katherine Pence and Paul Betts, "Introduction," in *Socialist Modern,* ed. idem, 12–13.
40. Uta G. Poiger, *Jazz, Rock, and Rebels: Cold War Politics and American Culture in a Divided Germany* (Berkeley, CA, 2000), 45–51. See also Mark Fenemore, *Sex, Thugs, and Rock 'n' Roll: Teenage Rebels in Cold-War East Germany* (New York, 2007).
41. Isabelle de Keghel, "Western in Style, Socialist in Content? Visual Representations of GDR Consumer Culture in the *Neue Berliner Illustrierte* (1953–64)," in *Winter Kept Us Warm: Cold War Interactions Reconsidered,* ed. Sari Autio-Sarasmo and Brendan Humphreys (Helsinki, 2010), 77.
42. "Jedem das Seine," *Neue Berliner Illustrierte* (*NBI*), no. 52, December 1950, 14–15.
43. "Wie du mich wünschst ... oder etwa nicht?," *Die Frau von heute,* no. 16, 9 June 1950, 6–7. See also "Signal auf Halt!," *Die Frau von heute,* no. 7, 7 April 1950, 4–5; "Amazonen in der Ami-Zone," *Die Frau von heute,* no. 13, 19 May 1950, 18–19; and "Sensationen oder Attraktionen," *Die Frau von heute,* no. 36, 27 October 1950, 10. See Maria Höhn, *GIs and Fräuleins: The German-American Encounter in 1950s West Germany* (Chapel Hill, NC, 2002), 126–34.
44. "Atombomben auf neckisch," *NBI,* no. 17, April 1953, 6.
45. See for example, "Atombomb," *NBI,* no. 24, June 1953, 8–9; and "Die Welt im Atomzeitalter," *NBI,* no. 45, November 1953, cover page and 8–9.
46. "Bonner Filmkloake," *NBI,* no. 19, May 1953, 7.
47. "Die Monroe-Invasion," *NBI,* no. 46, November 1953, 15.
48. "... die Ablenkungsmanöver," *NBI,* no. 8, February 1954, 9.
49. "Schaufenster der Entwürdigung," *Die Frau von heute,* no. 12, 21 March 1952, 8–9.
50. Ibid.
51. Ibid., 9. Also see "Zwei Welten im Spiegel der Presse," *NBI,* no. 19, March 1950, 6.
52. Carter, *How German Is She?*
53. Jennifer A. Loehlin, *From Rugs to Riches: Consumption and Modernity in Germany* (Oxford, 1999); Hanna Schissler, ed., *The Miracle Years: A Cultural History of West Germany, 1949–1968* (Princeton, NJ, 2001); Victoria de Grazia, *Irresistible Empire: America's Advance through Twentieth-Century Europe* (Cambridge, MA, 2005); and Swett et al., eds., *Selling Modernity.*
54. See Lynn, "Contested Femininities."
55. "Schöne Mädchen—Teure Kleider," *Die Frau von Heute,* no. 16, 19 April 1957, 10. See also "Warum müssen in Westdeutschland so viele Mütter sterben?," *Die Frau von heute,* no. 44, 31 October 1958.
56. Ibid.
57. Judd Stitziel, *Fashioning Socialism: Clothing, Politics and Consumer Culture in East Germany* (New York, 2005), 49–77.
58. Weitz, *Creating Communism*; Lynn, "Contested Femininities."

Selected Bibliography

Barck, Simone, Christoph Classen, and Thomas Heimann. "The Fettered Media: Controlling the Public Debate." In *Dictatorship as Experience: Towards a Socio-Cultural History of the GDR,* ed. Konrad H. Jarausch, 212–39. New York, 1999.

Bösch, Frank. *Mass Media and Historical Change: Germany in International Perspective, 1400 to the Present.* New York, 2015.

Bren, Paulina, and Mary Neuburger, eds. *Communism Unwrapped: Consumption in Cold War Eastern Europe.* Oxford, 2012.

Budde, Gunilla-Friederike. "Der Körper der 'sozialistischen Frauenpersönlichkeit': Weiblichkeits-Vorstellungen in der SBZ und der frühen DDR," *Geschichte und Gesellschaft* 26, no. 4 (2000): 602–28.

Carter, Erica. *How German Is She? Postwar West German Reconstruction and the Consuming Woman.* Ann Arbor, MI, 1997.

Evans, Jennifer. "Constructing Borders: Image and Identity in *Die Frau von heute,* 1945–49." In *Conquering Women: Women and War in the German Cultural Imagination,* ed. Hilary Collier Sy-Quia and Susanne Baackmann, 40–61. Berkeley, CA, 2000.

Fehrenbach, Heide, and Uta G. Poiger, eds. *Transactions, Transgressions, Transformations: American Culture in Western Europe and Japan.* New York, 2000.

Fenemore, Mark. *Sex, Thugs, and Rock 'n' Roll: Teenage Rebels in Cold-War East Germany.* New York, 2007.

Führer, Karl Christian, and Corey Ross eds. *Mass Media, Culture and Society in Twentieth Century Germany.* New York, 2006.

Grazia, Victoria de. *Irresistible Empire: America's Advance through Twentieth-Century Europe.* Cambridge, MA, 2005.

Harsch, Donna. *Revenge of the Domestic: Women, the Family, and Communism in the German Democratic Republic.* Princeton, NJ, 2007.

Harvey, Elizabeth, and Maiken Umbach. "Introduction: Photography and Twentieth Century German History." *Central European History* 48 no. 3 (2015): 287–99.

Hayes, Patricia, ed. *Visual Genders: Visual Histories.* Oxford, 2006.

Heineman, Elizabeth. *What Difference Does a Husband Make? Women and Marital Status in Nazi and Postwar Germany.* Berkeley, CA, 1999.

Höhn, Maria. *GIs and Fräuleins: The German-American Encounter in 1950s West Germany.* Chapel Hill, NC, 2002.

Horvath, Dora. *Bitte recht weiblich! Frauenleitbilder in der deutschen Zeitschrift "Brigitte" 1949–1982.* Zurich, 2000.

Ihle, Astrid. "Framing Socialist Reconstruction in the GDR: *Women under Socialism*—A Discussion of the Fragments of a Documentary Project by the Photographer Evelyn Richter." In *East Germany: Continuity and Change,* ed. Paul Cooke and Jonathan Grix, 45–56. Amsterdam, 2000.

Loehlin, Jennifer A. *From Rugs to Riches: Consumption and Modernity in Germany.* Oxford, 1999.

Merkel, Ina. . . . *und Du, Frau an der Werkbank: Die DDR in den 50er Jahren.* Berlin, 1990.

Moeller, Robert G., ed. *West Germany under Construction: Politics, Society, and Culture in the Adenauer Era.* Ann Arbor, MI, 1997.

Oertzen, Christine von. *The Pleasure of a Surplus Income: Part-Time Work, Gender Politics, and Social Change in West Germany, 1955–1969.* New York, 2007.
Pence, Katherine, and Paul Betts, eds. *Socialist Modern: East German Politics, Society and Culture.* Ann Arbor, MI, 2008.
Poiger, Uta G. *Jazz, Rock, and Rebels: Cold War Politics and American Culture in a Divided Germany.* Berkeley, CA, 2000.
Ross, Cory. *Media and the Making of Modern Germany: Mass Communications, Society, and Politics from the Empire to the Third Reich.* Oxford, 2008.
Schissler, Hanna, ed. *The Miracle Years: A Cultural History of West Germany, 1949–1968.* Princeton, NJ, 2001.
Stitziel, Judd. *Fashioning Socialism: Clothing, Politics and Consumer Culture in East Germany.* New York, 2005.
Swett, Pamela, S. Jonathan Wiesen, and Jonathan R. Zatlin, eds. *Selling Modernity: Advertising in Twentieth-Century Germany.* Durham, NC, 2007.

CHAPTER 16

Gendered Orientalism

Representations of "the Turkish" in the West German Press of the 1970s and 1980s

Brittany Lehman

In March 1983, the left-liberal weekly magazine *Der Spiegel* ran an article about the plight of Turkish women and girls in West Germany titled "Completely Powerless." The article described how in early March a young Turkish woman, Serife, had picked up her father from work and then shot him once in the back and twice in the head with a 6.35-millimeter pistol. The anonymous author condemned the murder but also argued that the deed was understandable: after enduring years of abuse, Serife could not take any more. The author claimed that, in addition, "Turks" were unable to cope with the unfamiliar West German environment. They were "extremely susceptible to spiritual illness on account of the cultural shock associated with the transition between the Orient and the West."[1] In response, "Anatolian patriarchs" took out their frustration and aggression on their daughters, as exhibited by Serife's father's "brutally grabbing her by the hair and beating her" when she was six years old. For years, Serife struggled against her father's domination, finding some freedom in her schooling. Yet, when she tried wearing miniskirts like her classmates, her father beat her with increasing frequency and called her a "whore."[2] In response to the escalating violence, Serife finally killed her father.

Press reports like this reflected and contributed to widespread Orientalist stereotypes of Turks, Muslims, and Arabs embedded in West German and Western discourse. As literary critic Edward Said first laid out in his pathbreaking 1978 book *Orientalism*, the West (Europe and the United States) looked at Arab and Muslim communities through an exaggerated and distorted lens, usually with the intention of exerting control.[3] The language of Orientalist discourse shifted in the postcolonial world as, in particular, the word "Oriental" fell out of use. Nonetheless the associated sentiments lingered, expressed in western media, society, and politics through pejorative stereotyping of individuals—particularly Muslims—from the Middle East, North Africa, and Asia as well as lingering beliefs in inherently inferior cultural behaviors and ethnic identity.

This stereotyping was gendered. Said and other postcolonial theorists demonstrated the ubiquity of a Western image of the Oriental man as a dangerous, backward, and uncivilized individual, prone to abuse and oppressing women. Building on Said's discussion, anthropologist Lila Abu-Lughod demonstrated in her 2013 book *Do Muslim Women Need Saving?* that the West tended to portray Muslim women as beautiful, veiled, and powerless. In the Orientalist narrative, Western men needed to save the wrapped Oriental woman and allow her to expose her body as an expression of freedom.[4] As these scholars and many others have shown since the 1970s, Western discourses were—and arguably still are—saturated with such images, often without realizing it.[5]

Drawing on evidence from the regional and national press, this chapter tracks the public evolution of gendered Orientalist stereotypes in the West German mainstream media between 1960 and 1989. It argues that the stereotypical depiction of Muslim men—particularly Turkish citizens—as probable criminals and Muslim women as their pitiable victims temporarily receded in the 1960s before reemerging by 1980. That claim comes out of research for a recent study of education policies related to non-German communities in the Federal Republic of Germany between 1949 and 1992.[6] In order to stay abreast of public responses to those policies, federal and state (*Länder*) education administrations collected regional and countrywide newspaper articles about the schooling of children with non-German citizenship. These collections included news stories about pitiable Turkish girls who were abused and suppressed by their patriarchal fathers and criminal boys who opposed their sisters and threatened the West German social order. Those articles motivated politicians in the federal and state parliaments to request information from state education administrations about the situation of Turkish children in public schools. The administrations' reports on headscarves and swimsuits fed additional news articles about the Turkish family, articles which often employed essentializing stereotypes.

In addition to the (West) German education administrations' collections, I conducted a series of targeted searches of two liberal weekly publications, *Der Spiegel* and *DIE ZEIT*, looking for references to Turkish women and schoolchildren. The analysis of the relevant articles demonstrates that *Der Spiegel* continuously presented an Orientalist depiction of Turkish girls and women. *DIE ZEIT*, in contrast, often provided a more positive representation of the German-Turkish population but was less likely to discuss gender. While journalists writing for *DIE ZEIT* typically suggested that multiple ethnic groups could live peaceably side by side, their articles, nonetheless, depicted Turkish citizens as non-German others.[7]

This chapter aims to contribute to the scholarship on Orientalism, on the one hand, and studies of stereotypes of Turks and Muslims in West Germany, on the other, by revealing the gendered continuities between them.[8] Literary scholars like Yasemin Yildiz have demonstrated the pervasive nature of a West German narrative that casts Turkish "women as foreign, deficient, and, most often, as pitiable victims of domestic abuse."[9] Sociologists Gökçe Yurdakul and Anna C. Korteweg have discussed the continued prevalence of essentialist images of the diverse cultures of Turkish, Kurdish, and Moroccan communities in Germany today.[10] The chapter looks back at the press of the 1960s through the 1980s in order to trace continuity and change in media imagery. The first section focuses on the discursive transition from the generically backward but hardworking male "foreigner" and "guest worker" to the essentially impoverished and criminal Turk" and, later, "Muslim." It then turns to the media's frequent depictions of Muslim—especially Turkish—girls whose state of dress allegedly demonstrated their victimhood in patriarchal families. These negative stereotypes, the chapter concludes, contributed to the widespread condemnation of Turkish culture and the Muslim faith in West Germany and, thus, to social segregation and individual suffering.

A note on language is necessary before continuing: Historians have yet to discover a good way to discuss different ethnic and citizenship groups. Individuals develop their own complex sense of identity that usually involves at least some level of hybridity. Yet, in order to discuss the past, scholars are forced to simplify and use labels like "German" or "Turkish."[11] While acknowledging that these are loaded terms that explicitly do violence to the very groups discussed, this chapter uses labels based on citizenship status to discuss individuals.

The Entanglement of Depictions of Muslim Boys and Men with Migration Policy

The 1983 *Spiegel* article on Serife's case described her father as a "patriarchal head of the family of a Turkish stamp" and a "particularly despotic man." According to the article, domestic abuse was a part of the family's Turkish cultural background. That background was supposedly particularly relevant as the family came from the southern Turkish region of Anatolia, where the author claimed that such proverbs as "whoever does not hit his daughter, hits himself" informed society and culture. Now that the family was in West Germany, confronted with a modern "industrial society" that conflicted with the "Oriental family spirit," the father's "abusive personality" became even more pronounced.¹²

This depiction of the abusive Muslim man reflected Western Orientalist assumptions about the Muslim world dating back to the fifteenth century and gender stereotypes from later eras, including the Enlightenment and Romantic periods.¹³ As literary scholars James R. Hodkinson and Jeff Morrison discussed in their 2009 volume *Encounters with Islam in German Literature and Culture,* eighteenth- and early nineteenth-century writers often depicted Muslim men as weak and more susceptible to rash behavior than their Occidental counterparts. Striving for power, they became abusive and wildly aggressive when faced with the stalwart West. According to Enlightenment and Romantic authors, that very weakness rendered Oriental men effeminate.¹⁴ Although grossly inaccurate, that representation of Muslim masculinity nonetheless became pervasive in German literature and culture.¹⁵

It was these very stereotypes about Muslim masculinity that many West German mainstream journalists used in the 1980s as they focused on Turkish men and boys as the largest "Oriental" citizenship group in West Germany. Superimposing Orientalist tropes on millions of people indiscriminately, many journalists tended to cast all adult Turkish men as inherent villains. The author of the 1983 *Spiegel* report on Serife's act of murder implied that her father's behavior was not singular but an example of a wider problem: Muslim men were criminally abusive due to their native culture and because they felt overpowered by a dominant West German culture. Thus, these men became victims of mental illness that turned them from domestic tyrants into outright monsters.

Although 1980s stereotypes of Turkish masculinity reflected Enlightenment depictions, there was actually a brief lull during the 1960s in the extremity of that imagery in favor of an emphasis on the necessity of foreign labor for West German economic development. During the 1950s and 1960s, western European economic expansion necessitated foreign labor recruitment to sustain explosive growth. Other European states relied on (former) colonies for labor. Until the construction of the Berlin Wall (1961), the booming West German industry used the stream of refugees from East Germany, but afterward it had to increase the recruitment of workers from southern and southeastern Europe as well as North Africa. Initially, in this first period of migration policy in West Germany from 1955 to 1973, Turkish citizens accounted for a small percentage of recruited labor in favor of workers from countries like Italy and Greece. The correspondingly sparse depictions of "Turks" in the press presented them as useful, hardworking male laborers, if inherently non-German others. Politicians and journalists assumed that the so-called guest workers were men, although one-third of the workers were women and there was a growing presence of children and elderly among the West German minority populations. As Ruth Mandel showed in her 2008 study *Cosmopolitan Anxieties: Turkish Challenges to Citizenship and Belonging in Germany*, West German government and media representations of Turkish workers often lumped them as ethnically and legally foreign "Southerners," whose otherness extended into their very bodies. In contrast with the restrained, clean masculinity of German workers, Southern (including Turkish) men possessed expressive emotions, a brute physicality, and frequently a strong smell of garlic.[16] That otherness was supposedly so inherent that the West German citizenry needed to understand that guest workers could never comprehend "Germanness." Nonetheless, even as those publications explicitly othered foreign labor, the government and most West German media informed citizens that they needed to welcome new workers as contributors to West German economic growth.[17]

That welcome was, however, supposed to be temporary. The West German government under the Christian-conservative chancellors Konrad Adenauer (1949–63) and Ludwig Erhard (1963–66) rendered mass immigration palatable by denying that the arrival of millions of people was in fact immigration. According to both chancellors, guest workers' residence would be short-term. These individuals were there to bolster the economy as it grew but were supposed to leave when the going got tough.[18] Many people across West Germany believed that claim, making the widespread dehumanization of recruited workers—seen in barrack-style housing and social exclusion—acceptable. As historian Ulrich Herbert pointed out in his *A History of Foreign Labor in Germany, 1880–1990: Seasonal Workers, Forced Laborers, Guest Workers,* treatment of post-1945 non-German labor was hardly equitable. Far from overcoming Nazi prejudice, ongoing discriminatory practices and semi-segregation contributed to the development of "ghettos" in many cities.[19] Recruited labor was welcomed as workers, not as people.[20]

When the economic miracle began to wear out in the late 1960s, when the West German economy suffered a recession in 1966–67, followed by the 1973 oil crisis, that emphasis on temporary male labor became even more of a problem. Now the West German government and society were forced to acknowledge that most of West Germany's foreign residents were de facto permanent. The second phase of post-1945 labor migration, family reunification, that started after 1973 underlined that point.[21] In November 1973, the governing coalition of the Social Democratic Party of Germany (Sozialdemokratische Partei Deutschlands, SPD) and the liberal Free Democratic Party (Freie Demokratische Partei, FDP), in power from 1969 to 1983, responded to rising unemployment with a "recruitment stop" (*Anwerbestopp*) to put a halt to bringing in new "guest workers."²² In 1973, about 2.6 million foreign workers were employed in the Federal Republic. Because of the previous recruitment policy, the proportion of foreigners living in Germany had grown from 1.2 percent in 1960 to over 4.9 percent in 1970. In total, the number of "foreigners" living in the FRG reached four million in 1973; 893,600 of them were Turkish citizens. This number included the women and children that the press had mostly long ignored.²³

The *Anwerbestopp* led to a second phase of German migration policy from 1973 to 1979, which was characterized primarily by the influx of family members, because the new law allowed family members to follow relatives (spouses and children of previously recruited workers) to West Germany. With this regulation the *Anwerbestopp* aimed at least at a temporary integration for the families of guest workers who wanted to settle permanently. On the basis of the *Ausländergesetz* of 1965, they received a residence permit or a permit to move there. The imposition of the recruitment stop virtually fostered family reunification: it was the only form of immigration still permitted. In addition, the federal government promised immigrant families that settled permanently a better integration policy.²⁴

Instead of leaving en masse, millions of male and female West German residents with foreign citizenship continued to build families or brought children and other family members to join them from abroad. Workers with Turkish citizenship were particularly likely to bring their families, as they did not have the protection of European Community membership.²⁵ The press and public finally acknowledged the permanence of immigrant communities and found their "ghettoized" situation inexcusable. West Germany was, after all, a welfare state described by political elites as having overcome classism and racism.²⁶ The existence of West German communities living below the social standard threatened the entire idea of a West German social order and inspired fears of social dissolution.²⁷

For many mainstream journalists and politicians, the realization that foreign workers were permanent members of West German society inspired discussions during the 1970s about possible integration. Those journalists and politicians became particularly interested in schoolchildren—initially without reference to gender. Born and raised in West Germany, children had the potential to bridge gaps between West Germany's minority and majority communities. Furthermore, through integration, those children had the potential to escape second-class existences, solving West German fears about ghettos. For both purposes, children with foreign citizenship—particularly Turkish—needed access to school and West German culture in order to rise above their heritage.²⁸ Yet, even as integration was paramount, most West German journalists felt that these children were too culturally different to ever be German or become German citizens. A few politicians suggested that full integration was possible, but their voices were largely drowned out in the public debate.[29] For the majority of West German politicians and journalists, schoolchildren with Turkish citizenship were still Turks regardless of where they were born and raised.

Those claims reflected in part the legal categorization imposed by West German law regarding both citizenship and religion. The West German Basic Law tied citizenship to ethnicity, which was supposedly dependent on ancestry. Thus ethnic German migrants, including 1.4 million migrants (*Aussiedler*) from Eastern Europe between 1950 and 1989, were entitled to citizenship. The children of West German residents with Turkish citizenship born and raised in country were, in contrast, legal foreigners.[30] Consequently, by 1973, the "Turks" in West Germany included not only new immigrants but second- and third-generation residents as well.[31] Furthermore, both the West German and the Turkish governments recorded Turkish citizens as Muslims regardless of personal belief or practice. Consequently, most West German politicians and journalists used "Turks" and "Muslims" as synonyms with little understanding of or reference to the diversity inherent in both labels. Reality, after all, dictated that each one of those more than 800,000 West German residents with Turkish citizenship was an individual.

Instead of acknowledging that individuality, many mainstream journalists emphasized West Germany's minority populations' supposed non-Germanness by increasingly resorting to Orientalist stereotypes. Those news articles focused in particular on supposedly innate poverty and criminality. An early example is a 1972 *Der Spiegel* article titled "The Turks Are Coming: Save Yourselves," which described the growing number of foreign, especially Turkish, families in large cities such as West Berlin, Frankfurt am Main, and Stuttgart, and criticized West Germany's migration policy. The unnamed author expressed pity for the deplorable situations of many Turkish families but at the same time stoked prejudices against Turks and their otherness. These foreigners were going to consume society and destroy Germanness due to criminality and poverty. Good Germans should flee, saving themselves even as they mourned the loss of once-German cities.[32]

The 1972 article in *Der Spiegel* would not be the last to make such claims, although the perception of appropriate responses differed, particularly with reference to whether or not such behavior was inherent to the group and how the state should react. Initially in the early and mid-1970s, as themes of desperation and criminalization became increasingly prevalent, many journalists claimed the government was liable for rectifying the situation. According to journalists like Ruth Lingenberg in her 1976 article for the daily *Kölnische Rundschau* based in Cologne, "For Foreign Children a 'Bomb Is Ticking': They Are Especially Threatened by Youth Unemployment," the government needed to step in to provide equal opportunities for children with non-German citizenship. If the government failed to act, Turkish boys would be doomed to unemployment and criminality, while girls would become prostitutes.[33] For Lingenberg and others, those fates were due to their circumstances and not inherent to the children's identities. Therefore, something could be done.

Disturbingly, the 1972 article in *Der Spiegel* with xenophobic depictions of Turkish citizens became a norm by the end of the 1970s as many journalists and politicians drew increasingly on Orientalist stereotypes. At the time and since, West German journalists and scholars have debated what drove the rise of xenophobia. They pointed to three causes in particular: racist stereotypes and social norms lingering from the Nazi period; economic recession; and cultural fears that Germany was no longer for "Germans."[34] Whatever the causes, sympathy for the situation of "foreign" male youths declined in the media by the late 1970s, shifting instead to xenophobic expressions and baseless accusations regarding criminal behavior. In February 1978, for example, the left-liberal daily *Frankfurter Rundschau* published an article titled "Foreigners at Risk— Associations: Without Help, Crime among Them Will Rise." The unnamed author reported that West German youth and welfare associations warned that criminality among male migrant youth was almost certain to rise.[35] Wielding stereotypes about dangerous difference, reports like these ignored statistical evidence that ethnic Germans were more likely than non-Germans to break the law. Instead, both the association reports and the news articles drew on biased public perceptions and prevailing stereotypes, reflecting and reinforcing xenophobic assumptions in the public.[36]

The perception of *the* "Turk" as a non-German "other" incapable of integration was based on negative perceptions of Islam. Where the "Oriental" had been the problem before, now the "Muslim" became a looming menace. That sentiment was reflected in the article "What Remains for Turks in the Foreign Land: Islam Can Mean Home, but also Encapsulate Intolerance" by Petra Kappert published in the *Frankfurter Allgemeine Zeitung* in September 1982. According to Kappert, the Muslim menace, coded male, drove a wedge between the local West German population and Turkish minority groups. The article furthered the idea that there was only one version of Islam and that version did not permit diversity or female emancipation.[37]

Articles like these suggested that Turks were to blame for any lack of integration as they refused to Germanize; its authors claimed that Islam made the situation worse. An article by Erich Wiedemann published in April 1983 in *Der Spiegel* under the title "When the Muftis Come, There'll be Trouble in the Pütt" (i.e., in the neighborhoods around the coal mines in the Ruhr area) underlined that sentiment, claiming that fifteen and more years of the "Turkish problem" had not resulted in integration. Wiedemann saw that separation in the use of different butchers, businesses, and clubs, and warned that increasing religious observance, driven by the arrival of Islamic religious leaders, would exacerbate the social divide instead of bringing them together. His tone suggested that "the Turkish" all shared identical beliefs and, seduced by "muftis," were becoming increasingly radical and an ever-greater problem.[38] These articles reflected and fed the rise of xenophobia directed toward "the Turkish" (now the country's largest national-minority group) and Muslims in West Germany with grossly inaccurate representations of the diverse group as an essentialized, monolithic other.

The West German public absorbed and reflected those sentiments to the extent that, in 1983, the majority supported the chancellorship of Helmut Kohl and his Christian Democratic Party of Germany (Christlich Demokratische Partei Deutschlands, CDU). Kohl had run his successful election campaign under the slogan of "Germany for the Germans" and propagated a German *Leitkultur* (the dominant culture). Toward that end, he demanded the assimilation of "foreigners" (as opposed to integration) and promised to reduce the number of Turkish citizens in West Germany.[39] Turkishness and, increasingly, Islam in general were supposedly antithetical to Christian Germanness and poised to destroy Western freedom.

Engaging these claims, news articles throughout the 1980s reflected and reinforced what became the negative West German stereotype of "the Turkish," which cast non-Germans, especially men and boys, as inherently non-German, Muslim villains. In her 2008 ethnography *Stolen Honor: Stigmatizing Muslim Men in Berlin,* cultural anthropologist Katherine Pratt Ewing described the lasting, detrimental power of that image.[40] She argued that the West German Oriental imagination of a "traditional" Muslim man contributed to the fears about what Muslim, including Turkish, men could become. The construct of a stereotypical and dangerous Muslim masculinity served as the other against which Germanness could be defined and from which Muslim women needed to be rescued.[41]

Unwrapping the Muslim Girl in the West German Imagination

During the 1980s, the widespread West German assumption that all Muslims shared a common, Oriental culture extended not only to men but also to women. In March 1989, for example, *Der Spiegel* published an article titled "He Was Not Able to Act Differently: Violence in Migrant Families—Motive: Culture Shock," about the death of a twelve-year-old from Morocco named Malika. The article's language recalled the rhetoric of the same magazine's 1983 story about Serife. But where the 1983 article suggested the depicted horrors were something new to West Germany, the 1989 article suggested these problems were ongoing and endemic. Furthermore, the image of the Oriental woman—now referred to as the Muslim woman—had become increasingly narrow over the 1980s. Where Serife had a limited agency to commit murder, Malika was supposedly killed for expressing herself physically while her German classmates could not understand why "she had to die" for "making her lips a little red, curling her eyelashes, and painting her nails." In Serife's story, the woman's right to undress and paint her body was becoming a symbolic marker of Western integration and supposed freedom. In Malika's case, makeup and a bared head was an assumed symbol of a Muslim woman's liberation.[42]

In equating the woman's physical exposure with freedom, articles like those in *Der Spiegel* mirrored nineteenth-century European gender norms and Orientalist stereotypes. German-speaking Romantics had portrayed Oriental women as passive victims in patriarchal societies. Supposedly, these women were forcibly kept at home, exposed in their private spaces while forbidden from and/or veiled in the public sphere.[43] These exotic, female victims needed and deserved rescue, even if they were always inferior to the German woman. In fact, to become like the German woman was to attain a form of liberation. Following that narrative, the act of unveiling became a common European fantasy to symbolize Western liberation of Oriental women.[44] Those depictions ignored women's agency and reality in favor of the torrid tale of oppression and victimization.

Buying into the assumption of Oriental women's captivity, liberal feminists and politicians across the West (including the FRG) in the 1980s cast themselves and West German society as saviors. As literary scholar Gayatri Chakravorty Spivak criticized in her pathbreaking 1983 article "Can the Subaltern Speak?," Western scholars, journalists, and politicians excused (post)colonial abuses because "white men [were] saving brown women from brown men."[45] One year later, in "Under Western Eyes: Feminist Scholarship and Colonial Discourses," sociologist Chandra Talpade Mohanty showed how Western feminists contributed to that stereotype by casting "Third World Women" as a "singular monolithic subject." Mohanty argued that Western feminists replaced the "white men" in Spivak's work with almost any contact to Western society. In so doing, these feminists and politicians adopted nineteenth-century claims of Western cultural superiority and the need for a civilizing mission.[46] Buying into those beliefs, German feminists promoted, in effect, the same image and, thus, indirectly collaborated with Christian-conservative politicians to fight against Turkish male oppression, as scholars like Patricia Ehrkamp or Rita Chin have shown.[47]

Many media outlets in the 1980s cast the school as the Western knight prepared to liberate Turkish and Moroccan girls. Reflecting widespread beliefs, the 1989 *Spiegel* article about Malika's case explained that viewpoint. It emphasized that universal compulsory schooling required all children—including Muslim girls—to attend public school.[48] Theoretically, in these public spaces non-German children would be acculturated to German ideals and taught choices outside of their oppressive, controlling homes. In school, Muslim (non-German) girls would be exposed to German (non-Muslim) girls. Here, they would learn about the liberty to be found in conformity to Western gender norms expressed in sport and fashion. In theory, Malika's exposure to a non-Muslim, semisecular German public sphere would have provided her salvation partly by offering a space for her to paint her lips.[49]

Even as those news articles presented the school as the Western liberator, many West German journalists cast the headscarf (usually *Kopftuch* in German and "veil" in English) as *the* symbol of patriarchal oppression. According to them, Muslim girls and women had to wear the headscarf to protect themselves from the prying male gaze. Following that belief, the removal of the headscarf, as the 1989 *Spiegel* report on Malika's story claimed, was a step toward female emancipation. Yet, most West German journalists did not differentiate between forced and voluntary use. Rather, reflecting Mohanty's argument, those writers essentialized women and cast them all as one monolithic bloc. The headscarf came to be seen, according to social scientists Neil Macmaster and Toni Lewis, as "the most public and visible signifier of radical sexual segregation, but also as a key marker of essential inferiority of Islamic societies." That often-colorful piece of cloth stood in for "Oriental despotism, sadism, and lasciviousness."[50]

That viewpoint led some West German politicians and school administrators to try to regulate girls' rights to choose their clothing in an attempt to force liberation. In March 1981, for example, the daily *Westdeutsche Allgemeine Zeitung* based in Essen reported a case in Baden-Württemberg in which a school principal attempted to forbid the headscarf. For him, the article explained, the headscarf was a symbol of Muslim repression and Turkish gender discrimination. The article's tone expressed sympathy for the principal's stand, unusual as it was at the beginning of the decade. The Standing Conference of the Ministers of Education and Cultural Affairs (Ständige Konferenz der Kultusminister, KMK) of the federal states, or *Länder,* of the Federal Republic of Germany, however, refused to regulate schoolchildren's clothing.[51] Nonetheless, as the headscarf's symbolic significance spread, several schools would claim that forcing young girls to bare their heads would teach them freedom. Following similar logic, some West German states in later years passed laws that prohibited teachers from donning the headscarf, as these women's choice to cover their head supposedly taught the children to be subservient. These prohibitions and bans were, however, challenged in court, usually with success.[52]

Even as many members of the West German press depicted Turkish and Moroccan girls as forced to cover their heads, the reality was that headscarves were an exception rather than the rule. Furthermore, many women who donned the headscarf did so voluntarily as an expression of self, choice, and belief, and often as a form of resistance. In 1980s West Germany, many women opted to cover their heads precisely because of West German othering. In Turkey, many women used the headscarf as an expression of faith in opposition to the secular state.[53] Thus, the symbolic value of the headscarf in the West German media became precisely the reason to embrace it.[54]

As the assumptions of Muslim women's oppression spread over the 1980s, some journalists began reflexively interpreting resistance to unwrapping as symbolic of ubiquitous patriarchal abuse. Thus in the mid-1980s, swim lessons became another site of symbolic conflict over the ownership of women's bodies between the German school and the Oriental man. Children across West Germany were supposed to learn to swim as part of the compulsory school curriculum. For those lessons, girls had to wear standardized, small bathing suits.[55] A few Turkish Muslim parents objected to their daughters' participation on the grounds that the required attire was too revealing. A handful of West German papers addressed the issue as one of religious conservatives trying to prevent their children from participating in West German society. In an August 1986 article in West Berlin's daily *Tagesspiegel*, for example, under the headline "Swimming Also Obligatory for Turks," the author described how a Turkish "father did not want to let his daughter participate in [swimming] instruction" and had to pay a penalty for preventing her participation.[56] As with the headscarf, the article implied that gender equality and a girl's personal liberty were practiced through the obligatory uncovering of the female body.[57] For the article's author, the compulsory act was representative of secular liberation. Furthermore, the exception was cast as a representation of a restrictive norm despite the fact that there were not "many such children," as the KMK's secretariat observed in October 1986.[58] Despite being uncommon, the imagery became part of a lingering perception of women's fashion as illustrating their freedom.

Through the 1980s, the use of the headscarf and the swimsuit became a common representation in the West German media of the oppression and abuse supposedly inherent in Muslim culture.[59] Scholars like the feminist historian Joan W. Scott criticized such positions. In her 2007 book *Politics of the Veil,* she discussed French feminists who could only accept expressions of physical liberation that corresponded to their own ideas of liberation. These feminists refused to acknowledge, Scott argued, that women's freedom could take different forms. They insisted that only through conformity to Western norms could a Muslim woman be free.[60] For these feminists, women could only reclaim themselves from their fathers, husbands, and brothers by bringing their private body into the public.[61] In West Germany, too, the right of these women to choose was refused on the grounds that only through Western conformity could a woman be free.

The emphasis on the exposed, painted body as a sign of liberation in 1980s West Germany fit precisely into Spivak, Mohanty, and later Scott's critiques of the West's depiction of Oriental or Muslim women. Here, only conformity to Western culture could be liberation. To save women from themselves, they had to be forced to comply. *Der Spiegel*'s articles about Serife and Malika criticized their fathers' imputed sense of ownership of their bodies. In taking away their sartorial choices, those men were inflicting violence on them that soon became literal. The West German response often suggested that an appropriate course of action was to move in the opposite direction: to compel exposure. Through both examples, the woman was ascribed little to no choice and cast instead as the suffering victim.

Conclusion

Many people across Germany and Europe continue to hold those gendered Orientalist stereotypes as true, as exhibited by recent debates about "Germaness" and "Turkishness."[62] The highly gendered forms of cultural and religious othering of Muslim minority groups, including "the Turkish," in West Germany have a long tradition, but the contemporary iterations took form in the 1980s. It was however after the fall of the wall in the 1990s that gendered Orientalist images became particularly widespread. Multiple scholars have discussed this development, including literature scholar Maria Stehle. She examined the ways in which the German popular image of the veil has forced Muslims to "inhabit a precarious space since the 1990s." Others, including political scientist Carola Richter, documented the "distortion" of "Islam in German public service television programmes" between 2005 and 2006 or, like Yasemin Yildiz, explored how West Germans took stereotypes of Turks and extended these essentialist images to all Muslims.[63] These studies and many others like them demonstrate that a large swath of the West German mainstream media, like many media elsewhere, has consistently denied that men and women with Turkish and Arab backgrounds can have individual equality, having instead clung to picturesque Oriental assumptions of inferiority and repression.

The reverberations of those distorted images affect daily lives as well as law and policy. In the last two decades, both scholars and ordinary women from Muslim groups have attested that "perceived ethnic discrimination" contributes to psychological distress. These studies show that othering and exclusion promote a sense of isolation and frequently lead to depression. In short, the myriad articles from the 1970s, 1980s, and later decades describing the unending horrors associated with a Muslim, Turkish, or Arab (including Moroccan) identity promoted the very problems they decried. The constant discussion of women's victimhood in fact victimized women. The very news articles that portrayed "Turkish women and girls" as requiring rescue contributed to these individuals' experience of social trauma.[64]

Brittany Lehman is senior liaison librarian for history and affiliated faculty with the History Department at Boston College. She received her Ph.D. in December 2015 from the University of North Carolina at Chapel Hill with a dissertation, which was published in 2019 under the title *Teaching Migrant Children in West Germany and Europe, 1945-1992* (Palgrave Macmillan, 2019). Her current research project focuses on the Federal Republic of Germany's involvement in decolonization in North Africa and the Middle East as well as the development of humanitarian organizations like Germany Amnesty International.

Notes

1. "Völlige Ohnmacht," *Der Spiegel*, no. 12, 21 March 1983, 81.
2. Ibid.
3. Edward W. Said, *Orientalism* (New York, 1978).
4. Lila Abu-Lughod, *Do Muslim Women Need Saving?* (Cambridge, 2013), 1, 3.
5. Edward W Said, *Culture and Imperialism* (New York, 1994), xi–xiii.
6. See Brittany Lehman, *Teaching Migrant Children in West Germany and Europe, 1949–1992* (New York: Palgrave MacMillan, 2018).
7. Patricia Ehrkamp, "The Limits of Multicultural Tolerance? Liberal Democracy and Media Portrayals of Muslim Migrant Women in Germany," *Space and Polity* 14, no. 1 (2010): 13–32.
8. On this history of German Orientalism, see Markus Meßling, "Wilhelm von Humboldt and the 'Orient': On Edward W. Said's Remarks on Humboldt's Orientalist Studies," *Language Sciences* 30, no. 5 (2008): 482–98; Suzanne L. Marchand, *German Orientalism in the Age of Empire: Religion, Race, and Scholarship* (Cambridge, MA, 2010); Felix Konrad, "From the 'Turkish Menace' to Exoticism and Orientalism: Islam as Antithesis of Europe (1453–1914)?," *European History Online*, 14 March 2011, ieg-ego.eu/en/threads/models-and-stereotypes/

from-the-turkish-menace-to-orientalism (accessed 30 May 2017); and John Phillip Short, *Magic Lantern Empire: Colonialism and Society in Germany* (Ithaca, NY, 2012).
9. Yasemin Yildiz, "Turkish Girls, Allah's Daughters, and the Contemporary German Subject: Itinerary of a Figure," *German Life and Letters* 62, no. 4 (2009): 465.
10. Anna C. Korteweg and Gökçe Yurdakul, "Gender Equality and Immigrant Integration: Honor Killing and Forced Marriage Debates in the Netherlands, Germany, and Britain," *Women's Studies International Forum* 41, part 3 (2013): 204–14.
11. Stephen Castles, *Challenges to National Identity and Citizenship: A Comparative Study of Immigration and Society in Germany, France and Australia* (Wollongong, NSW, 1999); and Stuart Hall, "The Question of Cultural Identity," in *Modernity and Its Futures*, ed. Stuart Hall et al. (Cambridge, 1992), 273–326.
12. "Völlige Ohnmacht."
13. D. A. F. Salama, "Forms and Functions of Oriental Bodies in the Parzival Wolframs von Eschenbach," *Archiv für das Studium der neueren Sprachen und Literaturen* 251, no. 1 (2014): 1–34; and Elena Pnevmonidou, "Veiled Narratives: Novalis' Heinrich von Ofterdingen as a Staging of Orientalist Discourse," *German Quarterly* 84, no. 1 (2011): 21–40.
14. James R. Hodkinson, "Moving Beyond the Binary: Christian-Islamic Encounters and Gender in the Thought and Literature of German Romanticism?," in *Encounters with Islam in German Literature and Culture*, ed. James R. Hodkinson and Jeff Morrison (Rochester, NY, 2009), 121.
15. See Hodkinson and Morrison, eds., *Encounters with Islam*.
16. Ruth Mandel, *Cosmopolitan Anxieties: Turkish Challenges to Citizenship and Belonging in Germany* (Durham, NC, 2008), 87, 136; and Lena Gorelik, *"Sie können aber gut Deutsch!": Warum ich nicht mehr dankbar sein will, dass ich hier leben darf, und Toleranz nicht weiterhilft* (Munich, 2012). On female guest workers, Monika Mattes, *"Gastarbeiterinnen" in der Bundesrepublik: Anwerbepolitik, Migration und Geschlecht in den 50er bis 70er Jahren* (Frankfurt/M., 2005), 9–25. The emphasis on smell would linger. See "Hier stinkt es nach Türken," *Der Spiegel*, no. 46, 15 November 1982, 90.
17. For example Giacomo Maturi, "Aus einer anderen Welt," *Die Welt*, 8 August 1964; "Bei Razzia in Gutsgebäude Gastarbeiter ohne Papiere entdeckt: Ausländeramt: 70 Marokkaner sollen so schnell wie möglich abgeschoben werden," *Bonner Rundschau*, 16 June 1965; and "1000 Marokkaner müssen wieder nach Hause: Illegal als 'Touristen' in die Bundesrepublik gekommen," *General Anzeiger*, 26 January 1966. The literature confirms my observation; see Alke Wierth, "Schwule Türken stinken nicht nach Knoblauch (Interview with Nurkan Erpulat)," *Die Tageszeitung*, 1 December 2008; Julia Woesthoff, "Ambiguities of Antiracism: Representations of Foreign Labourers and the West German Media, 1955–1990" (PhD diss., Michigan State University, 2004); Kiên Nghị Hà, *Ethnizität und Migration Reloaded: Kulturelle Identität, Differenz und Hybridität im postkolonialen Diskurs* (Berlin, 2004), 59; Mandel, *Cosmopolitan Anxieties*, 135–36; Maren Möhring, *Fremdes Essen: Die Geschichte der ausländischen Gastronomie in der Bundesrepublik Deutschland* (Munich, 2012); and Sarah Thomsen Vierra, "At Home in Almanya: Turkish-German Space of Belonging in West Germany, 1961-1990" (PhD diss., University of North Carolina at Chapel Hill, 2011).

18. Wolfgang Seifert, "Geschichte der Zuwanderung nach Deutschland nach 1950," Dossier, Bundeszentrale für politische Bildung, 31 May 2012, www.bpb.de/politik/grundfragen/deutsche-verhaeltnisse-eine-sozialkunde/138012/geschichte-der-zuwanderung-nach-deutschland-nach-1950 (accessed 17 May 2017).
19. Ulrich Herbert, *A History of Foreign Labor in Germany, 1880–1990: Seasonal Workers, Forced Laborers, Guest Workers,* trans. William Templer (Ann Arbor, MI, 1990).
20. Swiss author Max Frisch immortalized the West German citizens' collective shock with the observation "We asked for labor; we got people instead." Cited in Doris Meissner, "Managing Migrations," *Foreign Policy,* no. 86 (1992): 69; and Yannick Lemel and Heinz Herbert Noll, eds., *Changing Structures of Inequality: A Comparative Perspective* (Montréal, 2003), 288.
21. Christof Van Mol and Helga de Valk, "Migration and Immigrants in Europe: A Historical and Demographic Perspective," in *Integration Processes and Policies in Europe,* ed. Blanca Garcés-Mascareñas and Rinus Penninx (New York, 2016), 32–37.
22. Melanie Booth, "Die Entwicklung der Arbeitslosigkeit in Deutschland," Dossier "Der lange Weg zur politischen Einheit," 30 March 2010, Bundeszentrale für politische Bildung, http://www.bpb.de/geschichte/deutsche-einheit/lange-wege-der-deutschen-einheit/47242/arbeitslosigkeit?p=all.
23. Carolin Butterwegge, "Von der 'Gastarbeiter'-Anwerbung zum Zuwanderungsgesetz Migrationsgeschehen und Zuwanderungspolitik in der Bundesrepublik," Grundlagendossier "Migration," 15 March 2005, Bundeszentrale für politische Bildung, https://www.bpb.de/gesellschaft/migration/dossier-migration/56377/migrationspolitik-in-der-brd?p=all.
24. Ibid.
25. Technically, only Italy had that protection in 1973/74, but Greece, Spain, and Portugal were going through significant political changes and then a rapid process of accession to the European Community. Yugoslav, like Turkish, migration to West Germany would increase significantly with the recruitment stop.
26. M. K. Malhotra, "Die soziale Integration der Gastarbeiterkinder in die deutsche Schulklasse," *Kölner Zeitschrift für Soziologie und Sozialpsychologie,* no. 25 (1973): 104–21; Hartwig Suhrbier, "Bildungsplan für Ausländer: DGB fordert schulische Integration und Chancengleichheit," *Frankfurter Rundschau,* 2 June 1973; and Gert Bürgel, "Intensive Bemühungen um Ausländer-Integration: Kein Getto in Denkendorf: Ein Nahziel: Hauptschulabschluß für die Kinder," *Stuttgarter Nachrichten,* 13 September 1975.
27. Maria Stehle, *Ghetto Voices in Contemporary German Culture: Textscapes, Filmscapes, Soundscapes* (Rochester, NY, 2012).
28. Ulrich Bäder, "Hilfe für die 'Getto-Kinder': Opladen; Modellversuch soll Bildungschancen der ausländischen Schüler verbessern," *Neue Rhein Zeitung,* 25 May 1973; "Ausländische 'Problemkinder' in deutschen Schulen: Zahlen aus NRW/Sorgen und Teilerfolge," *Frankfurter Allgemeine,* 19 August 1975; "'Die Probleme beginnen in der 2. Generation': Wissenschaftler erforschen die Situation ausländischer Kinder: Die Volkswagenstiftung unterstützt das Projekt mit 500 000 Mark," *Badische Zeitung,* 3 July 1976.
29. Walter Fröhder, "Vom Gastarbeiter zum Mitbürger auf Zeit: Die Gewerkschaften wollen die Rechte der Ausländer erweitert sehen," *Frankfurter Allgemeine Zeitung,* 31 August 1972; Bayerisches Staatsministerium für Arbeit und Sozialordnung, "Sitzung der interministeriellen Arbeitsgruppe 'Ausländerpolitik' am 10.

Januar 1973 im Bayerischen Staatsministerium für Arbeit und Sozialordnung," Bayerisches Hauptstaatsarchiv, StK 14796; and Deutscher Bundestag [8.], 115. Sitzung, 10. November 1978, 9022A–9022C.

30. Rogers Brubaker, *Citizenship and Nationhood in France and Germany* (Cambridge, MA, 1992), 165–78; Patricia Ehrkamp, "Placing Identities: Transnational Practices and Local Attachments of Turkish Immigrants in Germany," *Journal of Ethnic and Migration Studies* 31, no. 2 (2005): 345–64; and Annemarie Sammartino, "After Brubaker: Citizenship in Modern Germany, 1848 to Today," *German History* 27, no. 4 (2009): 583–99.

31. Statistisches Bundesamt, ed., *Statistisches Jahrbuch für die Bundesrepublik Deutschland* (Stuttgart, 1978), 72; Douglas B. Klusmeyer and Thomas Alexander Aleinikoff, eds., *From Migrants to Citizens: Membership in a Changing World* (Washington, DC, 2000). Between those births and new migration, the number of non-German citizens living in West Germany reached 7.2 percent of the FRG's population or just under 4.5 million people in 1980. Statistisches Bundesamt, ed., *Statistisches Jahrbuch für die Bundesrepublik Deutschland* (Stuttgart, 1982), 50, 66; and Konrad H. Jarausch, *After Hitler: Recivilizing Germans, 1945–1995* (Oxford, 2008), 239–63.

32. "Die Türken kommen—rette sich wer kann," *Der Spiegel*, no. 31, 30 July 1973, 24–34.

33. Ruth Lingenberg, "Bei Ausländerkindern 'tickt eine Zeitbombe': Von der Jugendarbeitslosigkeit sind sie besonders bedroht," *Kölnische Rundschau*, 15 April 1976; and Nermin Abadan-Unat, *Turks in Europe: From Guest Worker to Transnational Citizen* (New York, 2011), 110–11.

34. See, for example, Heinz-Günter Kemmer, "Mit einem Koffer voller Geld: Rückkehr-Prämien für Türken?," *DIE ZEIT*, no. 40, 1 October 1982; and Irina Ludat, "Eine Frage der größeren Angst: Bilanz der 'Rückkehrförderung' ausländischer Arbeitskräfte," *DIE ZEIT*, no. 43, 18 October 1985.

35. "Ausländerkinder gefährdet—Verbände: Ohne Hilfe wird Kriminalität unter ihnen ansteigen," *Frankfurter Rundschau*, 21 February 1978; see also "Beratung der Großen Anfrage der Fraktionen der SPD und FDP: Zur Ausländerpolitik," Deutscher Bundestag [9.], 83. Sitzung, 4. Februar 1982, 4888–924, 4942–79; Thomas Faist, "From School to Work: Public Policy and Underclass Formation among Young Turks in Germany during the 1980s," *International Migration Review* 27, no. 2 (1993): 306–31; and Hans-Jörg Albrecht, "Ethnic Minorities, Crime, and Criminal Justice in Germany," *Crime and Justice* 21 (1997): 31–99.

36. See Rita Chin, *The Guest Worker Question in Postwar Germany* (New York, 2007), 117, 153.

37. Petra Kappert, "Was bleibt den Türken in der Fremde? Der Islam kann Heimat bedeuten, aber auch Abkapselung und Intoleranz," *Frankfurter Allgemeine Zeitung*, 25 September 1982.

38. Erich Wiedemann, "Wenn die Muftis kommen, gibt's Zoff im Pütt," *Der Spiegel*, no. 15, 11 April 1983, 86–101.

39. See Chin, *Guest Worker Question*, 30–191.

40. Katherine Pratt Ewing, *Stolen Honor: Stigmatizing Muslim Men in Berlin* (Stanford, CA, 2008).

41. Ibid., 52–93.

42. "'Er konnte gar nicht anders handeln': Gewalt in Einwandererfamilien—Tatmotiv: Kulturschock," *Der Spiegel*, no. 10, 6 March 1989, 96.

43. Pnevmonidou, "Veiled Narratives," 23.

44. See Claudia Mareike Katrin Schwabe, "Romanticism, Orientalism, and National Identity: German Literary Fairy Tales, 1795–1848" (PhD diss., University of Florida, 2012), 7–8, ufdc.ufl.edu/UFE0043960/00001 (accessed 17 May 2017).
45. Gayatri Chakravorty Spivak, "'Can the Subaltern Speak?' Revised Edition, from the 'History' Chapter of Critique of Postcolonial Reason," in *Can the Subaltern Speak? Reflections on the History of an Idea*, ed. Rosalind Morris (New York, 2010), 48–50; and Kwok Pui-lan, "Unbinding Our Feet: Saving Brown Women and Feminist Religious Discourse," in *Postcolonialism, Feminism and Religious Discourse*, ed. Laura E. Donaldson and Kwok Pui-lan (New York, 2002), 64.
46. Chandra Talpade Mohanty, "Under Western Eyes: Feminist Scholarship and Colonial Discourses," *Boundary 2* 12/13: 12, no. 3 and 13, no. 1 (1984): 333–58.
47. Ehrkamp, "Limits of Multicultural Tolerance?," 14–15; Rita Chin, "Turkish Women, West German Feminists, and the Gendered Discourse on Muslim Cultural Difference," *Public Culture* 22, no. 3 (2010): 557–81; and Claudia Diehl et al., "Religiosity and Gender Equality: Comparing Natives and Muslim Migrants in Germany," *Ethnic and Racial Studies* 32, no. 2 (2009): 278–301.
48. "Er konnte gar nicht anders handeln," *Der Spiegel*.
49. Landespresse- und Informationsamt, "Gleiche Bildungschancen für ausländische Kinder," 12. Dezember 1972, Landesarchiv NRW, NW 372-390; Suhrbier, "Bildungsplan für Ausländer"; Lutz-Rainer Reuter, *Das Recht auf chancengleiche Bildung: Ein Beitrag zur sozial ungleichen Bildungspartizipation und zu den Aufgaben und Grenzen der Rechtswissenschaft bei der Verwirklichung eines sozialen Grundrechts auf chancengleiche Bildung* (Ratingen, 1975); Marieke Boom, "Modellversuch für Lehrer: Deutsch als Fremdsprache: Ein Schritt zur Chancengleichheit für Ausländer-Kinder," *Westdeutsche Allgemeine*, 20 April 1979; Kate M. Wegmann, "Shaping a New Society: Immigration, Integration, and Schooling in Germany," *International Social Work* 57, no. 2 (2014): 131–42; and Andreas Hadjar and Rolf Becker, "Education Systems and Meritocracy: Social Origin, Educational and Status Attainment," in *Education Systems and Inequalities: International Comparisons*, ed. Andreas Hadjar and Christiane Gross (Chicago, 2016), 239.
50. Neil Macmaster and Toni Lewis, "Orientalism: From Unveiling to Hyperveiling," *Journal of European Studies* 28, no. 1 (1998): 121.
51. Müjgan Dericioglu an Schulamt Recklinghausen, "Türkische Mädchen mit Kopftüchern im Schulunterricht," 20. April 1981, Bundesarchiv Koblenz, B 304/6178; and Hermann, "Unterricht für türkische Schüler, hier: Antrittsbesuch der neuen Erziehungsrätin an der türkischen Botschaft beim Generalsekretär der Kultusministerkonferenz," Vermerk (Bonn: Sekretariat der Ständigen Konferenz der Kultusminister der Länder in der Bundesrepublik Deutschland, 25. Juni 1981), Bundesarchiv Koblenz, B 304/6178.
52. "Schulamt gibt Türkenmädchen recht—Grundgesetz wurde verletzt: Kopftücher ärgern Schulrektor," *Westdeutsche Allgemeine Zeitung*, 14 March 1981; "Mit Kopftuch in die Klasse," *Frankfurter Rundschau*, 19 March 1982. Interestingly, unlike the impression of the English and French "veil," the German verbal marker of the "headscarf" is less severe in tone. A headscarf was an article of clothing to cover the head, often with hair exposed, but in no way obstruct the face or hide identity. Hilal Elver, "Germany," in *The Headscarf Controversy: Secularism and Freedom of Religion* (New York, 2012), 129–52; Korteweg and Yurdakul, *Headscarf Debates*; and Haleh Chahrokh, *Discrimination in the Name of Neutrality: Headscarf Bans for Teachers and Civil Servants in Germany* (Berlin, 2009), 50.

53. Ruth Mandel, "Turkish Headscarves and the 'Foreigner Problem': Constructing Difference through Emblems of Identity," *New German Critique*, no. 46 (1989): 27–46; Wendy Pojmann, "The Political Participation of Berlin's Turkish Migrants in the Dual Citizenship and Headscarf Debates: A Multilevel Comparison," in *Migration and Activism in Europe Since 1945*, ed. Wendy Pojmann (New York, 2008), 209–32; and Feyzi Baban, "Secular Spaces and Religious Representations: Reading the Headscarf Debate in Turkey as Citizenship Politics," *Citizenship Studies* 18, no. 6–7 (2014): 644–46.
54. Magdalena Crăciun, "Aesthetics, Ethics and Fashionable Veiling: A Debate in Contemporary Turkey," *World Art* 7, no. 2 (2017): 329–52; Damani J. Partridge, *Hypersexuality and Headscarves: Race, Sex, and Citizenship in the New Germany* (Bloomington, IN, 2012), 131–40.
55. Hermann, "Antrittsbesuch der neuen Erziehungsrätin."
56. "Schwimmen auch für Türken Pflicht: Vater wollte Tochter nicht am Unterricht teilnehmen lassen—Geldbuße," *Tagesspiegel*, 23 August 1986.
57. Rogers Brubaker, "Language, Religion and the Politics of Difference," *Nations and Nationalism* 19, no. 1 (2013): 1–20.
58. Sekretariat der Kultusministerkonferenz, "25. Sitzung des Unterausschusses für ausländische Schüler," Ergebnisniederschrift (Bonn: Kultusministerkonferenz, 24. Oktober 1986), 28, Bundesarchiv Koblenz, B 304/7775.
59. Yasemin Yildiz, "Governing European Subjects: Tolerance and Guilt in the Discourse of 'Muslim Women,'" *Cultural Critique* 77 (2011): 70–101.
60. Joan Wallach Scott, *The Politics of the Veil* (Princeton, NJ, 2007), 21–41 and 151–74.
61. Ehrkamp, "Limits of Multicultural Tolerance?"
62. For example, Nora Schareika, "Deutschland und der Burkini: Schwimmbad taugt nicht zum Kulturkampf," *n-tv.de*, 11 June 2016, www.n-tv.de/politik/Schwimmbad-taugt-nicht-zum-Kulturkampf-article17916001.html (accessed 30 May 2017).
63. Maria Stehle, "Gender, Performance, and the Politics of Space: Germany and the Veil in Popular Culture," *Comparative Studies of South Asia, Africa and the Middle East* 32, no. 1 (2012): 89–101; Carola Richter and Kai Hafez, "The Image of Islam in German Public Service Television Programmes," *Journal of Arab and Muslim Media Research* 2, no. 3 (2009): 169–81; Yildiz, "Turkish Girls"; and Halyna Leontiy, "Deutsch-Türken und Spätaussiedler im Spiegel der Satire und Komik auf der Bühne," in *Fragiler Pluralismus*, ed. Hans-Georg Soeffner and Thea D. Boldt (Wiesbaden, 2014), 159–75.
64. Marion C. Aichberger et al., "Perceived Ethnic Discrimination, Acculturation, and Psychological Distress in Women of Turkish Origin in Germany," *Social Psychiatry and Psychiatric Epidemiology* 50, no. 11 (2015): 1691–700.

Selected Bibliography

Abu-Lughod, Lila. *Do Muslim Women Need Saving?* Cambridge, 2013.
Brubaker, Rogers. "Language, Religion and the Politics of Difference." *Nations and Nationalism* 19, no. 1 (2013): 1–20.
Chin, Rita. "Turkish Women, West German Feminists, and the Gendered Discourse on Muslim Cultural Difference." *Public Culture* 22, no 3 (2010): 557–81.
Ehrkamp, Patricia. "The Limits of Multicultural Tolerance? Liberal Democracy and

Media Portrayals of Muslim Migrant Women in Germany." *Space and Polity* 14, no. 1 (2010): 13–32.

Ewing, Katherine Pratt. *Stolen Honor: Stigmatizing Muslim Men in Berlin*. Stanford, CA, 2008.

Faist, Thomas. "From School to Work: Public Policy and Underclass Formation among Young Turks in Germany during the 1980s." *International Migration Review* 27, no. 2 (1993): 306–31.

Göktürk, Deniz, David Gramling, and Anton Kaes, eds. *Germany in Transit: Nation and Migration, 1955–2005*. Berkley, CA, 2007.

Hall, Stuart. "The Question of Cultural Identity." In *Modernity and Its Futures*, ed. Stuart Hall, David Held, and Tony McGrew, 273–326. Cambridge, MA, 1992.

Hodkinson, James R. "Moving Beyond the Binary: Christian-Islamic Encounters and Gender in the Thought and Literature of German Romanticism?" In *Encounters with Islam in German Literature and Culture*, ed. James R. Hodkinson and Jeffrey Morrison, 108–127. Rochester, NY, 2009.

Klusmeyer, Douglas B., and Thomas Alexander Aleinikoff, eds. *From Migrants to Citizens: Membership in a Changing World*. Washington, DC, 2000.

Konrad, Felix. "From the 'Turkish Menace' to Exoticism and Orientalism: Islam as Antithesis of Europe (1453–1914)?" *European History Online*, 14 March 2011, ieg-ego.eu/en/threads/models-and-stereotypes/from-the-turkish-menace-to-orientalism/.

Korteweg, Anna C., and Gökçe Yurdakul. *The Headscarf Debates: Conflicts of National Belonging*. Stanford, CA, 2014.

Macmaster, Neil, and Toni Lewis. "Orientalism: From Unveiling to Hyperveiling." *Journal of European Studies* 28, no. 1 (1998): 121–35.

Mandel, Ruth. *Cosmopolitan Anxieties: Turkish Challenges to Citizenship and Belonging in Germany*. Durham, NC, 2008.

Marchand, Suzanne L. *German Orientalism in the Age of Empire: Religion, Race, and Scholarship*. Cambridge, MA, 2009.

Mattes, Monika. *"Gastarbeiterinnen" in der Bundesrepublik: Anwerbepolitik, Migration und Geschlecht in den 50er bis 70er Jahren*. Frankfurt/M., 2005.

Mohanty, Chandra Talpade. "Under Western Eyes: Feminist Scholarship and Colonial Discourses." *Boundary 2* 12/13: 12, no. 3 and 13, no. 1 (1984): 333–58.

Morris, Rosalind, ed. *Can the Subaltern Speak? Reflections on the History of an Idea*. New York, 2010.

Pnevmonidou, Elena. "Veiled Narratives: Novalis' Heinrich von Ofterdingen as a Staging of Orientalist Discourse." *German Quarterly* 84, no. 1 (2011): 21–40.

Pui-lan, Kwok. "Unbinding Our Feet: Saving Brown Women and Feminist Religious Discourse." In *Postcolonialism, Feminism and Religious Discourse*, ed. Laura E. Donaldson and Kwok Pui-lan, 62–81. New York, 2002.

Richter, Carola, and Kai Hafez. "The Image of Islam in German Public Service Television Programmes." *Journal of Arab and Muslim Media Research* 2, no. 3 (2009): 169–81.

Said, Edward W. *Orientalism*. New York, 1978.

Scott, Joan Wallach. *The Politics of the Veil*. Princeton, NJ, 2007.

Stehle, Maria. "Gender, Performance, and the Politics of Space: Germany and the Veil in Popular Culture." *Comparative Studies of South Asia, Africa and the Middle East* 32, no. 1 (2012): 89–101.

Yildiz, Yasemin. "Governing European Subjects: Tolerance and Guilt in the Discourse of 'Muslim Women.'" *Cultural Critique* 77, no. 77 (2011): 70–101.

Index of Names

Adenauer, Konrad, 123, 125–27, 128, 278, 298, 299, 320, 366
Adorno, Theodor, 300
Bebel, August, 82, 257–58
Benjamin, Hilde, 117–19, 121–23
Blüher, Hans, 277–78
Brandt, Willy, 76, 192, 255, 304
Brüning, Elfriede, 321–22, 330–31
Bürger-Prinz, Hans, 284, 288
Dehler, Thomas, 124–25
Dibelius, Otto, 123, 124, 126
Eilers, Elfriede, 194
Erhard, Ludwig, 302, 366
Focke, Katharina, 265–66
Geißler, Heiner, 265–66
Giese, Hans, 277, 282–86, 290
Grotewohl, Otto, 121
Heinemann, Gustav, 302
Heuss, Theodor, 107
Hirschfeld, Magnus, 46, 274–75, 277–79, 281–83, 285, 287

Hitler, Adolf, 95, 330
Honecker, Erich, 80, 255
Kohl, Helmut, 108, 370
Langhans, Rainer, 209–10, 222–23
Lorde, Audre, 32, 229–36, 241–43
Mielke, Erich, 122–23
Neumayer, Fritz, 118–19
Oguntoye, Katharina, 230–31, 233, 234, 235, 239, 241–42
Radszuweit, Friedrich, 278–79, 280–82, 285, 286, 290
Reich, Wilhelm, 216, 275
Sander, Helke, 48, 74–76, 77, 78, 81–83
Schwarzer, Alice, 188, 190, 191
Schwarzhaupt, Elisabeth, 126
Stefan, Verena, 216
Strobel, Käte, 194
Ulbricht, Walter, 50, 255
Wex, Helga, 196
Zetkin, Clara, 257–58

Index of Subjects

abortion, 11, 34, 46, 48, 82, 146, 148, 149, 219, 220–21, 225
 movement against Paragraph 218, 30, 31, 82, 185, 194, 264
 Paragraph 218 of the Penal Code of the German Empire (*Reichsstrafgesetzbuch,* StGB), 30, 31, 147, 149
Action Council for the Liberation of Women (Aktionsrat zur Befreiung der Frauen) (FRG). *See under* women's movement, new
African diaspora, 232, 233, 236, 241
 diasporic politics, 32, 236–37, 243
Afro-Americanophilia, 238, 239
Afro-German. *See* Black German activism
Afro-German Women (Afrodeutsche Frauen, ADEFRA) (FRG). *See under* Black German activism
Air Protection Police (Luftschutzpolizei). *See under* Third Reich
Allied occupation of Germany
 Allied Control Council, 117, 118
 American occupation policy, 28, 98, 102, 105, 140–41, 322
 American Occupation Zone, 98, 102, 110, 319, 232, 323, 331
 British occupation policy, 28, 102, 104, 105, 140–41, 322
 British Occupation Zone, 102–3, 104, 340
 French occupation policy, 28, 105, 140–41, 322

 French Occupation Zone, 102, 104
 Soviet occupation policy, 28, 30, 98, 99–100, 101, 102, 104–5, 140–41, 164
 Soviet Occupation Zone (*Sowjetische Besatzungszone,* SBZ), 94, 98, 99, 106, 107, 109, 257, 318, 319, 320, 321–22, 325, 326
America. *See* United States
Anti-Fascist Committees (*Antifaschistische Komitees*), 97
Anti-Radical Decree (*Radikalenerlaß/ Berufsverbote*). *See under* Federal Republic of Germany (FRG)
Association of the German Press (Verband der Deutschen Presse, VDP) (GDR). *See under* media organizations

Berlin, 46, 49, 93, 94, 95, 96, 98, 99–101, 104, 105, 107, 108, 109, 121, 257, 274, 285, 319, 320, 325, 331, 340
 East, 24, 28, 33, 55, 82, 101–2, 106, 120, 164, 165, 168, 169, 170, 175, 176, 259–61, 262, 263, 318, 321, 325–29, 331, 340
 Wall, 23, 49, 55, 56, 78, 81, 162, 234, 253–54, 256, 258, 267–68, 365, 374
 West, 55, 74, 76, 81–82, 107, 109, 187–88, 189, 190, 192, 208, 209, 211, 214, 216, 217, 219, 222, 230–32, 234, 239–40, 242, 253, 255, 259, 260, 264–65,

267, 286, 317, 318, 321, 323–29, 331, 351, 368, 373
birth control, 30, 194. *See also* abortion
Pill, the (*Pille/Wunschkindpille*), 52, 75, 149, 150, 218–19
Black British women's activism
British Black Panthers, 237
Brixton Black Women's Group (BBWG), 237
Organization of Women of Asian and African Descent (OWAAD), 237
Black European / international activism, 241, 243
Cross-Cultural Black Women's Summer Institute, 241
Black German activism (FRG)
Afro-German Women (Afrodeutsche Frauen, ADEFRA), 10, 32, 229–31, 234, 235–43
Black German Movement, 230, 235, 240
Initiative of Black Germans (Initiative Schwarze Deutsche, ISD), 229, 230, 234, 235, 236, 239
Britain / United Kingdom, 2, 67, 94, 143, 190, 234, 237, 255, 259, 264, 285
Bundestag (Federal Parliament). *See* Federal Republic of Germany (FRG)

Catholicism
Caritas (*see under* welfare)
Catholic Church, 9, 28, 33–34, 50, 115–16, 119, 121, 124, 125–28, 161–79, 196, 257, 276, 320, 339
Catholic German Women's Union (Katholischer Deutscher Frauenbund) (FRG), 126
Center for Culture and Recreation (Cultuur en Ontsanningscentrum, COC) (Netherlands). *See under* gay/lesbian rights movement
Central Committee (Zentralkommitee, ZK, also Politburo). *See under* German Democratic Republic (GDR)
childcare. *See under* welfare

Christian conservatism
CDU Federal Women's Committee (CDU Bundesfrauenausschuss), 196
CDU Women's Union (CDU Frauenvereinigung) (FRG), 196
Christian Democratic Union of Germany (Christlich Demokratische Union Deutschlands, CDU) (FRG and GDR), 24, 31, 33, 35, 108, 115–16, 119, 121, 123, 125–26, 128, 137, 147, 186–87, 193–195, 196–98, 255, 257, 265–66, 298, 299, 302 320, 338–39, 370
Christian Social Union (Christlich-Soziale Union, CSU) (FRG), 24, 108, 115, 196, 298, 399
Civil Code (*Bürgerliches Gesetzbuch, BGB*) (German Empire). *See under* family law
clothing, contested (FRG)
headscarf, 363, 372–74, 379n52
swimwear, 363, 373–74
Club of Friends (Club der Freunde) (FRG). *See under* gay/lesbian rights movement
Cold War, 1, 3, 4–5, 6–7, 10–12, 22–23, 25, 26–27, 31, 32, 34–35, 48, 53, 56, 72, 76, 79, 105, 115–17, 126, 127–29, 136–37, 141, 146, 149, 150, 162, 167, 186, 192, 194, 199, 254, 256, 267, 276, 318, 322–23, 324, 326, 327, 331–32, 338, 348, 352
détente, 35, 76
communism
Communist Party of Germany (Kommunistische Partei Deutschlands, KPD), 25, 32–33, 123, 125, 321, 327
Free German Youth (Freie Deutsche Jugend, FDJ) (GDR), 263, 376
German Communist Party (Deutsche Kommunistische Partei, DKP) (FRG), 193, 220
Maoist Groups (K[ommunistische, Kader]-Gruppen) (FRG), 215, 220

Socialist Unity Party of Germany (Sozialistische Einheitspartei Deutschlands, SED) (GDR), 3, 8, 23–24, 28, 29, 33–34, 50, 56, 68, 73, 77, 80, 100, 115, 116, 117–20, 121–24, 127–28, 161, 163–67, 169, 171, 173, 178, 255, 258, 260, 262–63, 267, 321, 322, 324, 325, 326, 327, 328–29, 339, 341
Communist Party of Germany (Kommunistische Partei Deutschlands, KPD). *See under* communism
consumer/consumerism, 8, 11, 50, 72, 73, 80, 102, 162, 255, 337–38, 340, 341, 346, 352–53, 355–56
Cross-Cultural Black Women's Summer Institute. *See under* Black European / international activism
Cultural Union for the Democratic Renewal of Germany (Kulturbund zur demokratischen Erneuerung Deutschlands). *See under* German Democratic Republic (GDR)

Democratic Women's Initiative (Demokratische Fraueninitiative, DFI) (FRG). *See under* women's movement, new
Democratic Women's League of Germany (Demokratischer Frauenbund Deutschlands, DFB) (FRG and GDR). *See under* women's movement
discrimination
    antisemitism, 326
    class, 78, 144, 232, 345, 367
    homophobia, 46, 59, 232, 235, 243
    racism, 46, 47, 117, 137, 231–32, 233, 235, 237, 240, 243, 278, 367, 369
    sexism, 188, 231–32, 235, 237, 240, 243
    xenophobia, 369–70
disease
    cancer, 30, 136, 138, 139, 141–44, 145, 150
    cardiovascular disease (CVD), 139, 141, 143–44
    sexually transmitted diseases (STD), 140
    tuberculosis (TB), 30, 136, 138, 139, 141, 143, 285
    venereal disease (VD), 30, 48, 49, 136, 139, 140–41

East Germany. *See* German Democratic Republic (GDR)
education/schools/schooling, 11, 26, 27, 34, 50, 118, 119, 140, 141, 146, 150, 167, 169, 172, 173, 175, 178, 187, 189, 198, 210, 220, 255, 261, 263, 265, 277, 280, 281, 285, 286, 322, 346, 362–63, 367–68, 372–73
    Ministry of Education (Ministerium für Volksbildung) (GDR), 173
    national and federal education ministries and administrations (FRG), 363
    Standing Conference of the Ministers of Education and Cultural Affairs of the Länder in the Federal Republic of Germany (Ständige Konferenz der Kultusminister der Länder in der Bundesrepublik Deutschland, or Kultusministerkonferenz, KMK) (FRG), 372, 373
Equal Rights Act (*Gleichberechtigungsgesetz*) (FRG). *See under* family law
ethnicity, 2, 7, 57, 368. *See also* religion
    German/Germaness, 368
    Moroccan, 363, 372, 373, 375
    Turkish, 11, 79, 217, 242, 362–66, 367–70, 372–75
Extraparliamentary Opposition (*Außerparlamentarische Opposition*, APO) (FRG). *See under* New Left

family, 10, 12, 21, 22, 26, 34, 46, 50, 52, 105, 119, 120, 128, 171, 253–255, 262, 265, 300, 363–65
    family work, 5, 74, 107–8, 140, 144, 146, 196, 339

kinship, 229, 230, 237, 241
marriage, 7, 22, 26, 27, 34, 49, 52, 53, 73, 119, 120, 124, 253, 257, 258, 260, 261, 262, 276, 337, 341
  postwar crisis of the, 49, 108, 116, 256, 257, 276, 318, 320
  reconciling family and work, 23, 75, 107, 125, 184, 186, 187, 189, 190–92, 196–97, 198–99, 256, 318, 331, 341
family ideals, 5, 27–29, 56, 254, 260, 265–66, 267, 341
  dual-earner family, 27, 28, 100, 337, 339
  housewife marriage, 29, 107, 257, 352
  male-breadwinner / female-homemaker family, 21–22, 27, 28, 29, 31, 49, 102–3, 186, 194, 195, 197, 254, 337, 339, 341, 345, 352
family law, 27
  Civil Code (*Bürgerliches Gesetzbuch*, BGB) (German Empire, FRG), 28–29, 115–18, 123, 126–29, 150, 266
  Equal Rights Act (*Gesetz über die Gleichberechtigung von Mann und Frau auf dem Gebiet des bürgerlichen Rechts*) (FRG), 28, 116, 126, 128, 129
  Family Code (*Familiengesetzbuch*, FGB) (GDR), 28, 116–23, 127, 129, 255–56, 260
  First Law for the Reform of the Marriage and Family (*Erstes Gesetz zur Reform des Ehe- und Familienrechts*) (FRG), 29
  marriage law, 117, 118, 124, 150, 278
  reform of, 9, 28–29, 33, 51, 115–29, 150, 255
  Stichentscheid, 28–29, 117, 124–25, 127, 150, 257
family policy, 11, 21–22, 26, 27–29, 31, 37, 49, 103, 184–87, 194–199, 257, 259, 337, 367

Law for Child-Rearing Allowance and Parental Leave (*Gesetz zum Erziehungsgeld und zur Elternzeit*) (FRG), 197
maternity leave policy (*see under* motherhood / protection of maternity)
maternity protection policy (*see under* motherhood / protection of maternity)
fashion, 5, 69, 71, 73, 80, 208, 337, 341, 345–47, 352–53, 355, 372, 373
Federal Republic of Germany (FRG) / West Germany (Bundesrepublik Deutschland)
  Anti-Radical Decree (*Radikalenerlaß/Berufsverbote*), 192–93
  Basic Law (*Grundgesetz*), 119, 120, 123, 257, 266, 301, 368
  Federal Constitutional Court (Bundesverfassungsgericht), 30, 126
  Federal Ministry of All-German Affairs (Bundesministerium für gesamtdeutsche Fragen), 107
  Federal Ministry of Defence (Bundesministerium der Verteidigung), 57, 296, 298, 300–305, 308
  Federal Ministry of Family Affairs, Senior Citizens, Women, and Youth (Bundesministerium für Familie, Senioren, Frauen und Jugend), 259
  Federal Ministry of Health Care (Bundesministerium für Gesundheitswesen), 138, 147
  Federal Ministry of Justice (Bundesministerium der Justiz), 52, 118–19, 123–24, 301–2
  Federal Parliament (Bundestag), 24, 30, 116, 122, 123, 125–27, 128, 147–48, 150, 194, 198, 296, 302–3, 304
Federation for Human Rights (Bund für Menschenrecht). *See under* gay/lesbian rights movement

femininity, 9, 11, 30, 50, 69–70, 289, 331, 337, 338, 339, 341, 355
feminism
    autonomous, 31, 75, 184–86, 187–90, 191–96, 199–200
    Black, 10, 83, 230, 235–239
    individual, 194
    relational, 194, 196, 204n53
    socialist, 77, 182, 185, 186, 187–88, 190, 192–93
    transnational, 32, 230, 242–43
    West German (*see* women's movement, new)
foreign/foreigners, 95, 216, 238–39, 364–370. *See also* dicrimination: xenophibia
France, 47, 67, 94, 190, 274, 276, 285
Free Democratic Party (Freie Demokratische Partei, FDP) (FRG). *See under* liberalism
Free German Trade Union Federation (Freier Deutscher Gewerkschaftsbund, FDGB) (GDR). *See under* trade unions
Free German Youth (Freie Deutsche Jugend, FDJ) (GDR). *See under* communism

gay/lesbian/queer. *See also* sexuality
    gay, 26, 53–57, 58, 274–75, 278–80, 282, 284, 286, 288–89
    homophile, 10, 53–53, 275–277, 282, 285, 286–87, 289–90, 304
    homosexuality, 6, 7, 10, 11, 45, 46–47, 51, 55–57, 277–78, 280, 281, 282–83, 284, 295–98, 300–301, 304–6, 308
    lesbian, 6, 32, 45, 53–54, 55, 57, 58, 207, 218, 229–30, 231, 234, 235–37, 239–40, 241, 242, 243, 274, 275, 278, 279, 280, 281, 286, 288, 290, 302
    persecution, 6, 46, 54–56, 57, 277, 288, 298–300, 301–2, 305, 308
    queer, 45, 55–58
    rights, 22, 32, 45, 55, 57–58, 275, 281, 290, 295–98, 302, 307, 308
gay/lesbian rights movement
    Association for a Humane Way of Life (Verein für humanitäre Lebensgestaltung) (FRG), 286
    Center for Culture and Recreation (Cultuur en Ontsanningscentrum, COC) (Netherlands), 286
    Club of Friends (Club der Freunde) (FRG), 286
    Federation for Human Rights (Bund für Menschenrecht e.V.) (Weimar Germany), 278, 280–81, 290
    German Friendship Alliance (Deutscher Freundschafts-Verband) (Weimar Germany), 279, 280
    International Committee for Sexual Equality (Netherlands), 275, 286
    International Friendship Lodge (Internationale Freundschaftsloge, IFLO) (FRG), 286
    lesbian activism (FRG), 32, 45, 53–54, 55, 231, 234, 235, 237, 239–241, 243, 275
    Mattachine Society (USA), 276
    Scientific-Humanitarian Committee (Wissenschaftlich-humanitäres Komitee, WhK) (Weimar Germany), 274, 277–78, 281, 283, 285
    Society for Human Rights (Gesellschaft für Menschenrechte) (FRG), 286, 290
    Society for the Reform of Sexual Law (Gesellschaft für Reform des Sexualrechts) (FRG), 286
gender
    equality, 26, 28–29, 31, 33, 58, 67, 69–70, 78, 106, 107, 115, 118, 120, 126, 139, 151, 166, 184–85, 192, 255–56, 257–58, 259, 260–68, 321, 339, 342, 373
    images, 5, 11, 29, 69–72, 80, 83, 93, 107–8, 184, 279, 337–42, 348–49, 351–53, 355–56

order, 2, 21, 105, 121, 128, 191, 193, 197, 257, 266, 337–39
German Democratic Republic (GDR) / East Germany (Deutsche Demokratische Republik)
   Central Committee (Zentralkommitee, ZK) 23–24, 68, 122
   church policy, 164, 166
   Cultural Union for the Democratic Renewal of Germany (Kulturbund zur demokratischen Erneuerung Deutschlands), 321–22
   Ministers of the GDR (Ministerrat der DDR), 24
   Ministry for State Security (Ministerium für Staatssicherheit, MfS or Stasi), 4, 123, 165, 167, 169, 326
   Ministry of Health Care (Ministerium für Gesundheitswesen, MfG), 137, 140, 142, 146, 150, 167, 173
   Ministry of Justice (Ministerium der Justiz), 118, 119, 120, 121, 123
   Ministry of National Education (Ministerium für Volksbildung), 173
   People's Chamber (Volkskammer), 23
   State Secretariat for Church Affairs (Staatssekretär für Kirchenfragen), 167, 168, 169, 170
German Empire, 2, 6, 7, 117, 171, 257, 266, 297, 298
   Wilhelmine Empire, 7, 27, 29, 115, 185, 186, 342
German Film Company (Deutsche Film Aktiengesellschaft, DEFA) (GDR). *See under* media organizations
German Friendship Alliance (Deutscher Freundschafts-Verband). *See under* gay/lesbian rights movement
German Journalists Association (Deutscher Journalisten Verband) (FRG). *See under* media organizations
German Press Association (Reichsverband der deutschen Presse) (Third Reich). *See under* media organizations
German Trade Union Confederation (Deutscher Gewerkschaftsbund, DGB). *See under* trade unions
   DGB Women's Division (DGB Frauenabteilung). *See under* trade unions
German unification, 1, 4, 68, 118–22, 129, 242, 256
   Germans at one Table (Deutsche an einen Tisch) (GDR), 324–25
German Women's Circle (Deutscher Frauenring) (FRG). *See under* women's movement
German Women's Council (Deutscher Frauenrat) (FRG). *See under* women's movement
Germany
   East Germany (*see* German Democratic Republic [GDR])
   German Empire (*see* German Empire)
   Third/National Socialism (*see* Third Reich)
   Weimar Republic (*see* Weimar Germany)
   West Germany (*see* Federal Republic of Germany [FRG])
Gray Panthers (Graue Panther) (FRG), 108
Green Party (Die Grünen) (FRG), 108, 304
guest workers (*Gastarbeiter*) (FRG), 7, 364–67

Hamburg Institute for Sex Research (Hamburger Institut für Sexualforschung) (FRG). *See under* sexuality
headscarf (*Kopftuch*). *See under* clothing, contested
health, 6–7, 9, 11, 23, 27, 34, 35, 49, 56, 136–51, 166–67, 257, 279, 297, 353
   female/women's bodies, 29–30, 54, 136–37, 138–51, 213, 219, 353

Index of Subjects

German Hygiene Museum (Deutsches Hygiene Museum Dresden, DHMD) (GDR), 141–42, 148
healthcare system, 9, 29–30, 136–39, 146, 147–48, 151
  insurance, 142, 146–47
  physicians/doctors, 137–40, 142–44, 147–48, 149, 219, 253, 258, 286, 300
  social hygiene, 139–141, 145–47
historiography, 2–3, 5, 6, 25, 45, 47, 50, 76, 83–84, 93, 188, 192, 318
  Alltagsgeschichte, 5, 26
  histoire croisée (history of entanglements), 116, 127
  Historikerinnenstreit (quarrel between women historians), 3, 47–48, 109
  intersectionality, 7, 59, 80, 83, 87–88n40, 230, 233, 237–38, 242–43, 297, 338
  women's and gender history, 2, 3, 8, 22–23, 47–48, 109
Hitler Youth (Hitlerjugend, HJ). *See under* Third Reich
Holocaust, 3, 46
housework/housewife, 5, 26, 29, 82, 107, 108, 127, 188, 190–91, 196, 254, 257, 258, 337, 352–53

identity/belonging, 7, 57–58, 59, 78, 108, 162–63, 170, 176, 177–78, 179, 212, 229, 230, 236–37, 238, 240, 243, 295, 307, 318, 352–53, 363, 364, 375
Information Service for Women (Informationsdienst für die Frau) (FRG). *See under* women's movement
Initiative of Black Germans (Initiative Schwarze Deutsche, ISD). *See under* Black German activism
Institute of Sexual Research (Institut für Sexualwissenschaft) (Weimar Germany). *See under* sexuality
Interest Group for Women Married to Foreigners (Interessengemeinschaft der mit Ausländern verheirateten Frauen e.V., IAF) (FRG), 239
Islam/Muslim, 7, 11, 58, 79, 362–65, 368, 369–75

journals/magazines, gay and lesbian
  Die Blätter für Menschenrechte (Weimar Germany), 280
  Das dritte Geschlecht (Weimar Germany), 280, 281
  Der Eigene (Weimar Germany), 274
  Die Freunde (FRG), 286–87, 289
  Die Freundin (Weimar Germany), 280
  Die Freundschaft (Weimar Germany), 279–80
  Das Freundschaftsblatt (Weimar Germany), 280
  Der homosexuelle Mann in der Welt (FRG), 283, 284
  Die Insel (Weimar Germany), 280, 286, 288
  Der Kreis (Switzerland), 275, 283, 286, 288
journals/magazines, women's/feminist
  Afrekete/Farbe bekennen (FRG), 233–34, 236, 239, 241
  Courage (FRG), 187–88, 190–91, 207, 214, 218, 219, 221–22,
  Brigitte (FRG), 326, 338, 340–41, 346, 353, 355
  Constanze (FRG), 317, 338, 340–41, 345–47, 355
  Emma (FRG), 188, 190–91, 207
  Die Frau von heute (GDR), 338, 340
  Für Dich (GDR), 325, 329–30, 340
  Das Magazin (GDR), 50
  Sie (American zone), 319, 329

labor
  family work (*see under* family)
  forced labor, 96, 99, 317, 327
  gender division of, 31, 100, 188, 191, 339
  housework (*see* housework)
  labor duty (*Arbeitspflicht*), 98, 100
  labor policy, 29, 99, 257

paid labor, 137, 144, 190–91, 340, 341–43, 345, 352
public employment offices (*Arbeitsämter*), 98
state employment offices (*Landesarbeitsämter*), 103
liberalism
    Free Democratic Party (Freie Demokratische Partei, FDP) (FRG), 24, 28, 30, 31, 35, 107, 108, 119, 123–24, 125, 195, 196, 255, 258, 264, 265–66, 298, 302, 304, 366
    Liberal Democratic Party of Germany (Liberal-Demokratische Partei Deutschlands, LDPD) (GDR), 33

masculinity/men/male, 2, 3, 5–6, 7, 10, 11–12, 22, 24, 28, 29, 30, 31, 33, 49, 50, 56–57, 78, 80, 81–82, 96, 99, 100–101, 103–4, 106, 109, 136, 138, 139, 141–42, 143, 145, 150, 171, 186, 188, 189, 195, 210–11, 215, 256, 257, 260–61, 266, 267, 277–78, 280, 281, 287, 288–89, 295, 297, 299, 301, 305, 307–9, 342, 365–66, 370
    hegemonic, 57, 217, 297
    masculinists, 277, 278, 281
Mattachine Society (USA). *See under* gay/lesbian rights movement
media, 10–11, 27, 32, 53, 67–73, 76, 78–79, 80, 81, 82, 83–84, 93, 106, 107, 109, 136, 187, 191, 215, 220, 231, 260, 276, 287, 289, 295, 307, 324, 338, 339, 340, 341, 345, 347–48, 349, 351, 352, 355, 363, 364, 366, 369, 372, 373, 374
    film, 48, 68–69, 71–78, 79, 80, 81–82, 189, 191, 213, 214, 317, 326, 328, 339, 349, 352
    illustrated press, 11, 69–70, 71, 337–38, 339, 341, 346, 349, 355
    intermediality, 70, 339
    television, 10, 72, 78, 84, 93, 261, 352, 374

media organizations
    Association of the German Press (Verband der Deutschen Presse, VDP) (GDR), 72, 320–21, 322–24
    German Film Company (Deutsche Film-Aktiengesellschaft, DEFA) (GDR), 68, 73, 76, 77, 78, 317
    German Journalists Association (Deutscher Journalisten Verband, DJV) (FRG), 323
    German Press Association (Reichsverband der Deutschen Presse) (Third Reich), 319
memory, 49, 318
    collective memory, 28, 93–94, 107, 108, 109, 100
    public memory, 109
migration/migrants, 58, 83, 217, 238–39, 364–69, 371
    forced (*see* refugees)
Ministers of the GDR (Ministerrat der DDR). *See under* German Democratic Republic (GDR)
modern
    modern woman, 26, 337, 341, 342, 347, 352, 353, 355–56
    modernity, 22, 67, 69–70, 71, 73, 78, 138–39, 185, 196, 337, 338, 341, 342, 352, 353, 355
monasticism, 175, 178
    in Eastern Orthodoxy, 165
    in Roman Catholicism, 165–66, 168
Morocco, 371
motherhood / protection of maternity. *See also* pregnancy
    child-rearing allowance (*Erziehungsgeld*) (FRG), 196–97
    Law for Child-Rearing Allowance and Parental Leave (*Gesetz zum Erziehungsgeld und zur Elternzeit*) (FRG), 197
    Law for the Protection of Motherhood and Children and Rights of Women (*Gesetz über den Mutter- und Kinderschutz und die Rechte der Frau*) (GDR), 107, 117

Law for the Protection of Mothers at Work, in Training and Studies (*Gesetz zum Schutz von Müttern bei der Arbeit, in der Ausbildung und im Studium*) (FRG), 147
Maternal Leave Law (*Mutterschaftsurlaubgesetz*) (FRG), 195–96
maternity leave policy, 146–47, 149
maternity protection policy, 147, 148
natalism / natalist policy, 30, 139, 148–49

National Socialist German Workers' Party (Nationalsozialistische Deutsche Arbeiter Partei, NSDAP). *See under* Third Reich
New Left (FRG), 50–51, 193, 195, 213, 214, 220, 264, 304
    Extraparliamentary Opposition (*Außerparlamentarische Opposition*, APO), 31, 34, 207, 208–9
    Socialist German Student League (Sozialistischer Deutscher Studentenbund, SDS), 51, 82–83, 188, 209–13, 216, 220, 221–22
    student movement, 31, 34, 45, 51–52, 81–82, 188, 207, 208–10, 255

newspapers/magazines (general)
    Arbeiter Illustrierte Zeitung (Weimar Germany), 348
    Berliner Zeitung (GDR), 260, 325
    Deutsche Allgemeine Zeitung (Weimar Germany), 323
    Frankfurter Rundschau (FRG), 74, 93, 369
    graswurzelrevolution (FRG), 307
    Kurier (West Berlin), 320
    Nacht-Express (East Berlin), 321
    Neue Berliner Illustrierte, NBI (GDR), 319, 338, 340, 347, 348–51, 353, 355
    Die Neue Zeitung (FRG), 319, 323
    Neues Leben (GDR), 263
    Sonntag (FRG), 321–22, 325, 330
    Sozialdemokrat: Organ der Sozialdemokratie Groß-Berlin (West Berlin), 327
    Der Spiegel (FRG), 302, 303, 325, 349, 362, 363, 368–69, 370, 371, 374
    Stern (FRG), 188, 191, 317, 348
    Süddeutsche Zeitung (FRG), 331
    Tagesspiegel (West Berlin), 320, 323, 326, 330, 373
    Uhlenspiegel (GDR), 325
    Der Weg (FRG), 275, 286
    Weltbühne (GDR), 323, 325–26
    Weser-Kurier (FRG), 327–28
    Westdeutsche Allgemeine Zeitung (FRG), 372
nuns, 9
    Roman Catholic, 33–34, 161, 165, 169–77

occupation zones. *See* Allied occupation of Germany
Orientalism, 11, 79, 80, 362–65, 368, 369, 371, 374

Penal Code (*Reichsstrafgesetzbuch*, StGB), 30, 147, 274, 277, 295, 296, 298–99, 302
    Great Reform of the StGB (*Große Strafrechtsreform*) (FRG), 295–96, 299, 300, 301, 306, 308
    Reform of Paragraph 175 (FRG), 296, 297, 298–305 (*see also* gay: rights)
    Reform of Paragraph 175 (GDR), 296 (*see also* gay: rights)
    Reform of Paragraph 218/219 (FRG), 30, 31, 149 (*see also* abortion)
    Reform of Paragraph 218/219 (GDR), 30, 31 (*see also* abortion)
People's Chamber (Volkskammer). *See under* German Democratic Republic (GDR)
physicians/doctors. *See under* health

pregnancy, 30, 136–37, 145–51, 214, 218. *See also* birth control; motherhood
    clinic birth, 145–49
    infant mortality, 138, 146–48
    maternal mortality, 138, 146–48
    natalism / natalist policy, 30, 139, 148–49
    pregnancy counseling / prenatal exam
prisoners of war (POWs), 93, 95, 96–97, 99, 101, 109, 330, 140
prostitution, 46, 48, 49, 140–41, 280, 281, 284, 289, 300, 345, 369
Protestantism
    Eastern Conference of the Protestant Church in Germany (Kirchliche Ostkonferenz der Evangelischen Kirche in Deutschland, KO-EKD) (GDR), 120, 121–122, 123
    Federation of Protestant Churches in the GDR (Bund der Evangelischen Kirchen in der DDR), 163
    Protestant Church of Germany (Evangelische Kirche in Deutschland) (FRG and GDR), 28, 50, 116, 119, 120, 121, 126, 131, 163, 196, 257, 320, 339
    Protestant Churches in the GDR (Bund der Evangelischen Kirchen in der DDR), 163
public/private sphere, 22, 26, 52, 53, 57, 76, 142 174, 175, 199, 253, 255–56, 261, 262, 264, 267, 318, 319, 321, 323, 371, 372, 374

reconstruction of postwar Germany, 28, 94, 100, 103, 106, 107, 127, 256, 257
    construction businesses, 95, 97–99, 102
    construction offices (*Bauämter*), 99
    construction work, 100, 102–3, 106, 109
    rubble clearance / clearing, 9, 28, 34, 93–110, 330

refugees
    German, 104, 163, 330–31, 341, 365
Reich Labor Service (Reichsarbeitsdienst, RAD). *See under* Third Reich
religion. *See* Catholicism; Islam/Muslim; Protestanism; Russian Orthodox Church
religious institutes and societies
    orders (Order of Friars Minor; Order of Saint Benedict; Order of Ursulines; Priory of St. Gertrud, Alexanderdorf), 33–34, 161–78
    Society of Jesus (Jesuits, SJ), 167–68, 169, 175
Repair Service (Instandsetzungsdienst). *See under* Third Reich
rubble clearance. *See under* reconstruction of postwar Germany
rubble woman (*Trümmerfrau*), 9, 330
    memorial of the, 107
    myth of the, 28, 93–94, 106–10
Russian Orthodox Church, 164

schools/schooling. *See* education
Security and Aid Service (Sicherheits- und Hilfsdienst, SHD). *See under* Third Reich
sexuality. *See also* gay/lesbian/queer
    German Society for Sexual Research (Deutsche Gesellschaft für Sexualforschung, DGfS) (FRG), 283
    Hamburg Institute for Sex Research (Hamburger Institut für Sexualforschung) (FRG), 282–83, 295
    heterosexuality, 45, 50, 54–55, 56, 80, 284, 287, 289, 295, 297, 299–300, 301, 303, 304, 305, 306, 307, 308
    homosexuality (*see* gay)
    Institute of Sexual Research (Institut für Sexualwissenschaft) (Weimar Germany), 46, 274

Index of Subjects 393

shared apartments (*Wohngemeinschaften*, WGs), 184, 188, 212, 213
  communes (*Kommunen*); *Kommune 1, Kommune 2*, 213, 215, 220
social democracy / socialist
  Social Democratic Party of Germany (Sozialdemokratische Partei Deutschlands, SPD), 24, 28, 30, 31, 32–33, 35, 107, 108, 123, 125–26, 128, 137, 146, 147, 148, 186, 187, 192, 193–96, 197, 198, 199, 255, 258, 264, 265, 299, 302, 304, 321, 325, 327, 366
  Working Group of Social Democratic Women (Arbeitsgemeinschaft Sozialdemokratischer Frauen, ASF) (FRG), 194–95, 199
  Working Group of Young Socialists in the SPD (Arbeitsgemeinschaft der Jungsozialisten in der SPD, Jusos) (FRG), 195
Socialist German Student League (Sozialistischer Deutscher Studentenbund, SDS) (FRG). *See under* New Left
Socialist Unity Party of Germany (Sozialistische Einheitspartei Deutschlands, SED). *See under* communism
Socialist Women's Union West Berlin (Sozialistischer Frauenbund Westberlin, SFBW). *See under* women's movement, new
Soviet Union (USSR) / Soviet, 27, 67, 72, 99, 100, 164, 165, 215, 323, 327, 331
  Ministry of State Security, Soviet (MGB), 317, 327
  News Agency of the Soviet Military (SND), 321, 327
  Soviet law, 126
  Soviet Military Administration in Germany (Sowjetische Militäradministration in Deutschland, SMAD), 100

  (*see also* Allied occupation of Germany)
SS, Protection Squadron (*Schutzstaffel*). *See under* Third Reich
  SS Construction Brigades (*SS Baubrigaden*). *See under* Third Reich
storefront daycare (*Kinderläden*) (FRG), 189, 217
  movement (*Kinderladenbewegung*) (FRG), 189

Third Reich / National Socialism
  Air Protection Police (Luftschutzpolizei), 94
  concentration camps, 95–96
  Hitler Youth (Hitlerjugend, HJ), 95
  Holocaust (*see* Holocaust)
  National Socialism, 3, 47, 48, 51, 108–9, 188, 240, 318, 330
  National Socialist German Workers' Party (Nationalsozialistische Deutsche Arbeiter Partei, NSDAP), 95, 96, 99, 109, 145
  National Socialist Women's League (NS Frauenschaft), 329
  Reich Labor Service (Reichsarbeitsdienst, RAD), 95
  Repair Service (Instandsetzungsdienst), 94–95
  Security and Aid Service (Sicherheits- und Hilfsdienst, SHD), 94–95
  SS, Protection Squadron (Schutzstaffel), 95–96
  SS Construction Brigades (SS Baubrigaden), 95–96
trade unions
  DGB Federal Women's Committee (Bundesfrauenausschuß) (FRG), 197, 198, 199
  DGB Women's Division (DGB Frauenabteilung) (FRG), 24–25, 187, 191, 197–99
  Free German Trade Union Federation (Freier Deutscher

Gewerkschaftsbund, FDBG) (GDR), 24
German Trade Union Confederation (Deutscher Gewerkschaftsbund, DGB) (FRG), 24–25, 187, 191, 197–99
Turkey, 7, 373

United States / America, 52, 56, 67, 94, 138, 141, 145, 219, 232, 234, 236, 259, 264, 276, 283, 323, 337, 347–39, 355, 362
    Americanization, 72, 347–48
    US Military Government's Information Control Branch, 319

violence, 46, 78, 82, 348
    domestic abuse / violence, 54, 58, 185, 216, 253–68, 362, 371, 374
    women's shelter (*Frauenhaus*) (*see* women's shelter)

wage for housework movement (*Lohn für Hausarbeit*) (FRG). *See under* women's movement, new
    International Women's Collective, 190
War
    Cold War (*see* Cold War)
    First World War, 277, 278, 279
    Second World War, 7, 46, 53, 56, 68, 78, 93–96, 100, 102, 104, 108, 115, 117, 137, 141, 163, 164, 175, 184, 232, 256–57, 286
Weimar Germany, 27, 30, 54, 69, 186, 298, 348, 355
welfare
    Caritas, 166, 170, 173, 259, 263
    childcare, 11, 27, 34, 189, 191, 195, 198–99, 207, 213, 214, 217, 254, 258, 264, 345
    welfare organizations, 257
    welfare services, 52, 101
West German military (Bundeswehr) (FRG)
    Compulsory Military Service Act (*Wehrpflichtgesetz*), 301

Federal Ministry of Defense (Bundesministerium der Verteidigung), 57, 296, 298, 300–305, 308
    Lex Bundeswehr, 303
    Military Discipline Code, 305–6
West Germany. *See* Federal Republic of Germany (FRG)
women
    women's and gender history (*see under* historiography)
    women's center, 185, 193, 207, 213, 218, 259, 264
    women's emancipation, 5, 26, 75–76, 106, 117, 189, 190, 191, 257
    women's employment, 103, 144–45, 198, 256
    women's health, 136–39, 140–42, 144–51, 219, 353 (*see also* birth control)
    women's health center, 213, 219
    women's rights, 27, 116, 117, 127, 128, 150, 241
Women for Peace (Frauen für den Frieden) (FRG). *See under* women's movement, new
Women Helping Women (Frauen helfen Frauen) (FRG). *See under* women's movement, new
Women's Affairs Office (Büro der Frauenbeauftragten) (FRG), 197
women's and gender history. *See under* historiography
Women's Committees (*Kommunale Frauenausschüsse*). *See* women's movement
Women's Council Frankfurt (Weiberrat Frankfurt) (FRG). *See under* women's movement, new
Women's Forum Munich (Frauenforum München e.V.) (FRG). *See under* women's movement, new
women's movement
    Democratic Women's League (Demokratischer Frauenbund Deutschlands, DFD) (FRG and GDR), 24, 25, 340

German Women's Circle (Deutscher Frauenring) (FRG), 184
German Women's Council (Deutscher Frauenrat) (FRG), 184
Information Service for Women (Informationsdienst für die Frau) (FRG), 184
women's movement, new (FRG)
    Action Council for the Liberation of Women (Aktionsrat zur Befreiung der Frauen), 83, 187, 188, 189, 192, 193, 209, 210, 217, 264
    Democratic Women's Initiative (Demokratische Fraueninitiative, DFI), 187, 189, 192
    International Women's Collective, 190
    Socialist Women's Union West Berlin (Sozialistischer Frauenbund Westberlin, SFBW), 192, 193
    wages for housework movement (*Lohn für Hausarbeit*) (FRG), 190, 191
    Women for Peace (Frauen für den Frieden), 212
    Women Helping Women (Frauen helfen Frauen), 259, 264
    Women's Council Frankfurt (Weiberrat Frankfurt), 188, 209, 210–11, 212, 221
    Women's Forum Munich (Frauenforum München e.V.), 189
    Women's Self-Help—Women against Violence towards Women (Frauenselbsthilfe—Frauen gegen Gewalt an Frauen), 264
Women's Self-Help—Women against Violence towards Women (Frauenselbsthilfe—Frauen gegen Gewalt an Frauen). *See under* women's movement, new
women's shelter/house (Frauenhaus), 255, 258–59, 264
work. *See* labor; housework
Working Group of Social Democratic Women (Arbeitsgemeinschaft Sozialdemokratischer Frauen, ASF). *See under* social democracy (FRG)
Working Group of Young Socialists in the SPD (Arbeitsgemeinschaft der Jungsozialisten in der SPD, Jusos). *See under* social democracy (FRG)

youth welfare, 56
    Law against the Distribution of Written Material Endangering Youth (*Gesetz über die Verbreitung jugendgefährdender Schriften*) (FRG), 274–75

www.ingramcontent.com/pod-product-compliance
Lightning Source LLC
Chambersburg PA
CBHW072141100526
44589CB00015B/2034